Red Dot Design Yearbook 2019/2020

Edited by Peter Zec

About this book

"Doing" presents award-winning products for an active life. All of these products are of outstanding design quality and have been successful in one of the world's largest and most renowned design competitions, the Red Dot Design Award. This book documents the current results in the field of "Doing", and presents the most important players – the design team of the year, the designers of the best products and the jury members.

Über dieses Buch

„Doing" präsentiert ausgezeichnete Produkte für ein aktives Leben. All diese Produkte sind von herausragender gestalterischer Qualität, ausgezeichnet in einem der größten und renommiertesten Designwettbewerbe der Welt, dem Red Dot Design Award. Dieses Buch dokumentiert die aktuellen Ergebnisse im Bereich „Doing" und stellt zudem die wichtigsten Akteure vor – das Designteam des Jahres, die Designer der besten Produkte und die Jurymitglieder.

Contents
Inhalt

6	**Preface of the editor**
	Vorwort des Herausgebers
8	**Red Dot: Design Team of the Year 2019**
9	**Flavio Manzoni and Ferrari Design Team**
28	**The designers of the Red Dot: Best of the Best and their award-winning products**
	Die Designer der Red Dot: Best of the Best und ihre ausgezeichneten Produkte
30	Chin Ming Cheng – Joie Children's Products Co., Ltd.
32	Sanghyun Lee, Narae Yoon, Junghoo Hwang, Junghwan Park – JJOBI Company
34	Roland Heiler, Christian Schwamkrug, Steffen Ganz – Studio F. A. Porsche
36	Rick Hoobler, Insun Hong, Ben Schriesheim, Wes Johnson – iRobot
38	Tatsuya Kawai – Carozzeria Kawai
40	Richard Kappeller, Andreas Mathieson – Messermacher Kappeller GmbH
42	LARQ
44	Fiskars Finland Oy Ab
46	designaffairs
48	Blackmagic Design
50	Benjamin Sabourin, Nicolas Marquis – Ova Design
52	Igor Buturlia – VR Electronics Limited
54	Lenovo Experience Design Group
56	Kent Zeng – DTEN
58	Hyundai Robotics Hyundai Heavy Industries
60	Max Burton, Jonathan Mendoza, Frankie Vazquez, Kim Do – Fjord	Accenture Interactive

	The award-winning products of "Red Dot: Best of the Best", "Red Dot" and "Honourable Mention" distinctions
	Die Siegerprodukte der Auszeichnungen „Red Dot: Best of the Best", „Red Dot" und „Honourable Mention"
62	Babies and children
	Baby und Kind
106	Household
	Haushalt
132	Tableware and cooking utensils
	Tableware und Kochutensilien
164	Garden
	Garten
176	Tools
	Werkzeuge
200	Cameras
	Kameras
230	Communication
	Kommunikation
296	Robots
	Roboter
314	**The jurors of the Red Dot Award: Product Design**
	Die Juroren des Red Dot Award: Product Design
316	David Andersen
318	Prof. Masayo Ave
320	Martin Beeh
322	Gordon Bruce
324	Gisbert L. Brunner
326	Rüdiger Bucher
328	Prof. Jun Cai
330	Vivian Wai-kwan Cheng
332	Mårten Claesson
334	Vincent Créance
336	Martin Darbyshire
338	Katrin de Louw

340	Saskia Diez
342	Stefan Eckstein
344	Robin Edman
346	Prof. Lutz Fügener
348	Hideshi Hamaguchi
350	Prof. Renke He
352	Prof. Carlos Hinrichsen
354	Simon Husslein
356	Qiong Er Jiang
358	Prof. Cheng-Neng Kuan
360	Steve Leung
362	Dr. Thomas Lockwood
364	Wolfgang K. Meyer-Hayoz
366	Prof. Jure Miklavc
368	Adriana Monk
370	Prof. Dr. Ken Nah
372	Alexander Neumeister
374	Ken Okuyama
376	Simon Ong
378	Dr. Sascha Peters
380	Dirk Schumann
382	Prof. Song Kee Hong
384	Dick Spierenburg
386	Leon Sun
388	Kazuo Tanaka
390	Nils Toft
392	Prof. Danny Venlet
394	Dr. Joseph Francis Wong
	Alphabetical index
	Alphabetisches Register
396	Manufacturers and distributors
	Hersteller und Vertrieb
399	Designers
	Designer
408	Imprint
	Impressum

Professor Dr. Peter Zec
Preface of the editor
Vorwort des Herausgebers

Dear reader,
The Red Dot Design Yearbook with its four volumes "Living", "Doing", "Working" and "Enjoying" provides a comprehensive overview of the latest developments in product design. As you leaf through the books, you will notice some trends that run through all of the categories. In the competition year 2019/2020, one such trend is the clearly recognisable move toward more eco-friendly and sustainable products on the one hand and products that are more and more intelligent on the other. Other developments unfold within the narrow framework of a certain product segment or geographical region. Frequently, such developments are no less ground-breaking. On the contrary, they often indicate where future trends might lead. Embark on a journey of discovery, and be inspired by the many excellently designed products.

This year once again saw many well-known brands enter their products in the competition. This may come as an initial surprise, as one could be forgiven for thinking that these manufacturers don't need any more awards in order to sell their products or assure themselves of their own expertise. But the lesson to be learned from these companies that are successful as a brand through design is that this success has to be carefully earned – year after year. That's because the credibility of a brand is established by a company being visible over a longer period and also demonstrating a high level of continuity in its products, their design and quality. Many of the best-known brands internationally in the field of consumer and luxury goods have also been winning distinctions in the Red Dot Design Award for years, including Ferrari, Bosch, Apple, hansgrohe, Fiskars, LG Electronics, Lenovo and Sony. Not only are they some of this year's Red Dot: Best of the Best laureates, they can also look back at a consistent brand development. They have a striking corporate design, and above all else they stand for products with outstanding design and high quality.

In order to underscore and enhance the relevance of a comprehensive brand strategy (and ideally a related design strategy), brands have been accorded a larger platform in this year's Red Dot competition for communication design. Within an industry, companies can now enter the running for the distinction "Red Dot: Brand of the Year" in the Red Dot Award: Brands & Communication Design.

Without further ado, allow me to wish you an entertaining read!

Yours sincerely,
Peter Zec

Liebe Leserin, lieber Leser,
das Red Dot Design Yearbook gewährt Ihnen mit seinen vier Bänden „Living", „Doing", „Working" und „Enjoying" einen umfassenden Überblick über die neuesten Entwicklungen im Produktdesign. Wenn Sie durch die Bücher blättern, werden Sie den einen oder anderen Trend erkennen, der sich durch sämtliche Kategorien zieht – im Wettbewerbsjahr 2019/2020 ist dies etwa eine klar erkennbare Tendenz zu umweltfreundlicheren und nachhaltigeren Produkten einerseits sowie zu immer intelligenteren Produkten andererseits. Andere Entwicklungen spielen sich im engen Rahmen eines bestimmten Produktsegments oder einer geografischen Region ab, sind deswegen aber häufig nicht weniger richtungsweisend, sondern zeigen ganz im Gegenteil oft schon an, wohin der Trend in den nächsten Jahren gehen wird. Gehen Sie auf Entdeckungsreise und lassen Sie sich von den vielen ausgezeichnet gestalteten Produkten inspirieren.

Auch in diesem Jahr haben wieder viele bekannte Marken ihre Produkte zum Wettbewerb eingereicht. Auf den ersten Blick mag dies verwundern, denn man sollte meinen, dass diese Hersteller keine Auszeichnung mehr benötigen, um ihre Produkte zu verkaufen oder sich ihres eigenen Könnens zu versichern. Doch kann man von diesen Firmen, die als Marke mit Design erfolgreich sind, lernen, dass auch dieser Erfolg sorgfältig erarbeitet werden muss – Jahr für Jahr aufs Neue. Denn die Glaubwürdigkeit einer Marke kommt erst dadurch zustande, dass ein Unternehmen über einen längeren Zeitraum hinweg sichtbar ist und auch in seinen Produkten, deren Design und Qualität eine hohe Beständigkeit zeigt. Viele der international bekanntesten Marken im Bereich der Konsum- und Luxusgüter sind auch seit Jahren beim Red Dot Design Award erfolgreich, darunter Ferrari, Bosch, Apple, hansgrohe, Fiskars, LG Electronics, Lenovo oder Sony. Sie gehören nicht nur zu den diesjährigen Red Dot: Best of the Best-Preisträgern, sondern können auch auf eine kontinuierliche Markenentwicklung zurückblicken. Sie haben ein Corporate Design, das prägnant ist; vor allem aber stehen sie für Produkte mit herausragendem Design und hoher Qualität.

Um die Relevanz einer umfassenden Marken- und einer damit im Idealfall einhergehenden Designstrategie zu unterstreichen und zu stärken, erhalten Marken bei Red Dot ab diesem Jahr eine größere Plattform im Wettbewerb für Kommunikationsdesign: Beim Red Dot Award: Brands & Communication Design können sich Unternehmen jetzt innerhalb einer Branche um die Auszeichnung „Red Dot: Brand of the Year" bewerben.

Und nun wünsche ich Ihnen viel Vergnügen bei der Lektüre!

Ihr
Peter Zec

The title "Red Dot: Design Team of the Year" is bestowed on a design team that has garnered attention through its outstanding overall design achievements. This year, the title goes to Flavio Manzoni and the Ferrari Design Team. This award is the only one of its kind in the world and is extremely highly regarded even outside of the design scene.

Mit der Auszeichnung „Red Dot: Design Team of the Year" wird ein Designteam geehrt, das durch seine herausragende gestalterische Gesamtleistung auf sich aufmerksam gemacht hat. In diesem Jahr geht sie an Flavio Manzoni und das Ferrari Design Team. Diese Würdigung ist einzigartig auf der Welt und genießt über die Designszene hinaus höchstes Ansehen.

In recognition of its feat, the Red Dot: Design Team of the Year receives the "Radius" trophy. This sculpture was designed and crafted by the Weinstadt-Schnaidt based designer, Simon Peter Eiber.

Als Anerkennung erhält das Red Dot: Design Team of the Year den Wanderpokal „Radius". Die Skulptur wurde entworfen und angefertigt von dem Designer Simon Peter Eiber aus Weinstadt-Schnaidt.

2019	Flavio Manzoni & Ferrari Design Team
2018	Phoenix Design Team
2017	Canyon Design Team
2016	Blackmagic Industrial Design Team led by Simon Kidd
2015	Robert Sachon & Bosch Home Appliances Design Team
2014	Veryday
2013	Lenovo Design & User Experience Team
2012	Michael Mauer & Style Porsche
2011	The Grohe Design Team led by Paul Flowers
2010	Stephan Niehaus & Hilti Design Team
2009	Susan Perkins & Tupperware World Wide Design Team
2008	Michael Laude & Bose Design Team
2007	Chris Bangle & Design Team BMW Group
2006	LG Corporate Design Center
2005	Adidas Design Team
2004	Pininfarina Design Team
2003	Nokia Design Team
2002	Apple Industrial Design Team
2001	Festo Design Team
2000	Sony Design Team
1999	Audi Design Team
1998	Philips Design Team
1997	Michele De Lucchi Design Team
1996	Bill Moggridge & Ideo Design Team
1995	Herbert Schultes & Siemens Design Team
1994	Bruno Sacco & Mercedes-Benz Design Team
1993	Hartmut Esslinger & Frogdesign
1992	Alexander Neumeister & Neumeister Design
1991	Reiner Moll & Partner & Moll Design
1990	Slany Design Team
1989	Braun Design Team
1988	Leybold AG Design Team

Red Dot: Design Team of the Year 2019
Flavio Manzoni and Ferrari Design Team

This year's "Red Dot: Design Team of the Year" title goes to Flavio Manzoni and the Ferrari Design Team in Maranello. Flavio Manzoni became Senior Vice-President for Design at Ferrari in 2010. Since the Italian car manufacturer was founded in 1947, he is the first head designer to have succeeded in building a successful Ferrari Design Team.

This achievement is reflected not only in the new Centro Stile that opened in Maranello in 2018 but also in the Red Dot Award: Product Design. In the last five years, Manzoni and the Ferrari Design Team have won an accolade at the Red Dot Award 14 times and have five times been awarded the highest distinction the competition has to bestow, the Red Dot: Best of the Best.

Ferrari is the first car manufacturer in the history of the competition to win the top distinction five times in a row. Thanks to this achievement, the brand now also leads the Red Dot Ranking in the Automotive Design category for the first time. This is an outstanding accomplishment that will be recognised this year with the honorary title "Red Dot: Design Team of the Year".

Die Auszeichnung „Red Dot: Design Team of the Year" geht in diesem Jahr an Flavio Manzoni und das Ferrari Design Team in Maranello. 2010 wurde Flavio Manzoni Senior Vice-President for Design bei Ferrari. Seit der Gründung des italienischen Automobilherstellers im Jahr 1947 ist er der erste Chefdesigner, dem es gelungen ist, für Ferrari ein erfolgreiches Designteam aufzubauen.

Diese Leistung spiegelt sich nicht nur im neuen Centro Stile wider, das 2018 in Maranello eröffnet wurde, sondern auch im Red Dot Award: Product Design. Manzoni und das Ferrari Design Team wurden in den letzten fünf Jahren 14 Mal im Red Dot Award ausgezeichnet und erhielten fünf Mal die höchste Auszeichnung im Wettbewerb, den Red Dot: Best of the Best.

Ein Novum in der Geschichte des Wettbewerbs: Ferrari ist es als erstem Automobilhersteller gelungen, die höchste Auszeichnung fünf Mal in Folge zu gewinnen. Mit dieser Leistung führt die Marke erstmals auch das Red Dot Ranking im Automotive Design an. Eine herausragende Leistung, die in diesem Jahr mit der Ehrenauszeichnung „Red Dot: Design Team of the Year" gewürdigt wird.

Flavio Manzoni and the Ferrari Design Team of the Monza SP1 and Monza SP2.
Flavio Manzoni und das Ferrari Design Team des Monza SP1 und Monza SP2.

Flavio Manzoni, Senior Vice-President for Design; Matteo De Petris, Responsible Advanced Design;
Francesco Russo, Senior Exterior Designer; Alain Abramo, Senior Exterior Designer; Federico Acuto, Senior Exterior Designer;
Emanuel Salvatore, Responsible Virtual Modelling; Salvo Della Ventura, Responsible Advanced Virtual Modelling;
Luca Casarini, Responsible Interior Design; Fabio Massari, Senior Interior Designer; Guglielmo Galliano, Responsible Graphic & Visual

Designing Dreams
Flavio Manzoni and Ferrari Design Team

Maranello. The small Italian town in the Emilia-Romagna region is synonymous around the world with the brand and the myth that is Ferrari. This is where the dream cars of tomorrow are made, which feature technical innovations that shape our idea of the future and whose timeless language of form endures for generations. Ferrari's company premises are more than a mere ensemble of production halls, workshops and administrative buildings. Since the mid-1990s, site has transformed into a centre of modern industrial architecture. On Viale Enzo Ferrari, the campus street that bears the name of the company founder, a new dream factory that makes customers' dreams come true has emerged between the architectural gems designed by Jean Nouvel, Massimiliano Fuksas, Renzo Piano and Marco Visconti. Its name: Ferrari Centro Stile.

The dream factory

The architectural project of the new design centre was directed by the Ferrari Design Team under the guidance of architect Flavio Manzoni while the engineering project was developed in collaboration with the Design International studio of London and the Planning studio of Bologna. The building has brought together all design-related tasks and activities under one spectacular roof: a structure made from triangular glass and aluminium modules, the exterior of which is decorated with the cavallino rampante or 'prancing horse'. The geometric modules combine to form powerful and elegant areas reminiscent at their points of intersection of the dynamic lines of a Ferrari and that overlie the four-storey building like a wave.

What was once an old warehouse for prototypes is now a design dream factory. On a space of 5,000 square metres, a modern studio has been created for the designers and employees of the in-house design team in addition to a presentation room with a terrace for presenting new models and a Tailor Made area where the company's customers can configure their own customised dream car.

The Tailor Made area turns each Ferrari into a unique piece for its owner. The designers use virtual previews to show the customer his or her individually made vehicle in real time. For example, the aesthetic of the exterior and interior can be previewed on the display. With all of these possibilities for personalising their own Ferrari, customers are given a level of exclusivity that is unparalleled in the automotive sector.

The first floor of Centro Stile houses the Virtual Modelling department, where digital Ferrari models are created in 3D. Modelling involves using software to transform surface data into three-dimensional objects. Although the designers cannot touch or feel the virtual lines and edges, digital cavities and volumes with their hands, their professional eye takes

Maranello. Die kleine italienische Stadt in der Region Emilia-Romagna ist weltweit ein Synonym für die Marke und den Mythos Ferrari. Hier entstehen die Traumautos von morgen, deren technische Innovationen unsere Vorstellung von der Zukunft prägen und deren zeitlose Formensprache Generationen überdauert. Ferraris Betriebsgelände ist nicht nur ein Ensemble aus Fabrikhallen, Werkstätten und Verwaltungsgebäuden: Es hat sich seit Mitte der 1990er Jahre zu einem Zentrum moderner Industriearchitektur entwickelt. Auf dem Campus ist an der Viale Enzo Ferrari, der Straße, die den Namen des Firmengründers trägt, zwischen den architektonischen Glanzstücken von Jean Nouvel, Massimiliano Fuksas, Renzo Piano und Marco Visconti eine neue Traumfabrik entstanden, die die Wünsche der Kunden Wirklichkeit werden lässt: Ferrari Centro Stile.

Die Traumfabrik

Das architektonische Projekt für das neue Designzentrum wurde von dem Ferrari Design Team unter der Leitung des Architekten Flavio Manzoni gesteuert, während das bautechnische Projekt in Zusammenarbeit mit dem Design International Studio in London und dem Planning Studio in Bologna entwickelt wurde. Das Gebäude vereint alle designrelevanten Aufgaben- und Tätigkeitsbereiche unter einer spektakulären Dachkonstruktion: eine Struktur aus dreieckigen Glas- und Aluminiummodulen, deren Äußeres das Cavallino rampante, das sich aufbäumende Pferdchen ziert. Die geometrischen Module verbinden sich zu kraftvollen und eleganten Flächen, die dort, wo sie aufeinandertreffen, an die dynamischen Linien eines Ferrari erinnern und sich wie eine Welle über das vierstöckige Gebäude legen.

Was früher ein altes Lager für Prototypen war, ist heute eine Traumfabrik des Designs. Auf 5.000 m² Fläche ist ein modernes Studio für die Designer und Mitarbeiter des In-house Design Teams entstanden, ein Präsentationsraum mit Terrasse für die Vorstellung neuer Modelle und ein „Tailor Made"-Bereich, welcher den Kunden des Unternehmens erlaubt, ihr Traumauto individuell ausstatten zu lassen.

Im „Tailor Made"-Bereich wird jeder Ferrari zu einem Unikat für seinen Besitzer. In virtuellen Vorschauen präsentieren die Designer dem Kunden sein individuell gefertigtes Fahrzeug in Echtzeit. So lässt sich die Ästhetik des Exterieurs und Interieurs bereits am Monitor beurteilen. Mit all diesen Möglichkeiten zur persönlichen Gestaltung des eigenen Ferraris erhalten die Kunden einen Grad an Exklusivität, der in der Automobilbranche seinesgleichen sucht.

Auf der ersten Etage des Centro Stile befindet sich das Virtual Modelling. Hier entstehen digitale Ferrari-Modelle in 3D. Bei der Modellierung werden Daten der Oberflächen mithilfe von Software in dreidimensionale

in these features and 'touches' the surface with its convex and concave forms. This creative interplay with beauty, proportions, contrasts and colour hues is based on the designers' constantly alternating view of the details and the contours of the vehicle.

But alongside state-of-the-art technology, there is still a need for craftsmanship. That's because, in addition to sketches and computer models, Ferrari models are produced by hand. Flavio Manzoni places special emphasis on modelling, where scale models and original-size models are created by digitally controlled milling machines and are formed by a team of experienced artists before the meticulous manual finish. Flavio Manzoni brought the clay modelling approach from Germany in 2010. Particularly in the initial phase of the newly formed design team, Manzoni and his staff literally created new models with their hands. At that time, the Head of Design and his team worked like artists to connect surfaces with each other, to better assess forms and proportions and to refine the models step by step.

Like in many other design studios and in-house design teams, confidentiality was another top priority alongside creativity. Consequently, the geometric elements of the roof construction serve not only as an eye-catching feature but also as a privacy screen. The second skin of the roof construction works like a protective shield that allows daylight through while keeping out unwanted eyes. On the second floor of Centro Stile, which includes a terrace and a large conference and presentation room with a high-resolution LED wall, newly designed models can thus be presented in natural lighting conditions. Not only does Centro Stile make the professional work of the design team easier and more pleasant, it also makes it more effective and efficient for the company, as the draft and development phases are significantly shorter and it's possible to agree on improvements to the models with the engineers right up to the very last moment.

Start-up and warm-up

More than 100 designers work in the Centro Stile building today, but this was not always the case. When Flavio Manzoni was appointed Senior Vice-President for Design at Ferrari in 2010, there were just five people in a small team that lacked not only a structure but also tools and above all else a vision of the future of the Ferrari brand. When the decision was taken to create a dedicated in-house design team, Flavio Manzoni shared his vision with the small group of staff: "I saw their eyes light up, but nobody really believed in it," Flavio Manzoni remembers. "Everyone thought 'Manzoni is a dreamer'." Previously, the design activities were organised in collaboration with external partners such as Pininfarina.

Objekte verwandelt. Auch wenn die Designer die virtuellen Linien und Kanten, die digitalen Hohlräume und Volumen nicht mit den Händen berühren und ertasten können, fährt ihr professionelles Auge an ihnen entlang und berührt die Oberfläche aus konvexen und konkaven Formen. Das gestalterische Spiel mit der Schönheit, den Proportionen, den Kontrasten und Farbnuancen basiert auf dem ständig wechselnden Blick der Designer zwischen den Details und den Konturen des Autos.

Neben neuester Technologie ist aber nach wie vor handwerkliches Können gefragt. Denn neben Skizzen und Computermodellen werden Ferrari-Modelle von Hand gefertigt. Ein besonderes Augenmerk legt Flavio Manzoni auf den Modellbau, wo maßstabsgetreue Modelle und solche in Originalgröße von digital gesteuerten Fräsmaschinen entstehen und von einem Team aus erfahrenen Künstlern geformt werden, bevor dann das Finish sorgfältig von Hand erfolgt. Flavio Manzoni hat das Clay Modelling 2010 aus Deutschland mitgebracht. Insbesondere in der Anfangsphase des neu gebildeten Designteams formen Manzoni und seine Mitarbeiter neue Modelle buchstäblich mit ihren Händen. Der Designchef und sein Team arbeiten zu dieser Zeit wie Künstler, um Oberflächen miteinander zu verbinden, die Formen und Proportionen besser beurteilen zu können und die Modelle Schritt für Schritt weiterzuentwickeln.

Wie bei vielen anderen Designstudios und In-house Design Teams steht mit der Kreativität auch die Diskretion an oberster Stelle. Die geometrischen Elemente der Dachkonstruktion sind daher nicht nur Blickfang, sondern auch Blickschutz. Die zweite Haut der Dachkonstruktion funktioniert wie ein Schutzschild, der zwar Tageslicht hineinlässt, aber ungewünschte Blicke abhält. So können auf der zweiten Ebene des Centro Stile, wo sich eine Terrasse und ein großer Konferenz- und Präsentationsraum mit einer hochauflösenden LED-Wand befinden, neu konzipierte Modelle bei natürlichem Licht präsentiert werden. Das Centro Stile macht die professionelle Arbeit nicht nur für das Designteam angenehmer und leichter, sondern auch für das Unternehmen effektiver und effizienter, da sich die Entwurfs- und Entwicklungsphasen deutlich verkürzen und man in Abstimmung mit den Ingenieuren noch bis zur letzten Minute Verbesserungen an den Modellen vornehmen kann.

Start-up und Warm-up

In den Räumen des Centro Stile arbeiten heute mehr als 100 Designer. Das war nicht immer so. Als Flavio Manzoni im Jahr 2010 zum Senior Vice-President for Design bei Ferrari ernannt wird, bilden gerade einmal fünf Personen ein kleines Team, dem es nicht nur an Struktur fehlt, sondern auch an Werkzeugen, vor allem aber an einer Vorstellung von der Zukunft der Marke Ferrari. Als die Entscheidung fällt, ein eigenes In-house Design Team aufzubauen, teilt Flavio Manzoni mit der kleinen Gruppe von Mitarbeitern seine Vision: „Ich sah das Leuchten in ihren Augen, aber niemand glaubte wirklich daran", erinnert sich Flavio Manzoni. „Jeder dachte: Manzoni ist ein Träumer." Bisher waren Designaktivitäten in Zusammenarbeit mit externen Partnern wie Pininfarina organisiert worden.

The iconic shape of the Ferrari FXX K inspired by aircraft. The perfect fusion of form and function.
Von Flugzeugen inspirierte ikonische Form des Ferrari FXX K. Die perfekte Verschmelzung von Form und Funktion.

When Manzoni became Senior Vice-President for Design at Ferrari in 2010, an old storehouse that housed Ferrari prototypes initially had to be used as a temporary Design Center. And while Manzoni had to improvise on a daily basis, he worked tirelessly on designs for new models. Behind the scenes, he was interviewing hundreds of designers to find out who would fit in his team and be able to understand, reinterpret and transform the Ferrari brand and values.

In the beginning, it was difficult for Manzoni to judge who really understood the Ferrari brand and also fit in the team in terms of their social skills and attitudes. Manzoni quickly noticed that experience does not always pay off. Anyone who wanted to work as a designer for Ferrari would have to be able to approach the brand creatively without preconceptions and be willing to explore Ferrari's brand values again and again in a team with other designers, engineers and marketing experts. Too much experience could sometimes be a disadvantage in this regard. "It was like working in a start-up." That's how Manzoni describes the unimaginable dynamism of this new departure.

Als Manzoni 2010 Senior Vice-President for Design bei Ferrari wird, muss zunächst ein altes Lagerhaus, das Ferraris Prototypen beherbergt, als provisorisches Design Center genutzt werden. Und während Manzoni tagtäglich improvisieren muss, arbeitet er unermüdlich an Entwürfen für neue Modelle. Im Hintergrund führt er Hunderte von Bewerbungsgesprächen mit Designern, um herauszufinden, wer in sein Team passt und in der Lage sein könnte, die Marke und die Werte von Ferrari zu verstehen, sie neu zu interpretieren und zu transformieren.

Zu Beginn ist es für Manzoni schwierig zu beurteilen, wer die Marke Ferrari wirklich versteht und auch mit Blick auf seine sozialen Fähigkeiten und seine Lebenseinstellung ins Team passt. Manzoni merkt schnell, dass sich Erfahrung nicht immer auszahlt. Wer als Designer für Ferrari arbeiten will, muss in der Lage sein, sich auf die Marke einzulassen, und bereit sein, sich immer wieder aufs Neue kreativ und in einem Team mit anderen Designern, Ingenieuren und Marketingexperten mit den Werten, die Ferrari verkörpert, auseinanderzusetzen. Zu viel Erfahrung kann da bisweilen auch hinderlich sein. „Es herrschten Bedingungen wie in einem Start-up-Unternehmen", beschreibt Manzoni die unvorstellbare Dynamik des Neuanfangs.

Ferrari LaFerrari. The balance between organic form and the beauty of complexity.
Ferrari LaFerrari. Die Balance zwischen organischer Form und komplexer Schönheit.

The essence of the brand

The first model developed, designed and built entirely in-house was the LaFerrari, which was designed by the Ferrari Design Team in close cooperation with the technical and development department. The model won a Red Dot in 2015. It was the result of a sporting competition with Pininfarina, where the Ferrari Design Team ultimately emerged as the winner.

The profile of the new vehicle dipped down prominently at the nose and featured a low hood. The nose was reminiscent of the legendary shapes of the Ferrari sports prototypes from the 1960s, for example the "sharknose" of the Ferrari 156. There was a conceptual link between the two, but no formal connection. Of course Manzoni and his design team felt a loyalty to the brand and to Ferrari's mythical aura, but they didn't simply repeat individual elements nostalgically. For them, retro design was an expression of a lack of courage and creativity. With the Ferrari LaFerrari, the designers succeeded in recalling and reinterpreting milestones in the company and design history. Not only did the concave and convex surfaces provide a dramatic tension, they also ensured outstanding wind resistance and downforce values.

Manzoni and his design team have frequently been inspired by ideas and shapes from art and culture, for example the monumental sculptures and installations of the Indian-born British artist Anish Kapoor, whose Marsyas from 2002 was on display in the Turbine Hall of the Tate Modern in London. Like Anish Kapoor, Flavio Manzoni endeavours in his designs to answer the question of how to translate performance-based engineering

Die Essenz der Marke

Das erste Modell, das ausschließlich in-house entwickelt, gestaltet und gebaut wird, ist der LaFerrari, der in enger Zusammenarbeit des Ferrari Design Teams mit der Technik- und Entwicklungsabteilung entworfen wird. 2015 wird er mit dem Red Dot ausgezeichnet. Er geht aus einem sportlichen Wettbewerb mit Pininfarina hervor, bei dem das Ferrari Design Team am Ende als Sieger dasteht.

Im Profil hat das neue Fahrzeug eine scharf nach unten verlaufende Nase und eine tief sitzende Motorhaube. Die Nase erinnert an die legendären Formen der Ferrari Sport-Prototypen der 1960er Jahre, etwa an die „Haifischnase" des Ferrari 156. Zwischen beiden gibt es eine konzeptionelle, aber keine formale Verbindung. Natürlich fühlen sich Manzoni und sein Designteam der Marke und dem Mythos Ferrari verpflichtet, aber sie wiederholen nicht einfach einzelne Elemente in nostalgischer Weise. Für sie ist Retrodesign ein Ausdruck fehlenden Mutes und mangelnder Kreativität. Mit dem Ferrari LaFerrari gelingt es den Designern, Meilensteine der Unternehmens- und Designgeschichte in Erinnerung zu rufen und sie neu zu interpretieren. Die konkaven und konvexen Oberflächen sorgen nicht nur für eine wechselvolle Spannung, sie sorgen auch für herausragende Luftwiderstands- und Abtriebswerte.

Inspiriert werden Manzoni und sein Designteam nicht selten durch Ideen und Formen der Kunst und Kultur, wie etwa durch die monumentalen Skulpturen und Installationen des indisch-britischen Künstlers Anish Kapoor, dessen Marsyas aus dem Jahr 2002 in der Turbinenhalle der Tate Modern in London zu sehen war. Ähnlich wie Anish Kapoor geht

language into an aesthetic body language. "You can only design a Ferrari if you know what's under the surface." That's how Manzoni describes the interplay between technical complexity and aesthetic design.

Manzoni describes the design process as follows: "Designing a new car requires sensitivity, imagination, abstract thought and the ability to combine elements that do not appear to belong together, at least not intuitively." Ferrari endeavours to constantly redefine the limits of technology and design and to gradually push these boundaries towards the future without losing sight of the brand and its values. "Every Ferrari stands for innovation, beauty and driving thrill," says Manzoni, adding that "every model has to embody the essence of the brand."

Naturally, we always have to bear in mind the difference between a Gran Turismo and a supercar when considering the design of Ferrari models. While the Gran Turismo wins fans through its sporting elegance and luxury, a supercar that conveys the adrenaline of the racetrack calls for a higher degree of complexity. Its form hinges on the technical data and on performance. Yet what both of these models share is the idea "that a Ferrari always stems from a dream," says Flavio Manzoni.

One key difference between Ferrari and other manufacturers in automotive design is that the Italian sports car manufacturer does not feature a rhetorical evolution of form. Neither does Ferrari pursue the strategy adopted by other manufacturers that make the models belong to the brand by means of a similarity with other members of the brand family. Although there are lines that connect back to tradition, these are never for stylistic reasons. The focus is on state-of-the-art sports car technology, formal aestheticism and driving thrill. This is also exemplified by the new "Icona" model segment, the design of which draws inspiration from the open Barchettas from the 1950s that Scuderia Ferrari raced in at the time, in particular the 166 MM, but also the 750 Monza and the 860 Monza. The new limited production Monza SP1 and Monza SP2 models with their minimalistic silhouettes are the vanguard in this new series of design icons.

The Monza SP1, which won the Red Dot: Best of the Best in 2019, is designed as a single seater, while the Monza SP2 seats two. The carbon bodywork reduces the weight of the two vehicles to 1,500 kg each. The V12 6.5-litre engine has 810 hp and in both models accelerates from 0 to 100 in 2.9 seconds, reaching 200 km/h just 5 seconds later. Because neither model has a windscreen for the driver, the panelling includes a type of "bypass" that diverts the airflow away from the driver and creates a kind of "virtual windscreen" for the driver. Ferrari has registered a patent for this innovation. The two Monza models are an excellent example of how technology and design, innovation and aesthetics can all be channelled into a unique driving experience. This allows the driver to experience a feeling of speed that is otherwise known only to Formula 1 race drivers.

Flavio Manzoni bei seinen Entwürfen der Frage nach, wie eine leistungsorientierte Ingenieursprache in eine ästhetische Körpersprache umgeformt werden kann. „Man kann einen Ferrari nur gestalten, wenn man weiß, was unter der Oberfläche stattfindet", beschreibt Manzoni das Zusammenspiel von technischer Komplexität und ästhetischer Formgebung.

„Ein neues Auto zu gestalten, erfordert Einfühlungsvermögen, Vorstellungskraft, abstraktes Denken und die Fähigkeit, Elemente zu verbinden, die scheinbar nicht zusammengehören, zumindest nicht auf den ersten Blick", beschreibt Manzoni den Designprozess. Ferrari versucht, die Grenzen der Technik und Gestaltung immer wieder neu zu bestimmen und Schritt für Schritt in Richtung Zukunft zu verschieben, ohne die Marke und ihre Werte aus dem Auge zu verlieren. „Jeder Ferrari steht für Innovation, Schönheit und Fahrleidenschaft", sagt Manzoni und ergänzt, dass „jedes Modell die Essenz der Marke verkörpern muss."

Natürlich muss man bei der Gestaltung von Ferrari-Modellen immer auch den Unterschied zwischen einem Gran Turismo und einem Supersportwagen im Blick behalten. Während der Gran Turismo durch sportliche Eleganz und luxuriösen Komfort begeistert, erfordert ein Supersportwagen, der das Adrenalin der Rennstrecke versprüht, eine höhere Komplexität. Seine Form wird entscheidend von den technischen Daten und der Leistungsfähigkeit geprägt. Aber beide vereint, „dass ein Ferrari immer aus einem Traum entsteht", sagt Flavio Manzoni.

Ein wesentlicher Unterschied zwischen Ferrari und anderen Herstellern im Automobildesign besteht darin, dass es beim italienischen Sportwagenhersteller keine rhetorische Evolution der Form gibt. Ferrari folgt auch nicht der Strategie anderer Hersteller, die Markenzugehörigkeit der Modelle nach dem Vorbild von Familienähnlichkeit zu pflegen. Obgleich es Verbindungslinien zur Tradition gibt, werden diese niemals aus stilistischen Gründen gezogen. Modernste Sportwagentechnik, die Ästhetik der Form und die Fahrleidenschaft stehen im Vordergrund. So auch im neuen Modellsegment „Icona", dessen Design von den offenen Barchettas der 1950er Jahre inspiriert wurde, mit denen die Scuderia Ferrari damals an den Start ging, insbesondere von dem 166 MM, aber auch dem 750 Monza und dem 860 Monza. Die neuen Sondermodelle Monza SP1 und Monza SP2 mit ihren minimalistischen Silhouetten bilden den Auftakt zu dieser neuen Serie von Designikonen.

Der Monza SP1, im Jahr 2019 mit dem Red Dot: Best of the Best ausgezeichnet, ist als Einsitzer konzipiert, im Monza SP2 finden zwei Personen Platz. Die Karosserie aus Carbon drückt das Gewicht der beiden Fahrzeuge auf jeweils 1.500 kg. Der V12-Motor mit 6,5 Litern Hubraum leistet 810 PS und beschleunigt die beiden Fahrzeuge in 2,9 Sekunden aus dem Stand auf Tempo 100, nur 5 Sekunden später ist Tempo 200 erreicht. Da beiden Modellen eine Windschutzscheibe für den Fahrer fehlt, ist in der Verkleidung eine Art „Bypass" eingearbeitet, der den anströmenden Fahrtwind umlenkt und eine „virtuelle Windschutzscheibe" für den Fahrer erzeugt. Ferrari hat auf diese Innovation ein Patent angemeldet. Die beiden Monza-Modelle sind ein gelungenes Beispiel dafür, wie Technik und Design, Innovation und Ästhetik auf ein einzigartiges Fahrerlebnis ausgerichtet sind. So kommt der Fahrer in den Genuss eines Geschwindigkeitsgefühls, wie es sonst nur Formel-1-Fahrer erleben.

Designing values

The dream figures recorded by the sports cars from Maranello aren't limited to the race track – the company is also doing very well in terms of its profitability and share price and market value. The Italian car maker is the most profitable company in the automotive industry and the clear leader amongst premium and luxury car manufacturers. Ferrari understands better than any other company how to make luxury sports cars objects of desire by consistently focusing on the core of the brand and pursuing the strategy of always building one car less than the market requires. If ever any proof were needed that "Good design is good business," as former IBM President Thomas Watson Jr. once said, then Ferrari has delivered that proof impressively in recent years.

The models designed by Flavio Manzoni and the Ferrari Design Team won 14 awards in the Red Dot Design Award in the years 2015 to 2019 alone. Ferrari is the first car manufacturer in the history of the competition to win the top distinction five times in a row – for the Ferrari models FXX-K, 488 GTB, J50, Portofino and Monza SP1. Thanks to this achievement, the brand now also leads the Red Dot Ranking in the Automotive Design category for the first time.

By establishing a Ferrari in-house design team as well as Centro Stile in Maranello and the Ferrari models created under his leadership, Flavio Manzoni has succeeded in his pioneering work. He has created an open and trusting culture of communication, which is the basis for shared success. The further the team progresses together, the better the cars become.

Manzoni likes to compare his team to a jazz ensemble: everyone has his or her own personal strengths and individual skill set, but each person is willing to contribute his or her creativity and social skills to a shared objective and the future of the brand. As a result, the long journey from a blank sheet of paper to a finished car is a magical experience for Manzoni every single time. When a new idea is born and the first strokes and lines put an ideal scenario to paper, he dreams that this ideal and the creative fire that fanned the ideal can permeate the entire project – right through to the finished vehicle. And every new car, every new Ferrari should intuitively express the innovation and the emotion, the values and the philosophy of Ferrari. It has to be a moving sculpture that combines art and science, technology and design into something new and propels Ferrari's mythical aura into the future.

As we know, myths are stories with a significance based on uniquely lived lives that still fascinate us today. Outstanding products follow a similar pattern. They are visionary, stand out from the rest and tell us their story. Places can also carry this myth within them. Maranello is such a place.

Werte gestalten

Traumhafte Werte erzielen die Sportwagen aus Maranello nicht nur auf der Rennstrecke, traumhafte Werte erzielt das Unternehmen auch mit Blick auf die Profitabilität und seine Börsen- und Markenwerte. Der italienische Automobilhersteller ist das profitabelste Unternehmen der Autobranche und mit Abstand der Spitzenreiter unter den Premium- und Luxusherstellern. Kein anderes Unternehmen versteht es besser, luxuriöse Sportwagen zu Objekten der Begierde zu machen, indem man sich konsequent am Markenkern orientiert und der Strategie folgt, immer ein Auto weniger zu bauen, als der Markt verlangt. Wenn die Aussage „Good design is good business" des früheren IBM-Präsidenten, Thomas Watson Jr., noch irgendeines Beweises bedurft hätte, dann hat Ferrari ihn in den zurückliegenden Jahren auf eindrucksvolle Art und Weise geliefert.

Allein in den Jahren 2015–2019 werden die von Flavio Manzoni und dem Ferrari Design Team entworfenen Modelle vierzehn Mal im Red Dot Design Award ausgezeichnet. Ein Novum in der Geschichte des Wettbewerbs: Ferrari ist es als erstem Automobilhersteller gelungen, die höchste Auszeichnung fünf Mal in Folge zu gewinnen – für die Ferrari-Modelle FXX-K, 488 GTB, J50, Portofino und Monza SP1. Mit dieser Leistung führt die Marke erstmals auch das Red Dot Ranking im Automotive Design an.

Mit dem Aufbau eines Ferrari In-house Design Teams, dem Centro Stile in Maranello und den Ferrari-Modellen, die unter seiner Federführung entstanden sind, ist Flavio Manzoni eine Pionierleistung gelungen. Er hat eine offene und vertrauensvolle Kommunikationskultur geschaffen, die die Basis für den gemeinsamen Erfolg ist. Und je weiter das Team gemeinsam voranschreitet, desto besser werden die Autos.

Manzoni vergleicht sein Team gerne mit einem Jazzensemble: Jeder hat seine persönlichen Stärken und sein individuelles Qualifikationsprofil, aber jeder von ihnen ist bereit, seine Kreativität und seine sozialen Fähigkeiten für ein gemeinsames Ziel und die Zukunft der Marke einzubringen. Daher ist der lange Weg vom leeren Blatt Papier zum fertigen Auto für Manzoni jedes Mal und immer wieder ein magisches Ereignis. Wenn eine neue Idee geboren wird und die ersten Striche und Linien eine Idealvorstellung aufs Papier bringen, dann träumt er davon, dass dieses Ideal und das kreative Feuer, das dieses Ideal entfacht hat, das gesamte Projekt durchdringen kann – bis zum fertigen Auto. Und jedes neue Auto, jeder neue Ferrari sollte die Innovation und die Emotion, die Werte und die Philosophie von Ferrari wie selbstverständlich zum Ausdruck bringen. Es muss sich um eine Skulptur in Bewegung handeln, die Wissenschaft und Kunst, Technik und Design zu etwas Neuem verbindet und den Mythos Ferrari in die Zukunft trägt.

Mythen sind bekanntlich Erzählungen, deren Bedeutung auf einzigartigen Lebensgeschichten basiert, die uns heute noch faszinieren. Herausragende Produkte folgen einem ähnlichen Muster. Sie sind visionär, ragen aus der Masse heraus und erzählen uns ihre Geschichte. Auch Orte können diesen Mythos in sich tragen. Maranello ist so ein Ort.

Ferrari's premises are not just an ensemble of factory buildings, workshops and administrative buildings. It is also a center of modern industrial architecture.
Ferraris Betriebsgelände ist nicht nur ein Ensemble aus Fabrikhallen, Werkstätten und Verwaltungsgebäuden: Es ist auch ein Zentrum moderner Industriearchitektur.

Exceeding expectations
Interview with Flavio Manzoni
Senior Vice-President for Design at Ferrari

Flavio Manzoni was born in Sardinia in 1965 and studied architecture with a specialisation in industrial design at the University of Florence, where he graduated in 1993 under Professor Roberto Segoni. His first teacher, however, was his father, who taught him to draw and awakened in him a passion for art, architecture and design. He has been impressed by the approach of the Italian design masters: Bruno Munari, Joe Colombo, Achille Castiglioni, Marco Zanuso, Enzo Mari. In particular, he was fascinated by their attitude to exploring new materials and shapes, by their way of conceiving everyday objects and tools, and by the iconic power of their products. Manzoni's interdisciplinary creativity has accompanied him throughout his career in automotive design.

After graduating, he began his professional career at Lancia in Turin. In 1999, he moved to Seat in Barcelona as the Head of Interior Design before returning to Lancia as Design Director in 2001. In 2004, he took up the role of Design Director for Fiat, Lancia and LCV. From 2007 to 2010, he was Director of Creative Design in the Volkswagen Group, where he designed many of the most recent Škoda, Bentley, Bugatti and Volkswagen models and redefined the aesthetic of those brands.

Manzoni has been Senior Vice-President for Design at Ferrari since 2010. Prof. Dr. Peter Zec and Burkhard Jacob spoke with him in Maranello about design and Ferrari's brand values.

Mr. Manzoni, before joining Ferrari in 2010, you had already worked as a designer for many different automotive brands. Regardless of where and for whom you have already worked, what do you think should be important for a designer?

That's an important question, because there is one aspect that many designers fail to consider in their work, and that's respect for the brand. I think that every designer should first try to understand and interpret the brand rather than expressing himself or herself.

Flavio Manzoni, geboren 1965 auf Sardinien, studierte Architektur mit Spezialisierung auf Industriedesign an der Universität Florenz, wo er 1993 seinen Abschluss bei Professor Roberto Segoni machte. Sein erster Lehrer war indes sein Vater, von dem er das Zeichnen lernte und der in ihm die Leidenschaft für Kunst, Architektur und Design weckte. Er war beeindruckt vom Ansatz der italienischen Meister des Designs: Bruno Munari, Joe Colombo, Achille Castiglioni, Marco Zanuso und Enzo Mari. Insbesondere ihre Einstellung gegenüber neuen Materialien und Formen, ihre Art, alltägliche Gegenstände und Werkzeuge zu konzipieren, sowie die ikonische Kraft ihrer Produkte haben ihn fasziniert. Manzonis fachübergreifende Kreativität hat ihn über seine gesamte Karriere im Automobildesign begleitet.

Nach dem Studium begann Flavio Manzoni seine Laufbahn zunächst bei Lancia in Turin. Im Jahr 1999 wechselte er als Leiter Interior Design zu Seat nach Barcelona und kehrte 2001 als Design Director zu Lancia zurück. Ab 2004 übernahm er die Position des Design Directors von Fiat, Lancia und LCV. Von 2007 bis 2010 war er Director of Creative Design im Volkswagen-Konzern, wo er viele der jüngsten Autos von Škoda, Bentley, Bugatti und Volkswagen entwarf und die Ästhetik dieser Marken neu definierte.

Seit 2010 ist Manzoni Senior Vice-President for Design bei Ferrari. Prof. Dr. Peter Zec und Burkhard Jacob sprachen mit ihm in Maranello über das Design und die Markenwerte von Ferrari.

Herr Manzoni, bevor Sie 2010 zu Ferrari kamen, haben Sie als Designer bereits für viele verschiedene Automobilmarken gearbeitet. Unabhängig davon, wo und für wen Sie bereits gearbeitet haben: Was sollte aus Ihrer Sicht für einen Designer von Bedeutung sein?

Das ist eine wichtige Frage, denn es gibt einen Aspekt, den längst nicht alle Designer bei ihrer Arbeit berücksichtigen: Das ist der Respekt vor der Marke. Ich denke, dass jeder Designer zuerst versuchen sollte, die Marke zu verstehen und zu interpretieren und nicht sich selbst auszudrücken.

That's pretty surprising to hear, because it sounds very German!

Maybe it's what I learned during my time in Germany. I think it's important for a designer to experience the brand, to feel it and breathe it in, to absorb it and gauge and understand it better without being influenced by the typical design features that may have become embedded in the memory of a designer who has been in the profession for a long time. Together with my team, I try to understand, interpret and transform the Ferrari brand.

And how would you describe the Ferrari brand, its DNA?

There's a short and simple answer to that question. The Ferrari brand is based on three elements: innovation, driving thrill and beauty. These elements are key to understanding the brand. If one of the three is missing, then it's not a Ferrari.

So how do you marry these three aspects of innovation, driving enthusiasm and beauty?

If we think about very complex products like aircraft or cars, their form is heavily informed by the technical and aerodynamic conditions. The Concorde and the Ferrari FXX-K are good examples of this. They are shaped by hundreds of technical requirements, and yet there has always been and will always be a way to make these objects more beautiful without compromising on performance.

Sie sehen uns einigermaßen überrascht, denn das klingt sehr deutsch!

Vielleicht habe ich es während meiner Zeit in Deutschland gelernt. Ich denke, es ist wichtig für einen Designer, die Marke zu erleben, sie zu spüren, einzuatmen und zu absorbieren, um sie besser beurteilen und verstehen zu können, ohne dabei von den typischen Designmerkmalen beeinflusst zu werden, die sich nach einer langen Karriere vielleicht ins Gedächtnis eingebrannt haben. Zusammen mit meinem Team versuche ich, die Marke Ferrari zu verstehen, zu interpretieren und zu transformieren.

Wie würden Sie denn die Marke Ferrari, ihre DNA beschreiben?

Nun, darauf gibt es eine ebenso einfache wie kurze Antwort. Die Marke Ferrari basiert auf drei Elementen: Innovation, Fahrleidenschaft und Schönheit. Sie sind wesentlich für das Verständnis. Fehlt einer dieser drei Faktoren, ist es kein Ferrari.

Wie bringen Sie denn den Dreiklang aus Innovation, Fahrbegeisterung und Schönheit in Einklang?

Wenn wir über sehr komplexe Produkte wie Flugzeuge oder Autos nachdenken, dann wird deren Form stark von den technischen und aerodynamischen Bedingungen bestimmt. Die Concorde und der Ferrari FXX-K sind gute Beispiele dafür. Sie werden von Hunderten technischer Anforderungen bestimmt, und doch hat es und wird es immer einen Weg geben, diese Objekte schöner zu machen, ohne dass sie an Leistung verlieren.

"Every sketch already sets out a certain idea on paper."

„Mit jeder Skizze hält man bereits eine bestimmte Idee auf Papier fest."

Flavio Manzoni – Senior Vice-President for Design

This would mean that form does not necessarily follow function?

The solution has to lie in combining creativity with technology and art with science. In principle, then, form does follow function, but there will always be scope for creativity and aesthetics.

How do you manage to bridge the gap between the past and the future, between tradition and innovation?

Each new Ferrari opens up a whole new chapter and needs its own, independent form. But that doesn't mean our design team suddenly goes crazy and makes nonsensical design suggestions or interprets the product in an absurd way. There are certainly language codes that belong to the Ferrari brand and create a link between the past and the future. However, this is an unspoken, conceptual link rather than a repetition of stylistic features.

If the design of a new Ferrari means the start of a whole new design project, is it even possible to speak of a design language at Ferrari?

Absolutely. A design language does exist, but we do not pursue the strategy adopted by other car manufacturers that make their models belong to the brand by means of a similarity with other members of the brand family. We avoid this déjà vu effect. A new Ferrari always embodies our brand values, but it does not repeat any stylistic elements. That doesn't make any sense for Ferrari.

Die Form muss also nicht automatisch der Funktion folgen?

Die Lösung kann nur in der Verbindung von Kreativität und Technik, von Kunst und Wissenschaft liegen. Im Prinzip folgt die Form also der Funktion, aber es wird immer auch Raum für Kreativität und Ästhetik geben.

Wie gelingt Ihnen dann der Brückenschlag zwischen Vergangenheit und Zukunft, zwischen Tradition und Innovation?

Jeder neue Ferrari schlägt ein neues Kapitel auf und bedarf einer eigenständigen Form. Das bedeutet aber nicht, dass unser Designteam plötzlich verrücktspielt und unsinnige Gestaltungsvorschläge oder absurde Interpretationen macht. Es gibt durchaus Sprachcodes, die zur Marke Ferrari gehören und eine Verbindung zwischen Vergangenheit und Zukunft herstellen. Dies ist aber ein gedanklicher, konzeptioneller Zusammenhang, keine Wiederholung von stilistischen Merkmalen.

Wenn die Gestaltung eines neuen Ferrari gleichbedeutend mit dem Start eines neuen Designprojektes ist, lässt sich denn dann überhaupt von einer Designsprache bei Ferrari sprechen?

Absolut. Es gibt eine Designsprache. Wir folgen aber nicht der Strategie anderer Automobilhersteller, die die Markenzugehörigkeit ihrer Modelle nach dem Vorbild von Familienähnlichkeit pflegen. Wir vermeiden einen Déjà-vu-Effekt. Ein neuer Ferrari verkörpert immer unsere Markenwerte, aber er wiederholt keine stilistischen Elemente. Das macht für Ferrari keinen Sinn.

To what extent then do you even monitor the competition in your industry or compare Ferrari with other brands?

We don't compare ourselves with other brands. That's something we don't do. If we simply wanted to be different from the others, we would only have to add various distinctive elements to the interior or exterior of the car. But that's not Ferrari's approach. Otherwise I would contradict our principles and our understanding of the brand.

Can you describe to us how you and your team arrive at creative and aesthetic solutions?

The solution can either stem from the intuition of one individual or from a brainstorming session with the team. It's especially important to talk to the engineers. When we design a new Ferrari, we don't start with a blank sheet of paper, a stylistic idea or an existing form. Instead, we start with technical questions and content.

How do you start off a new project? Do you give your team a briefing, or do you use draft drawings to provide a certain direction?

Normally, I do not produce any draft drawings before my staff at the start of a new project, as I don't want to restrict the team's creativity. Because every sketch

Inwiefern beobachten Sie denn überhaupt die Konkurrenz in Ihrer Branche oder vergleichen Ferrari mit anderen Marken?

Wir vergleichen uns nicht mit anderen Marken. Das machen wir nicht. Wollten wir einfach nur anders sein als die anderen, müssten wir nur verschiedene, sich unterscheidende Elemente im oder am Auto hinzufügen. Dies ist aber nicht der Ansatz von Ferrari. Ansonsten würde ich unseren Grundsätzen und unserem Markenverständnis widersprechen.

Können Sie uns denn beschreiben, wie Sie und Ihr Team zu kreativen und ästhetischen Lösungen gelangen?

Die Lösung kann entweder in der Intuition eines Einzelnen liegen oder aus einem Brainstorming des Teams hervorgehen. Insbesondere das Gespräch mit Ingenieuren ist wichtig. Wenn wir einen neuen Ferrari gestalten, dann beginnen wir also nicht mit einem leeren Blatt Papier, einer stilistischen Idee oder einer bereits existierenden Form, sondern mit technischen Fragen und Inhalten.

Wie starten Sie in ein neues Projekt? Geben Sie Ihrem Team ein Briefing oder geben Sie durch Entwurfszeichnungen eine bestimmte Richtung vor?

Normalerweise mache ich zu Beginn eines neuen Projektes keine Entwurfszeichnungen vor meinen Mitarbeitern, weil ich die Kreativität des Teams nicht

"Every designer should first try to understand and interpret the brand."

„Jeder Designer sollte zuerst versuchen, die Marke zu verstehen und zu interpretieren."

Flavio Manzoni – Senior Vice-President for Design

already sets out a certain idea on paper. But certainly I sketch a lot, in my office, or during the development process, when it is necessary to converge and finalise ideas.

Is there internal competition in the team when designing a new model?

That's possible. But if there is internal competition, it is always fair and in good spirit. It's important to understand that the personal background and qualifications of each individual are different. That's why the composition of a team changes depending on the project.

What criteria do you use when deciding how to put a team together?

It depends on the project, the technical requirements and the timing. For example, we developed an Advanced Design Department that mainly comprises young designers and artists. Their task is to imagine the future of Ferrari and to sketch it up, far removed from technical specifications or economic restraints. They have to develop visionary ideas without any mental pressure, because the way in which they imagine the future is based on the conditions that we create here and the experiences they have here.

einschränken möchte. Denn mit jeder Skizze hält man bereits eine bestimmte Idee auf Papier fest. Aber ich fertige viele Skizzen in meinem Büro oder während des Entwicklungsprozesses an, wenn es darum geht, Ideen zusammenzuführen und zu finalisieren.

Gibt es denn innerhalb des Teams einen internen Wettbewerb, wenn es um die Gestaltung eines neuen Modells geht?

Das ist möglich. Aber wenn es einen internen Wettbewerb gibt, dann ist er immer fair und sportlich. Es ist wichtig zu verstehen, dass der persönliche Hintergrund und die Qualifikation jedes Einzelnen unterschiedlich sind. Deshalb ändert sich je nach Projekt die Zusammensetzung eines Teams.

Nach welchen Kriterien entscheiden Sie über die Zusammensetzung eines Teams?

Es hängt vom Projekt ab, den technischen Anforderungen und dem Zeitpunkt. Wir haben beispielsweise ein Advanced Design Department ins Leben gerufen, das im Wesentlichen aus jungen Designern und Künstlern besteht. Ihre Aufgabe ist es, sich die Zukunft von Ferrari vorzustellen und sie zu skizzieren, weit entfernt von technischen Vorgaben oder ökonomischen Bedingungen. Sie sollen visionäre Ideen entwickeln ohne mentalen Druck, denn die Art und Weise, wie sie sich die Zukunft vorstellen, basiert auf den Bedingungen, die wir hier schaffen, und den Erfahrungen, die sie hier machen.

You seem to have a very broad understanding of design and see it as more than just the task of finding an aesthetic form for a technical function.

In my view, design is a communicative and cultural process that culminates not just in a car but in a cultural object. I have developed this deeper understanding of design during my time at Ferrari.

If, as you say, design is a cultural process, is a Ferrari more than just a car?

A Ferrari is not just a car, it's an object of desire. We say that it's a dream, a dynamic sculpture. Something that goes far beyond a car. Maybe I'm not a typical car designer in this respect. I have always pursued a multidisciplinary approach, and I try to develop a much broader view of design, particularly automotive design.

Yet there are undeniable technical requirements that the design has to meet.

Of course. But we view the technical specifications or technical limitations as an opportunity for design, because there are limitations in all aspects of life. Limitations should inspire us to find new and unique solutions. We shift the boundaries of what is possible by transcending those boundaries time after time.

Sie scheinen ein sehr weites Verständnis von Design zu haben und sehen darin nicht nur die Aufgabe, eine ästhetische Form für eine technische Funktion zu finden.

Aus meiner Sicht ist Design ein kommunikativer und kultureller Prozess, an dessen Ende nicht einfach nur ein Auto, sondern ein Kulturobjekt steht. Während meiner Zeit bei Ferrari habe ich dieses tiefere Verständnis für Design entwickelt.

Wenn Design ein kultureller Prozess ist, wie Sie sagen: Ist dann ein Ferrari mehr als nur ein Auto?

Ein Ferrari ist nicht nur ein Auto, sondern ein Objekt der Begierde. Es ist ein Traum, wie wir zu sagen pflegen, eine dynamische Skulptur. Das geht weit über ein Auto hinaus. Vielleicht bin ich in dieser Hinsicht auch kein typischer Autodesigner. Ich habe schon immer einen multidisziplinären Ansatz verfolgt und versuche, eine viel breitere Sichtweise auf das Design, insbesondere auf das Automobildesign zu entwickeln.

Und doch gibt es unweigerlich technische Anforderungen, die das Design erfüllen muss.

Natürlich. Wir betrachten die technischen Bedingungen oder technischen Einschränkungen aber als Chance für das Design, denn Einschränkungen sind überall vorhanden. Einschränkungen sollten unsere Fantasie anregen, um neue und einzigartige Lösungen zu finden. Wir verschieben die Grenzen des Möglichen, indem wir sie immer wieder überschreiten.

"The Ferrari brand is based on three elements: innovation, driving thrill and beauty."
„Die Marke Ferrari basiert auf drei Elementen: Innovation, Fahrleidenschaft und Schönheit."

Flavio Manzoni – Senior Vice-President for Design

One of our jury members, Ken Okuyama, always used to say: "I design the cars that I can't afford myself." You and your team design luxury objects. But many of your designers are very young. How is it possible to design luxury that one can potentially not enjoy oneself?

There are different types of enjoyment. The enjoyment of owning a Ferrari, but also the enjoyment of creating a Ferrari.

Is that just a clever dodge?

Not at all. Designing a Ferrari means being allowed to dream and follow an idea that becomes a design object for our customers. Achilles Castiglioni once summarised this feeling very nicely when he said that design is like a delayed conversation with a customer. So there is also always a conversation about the design objects and symbols that we as designers create.

Is there a typical Ferrari customer or a typical Ferrari driver?

We always say: "Different Ferrari for different Ferraristi."

Einer unserer Juroren, Ken Okuyama, pflegte immer zu sagen: „Ich gestalte die Autos, die ich mir selbst nicht leisten kann." Sie und Ihr Team gestalten Luxusobjekte. Aber viele Ihrer Designer sind sehr jung. Wie kann man Luxus gestalten, den man selbst vielleicht nicht ausleben kann?

Nun, es gibt durchaus unterschiedliche Freuden. Die Freude, einen Ferrari zu besitzen, aber auch die Freude, einen Ferrari zu gestalten.

Ist das ein geschicktes Ausweichmanöver?

Keinesfalls. Die Gestaltung eines Ferrari bedeutet, träumen zu dürfen und einer Idee folgen zu können, die für unsere Kunden zu einem Designobjekt wird. Achilles Castiglioni hat dieses Gefühl einmal sehr schön zusammengefasst, indem er sagte, dass Design so etwas wie eine zeitversetzte Konversation mit einem Kunden sei. Es gibt also immer auch eine Konversation über die Designobjekte und Symbole, die wir als Designer schaffen.

Gibt es denn den typischen Ferrari-Kunden oder den typischen Fahrer eines Ferrari?

Wir pflegen immer zu sagen: „Different Ferrari for different Ferraristi."

"Design is a communicative and cultural process."
„Design ist ein kommunikativer und kultureller Prozess."

Flavio Manzoni – Senior Vice-President for Design

That's a clever answer!

It's the truth. The Ferraristi of a GT are not the same as the Ferraristi who drive an XX. They are entirely different people. They also have a completely different idea of what innovation, driving thrill and beauty mean. But ultimately every Ferrari will meet or exceed the different expectations.

How can these different perceptions of the Ferraristi be summed up in a design philosophy?

There's a wonderful quote that is said to have come from Plato: "Beauty is the splendour of truth." That basically explains and describes Ferrari. I think it fits perfectly.

Thank you for talking to us, Mr. Manzoni, and congratulations on winning the title "Red Dot: Design Team of the Year".

Das ist natürlich eine clevere Antwort!

Es ist die Wahrheit. Die Ferraristi eines GT sind nicht identisch mit den Ferraristi, die einen XX fahren. Es sind völlig verschiedene Menschen. Sie haben auch eine völlig unterschiedliche Vorstellung von Innovation, Fahrleidenschaft und Schönheit. Aber am Ende wird jeder Ferrari die unterschiedlichen Erwartungen erfüllen oder übertreffen.

Wie lassen sich denn diese unterschiedlichen Wahrnehmungen der Ferraristi in einer Designphilosophie zusammenfassen?

Es gibt dieses wunderbare Zitat, das angeblich auf Platon zurückgeht: „Schönheit ist der Glanz der Wahrheit." Im Grunde erklärt und beschreibt es Ferrari. Ich denke, es passt perfekt.

Vielen Dank für das Gespräch, Herr Manzoni, und herzlichen Glückwunsch zur Auszeichnung „Red Dot: Design Team of the Year".

Red Dot: Best of the Best
The best designers of their category
Die besten Designer ihrer Kategorie

The designers of the Red Dot: Best of the Best
Only a few products in the Red Dot Design Award receive the "Red Dot: Best of the Best" accolade. In each category, the jury can assign this award to products of outstanding design quality and innovative achievement. Exploring new paths, these products are all exemplary in their design and oriented towards the future.

The following chapter introduces the people who have received one of these prestigious awards. It features the best designers and design teams of the year 2019 together with their products, revealing in interviews and statements what drives these designers and what design means to them.

Die Designer der Red Dot: Best of the Best
Nur sehr wenige Produkte im Red Dot Design Award erhalten die Auszeichnung „Red Dot: Best of the Best". Die Jury kann mit dieser Auszeichnung in jeder Kategorie Design von außerordentlicher Qualität und Innovationsleistung besonders hervorheben. In jeder Hinsicht vorbildlich gestaltet, beschreiten diese Produkte neue Wege und sind zukunftsweisend.

Das folgende Kapitel stellt die Menschen vor, die diese besondere Auszeichnung erhalten haben. Es zeigt die besten Designer und Designteams des Jahres 2019 zusammen mit ihren Produkten. In Interviews und Statements wird deutlich, was diese Designer bewegt und was ihnen Design bedeutet.

Chin Ming Cheng
Joie Children's Products Co., Ltd.

"Making life easier for mother and safer for baby."
„Das Leben für die Mutter einfacher und für das Baby sicherer machen."

What was your goal when you designed your award-winning product?
Our products are designed to benefit not only the families that use them, but also the earth. The best baby gear is easy for parents to use and smart enough to grow with the family for years, helping to minimise waste.

Who or what inspires you?
My inspiration is the name and the essence of our brand: joy. Our constant aim is to contribute to the happiness of parents and little ones through clever designs – solutions that make everyday life simple and sweet.

How do you define design quality?
Design quality goes far beyond the way a product looks, and pulls together ease of manufacturing, simplicity for the end user, and longevity in one beautiful package.

Welches Ziel verfolgten Sie bei der Gestaltung Ihres ausgezeichneten Produktes?
Unsere Produkte sind darauf ausgelegt, nicht nur den Familien, die sie benutzen, zugutezukommen, sondern auch unserem Planeten. Die beste Babyausrüstung ist für Eltern leicht zu benutzen und clever genug, um mit der Familie über Jahre hinweg zu wachsen, und trägt so zur Verminderung von Abfall bei.

Wer oder was inspiriert Sie?
Meine Inspiration sind der Name und Kern unserer Marke: Freude. Unser ständiges Ziel ist es, Eltern und Kinder mithilfe cleverer Designs glücklich zu machen – mit Lösungen, die den Alltag einfach und angenehm machen.

Wie definieren Sie Designqualität?
Designqualität geht weit über das Aussehen eines Produktes hinaus und verbindet Fertigungsfreundlichkeit, Einfachheit für den Endverbraucher und Langlebigkeit in einem schönen Paket.

reddot award 2019
best of the best

Manufacturer
Joie Children's Products Co., Ltd.,
United Kingdom

versatrax™
Pushchair
Kinderwagen

See page 64
Siehe Seite 64

Sanghyun Lee, Narae Yoon, Junghoo Hwang, Junghwan Park
JJOBI Company

"Use good design to elegantly solve daily problems."
„Benutze gutes Design dazu, Alltagsprobleme elegant zu lösen."

Do you have a specific design approach for your work as a designer?
We tried to simplify the design by focusing on the problem. This makes our design more unique.

How do you define design quality?
It is a constant battle between too much or too little. If it is too much, then the product becomes too complicated for the user and/or the price of the product is too high. If it is too little, then the user will not be satisfied. We strive for the perfect balance.

Where will your industry be in ten years?
Taking care of children is a hard job. We are excited to see how various designs will help to reduce parents' mental and physical stress. In the future, we expect to see more children's products combined with sensor and AI technology.

Liegt Ihrer Arbeit als Designer ein bestimmter Gestaltungsansatz zugrunde?
Wir versuchen, das Design zu vereinfachen, indem wir uns auf das Problem konzentrieren. Das macht unsere Gestaltung einzigartig.

Wie definieren Sie Designqualität?
Es ist ein ständiger Kampf zwischen zu wenig oder zu viel. Wenn es zu viel ist, wird das Produkt für den Nutzer zu kompliziert und/oder der Preis des Produktes ist zu hoch. Wenn es zu wenig ist, wird der Nutzer nicht zufrieden sein. Wir bemühen uns, das perfekte Gleichgewicht zu finden.

Wo wird Ihre Branche in zehn Jahren stehen?
Für Kinder zu sorgen, ist harte Arbeit. Es begeistert uns zu sehen, wie unterschiedliche Gestaltungen dazu beitragen, die körperliche und mentale Belastung der Eltern zu reduzieren. Wir rechnen in Zukunft mit mehr Kinderprodukten, die Sensorik und KI nutzen.

reddot award 2019
best of the best

Manufacturer
JJOBI Company, Seoul, South Korea

JJOBI BOX
Toy Sterilisation Box
Spielzeug-Sterilisationsbox

See page 98
Siehe Seite 98

Roland Heiler, Christian Schwamkrug, Steffen Ganz
Studio F. A. Porsche

"A perfect symbiosis of technology and aesthetics."
„Eine perfekte Symbiose von Technologie und Ästhetik."

What was your goal when you designed your award-winning product?
With a user-first approach we aimed to provide the user with considerably improved and fascinating functionalities implemented in a superior quality. The ALPHA washing machine has a clean and minimalistic stainless steel exterior. This contrasts with refined details inside and the user interface to express its outstanding performance. With this washing machine, an innovative automatic load opening is introduced. Once a cycle is complete, the door opens, enabling natural airflow to pass through the appliance. This eliminates unpleasant odours and mould build-up. The design underlines the inherent character of the product: solidity, reliability and state-of-the-art technology.

When are you at your most creative?
In the company of other creative thinkers.

Welches Ziel verfolgten Sie bei der Gestaltung Ihres ausgezeichneten Produktes?
Unser Ansatz stellt den Nutzer in den Mittelpunkt. Unser Ziel war es daher, dem Nutzer in höchster Qualität ausgeführte, deutlich verbesserte und faszinierende Funktionalitäten zu bieten. Die ALPHA-Waschmaschine hat ein sauberes, minimalistisches Äußeres, das einen Kontrast zu den feinen Details im Inneren und dem Bedienfeld bildet, um so die überdurchschnittliche Leistung der Maschine hervorzuheben. Mit dieser Waschmaschine wird eine innovative, automatische Ladeöffnung eingeführt. Sobald ein Waschgang beendet ist, öffnet sich die Tür und eine natürliche Luftzufuhr strömt durch das Gerät, um unangenehme Gerüche und Schimmelbildung zu verhindern. Die Gestaltung betont den inhärenten Charakter des Produktes: Robustheit, Zuverlässigkeit und modernste Technologie.

Wann sind Sie besonders kreativ?
In der Umgebung anderer kreativer Denker.

reddot award 2019
best of the best

Manufacturer
Panasonic Appliances Washing Machine, Hangzhou, China

ALPHA Series (XQG100-P1DL)
Washing Machine
Waschmaschine

See page 108
Siehe Seite 108

Rick Hoobler, Insun Hong, Ben Schriesheim, Wes Johnson
iRobot

"We design and build robots that empower people to do more. We believe we are better together."

„Wir gestalten und bauen Roboter, die es Menschen erlauben, mehr zu leisten. Wir glauben, dass wir gemeinsam besser sind."

What was your goal when you designed your award-winning product?
Our goal with the i7+ was to create a product that marked the next step in consumer automation and efficacy, evolving the way we think about cleaning the home. With the i7+, we wanted a product that was not only functional but that also built upon the aesthetic that was defined with the Roomba series. With i7+, we've taken this further, creating a product that is sleek, powerful, and that integrates into the user's life seamlessly.

When are you at your most creative?
We're at our most creative when we're interacting and learning more about how we can create products that will address a consumer need.

Welches Ziel verfolgten Sie bei der Gestaltung Ihres ausgezeichneten Produktes?
Unser Ziel mit dem i7+ war, ein Produkt zu schaffen, das den nächsten Schritt in der Leistungsfähigkeit und Entwicklung der Automatisierungstechnik für Verbraucher darstellt, und die Art, wie wir über das Reinigen unseres Zuhauses denken, weiterentwickelt. Der i7+ sollte nicht nur ein funktionales Produkt sein, sondern auch auf der Ästhetik der Roomba-Serie aufbauen. Wir haben diese Ästhetik mit dem i7+ fortgeführt und ein Produkt gestaltet, das schnittig und kraftvoll ist und sich nahtlos in den Alltag des Benutzers integriert.

Wann sind Sie besonders kreativ?
Wir sind im Zusammenspiel am kreativsten, und wenn wir besser verstehen, wie wir Produkte gestalten können, die ein bestimmtes Kundenbedürfnis erfüllen.

reddot award 2019
best of the best

Manufacturer
iRobot, Boston, USA

Roomba® i7+ with Clean Base™ Automatic Dirt Disposal
Robot Vacuum Cleaner
Saugroboter

See page 120
Siehe Seite 120

Tatsuya Kawai
Carozzeria Kawai

"Science, art, design and fashion are branches of my creation tree."
„Wissenschaft, Kunst, Design und Mode sind die Zweige meiner Schöpfung."

What was your goal when you designed your award-winning product?
To maximise the function of carbon graphite and to produce various dishes of an easy-to-use size with great usability. The design is simple and has a presence like Japanese shrines and temples.

Who or what inspires you?
New science and materials, superior fashion and art, impressive natural environments, the mechanisms of the universe.

When are you at your most creative?
In an environment surrounded by nature, when I am alone.

What is your personal vision for the future?
My goal is to be a creator who will go down in history.

Welches Ziel verfolgten Sie bei der Gestaltung Ihres ausgezeichneten Produktes?
Die Funktionalität von Kohlenstoffgraphit zu maximieren und verschiedenes Geschirr in einer einfach zu gebrauchenden Größe zu schaffen. Die Gestaltung ist schlicht und erinnert in ihrer Ausstrahlung an japanische Schreine oder Tempel.

Wer oder was inspiriert Sie?
Neue wissenschaftliche Erkenntnisse und Materialien, außergewöhnliche Mode und Kunst, die eindrucksvolle Natur, die Mechanismen des Universums.

Wann sind Sie besonders kreativ?
In einer Umgebung in der Natur, wenn ich alleine bin.

Wie sieht Ihre persönliche Zukunftsvision aus?
Mein Ziel ist es, als ein Schöpfer in die Geschichte einzugehen.

reddot award 2019
best of the best

Manufacturer
Anaori Carbon Co., Ltd.,
Ibaraki City, Osaka Prefecture, Japan

DISC
Carbon Cooking Pot
Carbon-Kochtopf

See page 134
Siehe Seite 134

Richard Kappeller, Andreas Mathieson
Messermacher Kappeller GmbH

"Honouring the event through design and craftsmanship."
„Design und Handwerkskunst würdigen den Anlass."

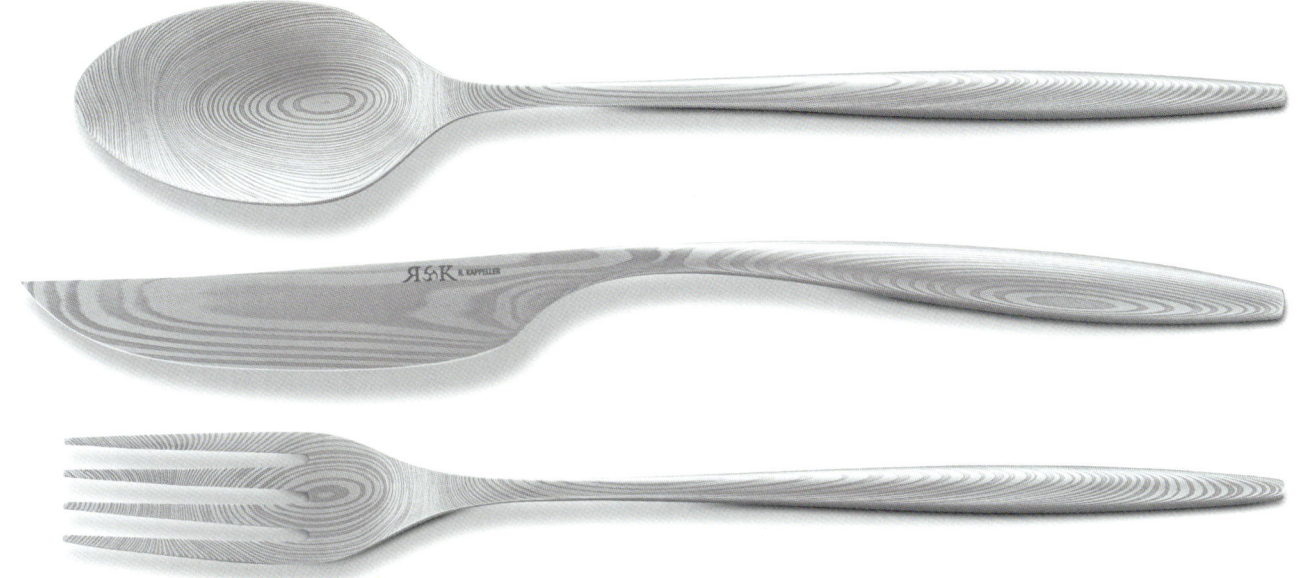

What was your goal when you designed your award-winning product?
Design is more than functionality and aesthetics; it bears responsibility for the future of mankind, for nature and for a healthy world. With every designed object, we not only determine its functionality and its appeal but also how durable and environmentally friendly it will be and how much satisfaction and joy it will bring. We created the Amenite table cutlery with that same commitment – to make something that will meet this goal.

Where will your industry be in ten years?
Automation and digitalisation will play an important role in the ordering process and in some parts of production. Nonetheless, in most processes manual work will be critical to achieve the best quality.

Welches Ziel verfolgten Sie bei der Gestaltung Ihres ausgezeichneten Produktes?
Design ist mehr als nur Funktionalität und Ästhetik. Es trägt auch Verantwortung für die Zukunft der Menschheit, für die Natur und für eine gesunde Welt. Bei jedem Stück, das wir gestalten, entscheiden wir nicht nur, wie funktional und ansprechend, sondern auch wie langlebig und umweltfreundlich es sein soll, und inwieweit es Freude bringt und zufriedenstellt. Mit diesem Ziel haben wir auch das Tischbesteck Amenite kreiert – um etwas zu erschaffen, das diesen Anspruch erfüllt.

Wo wird Ihre Branche in zehn Jahren stehen?
Automatisierung und Digitalisierung werden im Bestellprozess und in einigen Bereichen der Herstellung eine wichtige Rolle spielen. Dennoch wird Handarbeit die Hauptrolle bei den meisten Prozessen spielen, wenn höchste Qualität erzielt werden soll.

reddot award 2019
best of the best

Manufacturer
Messermacher Kappeller GmbH,
Salzburg, Austria

Amenite
Table Cutlery
Tischbesteck

See page 144
Siehe Seite 144

LARQ

"Let's make great products together."
„Lasst uns gemeinsam großartige Produkte machen."

What was your goal when you designed your award-winning product?
The LARQ Bottle has meaningful, unique functionality, so it didn't require an extroverted visual design to achieve differentiation. Our goal was to create a quiet design that is easy to fall in love with, and easy to live with for years to come.

When are you at your most creative?
First, in our studio, with a few team members and several cups of coffee in us. Second, while driving over the Manhattan Bridge. There's something about unfettered acceleration while suspended in space that frees the mind, and a solution to a problem we've been struggling with will simply present itself in that moment.

Where will your industry be in ten years?
Industrial design will be among the last of human activities that will be replaced by automation and AI.

Welches Ziel verfolgten Sie bei der Gestaltung Ihres ausgezeichneten Produktes?
Die Wasserflasche LARQ hat eine sinnvolle, einzigartige Funktionalität, sie brauchte zur Differenzierung also keine extrovertierte visuelle Gestaltung. Unser Ziel war es, ein dezentes Design zu schaffen, in das sich die Menschen einfach verlieben und mit dem sie jahrelang leicht leben können.

Wann sind Sie besonders kreativ?
Einerseits in unserem Studio mit einigen Teammitgliedern und mehreren Tassen Kaffee, andererseits während der Fahrt über die Manhattan Bridge. Irgendwie macht ungehinderte Beschleunigung, während man im Raum schwebt, den Kopf frei. Plötzlich präsentiert sich die Lösung zu einem Problem, an dem wir schon länger arbeiten, wie von selbst.

Wo wird Ihre Branche in zehn Jahren stehen?
Das Industriedesign wird eine der letzten menschlichen Tätigkeiten sein, die durch Automation und KI ersetzt werden.

red**dot** award 2019
best of the best

Manufacturer
LARQ, California, USA

LARQ Bottle
Water Bottle
Wasserflasche

See page 150
Siehe Seite 150

44

Fiskars Finland Oy Ab

"All things, even the simplest, can be made easier and smarter."
„Alle Dinge, selbst die simpelsten, können einfacher und intelligenter gemacht werden."

What was your goal when you designed your award-winning product?
High user experience and performance.

Who or what inspires you?
Nordic nature.

When are you at your most creative?
The invention of new technologies enables us to stay creative.

What is your personal vision for the future?
Making the everyday extraordinary.

What does winning the Red Dot: Best of the Best mean to you?
It is an indication of good design quality.

Welches Ziel verfolgten Sie bei der Gestaltung Ihres ausgezeichneten Produktes?
Hohe Benutzerfreundlichkeit und Leistung.

Wer oder was inspiriert Sie?
Die nordische Natur.

Wann sind Sie besonders kreativ?
Die Erfindung neuer Technologien erlaubt es uns, auch weiterhin kreativ zu bleiben.

Wie sieht Ihre persönliche Zukunftsvision aus?
Das Alltägliche außergewöhnlich zu machen.

Was bedeutet die Auszeichnung mit dem Red Dot: Best of the Best für Sie?
Es ist ein Zeichen guter Designqualität.

reddot award 2019
best of the best

Manufacturer
Fiskars Finland Oy Ab, Helsinki, Finland

Fiskars Waterwheel XL
Watering System
Bewässerungssystem

See page 166
Siehe Seite 166

designaffairs

"Creating change."
„Veränderung schaffen."

What was your goal when you designed your award-winning product?
As a newcomer in the domain of digital cameras, ZEISS has to make its mark with the ZX1. The focus for us was therefore on creating an icon that interprets the camera archetype in a modern and unique way. The bedrock for that is a straightforward and well-functioning user experience, which we managed to achieve through the perfect harmony of hard- and software.

How do you define design quality?
A well-designed product is the succinct response to a specific need, generally in a highly complex context. In an ideal world, it is also fun to create.

What does winning the Red Dot: Best of the Best mean to you?
For us, it is the perfect culmination of a process that lasted more than three years.

Welches Ziel verfolgten Sie bei der Gestaltung Ihres ausgezeichneten Produktes?
Als Neueinsteiger im Bereich der Digitalkameras muss ZEISS mit der ZX1 ein Zeichen setzen. Besonders im Fokus stand für uns deshalb das Schaffen einer Ikone, die den Archetyp Kamera auf eine moderne und einzigartige Weise interpretiert. Basis dafür war ein reibungsloses Nutzererlebnis, das wir durch perfekte Abstimmung von Hard- und Software erreicht haben.

Wie definieren Sie Designqualität?
Ein gut gestaltetes Produkt ist die prägnante Antwort auf ein spezifisches Bedürfnis in einem meist sehr komplexen Kontext. Im Idealfall macht es auch noch Spaß.

Was bedeutet die Auszeichnung mit dem Red Dot: Best of the Best für Sie?
Für uns ist sie der krönende Abschluss eines über dreijährigen Prozesses.

reddot award 2019
best of the best

Manufacturer
Carl Zeiss AG, Oberkochen, Germany

ZEISS ZX1
Digital Camera
Digitalkamera

See page 202
Siehe Seite 202

Blackmagic Design

"Fostering true creativity by making the highest quality video affordable to everyone."

„Echte Kreativität fördert man, indem die beste Videoqualität für jeden erschwinglich ist."

What was your goal when you designed your award-winning product?
Our aim was to deliver an affordable, professional camera control solution that empowers independent producers to create engaging live broadcasts, regardless of budget or technical expertise.

How do you define design quality?
For us, design quality is captured by a product's sense of clarity, visible purpose and high level of usability.

How do you keep abreast of new developments?
Our team is made up of people who are naturally inquisitive, and from varied backgrounds. We constantly learn and share ideas and influences in our studio, which informs the team as a whole.

Welches Ziel verfolgten Sie bei der Gestaltung Ihres ausgezeichneten Produktes?
Unser Ziel war es, eine erschwingliche, professionelle Kamerasteuerung anzubieten, die es unabhängigen Produzenten erlaubt, fesselnde Live-Übertragungen ungeachtet ihres Budgets oder technischen Know-hows zu machen.

Wie definieren Sie Designqualität?
Für uns kommt Designqualität durch formale Klarheit, einen erkennbaren Zweck und den hohen Nutzungsgrad eines Produktes zum Ausdruck.

Wie bleiben Sie über aktuelle Entwicklungen auf dem Laufenden?
Unser Team besteht aus Menschen, die von Natur aus neugierig sind und unterschiedliche Hintergründe haben. In unserem Studio lernen wir ständig. Wir tauschen uns über Ideen und Einflüsse aus, was unserem gesamten Team Anregungen gibt.

reddot award 2019
best of the best

Manufacturer
Blackmagic Design, Melbourne, Australia

Blackmagic Camera Control Panel
Remote Camera Control Unit
Bedienpult zur Fernsteuerung von Kameras

See page 222
Siehe Seite 222

Benjamin Sabourin, Nicolas Marquis
Ova Design

"Innovation comes from the study of uses and experiments."
„Innovation geht aus der Untersuchung von Anwendungen und Experimenten hervor."

What was your goal when you designed your award-winning product?
We wanted to break with conventional telescopes and create a unique form factor. When closed, Stellina has a refined and simple shape, which comes to life automatically as soon as the optic arm opens to position itself in the direction of the stars to be observed. We wanted to create a surprise when Stellina unfolds. The object wakes up and comes to life, the connected object becomes a companion to help its users have a new viewing experience.

Why did you become a designer?
It's the same story for both of us: our grandparents are makers or craftsmen. They passed on their passion for making things to us. We both loved drawing during our childhood. That is why we wanted to become designers, in order to design products needed by consumers.

Welches Ziel verfolgten Sie bei der Gestaltung Ihres ausgezeichneten Produktes?
Wir wollten mit dem traditionellen Teleskop brechen und einen einzigartigen Formfaktor schaffen. Wenn Stellina geschlossen ist, hat es eine edle und schlichte Form, die automatisch zum Leben erwacht, sobald sich die Optik in die Richtung der zu beobachtenden Sterne öffnet. Wir wollten in Erstaunen versetzen, wenn sich Stellina öffnet. Das Produkt erwacht und wird lebendig. Das vernetzte Objekt wird zum Gefährten und hilft seinen Nutzern, ein neuartiges Beobachtungserlebnis zu haben.

Warum sind Sie Designer geworden?
Wir haben beide den gleichen Beweggrund: Unsere Großeltern waren Fabrikanten oder Kunsthandwerker und haben ihre Begeisterung für das Herstellen von Dingen an uns weitergegeben. Da wir in der Kindheit beide Zeichnen geliebt haben, wollten wir Designer werden, um Produkte zu gestalten, die von Konsumenten gebraucht werden.

reddot award 2019
best of the best

Manufacturer
Vaonis, Clapiers, France

Stellina
Smart Telescope
Intelligentes Teleskop

See page 224
Siehe Seite 224

Igor Buturlia
VR Electronics Limited

"Do it, no matter what!"
„Tu es, egal was passiert!"

What was your goal when you designed your award-winning product?
The main goal was to create something entirely new: the new medium connecting human and technology in the digital world. Teslasuit promises deeper immersion with the transmission of touch, but the suit transcends that simple motion and becomes an early link in the symbiosis of humans and electronics.

Do you have a specific design approach for your work as a designer?
I always create a story in my head, to see who uses the product, when and how, and what it would change in people's lives. I look for ways to seamlessly integrate the product into real life. Functionality is paramount. Then I look at the tech that can tell this story.

Welches Ziel verfolgten Sie bei der Gestaltung Ihres ausgezeichneten Produktes?
Das Hauptziel war, etwas völlig Neues zu schaffen: das neue Medium, das den Menschen in der digitalen Welt mit der Technik verbindet. Der Teslasuit verspricht eine bessere Immersion durch die Übertragung von Berührungen, jedoch geht er über die einfache Bewegung hinaus und wird zu einem frühen Verbindungsglied in der Symbiose von Mensch und Elektronik.

Liegt Ihrer Arbeit als Designer ein bestimmter Gestaltungsansatz zugrunde?
Ich entwickele immer erst eine Geschichte in meinem Kopf, um zu verstehen, wer das Produkt wann und wie benutzen wird, und was es im Leben der Menschen verändern wird. Ich suche nach Möglichkeiten, das Produkt im wirklichen Leben zu integrieren. Funktionalität ist vorrangig. Dann schaue ich mir die Technik an, die diese Geschichte erzählen kann.

reddot award 2019
best of the best

Manufacturer
VR Electronics Limited,
London, United Kingdom

Teslasuit
Full-Body Haptics Suit
Haptischer Ganzkörperanzug

See page 240
Siehe Seite 240

Lenovo Experience Design Group

"We design for people."
„Wir gestalten für Menschen."

Do you have a specific design approach for your work as a designer?
We believe the designer's contribution to every project should strive for great design, flawless execution, quality build and a great product experience. If you consider this end-to-end spectrum, you can come up with products that serve the interests of the customers best possible and drive brand growth.

Who or what inspires you?
We look for inspiration from everywhere around us, but the end users are our true inspiration. A professional growth mindset brings continual improvements to our designs while the fusion of ideas makes our products unique and stand out from the crowd.

Liegt Ihrer Arbeit als Designer ein bestimmter Gestaltungsansatz zugrunde?
Wir glauben, dass der Beitrag eines Designers bei jedem Projekt darauf ausgerichtet sein sollte, einmalige Gestaltung, einwandfreie Umsetzung, Verarbeitungsqualität und ein großartiges Produkterlebnis zu bieten. Dieses End-to-End-Leistungsspektrum führt zu Produkten, die den Interessen der Kunden bestmöglich dienen und das Markenwachstum vorantreiben.

Wer oder was inspiriert Sie?
Wir suchen in unserer gesamten Umgebung nach Inspiration, doch sind die Endnutzer unsere wirkliche Inspiration. Professionelle Wachstumsorientierung sorgt für kontinuierliche Verbesserungen in der Designarbeit, während die Fusion von Ideen unsere Produkte so einzigartig macht, dass sie aus der Masse hervorstechen.

reddot award 2019
best of the best

Manufacturer
Lenovo, Morrisville, North Carolina, USA

ThinkReality A6
Augmented Reality Headset

See page 242
Siehe Seite 242

Kent Zeng
DTEN

"Innovation is the only path forward."
„Innovation ist der einzige Weg nach vorn."

Who or what inspires you?
Oddly, inspiration often comes from mediocre products found in the marketplace. I'm inspired to do better, design something that truly enhances our customers' experiences, to create something from my heart.

When are you at your most creative?
Curiosity is a major motivator. I like to find the current norm and then challenge myself to move beyond the status quo. What do customers want that they are not getting? What are new ways to advance their experience? How can we incorporate new materials and emerging technology? I always want to move the needle forward as far as possible.

Wer oder was inspiriert Sie?
Merkwürdigerweise kommt Inspiration oft von mittelmäßigen Produkten, die auf dem Markt zu finden sind. Das inspiriert mich, Besseres zu leisten und etwas zu gestalten, das die Erfahrungen unserer Kunden wirklich verbessert – etwas zu schaffen, das von Herzen kommt.

Wann sind Sie besonders kreativ?
Neugierde ist eine wesentliche Motivationsquelle. Ich finde gerne die aktuelle Norm und stelle mich dann der Herausforderung, über den Status quo hinauszugehen. Was wollen Kunden, das sie momentan nicht bekommen? Welche neuen Möglichkeiten gibt es, ihre Praxis zu verbessern? Wie können wir neue Materialien und neu entstehende Technologien einsetzen? Ich möchte immer eine möglichst große Veränderung bewirken.

reddot award 2019
best of the best

Manufacturer
DTEN, San Jose, California, USA

DTEN D7
AI-Powered Video Conference Board
KI-gestütztes Videokonferenz-Board

See page 268
Siehe Seite 268

Hyundai Robotics
Hyundai Heavy Industries

"Creating customer value and differentiating products through design thinking."
„Designorientiertes Denken führt zu Kundennutzen und sich unterscheidenden Produkten."

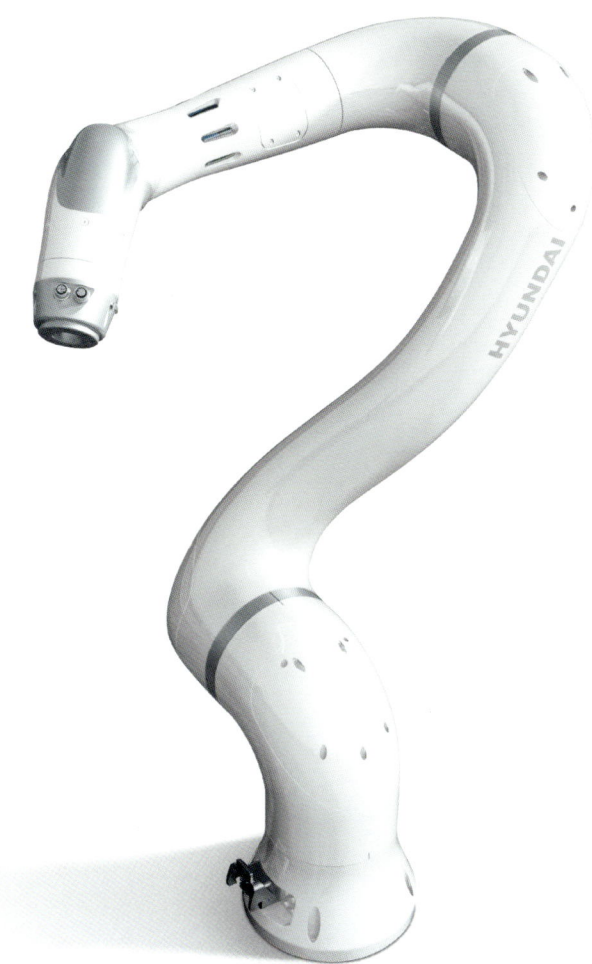

What was your goal when you designed your award-winning product?
Our goal is to create an attractive impression when our customers examine and use our robot. This goal helps us move forward towards becoming one of the global top brands.

Who or what inspires you?
Inspired by the dynamic energy and flexible movement that we see in nature, we try to reinterpret it in vibrant shapes and structures.

Where will your industry be in ten years?
The collaborative robot market is expected to grow exponentially in future. Because we will see increased demand in this industry, domestic and foreign robot companies are in a rush to launch their collaborative robots.

Welches Ziel verfolgten Sie bei der Gestaltung Ihres ausgezeichneten Produktes?
Unser Ziel war, unseren Roboter so zu gestalten, dass er auf Kunden einen ansprechenden Eindruck macht, wenn sie ihn in Augenschein nehmen und benutzen. Diese Zielsetzung hilft uns, einen weiteren Schritt in unserer Entwicklung hin zu einer führenden globalen Marke zu gehen.

Wer oder was inspiriert Sie?
Uns inspiriert die dynamische Energie und flexible Bewegung der Natur, die wir versuchen, in kraftvollen Formen und Strukturen wiederzugeben.

Wo wird Ihre Branche in zehn Jahren stehen?
Der Markt für kollaborative Roboter soll in Zukunft exponentiell wachsen. Da in dieser Branche mit einer zunehmenden Nachfrage gerechnet wird, beeilen sich nationale und internationale Hersteller, ihre kollaborativen Roboter auf den Markt zu bringen.

reddot award 2019
best of the best

Manufacturer
Hyundai Robotics, Daegu, South Korea

Hyundai Robot YL012
Collaborative Robot
Kollaborativer Roboter

See page 298
Siehe Seite 298

Max Burton, Jonathan Mendoza, Frankie Vazquez, Kim Do
Fjord | Accenture Interactive

What was your goal when you designed your award-winning product?
To bring bold advances in medical innovation to life and to allow all of the players who interact with the platform to not only see the bravery of the vision but to feel it through every interaction at every touchpoint.

When are you at your most creative?
We do our best work when we're solving problems with many constraints; when we are challenged to work together as effectively and efficiently as possible and we have a great groove going, the results can be incredible.

How do you define quality?
Since design is inherently subjective, we are dedicated to bringing structure to our thinking and our making so that what ultimately gets into the user's hands has a sense of purposeful meaning.

Welches Ziel verfolgten Sie bei der Gestaltung Ihres ausgezeichneten Produktes?
Mutige Fortschritte in einer medizinischen Innovation lebendig werden zu lassen. Alle Akteure, die mit der Plattform zu tun haben, sollten nicht nur den Mut der Vision erkennen können, sondern sie auch durch jede Interaktion bei jedem Berührungspunkt spüren.

Wann sind Sie besonders kreativ?
Wir leisten die beste Arbeit, wenn wir Probleme mit vielen Beschränkungen lösen sollen. Wenn wir vor der Herausforderung stehen, so wirkungsvoll und effizient wie möglich zusammenzuarbeiten, und in einem tollen Flow sind, können die Ergebnisse unglaublich sein.

Wie definieren Sie Qualität?
Da Design von Natur aus subjektiv ist, ist unser Anspruch, unserem Denken und Schaffen eine Struktur zu geben, damit das, was Nutzer am Ende in den Händen halten, einen zweckmäßigen Sinn hat.

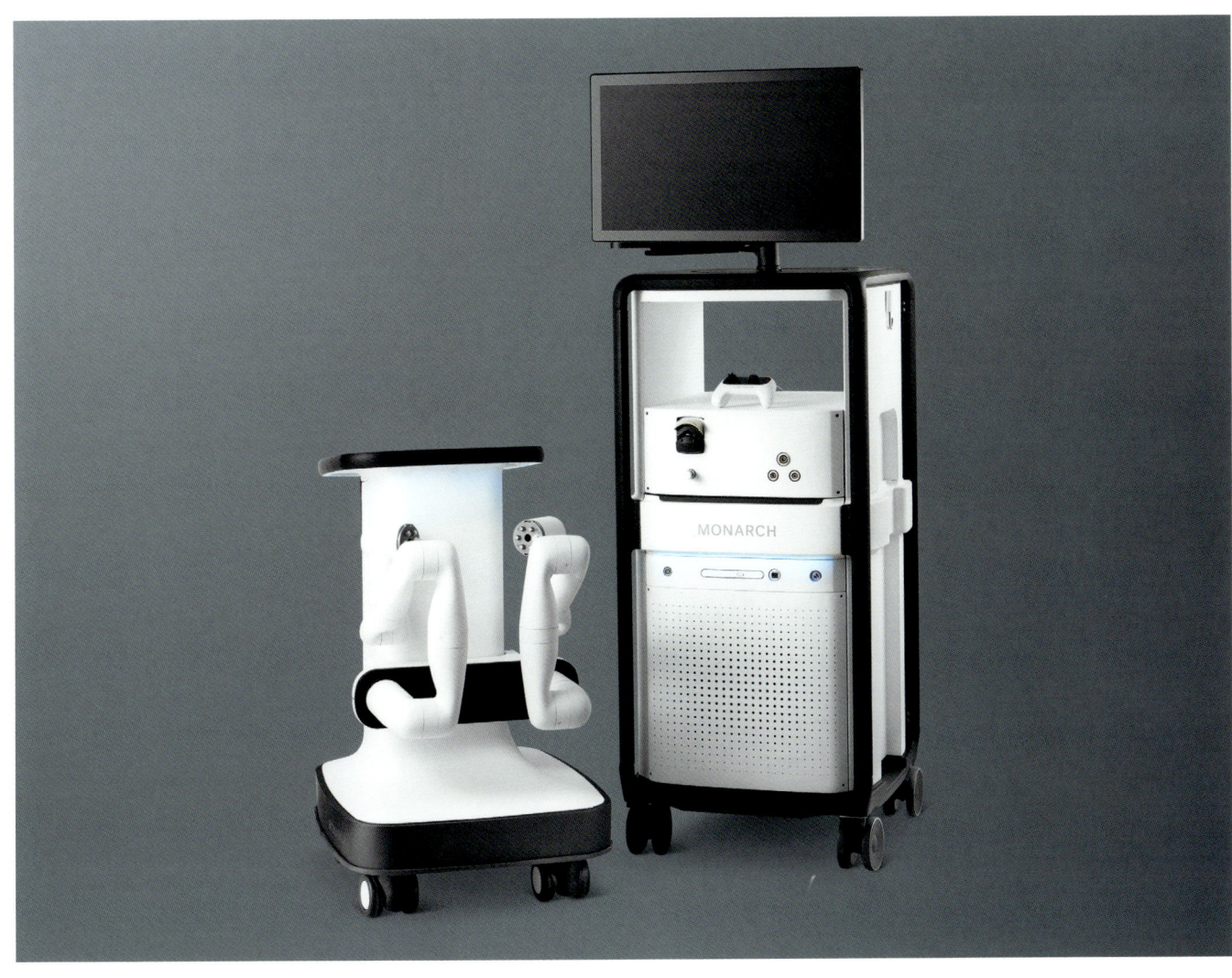

reddot award 2019
best of the best

Manufacturer
Auris Health,
Redwood City, California, USA

Auris Monarch
Endoscopic Robotic Platform
Endoskopie-Roboterplattform

See page 304
Siehe Seite 304

Babies and children
Baby und Kind

Accessories	Accessoires
Baby bottles	Babyflaschen
Baby carriers	Babyphones und -kameras
Baby phones and cameras	Babytragen
Breast pumps	Dreiräder
Child seats	Hygieneartikel
Children's bicycles	Kinderfahrräder
Children's furniture	Kindermöbel
Cradles	Kindersitze
Hygiene articles	Kinderwagen
Pregnancy and parenting articles	Milchpumpen
Soothers	Reisebetten
Strollers	Schnuller
Toys	Schwangerschaftsartikel
Travel cots	Spielzeuge
Tricycles	Wiegen

versatrax™
Pushchair
Kinderwagen

Manufacturer
Joie Children's Products Co., Ltd.,
United Kingdom

In-house design
Joie Children's Products Co., Ltd.

Web
www.joiebaby.com

reddot award 2019
best of the best

New possibilities
Since prams play a pivotal role in parent mobility, they should reflect the needs of both children and parents. Against this backdrop, the design of the Versatrax pushchair realises the concept of a full-featured pram. Based on a modularity that is perfectly adapted to life with children, it offers four different, easy-to-set modes as well as a quick and compact fold. It is compatible with both a carry cot and infant carrier, while the sports seat can be turned as needed, either rearward facing the parents or forward later to allow infants a view of the world. Thanks to a cleverly designed folding mechanism, this pushchair can be folded quickly and intuitively, regardless of the seat facing rearward or forward. To do so, users simply have to lower the seat back and pull up on a strap, making the pushchair fold into a neat, freestanding package with automatic locking. The pram is equipped with durable foam-filled tires to ensure smooth rides for the little ones, while the telescopic height-adjustable handle also ensures that parents can enjoy a comfortable stroll. The reclining sports seat can be folded completely flat and, together with a multi-position leg rest and a particularly large, expandable hood with a peekaboo window and mesh side panels, creates a cocooned area for sleeping babies. Single front swivel wheels, a practical single-touch brake and an outstandingly large shopping basket complement the package.

Neue Möglichkeiten
Da der Kinderwagen für die Mobilität eine entscheidende Rolle spielt, sollte er die Bedürfnisse von Kindern und Eltern widerspiegeln. Die Gestaltung von Versatrax verwirklicht das Konzept eines voll ausgestatteten Kinderwagens. Auf der Basis einer dem Leben mit Kindern nahtlos angepassten Modularität bietet er vier verschiedene, leicht einzustellende Modi und ein kompaktes Faltmaß. Er ist mit Babywanne oder Babyschale einsetzbar, und der Sportsitz lässt sich je nach Bedarf entweder zu den Eltern drehen oder später mit Blick in die Welt hinaus verwenden. Dank eines clever gestalteten Faltmechanismus kann dieser Kinderwagen unabhängig von der Sitzrichtung schnell und selbsterklärend zusammengeklappt werden. Dazu legt der Nutzer einfach den Sitz um und betätigt ein Zugband, woraufhin der Wagen unkompliziert zu einem freistehenden, kompakten Paket zusammenklappt. Ausgestattet mit widerstandsfähigen, schaumstoffgefüllten Reifen, ist für eine sanfte Fahrt gesorgt, und dank höhenverstellbarem Schiebebügel haben auch die Eltern Spaß bei allen Unternehmungen. Der Sportsitz lässt sich komplett flach umlegen, gemeinsam mit einem besonders groß gestalteten, erweiterbaren Verdeck mit Sichtfenster und seitlichen Mesh-Fenstern sowie einer verstellbaren Beinauflage schafft er einen gemütlichen Wohlfühlort für das Schlafen zwischendurch. Schwenk- und feststellbare Vorderräder, eine praktische One-Touch-Bremse und ein ausgesprochen großer Staukorb vervollständigen das Ausstattungspaket.

Statement by the jury
The Versatrax pushchair offers a versatile functionality that meets all scenarios of living with children. It convinces with a well-balanced overall design that allows easy folding up. Its intuitive comfort goes hand in hand with the use of high-quality materials and consistently integrated accessories. Adding to the beauty of it, this pushchair is highly robust after all, yet also imparts a sense of lightness.

Begründung der Jury
Der Kinderwagen Versatrax bietet eine vielseitige Funktionalität, mit der er allen Szenarien für das Leben mit Kindern gerecht wird. Er überzeugt durch seine ausgewogene Gestaltung und lässt sich auf einfache Weise zusammenklappen. Sein unkomplizierter Komfort geht einher mit der Wahl hochwertiger Materialien und schlüssig integrierten Accessoires. Die Schönheit dieses Kinderwagens liegt auch darin, dass er einerseits sehr robust ist und zugleich die Anmutung von Leichtigkeit vermittelt.

Designer portrait
See page 30
Siehe Seite 30

Tourist™
Pushchair

Kinderwagen

Manufacturer
Joie Children's Products Co.,
Limited, United Kingdom
In-house design
Web
www.joiebaby.com

Tourist was developed for parents who are frequently on the go; it combines a compact buggy and a pram in one product. The pushchair weighs only 6 kg. By means of a folding mechanism at the push-bar, it can be folded using one hand into a 24 × 66 cm package. Thanks to a carrying strap and tote bag, it is easy to transport. The frame is designed to hold an infant car seat and a carrycot. In buggy mode, the backrest and footrest can be adjusted. This pushchair also possesses independent wheel suspension, a single-step brake and a five-point safety belt.

Tourist wurde für Eltern entwickelt, die viel unterwegs sind, und verbindet Kompaktbuggy und Kinderwagen in einem Produkt. Der Kinderwagen wiegt nur 6 kg. Er lässt sich durch die Betätigung eines Klappmechanismus am Schiebebügel mit einer Hand zu einem 24 × 66 cm großen Paket zusammenfalten und dank Tragegurt und Tragetasche leicht transportieren. Das Gestell kann auch mit Babywanne und -schale genutzt werden, im Buggy-Modus können Rückenlehne und Beinauflage verstellt werden. Der Kinderwagen verfügt zudem über Einzelradfederung, eine Handbremse und einen 5-Punkt-Sicherheitsgurt.

Statement by the jury
The pushchair Tourist is a product that has been well considered down to the very last detail. It is flexibly adaptable to various scenarios and thus also very suitable for travel.

Begründung der Jury
Der Kinderwagen Tourist ist ein bis ins Detail durchdachtes Produkt, das an verschiedene Einsatzszenarien flexibel angepasst werden kann und sich dadurch sehr gut für Reisen eignet.

Anex Air-X
Pushchair
Kinderwagen

Manufacturer
Ideo Group LLC, Warsaw, Poland
In-house design
Design
Ergo Design, Krakow, Poland
Web
www.anexbaby.com
www.ergo.design

Air-X is a very light pushchair optimised for travelling. With its reduced weight and compact size, it can be taken aboard aircrafts as cabin luggage when folded. The innovative, one-stage folding mechanism may be operated with one hand. Thanks to its great manoeuvrability, the Air-X is easily guided through queues and the security zone in airports. Air-X is suitable for babies and toddlers due to its adjustable seat.

Statement by the jury
This purist buggy impresses with its distinct form. Due to its compact pack size and strong manoeuvrability, it is an ideal companion when travelling by air.

Air-X ist ein sehr leichter Kinderwagen, der für Reisen optimiert ist. Mit seinem geringen Gewicht und seiner kompakten Größe kann er auf Flügen zusammengeklappt als Kabinengepäck mitgeführt werden. Der innovative, einstufige Klappmechanismus lässt sich mit einer Hand bedienen. Dank seiner hohen Manövrierfähigkeit kann der Air-X entspannt durch Warteschlangen und den Sicherheitsbereich am Flughafen gelenkt werden. Mit seinem verstellbaren Sitz ist er für Babys und Kleinkinder geeignet.

Begründung der Jury
Dieser puristische Buggy besticht durch eine klare Formgebung und wird durch sein geringes Packmaß und seine gute Wendigkeit zum idealen Begleiter auf Flugreisen.

Anex Quant
Pushchair
Kinderwagen

Manufacturer
Ideo Group LLC, Warsaw, Poland
In-house design
Design
Ergo Design, Krakow, Poland
Web
www.anexbaby.com
www.ergo.design

Quant is a pushchair which combines a luxurious appearance with simple handling and functionality. Sport seat and carrycot are large and offer great comfort at a low weight. The seat elements are made of an airy mesh fabric. The carrycot has a hard shell, which makes it very safe and secure. The frame with sport seat can be folded up with one hand. Backrest and footrest are adjustable with a single button. The main hinge in the form of a Q is a concise design feature.

Statement by the jury
The Quant pushchair convinces from a functional viewpoint and particularly impresses in combination with the hardshell carrycot due to its elegant, classical and simultaneously modern appearance.

Quant ist ein Kinderwagen, der eine luxuriöse Anmutung mit einer einfachen Handhabung und Funktionalität kombiniert. Sportsitz und Babywanne sind groß und bieten hohen Komfort bei geringem Gewicht. Die Sitzelemente sind aus einem luftigen Mesh-Gewebe, die Wanne ist durch eine Hartschale sehr sicher. Das Gestell mit Sportsitz lässt sich mit einer Hand zusammenklappen, Rückenlehne und Fußstütze sind mit einem einzigen Knopf einstellbar. Das Hauptgelenk in Form eines Q ist prägnantes Designmerkmal.

Begründung der Jury
Der Kinderwagen Quant überzeugt in funktionaler Hinsicht und besticht insbesondere in Kombination mit der Hartschalen-Babywanne durch sein elegantes, klassisches und zugleich modernes Erscheinungsbild.

Eezy S+ Denim Edition
Pushchair
Kinderwagen

Manufacturer
Cybex GmbH, Bayreuth, Germany
In-house design
Ralf Holleis
Web
www.cybex-online.com

The Eezy S+ is a lightweight and versatile pushchair which can be easily stored in a practical way. With its one-hand folding mechanism, it can be quickly converted into a compact, self-standing package. The narrow, manoeuvrable urban pushchair offers comfort even on off-road paths thanks to its four-wheel suspension. The 2-in-1 travel system can be used with a carrycot and the integrated soft seat. Its appearance is characterised by reduced geometric forms and clear lines.

Statement by the jury
Reduced forms and high-quality materials lend the Eezy S+ a timeless appearance. Well-considered functions also ease handling and increase convenience and comfort for parents and child.

Der Eezy S+ ist ein leichter und vielseitiger Kinderwagen, der sich einfach und praktisch verstauen lässt. Mit seinem Einhand-Faltmechanismus kann er schnell in ein kompaktes, von selbst stehendes Paket verwandelt werden. Der schmale, wendige Stadtkinderwagen bietet dank Allradfederung auch jenseits der Straße Komfort. Dank des 2-in-1-Reisesystems kann er mit Babyschale und der komfortablen Sitzeinheit genutzt werden. Sein Erscheinungsbild ist durch reduzierte geometrische Formen und klare Linien geprägt.

Begründung der Jury
Reduzierte Formen und hochwertige Materialien verleihen dem Eezy S+ ein zeitloses Erscheinungsbild. Durchdachte Funktionen erleichtern die Handhabung und erhöhen den Komfort für Eltern und Kind.

MIXX
Pushchair
Kinderwagen

Manufacturer
Nuna International BV,
Leiderdorp, Netherlands
In-house design
Web
www.nuna.eu

MIXX is a versatile pushchair which offers four modes: it can be used with a carrycot or an infant car seat and as a forward or backward facing buggy. The pushchair has a one-touch brake and lockable front wheels; it can be easily steered with one hand and folded up quickly and compactly. The push bar and bumper bar are covered with hand-stitched, brandy-coloured artificial leather. MIXX also has a removable sun canopy with a UV protection factor of 50+ and a window of mesh fabric.

Der MIXX ist ein vielseitiger Kinderwagen, der vier Modi bietet: Er kann mit Babywanne oder Babyschale genutzt werden und als rückwärts- oder vorwärtsgerichteter Sportwagen. Der Kinderwagen hat eine One-Tip-Bremse und feststellbare Vorderräder, lässt sich problemlos mit einer Hand lenken und rasch kompakt zusammenfalten. Schiebe- und Spielbügel sind mit handgenähtem, cognacfarbenem Kunstleder ummantelt. Der MIXX besitzt zudem ein abnehmbares Sonnenverdeck mit UV-Schutz 50+ und einem Sichtfenster aus Meshgewebe.

Statement by the jury
This versatile pushchair impresses with its well-thought-out components and strong aesthetics characterised by artificial leather elements.

Begründung der Jury
Dieser vielseitige Kinderwagen besticht mit seinen durchdachten Komponenten und einer hochwertigen Ästhetik, die durch die Kunstlederelemente geprägt ist.

Mi Foldable Baby Stroller
Pushchair
Kinderwagen

Manufacturer
Xiaomi Inc., Beijing, China
In-house design
Design
Shanghai Baotung Tech Co., Ltd.,
Kunshan, China
Web
www.mi.com
www.baotung.com

The Mi Foldable Baby Stroller is a pushchair which can be very compactly folded, thanks to its frame with many folding possibilities and the collapsible rear wheels. The well-sprung stroller may be used from birth to 36 months of age. It has a freely adjustable backrest and footrest, as well as a reclining area, so that the spine is optimally supported at all times. The seat fabric is skin-friendly, breathable and antibacterial, while the push-bar has a pleasant feel.

Statement by the jury
This pushchair lends itself to impressively compact folding and is thus a good travel companion. When opened, it offers ergonomic seating and reclining for the child.

Mi Foldable Baby Stroller ist ein Buggy, der sich dank mehrfach klappbaren Rahmens sowie einklappbarer Hinterräder sehr kompakt zusammenfalten lässt. Der gut gefederte Wagen kann von der Geburt an bis zu einem Alter von 36 Monaten genutzt werden. Er hat eine frei verstellbare Rückenlehne und Fußstütze sowie steife Sitz- und Liegebereiche, sodass die Wirbelsäule jederzeit optimal gestützt wird. Das Sitzgewebe ist hautfreundlich, atmungsaktiv und antibakteriell, der Schiebebügel haptisch angenehm.

Begründung der Jury
Dieser Buggy lässt sich beeindruckend kompakt zusammenfalten und ist damit ein guter Reisebegleiter. Aufgeklappt bietet er wiederum eine ergonomische Sitz- bzw. Liegefläche fürs Kind.

Joolz Day³
Pushchair
Kinderwagen

Manufacturer
Joolz by Milk Design B.V.,
Amsterdam, Netherlands
In-house design
Stan Spangenberg, Michel Holper
Web
www.joolz.com

The Joolz Day³ combines functionality with ergonomics in a reduced, elegant appearance. Features include a large shopping basket, a high carrycot and a high seat. It has many well-considered properties, such as ventilation for the carrycot, soft suspension and a foot support adjustable with one hand. Equipped with swivel wheels, the pushchair is highly manoeuvrable and steerable with a single hand. It can also be compactly folded and stored vertically.

Statement by the jury
Compact dimensions and strong functionality make this elegant pushchair a dynamic companion in everyday family life.

Der Joolz Day³ verbindet Funktionalität und Ergonomie mit einem reduzierten, eleganten Erscheinungsbild. Zur Ausstattung gehören ein großer Einkaufskorb, eine hohe Wanne sowie ein hoher Sitz. Der Kinderwagen hat viele durchdachte Elemente wie eine Belüftung der Babywanne, eine weiche Federung oder eine einhändig verstellbare Fußstütze. Ausgestattet mit drehbaren Rädern ist er sehr wendig und lässt sich auch mit einer Hand lenken. Der Wagen kann zudem kompakt zusammengefaltet und aufrecht verstaut werden.

Begründung der Jury
Kompakte Maße und eine hohe Funktionalität machen diesen eleganten Kinderwagen zum dynamischen Begleiter im Familienalltag.

Quinny HUBB
Pushchair
Kinderwagen

Manufacturer
Quinny, Dorel Juvenile,
Helmond, Netherlands
In-house design
Design
Vanderveer Designers,
Geldermalsen, Netherlands
Web
www.quinny.com
www.vanderveerdesigners.nl

The Quinny HUBB is a roomy, comfortable and modular sibling pushchair tailored to the needs of new parents. Thanks to the modular frame with various slots, the pushchair provides effortless configuration – for example as pram with full-size carrycot or with one or two full-size seats positionable facing the front or rear. The large shopping basket is convenient to access and can carry up to 20 kg. The sun canopy has a peek-a-boo window. The narrow footprint makes the Quinny HUBB perfect for manoeuvring in urban environments.

Statement by the jury
With its modular design, this versatile sibling pushchair adapts to various scenarios of use and thus offers convenient handling.

Der Quinny HUBB ist ein geräumiger, komfortabler und modularer Geschwister-Kinderwagen, der auf die Bedürfnisse junger Eltern abgestimmt ist. Dank des modularen Rahmens mit verschiedenen Steckplätzen lässt sich der Kinderwagen mühelos konfigurieren – etwa als Wagen mit großer Babywanne oder mit einem oder zwei vorwärts oder rückwärts ausgerichteten Sitzen in voller Größe. Der große Einkaufskorb ist komfortabel erreichbar und kann bis zu 20 kg tragen, das Sonnenverdeck hat ein Sichtfenster. Der schmal gebaute Quinny HUBB lässt sich gut durch urbanes Umfeld manövrieren.

Begründung der Jury
Dieser vielseitige Geschwister-Kinderwagen passt sich aufgrund seiner Modularität an verschiedenste Nutzungsszenarien an und bietet dabei ein komfortables Handling.

Quintus DuetPro Stroller
Pushchair
Kinderwagen

Manufacturer
Stone (Shanghai) Juvenile Product Co., Ltd.,
Shanghai, China
In-house design
Prof. Chen Feng
Web
www.qtus.eu

The Quintus DuetPro Stroller is a convertible pushchair which can be easily adapted to various situations thanks to 17 possible seating configurations. It can be converted, for example, from a duo or twin version into a mono pushchair. Durable materials and high-quality fabrics were used to create an elegant carriage with a light and aerodynamic frame. The pushchair also offers a good deal of space, so that both children have enough room to settle in comfortably. The seats can be arranged independently, facing to the front or rear.

Der Quintus DuetPro Stroller ist ein umbaubarer Kinderwagen, der sich mit 17 möglichen Sitzkonfigurationen problemlos an verschiedene Situationen anpassen lässt. So kann er etwa von einem Duo- oder Zwillingswagen in einen Mono-Kinderwagen umgewandelt werden. Für den eleganten Wagen mit einem leichten und aerodynamischen Gestell wurden langlebige Materialien und hochwertige Stoffe verwendet. Der Kinderwagen bietet zudem so viel Raum, dass zwei Kinder komfortabel Platz haben. Die Sitze lassen sich unabhängig voneinander vor- oder rückwärts ausrichten.

Statement by the jury
This pushchair impresses with its combination of high flexibility and a straightforward, premium appearance meant to appeal to style-conscious parents.

Begründung der Jury
Dieser Kinderwagen besticht durch die Kombination von hoher Flexibilität und einem klaren, hochwertigen Erscheinungsbild, das stilbewusste Eltern anspricht.

MYTI
Child Car Seat
Kinderautositz

Manufacturer
Nuna International BV,
Leiderdorp, Netherlands
In-house design
Web
www.nuna.eu

The MYTI child car seat is characterised by its ability to accompany children from six months of age to around the size of 150 cm (approx. 12 years). Initially, it is used with a baby harness and a five-point belt, later without the harness and then eventually with the normal safety belt. The backrest is adjustable in five settings; the headrest can be simply pulled out and adjusted to the size of the child. The seat complies with the i-Size safety standards.

Der Kinderautositz MYTI ist dadurch gekennzeichnet, dass er Kinder ab sechs Monaten bis zu einer Größe von 150 cm (entspricht etwa 12 Jahren) begleiten kann. Zu Beginn wird er noch mit einem Babyeinsatz und 5-Punkt-Gurt verwendet, später dann ohne Einsatz und noch ein wenig später mit dem normalen Sicherheitsgurt. Die Rückenlehne ist in drei Stufen verstellbar, das Kopfteil lässt sich einfach herausziehen und an die Größe des Kindes anpassen. Der Sitz erfüllt den i-Size-Sicherheitsstandard.

Statement by the jury
The appearance of the MYTI child car seat indicates a high level of comfort. As an adjustable seat, it is also functionally sophisticated and thereby easily modified to the size of the child.

Begründung der Jury
Das Erscheinungsbild des Kindersitzes MYTI vermittelt hohen Komfort. Als mitwachsender Sitz ist er zudem funktional ausgereift und dadurch einfach an die Größe des Kindes anpassbar.

PIPA lite lx
Child Car Seat
Kinderautositz

Manufacturer
Nuna International BV,
Leiderdorp, Netherlands
In-house design
Web
www.nuna.eu

PIPA lite lx is a sturdy child car seat which is very light at the same time. The seat is manufactured in a proprietary production process using innovative materials, including special textiles like the environmentally friendly and particularly lightweight Lyocell fabric by the TENCEL brand. The extremely durable Aeroflex memory foam and a crush zone in the base both serve to minimise collision energy in case of an accident.

Die PIPA lite lx ist ein robuster und gleichzeitig sehr leichter Kindersitz. Der Sitz wird in einem eigens entwickelten Produktionsverfahren mit innovativen Materialien gefertigt, darunter spezielle Textilien wie Merinowolle und Lyocell-Gewebe der Marke TENCEL. Ein extrem widerstandsfähiger Aeroflex-Memoryschaum und eine Knautschzone im Stützfuß minimieren die Aufprallenergie im Falle eines Unfalls.

Statement by the jury
By using innovative materials, the PIPA lite lx has achieved a low weight and is also very safe, a relief for parents in their daily routine with the baby.

Begründung der Jury
Durch die Verwendung innovativer Materialien hat der PIPA lite lx ein geringes Gewicht und ist dabei sehr sicher, was Eltern den Alltag mit Baby erleichtert.

i-Spin 360™
Child Car Seat
Kinderautositz

Manufacturer
Joie Children's Products Co., Limited,
United Kingdom
In-house design
Web
www.joiebaby.com

The i-Spin 360 child car seat, when set facing backward, is suitable from birth to an age of about four years, whereby it offers a high degree of safety. When facing forward, it can be used for a child who is 76 cm or taller. A Tri-Protect headrest shields the head through a three-layer system and memory foam. Side impact protection elements, which are activated when the belt is tightened, add further shielding of the head area. The seat can be rotated after pressing a button on the side of the seat with one hand, making entry and exit effortless.

Rückwärtsgerichtet ist der Kinderautositz i-Spin 360 ab der Geburt und bis zu einem Alter von ca. vier Jahren verwendbar, wodurch er besonders viel Sicherheit bietet. Vorwärtsgerichtet kann er ab einer Größe von 76 cm genutzt werden. Eine Tri-Protect-Kopfstütze schützt den Kopf mithilfe eines Dreischicht-Systems und Memoryschaum. Seitenaufprallschutzelemente, die mit dem Festziehen des Gurtes aktiviert werden, schützen den Kopfbereich zusätzlich. Der Sitz lässt sich nach Aktivierung eines seitlichen Knopfs mit einer Hand auf der Basisstation drehen und erleichtert so Ein- und Ausstieg.

Statement by the jury
The i-Spin 360 is designed so that children up to four years of age are provided with the greatest possible safety. Convenient handling also makes it easy for parents to correctly adjust the seat.

Begründung der Jury
Der i-Spin 360 ist so gestaltet, dass er Kindern bis zu vier Jahren größtmögliche Sicherheit bietet. Eine komfortable Handhabung erleichtert zudem Eltern die korrekte Einstellung des Sitzes.

BeSafe iZi Twist
Child Car Seat
Kinderautositz

Manufacturer
HTS BeSafe AS, Krøderen, Norway
In-house design
Okke van Mourik, Erik van der Veer
Design
HTS BeSafe AS
(Hans Gutter, Joyce Smits),
Utrecht, Netherlands
Web
www.besafe.com

BeSafe iZi Twist is a child car seat which is optimised for safe transport in a rear-facing position from birth up to an age of around four years. It is horizontally positioned by means of an innovative installation method, facilitating the optimal angle for the backrest. An electronic display guides the user through the installation process. The seat can be rotated to the door side to help seat the child. An ergonomic baby insert substitutes for a separate baby shell.

Statement by the jury
This child seat gains merit with a construction that facilitates horizontal installation. Due to clear optical and acoustic signals, it is also easy to install.

Der Kindersitz BeSafe iZi Twist ist für den Transport in einer sicheren, rückwärtsgerichteten Position von Geburt an bis zu einem Alter von vier Jahren optimiert. Er wird durch eine innovative Montagemethode horizontal eingebaut, wodurch sichergestellt ist, dass die Rückenlehne immer den optimalen Neigungswinkel hat. Ein elektronisches Display führt durch die Installation. Der Sitz lässt sich zur Türseite drehen, um das Kind hineinzusetzen. Ein ergonomischer Babyeinsatz macht eine separate Babyschale überflüssig.

Begründung der Jury
Dieser Kindersitz punktet mit einer Konstruktion, die eine horizontale Installation ermöglicht. Durch deutliche optische und akustische Signale ist er zudem einfach zu montieren.

Genius R160A
Child Car Seat
Kinderautositz

Manufacturer
Max-Inf Baby Products Co., Ltd.,
Baby First, Ningbo, China
Design
D'Andrea & Evers Design,
Enter, Netherlands
Web
www.baby-first.cn
www.de-design.nl

R160A is a child car seat suitable for newborns and children up to around six years old. The design is inspired by a cocoon, with a hard-shell exterior and a soft interior. Both forward and reverse installation offer security thanks to a reinforced shell and a side-impact protection system. Moreover, the seat is easy to install and adjust to the size of the child. The ergonomic seat design and the angle adjustment system support various upright and reclining positions.

Statement by the jury
This child car seat is inspired by a cocoon in terms of form and functionality, thus visualising the safety and security that it offers.

R160A ist ein Kindersitz, der ab der Geburt bis zu einem Alter von etwa sechs Jahren genutzt werden kann. Seine Gestaltung ist von einem Kokon inspiriert, der außen eine harte Schale hat und innen weich ist. Rückwärts- wie vorwärtsgerichtet verwendbar, bietet er mit seiner verstärkten Schale und einem Seitenaufprallschutzsystem Sicherheit, ist einfach zu installieren und an die Größe des Kindes anzupassen. Sein ergonomisches Sitzdesign und ein Neigungsverstellsystem unterstützen verschiedene Sitz- oder Liegepositionen.

Begründung der Jury
Dieser mitwachsende Kindersitz ist in Formgebung und Funktionalität von einem Kokon inspiriert. Dies visualisiert die Sicherheit und Geborgenheit, die er bietet.

Cloud Z
Child Car Seat
Kinderautositz

Manufacturer
Cybex GmbH, Bayreuth, Germany
Design
Koncern Design Studio,
Prague, Czech Republic
Web
www.cybex-online.com
www.koncern.cz

As part of the Z-Line, the Cloud Z i-size infant car seat can be used on the base of the same series, allowing it to simply alternate between rear-facing and boarding position. The seat features an ergonomic reclining position on the pushchair. A removable inlay for newborns supports a safe position for the smallest ones. A linear side impact protection system, in combination with a shell made of energy-absorbing material, provides a high degree of safety.

Statement by the jury
This baby seat successfully unites an elegant form with great comfort and sophisticated safety features.

Als Teil des Z-Line kann die Babyschale Cloud Z mit der Basis der gleichen Reihe genutzt werden, die es ermöglicht, einfach zwischen rückwärtsgerichteter und Einstiegsposition zu wechseln. Der Sitz unterstützt eine ergonomische Liegeposition und kann auch auf dem Kinderwagen verwendet werden. Eine herausnehmbare Neugeboreneneinlage unterstützt eine sichere Position für die Kleinsten. Ein lineares Seitenaufprallschutzsystem sorgt in Verbindung mit der Schale, die aus einem energieabsorbierenden Material gefertigt ist, für hohe Sicherheit.

Begründung der Jury
Diese Babyschale verbindet auf gelungene Weise eine elegante Formgebung mit hohem Komfort und ausgefeilten Sicherheitsmerkmalen.

Solution Z-Fix
Child Car Seat
Kinderautositz

Manufacturer
Cybex GmbH, Bayreuth, Germany
Design
Koncern Design Studio,
Prague, Czech Republic
Web
www.cybex-online.com
www.koncern.cz

The Solution Z-Fix is a child car seat which grows with the child and can be used for children from three to twelve years old. With twelve height settings and automatic width adjustment, it is possible to move the head and shoulder protectors to the correct position for each child. This is achieved quickly and simply thanks to a one-handed setting mechanism. An adjustable headrest ensures that the head always remains in the safety zone. In addition, safety pads actively bring the head into a safe position in the case of an accident.

Statement by the jury
This especially long-term child seat convinces with an ergonomic design, high user-friendliness and optimised safety elements that, above all, protect the child's head.

Der Solution Z-Fix ist ein mitwachsender Kindersitz, der für Kinder von drei bis zwölf Jahren verwendet werden kann. Mit zwölf Höheneinstellungen und einer automatischen Breitenanpassung lassen sich Kopf- und Schulterprotektoren anpassen, was dank eines Einhand-Einstellmechanismus unkompliziert und schnell geht. Eine verstellbare Kopfstütze gewährleistet, dass sich der Kopf immer in der Sicherheitszone befindet. Zusätzlich bringen Sicherheitskissen den Kopf im Falle eines Unfalls aktiv in eine sichere Position.

Begründung der Jury
Dieser sehr lange einsetzbare Kindersitz überzeugt mit einer ergonomischen Gestaltung, einer hohen Benutzerfreundlichkeit und optimierten Sicherheitselementen, die vor allem den Kopf des Kindes schützen.

Advansafix IV
Child Car Seat
Kinderautositz

Manufacturer
Britax Römer Kindersicherheit GmbH,
Leipheim, Germany
In-house design
Cornelia Werth, Michael Fürstenberg
Web
www.britax-roemer.de

When designing the Advansafix IV, the aim was to create a product for the 1/2/3 market which combines a high level of safety, comfort and durability with an elegant appearance. Initially, the seat is used with a five-point harness. A later conversion to the 2/3 group child seat, thanks to the Flip&Grow function, is possible with just few hand movements. The integrated harness is stored behind the cover of the backrest and the shoulder pads are folded out. The side wings add strength to the side impact protection.

Statement by the jury
With its clear language of form, the Advansafix IV displays its high functionality and makes a safe and reliable impression, which in turn inspires confidence.

Ziel der Gestaltung des Advansafix IV war es, einen Kindersitz der Gruppe 1/2/3 zu schaffen, der hohe Sicherheit, Komfort, Langlebigkeit und ein elegantes Aussehen vereint. Der Sitz wird zunächst mit einem 5-Punkt-Gurt verwendet. Der spätere Umbau zum Kindersitz der Gruppe 2/3 ist dank Flip&Grow-Funktion mit wenigen Handgriffen möglich. Der integrierte Gurt wird hinter dem Bezug der Rückenlehne verstaut und die Schulterpolster werden aufgeklappt. Die Seitenflügel verstärken den Seitenaufprallschutz.

Begründung der Jury
Mit seiner klaren Formensprache transportiert der Advansafix IV seine hohe Funktionalität und wirkt sicher und zuverlässig, was wiederum Vertrauen schafft.

Urban Iki Front Seat
Bike Child Seat
Kinderfahrradsitz

Manufacturer
Urban Iki, OGK Europe BV,
Nijverdal, Netherlands
Design
Idenova BV Industrial Design,
Winterswijk, Netherlands
Web
www.urbaniki.com
www.idenova.nl

The Urban Iki Front Seat can be mounted on any standard bicycle in just five minutes. Also a UV filtered windscreen can be attached to the mounting block. To the seat a handlebar can be attached. The softly curved seats, featuring a wave pattern on the outside and waterproof upholstery, are available in the Japan-inspired colours of Bincho Black, Aotake Mint Blue, Sakura Pink and Shinju White. Individual colour combinations are also available.

Statement by the jury
With its soft form and fresh colours, this bicycle seat achieves an aesthetic which appeals to young urban parents. It gains further merit with well-considered functional features like simple mounting.

Der Urban Iki Front Seat lässt sich in nur fünf Minuten auf jedem Standardfahrrad montieren. An dem Montageblock kann zudem eine Windschutzscheibe mit UV-Filter und am Sitz selbst ein Kinderlenker angebracht werden. Den weich geschwungenen Sitz mit Wellenmuster an der Außenseite und wasserfester Polsterung gibt es in den von Japan inspirierten Farben Bincho Black, Aotake Mint Bleu, Sakura Pink und Shinju White. Individuelle Farbzusammenstellungen sind ebenfalls möglich.

Begründung der Jury
Mit seiner weichen Formgebung und den frischen Farben erzielt dieser Fahrradsitz eine Ästhetik, die junge urbane Eltern anspricht. Außerdem punktet er mit durchdachten funktionalen Aspekten wie einer einfachen Montage.

Urban Iki Rear Seat
Bike Child Seat
Kinderfahrradsitz

Manufacturer
Urban Iki, OGK Europe BV,
Nijverdal, Netherlands
Design
Idenova BV Industrial Design,
Winterswijk, Netherlands
Web
www.urbaniki.com
www.idenova.nl

The Urban Iki Rear Seat is a bike child seat that can be attached to any stable pannier rack. The seat support is quickly mountable, enabling the seat to be safely fitted in seconds, thanks to a self-locking click system. The five-point seatbelt with a buckle, which is effortlessly opened, offers security. With an additional base, the seat may also be used for another bicycle. The Urban Iki is available in many colour combinations.

Statement by the jury
This seat is convincing with a flexible base, allowing it to be removed without tools when not needed. Due to the many colour combinations, it may also be tailored to the user's personal taste.

Urban Iki Rear Seat ist ein Kinderfahrradsitz, der auf jedem stabilen Gepäckträger angebracht werden kann. Die Sitzhalterung lässt sich schnell montieren, und der Sitz kann dank eines selbstsperrenden Klicksystems in Sekundenschnelle sicher aufgesetzt werden. Ein 5-Punkt-Gurt mit einer Schnalle, die sich ohne Kraftaufwand öffnen lässt, bietet Sicherheit. Mit einer zusätzlichen Halterung kann der Sitz auch auf einem weiteren Fahrrad genutzt werden. Der Urban Iki ist in vielen Farbkombinationen erhältlich.

Begründung der Jury
Dieser Sitz überzeugt mit einer flexiblen Halterung, dank derer er ohne Werkzeug abgenommen werden kann, wenn er nicht gebraucht wird. Durch die vielen Farbkombinationen lässt er sich zudem an den persönlichen Geschmack anpassen.

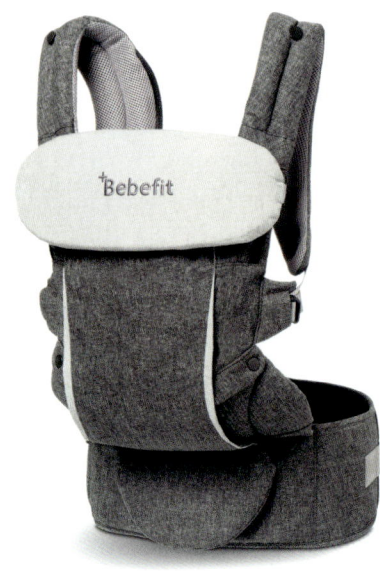

Bebefit
Baby Carrier
Babytrage

Manufacturer
Monit Corp., Seoul, South Korea
In-house design
Hyebin Lee, Jeonghoon Lee
Web
www.goodmonit.com

Bebefit is an ergonomic baby carrier which allows the wearer to transfer most of the baby's weight from the shoulder to the hip, and vice versa, with only one hand. This is made possible by a seat reinforcement mechanism which, when folded out, relieves the shoulders and, when folded in, relieves the waist. The hip seat can carry a weight of up to 50 kg. The lines of the baby carrier are soft and give the impression of comfort. The oval headrest is also a concise design element.

Statement by the jury
By adding a fold-out seat support, this baby carrier offers improved carrying comfort for parents. The soft, gender-neutral design is pleasing as well.

Bebefit ist eine ergonomische Babytrage, die es dem Tragenden erlaubt, das Hauptgewicht des Kindes mit einem Handgriff von der Schulter auf die Hüfte zu verlagern und umgekehrt. Ermöglicht wird dies durch eine mechanische Sitzverstärkung, die herausgeklappt die Schultern und eingeklappt die Hüfte entlastet. Der Hüftgurt kann ein Gewicht von bis zu 50 kg tragen. Die Linienführung der Trage ist weich und vermittelt den Eindruck von Komfort. Die ovale Kopfstütze ist zugleich prägnantes Designelement.

Begründung der Jury
Durch die Ergänzung einer ausklappbaren Sitzunterstützung bietet diese Babytrage Eltern einen verbesserten Tragekomfort. Zudem gefällt sie mit einer weichen, geschlechtsneutralen Gestaltung.

Carus Complete
Baby Carrier
Babytrage

Manufacturer
Diono, Sumner, Washington, USA
In-house design
Web
www.us.diono.com

Carus Complete combines baby carrier and daypack in one innovative product. It can be used in various ways: either as daypack or carrier in which the child can be carried facing forward or backward against the chest or on the back. Thanks to an insert for newborns in which babies can sit with the correct leg posture, Carus Complete can be used from birth onward. The integrated daypack offers a simple yet clever solution for carrying along the most important items.

Statement by the jury
This baby carrier delights with its clever combination of baby carrier and daypack, making it a flexible companion in the everyday family routine.

Carus Complete verbindet Babytrage und Rucksack in einem innovativen Produkt, das auf verschiedene Weise genutzt werden kann: als Rucksack oder als Trage, in der das Kind vorwärts oder rückwärts vor der Brust oder auf dem Rücken getragen wird. Dank einer Neugeboreneneinlage, in der Babys mit der richtigen Beinhaltung sitzen, kann Carus Complete von Geburt an eingesetzt werden. Der integrierte Rucksack bietet eine gleichermaßen einfache wie clevere Lösung, um das Nötigste mitzuführen.

Begründung der Jury
Diese Babytrage begeistert durch die clevere Kombination von Babytrage und Rucksack, was sie zu einem flexiblen Begleiter im Familienalltag macht.

LEAF™ grow
Bouncer & Children's Lounger
Babywippe & Kindersessel

Manufacturer
Nuna International BV,
Leiderdorp, Netherlands
In-house design
Web
www.nuna.eu

The bouncer LEAF grow can be used from birth on thanks to an insert for newborns. As the child grows, it can be easily transformed into a children's lounger. The seat unit is adjustable to three tilt angles. Both the shape and the functionality are inspired by a leaf rocking in the wind. If you give LEAF grow a push, it will rock gently back and forth for up to two minutes, while the elegantly curved foot guarantees a secure position.

Statement by the jury
The shape of this children's lounger is reminiscent of a soft nest, thus radiating a sense of security that is intensified by rocking. Especially convenient is how the chair grows with the child.

Die Babywippe LEAF grow kann dank eines Neugeboreneneinsatzes von Geburt des Kindes an genutzt und später einfach zum Kindersessel umgebaut werden. Die Sitzeinheit ist in drei Neigungswinkeln einstellbar. Die Formgebung ist ebenso wie die Funktionsweise von einem im Wind schaukelnden Blatt inspiriert. Stößt man die LEAF grow an, schwingt sie bis zu zwei Minuten lang sanft vor sich hin, wobei der elegant gebogene Fuß einen festen Stand garantiert.

Begründung der Jury
Dieser Kindersessel erinnert in seiner Formgebung an ein weiches Nest und strahlt eine Geborgenheit aus, die durch das Schwingen noch verstärkt wird. Besonders praktisch ist, dass der Sessel mitwächst.

Aristot
Convertible Bassinet
Stubenwagen

Manufacturer
Enfant Terrible Design AB,
Norrtälje, Sweden
In-house design
Lisa Furuland-Kotsianis
Web
https://aristot.com/

The design of the Aristot bassinet combines high comfort and functionality with versatility since it is based on a modular concept. Handcrafted by European artisans, Aristot offers interchangeable pedestals and bassinets crafted from various premium materials, for instance velvet fabrics or materials with a leather look, making them adaptable to interior furnishings. When the baby grows out of the bassinet, Aristot can be converted into high-quality furniture, such as a table, chair or stool.

Die Gestaltung des Stubenwagens Aristot verbindet hohen Komfort und Funktionalität mit Vielseitigkeit, denn ihm liegt ein modulares Konzept zugrunde: Von europäischen Kunsthandwerkern handgefertigt, bietet Aristot auswechselbare Podeste und Babykörbe in verschiedenen, hochwertigen Materialien an, z. B. mit Samtstoffen oder Materialien im Lederlook, sodass sie sich an die Einrichtung anpassen lassen. Ist das Baby aus dem Wagen herausgewachsen, kann Aristot in ein hochwertiges Möbel wie einen Tisch, einen Stuhl oder einen Hocker umgewandelt werden.

Statement by the jury
Aristot convinces with high-quality materiality and classical aesthetics which can be adapted to individual tastes. The fact that the bassinet can be used as household furniture later provides real added value.

Begründung der Jury
Aristot überzeugt mit einer hochwertigen Materialität und einer klassischen, auf den individuellen Geschmack anpassbaren Ästhetik. Ein echter Mehrwert liegt darin, dass der Stubenwagen später als Wohnmöbel weitergenutzt werden kann.

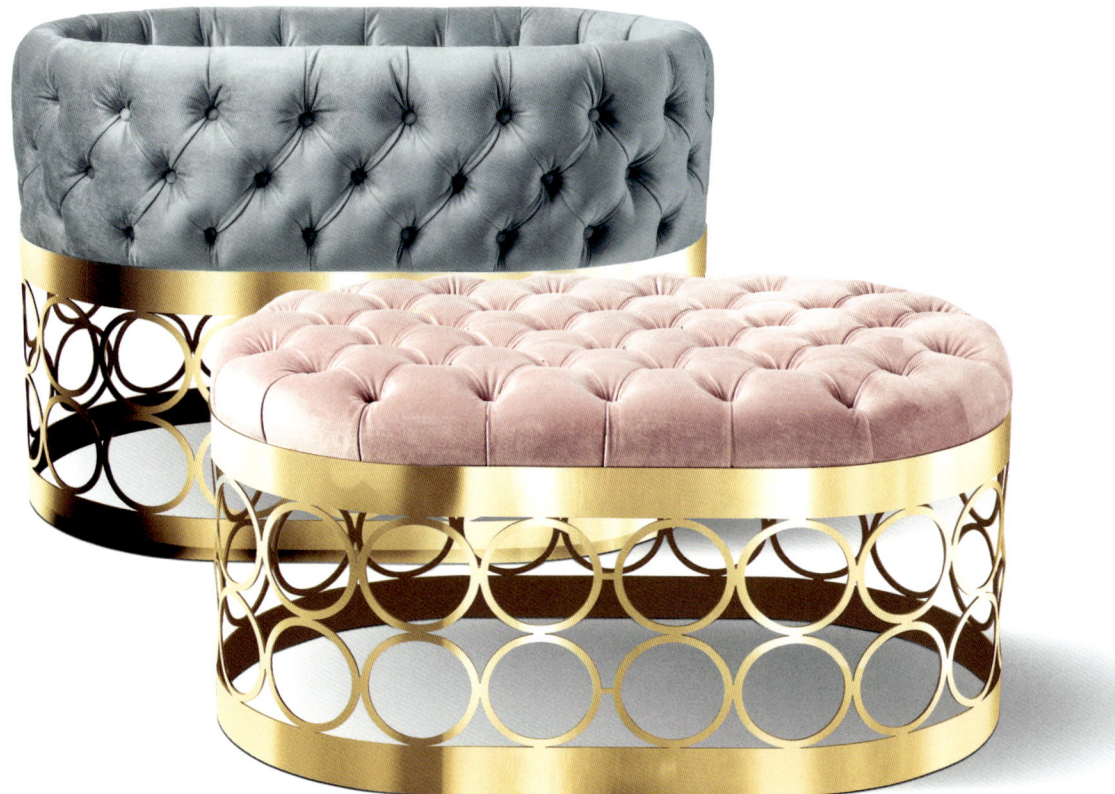

babybay® Boxspring Comfort
Co-Sleeper
Beistellbett

Manufacturer
Tobi Kindermöbel GmbH,
Inning, Germany
In-house design
Christian Pihale
Web
www.babybay.de

The babybay Boxspring Comfort is a co-sleeper solution for high-standing parental beds. With its elevated construction and variable height adjustability, the bed surface can be set at the height of frameless box-spring beds and fastened to them securely with a strap without the need for tools. Thanks to an integrated cot grille with snap lock, it is convertible from a co-sleeper to a bassinet. The bed is made of solid beech and available in various colours.

Statement by the jury
With its special design, this co-sleeper is optimally coordinated to box-spring beds, so that the baby bed is flush with the parents' mattress in terms of height.

Das babybay Boxspring Comfort ist eine Beistellbett-Lösung für hohe Elternbetten. Mit seiner hohen Bauweise und stufenlosen Höhenverstellung lässt sich die Liegefläche des Bettes an rahmenlose Boxspring-Betten anpassen und mit einem Gurt leicht, sicher und ohne Werkzeug an ihnen befestigen. Dank eines integrierten Gitters mit Schnappverschluss lässt sich das Beistellbett einfach in einen Stubenwagen verwandeln. Das Bett ist aus massivem Buchenholz gefertigt und in verschiedenen Farben erhältlich.

Begründung der Jury
Dieses Beistellbett passt sich mit seiner speziellen Gestaltung optimal an Boxspringbetten an, damit kein störender Höhenversatz zwischen elterlicher Matratze und Babybett entsteht.

Mickey, Tom and Zaya
Children's Beds
Kinderbetten

Manufacturer
Interia, Kyiv, Ukraine
Design
FORM bureau (Viktoriia Shkliar),
Kyiv, Ukraine
Web
www.interia.com.ua
www.form.house

The design of the Mickey, Tom und Zaya children's beds is inspired by animated cartoons. The headboards take the shape of animal heads and convey a happy impression. The bed frames, including the headboards, are covered with a deep black woollen fabric, so that the beds contrast with the surroundings while still making a soft impression. These beds are manufactured in a width of 90 or 120 cm and a length of 190 or 200 cm.

Statement by the jury
These children's beds combine a happy impression with a calm appearance, characterised by the black colouring. They thus blend harmoniously into children's colourful bedrooms.

Die Gestaltung der Kinderbetten Mickey, Tom und Zaya ist von Kindertrickfilmen inspiriert. Die Kopfenden haben die Form von Tierköpfen und vermitteln einen fröhlichen Eindruck. Die Bettgestelle inklusive der Kopfteile sind mit tiefschwarzem Wollstoff bespannt, sodass die Betten sich von ihrer Umgebung abheben, gleichzeitig jedoch weich wirken. Die Betten werden mit einer Breite von 90 oder 120 cm und einer Länge von 190 oder 200 cm hergestellt.

Begründung der Jury
Diese Kinderbetten verbinden eine fröhliche Anmutung mit einem ruhigen Erscheinungsbild, das durch die schwarze Farbgebung geprägt ist. Auf diese Weise fügen sie sich harmonisch in bunte Kinderzimmer ein.

FLEXA Birk
Children's Bed
Kinderbett

Manufacturer
Flexa4Dreams A/S,
Hornsyld, Denmark
In-house design
Markus Bangerter
Web
www.flexaworld.com

The children's bed Birk is made of solid birch wood and birch plywood. Its minimalist design with rounded corners and edges distinguishes the classical, timeless appearance of the bed. The light birch wood is durable; it ages with grace and gives the bed a natural, organic impression. Nordic woods served as inspiration for the design. The bed is produced in a normal and a mid high version.

Statement by the jury
The Birk children's bed delights with its durability, which is achieved by a calm, timeless design, high material quality and the careful, skilled craftsmanship.

Das Kinderbett Birk ist aus massivem Birkenholz sowie Birkenschichtholz gefertigt. Sein minimalistisches Design mit abgerundeten Ecken und Kanten prägt das klassische, zeitlose Erscheinungsbild des Bettes. Das helle Birkenholz ist langlebig, altert würdevoll und verleiht dem Bett eine natürliche, organische Anmutung. Inspiration für die Gestaltung waren die nordischen Wälder. Das Bett wird in einer normalen und einer halbhohen Variante hergestellt.

Begründung der Jury
Das Kinderbett Birk begeistert mit seiner Langlebigkeit, die durch eine ruhige, zeitlose Gestaltung, eine hohe Materialqualität und die sorgfältige, handwerkliche Fertigung erzielt wird.

Swing Pendulum 2in1
Rocker for Baby Cribs
Schaukelfunktion für Babybetten

Manufacturer
Olymp & Olipa GmbH, Frechen, Germany
In-house design
Andrej Olipa, Tatiana Olipa
Web
www.comfortbaby.global

Thanks to the Swing Pendulum 2in1 base, the SmartGrow 7in1 crib can be converted into a cradle. The stable, rocking base is made of solid beech. For this transformation, it is simply attached to the sides of the optionally round or oval cot, and the cot is rocked by giving it a gentle push. The rocking mechanism can be fixated when not in use.

Mit dem Untersatz Swing Pendulum 2in1 lässt sich das Babybett SmartGrow 7in1 in eine Wiege verwandeln. Der stabile, aus massivem Buchenholz gefertigte Schaukeluntersatz wird dafür einfach an den Seiten des wahlweise runden oder ovalen Babybetts befestigt, und das Bett kann mit einem leichten Stups angestoßen werden. Der Schaukelmechanismus lässt sich auch arretieren, wenn die Funktion nicht gebraucht wird.

Statement by the jury
The rocking base Swing Pendulum 2in1 convinces with its minimalist design and an impressively simple functionality, enabling the cot to be quickly converted into a cradle.

Begründung der Jury
Der Schaukeluntersatz Swing Pendulum 2in1 überzeugt mit seiner minimalistischen Gestaltung und einer bestechend einfachen Funktionsweise, durch die sich das Babybett schnell in eine Wiege verwandeln lässt.

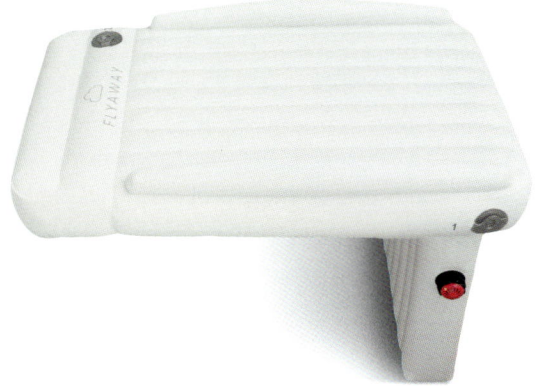

Flyaway Kids Bed
Children's Travel Bed for Flights
Kinderreisebett für Flüge

Manufacturer
Flyaway Designs, Forch, Switzerland
In-house design
Debra Pally
Web
www.flyawaydesigns.com
Honourable Mention

The Flyaway Kids Bed is an inflatable bed on which children can lie flat and sleep on an aeroplane. It can be inflated with a hand pump within 90 seconds and is compatible with any aircraft seat in the economy class, without blocking access to life vests, air vents or similar equipment. Thanks to an emergency pressure relief valve, air is automatically released if cabin pressure falls. The surface is wipeable and also grooved so that toys cannot roll off.

Statement by the jury
The Flyaway Kids Bed is based on a clever idea: making the time spent on longer flights more pleasant for children and parents.

Flyaway Kids Bed ist ein aufblasbares Bett, auf dem Kinder im Flugzeug flach liegen und schlafen können. Es lässt sich mit einer Handpumpe binnen 90 Sekunden aufblasen und ist mit jedem Flugzeugsitz der Economyclass kompatibel, ohne den Zugang zu Schwimmwesten, Lüftungsöffnungen o. Ä. zu blockieren. Dank eines Not-Überdruckventils lässt es die Luft automatisch ab, sobald der Druck in der Kabine abfällt. Die Oberfläche ist abwischbar und zudem geriffelt, sodass Spielzeug nicht so schnell herunterrollt.

Begründung der Jury
Mit dem Flyaway Kids Bed wurde eine smarte Idee umgesetzt: lange Flugzeiten für Kinder und Eltern angenehmer zu gestalten.

Aco
Children's Chair
Kindersessel

Manufacturer
iloom, Seoul, South Korea
In-house design
Yunsu Na
Web
www.iloom.com

The design of Aco pursues the objective of developing a sofa ideally suited to children. To this end, studies were conducted about their average body measurements and sitting behaviour. The result is a small sofa with an organic form inspired by the silhouette of a baby elephant. The ergonomic design requires good posture and offers comfort during activities while sitting. Aco is available in different versions which allude to animals or Disney characters.

Statement by the jury
With their simple language of form and cheerful colours, the small, ergonomic Aco sofas make a positive impression and appeal to children and parents alike.

Die Gestaltung von Aco hatte das Ziel, ein bestmöglich auf Kleinkinder abgestimmtes Sofa zu entwickeln. Dafür wurden Studien zu deren durchschnittlichen Körpermaßen und ihrem Sitzverhalten zugrunde gelegt. Das Ergebnis ist ein kleines Sofa, dessen organische Formgebung von der Silhouette eines Babyelefanten inspiriert ist. Das ergonomische Design fördert eine gute Haltung und bietet Komfort bei Aktivitäten im Sitzen. Aco gibt es in verschiedenen Versionen, die an Tiere oder Disney-Charaktere angelehnt sind.

Begründung der Jury
Mit ihrer einfachen Formensprache und den fröhlichen Farben haben die kleinen, ergonomischen Aco-Sofas eine positive Ausstrahlung und sprechen Kinder und Eltern gleichermaßen an.

MUtable
Play Table
Spieltisch

Manufacturer
Mukako, Milan, Italy
In-house design
Mukako Team
Web
www.mutable-design.com

MUtable is an all-in-one play table for children ages one to eight years old. Thanks to its adjustable leg heights, the table grows with the child. This multi-activity table comes with four double-sided play boards, including two bricks bases compatible with Lego and Lego Duplo, as well as two writing surfaces – a blackboard and a whiteboard. Every play board has a magic hole in the middle, so children can easily push all their toys into the Toy Storage Bag below. The wooden table is very solid and durable.

Statement by the jury
The MUtable all-in-one-play table ensures diversification and also more order in children's rooms. It is appealing with its multifunctional concept and its stable and loving design.

MUtable ist ein All-in-one-Spieltisch für Kinder im Alter von einem bis acht Jahren, der dank seiner höhenverstellbaren Beine mitwächst. Zu dem vielseitigen Spieltisch gehören vier doppelseitige Spielbretter, darunter zwei, die mit Lego und Lego Duplo kompatibel sind, sowie zwei Schreibflächen – eine Tafel und ein Whiteboard. Jedes Spielbrett hat in der Mitte ein „magisches Loch", durch das die Kinder das ihr Spielzeug in einen Beutel unter dem Tisch fallen lassen können. Der Holztisch ist solide und langlebig.

Begründung der Jury
Der All-in-one-Spieltisch MUtable sorgt für viel Abwechslung und gleichzeitig mehr Ordnung im Kinderzimmer. Er gefällt mit seinem multifunktionalen Konzept und einer stabilen und liebevollen Gestaltung.

ComfortBaby® SmartChair 2in1
High Chair
Hochstuhl

Manufacturer
Olymp & Olipa GmbH, Frechen, Germany
In-house design
Boris Arabadzhi, Andrej Olipa, Tatiana Olipa
Web
www.comfortbaby.global
Honourable Mention

ComfortBaby SmartChair 2in1 is a child's high chair which grows with the child. It has an ergonomic design combined with high-quality materials, manufactured with new woodworking technology. Completely rounded surfaces, a well-considered safety concept and an optional five-point seatbelt allow the chair to be used starting at six months of age, enabling the child to sit at the table and take part in family life. The chair is utilisable up to an age of ten years.

ComfortBaby SmartChair 2in1 ist ein mitwachsender Kinderhochstuhl, der ein ergonomisches Design mit hochwertigen Materialien kombiniert und bei dessen Fertigung eine neue Technologie der Holzverarbeitung angewandt wird. Komplett abgerundete Flächen, ein durchdachtes Sicherheitskonzept und ein optional erhältlicher 5-Punkt-Gurt erlauben eine Nutzung des Stuhls bereits ab dem sechsten Lebensmonat, sodass das Baby am Tisch sitzen und am Familienleben teilnehmen kann. Der Stuhl ist bis zu einem Alter von zehn Jahren verwendbar.

Statement by the jury
The ComfortBaby SmartChair 2in1 is attractive as a children's chair which grows with the child. The choice of beech gives it the necessary sturdiness and durability.

Begründung der Jury
Der ComfortBaby SmartChair 2in1 gefällt als mitwachsender Kinderstuhl. Die Wahl des Materials Buchenholz verleiht ihm die nötige Robustheit und Langlebigkeit.

bike8 R
Children's Vehicle
Kinderfahrzeug

Manufacturer
BA KE Technologies (Dongguan) Co., Ltd.,
Dongguan, China
In-house design
Da Ma
Web
www.bike8.bike

The bike8 R has been specially developed for children who take part in balance bike races. The bicycle is very aerodynamic and designed with a low centre of gravity, thus creating a very sporty bike with a stable frame and high manoeuvrability. Children thus find it easier to hold their balance and travel rapidly. Coloured rings are located on the seat post to record the race results.

Das bike8 R wurde speziell für Kinder entwickelt, die an Laufrad-Rennen teilnehmen. Das Laufrad ist sehr aerodynamisch und mit einem tiefen Schwerpunkt gestaltet, wodurch ein sehr sportliches Rad mit stabilem Rahmen und hoher Manövrierfähigkeit entstanden ist. Dadurch fällt es Kindern leichter, das Gleichgewicht zu halten und sich mit hoher Geschwindigkeit zu bewegen. An der Sattelstütze lassen sich bunte Ringe befestigen, die die Rennergebnisse dokumentieren.

Statement by the jury
With its aerodynamic and balanced construction, the bike8 R is fast and offers high safety. The coloured racing rings are a charming detail that suits the already sporty overall appearance.

Begründung der Jury
Mit seiner aerodynamischen und ausbalancierten Bauweise ist das bike8 R schnell und bietet hohe Sicherheit. Ein charmantes Detail, das schön zum sportlichen Gesamtbild passt, sind die bunten Rennringe.

No.3 Athlete Balance Bike
Children's Vehicle
Kinderfahrzeug

Manufacturer
Shenzhen Beite Industry Design Co., Ltd.,
Shenzhen, China
In-house design
He Chun Li, Si Hui Pang, Qing Song Liu,
Fei Shan, Yong Wang, Chang Qing Liu,
Qiao Wei Zhang, Yao Yao Huang
Web
www.cubho.com

No.3 Athlete is a balance bike whose sporty impression is characterised by smooth curves, dynamically arched lines and a frame with a single-arm dropout. A lamp is mounted on the steering head pipe which seamlessly blends into the design of the frame. Both the front and rear lights are controlled by a wireless, electronic regulator, thus enabling convenient operation. The balance bike also has a horn. Thanks to its clever construction, the frame is very light.

Statement by the jury
This balance bike combines a stable, sporty appearance with a lightweight construction. The harmonious integration of the front and rear lights is effectively implemented in the overall look.

No.3 Athlete ist ein Laufrad, dessen sportliche Anmutung von sanften Kurven, dynamisch geschwungenen Linien und einem Rahmen mit einarmigem Ausfallende geprägt ist. Am Steuerkopfrohr ist eine Leuchte montiert, die sich nahtlos in das Design des Rahmens einfügt. Sowohl dieses Vorderlicht als auch das Rücklicht werden über einen kabellosen elektronischen Regler gesteuert, was die Bedienung komfortabel macht. Das Laufrad hat zudem eine Hupe. Dank seiner raffinierten Bauweise ist der Rahmen sehr leicht.

Begründung der Jury
Dieses Laufrad verbindet ein stabiles, sportliches Erscheinungsbild mit einer leichten Bauweise. Gelungen ist auch die harmonische Integration von Vorder- und Rücklicht in das Gesamtbild.

sooibe
Children's Vehicle
Kinderfahrzeug

Manufacturer
SOOIBE Intelligent Technology
(Hangzhou) Co., Ltd.,
Hangzhou, China
In-house design
Yihang Pan
Web
www.sooibe.com

This balance bicycle is very light, with a weight of only 2.8 kg, and it trains the equilibrium and coordination of children between two and six years of age. The bike is made of hard aluminium and inspired by a sprinting cheetah. The lower pipe, the U-shaped fork and the three-cornered fork holder are interconnected and form a cone-shaped structure which protects the legs and feet of the child and improves the lateral vertical load.

Statement by the jury
With its dynamic design, sooibe imparts an impression of sportiness and thus awakens the ambitions of the child. The carefully considered construction is also convincing, as it ensures stability and safety.

Dieses gut ausbalancierte Laufrad ist mit einem Gewicht von 2,8 kg sehr leicht und schult Gleichgewichtssinn und Koordination von Kindern zwischen zwei und sechs Jahren. Die Formgebung des aus Hartaluminium gefertigten Rades ist von einem sprintenden Geparden inspiriert. Sein Unterrohr, die u-förmige Gabel und die dreieckige Gabelhalterung sind miteinander verbunden und bilden eine kegelförmige Struktur, die die Beine und Füße des Kindes schützt und die seitliche vertikale Belastung verbessert.

Begründung der Jury
sooibe vermittelt mit seiner dynamischen Gestaltung den Eindruck von Sportlichkeit und weckt so den Ehrgeiz der Kleinen. Überzeugend ist auch die sorgfältig durchdachte Konstruktion, die für Stabilität und Sicherheit sorgt.

BOO TRICYCLE.2
Children's Vehicle
Kinderfahrzeug

Manufacturer
LISLEI, Lda, Porto, Portugal
In-house design
Web
www.boo-kids.com
Honourable Mention

Tricycle.2 is a wooden tricycle designed for children 24 months and older, as evidenced by a simple language of form and an attractive appearance. The tricycle was developed by taking into account aesthetic, sensory and ecological aspects and manufactured of ash wood and Valchromat or coloured wood-fibre panels. With simple functionality and a pleasant feel, it supports children in developing coordination and a sense of balance.

Statement by the jury
This bicycle impresses with a consistent use of the material wood and with a clear language of form.

Tricycle.2 ist ein Dreirad aus Holz, das mit seiner einfachen Formensprache und seinem sympathischen Erscheinungsbild für Kinder ab einem Alter von 24 Monaten konzipiert ist. Das Dreirad wurde unter Berücksichtigung von ästhetischen, sensorischen und ökologischen Aspekten entwickelt und aus Eschenholz und Valchromat – farbigen Holzfaserplatten – gefertigt. Mit seiner einfachen Funktion und angenehmen Haptik unterstützt es Kinder bei der Entwicklung von Koordination und Gleichgewichtssinn.

Begründung der Jury
Dieses Dreirad besticht mit einer durchgängigen Verwendung des Materials Holz und einer klaren Formensprache.

BERG Reppy
Children's Vehicle
Kinderfahrzeug

Manufacturer
BERG Toys B.V., Ede, Netherlands
In-house design
Jord Mulder, Paul Scheurwater
Web
www.bergtoys.com

BERG Reppy is a pedal go-kart for children of ages between two and a half and six years old. It is attractive, light and has a compact design. The low positioned bucket seat can be easily adjusted to the body length. Pedalling is smooth thanks to the integrated direct drive, durable 10" EVA tyres and overall low weight of 9 kg. The go-kart is portable due to an integrated handle within the frame and can be easily stored.

Statement by the jury
This colourful vehicle convinces with a child-friendly design and is fun to ride. Thanks to its stable construction, the go-cart is safe and light to move.

Der BERG Reppy ist ein Pedal-Gokart für Kinder zwischen zweieinhalb und sechs Jahren. Er ist ansprechend, leicht und kompakt gestaltet. Der tief positionierte Schalensitz lässt sich einfach an die Körpergröße anpassen. Das Treten fällt dank integrierten Direktantriebs, 10"-EVA-Reifen und einem geringen Gesamtgewicht von 9 kg leicht. Der Pedal-Gokart ist mit seinem in den Rahmen integrierten Griff einfach zu tragen und lässt sich leicht verstauen.

Begründung der Jury
Dieses farbenfrohe Fahrzeug überzeugt mit einer kindgerechten Gestaltung und bringt Spaß. Dank seiner stabilen Konstruktion ist der Gokart sicher und leicht zu bewegen.

Drifter
Children's Vehicle
Kinderfahrzeug

Manufacturer
Goodbaby Child Products Co., Ltd., Kunshan, China
In-house design
David Alan Smith, Jinlong Lian
Web
www.haohaizi.com

The Drifter is a vehicle that enables children aged three to six years to learn drifting and thereby enhance their motor skills. The front bumper is angled aerodynamically at 37 degrees. A bucket seat ensures that the spine is protected during rapid drifting. There are three possible seating positions depending on the size of the child. The handles have deep grooves which offer good hold, even when drifting quickly around bends.

Statement by the jury
The children's vehicle Drifter gains merit with a shape that is functionally designed for safety and supports children in training their motor skills.

Der Drifter ist ein Fahrzeug, das Kindern zwischen drei und sechs Jahren ermöglicht, das Driften zu erlernen und dabei ihre motorischen Fähigkeiten zu verbessern. Die Lenkstange hat eine aerodynamische Neigung von 37 Grad. Ein Schalensitz stellt sicher, dass die Wirbelsäule auch bei rasantem Driften geschützt ist. Je nach Größe des Kindes können drei Sitzpositionen eingestellt werden. Die Griffe haben tiefe Rillen, die auch bei schnellen Kurvenfahrten viel Halt bieten.

Begründung der Jury
Das Kinderfahrzeug Drifter punktet mit einer funktionalen, auf Sicherheit ausgerichteten Formgebung und unterstützt Kinder beim Training ihrer motorischen Fähigkeiten.

700Kids Little Monster
In-Line Skates

Manufacturer
700Kids (Shenzhen) Technology Co., Ltd.,
Shenzhen, China
In-house design
Joey Li
Web
https://qixiaobai.tmall.com

The 700Kids Little Monster in-line skates attract attention due to their emotional and colourful design. Circular "eyes" are mounted on the sides of the skates, and their expression changes while skating. The shoes are softly rounded, avoiding sharp edges and corners. Plastic coatings also protect them from scratches. The inner shoe is made of breathable and comfortable foam material that is size-adjustable and can be removed for washing.

Statement by the jury
With its soft and colourful design, the 700Kids Little Monster appeals to children. Its size-adjustable and washable inner shoe also makes it very functional.

Die Inlineskates 700Kids Little Monster machen durch ihre emotionale und farbenfrohe Gestaltung auf sich aufmerksam. Seitlich am Schuh sind kreisrunde „Augen" angebracht, deren Ausdruck beim Skaten wechselt. Die Schuhe sind weich abgerundet, scharfe Kanten und Ecken wurden vermieden. Zudem schützen Kunststoffbeschichtungen vor Kratzern. Der Innenschuh aus einem atmungsaktiven und komfortablen Schaumstoffmaterial ist größenverstellbar und lässt sich zum Waschen herausnehmen.

Begründung der Jury
Mit seiner weichen und farbenfrohen Gestaltung spricht der 700Kids Little Monster Kinder an. Sein größenverstellbarer und waschbarer Innenschuh macht ihn zudem sehr funktional.

Mi Kids Scooter
Children's Vehicle
Kinderfahrzeug

Manufacturer
Xiaomi Inc., Beijing, China
In-house design
Web
www.mi.com

The Mi Kids Scooter for children is very safe. Its C-shaped rubber handle is ergonomic and designed with a buffer function. Metal parts and surfaces are entirely enclosed. The handlebar is easily dismantled and attached for transport under the wide, non-slip footboard. The front wheels are available in two modes: with a wide wheelbase the scooter runs slowly, and with the narrow version the steering is more sensitive and the speed greater. Flashing LEDs increase safety in traffic.

Statement by the jury
This scooter convinces with a design in which every detail is geared towards greatly minimising injury when children are riding the scooter.

Der Mi Kids Scooter für Kinder ist sehr sicher. Sein C-förmiger Gummigriff ist ergonomisch und mit Pufferfunktion gestaltet, Metallteile und -flächen sind vollständig ummantelt. Der Lenker lässt sich leicht demontieren und zum Transport unten am rutschfesten, breiten Fußbrett befestigen. Die Vorderräder sind in zwei Modi erhältlich: Mit breiter Achse gleitet der Roller langsam, mit schmaler ist die Lenkung schärfer und die Geschwindigkeit höher. Blinkende LED-Leuchten erhöhen die Verkehrssicherheit.

Begründung der Jury
Dieser Tretroller überzeugt mit einer Gestaltung, bei der in jedem Detail darauf geachtet wurde, dass Kinder sich beim Rollerfahren so wenig wie möglich verletzen.

Lelle
Children's Bicycle Helmet
Kinderfahrradhelm

Manufacturer
Cycleurope Sverige AB, Varberg, Sweden
Design
Idesign (Johan Larsvall, Nils Löventorn),
Stockholm, Sweden
Web
www.cycleurope.se
www.idesign.se

Lelle is a bicycle helmet for younger children which was developed especially for little heads and offers great comfort, aiming for children to accept the helmet and enjoy wearing it. The helmet expresses timeless aesthetics. The air holes ensure good ventilation, without disturbing the minimalist overall impression. The outer shell causes little friction and thus, in combination with the shock-absorbing EPS foam and the MIPS system, provides protection in the case of accidents. The front peak protects the face.

Statement by the jury
Due to its special fit to the form of children's heads, the Lelle helmet is comfortable and safe in equal measure. Furthermore, it appeals with its clear design.

Lelle ist ein Fahrradhelm für jüngere Kinder, der eigens für kleine Köpfe entwickelt wurde und viel Komfort bietet, sodass Kinder den Helm akzeptieren und gerne tragen. Der Helm hat eine zeitlose Ästhetik. Die Luftlöcher gewährleisten eine gute Belüftung, ohne den minimalistischen Gesamteindruck zu stören. Die Außenschale bietet geringen Reibungswiderstand und schützt so im Zusammenspiel mit dem stoßabsorbierenden EPS-Schaum und dem MIPS-System bei Unfällen. Die Frontspitze schützt das Gesicht.

Begründung der Jury
Durch seine spezielle Anpassung an die Form von Kinderköpfen ist der Helm Lelle gleichermaßen komfortabel wie sicher. Zudem gefällt er mit seiner klaren Gestaltung.

Horse
Rocking Horse
Schaukelpferd

Manufacturer
TrêsDê, Lda, Mafra, Portugal
In-house design
Rui Tomás
Web
www.ruitomas.pt

Horse is a minimalist reinterpretation of the rocking horse, whereby the appearance is characterised by Scandinavian aesthetics and formal simplicity. It was the objective of the design process to simplify the traditional rocking horse as far as possible. The result is a children's product which appears both contemporary and timeless in equal measure. Horse consists of the laminated material Corian and is shaped through a special bending process.

Horse ist eine minimalistische Neuinterpretation des Schaukelpferds, dessen Erscheinungsbild von skandinavischer Ästhetik und formaler Schlichtheit geprägt ist. Ziel des Gestaltungsprozesses war es, die Form des traditionellen Schaukelpferds so weit wie möglich zu vereinfachen. Das Ergebnis ist ein Kinderprodukt, das gleichermaßen zeitgemäß wie zeitlos wirkt. Horse besteht aus dem in einem speziellen Biegeverfahren geformten Verbundwerkstoff Corian.

Statement by the jury
This rocking horse impresses with its uncompromisingly reduced design, allowing it to blend in with the child's room and the living room equally well.

Begründung der Jury
Dieses Schaukelpferd besticht mit seiner kompromisslos reduzierten Gestaltung, durch die es sich ins Kinderzimmer ebenso gut einfügt wie ins Wohnzimmer.

Table Skill Mat
Handiwork Mat
Bastelunterlage

Manufacturer
Flying Tiger Copenhagen, Zebra A/S,
Copenhagen, Denmark
In-house design
Lovorika Banovic
Web
http://corporate.flyingtiger.com

This silicone handiwork mat helps to improve organisation for children when painting and crafting. In seven small, round storage compartments there is room for beads, modelling clay, paints and similar items. The handiwork materials can thus be clearly organised while the tabletop is protected. The mat is waterproof, non-slip and easily washed with soap and water. It can be hung out to dry and then rolled up or folded for space-saving storage.

Statement by the jury
The Table Skill Mat takes an amazing approach to combining a handiwork mat with an organising system and thus offers real added value.

Diese Bastelunterlage aus Silikon ermöglicht Kindern mehr Organisation beim Malen und Basteln. In sieben kleinen, runden Aufbewahrungsfächern finden Perlen, Knete, Malfarben u. Ä. Platz. Auf diese Weise können die Bastelmaterialien übersichtlich geordnet werden, zugleich ist die Tischoberfläche geschützt. Die Matte ist wasserdicht, rutschfest und lässt sich einfach mit Wasser und Seife reinigen. Zum Abtropfen und Trocknen kann sie aufgehängt und danach eingerollt oder gefaltet platzsparend verstaut werden.

Begründung der Jury
Table Skill Mat verbindet auf verblüffend einfache Weise eine Bastelunterlage mit einem Organisationssystem und bietet so einen echten Mehrwert.

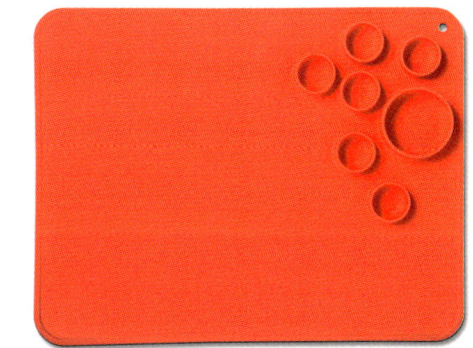

X Block
Construction Toy
Konstruktionsspielzeug

Manufacturer
X Block ApS, Copenhagen, Denmark
In-house design
Pascal Laraignou, Oliver Erritzøe
Web
www.xblock.dk

X Block is an innovative building block concept that supports children's fantasy-evoking games, creativity and motor skills. The building blocks made of impact-resistant plastic are manufactured in Denmark and were specially developed as playing options for childcare centres, schools, and so forth. Thanks to the special cross-shaped feature on the sides, the bricks are easy to assemble; when stacked in a brickwork pattern, stable constructions are built. The blocks are very robust, with a durability of up to 20 years.

Statement by the jury
X Block is convincing with its clear linearity and gives children a good deal of freedom when building. With its sturdy construction, this toy guarantees a long lifespan.

X Block ist ein innovatives Bausteinkonzept, das phantasievolles Spielen, Kreativität und Feinmotorik von Kindern fördert. Die Bauklötze aus stoßfestem Kunststoff werden in Dänemark gefertigt und wurden insbesondere als Spielmöglichkeit für Kindergärten, Schulen etc. entwickelt. Dank des speziellen Kreuzmusters an den Seiten lassen sich die Klötze einfach verbinden und bilden, versetzt gestapelt, stabile Bauwerke. Die Blöcke sind mit einer Lebensdauer von bis zu 20 Jahren sehr robust.

Begründung der Jury
X Block überzeugt mit seiner klaren Linienführung und gewährt Kindern viel Freiheit beim Bauen. Seine robuste Konstruktion garantiert dem Spielzeug eine lange Lebensdauer.

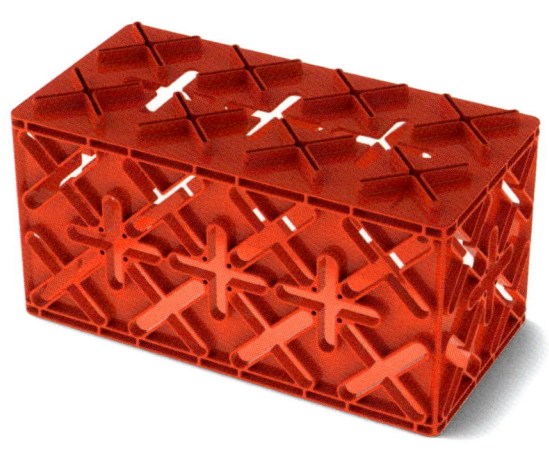

MURO
Activity Centre
Aktivitätsspielzeug

Manufacturer
Mymuro Ltd., London, United Kingdom
In-house design
Jeremy Bond
Web
www.mymuro.com

Muro is an activity and learning toy, developed in conjunction with school psychologists, which is meant to encourage children to play while applying all their senses. The Muro system is comprised of a base and various toys. The base, with its pattern of holes, serves as foundation. Thanks to a special connecter, various toys are simply pressed into the holes and fastened. Individual activity centres can thus be tailored to the development level of each child.

Statement by the jury
Muro is delightful with its system concept that offers great flexibility when creating ever-new play scenarios. The combination of a neutral wooden block and coloured accessories is also very attractive.

Muro ist ein mit Schulpsychologen entwickeltes Aktivitäts- und Lernspielzeug, das Kinder ermutigen soll, zu spielen und dabei all ihre Sinne einzusetzen. Das Muro-System setzt sich aus Basis und Spielzubehör zusammen. Die Basis dient mit ihrem Lochmuster als Fundament. Verschiedene Spielzeuge lassen sich dank spezieller Steckverbindungen einfach in die Löcher drücken und befestigen. So können individuelle Aktivitätszentren gestaltet werden, die zum jeweiligen Entwicklungsstand des Kindes passen.

Begründung der Jury
Muro begeistert mit seinem Systemgedanken, der eine hohe Flexibilität beim Erstellen von immer wieder neuen Spielszenarien bietet. Sehr schön ist auch die Kombination von neutralem Holzblock und farbigem Zubehör.

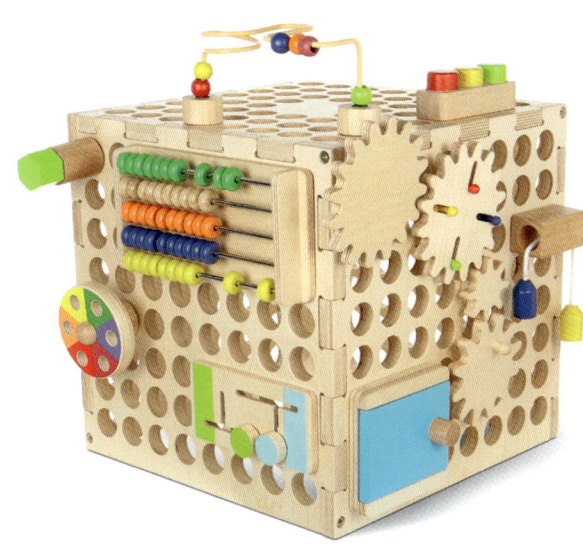

Wind Powered Motor Glider
Educational Toy
Lernspielzeug

Manufacturer
Hangzhou ZT Model Co., Ltd.,
Hangzhou, China
Design
Playsteam Education Limited,
London, United Kingdom
Web
www.ztmodel.com
www.playsteam.com

The wind powered glider is an innovative and fun toy that helps to represent a new age of modern energy. Designed for young children with a sleek, ergonomic style the glider is fully powered by wind energy through the mini-turbine which is sensitive enough to use when walking. In combination with the glider, the learning booklet helps inspire the child on the world of renewable energy. Through simple yet informative diagrams, the concept of 'green energy' and its vital importance for the planet earth becomes evident, even for a young person.

Dieser windbetriebene Motorsegler macht als innovatives Spielzeug Spaß und steht zugleich für das Zeitalter neuer Energien. Der für kleine Kinder entwickelte schlanke und ergonomische Gleiter wird von einer durch Windenergie gespeisten Miniturbine angetrieben, die so empfindlich ist, dass einfaches Gehen genügt, um Energie zu erzeugen. In Kombination mit einer dazugehörigen Broschüre lernen Kinder die Welt erneuerbarer Energien kennen. Anhand einfacher, informativer Diagramme werden das Konzept der erneuerbaren Energien und ihre Bedeutung für den Planeten Erde selbst kleinen Kindern verständlich.

Statement by the jury
The Wind Powered Motor Glider captivates by combining playful instinct in an age-appropriate manner with an acquisition of knowledge about regenerative energies.

Begründung der Jury
Der Wind Powered Motor Glider besticht, indem er den kindlichen Spieltrieb auf altersgerechte Weise mit dem Erwerb von Wissen über regenerative Energien verbindet.

MODU
Toy

Spielzeug

Manufacturer
MODU ApS, Copenhagen, Denmark
In-house design
Jonathan Rasmussen, Theo Ginman
Web
www.modutoy.com

Modu is a toy that allows children to build their own, life-sized creations from blocks of foam material. It is comprised of blocks, pegs and wheels which, thanks to an innovative construction system, can be simply interconnected. The toy is interesting for all ages: babies are able to observe and feel it, toddlers can build their first, simple constructions, such as cars, rocking animals or similar items, and with increasing age the objects become ever more complex.

Statement by the jury
Modu appeals with its minimalist design of components in contrasting colours. It is also fun since children can, on their own, fit together vehicles and the like – even ones large enough for their own use.

Modu ist ein Spielzeug, mit dem Kinder eigene lebensgroße Kreationen aus Schaumstoffblöcken bauen können. Es setzt sich aus Blöcken, Stiften und Rädern zusammen, die dank eines innovativen Konstruktionssystems einfach miteinander verbunden werden können. Das Spielzeug ist für alle Altersstufen interessant: Babys können es ansehen und betasten, Kleinkinder können erste einfache Bauwerke wie Fahrzeuge, Schaukeltiere o. Ä. bauen und mit zunehmendem Alter können die Werke immer komplexer werden.

Begründung der Jury
Modu gefällt mit minimalistisch gestalteten Bauteilen in Kontrastfarben und macht Spaß, da Kinder eigenständig Fahrzeuge und Ähnliches zusammenstecken können, die so groß sind, dass sie sie selbst nutzen können.

Itty Bitty Buggy
Educational Toy

Lernspielzeug

Manufacturer
Microduino, Beijing, China
In-house design
Zhenshan Wang, Xi Li, Bin Feng
Web
www.microduinoinc.com

Itty Bitty Buggy is a fun STEM educational toy that is programmable in Scratch, Python and Arduino offering innumerable playing possibilities. Accompanying explanations impart to children the logic behind the various functions while they build and play. Each project is controllable via Bluetooth and the corresponding app. Users can program various functions, including remote control, colour recognition and voice control. The basic package is extendable and compatible with Lego and electronic building blocks, providing endless possibilities.

Statement by the jury
This smart educational toy playfully imparts basic knowledge of programming. As a modular construction system, it also fosters creativity.

Das MINT-Lernspielzeug Itty Bitty Buggy kann in Scratch, Python und Arduino programmiert werden und bietet zahllose Spielmöglichkeiten. Begleitende Erklärungen vermitteln Kindern die Logik hinter den einzelnen Funktionen, während sie bauen und spielen. Jedes Projekt ist via Bluetooth über die dazugehörige App steuerbar. Benutzer können Fernbedienungs- und Farberkennungsfunktionen sowie Sprachsteuerung programmieren. Das Basispaket ist erweiterbar, mit Lego und elektronischen Bausteinen kompatibel und bietet so endlos viele Möglichkeiten.

Begründung der Jury
Dieses intelligente Lernspielzeug vermittelt auf spielerische Weise Basiswissen über Programmierung. Als modulares Baukastensystem fördert es zudem die Kreativität.

Nürburgring
Toy Car

Spielzeugauto

Manufacturer
Beijing Dynamics, Beijing, China
Design
Roci Design Technology Co., Ltd.
(Chang Qu, Weijun Huang),
Beijing, China
Web
www.beijingdynamics.com
www.rocidesign.com

Nürburgring is a remotely controlled toy car. Both elements – car and remote control – are characterised by a soft, organic language of form. With its curves and smooth surfaces, the car is pleasant to hold and also safe without a risk of injury to children. The two-part body structure is very stable. The car is made of environmentally friendly plastics. The remote control is durable and simple to operate.

Statement by the jury
The Nürburgring toy car impresses with its organic design vocabulary and sturdy construction. Thanks to the reduced operating surface, the remote control is easy for children to understand.

Nürburgring ist ein ferngesteuertes Spielzeugauto, bei dem beide Elemente – Auto und Fernbedienung – von einer weichen, organischen Formensprache geprägt sind. Mit seinen Rundungen und glatten Oberflächen ist das Auto haptisch angenehm und sicher, da Kinder sich nicht daran verletzen können. Die Karosseriestruktur setzt sich aus zwei Teilen zusammen und ist sehr stabil. Das Auto ist aus umweltschonenden Kunststoffen gefertigt. Das Fernsteuerungssystem ist robust und leicht zu bedienen.

Begründung der Jury
Das Spielzeugauto Nürburgring besticht mit seiner organischen Formensprache und seiner robusten Bauweise. Die Steuerung ist dank der reduzierten Bedienfläche der Fernbedienung für Kinder leicht verständlich.

G9 PRO
Educational Robot
Lernroboter

Manufacturer
Shenzhen Booyue Daily Necessities Co., Ltd.,
Shenzhen, China
In-house design
Zilun Zhang, Mifu Tao
Web
www.alilotoy.com

G9 pro is a robot for early education which attracts attention with its stylised bunny form. It uses intelligent voice interaction technology and thus supports two-way communication between child and robot. Thanks to extensive learning material, such as an encyclopaedia stored in the cloud, the G9 pro is able to answer many questions posed by children. By means of an integrated soft light, the robot can be illuminated at night in various colours.

Statement by the jury
The figurative design of this educational robot is reminiscent of a cuddly toy. Through speech interaction, the G9 pro eliminates any contact-related anxiety.

G9 pro ist ein Roboter für die Früherziehung, der mit seiner stilisierten Häschenform auf sich aufmerksam macht. Er nutzt intelligente Sprachinteraktionstechnologie und unterstützt so die wechselseitige Kommunikation zwischen Kind und Roboter. Dank umfangreichen Lernmaterials wie einer Enzyklopädie, die in der Cloud gespeichert ist, ist der G9 pro in der Lage, viele Kinderfragen zu beantworten. Mittels einer eingebauten Softlight-Lampe kann der Roboter nachts in verschiedenen Farben leuchten.

Begründung der Jury
Die figürliche Gestaltung dieses Lernroboters erinnert an ein Kuscheltier. Im Zusammenspiel mit der Sprachinteraktion eliminiert der G9 pro etwaige Berührungsängste.

J7
Educational Robot
Lernroboter

Manufacturer
Shenzhen Booyue Daily Necessities Co., Ltd.,
Shenzhen, China
In-house design
Zilun Zhang, Mifu Tao
Web
www.alilotoy.com

J7 is a bilingual educational robot in the form of a bunny. Its silicone ears light up softly when it is switched on, and the LED eyes make various expressions depending on interaction. The J7 uses intelligent voice interaction technology to answer children's questions. The robot can playfully mediate early language knowledge through foreign language learning content, such as nursery rhymes or other audio modules, and it also supports translation between Chinese and English.

Statement by the jury
The educational robot J7 supports the playful learning of a foreign language by means of artificial intelligence. Interaction through language and visual feedback through the eyes of the robotic bunny make it especially child-friendly.

J7 ist ein zweisprachiger Lernroboter in der Form eines Häschens. Seine Silikonohren leuchten sanft, wenn er eingeschaltet wird, und die LED-Augen zeigen je nach Interaktion unterschiedliche Ausdrücke. Der J7 nutzt eine intelligente Sprachinteraktionstechnologie, um Fragen von Kindern zu beantworten. Der Roboter kann mit Fremdsprachen-Lerninhalten wie Kinderreimen oder anderen Audiomodulen spielerisch erste Sprachkenntnisse vermitteln und unterstützt zudem Übersetzungen zwischen Chinesisch und Englisch.

Begründung der Jury
Der Lernroboter J7 unterstützt das spielerische Erlernen einer Fremdsprache mithilfe künstlicher Intelligenz. Die Interaktion über Sprache und ein visuelles Feedback über die Augen des Häschenroboters machen ihn besonders kindgerecht.

Luka Baby Reading Companion
Reading Robot
Vorleseroboter

Manufacturer
Ling Technology Co., Ltd., Beijing, China
In-house design
Jiabin He, Jinbo Huang, Xi Wang,
Jiawei Gu, Xiao Hong
Web
http://ling.ai
Honourable Mention

Luka Baby is a small, intelligent robot for reading aloud to children up to eight years old, helping them to develop their reading habits and to train their cognitive skills. The robot integrates sophisticated AI image-processing technology in order to recognise the content of picture books quickly and accurately and then read the corresponding page out loud. The design of Luka Baby is very compact and simultaneously robust, so that children can carry it anywhere.

Statement by the jury
Luka Baby captures the hearts of children with its cheerful design and intuitive, child-friendly interaction.

Luka Baby ist ein intelligenter kleiner Vorleseroboter für Kinder bis acht Jahre, der ihnen dabei hilft, Lesegewohnheiten zu entwickeln und ihre kognitiven Fähigkeiten zu schulen. Der Roboter integriert ausgereifte KI-Bildverarbeitungstechnologie, um die Inhalte von Bilderbüchern schnell und präzise zu erkennen und die jeweilige Seite dann vorlesen zu können. Luka Baby ist sehr kompakt und zugleich robust gestaltet, sodass Kinder ihn überall hin mitnehmen können.

Begründung der Jury
Luka Baby erobert Kinderherzen mit seiner fröhlichen Gestaltung und einer intuitiven, kindgerechten Interaktion.

Dinosaur Alarm Clock
Wecker

Manufacturer
Shenzhen Yuanguanghao
Electronics Co., Ltd., Shenzhen, China
In-house design
Shaohai Feng
Honourable Mention

The form of this alarm clock is reminiscent of dinosaurs and wakes up children to the call of dinosaurs. It has cheerful colours and is designed in soft forms. Small lamps light up in addition to the waking sound, which makes the clock more interactive and especially interesting to the child. With its figurative design, it evokes friendliness and blends in well with the environment of children's rooms.

Statement by the jury
The Dinosaur Alarm Clock, with its playful form, its shining colours and the unusual waking sounds, has a very cheerful effect and thus helps children to wake up easier in the mornings.

Dieser Wecker ist in seiner Formgebung von Dinosauriern inspiriert und weckt Kinder mit Dinosaurierlauten. Er ist in fröhlichen Farben und mit weichen Formen gestaltet. Zusammen mit den Wecktönen leuchten kleine Lampen auf, was den Wecker interaktiver und für Kinder noch interessanter macht. Mit seiner figürlichen Gestaltung weckt er Sympathien und fügt sich gut in das Kinderzimmer ein.

Begründung der Jury
Dinosaur Alarm Clock wirkt mit seiner verspielten Form, seinen leuchtenden Farben und ungewohnten Wecktönen sehr fröhlich und erleichtert Kindern so das morgendliche Aufwachen.

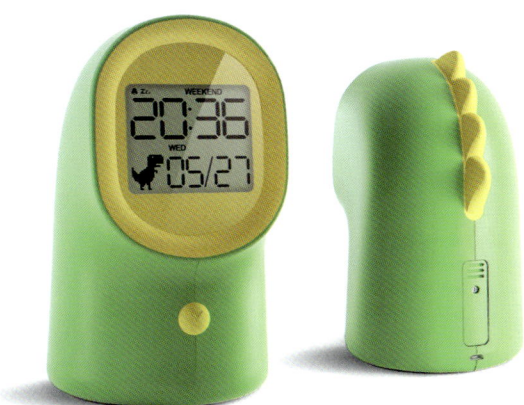

GoBot
Educational Toy
Lernspielzeug

Manufacturer
Xiamen Stoneware Technology Co., Ltd.,
Xiamen, China
In-house design
Ya Xu, Zhi Li, Ansheng Zhang
Web
www.stoneware.tech/en

GoBot is a child-friendly programmable robot which can be equipped with a relevant pen or bricks. The GoBot may be used in various ways: either playfully or through interaction with the programme via RFID. It can, however, be applied as a learning aid in subjects such as arithmetic, algebra, geometry, applied maths and statistics through use of the corresponding flashcards.

Statement by the jury
GoBot playfully supports the development of a basic comprehension of program processes. The individual elements are sturdy and clearly designed.

GoBot ist ein kindgerechter Programmierroboter, der mit dazugehörigen Stiften oder Steinen bestückt werden kann. Der GoBot lässt sich in unterschiedlicher Weise einsetzen: Er kann spielerisch verwendet werden und kommuniziert dann über RFID mit dem Spielplan. Mit den entsprechenden Lernkarten kann er aber auch als Lernhilfe in Fächern wie Arithmetik, Algebra, Geometrie, angewandte Mathematik und Statistik eingesetzt werden.

Begründung der Jury
GoBot unterstützt die Entwicklung eines Grundverständnisses für Programmierabläufe auf spielerische Weise. Die einzelnen Elemente sind klar gestaltet und robust.

Jornee
Baby Monitor
Babyfon

Manufacturer
inDare Design Strategy Limited,
Shenzhen, China
In-house design
Qinglang Chen, Fengming Chen,
Yujie Chen, Shaolong Chen, Huahui Lin
Web
www.indare.love

Jornee is an intelligent baby monitoring camera which attracts attention due to its unusual shape in the form of an aircraft. Networked with the parent's smartphone, it becomes a fully functional baby monitor with live streaming, allowing photos to be saved or shared. An integrated time function records sleep duration as well as feeding and nappy-changing times. Jornee also plays lullabies, monitors room temperature and has a two-way talking function.

Statement by the jury
This baby monitor impresses with a design that gives it the appearance of a toy. Jornee can thereby integrate harmoniously and unnoticeably in the child's room.

VA-IH006
Baby Monitor
Babyfon

Manufacturer
Shenzhen NearbyExpress
Technology Development Co., Ltd.,
Shenzhen, China
In-house design
Youlai Liang, Tianyu Xiao
Web
www.sunvalley-group.com

This baby monitor comprises a camera and a 5" screen that also serves as a remote control. The appearance is characterised by a glossy white finish. Thanks to interchangeable optical lenses, the camera covers various angles according to each room situation. With secure and stable 2.4GHz FHSS wireless connectivity, it transmits image and sound at high quality even in night mode. Innovative 24/7 sound and image monitoring provides round-the-clock information on what is happening in the child's room.

Dieses Babyfon umfasst eine Kamera und einen 5"-Monitor, der zugleich Fernbedienung ist. Das Erscheinungsbild ist von glänzend weißen, glatten Oberflächen geprägt. Dank der austauschbaren optischen Linse erlaubt die Kamera je nach Raumsituation verschiedene Blickwinkel. Mit einer sicheren und stabilen 2,4-GHz-FHSS-Funkverbindung überträgt sie Bild und Ton auch im Nachtmodus mit hoher Qualität. Eine innovative 24/7-Ton-und-Bild-Überwachung informiert rund um die Uhr über das Geschehen im Kinderzimmer.

Statement by the jury
The VA-IH006 makes it possible for parents to conveniently monitor their child thanks to its discreet appearance, extended functionality with interchangeable lenses and the remote control unit with monitor.

Begründung der Jury
Mit seinem dezenten Erscheinungsbild, einer dank austauschbarer Linsen erweiterten Funktionalität und einer Monitorfernbedienung ermöglicht das VA-IH006 Eltern eine komfortable Überwachung ihres Kindes.

JJOBI BOX
Toy Sterilisation Box
Spielzeug-Sterilisationsbox

Manufacturer
JJOBI Company,
Seoul, South Korea

In-house design
Sanghyun Lee, Narae Yoon,
Junghoo Hwang, Junghwan Park

Web
www.thejjobi.com

reddot award 2019
best of the best

Safely stored
Toys are often shared and passed through the hands of more than one child. However, toys can also easily collect germs and bacteria, contributing to an easy spread of infections and diseases. The JJOBI BOX is a toy storage box with UV LED eco-friendly sterilisation technology for keeping toys free of germs. The innovative system allows intuitive handling, as the sterilisation UV LED of the lid turns on automatically without requiring extra operation. When toys are put into the box, simply closing the lid is sufficient to immediately start the sterilisation process. It is very easy to operate the JJOBI BOX since it has the same user manual with the general toy storage box which has no sterilisation function. The JJOBI BOX also gives direct feedback. The indicator light on the lid keeps blinking during the sterilisation process and turns off once the sterilisation is completed. The sophisticated functionality of the JJOBI BOX goes hand in hand with an aesthetic use of shapes. Featuring a clear, well-proportioned design, the box adopts a friendly appearance that is further emphasised by the colour scheme in a soft pastel tone. Moreover, the height and size of the box is harmonious also with the house interior. In particular, the wooden legs and soft curved surface design help protect both children against injuries and the house against damages.

Sicher aufbewahrt
Da das Spielzeug von Kindern meist in engem Körperkontakt zu ihnen steht, wird es leicht zum Überträger von Krankheitserregern, mit denen sich auch andere Kinder anstecken können. Die JJOBI BOX für Kinderspielzeug arbeitet mit der umweltfreundlichen UV-LED-Sterilisationstechnik und hält so das Spielzeug keimfrei. Das innovative System erlaubt eine intuitive Handhabung, denn die im Deckel der Box befindliche UV-LED für die Sterilisation schaltet sich selbsttätig ein. Sobald Spielzeug in die Box gelegt wird, genügt es, den Deckel zu schließen, um den Sterilisationsvorgang zu starten. Die Bedienung der JJOBI BOX ist daher sehr einfach, da ihre Funktionsweise der des Vorgängermodells ohne Sterilisationstechnologie entspricht. Die JJOBI BOX gibt zudem ein direktes Feedback. Während der Sterilisation blinkt die Kontrollleuchte am Deckel und erlischt, sobald der Vorgang abgeschlossen ist. Die ausgereifte Funktionalität der JJOBI BOX geht einher mit einer ästhetischen Formensprache. Eine klare, gut proportionierte Gestaltung verleiht ihr eine freundliche Anmutung, die durch die Farbgebung in einem sanften Pastellton noch unterstrichen wird. Auch in Höhe und Größe harmoniert die Box gut mit dem übrigen Interieur. Insbesondere ihre Holzbeine und die weich geschwungene Oberfläche tragen zum Schutz der Kinder bei und helfen, Beschädigungen im Haus zu vermeiden.

Statement by the jury
The JJOBI BOX is a sophisticated solution that realises the idea of using UV LED technology for the sterilisation of children's toys. Extremely useful in everyday use, this functional storage box effectively protects children against picking up infections. It is made of durable, high-quality materials and showcases a very well-balanced design in a soft pastel colour scheme. Thanks to its clear and purist style, the box easily blends in almost anywhere.

Begründung der Jury
Mit der JJOBI BOX wurde auf intelligente Weise die Idee verwirklicht, die UV-LED-Technologie für die Sterilisation von Spielzeug einzusetzen. Als funktionale Aufbewahrungsbox ausgesprochen nützlich für den täglichen Gebrauch, schützt sie die Kinder sicher vor Infektionen. Sie ist sehr ausgewogen gestaltet in einem zarten Pastellton und besteht aus hochwertigen, langlebigen Materialien. Durch ihre klare und puristische Formensprache fügt sie sich überall gut ein.

Designer portrait
See page 32
Siehe Seite 32

JJOBI
Portable Pacifier Steriliser
Tragbarer Schnuller-Sterilisator

Manufacturer
JJOBI Company, Seoul, South Korea
In-house design
Sanghyun Lee, Junghoo Hwang, Narae Yoon, Junghwan Park
Web
www.thejjobi.com

JJOBI is a portable steriliser for baby pacifiers that works with eco-friendly sterilisation technology on a UV-LED basis. The soft, figurative shape is inspired by trolls, and the colour by the clean waters of Iceland. JJOBI is made of soft silicone, which has a pleasant feel and conforms to the safety requirements of products for children. Operation is simple and intuitive: the front light flashes during sterilisation and turns off as soon as it is finished.

Statement by the jury
JJOBI charmingly combines its function as a steriliser for pacifiers with a design and materiality that are reminiscent of a toy.

JJOBI ist ein tragbarer Sterilisator für Schnuller, der mit einer umweltfreundlichen Sterilisationstechnik auf UV-LED-Basis arbeitet. Die weiche, figürliche Formensprache ist von Trollen inspiriert, die Farbgebung von den sauberen Gewässern Islands. Gefertigt ist JJOBI aus weichem Silikon, das haptisch angenehm ist und den Sicherheitsanforderungen an Kinderprodukte entspricht. Die Bedienung ist einfach und intuitiv: Die Frontleuchte blinkt während der Sterilisation und erlischt, sobald sie abgeschlossen ist.

Begründung der Jury
JJOBI verbindet seine Funktion als Sterilisator für Schnuller auf charmante Weise mit einer Gestaltung und Materialität, die an Spielzeug erinnern.

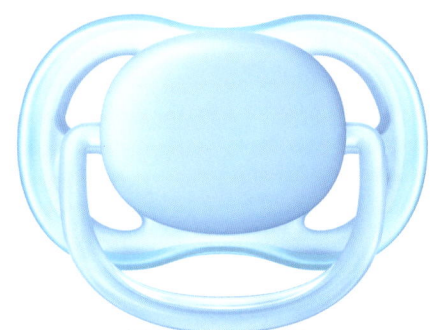

Philips Avent Ultra Air Soother SCF24X
Schnuller

Manufacturer
Philips, Eindhoven, Netherlands
In-house design
Philips Design
Web
www.philips.com

This soother is designed in such a way that it allows as much air as possible on the baby's skin. Hardly any saliva can collect under the shield when sucking, so that the sensitive skin remains dry and soft. The appearance of the soother is contemporary, friendly and airy. By means of the translucent front – with large openings and soft edges manufactured by 2K injection moulding – the face is hardly covered. The soother is available with various illustrations on the knob.

Statement by the jury
The open design of this soother facilitates good air circulation and thus prevents irritated skin. Translucent elements emphasise its visual lightness.

Dieser Schnuller ist so gestaltet, dass er möglichst viel Luft an die Babyhaut lässt. Dadurch sammelt sich unter dem Saugerschild beim Saugen kaum Speichel an und die empfindliche Haut bleibt trocken und weich. Das Erscheinungsbild des Schnullers ist zeitgemäß, freundlich und luftig. Durch die transluzente, mit großen Öffnungen und weichen Rändern im 2K-Spritzguss hergestellte Vorderseite wird das Gesicht kaum verdeckt. Der Schnuller ist mit verschiedenen Illustrationen auf dem Knopf erhältlich.

Begründung der Jury
Die offene Gestaltung dieses Schnullers ermöglicht eine gute Luftzirkulation und verhindert dadurch wunde Stellen. Transluzente Elemente verstärken seine visuelle Leichtigkeit.

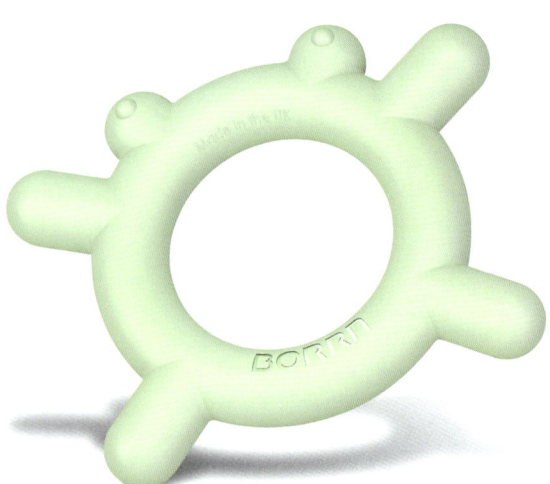

BORRN Teethers
Beißringe

Manufacturer
BORRN UK, London, United Kingdom
Design
Blond Ltd., London, United Kingdom
Web
www.borrn.com
www.blond.cc

When designing these teethers, the thickness of the rings was taken from the diameter of a baby's finger, in order to promote the natural teething process. The selected material is medical-grade, BPA-free silicone, which is very hygienic. The teething rings are also characterised by a simple and playful form: the collection consists of nine animals in a circular shape, differentiated by the straight lines emanating from the body.

Statement by the jury
These teethers delight with their successful combination of playfulness and simplicity, as well as with an ergonomic design oriented to a baby's fingers.

Bei der Gestaltung dieser Beißringe diente der Durchmesser eines Babyfingers als Orientierung für die Dicke der Beißringe, um so den natürlichen Zahnungsprozess zu fördern. Als Material wurde BPA-freies, medizinisches Silikon gewählt, das sehr hygienisch ist. Die Beißringe sind zudem durch eine einfache und verspielte Formgebung gekennzeichnet: Die Serie setzt sich aus neun Tieren mit kreisförmigen Körpern zusammen, die sich in den geraden Elementen unterscheiden, die aus dem Kreis herausragen.

Begründung der Jury
Diese Beißringe begeistern mit einer geglückten Kombination aus Verspieltheit und Einfachheit sowie einer ergonomischen Gestaltung, die sich an Babyfingern orientiert.

Softmate one step case
Wipes Case
Wischtücherbox

Manufacturer
Suomi, Seoul, South Korea
In-house design
Suomi Design Team
Design
3D Connection, Seoul, South Korea
Web
www.suomi.co.kr

The Softmate one step case is a box for wipes in the form of a gently rounded cradle. The box reduces the noise produced by the package when wipes are removed. It also enhances user convenience by combining three steps into one: opening the package, pulling out a wipe, and closing the box. The removable lid with its cross-shaped opening is made of environmentally friendly silicone. A stainless-steel stopper ensures that only one wipe at a time is pulled out.

Statement by the jury
With its soft linearity and pastel design, the Softmate one step case blends harmoniously into the environment of the baby's nappy-changing table.

Softmate one step case ist eine Wischtücherbox in Form einer sanft gerundeten Babywiege. Die Box reduziert die Geräusche, die die Verpackung beim Herausziehen der Tücher macht, und verbessert den Benutzerkomfort, indem sie das Öffnen der Box, das Herausziehen des Tuchs und das Wiederverschließen in einem einzigen Schritt zusammenfasst. Die abnehmbare Oberseite mit kreuzförmiger Öffnung besteht aus umweltfreundlichem Silikon. Ein Edelstahl-Stopper sorgt dafür, dass immer nur ein Tuch herausgezogen wird.

Begründung der Jury
Mit ihrer weichen Linienführung und ihrer Gestaltung in Pastellfarben fügt sich Softmate one step case harmonisch in die Wickeltischumgebung ein.

BABYBJÖRN Small Baby Bib
BABYBJÖRN Kleines Lätzchen

Manufacturer
BabyBjörn AB, Solna, Sweden
In-house design
Malin Henrikson
Design
McKinsey Design (Peter Ejvinsson, Elisabeth Ramel-Wåhrberg, David Crafoord), Bromma, Sweden
Web
www.babybjorn.com
www.veryday.com

This baby bib catches dropped food and is waterproof, so that food and liquids do not soil the clothes. It is designed for small babies, enabling the infant to move its arms freely. The bib's soft neck opening is continuously adjustable. If the bib gets caught on anything, then the neckband's fastening will open. The bib is made of BPA-free, biological plastic, which contains 45 per cent renewable material, and is dishwasher-safe.

Statement by the jury
With a functionally well-considered design that is ergonomically suited to the baby, the Small Baby Bib makes meals more convenient for both baby and parents alike.

Dieses Lätzchen für Babys fängt herunterfallendes Essen auf und ist wasserdicht, sodass Speisen und Flüssigkeiten keine Flecken auf der Kleidung hinterlassen. Es ist auf kleine Babys zugeschnitten, so kann das Kind die Arme frei bewegen und die weiche Halsöffnung ist stufenlos verstellbar. Bleibt das Lätzchen an etwas hängen, öffnet sich der Verschluss. Das Lätzchen ist aus BPA-freiem, biobasiertem Kunststoff gefertigt, der zu 45 Prozent aus erneuerbarem Material besteht und spülmaschinenfest ist.

Begründung der Jury
Mit seiner funktional durchdachten und ergonomisch an den Babykörper angepassten Gestaltung macht das Kleine Lätzchen die Mahlzeiten für das Baby und die Eltern komfortabler.

milkymeter
Microwave Thermometer for Baby Bottles
Mikrowellen-Thermometer für Babyflaschen

Manufacturer
Senserna A/S, Herlev, Denmark
In-house design
Henrik Schneider,
Kristian Lindberg-Poulsen
Design
Above Agency AB (Ellen Lynghed, Victor Johansson), Malmö, Sweden
Web
www.milkymeter.com

The milkymeter measures the temperature of milk in a baby bottle while being warmed in a microwave. This avoids an overheating of the milk and prevents a loss of nutrients. The minimalist thermometer is waterproof and airtight, thus allowing the use of the electronics in the microwave. An easily read signal light gives a clear indication of the temperature. The milkymeter uses new Microweter technology, which converts microwaves into electricity and thereby makes it possible to take real-time temperature readings without a battery or cable.

Statement by the jury
The milkymeter microwave thermometer combines a minimalist appearance with sophisticated functionality.

milkymeter misst die Temperatur der Milch in einer Babyflasche, während sie in der Mikrowelle erwärmt wird. So wird Überhitzung und der Verlust von Nährstoffen vermieden. Das minimalistische Thermometer ist wasser- und luftdicht und ermöglicht so die Verwendung der Elektronik in der Mikrowelle. Eine Signalleuchte zeigt die Temperatur gut erkennbar an. milkymeter nutzt eine neue Microweter-Technologie, die Mikrowellen in Strom umwandelt und dabei Temperaturmessungen in Echtzeit ohne Batterie oder Kabel ermöglicht.

Begründung der Jury
Das Mikrowellen-Thermometer milkymeter verbindet ein minimalistisches Erscheinungsbild mit einer ausgereiften Funktionalität.

Pigeon GoMini™
Electric Breast Pump
Elektrische Milchpumpe

Manufacturer
Pigeon, Singapore
In-house Design
Design
Orcadesign Consultants, Singapore
Web
www.pigeon.com.sg
www.orcadesign.net

The electric GoMini breast milk pump has a small and light motor pump unit, making it compact, easy to store and light to carry around. With its slender form and soft contours, it rests pleasantly in the hand. Ergonomic buttons facilitate simple and intuitive operation with one hand. The pump prevents a backflow of milk, and the positioning of the tube holder eases handling when in operation. The user can choose between single or double pump mode as well as five levels of preferred pumping power.

Die elektrische Milchpumpe GoMini hat eine kleine und leichte Motorpumpeneinheit, wodurch sie kompakt, gut verstaubar und leicht mitzunehmen ist. Mit ihrer schlanken Form und ihren weichen Konturen liegt sie angenehm in der Hand. Ergonomische Tasten ermöglichen eine einfache und intuitive Bedienung mit einer Hand. Die Pumpe verhindert den Rückfluss der Milch, und die Ausrichtung des Schlauchhalters erleichtert die Handhabung während des Betriebs. Die Benutzerin kann zwischen Einzel- und Doppelpumpmodus sowie aus fünf Stufen die bevorzugte Pumpleistung wählen.

Statement by the jury
With its soft language of form, pleasant feel and clever functionality, the GoMini makes pumping breast milk as pleasant as possible.

Begründung der Jury
Mit ihrer weichen Formensprache, ihrer angenehmen Haptik und einer durchdachten Funktionalität macht die GoMini das Abpumpen der Milch so angenehm wie möglich.

BORRN Feeding Bottle
Babyflasche

Manufacturer
BORRN UK, London,
United Kingdom
Design
Blond Ltd. (James Melia),
London, United Kingdom
Web
www.borrn.com
www.blond.cc

The design of this feeding bottle is characterised by purist aesthetics oriented towards tableware and home accessories. Its form – oval at the bottom and circular at the top – is ergonomic and rests pleasantly in the hand. The materials used meet high hygienic standards. The content of the bottle, for example, only comes into contact with temperature-resistant, medical-grade silicone that is BPA-free. The body features a thicker design, which increases durability.

Statement by the jury
The Borrn Feeding Bottle is convincing with a minimalist design characterised by clear-cut basic forms. A translucent body and pastel-coloured elements characterise its contemporary overall appearance.

Das Design der Babyflasche ist durch eine puristische Ästhetik gekennzeichnet, die sich an Tableware und Wohnaccessoires orientiert. Ihre Formgebung – am Boden oval und oben rund – ist ergonomisch und die Flasche liegt angenehm in der Hand. Die verwendeten Materialien erfüllen hohe Anforderungen an Hygiene; so kommt der Flascheninhalt nur mit temperaturbeständigem, BPA-freiem, medizinischem Silikon in Berührung. Die Flaschenwand ist etwas dicker gestaltet, was die Langlebigkeit erhöht.

Begründung der Jury
Die Borrn Feeding Bottle überzeugt mit ihrer minimalistischen Gestaltung, die durch klare Grundformen geprägt ist. Ein transluzenter Korpus und pastellfarbene Elemente prägen ihr zeitgemäßes Gesamtbild.

Philips Avent Smart Baby Bottle
Babyflasche

Manufacturer
Philips, Eindhoven, Netherlands
In-house design
Philips Design
Web
www.philips.com

This baby bottle is a combination of a 125 ml bottle and an intelligent sleeve. The sleeve is activated via simple one-button interaction and records quantity, time, duration and interruptions of a bottle-feed. The data are transmitted to the smart baby bottle app and automatically archived. The sleeve is light, pleasant to hold thanks to soft-touch materials and also easy to remove.

Statement by the jury
This clever additional feature for the baby bottle simplifies documentation of the drinking behaviour and thus remains visually discreet in the background.

Diese Babyflasche ist eine Kombination aus einer Flasche mit ca. 125 ml Fassungsvermögen und einer intelligenten Manschette. Letztere wird über eine einfache Ein-Tasten-Interaktion aktiviert und erfasst dann Menge, Uhrzeit, Dauer und Unterbrechungen einer Flaschenfütterung. Diese Daten werden an die „Smart Baby Bottle"-App gesendet und automatisch archiviert. Die Manschette ist leicht, dank Soft-Touch-Materials angenehm zu halten und lässt sich einfach abnehmen.

Begründung der Jury
Die smarte Ergänzung dieser Babyflasche erleichtert die Dokumentation des Trinkverhaltens und hält sich dabei visuell dezent im Hintergrund.

Baby Diamond Nursing Bottle
Babyflasche

Manufacturer
Taizhou Howawa Baby Products Co., Ltd.,
Taizhou, China
In-house design
Henglu Xia
Design
Design To Product Ltd.
(Roberto Pauli), Turin, Italy
Web
www.howawa.cc
www.designtoproduct.it

The design idea behind this nursing bottle for babies was to create a stylish product resembling a water glass which can be harmoniously combined with other everyday items, such as glasses, bottles or dishes. The bottle takes the form of an hourglass, enabling it to be grasped and held by the baby. With a shape inspired by the iconic Gibraltar glass, the bottle is reminiscent of tableware and presents a friendly and natural appearance.

Statement by the jury
The Baby Diamond Nursing Bottle appeals with a form inspired by drinking glasses which is elegant and ergonomic at the same time.

Die Gestaltungsidee dieser Babyflasche war, ein stilvolles Produkt zu entwerfen, das die Anmutung eines Wasserglases hat und sich harmonisch mit anderen Alltagsgegenständen wie Gläsern, Flaschen oder Geschirr kombinieren lässt. Die Flasche hat die Form einer Sanduhr und kann so auch vom Baby selbst gehalten werden. Die Formgebung ist von dem ikonischen Gibraltar-Glas inspiriert, wodurch die Flasche an Tableware erinnert, Reinheit ausstrahlt, freundlich und natürlich wirkt.

Begründung der Jury
Die Baby Diamond Nursing Bottle gefällt mit einer eleganten und zugleich ergonomischen Formgebung, die von Trinkgläsern inspiriert ist.

Milly PRO
Nursing Bra
Still-BH

Manufacturer
YAHUI Fashion & Technology (Shanghai) Co., Ltd.,
Shanghai, China
In-house design
Wukun Dong, Roger Gu
Web
www.infansy.com

Milly PRO is a functional nursing bra with innovative four-way adjustable crossover design. It provides adaptive wearing experience, maximising breast feeding space for the baby and enhancing intimacy between mother and child. Thanks to the flexible cup design and non e-band technique, Milly PRO easily accommodates mothers' changing body shape, offers good wearing comfort and provides anti-sagging support to the breasts. More importantly, this nursing bra is manufactured in an eco-friendly and energy-saving way.

Milly PRO ist ein funktionaler Still-BH mit einem innovativen Vierfach-Crossover-Design. Er bietet flexible Tragevarianten, um den Platz für das Stillen des Babys zu maximieren und die Intimität zwischen Mutter und Kind zu verbessern. Dank des flexiblen Cup-Designs und des Verzichts auf Gummibänder passt sich Milly PRO den sich verändernden Körperformen der Mutter an, bietet hohen Tragekomfort und unterstützt die Brüste nachhaltig. Der Still-BH wird ökologisch und energiesparend hergestellt.

Statement by the jury
The Milly PRO nursing bra is convincing with a well-considered functionality, offering great flexibility and comfort during wear and nursing.

Begründung der Jury
Der Still-BH Milly PRO überzeugt mit einer durchdachten Funktionalität, die viel Flexibilität und Komfort beim Tragen und Stillen bietet.

Loveincolors belly-lift sport trousers for moms-to-be
Schwangerschaftssporthose

Manufacturer
Hangzhou Xingshangzhongzhi
Clothing Co., Ltd., Hangzhou, China
In-house design
Li Li, Shen Zheying
Web
www.loveincolors.com

These sport trousers were specially developed for pregnant women. Due to a good fit and strong resilience, they are comfortable while simultaneously supporting muscles, bones and knees. For the trouser leg, Lycra Sport fabric is used in order to enhance comfort, fit and hold. Due to triple seamless weaving technology, the waist and stomach are fully protected. At the same time, the simple weave at the front is stretchable and adjusts to the growing baby.

Statement by the jury
The design of these sport trousers assures that the body of pregnant women is supported in all the right places. The trousers provide support and promote free movement at the same time.

Diese Sporthose wurde speziell für schwangere Frauen entwickelt. Durch ihre Passform und Widerstandsfähigkeit ist sie komfortabel und unterstützt zugleich Muskeln, Knochen und Knie. In den Beinteilen der Hose kommt ein Lycra-Sport-Gewebe zum Einsatz, um Komfort, Passform und Halt zu verbessern. Mit einer dreifachen Nahtlos-Webtechnik werden Taille und Bauch vollständig geschützt, gleichzeitig ist das einfache Gewebe im vorderen Bereich dehnbar und passt sich dem wachsenden Babybauch an.

Begründung der Jury
Das Design dieser Sporthose sorgt dafür, dass der Körper von Schwangeren an den richtigen Stellen unterstützt wird. Die Hose gibt Halt und fördert zugleich die Bewegungsfreiheit.

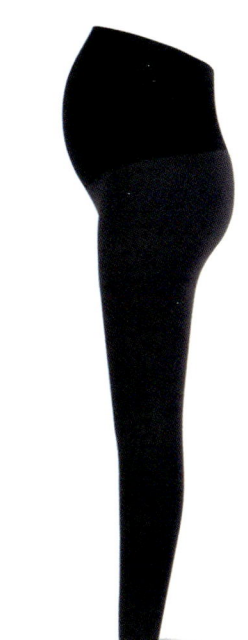

LÄSSIG Green Label Adventure Backpack
Diaper Bag
Wickeltasche

Manufacturer
Lässig GmbH, Babenhausen, Germany
In-house design
Christina Driessen, Claudia Lässig
Web
www.laessig-fashion.de

The Green Label Adventure Backpack is a diaper bag that combines clear design language and high functionality with a young, timeless appearance. The outer material is an easy-care and highly resistant canvas made from Cyclepet material, which is manufactured entirely from recycled PET bottles. The backpack has a large main compartment, two pockets, a water-repelling wet pouch and many inside pockets as well as practical accessories like a changing mat.

Statement by the jury
Functional design and durability turn this diaper bag made of recycled PET bottles into a contemporary product for modern parents.

Der Green Label Adventure Backpack ist ein Wickelrucksack, der eine klare Formensprache und hohe Funktionalität mit einer jungen, zeitlosen Anmutung verbindet. Das Außenmaterial ist ein pflegeleichter und strapazierfähiger Canvas-Stoff aus dem Material Cyclepet, das vollständig aus wiederaufbereiteten PET-Flaschen hergestellt wird. Der Rucksack besitzt ein großes Hauptfach, zwei Steckfächer, ein wasserabweisendes Feuchtfach und viele Innenfächer sowie praktisches Zubehör wie eine Wickelunterlage.

Begründung der Jury
Diesen Wickelrucksack aus recycelten PET-Flaschen machen seine funktionale Gestaltung sowie seine Nachhaltigkeit zu einem zeitgemäßen Produkt für moderne Eltern.

Household
Haushalt

Cleaning accessories	Abfallsysteme
Cleaning devices	Bügelsysteme
Fans	Feuerlöscher
Fire extinguisher	Reinigungsgeräte
Ironing systems	Reinigungszubehör
Tumble dryers	Staubsauger
Vacuum cleaners	Trockner
Washing machines	Ventilatoren
Waste systems	Waschmaschinen

ALPHA Series (XQG100-P1DL)
Washing Machine
Waschmaschine

Manufacturer
Panasonic Appliances Washing Machine, Hangzhou, China

In-house design
Panasonic Design Center

Design
Studio F. A. Porsche, Zell am See, Austria

Web
http://wm.panasonic.cn

reddot award 2019
best of the best

Design and inspiration
The Panasonic ALPHA washing machine, which has been developed in cooperation with the Studio F. A. Porsche, shows a minimalist design based on Bauhaus maxims. It aims at breaking the design limitation of traditional washing machines and bringing a comprehensive improvement of quality, value and practicability. Designed with a wheel housing shaped drum, its robust construction allows a speed of up to 1,600 rounds per minute, which makes for excellent washing results. The self-explanatory arrangement and stylistic idiom of the clear user interface gives a professional reading performance and lends this washing machine a classic and elegant appearance. Moreover, the Panasonic ALPHA washing machine also features a five-point suspension shockproof system, carrying a CBB ball centrifugal balance wheel and integrating the shock absorber principle of a metal balance block. This system can effectively filter vibrations and deliver stable and quiet operation even at maximum spin speed. A special high-quality aluminium-blended rotary knob for setting the machine follows the logic of a professional control system, while using the infinite damping design of a high-end audio knob. Thus, the turning process promotes an enhanced user comfort and delivers a high-quality experience, showcasing pre-eminent taste.

Design und Inspiration
Die Panasonic ALPHA-Waschmaschine, die in Zusammenarbeit mit dem Studio F. A. Porsche entwickelt wurde, zeigt ein klares, an den Maximen des Bauhauses orientiertes Design. Ziel war es, die gestalterischen Grenzen traditioneller Waschmaschinen zu überwinden und eine umfassende Verbesserung hinsichtlich Qualität, Wert und Praktikabilität zu erreichen. Gestaltet mit einer Waschtrommel in Form eines Radgehäuses, erlaubt die robuste Konstruktion eine Drehzahl von bis zu 1.600 Umdrehungen pro Minute, was für ausgezeichnete Waschergebnisse sorgt. Das in seiner Formensprache und Aufteilung klare, selbsterklärende Bedieninterface bietet eine professionelle Lesequalität und verleiht dieser Waschmaschine ein klassisches, elegantes Aussehen. Die Panasonic ALPHA-Waschmaschine verfügt darüber hinaus über ein Fünf-Punkt-Federungssystem für die Stoßdämpfung, das mit einem CBB-Kugellager und einem Ausgleichsblock aus Metall der Stoßabsorption dient. Dieses System kann Vibrationen effektiv abfangen und gewährleistet einen stabilen, leisen Betrieb selbst bei Höchstgeschwindigkeit des Schleudervorgangs. Ein hochwertiger Drehknopf aus Aluminium für die Bedienung wurde im Sinne einer professionellen Steuerungslogik entworfen, unter Nutzung der stufenlosen Dämpfung ähnlich eines High-End-Audioreglers. Der Drehvorgang bietet dadurch einen angenehmen Komfort und ein hochwertiges Nutzererlebnis, das die ausgezeichnete Qualität unterstreicht.

Statement by the jury
This washing machine impresses with its focused design. It showcases aesthetic clarity and a conclusively defined functionality in harmony with beautiful materials. Both the overall style and the reduced interface lend it an air of exclusivity. Operation is intuitive and comfortable by means of a single rotary knob. The information shown on the TFT display provides direct status feedback.

Begründung der Jury
Diese Waschmaschine beeindruckt durch ihr fokussiertes Design. Sie zeigt eine klare Ästhetik und schlüssig definierte Funktionalität im Einklang mit schönen Materialien. Sowohl die Formgebung wie auch das reduzierte Interface verleihen ihr die Anmutung von Exklusivität. Der Nutzer kann diese Waschmaschine intuitiv mittels eines komfortablen Drehknopfs aktivieren. Die Informationen auf dem TFT-Display geben dabei ein direktes Feedback.

Designer portrait
See page 34
Siehe Seite 34

Casarte C1 HD10G6LU1 Washer
Washing Machine
Waschmaschine

Manufacturer
Haier Group, Qingdao, China
Design
Haier Innovation Design Center
(Li Shenghua, Kong Zhi, Sun Xiaoli),
Qingdao, China
Web
www.haier.com

This washing machine, which is equipped with an automatic dosage system, has been especially developed to wash high-end clothing: it not only allows to clean textiles with the conventional washing programmes but also with micro-steam, which gently permeates and refreshes sensitive fibres. The slim display, with its 25-degree angle, is convenient to use while standing. When touching the control panel, its tempered glass surface exudes a pleasant feel. The generous glass door, with a diameter of 525 mm, opens and closes upon a slight push.

Die Waschmaschine mit automatischer Waschmitteldosierung wurde speziell für die Reinigung hochwertiger Kleidung entwickelt: Textilien können nicht nur mit den gängigen Waschprogrammen bearbeitet werden, sondern auch mit Mikrodampf, der empfindliche Fasern schonend durchdringt und auffrischt. Das schlanke Display mit einem 25-Grad-Winkel ist bequem im Stehen zu bedienen. Seine gehärtete Glasoberfläche vermittelt ein angenehmes Gefühl beim Berühren des Bedienfelds. Die großzügige Glastür mit einem Durchmesser von 525 mm öffnet und schließt sich bereits durch leichtes Drücken.

Statement by the jury
Delicate materials in combination with harmonious proportions and appealing design details convey a high-quality standard.

Begründung der Jury
Edel anmutende Materialien vermitteln hier in Verbindung mit ausgewogenen Proportionen und ansprechenden Gestaltungsdetails einen hohen Qualitätsanspruch.

Casarte Wall-Mounted Washer
Washing Machine
Waschmaschine

Manufacturer
Haier Group, Qingdao, China
Design
Haier Innovation Design Center
(Sun Peng, Zhu Bingyue, Kong Zhi),
Qingdao, China
Web
www.haier.com

Designed to serve as a second washing machine, this wall-mounted device meets the demand to wash baby clothes, underwear or individual textiles separately. The compact device only takes up little space due to its small volume. Being wall-mounted, it can be loaded and unloaded at eye level. The integrated glass door opens conveniently at different angles. A transparent acrylic glass front panel lets the white body shine through and features an elegant decorative strip.

Konzipiert als Zweitgerät, erfüllt diese wandmontierte Waschmaschine das Bedürfnis, Babykleidung, Unterwäsche oder einzelne Textilien separat zu waschen. Das kompakte Gerät nimmt mit seinem geringen Volumen nur wenig Platz ein. Seine Wandmontage erlaubt das Befüllen und Entleeren auf Augenhöhe. Die integrierte Glastür lässt sich komfortabel in unterschiedlichen Winkeln öffnen. Eine transparente Acrylglas-Frontplatte, die den weißen Korpus durchscheinen lässt, ist mit einem eleganten Dekorstreifen verziert.

Statement by the jury
The elegant look of the materials used lend the wall-mounted washing machine a uniform overall appearance.

Begründung der Jury
Unter Verwendung elegant wirkender Materialien erreicht die wandmontierte Waschmaschine ein homogenes Gesamtbild.

Bosch WxUM4x
Washing Machine Series 4
Waschmaschinen-Serie 4

Manufacturer
BSH Home Appliances (China) Co., Ltd., Nanjing, China
In-house design
Florian Metz, Carsten Weber, Raphael Krug, Zhou Xuqi
Web
www.bsh-group.com

With its body made of matte brushed stainless steel, this washing machine series continues the specific design idiom of the manufacturer, complementing it with new details. The redesigned control panel includes an intuitive rotary control and a full-touch control panel, which, among other things, displays the remaining time of the washing programme. The large porthole with its chrome frame stands in contrast to the shimmering gold and silver of the body and facilitates access to the 10 kg washing drum.

Statement by the jury
As an expression of high commitment to quality, this washing machine showcases an utterly characteristic design which captures the zeitgeist.

Mit ihrem Korpus aus matt gebürstetem Edelstahl greift diese Waschmaschinen-Serie eine herstellertypische Formensprache auf, die um neue gestalterische Details ergänzt wurde. Die überarbeitete Bedienkonsole umfasst neben dem intuitiv bedienbaren Drehring ein Full-Touch-Bedienfeld, das u. a. die verbleibende Laufzeit des Waschprogramms anzeigt. Das große Bullauge mit Chromrahmen setzt einen Kontrast zum goldsilbrig schimmernden Korpus und erleichtert den Zugriff zur 10 kg fassenden Waschtrommel.

Begründung der Jury
Als Ausdruck eines gehobenen Qualitätsanspruchs zeigt diese Waschmaschine eine äußerst charakteristische Gestaltung, die den Zeitgeist trifft.

Toshiba combo
Washer-Dryer
Waschtrockner

Manufacturer
Little Swan, Wuxi, China
In-house design
Web
www.littleswan.com

This washer-dryer can be operated via an innovative metal slider, which makes selecting programmes and setting parameters easy. In addition, the device control supports individual adjustment via voice control or a mobile app. The control panel tilts at an angle of 30 degrees to meet ergonomic criteria. Equipped with a nanosilver ion chamber, the washer-dryer kills bacteria effectively.

Statement by the jury
This contemporary washer-dryer combines high ease of use with an expressive design of the front panel.

Dieser Waschtrockner erlaubt eine innovative Bedienung über einen Metall-Schieber, wodurch die Programmauswahl sowie das Einstellen weiterer Parameter auf einfache Weise erfolgt. Zudem unterstützt die Gerätesteuerung individuelle Anpassungen, die per Sprachsteuerung oder Eingabe über eine mobile App vorgenommen werden. Das Bedienfeld ist um 30 Grad geneigt, um ergonomischen Kriterien gerecht zu werden. Ausgestattet mit einer Nanosilberionen-Kammer optimiert der Waschtrockner die Bekämpfung von Bakterien.

Begründung der Jury
Ein zeitgemäß hohes Maß an Bedienkomfort vereint sich bei diesem Waschtrockner mit einer ausdrucksvoll gestalteten Gerätefront.

Beverly
Washing Machine
Waschmaschine

Manufacturer
Little Swan, Wuxi, China
In-house design
Web
www.littleswan.com

In order to provide maximum operating comfort, this washing machine employs a double touch screen. The top panel allows easy selection of the most common wash programmes while the bottom panel enables more detailed settings. Users can easily set parameters to their individual needs, which are then saved by the machine for future washes. The base of the device features a drawer with additional storage space.

Statement by the jury
The Beverly washing machine delivers a functionality which has been thought out down to the minutest detail, achieving a high ease of use and allowing customisation.

Um eine möglichst komfortable Bedienung zu ermöglichen, wurde diese Waschmaschine mit einem zweifachen Touchscreen ausgestattet. Das obere Bedienfeld erlaubt eine unkomplizierte Auswahl der gängigsten Waschprogramme, während das untere eine detailliertere Steuerung erlaubt. Dabei legen die Benutzer Parameter fest, die ihren Bedürfnissen entsprechen, die dann vom Gerät für künftige Waschgänge gespeichert werden. Im Sockel des Geräts befindet sich eine Schublade als zusätzlicher Stauraum.

Begründung der Jury
Eine bis ins Detail durchdachte Funktionalität erreicht bei der Waschmaschine Beverly ein hohes Maß an Bedienkomfort, der sich zudem individualisieren lässt.

Midea
Top-Loading Washing Machine
Toplader-Waschmaschine

Manufacturer
Little Swan, Wuxi, China
In-house design
Web
www.littleswan.com
Honourable Mention

Midea is a small-sized top-loading washing machine with a capacity of 3 kg. The slim, 42 cm high device takes up very little space and, with its matte white body, discreetly blends into most interiors. It is mainly targeted at young families who prefer to wash the clothing of children and adults separately. The washing machine offers special programmes which are perfect for the hygienic and efficient cleaning of, for example, baby clothes.

Statement by the jury
Using a clear, independent design language, this top-loading washing machine allows a needs-oriented use.

Midea ist eine kleinformatige Toplader-Waschmaschine mit einem Fassungsvermögen von 3 kg. Das schlanke, 42 cm hohe Gerät beansprucht nur wenig Platz und fügt sich mit seinem mattweißen Korpus dezent ins Interieur ein. Zur Hauptzielgruppe zählen junge Familien, die es bevorzugen, die Bekleidung von Kindern und Erwachsenen getrennt voneinander zu waschen. Die Waschmaschine bietet spezielle Waschprogramme, die beispielsweise verschmutzte Babybekleidung hygienisch einwandfrei reinigen.

Begründung der Jury
Unter Einsatz einer klaren, eigenständigen Formensprache ermöglicht diese Toplader-Waschmaschine einen bedarfsgerechten Gebrauch.

Little Swan
Top-Loading Washing Machine
Toplader-Waschmaschine

Manufacturer
Little Swan, Wuxi, China
In-house design
Web
www.littleswan.com
Honourable Mention

The top-loading washing machine showcases a contemporary minimalist design with gently rounded edges. The consistently embedded body is mainly made of environmentally friendly materials. The interactive controls are integrated into the front section of the body, which ensures that the washing machine is easy to operate. This new generation of devices is also equipped with an automatic detergent dosing technology and a variable pre-wash cycle.

Statement by the jury
This space-saving top-loading washing machine, which is geared towards the Asian market, stands out due to its operating comfort and convenience.

Die Toplader-Waschmaschine zeigt mit ihren sanft abgerundeten Ecken eine zeitgemäß minimalistische Gestaltung. Der formschlüssig eingebettete Korpus besteht überwiegend aus umweltschonend hergestellten Materialien. Die interaktiven Bedienelemente wurden im vorderen Bereich des Korpus integriert, was die Steuerung der Waschmaschine komfortabel gestaltet. Diese neue Gerätegeneration bietet zudem eine automatische Waschmitteldosierung sowie einen variablen Vorwaschgang.

Begründung der Jury
Ein auf den asiatischen Markt ausgerichteter Bedienkomfort zeichnet diese platzsparende Toplader-Waschmaschine aus.

Colmo
Washing Machine
Waschmaschine

Manufacturer
Little Swan, Wuxi, China
In-house design
Web
www.littleswan.com

Via an integrated camera, this washing machine recognises clothes and their materials in order to select and set an appropriate washing programme for the respective laundry load. Made of brushed stainless steel, the body with its rounded edges conveys a homogeneous overall image. The flush-integrated touch control panel with 3D effect is at a comfortable height. The large drawer in the base can be opened and closed via a push function.

Statement by the jury
This visually striking washing machine successfully integrates innovative technology in a convincing manner.

Mithilfe einer integrierten Kamera erkennt diese Waschmaschine Kleidungsstücke und deren Materialien, um die Auswahl der Waschprogramme bedarfsgerecht auf die jeweilige Waschladung abzustimmen. Der Korpus aus gebürstetem Edelstahl vermittelt mit seinen abgerundeten Kanten ein homogenes Gesamtbild. In komfortabler Höhe befindet sich das flächenbündig integrierte Touch-Bedienfeld mit 3D-Effekt. Die große Schublade im Sockel lässt sich per Push-Funktion öffnen und schließen.

Begründung der Jury
Bei dieser visuell prägnant wirkenden Waschmaschine gelingt die Integration einer innovativen Technologie auf überzeugende Weise.

Laundry Center
Washing Machine and Trumble Dryer
Waschmaschine und Trockner

Manufacturer
Little Swan, Wuxi, China
In-house design
Web
www.littleswan.com

As a pioneering combination of devices, Laundry Center comprises a washing machine and a dryer stacked on top of each other to save space. The two transparent full-surface doors are made of tempered glass and allow a view into the 12 kg washing and drying drums. An eye-level TFT screen enables intuitive control of both devices, which are equipped, among other things, with a high-heat sterilisation and a steam ironing function.

Statement by the jury
With its high-quality glass door and minimalist style, the Laundry Center exudes an elegant appeal.

Als zukunftsweisende Gerätekombination umfasst das Laundry Center eine Waschmaschine und einen Trockner, die platzsparend aufeinandergestapelt werden. Die beiden vollflächigen Türen aus transparentem, thermisch gehärtetem Glas erlauben den Blick in die 12 kg fassende Waschbzw. Trocknertrommel. Ein auf Augenhöhe platzierter TFT-Bildschirm erlaubt die intuitive Steuerung beider Geräte, die u. a. eine Hochtemperatur-Sterilisation sowie eine Dampfbügelfunktion bieten.

Begründung der Jury
Aufgrund seiner hochwertigen Glastür und einer minimalistischen Formensprache erreicht das Laundry Center eine elegante Anmutung.

Mi Front-Load Washer and Dryer Pro
Washer-Dryer
Waschtrockner

Manufacturer
Xiaomi Inc., Beijing, China
In-house design
Web
www.mi.com

This washer-dryer is equipped with an automatic dosing system which allows the precise dispensing of detergent and softener, considering not only the selected programme but also additional settings and the weight of the load. Detergents need to be added only every three months. The centrally integrated rotary control is equipped with an OLED screen. The large door features an intuitive push-to-open mechanism.

Statement by the jury
This washer-dryer combines a purist body design with convenient and contemporary functionality.

Dieser Waschtrockner ist mit einem automatischen Dosiersystem ausgestattet, das eine präzise Abgabe von Waschmittel und Weichspüler ermöglicht. Dabei werden nicht nur das gewählte Programm, sondern auch zusätzliche Einstellungen sowie das Gewicht der Ladung berücksichtigt. Die Waschmaschine muss nur ca. alle drei Monate mit Waschmittel aufgefüllt werden. Das mittig integrierte Drehrad ist mit einem OLED-Bildschirm versehen. Die große Tür lässt sich per Push-Effekt betätigen.

Begründung der Jury
Eine puristisch anmutende Korpusgestaltung vereint sich bei diesem Waschtrockner mit einer sehr komfortablen und zeitgemäßen Funktionalität.

ASKO T600HX
Tumble Dryer Series
Trockner-Serie

Manufacturer
Asko Appliances AB, Lidköping, Sweden
In-house design
ASKO Design Centre, Lidköping, Sweden
Gorenje Design Studio, Velenje, Slovenia
Web
www.asko.com

Following a minimalist design approach, the front of the dryer was manufactured from a single piece of sheet steel. The controls, including the inlay, the dial and the buttons, are made of solid metal as well. The heat pump dryer is energy-efficient and reliably dries the laundry, even at lower temperatures. The steam function prevents creasing and can also be used to refresh clothes which do not yet need to be washed.

Statement by the jury
In addition to its convincing functionality, this energy-efficient dryer is characterised by a clear design vocabulary and robust materials.

Einem minimalistischen Gestaltungsansatz folgend, wurde die Front des Trockners aus einem einzigen Stück Stahlblech gefertigt. Auch die Bedienelemente wie das Inlay, das Ziffernblatt und die Tasten sind aus massivem Metall. Als Wärmepumpentrockner arbeitet das Gerät energieeffizient und trocknet die Wäsche auch bei niedrigeren Temperaturen zuverlässig. Die Dampffunktion verhindert die Knitterbildung und lässt sich zudem nutzen, um Kleidungsstücke, die noch nicht gewaschen werden müssen, aufzufrischen.

Begründung der Jury
Neben seiner überzeugenden Funktionalität zeichnet sich dieser energieeffiziente Trockner durch eine klare Formensprache und robuste Materialien aus.

Morus Zero
Tumble Dryer
Wäschetrockner

Manufacturer
Morus Technology (Shenzhen) Co., Ltd., Shenzhen, China
In-house design
Axe Yi, Roy Yan, SK Chen
Web
www.morustech.com
Honourable Mention

Morus Zero is an innovative tumble dryer which reduces the drying time per load to 15 minutes using vacuum technology. The laundry is dried at 37 degrees centigrade; this relatively low temperature is easy on the fabric and prevents shrinkage. Inspired by aerospace technology, the design concept follows a minimalist approach. The energy-saving device switches off automatically as soon as the drying process is completed.

Statement by the jury
The innovative quality of this energy-efficient tumble dryer is emphasised by its appealingly unconventional overall image.

Morus Zero ist ein innovativer Wäschetrockner, der durch den Einsatz einer Vakuum-Technologie die Trocknungszeit pro Ladung auf 15 Minuten reduziert. Getrocknet wird die Wäsche bei 37 Grad Celsius, da diese relativ niedrige Temperatur das Gewebe schont und vor dem Einlaufen schützt. Inspiriert von Raumfahrttechnologie, folgt das Gestaltungskonzept einem minimalistischen Ansatz. Das energiesparsame Gerät schaltet sich automatisch aus, sobald die Trocknung abgeschlossen ist.

Begründung der Jury
Sein ansprechend unkonventionelles Gesamtbild betont die innovative Qualität dieses energiesparsamen Wäschetrockners.

Mr. Bond M1xpro
Clothes Airer
Wäschetrockner

Manufacturer
Hangzhou Mr. Bond Technology Co., Ltd.,
Hangzhou, China
In-house design
Design
Hangzhou Bole Industrial Design
(Mandy Wang, Ligang Zhou),
Hangzhou, China
Web
www.mrbond.cn
www.hzbole.cn

This patented clothes airer is mounted to the ceiling and creates a warm airflow which dries hanging laundry within two hours. Rods and hooks allow the flexible hanging of various textiles. The capacity of the laundry rack, which can carry up to 30 kg, can be increased by additional hooks. The airer can be controlled via an app and is also equipped with light panels which illuminate the area underneath. After use, the rack can be lifted up to the ceiling.

Statement by the jury
A space-saving product solution, this clothes airer provides superior comfort paired with contemporary technical features.

Dieser patentierte Wäschetrockner wird an der Zimmerdecke montiert und erzeugt einen warmen Luftstrom, der Wäsche hängend innerhalb von zwei Stunden trocknet. Stangen und Haken erlauben das flexible Aufhängen von diversen Textilien. Die Kapazität des Wäschegitters mit einer Tragfähigkeit von 30 kg kann mit zusätzlichen Haken vergrößert werden. Das über eine App steuerbare Gestell ist zudem mit Lichtpaneelen ausgestattet, die den Arbeitsbereich darunter beleuchten. Nach dem Gebrauch lässt sich das Gitter bis zur Decke emporheben.

Begründung der Jury
Als platzsparende Produktlösung bietet dieser Wäschetrockner einen gehobenen Komfort, der mit einer zeitgemäßen technischen Ausstattung einhergeht.

BONECO F-Series
BONECO F-Serie Fans
Ventilatoren

Manufacturer
BONECO AG, Widnau, Switzerland
In-house design
Manfred Fitsch
Design
Studio Volpi S.r.l. (Roberto Manzari),
Carnago (Varese), Italy
Web
www.boneco.com
www.studiovolpi.com

The asymmetrically designed fans of the F-Series comprise the small F50 USB fan, the F100 desktop fan, as well as the large F230 pedestal fan, covering different needs in homes and living areas. The models with a stand allow an indirect air circulation thanks to their 270-degree swivelling heads, resulting in a pleasant circulation of the ambient air. Various settings can be selected via a colour-coded button which is perfectly integrated into the product.

Statement by the jury
Using precise technology, these fans achieve high efficiency and set architectural accents through their asymmetry.

Die asymmetrisch gestalteten Ventilatoren der F-Serie reichen vom kleinen USB-Lüfter F50 über den Tischventilator F100 bis hin zum großen Standlüfter F230; sie decken somit unterschiedliche Bedürfnisse im Wohnbereich ab. Die Ausführungen mit Fuß ermöglichen durch einen um 270 Grad schwenkbaren Kopf eine indirekte Luftzirkulation, was zu einer angenehmen Durchmischung der Raumluft führt. Diverse Einstellungen lassen sich über einen farblich markierten Knopf wählen, der formschlüssig integriert ist.

Begründung der Jury
Unter Einsatz einer präzisen Technik erreichen diese Ventilatoren einen hohen Wirkungsgrad und setzen durch ihre Asymmetrie architektonische Akzente.

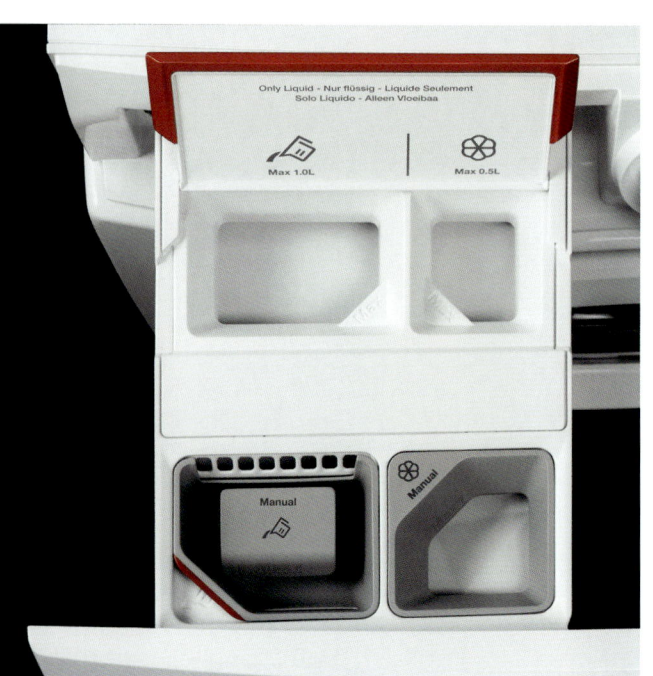

AEG Autodose
Washing Machine Drawer
Waschmaschinenschublade

Manufacturer
AB Electrolux, Stockholm, Sweden
In-house design
Web
www.electrolux.com

Autodose is a detergent drawer with an automatic dosage system. During the washing process, a sensor measures the weight of the current laundry load and ensures that the correct amount of detergent is added, and thus effectively prevents overdosing. If required, the device also allows flexible, manual dosing. Symbols and terms which are easy to understand as well as the colour-code of the compartments facilitate intuitive handling.

Statement by the jury
With regard to the increasing pollution of water, Autodose makes an advanced contribution to an environ-mentally sound use of detergents.

Autodose ist eine Waschmaschinenschublade, die der automatischen Dosierung von Waschmittel dient. Während des Betriebs misst ein Sensor das aktuelle Ladungsgewicht und stellt eine angemessene Waschmittelabgabe sicher. Auf diese Weise wird eine Überdosierung verhindert. Im Bedarfsfall ist zudem eine flexible, manuelle Dosierung von Waschmittel möglich. Mit klar verständlichen Symbolen sowie farblich gekennzeichneten Kammern wird den Benutzern eine intuitive Handhabung ermöglicht.

Begründung der Jury
Im Hinblick auf die zunehmende Gewässerbelastung leistet Autodose einen fortschrittlichen Beitrag zur ökologisch sinnvollen Waschmitteldosierung.

GS2
Clothes Steamer
Dampfglätter

Manufacturer
Hangzhou Rosou Electronic
Technology Co., Ltd.,
Hangzhou, China
In-house design
Chang Jin
Web
https://zhibai.tmall.com

In order to extend the operating time, this clothes steamer has been equipped with a comparatively large water tank. The tank also serves as its handle and is positioned at an ergonomic angle to facilitate the handling of the device. The on/off button is easy to reach with the thumb. After use, the device can be disassembled: in order to reduce the required space, especially when traveling, the water tank can be removed from the steaming unit via a turn-lock.

Statement by the jury
Thanks to a minimalist design, this clothes steamer showcases a contemporary aesthetics which conveys clarity and cleanliness.

Um die Betriebsdauer zu verlängern, wurde dieser Dampfglätter mit einem vergleichsweise großen Wassertank ausgestattet. Der Tank dient zugleich als Griff und ist in einem ergonomisch sinnvollen Winkel angebracht, um die Handhabung des Geräts zu erleichtern. Die Ein-/Aus-Taste befindet sich an einer Position, die der Daumen gut erreicht. Nach dem Gebrauch kann das Gerät zerlegt werden: Um den Platzbedarf insbesondere auf Reisen zu reduzieren, lässt sich der Wassertank per Drehverschluss vom Glättaufsatz trennen.

Begründung der Jury
Dank einer minimalistischen Gestaltung zeigt dieser Dampfglätter eine zeitgemäße Ästhetik, die zugleich Klarheit und Sauberkeit vermittelt.

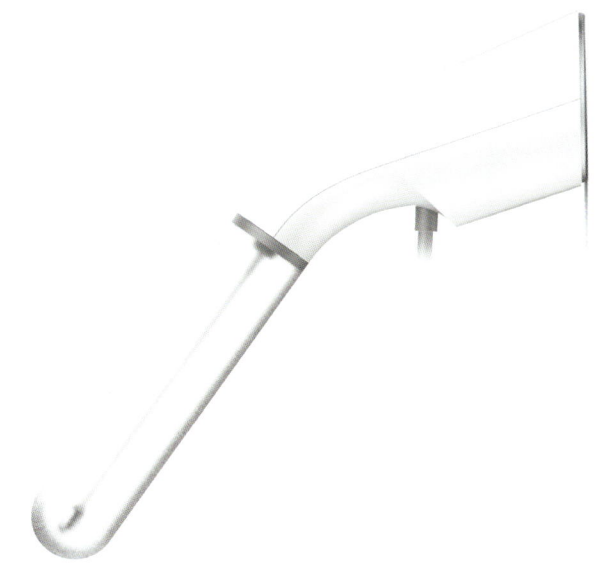

PerfectCare Expert Plus Range
Steam Generator Iron
Dampfbügelstation

Manufacturer
Philips, Eindhoven, Netherlands
In-house design
Philips Design
Web
www.philips.com

This steam generator iron was developed with the objective of easy handling. Its light weight is built on a sophisticated design which is reduced to the basics. The elimination of excess material and unnecessary control elements has made the ironing process much faster and easier. The iron glides smoothly over the clothes, reducing strain on the wrist. The 1.8-litre water tank of the steam generator station allows ironing for up to two hours.

Statement by the jury
This steam generator iron blends a high degree of operating comfort with sophisticated functionality and distinctive aesthetics.

Unter der Prämisse einer einfachen Handhabung wurde diese Dampfbügelstation entwickelt. Ihr geringes Gewicht basiert auf einer gut durchdachten Konstruktion, die auf das Wesentliche reduziert wurde. Der Verzicht auf überschüssiges Material und unnötige Bedienelemente beschleunigt und vereinfacht den Bügelvorgang. Das Bügeleisen gleitet leichtgängig über die Kleidung und verringert somit die Belastung des Handgelenks. Der 1,8 Liter fassende Wasserbehälter der Dampfbügelstation ermöglicht ein Bügeln von bis zu zwei Stunden.

Begründung der Jury
Ein hohes Maß an Bedienkomfort vereint sich bei dieser Dampfbügelstation mit einer ausgereiften Funktionalität sowie einer markanten Ästhetik.

FAD-01/02
Clothes Purifier
Bekleidungslüfter

Manufacturer
Coway, Seoul, South Korea
In-house design
Bo Seong Seo, Kyoung Hwa Maeng
Web
www.coway.co.kr

This purifier removes dust and pollen from clothes. After use, they are hung into the cabinet-like floor unit to be cleaned by precise air blasts. Integrated invisibly into the large mirrored door, the control elements only light up during operation and can be used. Animation graphics illustrate the progress of the cleaning process. When the door is open, the purifier can also serve to clean the air in the room.

Statement by the jury
In view of increasing dust pollution, this technically sophisticated clothes purifier offers a high utility value.

Dieser Bekleidungslüfter befreit Kleidungsstücke von Staub und Pollen. Dazu werden diese nach dem Tragen in das schrankähnliche Standgerät gehängt, um von gezielten Luftstößen gereinigt zu werden. Die unsichtbar in die großflächige Spiegeltür integrierten Bedienelemente leuchten nur während des Betriebs auf und erlauben eine intuitive Steuerung. Dabei veranschaulichen Animationsgrafiken das Voranschreiten des Reinigungsprozesses. Bei geöffneter Tür kann zudem eine Raumluftreinigung aktiviert werden.

Begründung der Jury
Angesichts einer zunehmenden Staubbelastung bietet dieser technisch ausgereifte Bekleidungslüfter einen hohen Gebrauchswert.

FC 3 Cordless Premium
Floor Cleaner
Hartbodenreiniger

Manufacturer
Alfred Kärcher SE & Co. KG, Winnenden, Germany
In-house design
Michael Meyer, Felix Schneider, Matthias Helfert
Design
Pearl Creative (Christian Rummel), Ludwigsburg, Germany
Web
www.kaercher.de
www.pearlcreative.com

Thanks to its innovative roller self-cleaning function, the FC 3 Cordless Premium wipes floors always with fresh water. During the cleaning process, the two rotating microfibre rollers are continuously moistened with a mixture of water and detergent. The dirt is removed from the rollers by a special blade and collected in a separate tank. Hard floors, such as tiles and vinyl as well as parquet or laminate, are thus cleaned thoroughly and gently. The slim device reaches under furniture and into corners.

Dank seiner innovativen Walzen-Selbstreinigungsfunktion wischt der FC 3 Cordless Premium Böden immer mit frischem Wasser. Während der Bodenreinigung werden die beiden rotierenden Mikrofaserwalzen kontinuierlich mit einem Gemisch aus Wasser und Reinigungsmittel befeuchtet. Der aufgenommene Schmutz wird durch eine Abstreifkante von den Walzen entfernt und in einem separaten Auffangbehälter gesammelt. Hartböden wie Fliesen und Vinyl, aber auch Parkett oder Laminat lassen sich somit gründlich und schonend reinigen. Das schmale Gerät gelangt unter Möbelstücke und in Ecken.

Statement by the jury
As a contemporary alternative to wet mops, the distinctive FC 3 Cordless Premium hard floor cleaner convinces with a high quality of use.

Begründung der Jury
Als zeitgemäße Alternative zum Wischmopp überzeugt der markante Hartbodenreiniger FC 3 Cordless Premium mit einer hohen Gebrauchsqualität.

EVERYBOT EDGE
Mopping Robot
Wischroboter

Manufacturer
Everybot Inc., Seongnam, South Korea
In-house design
Bong Yun Kim, Tae Wan Kim
Web
www.everybotweb.com

Everybot Edge is a mopping robot suitable for wet and dry cleaning of hard floors and can also be used in handheld mode. The compact device manoeuvres without wheels. Instead, it runs on two round, rotating microfibre pads, which are driven by two separate motors; so the robot cleans the floor while moving. Two containers constantly supply the pads with water. Thanks to the fact that they are protruding, the device also reaches into corners. In addition, it is equipped with anti-collision and fallprotection sensors.

Statement by the jury
This mopping robot conceals a high level of functionality in a compact body. It is versatile and flexible in everyday use.

Everybot Edge ist ein Wischroboter, der sich sowohl für die feuchte als auch für die trockene Reinigung von Hartböden eignet und zudem im Handbetrieb nutzbar ist. Das kompakt konstruierte Gerät bewegt sich ohne Räder, stattdessen betreiben zwei Motoren die mit Mikrofasertüchern versehenen Scheiben und ermöglichen somit ein gleichzeitiges Gleiten und Wischen. Zwei Behälter versorgen die Mikrofasertücher konstant mit Wasser. Das Gerät erreicht mithilfe hervorstehender Tücher auch Ecken und ist mit Antikollisions- und Fallschutzsensoren ausgestattet.

Begründung der Jury
Dieser Wischroboter verbirgt eine hochgradige Funktionalität in einem handlichen Gerätekorpus.

GlassVAC
Window Vacuum Cleaner
Fenstersauger

Manufacturer
Robert Bosch GmbH, Power Tools Division, Leinfelden-Echterdingen, Germany
Design
Tatic Designstudio S.r.l.
(Aleks Tatic, Patrick Heutschi, Laura Haas), Milan, Italy
Web
www.bosch-pt.com
www.taticdesignstudio.com

Thanks to its patented rubber coating, this window vacuum cleaner ensures a particularly easy glide over glass panes, thus shortening the cleaning process. Its compact design allows streak-free results and cleans the surface right up to the edge. The accessories comprise large and small attachments for a variety of applications such as cleaning windows, mirrors and shower walls. The integrated LED indicator shows the battery level and charging status.

Statement by the jury
This window vacuum cleaner is characterised by a high degree of functionality. In addition, GlassVAC convinces with comfortable handling.

Dank seiner patentierten Gummibeschichtung ermöglicht dieser Fenstersauger ein besonders leichtes Gleiten über die Glasscheibe und verkürzt somit den Reinigungsvorgang. Seine kompakte Bauweise erlaubt eine streifenfreie Reinigung bis zur Oberflächenkante. Das Zubehör umfasst große und kleine Aufsätze für eine Vielzahl von Anwendungen wie die Säuberung von Fenstern, Spiegeln oder Duschwänden. Der integrierte LED-Leuchtmelder zeigt den Verbrauch des Akkus an und macht auf einen zu niedrigen Ladezustand aufmerksam.

Begründung der Jury
Ein hohes Maß an Funktionalität zeichnet den Fenstersauger aus. GlassVAC überzeugt zudem durch seine komfortable Handhabung.

Roomba® i7+ with Clean Base™ Automatic Dirt Disposal
Robot Vacuum Cleaner
Saugroboter

Manufacturer
iRobot, Boston, USA

In-house design
iRobot

Web
www.irobot.com

reddot award 2019
best of the best

Intelligently advanced
Robot vacuum cleaners have established themselves firmly in households, saving residents a lot of work. Following an innovative approach, the design of the Roomba i7+ extends the capabilities of such devices in terms of intelligence and automation. This appealingly designed robot offers the ability to "learn" by mapping a home's floor plan and adapts itself accordingly in its cleaning actions. Featuring the new Imprint Smart Mapping technology, the robot can map up to ten different floor plans, remembering the rooms of each floor by name. The robot can then start to act self-sufficiently, eliminating the need for human interaction for weeks at a time. In addition, it also allows users to control which specific rooms are to be cleaned and when, as it features full connectivity to Alexa-enabled devices and the Google Assistant. This allows users to order the robot to clean specific rooms by name with a voice command. Also highly convenient is the Clean Base Automatic Dirt Disposal, which empties the contents of the vacuum's dust bin automatically and hygienically into the Clean Base, while also serving as a charging dock. Thanks to this automatic emptying, the robot can do its job maintenance-free over a long period. With its innovative features, the Roomba i7+ makes everyday life much easier.

Intelligent weiterentwickelt
Saugroboter haben mittlerweile ihren festen Platz in den Haushalten, da sie den Bewohnern viel Arbeit ersparen. Auf innovative Weise erweitert die Gestaltung des Roomba i7+ die Möglichkeiten eines solchen Geräts hinsichtlich seiner Intelligenz und Automatisierung. Dieser ansprechend gestaltete Roboter kann den Grundriss der vorhandenen Wohnräume „erlernen" und sich in seinen Aktionen entsprechend anpassen. Ausgestattet mit der innovativen Imprint Smart Mapping-Technologie, erfasst er bis zu zehn verschiedene Grundrisse. Die jeweiligen Räume werden dabei mit Namen gespeichert. Da der Roboter selbst unabhängig agiert, erübrigt sich die Interaktion mit dem Nutzer auch über Wochen. Es kann zudem genau gesteuert werden, welche Räume zu welchem Zeitpunkt gereinigt werden sollen. Der i7+ bietet dafür volle Konnektivität zu Alexa-fähigen Geräten sowie dem Google Assistant. Mit einem einfachen Sprachbefehl können Nutzer so den Roboter gezielt anweisen, einen bestimmten Raum zu reinigen. Überaus komfortabel ist außerdem die Clean Base-Absaugstation, die auf praktische, hygienische Weise den Inhalt des Staubsaugers aufnimmt und zugleich als Ladestation dient. Dank dieser automatischen Entleerung kann der Saugroboter über längere Zeit selbständig seine Arbeit verrichten. Mit seinen innovativen Eigenschaften erleichtert der Roomba i7+ damit in hohem Maße den Alltag.

Statement by the jury
Thanks to its innovative functionality and intelligent features, the Roomba i7+ can perfectly adapt to the floor plan of its environment. And when combined with the Clean Base vacuum and charging station, which automatically absorbs the collected dirt, the unit delivers a new level of self-sufficiency and hygiene. An outstanding design solution, the robot vacuum cleaner impresses with its advanced technology and elegant, consistent use of forms.

Begründung der Jury
Mittels seiner innovativen Funktionalität und intelligenten Eigenschaften kann sich der Roomba i7+ perfekt den Gegebenheiten seiner Umgebung anpassen. Auch durch die Kombination mit der Clean Base-Absaug- und Ladestation, die den Schmutz selbsttätig aufnimmt, erreicht dieses Gerät ein neues Level hinsichtlich Autarkie und Hygiene. Gestalterisch hervorragend gelöst, überzeugt der Saugroboter durch seine fortschrittliche Technologie und elegante, einheitliche Formensprache.

Designer portrait
See page 36
Siehe Seite 36

DEEBOT OZMO 960
Floor-Cleaning Robot
Bodenreinigungsroboter

Manufacturer
Ecovacs Robotics Co., Ltd.,
Suzhou, China
In-house design
Ecovacs Design Team
Web
www.ecovacs.cn

The OZMO 960 is a floor cleaning robot with a mounted AI camera. By means of artificial intelligence and visual interpretation technology, the device recognises and avoids obstacles such as cables, slippers, etc. Each time it is used, the robot records the position of the items in order to plan the next cleaning run more efficiently. The integrated cleaning system combines the functions of sweeping, vacuuming and mopping, depending on the amount of dirt.

Statement by the jury
This floor cleaning robot owes its high quality of use to the consistent implementation of a user-friendly product concept.

Der OZMO 960 ist ein Bodenreinigungsroboter mit aufmontierter KI-Kamera. Somit erkennt das Gerät mittels künstlicher Intelligenz und visueller Interpretationstechnologie Hindernisse wie Kabel, Hausschuhe etc. und weicht ihnen aus. Bei jedem Gebrauch speichert der Roboter die Position der Gegenstände ab, um die nächste Reinigung effizienter planen zu können. Das integrierte Reinigungssystem kombiniert je nach Schmutzaufkommen die Funktionen Kehren, Staubsaugen und Wischen miteinander.

Begründung der Jury
Der stringenten Umsetzung eines bedienungsfreundlichen Produktkonzepts verdankt dieser Bodenreinigungsroboter seine hohe Gebrauchsqualität.

DEEBOT DX Series
DEEBOT DX-Serie
Floor-Cleaning Robot
Bodenreinigungsroboter

Manufacturer
Ecovacs Robotics Co., Ltd.,
Suzhou, China
In-house design
Ecovacs Design Team
Web
www.ecovacs.cn

The DX series includes an app-controlled floor cleaning robot featuring an LDS system and SLAM based navigation. This enables an appropriate combination of sweeping, vacuuming and mopping in medium-to-large-sized homes and multi-storey buildings. For orientation, the device creates and saves maps of the floors and rooms to be cleaned. On these maps, users can specify areas, such as no-mopping areas, using an app.

Statement by the jury
Technically sophisticated, this minimalist floor cleaning robot impresses as a highly user-friendly device.

Die DX-Serie umfasst einen mobil steuerbaren Bodenreinigungsroboter, der mit einem LDS-System sowie einem SLAM-Algorithmus ausgestattet ist. Dies ermöglicht eine bedarfsgerechte Kombination von Kehren, Staubsaugen und Wischen in größeren Haushalten oder Mehrfamilienhäusern. Zur eigenen Orientierung erstellt das Gerät Karten von den zu reinigenden Stockwerken und Räumen und speichert diese ab. Per App können die Nutzer in diesen Karten die Bereiche festlegen, die beispielsweise nicht gewischt werden sollen.

Begründung der Jury
Technisch ausgereift, beeindruckt dieser minimalistisch anmutende Bodenreinigungsroboter als sehr bedienungsfreundliches Gerät.

DEEBOT DV Series
DEEBOT DV-Serie
Floor-Cleaning Robot
Bodenreinigungsroboter

Manufacturer
Ecovacs Robotics Co., Ltd.,
Suzhou, China
In-house design
Ecovacs Design Team
Web
www.ecovacs.cn

This floor cleaning robot recognises the areas to be cleaned with the help of a camera and infrared sensors. The robot features a technology which, if a user has moved the device during the cleaning process, allows to relocate its position in order to seamlessly complete the cleaning task. The body, with a height of only 77 mm, can reach the area under furniture. The functionality of the removable parts, such as the dust container and roller brushes, has also been optimised for enhanced user friendliness.

Statement by the jury
An elegant, flat body design underlines the high functionality of this floor cleaning robot.

Dieser Bodenreinigungsroboter erkennt die zu reinigenden Flächen mithilfe einer Kamera und Infrarotsensoren. Sollten die Nutzer das Gerät während der Reinigung woanders einsetzen, erlaubt eine Technologie die anschließende Bestimmung der ursprünglichen Position, um die Aufgabe lückenlos fortzuführen. Der Korpus mit einer Höhe von nur 77 mm erreicht den Bereich unterhalb der Möbel. Auch die Funktionsweise der abnehmbaren Teile, wie Staubbehälter und Walzenbürsten, wurde bedienungsfreundlich optimiert.

Begründung der Jury
Eine elegant anmutende, flache Korpusgestaltung untermalt die hohe Funktionalität dieses Bodenreinigungsroboters.

Vileda VR102 & VR201 PetPro
Cleaning Robots
Saugroboter

Manufacturer
Freudenberg Home and
Cleaning Solutions GmbH,
Weinheim, Germany
In-house design
Christian Stenglein, Willem Lijmbach
Design
Luca Casini Design Studio and
Casini Studio Industrial Design (Luca Casini),
Milan, Italy
Web
www.vileda.com
www.lucacasini.com

These two newly developed vacuum robots feature an elegant body, showcasing balanced colour combination. The VR 201 PetPro is equipped with a patented pet hair brush, while the VR 102 delivers particularly strong suction performance. They do the cleaning autonomously for up to 90 minutes and, thanks to their low height of 8 cm, also reach under furniture. Both devices come with an active sound control and a 60-decibel silent mode for low-noise operation. The 500 ml dust box is equipped with an allergen filter system.

Statement by the jury
Thought through to the last detail, the product design of these vacuum robots underlines their contemporary functionality to emotionally appealing effect.

Die beiden neu entwickelten Saugroboter zeigen einen eleganten Korpus mit einer ausgewogenen Farbkombination. Der VR 201 PetPro ist mit einer patentierten Tierhaarbürste ausgestattet, während der VR 102 eine besonders starke Saugkraft bietet. Dank ihrer geringen Höhe von 8 cm gelangen die Roboter auch unter Möbelstücke, sie reinigen autark bis zu 90 Minuten. Beide Geräte verfügen über eine aktive Klangsteuerung und einen Silent Mode mit 60 Dezibel für einen geräuscharmen Betrieb. Die 500 ml fassende Staub-Box ist mit einem Allergenschutzfiltersystem versehen.

Begründung der Jury
Eine bis ins Detail durchdachte Produktgestaltung betont auf emotional ansprechende Weise die zeitgemäße Funktionalität dieser Saugroboter.

Vorwerk Kobold VR300
Robot Vacuum Cleaner
Saugroboter

Manufacturer
Vorwerk Elektrowerke GmbH & Co. KG,
Wuppertal, Germany
In-house design
Uwe Kemker
Design
Phoenix Design GmbH + Co. KG,
Stuttgart, Germany
Web
www.vorwerk-kobold.de
www.phoenixdesign.com

The Kobold VR300 robot vacuum cleaner can be conveniently controlled via smartphone. An app offers many advanced features, such as easy switching between cleaning programmes or limiting the workspace by setting boundary lines. The flat design in combination with the intelligent navigation ensures independent and thorough cleaning. Thanks to the sophisticated laser navigation and ultrasonic sensors, it can avoid obstacles such as furniture or objects lying on the floor.

Statement by the jury
With its contemporary app control, the Kobold VR300 vacuum robot offers a high level of user-friendliness and an impressive cleaning performance.

Der Kobold VR300 Saugroboter lässt sich komfortabel über das Smartphone steuern. Eine App ermöglicht zahlreiche erweiterte Funktionen, wie beispielsweise den einfachen Wechsel zwischen den Reinigungsprogrammen oder die Begrenzung des Arbeitsbereichs durch das Festlegen von No-Go-Linien. Die flache Bauweise sorgt in Verbindung mit der intelligenten Navigation dafür, dass der Saugroboter selbständig und sorgfältig reinigt. Dank einer ausgefeilten Lasernavigation und Ultraschallsensoren umfährt er dabei Hindernisse wie Möbel oder herumliegende Gegenstände.

Begründung der Jury
Mit seiner zeitgemäßen App-Steuerung bietet der Kobold VR300 ein hohes Maß an Bedienkomfort, zudem überzeugt die Leistungsstärke des Saugroboters.

Vorwerk Kobold VB100
Cordless Vacuum Cleaner
Akku-Staubsauger

Manufacturer
Vorwerk Elektrowerke GmbH & Co. KG,
Wuppertal, Germany
In-house design
Uwe Kemker, Felix Thies
Web
www.vorwerk-kobold.de

The Kobold VB100 is a cordless stick vacuum cleaner which offers fast and easy floor cleaning. With its two-motor technology, it provides strong suction power on both carpets and hard floors. In order to collect dirt particles, the device is equipped with premium filter bags which can easily be replaced. Its compact dimensions and low weight ensure comfortable handling. The slim silhouette of the vacuum cleaner shows the typical colour accents of the manufacturer's corporate identity.

Statement by the jury
A technically sophisticated device, the Kobold VB100 is characterised by comfortable handling and formal independence.

Der Kobold VB100 ist ein Akku-Staubsauger, der aufgrund seines kabellosen Gebrauchs eine unkomplizierte Bodenreinigung ermöglicht. Dank seiner Zwei-Motoren-Technologie bietet er sowohl auf Teppichen als auch auf Hartböden eine starke Saugleistung. Zur Aufnahme der Schmutzpartikel wird der Akku-Staubsauger mit hochwertigen, einfach zu wechselnden Filtertüten ausgestattet. Aufgrund seiner kompakten Maße und des geringen Gewichts ist die Handhabung des Geräts komfortabel. Die schlanke Silhouette des Staubsaugers zeigt herstellertypische Farbakzente.

Begründung der Jury
Technisch ausgereift zeichnet sich der Kobold VB100 durch seine komfortable Handhabung aus und erreicht zudem formale Eigenständigkeit.

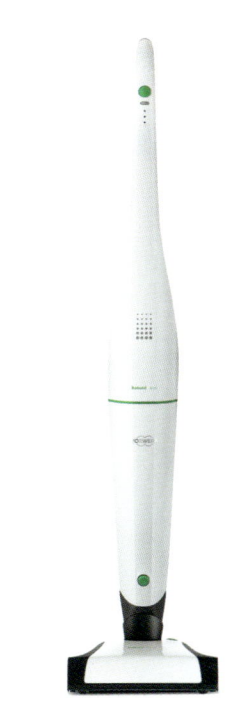

Pure F9
Cordless Vacuum Cleaner
Akku-Staubsauger

Manufacturer
AB Electrolux, Stockholm, Sweden
In-house design
Web
www.electrolux.com

With a battery life of up to 60 minutes, the Pure F9 allows thorough cleaning of an area of up to 270 sqm. The main unit is height-adjustable: in the upper position, it can reach under low furniture, while in the low position, the centre of gravity shifts closer to the floor, making the vacuum cleaner easier to manoeuvre. A pullout hose in combination with a 3-in-1, multi-function nozzle allows easy cleaning of upholstery and delicate surfaces as well as reaching narrow areas. The height of the robust telescopic tube can be adapted to the user.

Mit einer Akku-Laufzeit von bis zu 60 Minuten ermöglicht der Pure F9 die gründliche Reinigung einer Fläche von bis zu 270 qm. Die Motoreinheit lässt sich verschieben: In der höheren Position können Bereiche unterhalb von Möbeln bearbeitet werden. In der niedrigen Position verlagert sich der Schwerpunkt in Bodennähe, wodurch der Staubsauger besser manövrierbar ist. Ein herausziehbarer Saugschlauch erleichtert in Kombination mit einer 3-in-1-Multifunktionsdüse die Reinigung von empfindlichen Flächen, Nischen und Polstern. Das robuste Teleskoprohr lässt sich der jeweiligen Körpergröße anpassen.

Statement by the jury
The easy-to-manoeuvre Pure F9 offers a high ease of use and is a powerful cordless vacuum cleaner for everyday use at home.

Begründung der Jury
Der leicht manövrierbare Pure F9 bietet ein hohes Maß an Bedienkomfort und überzeugt im häuslichen Alltag als leistungsstarker Akku-Staubsauger.

BOSCH Flexxo Serie 4
2 in 1 Cordless Vacuum Cleaner
2-in-1-Akku-Staubsauger

Manufacturer
Robert Bosch Hausgeräte GmbH,
Munich, Germany
In-house design
Daniel Dockner
Design
BRANDIS Industrial Design,
Nuremberg, Germany
Web
www.bsh-group.com
www.brandis-design.de

The Flexxo 2-in-1 cordless vacuum cleaner has an integrated detachable hand unit and fulfils a variety of needs in one device: cleaning carpets, smooth surfaces and corners is just as possible as selective cleaning with the hand unit. All accessories are integrated into the body of the vacuum and are thus readily at hand when needed. The soft furniture dust brush offers versatility, while the flexible, extendable crevice tool cleans hard-to-reach areas in drawers or between seat upholstery. The ergonomically sophisticated design is complemented by intuitive operation.

Statement by the jury
This 2-in-1 cordless vacuum cleaner combines a compact layout with a balanced design vocabulary, which underlines its high-quality standard.

Der Flexxo 2-in-1-Akku-Staubsauger mit integriertem Handstaubsauger erfüllt unterschiedliche Anforderungen in einem Gerät: von der Reinigung von Teppichen, glatten Oberflächen und Ecken bis hin zum punktuellen Saugen mittels abnehmbarem Handmodul. Sämtliche Zubehörteile sind im Korpus integriert und daher bei Bedarf schnell griffbereit. Die weiche Möbelstaubbürste bietet Vielseitigkeit, während die biegsame, ausziehbare Fugendüse schwer zugängliche Stellen in Schubladen oder zwischen Sitzpolstern erreicht. Eine intuitive Bedienung rundet die ergonomisch durchdachte Konstruktion ab.

Begründung der Jury
Eine kompakte Bauweise vereint sich bei diesem 2-in-1-Akku-Staubsauger mit einer ausgewogenen Formensprache, die einen hohen Qualitätsanspruch untermalt.

Philips SpeedPro Max Aqua FC690X
Cordless Vacuum Cleaner
Akku-Staubsauger

Manufacturer
Philips, Eindhoven, Netherlands
In-house design
Philips Design
Web
www.philips.com

The cordless SpeedPro Max Aqua FC690X is a combined vacuum mop system and was developed to save time when cleaning the floor. A detergent can be added, if necessary, while the boost function helps with stubborn stains. The dynamic silhouette of the vacuum cleaner is highlighted by lines full of suspense and a flowing surface design. Accent colours underline the user-friendly display, which indicates the battery level, the currently selected mode and when the filter should be cleaned.

Statement by the jury
High ease of use characterises the SpeedPro Max Aqua FC690X, the multifunctionality of which is emphasised by its concise design.

Als Kombination eines kabellosen Staubsaugers mit einem Wischelement wurde der SpeedPro Max Aqua FC690X für eine zeitsparende Bodenreinigung ent-wickelt. Bei Bedarf kann eine Reinigungsflüssigkeit hinzugegeben werden, zudem hilft eine Boost-Funktion bei hartnäckigen Flecken. Spannungsvoll verlaufende Linien und die fließende Oberflächengestaltung heben die dynamische Silhouette des Staubsaugers hervor. Akzentfarben unterstreichen das benutzerfreundliche Display, welches den Batteriestatus, den jeweiligen Modus und eine Erinnerung an die Filterreinigung anzeigt.

Begründung der Jury
Ein hohes Maß an Bedienkomfort zeichnet den SpeedPro Max Aqua FC690X aus, dessen Multifunktionalität von einer prägnanten Gestaltung betont wird.

Shark ION™ W1
Handheld Vacuum Cleaner
Handstaubsauger

Manufacturer
SharkNinja, Needham, Massachusetts, USA
In-house design
Scott Niedzwecki
Web
www.sharkninja.com

The Shark ION W1 is, with an overall weight of 635 grams, a remarkable light handheld vacuum cleaner. It was designed to be placed within easy reach and clearly visible on a kitchen worktop or in the living room. Its brushless motor delivers powerful suction to pick up everyday dirt, while attachable accessories facilitate the cleaning of hard-to-reach places and upholstery. A one-touch system allows the quick and easy emptying of the vacuum cleaner.

Statement by the jury
Thanks to its compact design, suction power and low weight, this handheld vacuum cleaner scores as a well thought-out product solution.

Der Shark ION W1 ist mit seinem Gesamtgewicht von 635 Gramm ein auffallend leichter Handstaubsauger. Er wurde entwickelt, um auf der Küchenarbeitsplatte oder in Wohnräumen für alle sichtbar und griffbereit platziert zu werden. Sein bürstenloser Motor erreicht eine leistungsstarke Absaugung von alltäglichem Schmutz, wobei das integrierte Zubehör die Reinigung von schwer zugänglichen Stellen sowie Polstern erleichtert. Nach dem Gebrauch ermöglicht ein One-Touch-System die schnelle und einfache Entleerung des Staubsaugers.

Begründung der Jury
Dank seiner kompakten Bauweise, der Saugleistung und des geringen Gewichts punktet dieser Handstaubsauger als gut durchdachte Produktlösung.

LEXY Magic M12
Cordless Vacuum Cleaner
Akku-Staubsauger

Manufacturer
Kingclean Electric Co., Ltd.,
Jiangsu, China
In-house design
Jingzhe Li, Ruoya Zhou
Web
www.lexy.cn

This cordless device can be used as both a stick and a handheld vacuum cleaner. Thanks to a variety of brush heads, it can not only be used for the thorough cleaning of floors and upholstered furniture but also for curtains and hard-to-reach areas. Its compact body features a brushless 450-watt motor with a battery which offers a usage time of up to 70 minutes, providing a high suction power at 100,000 rpm. The specially developed, three-stage filter technology achieves a dust-air separation efficiency of 99.9 per cent.

Statement by the jury
With its convincing functionality and high efficiency, this cordless vacuum cleaner embodies a successful product development.

Dieser kabellose Akku-Staubsauger lässt sich sowohl als Stiel- wie auch als Handstaubsauger einsetzen. Dank einer Vielzahl von Bürstenköpfen können neben Böden und Polstermöbeln auch Vorhänge sowie schwer erreichbare Stellen gründlich gereinigt werden. Das kompakte Gehäuse ist mit einem bürstenlosen 450-Watt-Motor ausgestattet, der mit 100.000 U/min eine große Saugkraft ermöglicht. Der Akku erlaubt eine Einsatzdauer von bis zu 70 Minuten. Die eigens entwickelte, dreistufige Filtertechnologie erreicht einen Staub-Abscheidegrad von 99,9 Prozent.

Begründung der Jury
Aufgrund seiner überzeugenden Funktionalität und hohen Effektivität stellt dieser Akku-Staubsauger eine gelungene Produktentwicklung dar.

Concelo®
Kitchen Waste Bin
Küchenabfallbehälter

Manufacturer
Kitchen King Limited, Auckland, New Zealand
In-house design
Allen Bertelsen, Jamie Bertelsen,
David Howse, Steve Woodall, Jesse Staines
Web
www.concelo.com

Concelo is a waste bin which can be discreetly integrated into kitchen units. Conveniently mounted at about the same height as the worktop, it has two containers which pull out like drawers. In order to reduce unpleasant odours, it features an active lid, which remains hidden inside the cabinet when pulling out the waste container. The hands-free operation of the lid is synchronised with the opening and closing of the waste bins. The clip and clean components allow the bin to be cleaned easily eliminating potential dirt traps in difficult spaces.

Concelo ist ein Abfallbehälter, der sich dezent in Küchenzeilen integrieren lässt. Auf komfortabler Arbeitsplattenhöhe bietet er zwei Behälter, die sich wie Schubladen herausziehen lassen. Um unangenehme Gerüche einzudämmen, verfügt er über einen automatischen Deckel, der beim Herausziehen des Abfallbehälters im Schrank verborgen bleibt. Die freihändige Bedienung des Deckels ist mit dem Öffnen und Schließen der Abfallbehälter synchronisiert. Die Clip-and-Clean-Komponenten ermöglichen eine einfache Reinigung der Behälter und verhindert Schmutz in problematischen Stellen.

Statement by the jury
A sophisticated product solution, this kitchen waste bin convinces thanks to its automatic, odour controlling closing mechanism.

Begründung der Jury
Als durchdachte Produktlösung überzeugt dieser Küchenabfallbehälter auch aufgrund seiner automatischen Schließvorrichtung zur Geruchseindämmung.

Bokashi Organko 2
Kitchen Composter
Küchenkomposter

Manufacturer
Plastika Skaza d.o.o., Velenje, Slovenia
Design
Gigodesign d.o.o., Ljubljana, Slovenia
Kabinet 01 d.o.o., Ljubljana, Slovenia
Web
www.skaza.com
www.gigodesign.com
www.kabinet01.ne

Bokashi Organko 2 was developed to facilitate the collection of organic waste. The kitchen composter is equipped with a lid which is easy to open and offers a capacity of 9.6 litres. Thanks to its slim silhouette and unobtrusive colouring, it can be placed in any kitchen. The environmentally friendly composter is manufactured from recycled material. In addition, it can be recycled. With the use of bran, the waste can be fermented and then be used as a fertiliser.

Statement by the jury
The functionally sophisticated kitchen composter impresses as a sustainable product solution as well as with its subtle form and colour scheme.

Bokashi Organko 2 wurde entwickelt, um das Sammeln von organischem Abfall zu vereinfachen. Der mit einem leicht zu öffnenden Deckel ausgestattete Küchenkomposter bietet ein Fassungsvermögen von 9,6 Litern. Dank seiner schlanken Silhouette und unauffälligen Farbgebung lässt er sich in jeder Küche platzieren. Bestehend aus recyceltem Material, wird der Komposter umweltfreundlich gefertigt und ist zudem recyclebar. Die Abfälle vergären unter Einsatz von Kleie und eignen sich als Pflanzendünger.

Begründung der Jury
Der funktional ausgereifte Küchenkomposter überzeugt als nachhaltige Produktlösung sowie durch seine dezente Form- und Farbgebung.

Luna
Sensor Waste Bin
Sensor-Abfalleimer

Manufacturer
Top Profit Manufacturing Co., Ltd., Foshan, China
In-house design
Lesley Lai
Web
www.upella.com

Luna is a sensor waste bin with a stainless steel surface, the glossy finish of which is inspired by the light of the moon. Using a sensor-controlled mechanism, the lid opens swiftly and then closes slowly and quietly. Thanks to its height, the bin offers a large capacity and can easily be emptied. The bottom insert prevents the buildup of moisture and features an insecticide trap for cockroaches.

Statement by the jury
This sensor waste bin merges an elegant surface design with functionality which has been well thought-out down to the detail.

Luna ist ein Sensor-Abfalleimer mit einer Edelstahloberfläche, deren schimmernder Glanz dem Mondlicht nachempfunden wurde. Der Deckel wird durch einen sensorgesteuerten Mechanismus schnell geöffnet, um sich danach langsam und leise zu schließen. Aufgrund seiner Höhe bietet der Abfalleimer ein großes Fassungsvermögen und lässt sich einfach entleeren. Der Bodeneinsatz verhindert die Ansammlung von Feuchtigkeit und birgt darüber hinaus eine mit Insektiziden versehene Falle für Schaben.

Begründung der Jury
Eine bis ins Detail durchdachte Funktionalität vereint sich bei diesem Sensor-Abfalleimer mit einer edel anmutenden Oberflächengestaltung.

Teza
Sensor Waste Bin
Sensor-Abfalleimer

Manufacturer
Top Profit Manufacturing Co., Ltd., Foshan, China
In-house design
Lesley Lai
Web
www.upella.com

Showcasing rounded edges, the design idiom of this sensor waste bin strives for the right balance between hard and soft contours. Available in four colours, Teza harmoniously blends into the environment. The dark, drain-strainer-shaped bottom insert is equipped with a bait compartment which attracts cockroaches but prevents children from getting in contact with the insecticides. The sensor-controlled lid opens swiftly and closes silently.

Statement by the jury
Visually appealing as well as functionally sophisticated, the Teza sensor waste bin delivers high utility value.

Die Formensprache des Sensor-Mülleimers strebt mit ihren abgerundeten Ecken ein Gleichgewicht zwischen harten und weichen Konturen an. Erhältlich in vier Farbausführungen, fügt sich Teza harmonisch in sein Umfeld ein. Der dunkle Bodeneinsatz in Form eines Drainage-Siebs ist mit einem Köderfach für Schaben ausgestattet. Es lockt diese an und verhindert, dass Kinder mit den Insektiziden in Berührung kommen. Per Sensorsteuerung öffnet sich der Deckel zügig und schließt sich auf geräuscharme Weise.

Begründung der Jury
Sowohl visuell ansprechend als auch funktional ausgereift, erreicht der Sensor-Abfalleimer Teza einen hohen Gebrauchswert

ALBULA
Recycling Waste Bin System
Recycling-Müllbehältersystem

Manufacturer
Rotho Kunststoff AG,
Würenlingen, Switzerland
In-house design
Marc Binder, Marcus Brunner
Web
www.rotho.com

Albula has been developed to meet the growing demand for space-efficient waste separation. The modular system comprises stackable containers with lids, including a front opening allowing convenient disposal of paper, cardboard, glass and plastic bottles. The containers can be customised with attached stickers for clear identification of its function. The product is made from recycled plastics and, thanks to its smooth surface, easy to clean. The handles ensure effortless carrying and support up to 40 kg.

Statement by the jury
The clear structure of its functional design lends this stackable recycling waste bin system an independent overall appearance.

Albula wurde im Hinblick auf eine wachsende Nachfrage nach platzsparender Mülltrennung entwickelt. Das modulare System umfasst stapelbare Behälter samt Deckel, deren vordere Öffnung eine bequeme Entsorgung von Papier, Karton, Glas und Plastikflaschen ermöglicht. Zur besseren Übersicht können die Behälter mit Aufklebern gekennzeichnet werden. Die aus recycelten Kunststoffen hergestellten Behälter sind dank ihrer glatten Oberfläche gut zu reinigen. Die Griffe vereinfachen den Transport und tragen bis zu 40 kg.

Begründung der Jury
Eine klar strukturierte, zweckgerichtete Gestaltung verleiht diesem stapelbaren Recycling-Müllbehältersystem ein eigenständiges Gesamtbild.

BRISEN
Storage Boxes
Aufbewahrungsboxen

Manufacturer
Rotho Kunststoff AG,
Würenlingen, Switzerland
In-house design
Marc Binder, Bruno Meier
Web
www.rotho.com

Inspired by perforated metal, the appearance of these storage boxes showcases a timeless look. The discreet design vocabulary blends into different home styles and is also aimed to appeal to users of all ages. BRISEN follows the idea of designing stylish boxes of well thought-out sizes so that they can be used both for storage and laundry. There is a choice of boxes with 4.5, 7, 16 and 18 litres, as well as a 41-litre laundry basket and a 50-litre laundry hamper.

Statement by the jury
Well thought-out to the last detail, the BRISEN storage boxes impress with durable materials and a high quality of use.

Die von perforierten Metallen inspirierte Gestaltung dieser Aufbewahrungsboxen folgt einem zeitlosen Look. Die dezente Formensprache fügt sich in unterschiedliche Wohnstile ein und soll zudem Nutzer jeden Alters ansprechen. BRISEN folgt der Idee, stilvolle Boxen in gut durchdachten Größen zu entwerfen, um diese sowohl zur Aufbewahrung als auch für die Wäsche nutzen zu können. Zur Auswahl stehen Boxen mit einem Fassungsvermögen von 4,5 sowie 7, 16, und 18 Litern, ein 41-L-Wäschekorb und ein 50-L-Wäschesammler.

Begründung der Jury
Die bis ins Detail durchdachten Aufbewahrungsboxen BRISEN überzeugen durch hohe Gebrauchsqualität und langlebige Materialien.

Compact Stool
Step Stool
Klapphocker

Manufacturer
Casa Vigar S.L.,
Gata de Gorgos (Alicante), Spain
In-house design
Design
LÚCID Design Agency,
Terrassa (Barcelona), Spain
Web
www.vigar.com
www.lucid.pro/en

This space-saving step stool is sturdy enough to support up to 150 kg. With a single movement of the hand, by pulling up the recessed handles in its centre, it folds up to a flat, easily storable household tool. The stool is available in three different sizes, depending on needs and application. The design concept attaches importance to a colourful implementation with bright colours, which are aimed at expressing the zest for life.

Statement by the jury
This sturdy step stool combines a meticulously thought-out design with an emotionally appealing colour scheme.

Dieser platzsparende Klapphocker ist stabil genug, um ein Gewicht von bis zu 150 kg tragen zu können. Er lässt sich durch einen einfachen Handgriff zu einem flachen, leicht verstaubaren Haushaltsutensil zusammenklappen, wobei die mittig platzierten Griffmulden nach oben gezogen werden. Der Klapphocker ist je nach Bedarf in drei unterschiedlichen Größen erhältlich. Das Gestaltungskonzept legt Wert auf eine farbenfrohe Umsetzung mit hellen Farben, die den Nutzern Lebensfreude vermitteln sollen.

Begründung der Jury
Bei diesem stabilen Klapphocker vereinen sich eine schlüssig durchdachte Konstruktion mit einer emotional ansprechenden Farbgebung.

ERIF
Fire Extinguisher
Feuerlöscher

Manufacturer
Samwoo Instrument, Inc.,
Chungcheongbuk Province, South Korea
In-house design
Design
RND PLUS, Seoul, South Korea
Web
www.erif.co.kr
www.rndplus.co.kr

The Erif fire extinguisher – the name is an anagram of "fire" – is the result of the comprehensive development of a new product. Boasting a striking colour, the extinguisher features a design which has been reduced to the essential. In order to facilitate operation as much as possible, the conventional safety pin and seal were replaced by a safety bar. Thanks to this easy and intuitive mechanism, paired with a funnel-shaped aiming device which gives off the extinguishing foam, even inexperienced users can put out a a fire quickly.

Statement by the jury
This fire extinguisher achieves concision through its purist design language. It features a very well thought-out safety concept and is easy to operate.

Der Feuerlöscher Erif – der Name ist ein Anagramm für „fire" (englisch Feuer) – ist das Ergebnis einer umfassenden Produktneuentwicklung. Neben der auffallenden Farbgebung zeigt der Feuerlöscher eine auf das Wesentliche reduzierte Ausstattung. Im Hinblick auf eine möglichst einfache Bedienung wurde der herkömmliche Sicherheitsstift samt Dichtung durch einen Sicherheitsbügel ersetzt. Aufgrund dieses leicht verständlichen Mechanismus sowie einer trichterförmigen Zielapparatur, aus der der Löschschaum austritt, können auch Ungeübte ein Feuer schnell löschen.

Begründung der Jury
Eine puristische Formensprache verleiht diesem Feuerlöscher Prägnanz. Er verfügt über ein sehr durchdachtes Sicherheitskonzept und ist leicht bedienbar.

Cuffy
Multipurpose Sterilising Lid
Mehrzweck-Desinfektionsdeckel

Manufacturer
Shenzhen UVLED Optical Technology Co., Ltd., Shenzhen UV Guard Technology Co., Ltd., Shenzhen, China
In-house design
Prof. Dehua Liu, Prof. Yi Tang, Wensheng Zhou
Design
Shenzhen EEDesign Co., Ltd. (Tian Gao), Shenzhen, China
Web
www.59s.com
www.eedesign.net.cn

Cuffy is a multipurpose sterilising lid which uses UVC rays to sanitise the inner surfaces of drinking and eating utensils. Pathogenic bacteria are killed within 19 seconds by intense light exposure. Silicone parts reminiscent of water waves ensure that the lid closes tightly and no UVC light can leak out. The childproof device is made of environmentally friendly materials. The integrated battery charges via USB connection.

Statement by the jury
In combination with an emotionally appealing design idiom, the high functionality of Cuffy establishes high user trust.

Cuffy ist ein Mehrzweck-Desinfektionsdeckel, der durch UV-C-Strahlung die Innenflächen von Trink- oder Essgeschirr entkeimt. Krankheitserregende Bakterien werden durch eine intensive Lichtex-position innerhalb von 19 Sekunden abgetötet. An Wasserwellen erinnernde Silikonteile sorgen dafür, dass der Deckel dicht abschließt und kein UV-C-Licht nach außen dringt. Das aus umweltfreundlichen Materialien gefertigte Gerät ist zudem kindersicher. Über einen USB-Anschluss wird der integrierte Akku aufgeladen.

Begründung der Jury
In Kombination mit einer emotional ansprechenden Formensprache erweckt die hohe Funktionalität von Cuffy das Vertrauen der Nutzer.

cooking utensils
Tableware und Kochutensilien

Baking utensils	Backutensilien
Bottles	Becher
Cans	Besteck-Sets
Carafes	Flaschen
Cutlery sets	Geschirr
Dishes	Gläser
Glasses	Kannen
Kitchenware	Karaffen
Knives	Küchengeschirr
Pan sets	Messer
Pans	Pfannen
Porcelain	Pfannen-Sets
Pot sets	Porzellan
Pots	Spezialbestecke
Special cutleries	Thermobecher
Teapots / Coffee pots	Thermoskannen
Thermos flasks	Töpfe
Travel mugs	Topf-Sets
Vases	Vasen

DISC
Carbon Cooking Pot
Carbon-Kochtopf

Manufacturer
Anaori Carbon Co., Ltd.,
Ibaraki City, Osaka Prefecture,
Japan

Design
Carozzeria Kawai,
Tajimi City, Gifu Prefecture,
Japan

Web
www.anaori.co.jp
www.ccc-japan.com

reddot award 2019
best of the best

The fascination of form and material
Carbon fibre reinforced composites possess astonishing properties that offer many design possibilities that are still far from having been exhausted. In this sense, the design of the DISC cooking pot breaks new ground. This cooking pot is made of 99.9 per cent industrial grade pure carbon that is otherwise also used in space technology. The material is characterised by its special far-infrared properties and excellent heat distribution effect. The design quality is also reflected in the outstanding shape the pot has adopted. Inspired in name and design by the circular shape that is found in music and race cars, whereas the side view of the cooking pot astonishes with its continuous triangular shape. Fitting well in the hands, the overall sharp lines and delicate curves are made possible because the product is carved out, while the sides serve as handles so that the fingers can easily grip and hold the pot. The basic structure is intended to reflect the simplicity and elegance seen in the appearance of Japanese shrines and temples. The innovative form goes hand in hand with enhanced functionality. The steam holes can be opened and closed by simply turning the lid. Closing the steam holes is good for both condensed cooking, which eliminates the need to add water, or for pressure cooking. With open holes the pot is ideal for cooking rice or stews.

Die Faszination von Form und Material
Kohlenstofffaserverstärkte Verbundwerkstoffe besitzen erstaunliche Eigenschaften, die noch lange nicht ausgereizt sind und viele Möglichkeiten bieten. Die Gestaltung des Kochtopfs DISC schlägt hier neue Wege ein. Dieser Kochtopf wird aus 99,9 Prozent reinem Kohlenstoffgraphit industrieller Qualität hergestellt, wie er auch in der Weltraumtechnik eingesetzt wird. Das Material zeichnet sich durch besondere Ferninfrarot-Eigenschaften und eine hervorragende Wärmeverteilung aus. Die Qualität der Gestaltung zeigt sich auch in der bemerkenswerten Formgebung. Inspiriert in Name und Design von der im Musik- und Rennwagenbereich anzutreffenden Kreisform, verblüfft der Kochtopf in der Seitenansicht hingegen mit seiner dreieckigen Silhouette. Gestaltet mit aus dem Material herausgearbeiteten klaren Linien und sanften Rundungen, lässt er sich gut handhaben, wobei der als Griff dienende Randbereich ein leichtes Greifen und Halten ermöglicht. Die Grundstruktur soll dabei die Einfachheit und Eleganz widerspiegeln, die sich in japanischen Schreinen und Tempeln finden lässt. Die innovative Form geht mit einer hohen Funktionalität einher. Die Dampföffnungen können durch einfaches Drehen des Deckels geöffnet oder geschlossen werden. Bei geschlossenen Öffnungen eignet sich der Topf gut etwa für das Kochen mit Kondensat, ohne dass Wasser hinzugefügt werden müsste, oder auch zum Druckgaren. Mit geöffneten Schlitzen kann er perfekt zum Kochen von Reis oder Eintöpfen genutzt werden.

Statement by the jury
The design of DISC takes advantage of the properties of carbon fibre that have been proven in areas such as aerospace and motor sports, utilising them in the innovative development of a cooking pot. Highly contemporary, simple and clear in expression, the pot impresses with its high production quality and functionality. Created for professional use, it lends itself perfectly for serving directly at the table, promoting a new paradigm in culinary culture.

Begründung der Jury
Die Gestaltung von DISC nutzte die in anderen Bereichen, wie etwa der Raumfahrt oder dem Motorsport, erprobten Eigenschaften der Carbonfaser für die innovative Entwicklung eines Kochtopfs. Sehr zeitgemäß, einfach und klar in seinem Ausdruck, begeistert dieser mit seiner hohen Fertigungsqualität und Funktionalität. Kreiert für den professionellen Einsatz, eignet er sich auch perfekt für das Servieren direkt am Tisch und verkörpert so eine neue Denkweise in der Tischkultur.

Designer portrait
See page 38
Siehe Seite 38

GALAXY
Pressure Cooker
Schnellkochtopf

Manufacturer
Guangdong Linkfair Group Co., Ltd.,
Yunfu, China
Design
LINKFAIR Industrial Design Centre
(Liang Jianxiu, Huang Zhirong, Wu Shangkai),
Yunfu, China
Kurz Kurz Design China
(Xiong Hao, Yue Long, Zuo Xu),
Foshan, China
Web
www.linkfair.com.cn
www.kkdesign.cn

In order to improve safety for the use of pressure cookers, GALAXY follows a new design concept: the recessed grips as well as the lid and other heat-conducting components are completely covered with plastic. In addition, the easy-to-clean steam valve is placed at 45 degrees to the handles to prevent scalding. The stainless steel pressure cooker is available with two different lids in various colours.

Statement by the jury
The appealing combination of plastic and purist stainless steel underlines the high quality of use of this pressure cooker.

Um die Sicherheit bei der Handhabung des Schnellkochtopfs zu erhöhen, folgt GALAXY einem neuen Gestaltungskonzept: Sowohl die Griffmulden als auch der Deckel und weitere wärmeleitende Komponenten sind vollständig mit Kunststoff verkleidet. Zudem wurde das leicht zu reinigende Dampfablassventil um 45 Grad versetzt zu den Griffmulden angeordnet, um Verbrühungen zu verhindern. Der Schnellkochtopf aus Edelstahl ist mit zwei Deckelvarianten in diversen Farben erhältlich.

Begründung der Jury
Die ansprechende Kombination von puristisch wirkendem Edelstahl und Kunststoff betont bei diesem Schnellkochtopf eine hohe Gebrauchsqualität.

Maho Nabé
Cooking Pot
Kochtopf

Manufacturer
Tiger Corporation,
Kadoma, Osaka Prefecture, Japan
In-house design
Atsuko Mori, Masahiro Watanabe
Design
Kanae Design Labo (Kanae Tsukamoto),
Kyoto, Japan
Web
www.tiger.jp
www.kanaedesignlabo.com

Thanks to its double-walled vacuum structure, this cooking pot seals the heat inside very effectively, keeping cooked food warm for a long time. In addition, the pot requires comparatively little energy during cooking. The trivet precisely encloses the bottom of the pot and thus further improves thermal insulation. Available in five traditional Japanese colours, the decorative Maho Nabé pot can also be used to serve food at the table.

Statement by the jury
Showcasing a keen sense for design details, this cooking pot not only exudes a traditional aesthetic appeal but also convinces with a high level of operating comfort.

Dank seiner doppelwandigen Vakuum-Struktur speichert dieser Kochtopf die Hitze so effektiv, dass gekochte Speisen über längere Zeit warm bleiben. Zudem benötigt der Topf vergleichsweise wenig Energie beim Kochen. Der Topfuntersetzer umschließ den Boden des Kochtopfs passgenau und trägt auf diese Weise zur Wärmedämmung bei. Erhältlich in fünf traditionellen japanischen Farben, lässt sich Maho Nabé zudem als dekorativer Serviertopf am Esstisch einsetzen.

Begründung der Jury
Mit viel Gespür für gestalterische Details zeigt dieser Kochtopf eine traditionell anmutende Ästhetik, zudem überzeugt der hohe Bedienkomfort.

Leo
Cookware Series
Kochgeschirr-Serie

Manufacturer
BergHOFF Worldwide,
Heusden-Zolder, Belgium
In-house design
Pieter Roex
Web
www.berghoffworldwide.com

This cookware is made of cast aluminium to ensure an energy-efficient and even heat distribution. Nevertheless, the handles stay cool and allow easy handling thanks to their good tactile qualities. The non-stick coating promotes cooking with only little or no oil. The large glass lids have an integrated vent hole and allow users to see the inside of the pot. Versatile accessories including a steamer basket, pasta strainer and a splash guard lid complement the series.

Statement by the jury
This well thought-out cookware series is characterised by energy efficiency, outstanding workmanship and stylish accessories.

Dieses Kochgeschirr ist aus Aluminiumguss gefertigt und bietet somit eine energieeffiziente und gleichmäßige Hitzeverteilung. Dennoch bleiben die Griffe kühl und erlauben dank guter Haptik eine leichte Handhabung. Die Antihaftbeschichtung begünstigt eine fettarme bis fettfreie Zubereitung von Speisen. Die großflächigen Glasdeckel mit einem integrierten Abzugsloch geben Einblicke ins Topfinnere. Vielseitiges Zubehör wie der Dämpfeinsatz, das Nudelsieb oder der Spritzschutzdeckel runden die Serie ab.

Begründung der Jury
Diese bis ins Detail durchdachte Kochgeschirr-Serie zeichnet sich durch Energieeffizienz, gute Verarbeitung sowie stilvolles Zubehör aus.

Diamond XR Logic
Cookware Series
Kochgeschirr-Serie

Manufacturer
Norbert Woll GmbH, Saarbrücken, Germany
In-house design
Web
www.woll-cookware.com

This cookware series shows an exceptionally robust sealing with a rough surface. All pots and pans are made by hand and feature three layers: a plasma-hardened base as well as a PEEK intermediate layer and a diamond-reinforced finish with an abrasion-resistant non-stick coating. The cookware is optionally available with phenolic or stainless steel handles which are either fixed or detachable. It also includes matching lids for all sizes. They are made of safety glass or stainless steel and equipped with a vent.

Diese Kochgeschirr-Serie zeigt eine außergewöhnlich robuste Versiegelung mit rauer Oberfläche. Alle Töpfe und Pfannen werden von Hand gefertigt und bestehen aus einer plasmagehärteten Basisschicht, einer PEEK-Zwischenschicht sowie einer diamantverstärkten Oberschicht samt abriebfester Antihaftversiegelung. Das Kochgeschirr ist optional mit festen oder abnehmbaren Phenol- oder Edelstahlgriffen erhältlich. Zudem gibt es für alle Größen passende Deckel aus Sicherheitsglas oder Edelstahl, die mit einer Entlüftung ausgestattet sind.

Statement by the jury
Following a modular design concept and striving for excellent quality, this cookware series offers a high utility value.

Begründung der Jury
Einem modularen Gestaltungskonzept und einem gehobenen Qualitätsanspruch folgend, bietet diese Kochgeschirr-Serie einen hohen Gebrauchswert.

Le Kitchen
Cookware Series
Kochgeschirr-Serie

Manufacturer
Guangdong Master Group Co., Ltd., Yunfu, China
In-house design
Yanming Liang, Guoxing Liang
Web
www.mastergroup.com.cn

This non-stick cookware series is made of food-safe aluminum alloy and allows for the preparation of food without using fat. In order to realise the concept of a contemporary look, the outer surfaces showcase a silver-black high-temperature coating. The particularly tight-closing lids are made of food-grade silicone and glass. The cookware also includes a spatula and a perforated cooking spoon made of non-abrasive nylon, both of which can be placed between the handle and the lid during cooking to save space.

Diese antihaftbeschichtete Kochgeschirr-Serie aus einer lebensmittelechten Aluminiumlegierung ermöglicht die fettfreie Zubereitung von Speisen. Um dem Konzept eines zeitgemäßen Looks zu folgen, sind die Außenflächen mit einer silberschwarzen Hochtemperaturfarbe versehen. Die besonders dicht schließenden Deckel sind aus lebensmittelechtem Silikon und Glas gefertigt. Zum Kochgeschirr gehören zudem ein Spachtel sowie ein perforierter Kochlöffel aus nicht kratzendem Nylon, die beide während des Kochens platzsparend zwischen Griff und Deckel abgelegt werden können.

Statement by the jury
Le Kitchen especially scores with the appealing combination of high-quality materials and the practical positioning of the spoon and the spatula.

Begründung der Jury
Le Kitchen punktet vor allem mit der ansprechenden Kombination hochwertiger Materialen sowie der praktischen Platzierung von Kochlöffel und Spachtel.

Pure Steel
Fryware
Bratpfannen

Manufacturer
BK Cookware BV, Delft, Netherlands
In-house design
Nadia Bartels-Wijstma
Web
www.bk.nl

These 2 mm thick, uncoated carbon steel frying pans are energy-efficient and, with every use, develop a natural non-stick layer, called patina. The darker the patina, the better the non-stick properties – a process that makes the pan especially durable. The long handle, attached with stainless steel rivets to the pan, allows the space-saving stacking of different sized pans. In order to ensure that the heat of the pan is not transferred to the cast handle, the handle forks out and tapers toward the rim of the pan.

Diese 2 mm dicken, unbeschichteten Bratpfannen aus Kohlenstoffstahl sind energieeffizient und entwickeln bei jedem Gebrauch eine natürliche Antihaftbeschichtung, die sogenannte Patina. Je dunkler die Patina, desto besser sind die Antihafteigenschaften – dieser Prozess macht die Pfanne besonders langlebig. Der lange, mit Edelstahlnieten befestigte Griff erlaubt das platzsparende Stapeln von unterschiedlich großen Pfannen. Damit die Hitze der Pfanne nicht auf den gegossenen Griff übergeht, teilt sich dieser zum Pfannenrand hin und wird schmaler.

Statement by the jury
These frying pans owe their puristic appearance to a consistent design, showcasing the material properties of carbon steel.

Begründung der Jury
Ihre puristische Anmutung verdanken diese Bratpfannen einer stringenten Gestaltung, die auf die Materialeigenschaften von Kohlenstoffstahl setzt.

Colander and Bowl
Sieb- und Schüssel-Set

Manufacturer
Like-it Co., Ltd., Katsuragi, Nara, Japan
Design
RKDS (Ryuichi Kozeki), Shinjuku, Tokyo, Japan
Web
www.like-it.jp/en
www.ryuichikozeki.com

Inspired by the Japanese way of preparing rice, this set includes a colander and a mixing bowl, which fit together precisely. The flexible colander allows comfortable straining: the 1 mm wide draining slots drain water quickly. Their edges are very smooth, allowing even delicate foods to be rinsed off without getting damaged. The sturdy bowl is suitable for both preparing and serving food.

Statement by the jury
This colander and bowl set merges comfortable handling with timeless elegance.

Inspiriert von der japanischen Reiszubereitung umfasst dieses Set ein Sieb und eine Rührschüssel, die präzise zusammenpassen. Das biegsame Sieb ermöglicht ein komfortables Abseihen: Die 1 mm breiten Ausgussschlitze leiten die Flüssigkeit schnell ab. Ihre Ränder sind so glatt, dass selbst empfindliche Lebensmittel ohne Beschädigung abgespült werden können. Die stabile Schale eignet sich sowohl zur Zubereitung als auch zum Servieren von Speisen.

Begründung der Jury
Bei diesem Sieb- und Schüssel-Set verbindet sich eine komfortable Handhabung mit einer zeitlosen Eleganz.

Ortwo
Pepper Mill
Pfeffermühle

Manufacturer
Dreamfarm, Brisbane, Australia
In-house design
Philip Howieson, Thomas Schuster, Alexander Gransbury
Web
www.dreamfarm.com

Ortwo is an innovative pepper mill which combines the convenience of one-handed grinding with the output of mills which are operated using two hands. The positioning of the handles enables users to apply more leverage, allowing the ceramic grinding mechanism to be exceptionally efficient. The mechanism is suitable for all types of spices, salt as well as seeds, and is fully adjustable offering six grind settings. Thanks to its wide opening, the borosilicate glass jar allows easy refilling.

Statement by the jury
This decorative pepper mill stands out as a product solution with a high ease of use, flexibility and efficiency.

Ortwo ist eine neuartige Pfeffermühle, die den Komfort der Einhandbedienung mit der Leistung beidhändig betriebener Mühlen kombiniert. Die Anordnung der Griffe ermöglicht es dem Anwender, eine höhere Hebelwirkung auszuüben, was das Keramikmahlwerk außergewöhnlich effizient arbeiten lässt. Der Mechanismus eignet sich für alle Arten von Gewürzen, Salz und Samen und ist in sechs Mahlgraden flexibel einstellbar. Der Behälter aus Borosilikatglas lässt sich dank seiner großen Öffnung leicht nachfüllen.

Begründung der Jury
Als Produktlösung mit einem hohen Maß an Bedienkomfort, Flexibilität und Effizienz zeichnet sich diese dekorative Pfeffermühle aus.

Twister
Bundt Pan
Bundform

Manufacturer
W. F. Kaiser u. Co. GmbH, Diez, Germany
Design
Rudolph Schelling Webermann, Product Design & Innovation Consultancy, Hannover, Germany
Web
www.wmf-group.com
www.rsw.design

Twister is a spiral-shaped Bundt pan for baking dynamic-looking cakes. On the outside, the spiral runs from the base up to the top, before continuing downwards along the inside. As a result, cakes can be decorated not only on top, but also on the inside and outside. Even without decoration, the pan helps produce appealing cakes, lending every piece of cake an interesting contour.

Statement by the jury
The stringent implementation of a creative idea has been particularly successful with Twister. The sculptural appearance of this bundt pan produces elegant cakes.

Twister ist eine spiralförmige Bundform, mit der sich dynamisch wirkende Kuchen backen lassen. An der Außenseite zieht sich die Spirale von unten beginnend über die gesamte Höhe nach oben und führt innen fortlaufend abwärts. Dadurch lässt sich der Kuchen nicht nur auf der Oberseite, sondern auch auf seiner Innen- und Außenseite dekorieren. Er vermag aber auch ohne Dekoration zu gefallen und zeigt als geschnittenes Kuchenstück eine interessante Kontur.

Begründung der Jury
Die stringente Umsetzung einer kreativen Idee ist bei Twister besonders gelungen. Die skulpturale Anmutung dieser Bundform bringt formschöne Kuchen hervor.

UBRD Bevel
Cutting Board
Schneidbrett

Manufacturer
Check Roots s.r.o.,
Rožmitál pod Tremšínem, Czech Republic
Design
Novague, Prague, Czech Republic
Web
www.ubrd.cz
www.novague.com

This cutting board, made of solid walnut, features a striking contour which emphasises the elegant appeal of the wood grain. Precisely skewed edges allow the user to drain liquids and specifically slip off finely chopped food. An inversely shaped bevel on the reverse enables users to easily lift the cutting board off the worktop.

Statement by the jury
This visually appealing cutting board combines quality workmanship with wooden surfaces which provide for pleasing haptics.

Dieses Schneidbrett aus massivem Nussbaum zeigt eine auffallende Kontur, welche die edel anmutende Holzmaserung betont. Präzise abgeschrägte Kanten erlauben sowohl das Abfließen von Flüssigkeiten als auch das gezielte Abgleiten der kleingeschnittenen Lebensmittel. Da sich die Abschrägung spiegelverkehrt auf der Rückseite des Schneidbretts wiederfindet, lässt sich das Brett an dieser Stelle komfortabel von der Arbeitsplatte abheben.

Begründung der Jury
Bei diesem visuell ansprechenden Schneidbrett vereint sich eine präzise Verarbeitung mit einer haptisch angenehmen Holzoberfläche.

AnySharp™ X-Blade
Knife Sharpener
Messerschärfer

Manufacturer
Aydya Limited, Dundee, United Kingdom
In-house design
Yusuf Okhai
Web
www.aydya.co.uk

The AnySharp X-Blade is a manual knife sharpener for private households. With a suction cup especially developed by the manufacturer, it attaches securely to any flat surface, guaranteeing safe handling. Its bespoke self-adjusting sharpening tool angle allows to sharpen steel knives varying from 12.5 to 22.5 degrees blade angle. Enclosed by red protective plates, the tungsten carbide blades are so sharp that even an inexperienced user, left- or right-handed, can achieve good results.

Statement by the jury
The functional elements of the AnySharp X-Blade in combination with clear contours and high contrast colours yield a characteristic overall appearance.

Der AnySharp X-Blade ist ein Messerschärfer für den manuellen Gebrauch in Privathaushalten. Für die nötige Sicherheit sorgt ein vom Hersteller entwickelter Saugnapf, der eine zuverlässige Standfestigkeit bietet. Dank seiner speziellen, sich automatisch einstellenden Schärfwinkel können unterschiedliche Stahlmesser mit einem Klingenwinkel von 12,5 bis 22,5 Grad geschärft werden. Rote Schutzplatten umgeben die Klingen aus Wolframcarbid, die so scharf sind, dass selbst ungeübte Nutzer, egal ob Links- oder Rechtshänder, gute Ergebnisse erzielen.

Begründung der Jury
Die funktionalen Elemente des AnySharp X-Blade schaffen in Kombination mit klaren Konturen und kontrastreichen Farben ein charakteristisches Gesamtbild.

Thomas Keller Signature Collection
Kitchen Knifes
Küchenmesser

Manufacturer
Cangshan Cutlery Company,
Chino, California, USA
In-house design
Design
Thomas Keller, Yountville,
California, USA
Web
www.cangshancutlery.com/en

These kitchen knives were developed in cooperation with the renowned American chef Thomas Keller. They are forged from Swedish RWL34 Powdered Steel; a high alloy steel known for its excellent edge strength, hardness and corrosion resistance. After a precise heat treatment, these knives achieve a Rockwell Hardness Rating of 62 +/- 2. The structure of the steel gives the knives remarkable edge retention. Bold angles create a focus on the minimalist silhouette.

Statement by the jury
With a design which has been thought out down to the smallest detail, these kitchen knives display a well-balanced, consistent aesthetic.

Diese Küchenmesser wurden gemeinsam mit dem amerikanischen Sternekoch Thomas Keller entwickelt. Gefertigt sind sie aus dem schwedischen Pulverstahl RWL34 – einem hochlegierten Stahl, der für seine Kantenfestigkeit, Härte und Korrosionsbeständigkeit bekannt ist. Nach einem präzisen thermischen Verfahren erreichen die Messer eine Rockwell-Härte von 62 +/– 2. Die Struktur des Stahls verleiht den Messern eine hohe Kantenstabilität. Kühne Winkel legen den Fokus auf eine minimalistisch anmutende Silhouette.

Begründung der Jury
Mit ihrer bis ins Detail durchdachten Gestaltung zeigen diese Küchenmesser eine ausgewogene, stimmige Ästhetik.

Fresh
Kitchen Knives Series
Küchenmesser-Serie

Manufacturer
Groupe SEB, Rumilly, France
In-house design
Philippe de la Coussaye
Design
Bradshaw Home, Pennsylvania, USA
Web
www.groupeseb.com
www.bradshawhome.com

The strong stainless steel blades of this kitchen knife series are coated with a titanium-reinforced non-stick coating, which ensures durability and easy cleaning. The coating also delivers long-term protection from corrosion and abrasion. The ergonomically shaped handles facilitate precise cutting. The knives come with translucent blade covers in different colours for safe storage.

Statement by the jury
This kitchen knife series stands out with a high degree of durability and functionality. Trendy colours lend it a contemporary appearance.

Bei dieser Küchenmesser-Serie sind die robusten Edelstahlklingen mit einer titanverstärkten Antihaftbeschichtung versehen, die Langlebigkeit und eine einfache Reinigung gewährleistet. Die Beschichtung schützt die Messer auch langfristig vor Korrosion und Abrieb. Die nach ergonomischen Gesichtspunkten geformten Griffe ermöglichen ein kontrolliertes Schneiden. Zur sicheren Aufbewahrung werden alle Messer mit einer lichtdurchlässigen Klingenabdeckung in unterschiedlichen Farben geliefert.

Begründung der Jury
Ein hohes Maß an Haltbarkeit und Funktionalität zeichnet diese Küchenmesser-Serie aus. Trendige Farben verleihen ihr eine zeitgemäße Anmutung.

Amenite
Table Cutlery
Tischbesteck

Manufacturer
Messermacher Kappeller GmbH,
Salzburg, Austria

In-house design
Richard Kappeller,
Andreas Mathieson

Web
www.messermacher.at

reddot award 2019
best of the best

Distinctively pleasant to the touch
Damascus steel has been appreciated throughout history not only for its special properties, but above all, for its decorative patterns. Produced in a composite steel process, the blades stand out due to high quality and individuality. The Amenite table cutlery has been designed using this traditional craftsmanship approach in combination with modern technology. The product series is manufactured in the Richard Kappeller workshop, located in the old town of Salzburg, and is targeted at both upscale restaurants and for use at home. The aim was to appeal to a wider circle of customers and promote Salzburg-based craftsmanship as the source of a unique experience. This table cutlery exudes a modern, yet elegant and light appearance. It rests well in the hand and is highly pleasing to the touch. The concept behind its sophisticated functionality consists of being able to accompany guests through the entire menu. It is made of high-quality stainless Damascus steel, which is forged, milled, thermally hardened and finished by hand, which makes it highly durable. In addition, the combination of modern CNC technology and skilled handwork in the production of the cutlery also allows customers to specify individual wishes and decorative needs, with a portfolio that embraces the use of different materials or customised engravings such as in the form of a restaurant logo.

Exklusiver Handschmeichler
Damaststahl wird seiner speziellen Eigenschaften und vor allem seiner dekorativen Musterung wegen seit jeher besonders geschätzt. Die in einem Verbundstahl-Verfahren hergestellten Klingen zeichnen sich durch ihre hohe Qualität und Individualität aus. Bei der Gestaltung des Tischbestecks Amenite kommt dieses traditionelle Handwerk in Kombination mit moderner Technologie zum Einsatz. Die Produktserie entsteht in der Werkstatt von Richard Kappeller in der Salzburger Altstadt und wurde entworfen für die gehobene Gastronomie und den edlen Tisch zu Hause. Ziel war es, den Kundenkreis auf ein neues Gebiet auszuweiten und die Geschichte der Salzburger Handwerkskunst in exklusiven Restaurants zu einem Erlebnis zu machen. Dieses Tischbesteck hat eine moderne Anmutung, es ist elegant und leicht. Gut austariert, liegt es auch haptisch angenehm in der Hand. Das Konzept seiner ausgereiften Funktionalität besteht darin, den Gast durch die gesamte Speisekarte begleiten zu können. Gefertigt ist es aus hochwertigem Damaststahl, der geschmiedet, gefräst, thermisch gehärtet und von Hand geschliffen wird. Dieses Besteck ist deshalb sehr langlebig. Seine Herstellung mithilfe moderner CNC-Technologie, kombiniert mit geübtem Handwerk, ermöglicht es zudem, individuelle Wünsche und Details in die Gestaltung mit einzubringen. Das Portfolio umfasst dabei die Verwendung unterschiedlicher Materialien oder etwa auch eine Gravur in Form eines Restaurant-Logos.

Statement by the jury
The Amenite table cutlery managed in a fascinating manner to transform Damascus steel into an outstanding elegant design. Otherwise known rather from the area of knife production, the material opens up a new field of application targeted at the upscale gastronomy. Light and perfectly balanced, this table cutlery rests well in the hands of users. Also outstanding are its quality craftsmanship and the distinctive finish with its sensually appealing feel.

Begründung der Jury
Mit dem Tischbesteck Amenite wurde auf faszinierende Weise Damaststahl in eine überaus elegante Formgebung überführt. Das Material, sonst eher aus dem Bereich der Messerherstellung bekannt, erschließt sich so einen neuen Einsatzbereich in der gehobenen Gastronomie. Leicht und perfekt ausbalanciert, liegt dieses Tischbesteck in der Hand des Nutzers. Herausragend sind seine handwerkliche Qualität sowie das besondere Finish mit einer sinnlich ansprechenden Haptik.

Designer portrait
See page 40
Siehe Seite 40

TABLE NOIR
Cutlery
Besteck

Manufacturer
Table Noir A/S, Copenhagen, Denmark
In-house design
Benjamin Folkmann Hansen
Design
Snøhetta Design AS (Marius Myking, Martin Nichols), Oslo, Norway
Web
www.tablenoir.com
www.snohetta.com

The Table Noir cutlery was designed with the aim to complement the dining with a unique tactile experience. Its rough surface is caused by a stone-washed finish, lending it contrast and a natural appeal. All edges are rounded while a distinct groove ensures a comfortable and sturdy grip. The contours are harmoniously coordinated so that the cutlery sits perfectly balanced in the hand. Carefully aligned shapes create harmony between the individual pieces of cutlery. The lettering on the handle's upper surface underlines the distinctive appearance.

Das Besteck Table Noir wurde mit dem Ziel entworfen, ein Essen auch haptisch zu etwas Besonderem zu machen. Seine raue Oberfläche entsteht durch ein Stonewash-Finish, welches dem Besteck Kontraste und eine natürliche Anmutung verleiht. Alle Kanten sind abgerundet, wobei eine ausgeprägte Nut für einen komfortablen und stabilen Griff sorgt. Dank ausgewogener Konturen liegt das Besteck ausbalanciert in der Hand. Sogfältig abgestimmte Formen schaffen Harmonie zwischen den Teilen. Die Beschriftung auf der Oberseite des Griffs unterstreicht das unverwechselbare Erscheinungsbild.

Statement by the jury
A novel surface design lends this cutlery extraordinary haptic properties, perfectly matching its characteristic lines.

Begründung der Jury
Eine neuartige Oberflächengestaltung erzeugt bei diesem Besteck eine ungewohnte Haptik, die zur charakteristischen Linienführung passt.

Shiny & Happy
Tableware Collections
Geschirr-Kollektionen

Manufacturer
colarty GmbH & Co. KG, Essen, Germany
In-house design
Nadin Ostendorf, Nicole Nusser
Web
www.colarty.com

The two tableware collections Shiny and Happy comprise cups, glasses, bowls, plates, trays, carafes and bottle coolers, all of which are made of unbreakable and fully recyclable aluminium. According to the motto "Color your heart!", the unique shimmering tableware is available in numerous trend colours. A clear design language reduced to the essentials characterises the overall image of these collections.

Statement by the jury
With a pronounced love for colours and shapes, the design of these tableware collections exudes a refreshingly unconventional overall image.

Die beiden Geschirr-Kollektionen Shiny und Happy umfassen Becher, Gläser, Schalen, Teller, Tabletts, Karaffen und Flaschenkühler, die allesamt aus unzerbrechlichem und vollständig recyclebarem Aluminium gefertigt sind. Gemäß dem Motto „Color your heart!" ist das schimmernde Geschirr in zahlreichen Trendfarben erhältlich. Eine klare, auf das Wesentliche reduzierte Formensprache prägt das Gesamtbild dieser Kollektionen.

Begründung der Jury
Mit einer ausgeprägten Liebe zu Farben und Formen erreicht die Gestaltung dieser Geschirr-Kollektionen ein erfrischend unkonventionelles Gesamtbild.

HIDE
Tableware
Geschirr

Manufacturer
RAK Porcelain Europe, Windhof, Luxembourg
Design
Gemma Bernal, Rubí (Barcelona), Spain
Web
www.rakporcelain.eu
www.gemmabernal.com

HIDE is a set of tableware which combines dinner plates of versatile designs with matching porcelain lids. In this way, food can be decoratively concealed while serving to increase the joyful anticipation of a delicious dish. The food unfolds its full flavour at the table, not until the guests lift the covers. In addition, the tableware keeps dishes hot and juicy for a long time. Each of the differently shaped lids features an easy-to-grab tip.

Statement by the jury
This tableware distinguishes itself through a remarkably outstanding design and convinces with both functionality and versatility.

HIDE ist ein Geschirr, das vielfältig gestaltete Essteller mit passenden Porzellandeckeln kombiniert. Somit lassen sich Speisen beim Servieren dekorativ verbergen, um die Vorfreude auf das Essen zu steigern. Die Aromen der Speisen entfalten sich erst vollends am Tisch, sobald die Gäste die Deckel lüften. Zudem bleiben die Gerichte dank dieses Geschirrs länger heiß und saftig. Die unterschiedlich geformten Deckel sind jeweils mit einer griffigen Spitze versehen.

Begründung der Jury
Eine bemerkenswert unverwechselbare Gestaltung zeichnet dieses Geschirr aus, das aufgrund seiner Variabilität und Funktionalität überzeugt.

Lufthansa First Class Dining Experience
Tableware
Geschirr

Manufacturer
Dibbern GmbH, Bargteheide, Germany
uccellino, Hamburg, Germany
Design
Deutsche Lufthansa AG, Frankfurt/Main, Germany
Web
www.dibbern.de
www.uccellino-shop.de
www.lufthansa.com

This timeless tableware features a combination of fine bone china and rustic ash wood. The serving plate with three integrated bowls and the matching Jausenplatte are part of the airline's Dine on Demand concept. Passengers can choose and combine their individual appetizer selection. Since hygienic regulations do not allow wooden plates in airline catering, a flat porcelain plate was developed and combined with a wooden tray in order to create the authentic look of a German Jausenplatte (traditional or hearty snacks on a plate).

Statement by the jury
This tableware owes its self-reliant, elegant aesthetics to the consistent implementation of a modular product concept.

Por-Dee
Dinnerware
Essgeschirr

Manufacturer
Tanya Ceramic, Bangkok, Thailand
Design
Pimsiri Nilkositya, Bangkok, Thailand
Web
www.tanyaceramic.com
www.pimsirinil.com
Honourable Mention

This dinnerware has been developed for people with type 2 diabetes. The graphic design aims to support a balanced diet which keeps the blood sugar at a normal level. The decor of the dining plate shows a reasonable portioning of rice, meat and vegetables at a ratio of 1:1:2. In order to reduce the consumption of carbohydrates, the design concept uses the Delboeuf illusion, according to which a circle appears optically larger if it is surrounded by another circle.

Statement by the jury
Por-Dee is a successful implementation of an astounding graphic concept which, in a creative and appealing way, motivates people to keep a healthy diet.

Dieses Geschirr wurde für Menschen mit Typ-2-Diabetes entwickelt. Die grafische Gestaltung soll eine ausgewogene Ernährung unterstützen, die den Blutzuckerspiegel auf einem normalen Niveau hält. Dazu zeigt das Dekor des Esstellers eine angemessene Portionierung von Reis, Fleisch und Gemüse im Verhältnis 1:1:2 an. Um den Verzehr von Kohlehydraten zu reduzieren, nutzt das Gestaltungskonzept die Delboeuf-Täuschung, wonach ein Kreis optisch größer erscheint, wenn er von einem weiteren Kreis umgeben ist.

Begründung der Jury
Bei Por-Dee gelingt die Umsetzung eines verblüffenden Grafikkonzepts, das auf kreative und ansprechende Weise zu einer gesunden Ernährung motiviert.

it's my match
Tableware Collection
Geschirr-Kollektion

Manufacturer
Villeroy & Boch AG, Mettlach, Germany
In-house design
Helena Boddenberg
Web
www.villeroy-boch.com

The "it's my match" tableware collection supports the personal style of a young target group, with four multi-functional products which can be used at any meal, whether breakfast, lunch or dinner. Different relief structures and coloured glazes, which are based on current interior and fashion trends, offer a variety of possibilities for individual table designs. Thanks to structures inspired by nature and a trend-oriented mix of surfaces, each tableware piece is unique.

Statement by the jury
With a keen sense of trendy colours, materials and structures, "it's my match" achieves a harmonious overall appearance and comes to life through its versatility.

Die Geschirr-Kollektion „it's my match" unterstützt den persönlichen Stil einer jungen Zielgruppe, indem sie mit vier multifunktional nutzbaren Produkten für jede Mahlzeit morgens, mittags und abends eingesetzt werden kann. Unterschiedliche Reliefstrukturen und Glasurfarben, die auf aktuellen Interior- und Modetrends basieren, bieten vielfältige Möglichkeiten zur individuellen Tischgestaltung. Dank trendorientierter Oberflächen und von der Natur inspirierte Strukturen ist jedes Geschirrteil besonders.

Begründung der Jury
Mit Gespür für aktuell gefragte Farben, Materialien und Strukturen erreicht „it's my match" ein stimmiges Gesamtbild, das von seiner Variabilität lebt.

Gastroline
Hospitality Tableware
Gastronomie-Geschirr

Manufacturer
Minh Long I Co., Ltd.,
Binh Duong Province, Vietnam
Design
Design Studio Hans-Wilhelm Seitz
(Hans-Wilhelm Seitz),
Marktredwitz, Germany
Web
www.minhlong.com
www.design-seitz.de

Gastroline was developed to meet the needs of different businesses. The multi-piece hospitality tableware offers a wide range of plates, bowls, cups and jugs, which can be individually selected and combined. The classic tableware comes in pure white and exudes a timeless, elegant look, yet it is highly robust. Most pieces can be stacked to save space, with discreet spacers, placed at the bottom to protect the surfaces from scratches.

Statement by the jury
With its clear, self-contained design, Gastroline exudes a characteristic overall image which meets high standards.

Gastroline wurde entwickelt, um den Bedürfnissen unterschiedlicher Betriebe gerecht zu werden. Das mehrteilige Gastronomie-Geschirr bietet eine große Auswahl an Tellern, Schüsseln, Tassen und Kannen, die bedarfsgerecht zusammengestellt werden können. Das klassische Geschirr in Reinweiß wirkt zeitlos elegant und ist dennoch robust. Die meisten Einzelteile lassen sich platzsparend stapeln, wobei dezent an der Unterseite platzierte Abstandhalter die Oberflächen vor Kratzern schützen.

Begründung der Jury
Mit seiner klaren, eigenständigen Gestaltung zeigt Gastroline ein charakteristisches Gesamtbild, das gehobene Ansprüche erfüllt.

LARQ Bottle
Water Bottle
Wasserflasche

Manufacturer
LARQ,
California, USA

In-house design
LARQ

Web
www.livelarq.com

reddot award 2019
best of the best

Design and responsibility
Good quality drinking water is vital for people worldwide; however, in many parts of the world, it is not always readily available. Against this backdrop, LARQ represents an impressively innovative development, as this system is capable of automatically cleaning water anywhere. By means of proprietary LED technology, the bottle makes it possible to easily access clean water while on the move. The cleaning process is based on the emission of ultraviolet light in the UV-C range, which instantly destroys bacteria and viruses inside the water. In addition, this technology also prevents musty odours without the need for chemical treatment or otherwise onerous filtration processes. The design of the reusable LARQ Bottle is an answer not only to the problem of wasteful, single-use water bottles, but also to the fact that many people around the world lack access to clean water that is free of disease-causing waterborne microbes. Thus, this water bottle combines sophisticated functionality with clear lines and a stylish design vocabulary. Made of high-quality materials, its outer shell is made up of two sturdy layers that make it robust and highly durable. LARQ also impresses with an attractive colour scheme with a fresh appearance achieved through a two-tone powder-coated finish.

Design und Verantwortung
Trinkwasser in einer guten Qualität ist für jeden Menschen lebensnotwendig, jedoch in vielen Teilen der Welt nicht leicht verfügbar. LARQ stellt hier eine beeindruckend innovative Entwicklung dar, da dieses System in der Lage ist, Wasser vor Ort selbsttätig zu reinigen. Mittels einer eigens entwickelten LED-Technologie ist es möglich, auch unterwegs unkompliziert auf sauberes Wasser zugreifen zu können. Der Reinigungsvorgang beruht darauf, dass ultraviolette Strahlung im UV-C-Bereich abgegeben wird, welche mögliche Bakterien und Viren im Wasser zerstört. Diese Technologie verhindert zudem das Entstehen muffiger Gerüche, ohne dass chemische Mittel eingesetzt werden müssten oder lästige Filtrationsvorgänge vonnöten wären. Die Gestaltung von LARQ versteht sich als Antwort auf die Problematik der Einweg-Wasserflaschen. Sie begegnet aber auch der Tatsache, dass viele Menschen keinen Zugang zu nicht von krankheitserregenden Mikroben befallenem Wasser haben. Bei dieser Wasserflasche verbindet sich so eine hochentwickelte Funktionalität mit einer stilvollen Formensprache und klaren Linienführung. Gefertigt aus hochwertigen Materialien, besteht ihre äußere Hülle aus zwei stabilen Schichten. Sie ist deshalb robust und sehr langlebig. LARQ beeindruckt auch durch eine attraktive Farbgebung, deren frische Anmutung durch ein zweifarbiges, pulverbeschichtetes Finish erzeugt wird.

Statement by the jury
Based on an innovative LED technology, the LARQ water bottle offers the fascinating possibility to easily produce neutral tasting, sterilised drinking water. Thus increasing the quality of life, it represents a trendsetting way to maintain the health of people. Elegant in shape and highly durable, it has adopted a simple construction and does without moving parts or filters that would otherwise need to be changed.

Begründung der Jury
Auf der Basis einer innovativen LED-Technologie bietet die Wasserflasche LARQ eine faszinierende Möglichkeit, unkompliziert an geschmacklich einwandfreies, sterilisiertes Trinkwasser zu gelangen. Sie erhöht damit die Lebensqualität und stellt einen zukunftsweisenden Weg dar, die Gesundheit der Menschen zu erhalten. Elegant in ihrer Form und sehr langlebig, ist sie einfach in ihrem Aufbau und verzichtet auf bewegliche Teile oder Filter, die gewechselt werden müssten.

Designer portrait
See page 42
Siehe Seite 42

Vacuum Bottles
Isolierflaschen

Manufacturer
Hefei Yiso Product Design Co., Ltd.,
Hefei, China
In-house design
Gang Hu, Likun Dai, Zhefeng Hu,
Chuanzhu Zhang, Wei Jiang,
Yidan Zhuge, Jie Chen, Yanxue Zhang,
Zhihui Guo, Miaojun Guo
Web
www.yisodesign.com

These vacuum bottles project a minimalist design language to meet the taste of outdoor and sports enthusiasts. The bottles' flowing contour, which provides for better grip, is achieved by using spray moulding technology. Made of corrosion-resistant stainless steel, the product is available in two sizes, each model with a coated or uncoated finish. The double-walled stainless steel lid can serve as a drinking cup.

Statement by the jury
The purist character of these vacuum bottles is marked by a self-reliant design, a concept which is consistently rounded off by appealing details.

Diese Isolierflaschen folgen einer minimalistischen Formensprache, um dem Geschmack von Outdoor- und Sportinteressierten zu entsprechen. Die geschwungene Kontur der Flaschen, die der besseren Griffigkeit dient, wird durch eine Sprühformtechnologie ermöglicht. Das Produkt aus korrosionsbeständigem Edelstahl ist sowohl in einer unbeschichteten als auch in einer beschichteten Variante sowie in zwei Größen erhältlich. Der doppelwandige Deckel aus Edelstahl kann als Trinkbecher verwendet werden.

Begründung der Jury
Eine eigenständige Gestaltung prägt den puristischen Charakter dieser Isolierflaschen, zudem runden ansprechende Details das Konzept stimmig ab.

MOTION
Vacuum Flask Series
Isolierflaschen-Serie

Manufacturer
WMF Group GmbH, Geislingen/Steige,
Germany
In-house design
Ernst Köhler
Web
www.wmf-group.com

This vacuum flask series merges minimalism with functionality. The flasks feature a smooth, polished metal surface, which, in some models, is coated with durable resin. The double-walled stainless steel cup and the seamless body aim to prevent dirt from adhering. A recess for the thumb, the push-to-open stopper and a spout which allows pouring in any direction ensure comfortable handling.

Statement by the jury
Using sturdy materials, this vacuum flask series showcases an appealing design and a high level of user-friendliness.

Diese Isolierflaschen-Serie verbindet Minimalismus mit Funktionalität: Die Flaschen zeigen eine glattpolierte Metalloberfläche, die in einigen Versionen mit einer langlebigen Harzbeschichtung versehen ist. Der doppelwandige Edelstahlbecher und der nahtlos gefertigte Korpus zielen darauf ab, dass sich nirgendwo Schmutz festsetzen kann. Die griffige Vertiefung für den Daumen, der Push-to-Open-Stopfen und ein Ausguss, der das Ausgießen in jede Richtung ermöglicht, gestalten die Handhabung komfortabel.

Begründung der Jury
Unter Verwendung von robusten Materialien zeigt diese Isolierflaschen-Serie eine ansprechende Gestaltung und einen hohen Bedienkomfort.

Max
Vacuum Mug
Isolierbecher

Manufacturer
Guangzhou Kemei Commodity Co., Ltd.,
Guangzhou, China
In-house design
Pei Wen Huang
Web
www.3cmsh.com
Honourable Mention

Max is an insulated stainless steel cup which maintains the beverage temperature for approximately two hours. The lid can easily be opened and closed using a specially developed mechanism: an iron spring, wrapped in soft rubber, connects the lid and handle. The spring, marked with a striking colour, responds to a light touch and causes the lid to spring open at a wide angle. The insulated cup is also equipped with an integrated tea strainer.

Statement by the jury
With its innovative mechanism, this vacuum mug can be opened and closed in a particularly comfortable way.

Max ist ein Isolierbecher aus Edelstahl, der die jeweilige Getränke-Temperatur für circa zwei Stunden beibehält. Mithilfe einer eigens entwickelten Mechanik lässt sich der Deckel leichtgängig öffnen und schließen: Dazu verbindet eine mit Weichgummi umwickelte Eisenfeder Deckel und Griff. Die farblich prägnant gekennzeichnete Feder reagiert bereits auf eine leichte Berührung und lässt den Deckel in einem weiten Winkel aufspringen. Der Isolierbecher ist zudem mit einem integrierten Teesieb ausgestattet.

Begründung der Jury
Mit seiner innovativen Mechanik lässt sich dieser Isolierbecher auf besonders komfortable Weise öffnen und schließen.

Dolphin
Vacuum Bottle Series
Isolierkannen-Serie

Manufacturer
Jieyang Xingcai Industrial Co., Ltd.,
Jieyang, China
Design
AKS Design Studio (Lewis Wong, Alex Lin, Zizhe Lin), Hong Kong
Web
www.xingcai.com
www.aks.hk
Honourable Mention

Dolphin is a series of stainless steel vacuum bottles, comprising three different versions. Dolphin for Tea is equipped with a satin tea strainer. "Dolphin for Easy Drink" offers a drinking stopper which can easily be opened and closed with one hand, as well as unscrewed for thorough cleaning. Finally, there is the "Dolphin for Fun" model, which has a ball-shaped handle especially developed for the needs of mother and child. In contrast, the other bottles are equipped with carrying loops.

Statement by the jury
These vacuum bottles showcase a sound quality, while the distinctive colour scheme lends the series an independent character.

Dolphin ist eine Serie von Isolierkannen aus Edelstahl, die drei Produktausführungen umfasst: „Dolphin for tea" ist mit einem Satin-Teesieb ausgestattet, während „Dolphin for easy drinking" einen Trinkstopper bietet, der sich leicht mit einer Hand öffnen und schließen lässt. Zur gründlichen Reinigung lässt er sich einfach abschrauben. Die Variante „Dolphin for fun" wurde mit seinem kugelförmigen Griff speziell für die Bedürfnisse von Mutter und Kind entwickelt. Hingegen haben die anderen Kannen Griffschlaufen.

Begründung der Jury
Diese Isolierkannen zeigen eine gute Qualität, zudem verleiht die auffallende Farbgebung der Serie einen eigenständigen Charakter.

ACERA
Vacuum Bottle
Isolierflasche

Manufacturer
ACERA, Brand LIVEN, Taoyuan, Taiwan
In-house design
Kang Zhen Hui
Web
www.aceraliven.com
Honourable Mention

This vacuum bottle showcases a stainless steel exterior and a ceramic interior. The shock-absorbing structure makes it possible to use mineral compounds inside the bottle. The joints between the two materials for the interior and exterior have been precisely aligned using a special technique. ACERA is available in four different colours and suitable for both hot and cold drinks.

Statement by the jury
Thanks to the integration of a ceramic interieur, this vacuum bottle offers a high ease of use.

Diese Isolierflasche hat eine Innenwand aus Keramik und eine Außenhülle aus Edelstahl. Eine Verwendung von Mineralwerkstoffen im Innern wird durch die stoßdämpfende Struktur der Flasche ermöglicht. Die Fugen zwischen den beiden Materialien des Innen- und Außenbereichs sind durch eine spezielle Technik exakt ausgerichtet. ACERA ist in vier unterschiedlichen Farben erhältlich und sowohl für heiße als auch für kalte Getränke geeignet.

Begründung der Jury
Aufgrund der Integration einer Keramikinnenfläche bietet diese Isolierflasche ein hohes Maß an Gebrauchskomfort.

Halo
Vacuum Bottle
Isolierflasche

Manufacturer
Shenzhen 55° Innovation Technology Co., Ltd.,
Shenzhen, China
In-house design
Taorong Liu
Web
www.55du.cc

Halo is a vacuum bottle which can be controlled via an app. A circle of light, integrated into the rim of the lid, flashes at given times, in order to, for example, remind the user to drink water regularly. An intelligent probe measures the water temperature and indicates it in the lid using colour signals. Thanks to its three-layered structure, Halo can cool down 100 degree hot drinks to 55 degrees centigrade in one minute and maintain that temperature for more than three hours.

Statement by the jury
Using contemporary technology, this elegant vacuum bottle convinces as an alternative product which is highly customisable.

Halo ist eine Isolierflasche, die sich per App kontrollieren lässt. Am Deckelrand ist ein Lichtkreis integriert, der zu vorgegebenen Zeiten aufblinkt, um z. B. ans regelmäßige Trinken zu erinnern. Eine intelligente Temperatursonde erfasst die Wassertemperatur in der Flasche und lässt diese durch Farbsignale im Deckel anzeigen. Aufgrund eines dreilagigen Aufbaus kann Halo 100 Grad heiße Getränke innerhalb von einer Minute auf 55 Grad herunterkühlen und diese Temperatur länger als drei Stunden beibehalten.

Begründung der Jury
Unter Einsatz einer zeitgemäßen Technologie überzeugt diese elegante Isolierflasche als eine individuell anpassbare Produktalternative.

Mose
Vacuum Tumbler
Isolierbecher

Manufacturer
Shenzhen 55° Innovation Technology Co., Ltd.,
Shenzhen, China
In-house design
Tom Tam
Web
www.55du.cc

Mose is a vacuum tumbler which cools hot drinks down to approximately 55 degrees centigrade. In order to cool down boiling water, users simply have to shake the tumbler for one minute. An LED system with three different colours is integrated in the lid and indicates whether the drink is too hot, too cold or has reached the optimum drinking temperature. The thermal sensor is activated as soon as the illuminated control symbol is touched. The tumbler is made of three stainless steel layers, the inner layer filled with cooling material.

Statement by the jury
With its clear aesthetics and contemporary ease of use, this vacuum tumbler is convincing in terms of both form and function.

Mose ist ein Isolierbecher, mit dem sich heiße Getränke auf ca. 55 Grad herunterkühlen lassen. Die Benutzer müssen dazu den Becher eine Minute lang schütteln. Ein im Deckel integriertes LED-Licht zeigt durch drei Farben an, ob das Getränk zu heiß oder zu kalt ist und wann es die optimale Trinktemperatur erreicht hat. Der Temperatursensor ist aktiviert, sobald das illuminierte Bediensymbol berührt wird. Der Becher aus drei Edelstahlschichten birgt eine Innenschicht, die mit Kühlmaterial gefüllt ist.

Begründung der Jury
Mit seiner klaren Ästhetik und seinem zeitgemäßen Bedienkomfort überzeugt dieser Isolierbecher sowohl formal als auch funktional.

muki
Vacuum Snack Pot
Vakuum-Snackpot

Manufacturer
FLSK Products GmbH, Munich, Germany
In-house design
Web
www.flsk.de

muki is a stylish snack pot which allows users to take their food wherever they go. It features a compact design, fits easily into any bag and does not leak. Thanks to its good insulation properties, it keeps snacks hot or cold for several hours. The snack pot is divided into two compartments by an intermediate lid and thus allows the separate transport of foods which are supposed to be combined only when consumed, such as milk with cereals, vegetable sticks with dips or coffee with biscuits.

muki ist ein stilvoller Snackpot, der das Mitnehmen von Speisen ermöglicht. Er ist kompakt gestaltet, lässt sich leicht verstauen und läuft nicht aus. Dank seiner guten Isolierung halten heiße und kalte Speisen über mehrere Stunden ihre Temperatur. Das durch einen Zwischendeckel zweigeteilte Gefäß ermöglicht den getrennten Transport von Lebensmitteln, die man erst beim Verzehren kombinieren möchte, wie beispielsweise Milch mit Müsli, Gemüsesticks mit Dips oder Kaffee mit Keksen.

Statement by the jury
Presenting a trend-oriented colour concept and an appealingly tactile surface, this snack pot constitutes a fascinating contemporary product.

Begründung der Jury
Mit einem trendorientierten Farbkonzept und einer haptisch reizvoll gestalteten Oberfläche begeistert dieser Snackpot als zeitgemäßes Produkt.

BISTRO
Vacuum Bottle
Isolierkanne

Manufacturer
Bodum AG, Triengen, Switzerland
Design
Pi-Design AG, Triengen, Switzerland
Web
www.bodum.com

This 1.5 litre vacuum bottle keeps hot and cold drinks at a constant temperature. The lid and a distinctive black plastic banderole create a contrast to the glossy stainless steel surface of the bottle. A simple push on the lid opens the bottle for pouring out the drinks. Immediately after that, the lid closes automatically to prevent heat exchange and ensure that the drink keeps its temperature.

Statement by the jury
The design language of this vacuum bottle convinces with elegant, brand-typical lines and an appealing material mix.

Diese 1,5 Liter fassende Isolierkanne hält die Temperatur von heißen und kalten Getränken konstant. Der Deckel und eine markante Banderole aus schwarzem Kunststoff stehen im Kontrast zur glänzenden Edelstahloberfläche der Kanne. Ein einfacher Druck auf den Deckel öffnet die Kanne und ermöglicht das Ausschenken der Getränke. Danach schließt sich der Deckel sofort automatisch, sodass der Wärmeaustausch unterbunden ist und das jeweilige Getränk heiß oder kalt bleibt.

Begründung der Jury
Die Formensprache dieser Isolierkanne überzeugt mit einer eleganten, markentypischen Linienführung. Auch der Materialmix gefällt.

Minimal
Travel Coffee Set
Reise-Kaffeeset

Manufacturer
Eilong Enterprise Co., Ltd.,
New Taipei City, Taiwan
In-house design
Chi-Ya Chien
Web
www.eilong.com

This travel coffee set comprises a heat-resistant glass mug, a coffee filter and a wooden lid which can also be used as a coaster. Each of the three items can be carried in a protective bag, with the filter being stored inside the mug. For preparing a cup of coffee, the funnel-shaped filter attaches simply and firmly to the wooden lid. The mug with a capacity of 280 ml is enclosed by a leather banderole, protecting against burns.

Statement by the jury
Natural materials promote a way of preparing coffee which is perceived as highly original. The astonishing functionality of this set is highly convincing.

Dieses Reise-Kaffeeset umfasst einen Becher aus hitzebeständigem Glas, einen Kaffeefilter sowie einen Holzdeckel, der zudem als Untersetzer genutzt werden kann. Alle drei Einzelteile lassen sich in einer schützenden Tasche verstauen, wobei der Filter im Becher Platz findet. Zur Kaffeezubereitung wird der trichterförmige Filter einfach standfest in den Holzdeckel gesteckt. Der Becher mit einem Fassungsvermögen von 280 ml ist von einer Lederbanderole umfasst, die beim Hochheben vor Verbrennungen schützt.

Begründung der Jury
Natürliche Materialien betonen die als ursprünglich empfundene Zubereitungsart, zudem überzeugt die verblüffende Funktionalität des Sets.

Drift Beverage Collection
Bar and Teaware
Bar- und Teegeschirr

Manufacturer
Robert Welch Designs Ltd.,
Gloucestershire, United Kingdom
In-house design
Robert Welch Design Team
Web
www.robertwelch.com

The Drift Beverage Collection was inspired by nature, with graceful, flowing lines becoming the design principle of the entire collection. A single flowing stroke became the main feature and finding the right curve and proportion was the defining moment for every piece in the range. All the components are made of 18/10 stainless steel and features a mirror polish. The Grand champagne cooler, made from a single sheet of stainless steel, is the heart of the collection.

Statement by the jury
The Drift Beverage Collection is marked by its unique and distinctive lines. It furthermore convinces with precisely processed stainless steel.

Inspiriert von der Natur folgt die Drift Beverage Collection einer grazilen, fließenden Linienführung, welche sich durch die gesamten Kollektion zieht: Eine einzige fließende Linie wird zum Hauptmerkmal, während das Finden einer passenden Kontur und Proportion jedes einzelne Stück ausmacht. Sämtliche Bestandteile sind aus Edelstahl 18/10 gefertigt und mit einer Hochglanzpolitur veredelt. Der Champagnerkühler Grand, gefertigt aus einem einzigen Edelstahlblech, ist das Herzstück der Kollektion.

Begründung der Jury
Eine unverwechselbar charakteristische Linienführung zeichnet die Drift Beverage Collection aus, zudem überzeugt die präzise Verarbeitung des Edelstahls.

DOURO
Tea Press
Teekanne

Manufacturer
Bodum AG, Triengen, Switzerland
Design
Pi-Design AG, Triengen, Switzerland
Web
www.bodum.com

In order to control the preparation of tea precisely, the DOURO tea press features a brewing system similar to what is used with a French press. Once brewing is complete, a silicone plunger locks in the tea leaves at the bottom of the filter, stopping the tea from steeping. Both the 1.5-litre can and the lid are manufactured of matte black porcelain. The handle, made of bright, smooth-cut wood, rests comfortably in the hand. The silicone rim of the filter makes sure it stays in place and remains cool, allowing the filter to be removed safely.

Um die Teezubereitung präzise zu kontrollieren, bietet die Teekanne DOURO ein Brühsystem wie bei französischen Teepressen. Nach Beendigung des Brühvorgangs umschließt ein Kolben aus Silikon die Teeblätter am Boden des Filters und unterbricht ein fortdauerndes Ziehen des Tees. Sowohl die 1,5 Liter fassende Kanne als auch der Deckel sind aus mattschwarzem Porzellan gefertigt. Der Griff aus hellem, glatt geschliffenem Holz liegt angenehm in der Hand. Der Silikonrand des Filters stabilisiert dessen Position und bleibt kühl für ein sicheres Herausnehmen des Filters.

Statement by the jury
The balanced design language lends this tea press a strong visual presence. In addition, its high quality of use is convincing.

Begründung der Jury
Eine ausgewogene Formensprache verleiht dieser Teekanne eine starke visuelle Präsenz. Zudem überzeugt die hohe Gebrauchsqualität.

FORLIGHT AIR
Portable Tea Set
Tragbares Teeset

Manufacturer
Jingdezhen Tongzao Trade Co., Ltd.,
Jingdezhen, China
In-house design
Xiaonan Wang, Pengfei Chen
Web
fineth.jiyoujia.com

FORLIGHT AIR is a portable tea set which allows users to enjoy tea on the go or when travelling. The compact, easy-to-store bag contains a teapot, two small cups and a tea filter. The particularly flat pot offers a small packing size. The thin-walled ceramic is manufactured with traditional craftsmanship. Made of bamboo, the insulated area of the handle protects against burns and allows effortless handling.

Statement by the jury
This portable tea set owes its functional and aesthetic quality to the consistent implementation of a space-saving product solution.

FORLIGHT AIR ist ein tragbares Teeset, das unterwegs oder auf Reisen den Genuss von Tee ermöglicht. In einer kompakten, leicht zu verstauenden Tasche finden sowohl eine Teekanne als auch zwei kleine Tassen und ein Teefilter Platz. Die ungewohnt flache Teekanne erlaubt ein platzsparendes Packmaß, wobei die dünnwandige Keramik in traditioneller Handwerkskunst gefertigt wird. Eine isolierende Griffleiste aus Bambus schützt vor Verbrennungen und ermöglicht die komfortable Handhabung der Teekanne.

Begründung der Jury
Der stringenten Umsetzung einer platzsparenden Produktlösung verdankt dieses tragbare Teeset seine funktionale und ästhetische Qualität.

Mini Dome
Tea Set
Teeset

Manufacturer
Xiamen XiaoPaoDan Technology,
Xiamen, China
Design
Balance Design, Tokyo, Japan
Web
www.pertouch.cn
www.jinkuramoto.com

Mini Dome is a compact tea set for two people which aims to simplify the traditional preparation of tea. Dispensing with the need for further accessories, the decorative, oval box contains only a teapot with an integrated stainless steel tea filter and two cups. The lid of the plastic box also serves as a tray while its diagonal surface structure ensures slip resistance. The tea pot and the cups are made of ceramics, hand-glazed and enhanced by a black sandstone coating.

Statement by the jury
Featuring minimalist contours paired with a classic black-and-white contrast, this tea set exudes a timeless, elegant aesthetic.

Mini Dome ist ein kompaktes Teeset für zwei Personen, das die traditionelle Zubereitung von Tee vereinfachen möchte. Da auf weiteres Zubehör verzichtet wird, beinhaltet die dekorative, ovale Box nur eine Teekanne mit integriertem Teefilter aus Edelstahl sowie zwei Tassen. Der Deckel der Kunststoffbox dient zugleich als Tablett; seine diagonale Oberflächenstruktur sorgt für Rutschfestigkeit. Die Kanne und die Tassen bestehen aus Keramik und werden von Hand mit einer schwarzen Sandsteinglasur versehen.

Begründung der Jury
Aufgrund eines klassischen Schwarz-Weiß-Kontrasts und minimalistischer Konturen entsteht bei diesem Teeset eine zeitlos-elegante Ästhetik.

RÖSLE Aroma Egg
RÖSLE Aroma-Ei
Kitchen Utensil
Küchenutensil

Manufacturer
Rösle GmbH & Co. KG,
Marktoberdorf, Germany
Design
Elbe Eichhorn (Reiner Wallbaum),
Düsseldorf, Germany
Web
www.roesle.com
www.elbeeichhorn.de

The Aroma Egg allows cooking herbs and spices such as bay leaves, cardamom pods or juniper berries in a saucepan and have them unfold their full aroma. Using its integrated air cushion, the Aroma Egg floats on top of liquids. At the end of the cooking time, it can easily be removed. Made of a stainless steel strainer with a bayonet lock and a black plastic handle, this kitchen utensil is also suitable for teas or fresh mint.

Statement by the jury
The Aroma Egg offers a high ease of use and impresses as a functionally and formally well thought-out product solution.

Mit dem Aroma-Ei können Kräuter und Gewürze wie Lorbeerblätter, Kardamomkapseln oder Wacholderbeeren im Kochtopf mitgekocht werden und dabei ihr volles Aroma entfalten. Durch ein integriertes Luftpolster schwimmt das Aroma-Ei in Flüssigkeiten obenauf. Am Ende der Garzeit kann es samt Inhalt einfach mit einem Griff aus dem Topf gefischt werden. Das aus einem Edelstahl-Siebkorb mit Bajonettverschluss und einem schwarzem Kunststoffgriff bestehende Utensil eignet sich auch für Tees oder frische Minze.

Begründung der Jury
Das Aroma-Ei bietet einen hohen Bedienkomfort und begeistert sowohl funktional als auch formal als gut durchdachte Produktlösung.

Capsule Cup
Portable Teaset
Tragbares Teeset

Manufacturer
Fuyu Blue and White Rice-Pattern
Porcelain Co., Ltd., Jingdezhen, China
Design
LKKer Technology Co., Ltd.
(Jing Zhu), Jingdezhen, China
Web
www.0798fytc.com
www.lkker.com

This portable tea set has been designed to promote the calming ritual of making tea not only in the office but also when travelling. The modular concept assigns flexible functions to the individual components of the product. The set comprises one cup lid, two cups, a strainer, a tea tin and a wooden vessel for the brewed tea. The parts can be stacked in a space-saving arrangement for transport. The outer packaging can be either reused or recycled.

Statement by the jury
Thanks to an appealing combination of wood and white porcelain, this portable tea set exudes a sophisticated and elegant appeal.

Dieses tragbare Teeset wurde entwickelt, um auch auf Reisen oder im Büro das beruhigende Ritual einer Teezubereitung genießen zu können. Das modulare Produktkonzept weist den einzelnen Bestandteilen flexible Funktionen zu. Das Set umfasst einen Tassendeckel, zwei Teetassen, ein Teesieb, eine Teedose sowie einen Holzbehälter für den aufgebrühten Tee. Zum Transport lassen sich alle Teile platzsparend stapeln. Die Umverpackung kann entweder recycelt oder wiederverwendet werden.

Begründung der Jury
Dank einer ansprechenden Kombination aus Holz und weißem Porzellan wirkt dieses tragbare Teeset hochwertig und elegant.

Bamboo Fibre Drinking Straws
Bambusfaser-Trinkhalme

Manufacturer
Plant Fiber International Incorporation, New Taipei City, Taiwan
In-house design
Web
www.yollyware.com

These bamboo fibre drinking straws have been designed as a sustainable product solution. In a specially developed manufacturing process, bamboo is ground and the powder is used to produce drinking straws of different diameters. The drinking straws can be left in drinks for up to 24 hours without them swelling. In addition, they withstand temperatures from −20 to +100 degrees centigrade. The drinking straws can be disposed as general waste, or be composted, decomposing completely within months.

Statement by the jury
From cultivation and processing to disposal, the production of these bamboo fibre drinking straws is based on an ecologically sound concept.

Diese Trinkhalme aus Bambusfasern wurden kreiert, um eine nachhaltige Produktlösung anzubieten. Mithilfe eines eigens entwickelten Fertigungsprozesses wird Bambusrohr zu Pulver gemahlen, woraus Trinkhalme mit verschiedenen Durchmessern gefertigt werden. Ohne dabei aufzuquellen, können die Halme bis zu 24 Stunden in den Getränken verbleiben. Zudem halten sie Temperaturen von −20 bis +100 Grad stand. Die Trinkhalme können als Restmüll entsorgt oder auf dem Kompost innerhalb von Monaten abgebaut werden.

Begründung der Jury
Vom Anbau über die Verarbeitung bis hin zur Entsorgung folgt die Produktion dieser Trinkhalme aus Bambusfasern einem ökologisch sinnvollen Konzept.

SliderStraw
Drinking Straw
Trinkhalm

Manufacturer
Brainchildren GmbH, Berlin, Germany
Design
Emami Design (Arman Emami), Berlin, Germany
Web
www.sliderstraw.com
www.emamidesign.de

SliderStraw is a reusable drinking straw made of robust plastics. Thanks to its patented design, each straw consists of two parts which can easily be connected. After use, the two parts can be put into the dishwasher individually for perfectly hygienic cleaning – something that is not possible with conventional disposable straws due to their small diameter. The oval drinking straws are available in light summer colours.

Statement by the jury
As an environmentally responsible product solution, SliderStraw offers a high utility value and shows an appealing formal quality.

SliderStraw ist ein wiederverwendbarer Trinkhalm aus robustem Kunststoff. Dank einer patentierten Konstruktion besteht jeder Strohhalm aus zwei Teilen, die einfach in- oder auseinandergeschoben werden können. Nach der Benutzung können beide Teile einzeln in den Geschirrspüler gesteckt und hygienisch einwandfrei gereinigt werden – was bei herkömmlichen Einwegtrinkhalmen aufgrund ihres geringen Durchmessers nicht möglich ist. Die ovalen Trinkhalme sind in sommerlichen Farben erhältlich.

Begründung der Jury
Als umweltbewusste Produktlösung bietet SliderStraw einen hohen Gebrauchsnutzen und zeigt darüber hinaus eine ansprechende formale Qualität.

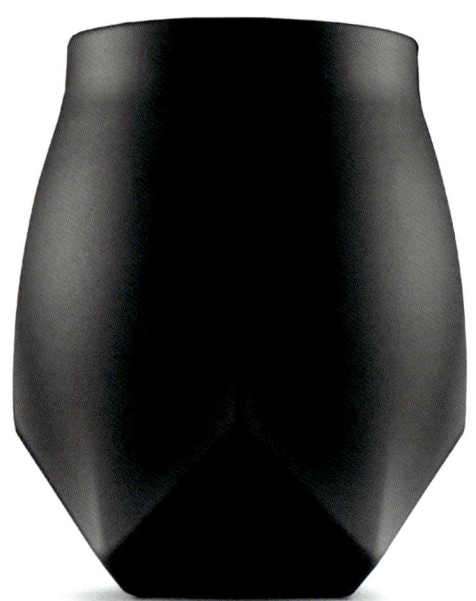

Norlan Whisky Glass VAILD
Whisky Glass
Whiskyglas

Manufacturer
Serial Future Visions, Inc., Norlan, New York, USA
In-house design
Sruli Recht
Web
www.norlanglass.com
Honourable Mention

This whisky glass has been developed to capture the spirit's distinctive flavours and concentrate them for enhanced olfactory enjoyment. The double-walled structure creates a high-contrast between the inner and outer glass surfaces. While the matte black exterior conceals the whisky when viewed from the side, the inner surface allows for light reflections within, highlighting the spirit when viewed from above.

Statement by the jury
The interplay of unique colouring and distinctive contours lends this whisky glass its self-reliant character.

Dieses Whiskyglas wurde entwickelt, um die Aromen der Spirituose einzufangen und diese für einen verstärkten olfaktorischen Genuss aufsteigend zu bündeln. Die doppelwandige Struktur ermöglicht eine kontrastreiche Gestaltung der inneren und äußeren Glasflächen: Während die mattschwarze Außenfläche den seitlichen Einblick verwehrt, erlaubt die Innenfläche Lichtreflektionen im Glas und setzt somit das Getränk in Szene, wenn es von oben betrachtet wird.

Begründung der Jury
Das Zusammenspiel einer prägnanten Farbgebung mit charakteristischen Konturen lässt bei diesem Whiskyglas einen eigenständigen Charakter entstehen.

Praha
Tankard
Bierkrug

Manufacturer
Sahm GmbH & Co. KG,
Höhr-Grenzhausen, Germany
In-house design
Rony Plesl
Web
www.sahm.de

Inspired by traditional Czech glassmaking, this tankard is a homage to the baroque architecture of Prague. In order to make the beer appear brighter and more sparkling, the design uses an optical effect created by elliptical recesses ground into the glass. These recesses also provide an easier and firmer grip. For comfortable serving, the handle has been ergonomically tailored to the two glass sizes of 0.3 and 0.5 litres.

Statement by the jury
Praha showcases a skilful contemporary interpretation of a traditional design language. The handy tankard promotes the appeal of its refreshing content.

Dieser von der traditionellen tschechischen Glasherstellung inspirierte Bierkrug ist eine Hommage an die Barockarchitektur Prags. Um das Bier heller und perlender erscheinen zu lassen, bedient sich die Gestaltung eines optischen Effekts, für den ellipsenförmige Vertiefungen ins Glas geschliffen wurden. Diese Vertiefungen ermöglichen zudem eine griffigere Handhabung. Zum komfortablen Servieren wurde der Henkel ergonomisch auf die beiden Glasgrößen 0,3 und 0,5 Liter abgestimmt.

Begründung der Jury
Bei Praha gelingt die zeitgemäße Interpretation einer traditionellen Formensprache. Der handliche Bierkrug setzt seinen Inhalt verlockend in Szene.

Paris
Whiskey Glass Series
Whiskyglas-Serie

Manufacturer
Nude, Istanbul, Turkey
In-house design
Umut Sinan Karaca
Web
www.nudeglass.com

Paris is a whiskey glass series made of mouth-blown crystal glass. Each glass is based on a thick-walled bottom, with the glass carefully tapering towards the brim. This contour aims to prevent the aromas from escaping. Thanks to its heavy weight, the glass invites users to swirl the whiskey with pleasure. The specially developed bottom provides a surface for hand-made engravings which may lend each glass a unique appearance.

Statement by the jury
This whiskey glass series owes its overall high-quality appearance to sophisticated manufacturing techniques which are characterised by a great sense for details.

Paris ist eine Whiskyglas-Serie aus mundgeblasenem Kristallglas. Jedes Glas basiert auf einem dickwandigen Boden, wobei sich die Form nach oben sanft zu einem dünnen Rand hin verjüngt. Diese Kontur soll das Entweichen der Aromen verhindern. Aufgrund seines hohen Gewichts lädt das Glas dazu ein, den Whisky genussvoll zu schwenken. Der speziell entwickelte Boden ermöglicht eine variantenreiche Umsetzung von handgefertigten Gravuren, die jedes Glas besonders erscheinen lassen.

Begründung der Jury
Ihr wertiges Gesamtbild verdankt diese Whiskyglas-Serie einer handwerklich anspruchsvollen Fertigung, die viel Gespür für Details zeigt.

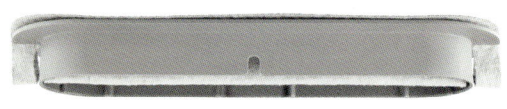

Self-Watering Herb Organiser
Herb Pot
Kräuterpflanztopf

Manufacturer
Eva Solo A/S, Måløv, Denmark
Design
Tools Design, Copenhagen, Denmark
Web
www.evasolo.com
www.toolsdesign.com

The herb pot is equipped with a sophisticated self-watering system which keeps herbs fresh for several days, providing good growing conditions without daily watering. The water reservoir at the bottom of the ceramic pot holds up to 500 ml of water and thus only needs to be refilled from time to time. An integrated capillary mat transports the water from the reservoir to the roots. Available in different colours, the herb organiser may accommodate three standard-sized herbal pots.

Statement by the jury
In addition to its convincing functionality, this herb pot is characterised by an elegant appearance and high-quality materials.

Der Kräuterpflanztopf ist mit einem raffinierten Selbstbewässerungssystem ausgestattet, sodass Kräuter einige Tage ohne Gießen auskommen und dennoch gute Wachstumsbedingungen vorfinden. Das Wasserreservoir am Boden des Keramiktopfs fasst bis zu 0,5 Liter und braucht deshalb nur ab und an aufgefüllt zu werden. Eine integrierte Kapillarmatte transportiert das Wasser aus dem Reservoir zu den Wurzeln. Das in unterschiedlichen Farben erhältliche Gefäß bietet Platz für drei handelsübliche Kräutertöpfe.

Begründung der Jury
Neben seiner überzeugenden Funktionalität zeichnet sich dieser Kräuterpflanztopf durch eine edle Anmutung und hochwertige Materialien aus.

LifeStraw® Home
Water Filter Pitcher
Wasserfilterkaraffe

Manufacturer
LifeStraw, Vestergaard S.A., Lausanne, Switzerland
In-house design
Jean Luc Madier, Alison Hill
Design
Soren Rose Studio, Hellerup, Denmark
Web
www.lifestraw.com
www.sorenrose.com

LifeStraw Home is a slender, purist water filter pitcher made from borosilicate glass, which enhances the quality and taste of tap water. By means of a specially developed water filtration technology, it removes microplastics, bacteria and parasites from the water while also reducing heavy metals and chemicals – a process which combines a long-lasting, hollow fibre membrane microfilter with an activated carbon and ion exchange filter. Every product sold provides a school child in need with safe drinking water for a year.

Statement by the jury
The LifeStraw Home delights with a successful combination of the classically elegant carafe shape and high filtration efficiency.

LifeStraw Home ist eine schlanke, puristische Wasserfilterkaraffe aus Borosilikatglas, die Qualität und Geschmack von Leitungswasser verbessert. Sie entfernt mithilfe einer speziell entwickelten Wasserfiltration Mikroplastik, Bakterien und Parasiten aus dem Wasser und reduziert die Anteile an Schwermetallen und Chemikalien – ein Prozess, der einen langlebigen Hohlfasermembran-Mikrofilter mit Aktivkohle und einem Ionenaustauschfilter kombiniert. Pro Produktverkauf wird ein bedürftiges Schulkind für ein Jahr mit sauberem Trinkwasser versorgt.

Begründung der Jury
Die LifeStraw Home begeistert mit einer gelungenen Kombination aus klassisch-eleganter Karaffenform und hoher Filtrationsleistung.

PlusMinus Vases
Vases Series
Vasen-Serie

Manufacturer
KAHLA/Thüringen Porzellan GmbH,
Kahla, Germany
Design
Studio Jonathan Radetz (Jonathan Radetz),
Frankfurt/Main, Germany
Web
www.kahlaporzellan.com
www.jonathanradetz.com

This series of vases was created in the course of an international porcelain workshop initiated by the manufacturer. The geometric contours of the vase openings symbolise the themes of abundance and shortage, as well as the contrast of give and take. In addition to being committed to a purist design, they also communicate a discreet appeal to society, inviting people to reflect about these topics. The porcelain vases are hand cast and available with glazed or matte finishes.

Statement by the jury
This vases series owes its distinctive overall image to the consistent implementation of a creative and at the same time ambitious design idea.

Diese Vasen-Serie entstand im Rahmen eines vom Hersteller initiierten, internationalen Porzellanworkshops. Die geometrischen Konturen ihrer Öffnungen sollen die Themen Überfluss und Mangel sowie Geben und Nehmen symbolisieren. Neben einem Bekenntnis zu puristischer Gestaltung vermitteln sie auf diese Weise auch einen dezenten Appell an die Gesellschaft, sich mit diesen Themen auseinanderzusetzen. Die Vasen aus Porzellan werden von Hand gegossen und sind in glasierter oder matter Ausführung erhältlich.

Begründung der Jury
Der stringenten Umsetzung einer kreativen und zugleich ambitionierten Gestaltungsidee verdankt diese Vasen-Serie ihr charakteristisches Gesamtbild.

Bloom
Serving Stand
Servierständer

Manufacturer
Nude, Istanbul, Turkey
In-house design
Hazal Balasar, Sevgi Kes
Web
www.nudeglass.com

Bloom is a multifunctional serving stand which combines the decorative serving of cakes and pastries with floral arrangements. The set comprises a glass plate and an opal glass base, which can be placed flexibly into each other. The opal glass vessel flows into a coated stainless steel plate, which allows it to be used either as a vase, a tray or as a base for a multi-tier cake stand. In addition, the glass vessel can also be used as a vase or glass lid.

Statement by the jury
In a surprising manner, Bloom allows for a variety of aesthetic table decorations – a creative and emotionally appealing design idea.

Bloom ist ein multifunktionaler Servierständer, der das dekorative Servieren von Backwaren mit Blumenarrangements verbindet. Das Set besteht aus einer Glasplatte und einem Opalglasfuß, die variabel ineinander gestellt werden können. Das Opalglasgefäß mündet in einer beschichteten Edelstahlplatte, wodurch es sowohl als Vase, als Tablett oder als Basis einer Etagere verwendet werden kann. Auch das Glasgefäß lässt sich als Vase oder Glasdeckel nutzen.

Begründung der Jury
Auf überraschende Weise ermöglicht Bloom eine Vielzahl an ästhetischen Tischdekorationen – eine kreative und emotional ansprechende Gestaltungsidee.

Garden
Garten

Accessories	Accessoires
BBQ equipment	Garten- und Outdoormöbel
Garden and outdoor furniture	Gartengeräte
Garden appliances	Gartenwerkzeuge
Garden tool sets	Gartenwerkzeugsets
Garden tools	Grillzubehör
Lounge furniture	Loungemöbel
Terrace and balcony furniture	Terrassen- und Balkonmöbel

Fiskars Waterwheel XL
Watering System
Bewässerungssystem

Manufacturer
Fiskars Finland Oy Ab,
Helsinki, Finland

In-house design
Fiskars Finland Oy Ab

Web
www.fiskars.com
www.fiskarsgroup.com

reddot award 2019
best of the best

Mobile aesthetics
The complicated handling of hoses makes watering the garden an often strenuous undertaking not only in hot summers. The Fiskars Waterwheel XL watering system has been optimised especially for work in large gardens where long distances have to be bridged. Expanded with an automatic reel-in function, the design has pursued the main goal of raising the ease of watering to a new level. This has led to giving it the compact form of a circular reel that is geared towards satisfying the needs of a wide variety of users in terms of aesthetics and usability. This elegant system impresses with both enhanced mobility and sophisticated functionality. It is ergonomically designed, easy to carry and requires no wall mounting. The hose system has been integrated into the lightweight housing, eliminating the need to lift heavy hoses. Handling the device is easy and self-explanatory. The most distinctive feature is that this watering system can be placed anywhere in the garden in a horizontal position, which means that it cannot tip over. Equipped with large, smooth sliding wheels, the system provides high manoeuvrability without having to lift it. It can be placed freely in the garden and enables watering within a rotation radius of 360 degrees – meaning that it allows even hard-to-reach corners to be watered easily and efficiently.

Mobile Ästhetik
Das komplizierte Hantieren mit Schläuchen macht die Bewässerung des Gartens nicht nur in heißen Sommern zu einem oft anstrengenden Unterfangen. Das Bewässerungssystem Fiskars Waterwheel XL wurde hier insbesondere für die Arbeit in großen Gärten optimiert, in denen weite Strecken zu bewältigen sind. Mit der Erweiterung um eine automatische Aufrollfunktion verfolgte die Gestaltung dabei vor allem das Ziel, die Leichtigkeit der Bewässerung auf eine neue Ebene zu heben. Daraus resultierte die Form einer kompakten kreisförmigen Trommel, deren Ästhetik und Gebrauch auf die Ansprüche unterschiedlichster Nutzer ausgerichtet sind. Dieses elegant anmutende System beeindruckt durch seine Mobilität und ausgereifte Funktionalität. Es ist ergonomisch gestaltet, lässt sich gut transportieren und erfordert keine Wandmontage. In das leichte Gehäuse wurde ein Schlauchsystem integriert, wodurch das Heben schwerer Schläuche entfällt. Die Handhabung ist selbsterklärend und komfortabel. Das hervorstechendste Merkmal ist dabei, dass sich dieses Bewässerungssystem überall im Garten horizontal aufstellen lässt und deshalb auch nicht kippen kann. Die Ausstattung mit großen, angenehm gleitenden Rädern verleiht ihm viel Manövrierfähigkeit, ohne dass man es anheben muss. Es ist frei im Garten platzierbar und bietet eine Bewässerungsmöglichkeit in einem Radius von 360 Grad – auf diese Weise können auch schwer zugängliche Bereiche problemlos bewässert werden.

Statement by the jury
The Fiskars Waterwheel XL watering system impresses with its elegant and purist design. Featuring soft surfaces, ergonomically shaped handles and other carefully designed details, it possesses a highly aesthetic appearance. Delivering a sophisticated system in a compact housing, it can be easily moved around even in large gardens for effortless watering in a 360-degree rotation radius. Another benefit is that its horizontal positioning prevents it from tipping over.

Begründung der Jury
Das Bewässerungssystem Fiskars Waterwheel XL beeindruckt mit seiner puristischen und eleganten Gestaltung. Im Einklang mit weichen Oberflächen, ergonomischen Griffen und sorgfältig ausgeführten Details besitzt es eine sehr ansprechende Ästhetik. Da dieses durchdachte System mit seinem kompakten Gehäuse leicht bewegt werden kann, erlaubt es das mühelose Bewässern großer Gärten in einem 360-Grad-Radius. Ein großer Vorteil ist dabei auch, dass es nicht umkippen kann.

Designer portrait
See page 44
Siehe Seite 44

Bosch Fontus
Low Pressure Cleaner
Niedrigdruckreiniger

Manufacturer
Robert Bosch GmbH, Power Tools Division, Leinfelden-Echterdingen, Germany
Design
Tatic Designstudio S.r.l. (Aleks Tatic, Alessandro Cereda, Thomas Gemperle), Milan, Italy
Web
www.bosch-pt.com
www.taticdesignstudio.com

Fontus is a battery powered low-pressure cleaner designed for use in home gardens and on the go. It offers three pressure levels with a maximum water pressure of 15 bar. In addition, the spray pattern can be adjusted as required. Thus, the water jet can be gentle enough for a dog shower and powerful enough to remove stubborn dirt from a bike. The 15-litre water tank and the 18-volt battery allow operation of up to one hour.

Statement by the jury
With its distinctive design idiom and sophisticated technology, Fontus convinces as a convenient and versatile product solution.

Fontus ist ein akkubetriebener Niedrigdruckreiniger, der für den Einsatz im heimischen Garten oder unterwegs konzipiert wurde. Es stehen drei Druckstufen mit einem maximalen Wasserdruck von 15 bar zur Auswahl. Zudem lässt sich das Sprühmuster bedarfsgerecht anpassen: So ist der Wasserstrahl sanft genug für eine Hundedusche und ausreichend kraftvoll, um hartnäckigen Schmutz vom Fahrrad zu entfernen. Der 15 Liter fassende Wassertank sowie der 18-Volt-Akku erlauben einen Gebrauch von bis zu einer Stunde.

Begründung der Jury
Mit seiner markanten Formensprache und ausgereiften Technik überzeugt Fontus als komfortable und vielseitige Produktlösung.

FISKARS®
Watering Connectors
FISKARS® Schlauchverbinder

Manufacturer
Fiskars Finland Oy Ab, Helsinki, Finland
In-house design
Web
www.fiskars.com
www.fiskarsgroup.com

These colour-coded hose connectors have been developed to simplify the selection of matching watering connectors. While consumers are often not aware that hoses and connectors come in different sizes, they can now simply follow the colour coding. The hose connector features the same colour as the matching hose to facilitate intuitive pairing: blue for 1/2"–5/8", red for 3/4" and yellow for 3/8". In addition, coated gripping surfaces serve to make the overall handling easier, even when hands are wet.

Statement by the jury
These functional hose connectors offer a high utility value. In particular, it is their self-explanatory colour concept which ensures hassle-free application.

Um die Auswahl passender Bewässerungsanschlüsse zu vereinfachen, wurden diese Schlauchverbinder mit farblicher Kennung entwickelt. Ohne die genaue Größe der Schläuche und Anschlüsse zu kennen, können sich die Nutzer einfach an deren Farben orientieren. So hat der Schlauchverbinder die gleiche Farbkennzeichnung wie der passende Schlauch, was die Paarung erleichtert: Blau für 1/2"–5/8", Rot für 3/4" und Gelb für 3/8". Zudem erleichtern beschichtete Griffflächen die Handhabung, selbst bei nassen Händen.

Begründung der Jury
Diese funktionalen Schlauchverbinder bieten einen hohen Gebrauchswert. Insbesondere ihr selbsterklärendes Farbkonzept vereinfacht die Anwendung.

FISKARS® Xact™
Gardening Tool Series
Gartenhandgeräte-Serie

Manufacturer
Fiskars Finland Oy Ab, Helsinki, Finland
In-house design
Web
www.fiskars.com
www.fiskarsgroup.com

This gardening tool series has been conceived to provide proper tools, optimised in terms of weight and balance, for a variety of tasks. The ergonomically designed ends of the handles provide support during both push and pull motions, while the gripping surfaces feature a soft coating. A hardened connection between the blade and the shaft ensures stability. Made of high-quality materials, the gardening tools have been honed for high durability.

Statement by the jury
The Xact gardening tool series combines sophisticated functionality and ergonomics with an expressive colour and material design.

Diese Gartengeräte-Serie wurde so konzipiert, dass sie für diverse Einsatzzwecke ein passendes Werkzeug mit optimiertem Gewicht und Gleichgewicht bietet. Alle Druck- und Zugbewegungen werden von den ergonomisch sinnvoll gestalteten Griffenden unterstützt, während die Griffflächen weich beschichtet sind. Zwischen Klinge und eloxiertem Aluminiumschaft befindet sich eine gehärtete Verbindung. Hergestellt aus hochwertigen Materialien, sind die Handgeräte auf eine lange Lebensdauer ausgelegt.

Begründung der Jury
Die Gartenhandgeräte der Serie Xact verbinden ihre ausgereifte Funktionalität und Ergonomie mit einer ausdrucksstarken Farb- und Materialgestaltung.

FISKARS® Garden Snips
FISKARS® Gartenscheren

Manufacturer
Fiskars Brands Inc.,
Middleton, Wisconsin, USA
In-house design
Emery Weber, Nicholas Vallo
Web
www.fiskars.com

Featuring a special spring, the blades of these garden snips open particularly gently after each cut to reduce the fatigue of the hand. In addition, soft-coated handles facilitate easy use. The pruning shears are characterised by extra-large handle loops for working with gloves. All garden snips feature serrated and straight edges for cutting various materials, while the pruning snips have curved blades for improved reach and precision.

Statement by the jury
These garden snips owe their high utility value to a design which focuses on both functionality and ergonomics.

Mithilfe einer speziellen Feder öffnen sich die Klingen dieser Gartenscheren nach jedem Schnitt besonders sanft, um einer Ermüdung der Hand entgegenzuwirken. Zudem erleichtern weich beschichtete Griffe die Handhabung. Extra große Griffschlaufen für das Arbeiten mit Handschuhen zeichnen die Astschere aus. Die robuste Gartenschere eignet sich mit ihren gezahnten und geraden Kanten zum Zerschneiden von diversen Materialien. Hingegen verleihen gebogene Klingen der Astschere genügend Reichweite und Präzision.

Begründung der Jury
Einer gleichermaßen auf Funktionalität und Ergonomie ausgerichteten Gestaltung verdanken diese Gartenscheren ihren hohen Gebrauchswert.

FISKARS® Pro Cutting Tools
FISKARS® Pro Schneidwerkzeuge

Manufacturer
Fiskars Brands Inc.,
Middleton, Wisconsin, USA
In-house design
Colin Roberts, Emery Weber
Web
www.fiskars.com

These cutting tools enable a simplified handling. While the lever technique of the loppers increases the cutting power by about 30 per cent, the pruner features intelligently curved blades for 20 per cent easier cuts. The hedge shears also feature a special lever technology and serrated blades for firmly gripping hedges and stems. All three tools are equipped with easy-to-sharpen, replaceable, high carbon steel blades with a non-stick coating.

Statement by the jury
These ergonomically sophisticated cutting tools fascinate with smooth handling and the use of durable materials.

Diese Schneidwerkzeuge ermöglichen eine vereinfachte Handhabung: Während die Hebeltechnik der Astschere die Schneidkraft um rund 30 Prozent verstärkt, verringert die Gartenschere mit ihren gebogenen Klingen den Kraftaufwand um ca. 20 Prozent. Auch die Heckenschere ist mit einer speziellen Hebeltechnologie ausgestattet; sie weist gezahnte Klingen zum Fixieren der Äste auf. Alle drei Werkzeuge verfügen über leicht zu schärfende, austauschbare Klingen aus kohlenstoffreichem Stahl mit Antihaftbeschichtung.

Begründung der Jury
Diese ergonomisch durchdachten Schneidwerkzeuge begeistern mit ihrer leichtgängigen Handhabung und der Verwendung langlebiger Materialien.

FISKARS® Pro Shovels
FISKARS® Pro Schaufeln

Manufacturer
Fiskars Brands Inc.,
Middleton, Wisconsin, USA
In-house design
Colin Roberts, Emery Weber
Web
www.fiskars.com

Designed for durability, these shovels are equipped with extended shanks, extruded aluminium handles and double-bolted connections. The ergonomically shaped shafts and handles allow comfortable handling with Softgrip touchpoints. The digging shovel features sharpened edges for easier digging, chopping and prying, while the transfer shovel is angled for transferring heavy loads. The shorter shovels facilitate work in tight spaces.

Statement by the jury
A distinctive design with an appealing colour accent emphasises the high ease of use and functionality of these robust shovels.

Auf Langlebigkeit ausgerichtet, wurden diese Schaufeln mit verlängerten Schäften, stranggepressten Aluminiumgriffen und doppelt verschraubten Verbindungen ausgestattet. Die ergonomisch geformten Stiele und Griffe ermöglichen mit Softgrip-Flächen eine komfortable Handhabung. Der Spaten bietet geschärfte Kanten zum leichteren Graben, Häckseln und Brechen, während die Schaufel zum Transport schwerer Lasten abgewinkelt ist. Die kürzeren Schaufeln erleichtern das Arbeiten auf engstem Raum.

Begründung der Jury
Eine markante Gestaltung mit ansprechendem Farbakzent betont den Bedienkomfort und die Funktionalität der robusten Schaufeln.

GARDENA Lopper Series
GARDENA Astscheren-Serie

Manufacturer
GARDENA GmbH, Ulm, Germany
In-house design
Martin Rauch, Nilas Pleje
Web
www.gardena.com

With various common parts shared across the range, this lopper series fulfils a variety of requirements: the EasyCut shears have been designed for compactness and lightness, while the EnergyCut models, with an integrated gear unit, deliver a particularly high cutting force. The telescopic TeleCut loppers allow the precise cutting of distant branches thanks to their length-adjustable lever arms. All models feature soft stop buffers to protect the wrists.

Statement by the jury
This lopper series is characterised by durability and a high ease of use. It has emerged with a consistent design vocabulary which projects an overall image of precision.

Unter Verwendung linienübergreifender Gleichteile deckt diese Astscheren-Serie verschiedene Anforderungen ab: Die EasyCut-Scheren wurden im Hinblick auf Kompaktheit und Leichtigkeit entwickelt, während die EnergyCut-Modelle dank integriertem Getriebe eine besonders hohe Schneidkraft erreichen. Durch längenverstellbare Hebelarme erlauben die teleskopierbaren TeleCut-Scheren den präzisen Schnitt von weiter entfernten Ästen. Bei allen Modellen werden die Handgelenke durch weiche Anschlagspuffer geschont.

Begründung der Jury
Bedienkomfort und Langlebigkeit zeichnen diese Astscheren-Serie aus. Zudem lässt eine stringente Formensprache ein schlüssiges Gesamtbild entstehen.

GARDENA ClassicCut Li & ComfortCut Li
Battery Grass Shears
Akku-Grasscheren

Manufacturer
GARDENA GmbH, Ulm, Germany
In-house design
Martin Rauch, Mait Mahlapuu
Web
www.gardena.com

The battery grass shears ClassicCut Li and ComfortCut Li serve to cut lawn edges accurately. Thanks to their ergonomic handles, both shears are comfortable to hold. They can be bent and thus adapt to the natural position of the hand. The high-quality blades can be easily released and exchanged at the touch of a button, with no tools required. In this way, the tool can be easily converted into shrub shears. There is also a telescopic handle available.

Statement by the jury
As an expression of high-quality standards, these battery-powered grass shears showcase a distinctive design language which emphasises individual operating elements.

Mit den Akku-Grasscheren ClassicCut Li und ComfortCut Li können Rasenkanten präzise geschnitten werden. Dank ihrer ergonomischen Handgriffe liegen beide Scheren gut in der Hand. Der Griff der ComfortCut Li lässt sich zudem abwinkeln und passt sich so der natürlichen Handhaltung an. Die hochwertigen Messer lassen sich mit einem Knopfdruck lösen und werkzeugfrei austauschen. So kann das Gerät unkompliziert zur Strauchschere umgerüstet werden. Zudem ist ein komfortabler Teleskopstiel erhältlich.

Begründung der Jury
Als Ausdruck eines gehobenen Qualitätsanspruchs zeigen diese Akku-Grasscheren eine prägnante Formensprache, die einzelne Bedienelemente betont.

SILENO life
Robotic Lawnmower
Mähroboter

Manufacturer
GARDENA GmbH, Ulm, Germany
In-house design
Martin Rauch, Alexander Turesson
Web
www.gardena.com

The SILENO life has been especially developed for medium-sized gardens with an area of up to 1,250 sqm. The clear structure of the device, with its flowing contours, follows the objective of giving the robotic lawn mower a friendly appearance. At the top of the mower, the main controls are grouped in an interaction zone to make them easy to see for users. The device can be controlled either via a control panel, which is protected by a cover, or optionally via a smartphone app.

Statement by the jury
This robotic lawn mower impresses with a distinctive, yet emotionally appealing design language. It offers a high degree of quality and ease of use.

Der SILENO life wurde speziell für mittelgroße Gärten mit einer Fläche von bis zu 1.250 qm entwickelt. Eine klare Gerätestruktur mit fließenden Konturen folgt der Zielsetzung, dem Mähroboter eine freundliche Anmutung zu verleihen. Auf der Oberseite sind die wesentlichen Bedienelemente in einer Interaktionszone zusammengefasst, um sie den Nutzern ersichtlich zu machen. Steuern lässt sich das Gerät über ein Bedienpanel, welches durch eine Klappe geschützt ist, sowie optional per Smartphone-App.

Begründung der Jury
Dieser Mähroboter gefällt mit einer markanten und zugleich emotional ansprechenden Formensprache. Er bietet ein hohes Maß an Qualität und Bedienfreundlichkeit.

SPIN
Lantern
Windlicht

Manufacturer
höfats GmbH, Kempten, Germany
In-house design
Christian Wassermann, Thomas Kaiser
Web
www.hoefats.com

SPIN creates a campfire atmosphere on balconies and terraces with an impressive dance of flames based on bioethanol. A can of bioethanol is simply placed in the stainless steel footing and ignited. After this, the glass cylinder, made of high-quality borosilicate glass, is put on top of it, allowing users to enjoy the fire vortex for about one and a half hours. If required, the cylinder can be sealed airtight with the appropriate accessory to extinguish the flames. In combination with a rod, the lantern can also serve as a torch.

Statement by the jury
This versatile lantern is a stylish eye-catcher which also convinces with high ease of use.

SPIN schafft eine Lagerfeueratmosphäre auf Balkon und Terrasse, wobei sein eindrucksvolles Flammenspiel auf Bioethanol basiert. Dazu wird eine Dose Bioethanol einfach in den Edelstahlfuß eingesetzt und entzündet. Der Glaszylinder aus hochwertigem Borosilikatglas wird anschließend aufgesetzt, und so kann der Feuerwirbel für rund anderthalb Stunden genossen werden. Bei Bedarf lässt sich der Zylinder mit dem passenden Zubehör luftdicht verschließen, um die Flamme zu löschen. In Verbindung mit dem Bodenspieß dient das Windlicht als Fackel.

Begründung der Jury
Dieses variabel nutzbare Windlicht ist ein stilvoller Blickfang und überzeugt zudem mit einem hohem Bedienkomfort.

Everdure by Heston Blumenthal 4K
Charcoal Barbeque
Holzkohlegrill

Manufacturer
Everdure by Heston Blumenthal, Sydney, Australia
Design
Design + Industry, Sydney, Australia
Web
www.everdurebyheston.com
www.design-industry.com.au

Inspired by the Japanese Kamado tradition, the charcoal barbeque uses the benefits of this cooking technique and combines them with contemporary ease of use. It features multiple temperature probes which relay the temperature data to the controller display or directly to the smartphone, allowing users to increase or decrease the grilling heat through precise airflow control. The die-cast aluminium construction delivers high heat retention, while its double-walled structure keeps the outside surfaces cool.

Statement by the jury
This charcoal barbeque impresses with its high level of efficiency and ease of use. Formally, it is inspired by a traditional design language.

Inspiriert von der japanischen Kamado-Tradition nutzt der Holzkohlegrill die Vorteile dieser Gartechnik und kombiniert sie mit einem zeitgemäßen Bedienkomfort. Mehrere Temperatursonden leiten Messdaten an die Steuerungsanzeige oder ans Smartphone weiter, sodass die Nutzer die Grillhitze über eine präzise Luftstromregelung steigern oder verringern können. Der Kessel aus Aluminiumdruckguss bietet eine hohe Wärmerückhaltung, während seine doppelwandige Struktur die Außenflächen kühl hält.

Begründung der Jury
Dieser Holzkohlegrill überzeugt mit seiner Effektivität und einem Bedienkomfort auf hohem Niveau. Formal lehnt er sich an eine traditionelle Formensprache an.

Husqvarna Automower 435X AWD
Robotic Lawn Mower
Mähroboter

Manufacturer
Husqvarna AB (publ.), Stockholm, Sweden
In-house design
Web
www.husqvarnagroup.com

Automower 435X AWD is an innovative, connected all-wheel drive robotic lawn mower. It can be operated via mobile app or its novel intuitive interface. Dynamic lines underline the connected body of the device, which is equipped with an ergonomic handle. Thanks to its all-wheel drive and articulated steering, the robotic mows tough terrain and even slopes with an incline of up to 70 per cent. With its battery drive, the robot runs silent and without exhaust emissions.

Statement by the jury
This distinctive robotic lawn mower owes its remarkable all-terrain manoeuvrability to a sophisticated mobility concept.

Der Automower 435X AWD ist ein innovativer Allrad-Mähroboter mit serienmäßiger Konnektivität. Er lässt sich mobil per App oder mithilfe eines neuen Interface intuitiv bedienen. Dynamische Linien unterstreichen die zweigeteilte Struktur des Geräts, in das ein bequemer Tragegriff integriert wurde. Dank Allrad-Antrieb und Knicklenkung meistert der Mähroboter selbst unwegsames Gelände und mäht Steigungen von bis zu 70 Prozent. Aufgrund des Akku-Antriebs arbeitet der Roboter abgasfrei und geräuscharm.

Begründung der Jury
Seine bemerkenswerte Geländegängigkeit und Wendigkeit verdankt dieser charakteristische Mähroboter einem durchdachten Mobilitätskonzept.

SO!
Pergola

Manufacturer
Winsol, Aalter, Belgium
In-house design
Gwenn Vanthournout
Web
www.winsol.eu

In combination with a concise design, this pergola offers state-of-the-art technology. The LED lights, the audio system and the wall plugs are fully integrated into its linear structure. All functions can be easily controlled via smartphone or tablet. The patented motorisation ensures that the louvres automatically align themselves according to the position of the sun and the weather conditions. The optionally available starlight, coloured LEDs and video projection complement the product.

Statement by the jury
The SO! pergola fascinates with technical refinements, projecting a formal quality which lends it a self-reliant overall image.

Bahama Easy
Parasol
Sonnenschirm

Manufacturer
Bahama GmbH, Reichshof, Germany
In-house design
Web
www.bahama.de

As the name suggests, the large-sized Easy parasol offers convenient handling. Its smooth-running mechanism allows for quick opening and closing with only one hand. Its waterproof fabric provides reliable UPF 50+ sun protection and is free of harmful substances. Easy is available in contemporary colours and measures up to 16 sqm in the square model and up to 12 sqm in the round version. The parasol can be optionally equipped with anti-theft protection.

Statement by the jury
With its elegant silhouette, this parasol not only blends harmoniously into public areas, it also impresses with a high level of operating comfort.

Wie der Name des großflächigen Sonnenschirms andeutet, bietet Easy eine komfortable Handhabung: Seine leichtgängige Mechanik erlaubt ein schnelles Öffnen und Schließen mit nur einem Handgriff. Der wasserdichte Schirmstoff bietet einen zuverlässigen Sonnenschutz von UPF 50+ und ist zudem schadstoffgeprüft. Easy ist in zeitgemäßen Farben erhältlich und misst maximal 16 qm in der quadratischen Ausführung sowie maximal 12 qm in seiner runden Version. Der Sonnenschirm kann u. a. optional mit einer Diebstahlsicherung versehen werden.

Begründung der Jury
Dieser Sonnenschirm fügt sich mit seiner eleganten Silhouette harmonisch in öffentliche Bereiche ein und begeistert mit einem hohen Bedienkomfort.

Bistroo
Bistro Furniture
Bistromöbel

Manufacturer
Extremis NV, Poperinge, Belgium
Design
Dirk Wynants Design Works, Poperinge, Belgium
Web
www.extremis.be

Instead of sitting opposite each other, Bistroo invites people to sit side by side, allowing them to watch the surroundings together, as if in a bistro in Paris. The sturdy construction combines two seats and a table into a space-saving piece of bistro furniture. Standing firmly on only three legs, it grants guests more legroom and allows restaurant and bistro owners comparatively quick stacking. The double "o" in the product name refers to the two circular backrests.

Statement by the jury
In a creative manner, this bistro furniture manages to merge two seats and a table into a formal and functional unit.

Auf dem Bistroo sitzt man sich nicht gegenüber, sondern nebeneinander, um wie in einem Pariser Bistro die Blicke auf die Umgebung richten zu können. Die robuste Konstruktion verbindet zwei Sitze und einen Tisch zu einem platzsparenden Bistromöbel. Der stabile Stand auf nur drei Beinen gewährt den Gästen mehr Beinfreiheit und erlaubt den Gastronomen ein vergleichsweise schnelles Stapeln. Das doppelte „O" im Produktnamen bezieht sich auf die beiden kreisrunden Rückenlehnen.

Begründung der Jury
Auf kreative Weise gelingt bei diesem Bistro-Möbel, zwei Sitze und einen Tisch zu einer gleichsam formalen und funktionalen Einheit zu vereinen.

BRUSEN
Outdoor Sofa

Manufacturer
IKEA of Sweden, Älmhult, Sweden
In-house design
Ola Wihlborg
Web
www.ikea.com

BRUSEN is an outdoor metal sofa with a bold accent colour which makes it stand out in the garden, on the terrace, the balcony or by the front door. The aim of the design concept was to take maximum advantage of materials and production methods in order to create a highly distinctive overall appearance. The sturdy frame provides enough space for three people and the sofa can be personalised with cushions for added comfort.

Statement by the jury
This sturdy outdoor sofa catches the eye with its curved design language and red accent colour.

BRUSEN ist ein Outdoor-Sofa aus Metall, das mit seiner kräftigen Akzentfarbe sowohl im Garten als auch auf der Terrasse, dem Balkon oder neben der Haustür auffällt. Ziel des Gestaltungskonzepts war es, einen maximalen Vorteil aus Material und Fertigungsmethoden zu ziehen, um ein unverwechselbares Gesamtbild zu schaffen. Der stabile Rahmen bietet genügend Sitzfläche für drei Personen, für zusätzlichen Komfort kann das Sofa mit Kissen individuell ausgestattet werden.

Begründung der Jury
Aufgrund seiner geschwungenen Formensprache und der Signalfarbe Rot erregt dieses robuste Outdoor-Sofa hohe Aufmerksamkeit.

Gina
Recamier
Liegesofa

Manufacturer
JANUS et Cie, Milan, Italy
Design
Lissoni Associati (Piero Lissoni), Milan, Italy
Web
www.janusetcie.com
www.lissoniassociati.com

The Gina Recamier is part of an extensive collection designed for contemporary living – mixing tactile materials and plush seating with durability and modern silhouettes. It is impeccably engineered for outdoor living with a solid aluminium frame and a seat made of handwoven polyolefin rope. Finished with a thick cushion and pillows, the furniture's beautiful contours offer visual interest. Gina can be used alone or can be combined with modular seating to create a sofa.

Das Liegesofa Gina ist Teil einer umfangreichen Kollektion, die für ein zeitgemäßes Wohnen geschaffen wurde – es kombiniert taktile Materialien und üppige Polster mit Haltbarkeit und modernen Silhouetten. Mit einem soliden Aluminiumrahmen und einer Sitzfläche aus handgewebten Polyolefin-Seilen, eignet es sich für den Einsatz im Freien. Vervollständigt mit dicken Polstern und Kissen, wecken die schönen Konturen des Möbels visuelle Aufmerksamkeit. Gina kann ohne Auflagen genutzt werden oder in Kombination mit modularen Polstern zum Sofa umgestaltet werden.

Statement by the jury
This comfortable Recamier is characterised by a harmonious combination of a purist metal frame and natural materials.

Begründung der Jury
Eine stimmige Kombination natürlicher Materialien mit einem puristisch anmutenden Metallgestell zeichnet dieses bequeme Liegesofa aus.

Tools
Werkzeuge

Construction equipment	Arbeitsschutz
Electronic tools	Baugeräte
Hand tools	Elektrowerkzeuge
Industrial tools	Handwerkzeuge
Measurement	Industriewerkzeuge
Safety clothing	Sicherheitskleidung
Tool cabinets	Vermessung
Tools accessories	Werkzeugschränke
Work protection	Werkzeugzubehör

SC 60W-A36
Cordless Circular Saw
Akku-Handkreissäge

Manufacturer
Hilti Corporation, Schaan, Liechtenstein
In-house design
Web
www.hilti.group

The SC 60W-A36 is a cordless circular saw guaranteeing comfortable handling with its ergonomically sophisticated shape, a low weight of merely 5.8 kg and a recessed rear handle. These properties ensure that precise operation is possible even over long periods of continuous use. With the 36 V rechargeable batteries, the saw delivers a cutting performance comparable to that of traditional corded saws, without neglecting ergonomics. The fast-acting blade brake and minimised kickback provide additional security.

Die SC 60W-A36 ist eine Akku-Handkreissäge, die mit ihrer ergonomisch ausgereiften Form, dem geringen Gewicht von 5,8 kg und der zurückgesetzten Position des Griffs eine komfortable Handhabung gewährleistet und dafür sorgt, dass selbst bei längerem Einsatz ein präzises Arbeiten möglich ist. Die 36 V-Akkus erreichen eine Schnittleistung, die mit der Leistung kabelgebundener Kreissägen vergleichbar ist, ohne dabei die Ergonomie zu vernachlässigen. Der schnelle Sägeblattstopp und die Minimierung der Rückschläge sorgen obendrein für mehr Sicherheit.

Statement by the jury
The design of this cordless circular saw, with emphasis on safety and productivity, also enhances its ergonomic properties.

Begründung der Jury
Die Formgebung dieser auf Sicherheit und Produktivität bedachten Akku-Handkreissäge verbessert auch ihre ergonomischen Eigenschaften.

Milwaukee M12 FUEL™ 3" Compact Cut Off Tool
Cutting Power Tool
Multimaterialschneider

Manufacturer
Techtronic Industries (Dongguan) Co., Ltd., Dongguan, China
In-house design
Techtronic Design (Vincent Ng), Hong Kong
Milwaukee Tool (Robert Jensen), Brookfield, Wisconsin, USA
Web
www.ttigroup.com
www.milwaukeetool.com

The Milwaukee M12 FUEL 3" Compact Cut Off Tool is a multi-material cutting tool with sophisticated ergonomics for one-handed use. Its Powerstate brushless motor enables fast and accurate cutting of many different materials. A remarkable feature is the reversible blade rotation with adjustable rotational speed, allowing for even more precise working. Cut-off wheels for metal and tile, a grinding disk, an easily adjustable protective cover and a detachable suction unit complement the hand held tool.

Bei dem Milwaukee M12 FUEL 3" Compact Cut Off Tool handelt es sich um einen Multimaterialschneider mit ausgefeilter Ergonomie für den Einhandgebrauch. Sein bürstenloser Powerstate Motor ermöglicht ein schnelles und akkurates Schneiden einer Vielzahl verschiedener Materialien. Bemerkenswert ist die reversible Rotationsrichtung mit einstellbarer Rotationsgeschwindigkeit, die noch präziseres Arbeiten erlaubt. Trennscheiben für Metall und Fliesen, ein Schleifteller sowie eine einfach verstellbare Schutzhaube und ein abnehmbarer Absaugschuh ergänzen die Ausstattung.

Statement by the jury
The Milwaukee M12 FUEL 3" Compact Cut Off Tool combines ergonomic and functional aspects with precision and high performance in a harmonious way.

Begründung der Jury
In dem Milwaukee M12 FUEL 3" Compact Cut Off Tool sind ergonomische und funktionale Gesichtspunkte auf harmonische Weise mit Präzision und Leistungsfähigkeit vereint.

Kress 20V BL LI Brushless Motor Impact Wrench
Impact Wrench
Schlagschrauber

Manufacturer
Positec Technology, Suzhou, China
In-house design
Jinping Zhang
Web
www.positecgroup.com

The Kress 20V BL LI is equipped with a brushless electric motor reaching a high torque of 300 Nm, yet reducing wear and improving durability. With its compact design, the tool is suitable for work in the tightest of spaces. Its auto-stop technology ensures safe driving and loosening of screws. The surface texture of the materials applied guarantees longevity, facilitates handling and also gives the wrench a contemporary appearance.

Statement by the jury
The application-oriented design of the 20V BL LI impact wrench stands out thanks to its well-conceived ergonomic properties and an up-to-date appearance.

Der Schlagschrauber Kress 20V BL LI ist mit einem bürstenlosen Elektromotor ausgestattet, der mit 300 Nm ein hohes Drehmoment erreicht, dabei jedoch Verschleiß reduziert und die Haltbarkeit erhöht. Dank der kompakten Bauweise eignet sich das Werkzeug für Arbeiten auf engstem Raum. Seine Autostopp-Technologie stellt sicher, dass das Anziehen und Lösen der Schrauben sicher vonstattengeht. Die Oberflächentextur der verwendeten Materialien garantiert Langlebigkeit, erleichtert die Handhabung und verleiht dem Schrauber zudem ein aktuelles Erscheinungsbild.

Begründung der Jury
Die anwendungsorientierte Gestaltung des Schlagschraubers 20V BL LI besticht mit klug durchdachten ergonomischen Eigenschaften und einem zeitgemäßen Äußeren.

Kress-KU340
Demolition Hammer
Abbruchbohrer

Manufacturer
Positec Technology,
Suzhou, China
In-house design
Jinping Zhang
Web
www.positecgroup.com

The design of the Kress-KU340 demolition hammer primarily follows functional principles, whereby it displays a technical impression. The use of state-of-the-art laser technology gives the machine a high-grade texture. The softly contoured grip is equipped with a user-friendly profile, guaranteeing safe handling. The integrated cooling and vibration-reducing system tackles two major problems of a demolition hammer: overheating and excessive vibration.

Statement by the jury
The design of this demolition hammer is geared to adequate applicability, leading to a technically advanced solution of practical problems.

Die Gestaltung des Abbruchbohrers Kress-KU340 folgt in erster Linie funktionalen Prinzipien, wodurch er eine technische Anmutung erhält. Die Verwendung zeitgemäßer Lasertechnik verleiht der Maschine eine qualitativ hochwertige Textur. Der sanft konturierte Griff ist mit einem benutzerfreundlichen Profil ausgestattet, das eine sichere Handhabung garantiert. Die integrierte Kühlung und das Vibrationsdämpfungssystem lösen zwei große Probleme eines Abbruchbohrers: das Überhitzen und das Entstehen starker Schwingungen.

Begründung der Jury
Ein auf adäquate Anwendbarkeit angelegter Entwurf führt bei diesem Abbruchbohrer zu einer technisch fortschrittlichen Lösung praktischer Probleme.

20V BL
Impact Drill
Schlagbohrmaschine

Manufacturer
Positec Technology,
Suzhou, China
In-house design
Haibo Zhou
Web
www.positecgroup.com

Equipped with a brushless motor which features an automatic, torque-dependent switch-off function, this 20 volt impact drill is a highly efficient, durable tool which can be handled safely. With its smart power-saving technology, it is economical as well. The pulse technology employed enables the user to easily drill holes in ceramic tiles without breakage. The machine is lightweight, compact and equipped with a shock-absorbing mechanism so that it may be comfortably operated with just one hand.

Statement by the jury
The 20V BL is a power-saving impact drill which is highly durable and, thanks to its compactness, also very user-friendly.

Ausgerüstet mit einem bürstenlosen Motor mit automatischer drehmomentabhängiger Abschaltung, ist diese 20-Volt-Schlagbohrmaschine ein hocheffizientes, langlebiges Werkzeug, das sich sicher handhaben lässt und dank seiner intelligenten Stromspartechnologie auch ökonomisch ist. Die zum Einsatz kommende Impulstechnologie ermöglicht es, selbst Keramikfliesen bruchfrei zu bohren. Die Maschine ist leicht, kompakt und mit einem stoßdämpfenden Mechanismus ausgestattet, sodass sie bequem mit einer Hand bedient werden kann.

Begründung der Jury
Der 20V BL ist eine stromsparende Schlagbohrmaschine, die sehr langlebig und dank ihrer Kompaktheit sehr benutzerfreundlich ist.

TE 60-A36
Cordless Combihammer
Akku-Kombihammer

Manufacturer
Hilti Corporation, Schaan, Liechtenstein
In-house design
Design
Matuschek Design & Management,
Aalen, Germany
Web
www.hilti.group
www.matuschekdesign.de

By putting emphasis on comfortable and fatigue-free work, this high-performance combihammer with a weight of only 7.9 kg was designed for heavy-duty concrete drilling and hammering. A low vibration level enables particularly precise handling. The cordless operation of the device offers advantages with regard to mobility and ergonomics, while ensuring the same performance as wired solutions. With eight joules of impact energy, the TE 60-A36 is an extremely powerful tool.

Das Augenmerk auf angenehmes und ermüdungsarmes Arbeiten gerichtet, wurde dieser leistungsstarke und, mit einem Gewicht von 7,9 kg, leichte Kombihammer für schwere Bohr- und Meißelarbeiten in Beton entworfen. Ein niedriges Vibrationsniveau macht besonders präzises Arbeiten möglich. Die kabellose Bedienung des Geräts bietet darüber hinaus Vorteile im Hinblick auf Mobilität und Ergonomie, ohne dabei hinter die Leistungsfähigkeit kabelgebundener Lösungen zurückzufallen. Mit acht Joules ist der TE 60-A36 ein äußerst kraftvolles Werkzeug.

Statement by the jury
The TE 60-A36 succeeds in facilitating work in terms of mobility and ergonomics, while simultaneously optimising performance.

Begründung der Jury
Dem TE 60-A36 gelingt es, die Arbeit im Hinblick auf Mobilität und Ergonomie zu erleichtern und gleichzeitig die Leistungsfähigkeit zu optimieren.

DX 9
Powder-Actuated Nailer
Bolzensetzgerät

Manufacturer
Hilti Corporation, Schaan, Liechtenstein
In-house design
Design
Matuschek Design & Management,
Aalen, Germany
Web
www.hilti.group
www.matuschekdesign.de

The DX 9 fully automatic powder-actuated nailer is used for fixing profile sheet metal to steel beams. It includes a maintenance indicator which minimises downtime and particularly shows its advantages with regard to ergonomics and productivity. The device allows for an upright working position, reducing back strain and stress on wrists, elbows and shoulders by employing a grip which absorbs recoils. Moreover, the unit's direct mounting method is characterised by a high working speed.

Statement by the jury
The functional design of the efficient and durable DX 9 powder-actuated nailer is a successful approach, particularly due to its easy operability.

Das vollautomatische Bolzensetzgerät DX 9 dient zur Befestigung von Profilblechen an Stahlträgern. Es verfügt über eine Wartungsanzeige, die Ausfallzeiten minimiert, und zeigt seine Vorzüge vor allem im Hinblick auf Ergonomie und Produktivität. So erlaubt das Gerät eine aufrechte, den Rücken schonende Arbeitsposition und ist zur Entlastung von Handgelenken, Ellenbogen und Schultern mit einem Griff ausgestattet, der Rückstöße absorbiert. Außerdem zeichnet sich die angewandte Direktmontagemethode durch ihr hohes Arbeitstempo aus.

Begründung der Jury
Die funktionale Gestaltung des effizienten und langlebigen Bolzensetzgeräts DX 9 ist insbesondere im Hinblick auf seine einfache Anwendung gelungen.

TE-SPX
Wave Polygon Chisel
Meißel im Polygon-Wellendesign

Manufacturer
Hilti Corporation, Schaan, Liechtenstein
In-house design
Web
www.hilti.group

The TE-SPX is a robust chisel for high-performance demolition hammers. Its fundamentally new design offers a solution for several problems complicating demolition work. On the one hand, the strong flanks help to prevent the chisel from getting stuck in the concrete. On the other hand, the wave design reduces by 35 per cent the danger of the chisel getting broken, while increasing performance by 15 per cent. In addition, the flower-shaped cross section prevents dust from becoming airborne, significantly enhancing the working environment.

Statement by the jury
The well-conceived form of the TE-SPX has a positive effect on longevity and performance capacity, as well as on safety-related aspects.

Der TE-SPX ist ein robuster Meißel für Hochleistungs-Abbruchhämmer. Seine grundlegend neue Formgebung bietet gleich für mehrere Probleme, die Abbrucharbeiten komplizieren, eine Lösung. Zum einen verhindern die starken Flanken ein Verklemmen des Meißels. Zum anderen reduziert das Wellendesign die Gefahr eines Meißelbruchs um 35 Prozent bei gleichzeitiger Erhöhung der Arbeitsleistung um 15 Prozent. Zusätzlich verhindert der blütenförmige Querschnitt, dass Staub in die Luft gelangt, was die Arbeitsumgebung erheblich verbessert.

Begründung der Jury
Die wohldurchdachte Form des TE-SPX wirkt sich positiv auf Langlebigkeit und Leistungsvermögen sowie auf sicherheitstechnische Aspekte aus.

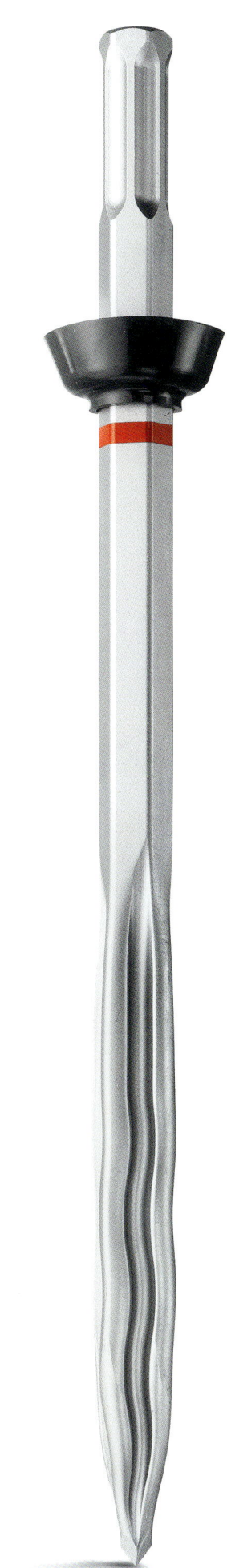

TENZ® Low-Energy Screw
Wood Screw
Holzschraube

Manufacturer
TENZ GmbH, Graz, Austria
Design
AVVIO GmbH & Co KG, Graz, Austria
Web
www.tenz.at
www.avvio.at

The design of the TENZ Low-Energy Screw contributes to environmental protection by employing advanced, patented thread technology. Thanks to its geometry, this wood screw displaces the wood fibres gently rather than drilling or milling into them. This facilitates work considerably and reduces energy input by up to 60 per cent, resulting in high efficiency and increasing the service life of the tools used.

Statement by the jury
With its innovative design, the TENZ Low-Energy Screw is eco-friendly and future-oriented. It reflects the consistent implementation of the need for a resource-saving wood screw.

Bei der Gestaltung der TENZ Low-Energy Screw ist es gelungen, durch Einsatz einer fortschrittlichen, patentierten Gewindetechnologie einen Beitrag zur Schonung der Umwelt zu leisten. Dank ihrer Geometrie dringt die Holzschraube sanft in das Holz ein, indem sie seine Fasern eher verdrängt, als sich hineinzubohren oder hineinzufräsen. Das erleichtert die Arbeit beträchtlich und reduziert den Energieeinsatz um bis zu 60 Prozent, was zu hoher Effizienz führt und zudem den Verschleiß der verwendeten Werkzeuge verringert.

Begründung der Jury
Umweltfreundlich und zukunftsorientiert ist die innovativ gestaltete TENZ Low-Energy Screw eine konsequente Umsetzung des Wunsches nach einer ressourcenschonenden Holzschraube.

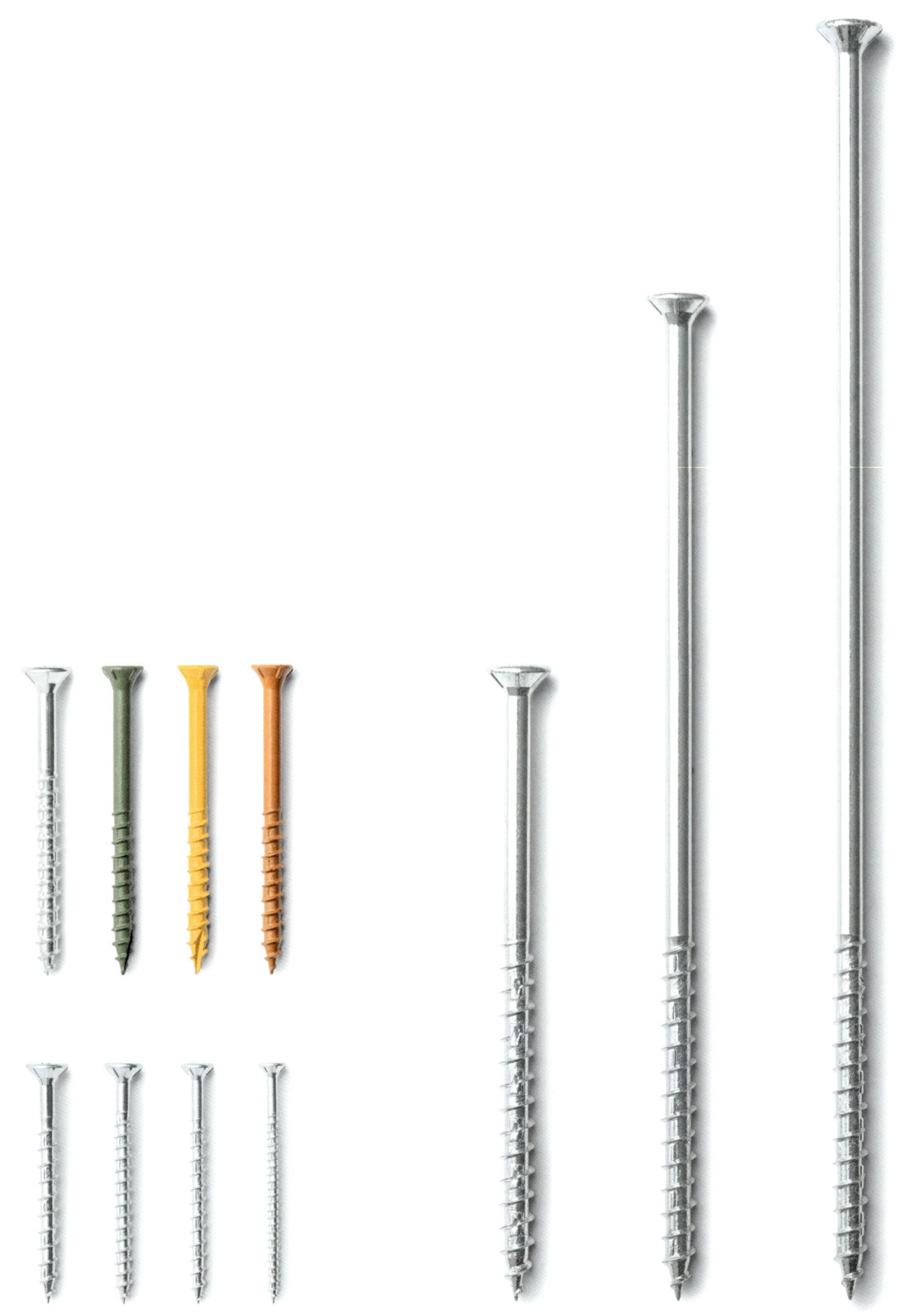

AXILO®
Plinth Adjustment System
Sockelverstellsystem

Manufacturer
Häfele GmbH & Co KG, Nagold, Germany
Paul Henke GmbH & Co. KG, Löhne, Germany
Wuro GmbH & Co. KG, Freudenberg, Germany

Design
Designerscope Limited
(Wim de Bruin, Robyn de Bruin-Judge, Roseanne de Bruin),
Auckland, New Zealand

Web
www.haefele.de
www.henke-beschlaege.de
www.wuro.de
www.designerscope.co.nz

AXILO is a cabinet levelling system for kitchens and cabinets. It consists of an adjustment tool and plastic legs which are positioned under the cabinets at hand and engage with the tool. The adjustment is done sitting upright, enabling easy reading of the spirit level. Changes in position during the adjustment are not necessary. The tool can be extended in length to reach the farthest corners under cabinets reducing working time and risk of injury. It can also be motorised by using a cordless screwdriver or drill.

AXILO ist ein Sockelverstellsystem für Küchen und Schränke. Es besteht aus dem Verstellwerkzeug und Kunststoffbeinen, die unter dem jeweiligen Möbel positioniert und mit dem Werkzeug verbunden werden. Die Justage erfolgt aufrecht sitzend, wobei das Ablesen der Wasserwaage möglich ist. Positionswechsel während des Einstellens sind nicht nötig. Das Werkzeug kann verlängert werden, um auch die hintersten Ecken unter Schränken zu erreichen. Das verringert die Arbeitszeit und das Verletzungsrisiko. Durch den Einsatz eines Akkuschraubers oder -bohrers kann das Werkzeug zudem motorisiert werden.

Statement by the jury
The AXILO plinth adjustment system may be operated intuitively and, with its simple and clever design, results in noticeable relief in daily work.

Begründung der Jury
Das intuitiv bedienbare Sockelverstellsystem AXILO stellt mit seiner einfachen wie klugen Gestaltung eine spürbare Erleichterung für den Arbeitsalltag dar.

slimBit-Box
slimBit-Box with Belt Holder
slimBit-Box mit Gürtelclip

Manufacturer
Wiha Werkzeuge GmbH,
Schonach, Germany
In-house design
Web
www.wiha.com

With its high-grade workmanship, the slimBit-Box shows a modern and clear design. It comprises a compact, clearly arranged storage and transport case for sets with either 6 or 12 Wiha slimBits. Both versions display a practical orientation and can be attached to a belt with a clip. The slimBits, which are characterised by their elongated and slim shape, as well as their voltage protection of up to 1,000 volts, may easily be removed and replaced with just one hand.

Statement by the jury
The slimBit-Box presents itself as a working aid in a contemporary design, with practical orientation as the topmost design principle.

Die hochwertig verarbeitete slimBit-Box zeigt eine moderne und klare Formensprache und umfasst ein kompaktes, übersichtlich angeordnetes Aufbewahrungs- und Transportetui für sechs oder zwölf Wiha slimBits. Beide Versionen präsentieren sich praxisnah und lassen sich mit einem Clip am Gürtel befestigen. Dabei können die slimBits ganz unkompliziert mit einer Hand entnommen und wieder zurückgesteckt werden. Sie sind durch ihre länglich schmale Form gekennzeichnet und besitzen eine Spannungssicherheit bis 1.000 Volt.

Begründung der Jury
Die slimBit-Box präsentiert sich in einer zeitgemäßen Formensprache als Arbeitshilfsmittel, dessen oberstes Gestaltungsprinzip ihre Praxisnähe ist.

DUOBLADE
Plasterboard Anchor
Gipskartondübel

Manufacturer
fischerwerke GmbH & Co. KG,
Waldachtal, Germany
In-house design
Web
www.fischer.de

The DUOBLADE is a novel, self-drilling plasterboard anchor enabling fast and easy installation in plasterboard, gypsum fibreboard and light cement board. It consists of a carefully chosen material blend of two plastic components, thus guaranteeing more grip and giving the plug its extraordinary look. The heat-resistant black metal tip creates an additional contrast. The high torque when bearing against the edge of the anchor provides a strong sense of stability.

Statement by the jury
The DUOBLADE is characterised by user-friendly reliability and, with its original three-colour optics, has a high recognition value.

Der DUOBLADE ist ein neuartiger, selbstbohrender Dübel, der eine schnelle, montagefreundliche Anbringung von Lasten in Gipskarton-, Gipsfaser- und leichten Zementbauplatten ermöglicht. Er besteht aus einer mit Bedacht gewählten Materialkombination zweier Kunststoff-Komponenten, die mehr Halt gewährleistet und dem Dübel gleichzeitig sein außergewöhnliches Aus_ hen verleiht. Die hitzebeständige schwarze Metallspitze bildet einen zusätzlichen Kontrast. Das hohe Drehmoment beim Anlegen des Dübelrandes sorgt für einen hohen Grad an Stabilität.

Begründung der Jury
Der sich durch benutzerfreundliche Zuverlässigkeit auszeichnende DUOBLADE gewährleistet mit seiner originellen Dreifarbenoptik einen hohen Wiedererkennungswert.

DC-Plus
Hammer Drill Bit
Hammerbohrer

Manufacturer
DreBo Werkzeugfabrik GmbH,
Altshausen, Germany
In-house design
Web
www.drebo.de

The DC-Plus hammer drill bit consists of a two-part system combining a drill body and an SDS-plus insertion end with suction adapter. With the adapter, drill holes are automatically cleaned during drilling by directly vacuuming out the stone dust. In this way, drilling work is nearly dust-free, even in small diameter ranges, and health risks are considerably reduced. The active air cooling of the robust head geometry of the machine also provides the durability required.

Statement by the jury
The design of this hammer drill bit reflects a successful combination of functionality, resilience, ergonomics, extended service life and preventive health protection.

Der Hammerbohrer DC-Plus besteht aus einem zweiteiligen System mit Bohrkörper und SDS-plus-Einsteckende mit Saugadapter. Mit dem Adapter werden Bohrlöcher beim Bohren automatisch gereinigt, indem der Steinstaub direkt beim Ansaugen auch abgesaugt wird. Dies schafft die Voraussetzung für ein nahezu staubfreies Bohren, auch in kleinen Durchmesserbereichen, und reduziert die Gesundheitsrisiken während der Anwendung beträchtlich. Die aktive Luftkühlung der stabilen Kopfgeometrie der Maschine sorgt außerdem für die nötige Strapazierfähigkeit.

Begründung der Jury
Bei der Gestaltung des Bohrers ist es gelungen, Funktionalität, Belastbarkeit, Ergonomie und lange Betriebsdauer mit präventivem Gesundheitsschutz zu vereinen.

RICHARTZ KEY tool®
Pocket Tool Series
Taschenwerkzeugserie

Manufacturer
Richartz GmbH, Solingen, Germany
Design
Klamer Productdesign (Marcel Klamer), Hamburg, Germany
Web
www.richartz.com
www.pockettools.richartz.com
www.klamerdesign.com

The small compact multifunctional RICHARTZ KEY tools are precisely manufactured from high-grade, matt blasted stainless steel. The versatile pocket tools provide numerous useful functions featuring, for instance, those of a cap lifter, a screwdriver, a shopping cart chip, a bicycle spoke key and a parcel opener. In a small amount of space, the compact tool offers outstandingly high functionality and also fits to any key ring.

Die kleinen kompakten Multifunktionswerkzeuge RICHARTZ KEY tools sind präzise aus hochwertigem, matt gestrahltem Edelstahl gefertigt. Die vielseitigen Taschenwerkzeuge halten zahlreiche nützliche Funktionen, wie z. B. die eines Kapselhebers, Schraubendrehers, Einkaufswagenlösers, Fahrradspeichenschlüssels und Paketöffners bereit. Das kompakte Werkzeug bietet auf kleinem Raum eine ausgesprochen hohe Funktionalität und passt dabei an jeden Schlüsselbund.

Statement by the jury
The RICHARTZ KEY tool series offers intelligent and well-designed tools, putting emphasis on practical functionality.

Begründung der Jury
Die Serie RICHARTZ KEY tool bietet intelligentes und formschönes Werkzeug, das seinen Schwerpunkt auf praxisnahe Funktionalität legt.

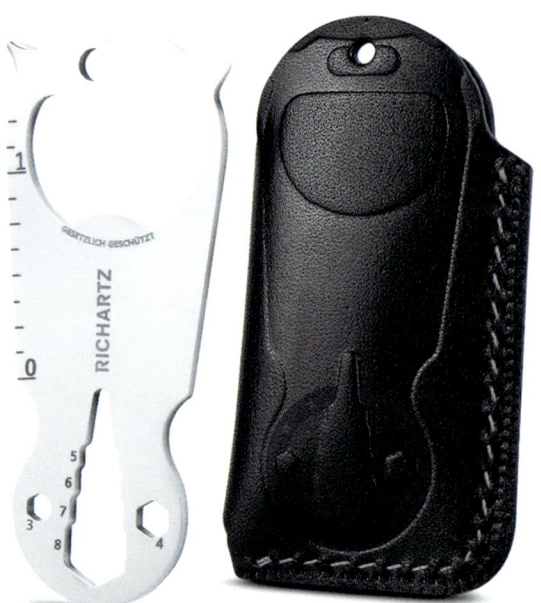

GARANT 41 2690 IP67
Digital Caliper
Digitaler Messschieber

Manufacturer
Hoffmann GmbH Qualitätswerkzeuge,
Munich, Germany
Design
Böhler GmbH, Corporate Industrial Design
(Christoph Böhler, Simon Müller),
Fürth, Germany
Web
www.hoffmann-group.com
www.boehler-design.de

The reduced structure of the large, easily readable digital display and the finely lapped measuring surfaces of the GARANT caliper allow for precise, effortless work. The device is equipped with an automatic idle mode guaranteeing low energy consumption. Simply moving the slider turns it back on, retaining the measuring values. The unit displays high-grade workmanship and is resistant to water, coolants, oil and dust, rendering it a reliable tool.

Statement by the jury
The GARANT caliper impresses with a straightforward design, which lends it clarity, and low energy consumption.

Die reduzierte Struktur der großen, gut ablesbaren Digitalanzeige und die feinstgeläppten Messflächen des GARANT Messschiebers gewährleisten ein präzises, müheloses Arbeiten. Das Gerät ist mit einem automatischen Ruhemodus ausgestattet, der für einen niedrigen Energieverbrauch bürgt. Einfaches Bewegen des Schiebers aktiviert es anschließend wieder, wobei die Messwerte erhalten bleiben. Die Schieblehre ist qualitativ hochwertig verarbeitet und unempfindlich gegen Wasser, Kühlmittel, Öl und Staub, was sie zu einem zuverlässigen Werkzeug macht.

Begründung der Jury
Der GARANT Messschieber punktet sowohl mit einer klaren Gestaltung, die ihm eine beeindruckende Übersichtlichkeit verleiht, als auch mit einem sparsamen Energieverbrauch.

VTD Torque Limiting Knob
Clamping Knob
Drehmoment-Griff

Manufacturer
Elesa S.p.A., Monza, Italy
In-house design
Web
www.elesa.com

The design of the VTD Torque Limiting Knob, which, due to its ergonomic balance, rests well in the hand, places particular focus on limiting tightening torque. This is done by a spring system which releases the grip after the desired torque is reached, signalled by a clearly audible click sound. By turning the knob anticlockwise, the patented mechanism unlocks automatically. The matte black, glass fibre reinforced thermoplastic knob is available with different torque values.

Statement by the jury
The design of this clamping knob convinces with its sophisticated functionality and ergonomics enabling fatigue-free work.

Die Gestaltung des VTD-Drehmoment-Griffs, der aufgrund seiner ergonomischen Ausgewogenheit gut in der Hand liegt, legt besonderes Augenmerk auf die Begrenzung der Drehkraft. Dafür sorgt ein Springfedersystem, das den Griff nach Erreichen des gewünschten Drehmomentes freigibt, was durch ein klar vernehmbares Klickgeräusch signalisiert wird. Beim Drehen gegen den Uhrzeigersinn öffnet sich der patentierte Mechanismus automatisch. Den Griff, der aus mattschwarzem, glasfaserverstärktem Thermoplast besteht, gibt es mit unterschiedlichen Drehmomenten.

Begründung der Jury
Die Gestaltung des Drehmoment-Griffs überzeugt durch ausgereifte Funktionalität sowie eine Ergonomie, die ermüdungsfreies Arbeiten erlaubt.

Toolex TMC-SYS
Mobile Cabinet for Systainers
Werkzeugwagen

Manufacturer
Toolex AB, Bunkeflostrand, Sweden
In-house design
Tony Andersson
Web
www.toolex.net

TMC-SYS is a high-grade mobile cabinet with a minimalist design for arranging, storing and transporting tools. With its shape based on the principle of modularity, the cabinet is manufactured from scratch-free, slightly textured veneer panels with glazed massive wood corners and anodised aluminium fittings. It is available in more than 300 potential basic configurations for workshops and customer service vehicles, and can easily be adapted to individual needs and requirements.

Statement by the jury
This mobile tool cabinet combines a design oriented to flexibility with an appealingly plain shape.

Der TMC-SYS ist ein hochwertig gestalteter, minimalistisch gehaltener Rollwagen zum Ordnen, Lagern und Transportieren von Werkzeugen. Die Formgebung des aus kratzfesten, leicht texturierten Furnierplatten gefertigten Wagens mit seinen lasierten Massivholzecken und eloxierten Aluminiumeinbauten beruht auf dem Prinzip der Modularität. Er ist in über 300 möglichen Grundkonfigurationen für Werkstätten und Kundendienstfahrzeuge erhältlich und kann ohne großen Aufwand an individuelle Bedürfnisse angepasst werden.

Begründung der Jury
Eine auf Flexibilität ausgerichtete Gestaltung vereint sich bei diesem Werkzeugwagen stimmig mit einer auf ansprechender Schlichtheit beruhenden Formgebung.

VB.839
Three-Arm Knob
Dreisterngriff

Manufacturer
Elesa S.p.A., Monza, Italy
In-house design
Web
www.elesa.com

The VB.839 three-arm knob provides a direct torque transmission. With its form characterised by two overlapping triangles shifted by an angle of eight degrees, it ensures a safe and comfortable grip. By using smooth surfaces and dispensing with cavities, dirt deposits are largely avoided, simplifying the cleaning of the thermoplastic knob. The centre cover cap is available in a variety of colours so that the knob may be adapted, in terms of appearance, to different environments.

Statement by the jury
The VB.839 is an ergonomic three-arm knob with a maintenance-friendly design, distinguished by its adaptability with regard to colour.

Der Dreisterngriff VB.839 bietet eine sehr direkte Übertragung des Drehmoments und sorgt mit seiner Form, die durch zwei sich in einem Winkel von acht Grad überlagernde Dreiecke gekennzeichnet ist, für sicheren und angenehmen Halt. Durch glatte Oberflächen und den Verzicht auf Aussparungen werden Schmutzablagerungen weitestgehend vermieden und die Reinigung des aus Thermoplast hergestellten Griffs wird vereinfacht. Die zentrale Abdeckkappe ist in verschiedenen Farben erhältlich, sodass der Griff in seinem Erscheinungsbild auf verschiedene Umgebungen abgestimmt werden kann.

Begründung der Jury
Der VB.839 ist ein wartungsfreundlich gestalteter, ergonomisch gut durchdachter Dreisterngriff, den zudem seine farbliche Anpassungsfähigkeit auszeichnet.

PM 40-MG
Multiline Laser
Multilinienlaser

Manufacturer
Hilti Corporation, Schaan, Liechtenstein
In-house design
Design
Matuschek Design & Management, Aalen, Germany
Web
www.hilti.group
www.matuschekdesign.de

The PM 40-MG is a multiline laser used for the adjustment of walls in drywall construction as well as supply lines and cable runs. It operates with a green laser beam, which offers better visibility than traditional red lasers. Even in bright daylight, it is clearly visible from over 25 metres away. To guarantee durability, diodes and prisms are protected against damage and rough handling by the Metal Blade Axicon technology. The rechargeable battery is also compatible with all other 12 volt devices by the manufacturer.

Der PM 40-MG ist ein Multilinienlaser zum Ausrichten von Trockenbauwänden sowie Versorgungsleitungen und Kabeltrassen. Er operiert mit einem grünen Laserstrahl, der eine bessere Sichtbarkeit als gewöhnliche rote Laserstrahlen bietet und selbst bei Tageslicht aus einer Entfernung von mehr als 25 Metern erkennbar ist. Um Langlebigkeit zu garantieren, werden Dioden und Prismen durch die Metal-Blade-Axicon-Technologie selbst bei Stürzen und grober Handhabung geschützt. Der verwendete Akku ist zudem mit allen anderen 12-Volt-Geräten des Herstellers kompatibel.

Statement by the jury
The use of innovative technologies in the manufacture of the PM 40-MG multiline laser guarantees both flexible applicability and high durability.

Begründung der Jury
Der Einsatz innovativer Technologien garantiert bei dem Multilinienlaser PM 40-MG sowohl flexible Anwendbarkeit als auch hohe Robustheit.

LS1
Laser Rangefinder
Laser-Entfernungsmesser

Manufacturer
Shenzhen Atuman Precision Machinery Technology Co., Ltd., Shenzhen, China
In-house design
Web
www.atuman.com

The LS1 is an easy-to-use laser rangefinder and its different functions can be controlled with just one button. With a weight of merely 27 grams, it is comparatively light, and its aluminium casing gives it the impact and scratch resistance required. Once the device is completely charged, up to 2,000 measurements can be taken. The product, which is capable of measuring distances of up to 40 metres and thus meets professional demands, also has a coherent aesthetic appearance.

Statement by the jury
This measuring device convinces with easy operability and durable materials, lending it a sense of elegant lightness.

Der LS1 ist ein leicht zu handhabender Laser-Entfernungsmesser, dessen verschiedene Funktionen mit nur einem einzigen Knopf zu bedienen sind. Mit seinen 27 Gramm ist er vergleichsweise leicht, und sein Aluminiumgehäuse verleiht ihm die nötige Stoß- und Kratzfestigkeit. Ist das Gerät vollständig aufgeladen, sind bis zu 2.000 Anwendungen möglich. Zudem besitzt das Produkt, das Entfernungen bis zu 40 Metern messen kann und dabei professionellen Ansprüchen genügt, eine gelungene ästhetische Anmutung.

Begründung der Jury
Dieses Messgerät überzeugt mit einfacher Bedienbarkeit und belastbaren Materialien, die ihm eine formschöne Leichtigkeit verleihen.

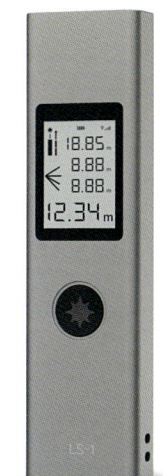

Leica BLK3D
Measuring Camera
Messkamera

Manufacturer
Leica Geosystems AG, Heerbrugg, Switzerland
Design
Platinumdesign, Stuttgart, Germany
Web
www.leica-geosystems.com
www.platinumdesign.com

The Leica BLK3D is an innovative camera for three-dimensional measurements. Its handheld image measurement system allows for precise in-picture measurements immediately after the shot. The high-resolution display is another technical equipment feature underlining the high demands placed on this camera. The compact design is clear and supports intuitive handling. With its robustness, the camera is predestined for use in rough environments, for instance construction sites.

Statement by the jury
With its high-grade workmanship, the easy-to-use Leica BLK3D reflects a symbiosis of practice-oriented robustness and metrological innovation.

Die Leica BLK3D ist eine innovative Messkamera für dreidimensionale Messungen. Ihr handgeführtes Bildmesssystem macht es möglich, unmittelbar nach der Aufnahme innerhalb des Bildes präzise Messungen durchzuführen. Das hochauflösende Display ist ein weiteres technisches Ausstattungsmerkmal, das die hohen Ansprüche an die Kamera unterstreicht. Die kompakte Gestaltung ist klar und unterstützt eine intuitive Bedienung. Durch ihre Unempfindlichkeit ist die Kamera für den Einsatz in rauen Umgebungen, wie beispielsweise Baustellen, prädestiniert.

Begründung der Jury
Die hochwertig verarbeitete und einfach zu bedienende Leica BLK3D ist eine Symbiose aus praxisorientierter Robustheit und messtechnischem Fortschritt.

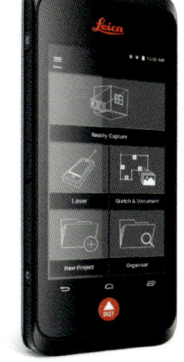

Zamo
Laser Rangefinder
Laser-Entfernungsmesser

Manufacturer
Robert Bosch Power Tools GmbH, Leinfelden-Echterdingen, Germany
In-house design
Web
www.bosch-pt.com

The easily operated Zamo laser rangefinder includes an innovative interface for different adapters. They enable the measurement of long and short distances, ranges, curves and uneven surfaces, as well as precise determination of the dimensions of round surfaces. A laser line serves to quickly align objects. The integrated square meter function helps to determine the amount of wall paint required. This functional diversity is combined with a premium, elegant appearance.

Statement by the jury
Aside from providing a wide range of functions, the Zamo laser rangefinder offers appealing aesthetics, giving the device a rather sensual quality.

Der einfach zu bedienende Laser-Entfernungsmesser Zamo verfügt über eine innovative Schnittstelle für verschiedene Aufsätze. Sie ermöglichen sowohl die Messung langer und kurzer Abstände, Strecken, Kurven und unebener Flächen als auch die präzise Bestimmung der Ausmaße runder Flächen. Eine Laserlinie dient dazu, Objekte schnell auszurichten. Die integrierte Flächenfunktion hilft den Bedarf an Wandfarbe zu ermitteln. Diese funktionale Vielfalt geht einher mit einem hochwertigen, eleganten Erscheinungsbild.

Begründung der Jury
Neben einer Vielzahl von Funktionen bietet der Entfernungsmesser Zamo auch eine ansprechende Ästhetik, die ihm eine durchaus sinnliche Qualität verleiht.

Dolphin™ CT40
Handheld Computer

Manufacturer
Honeywell China, Shanghai, China
In-house design
SPS HUE Design Studio
Web
www.honeywell.com

The Dolphin CT40 mobile computer is designed for retail store associates and other highly mobile workers. It contains everything that businesses require to accomplish their everyday tasks. It can easily be operated with both in-house and third-party software and may also be connected with a wide range of accessory devices. The lightweight CT40 is thus a high-performance, ergonomic tool contributing to enhanced productivity.

Der Dolphin CT40 ist ein mobiler Computer, der für den Einzelhandel oder im Umfeld mobiler Außendiensttätigkeiten vorgesehen ist. Er bringt alles mit, was Unternehmen zur Erledigung ihrer alltäglichen Aufgaben benötigen, da er sich problemlos mit hauseigener wie auch fremder Software betreiben und mit einer ganzen Reihe von Zusatzgeräten verbinden lässt. Der leichtgewichtige CT40 ist damit ein leistungsfähiges, ergonomisch durchdachtes Utensil, das zur Erhöhung der Produktivität beiträgt.

Statement by the jury
The Dolphin CT40 integrates flexibly into different work environments and, with its compatibility, offers enormous performance efficiency.

Begründung der Jury
Der Dolphin CT40 fügt sich flexibel in verschiedene Arbeitsumfelder ein und bietet dank seiner Kompatibilität eine enorme Leistungsfähigkeit.

GemPen®
Screening Tool for Gemstones
Edelstein-Prüfgerät

Manufacturer
Gemometrics AB, Luleå, Sweden
Design
Studio Doms AB, Visby, Sweden
Web
www.gemometrics.com
www.studiodoms.com

With this screening tool, it is possible to reliably determine whether diamonds, rubies and sapphires are of natural origin or synthetically produced gems, and whether they were subjected to value-enhancing measures. The device operates with four different filters to determine the value of the test specimen at hand. The battery-powered GemPen is resilient and comes with a travel case which, like the tool itself, guarantees safe and correct usage due to its shapes, surfaces and graphics.

Mit diesem Prüfgerät lässt sich zuverlässig feststellen, ob es sich bei Diamanten, Rubinen und Saphiren um natürliche oder synthetisch hergestellte Edelsteine handelt und ob sie einer wertsteigernden Behandlung unterzogen wurden. Das Gerät bedient sich vier verschiedener Filter, um den Wert des jeweiligen Prüflings zu bestimmen. Der akkubetriebene GemPen ist strapazierfähig und wird mit einem Reiseetui angeboten, das, so wie das Prüfgerät selbst, durch seine Formen, Oberflächen und Grafiken einen sicheren und korrekten Gebrauch garantiert.

Statement by the jury
The GemPen screening tool for gemstones is characterised by an elegant design reflecting its purpose and enhancing intuitive handling.

Begründung der Jury
Das Edelstein-Prüfgerät GemPen ist durch eine gestalterische Eleganz gekennzeichnet, die auf seine Aufgabe hindeutet und eine intuitive Handhabung begünstigt.

AVA Master Series
High-Pressure Washer
Hochdruckreiniger

Manufacturer
Swantech AS, Kleppestoe, Norway
In-house design
Are-Dag Wagtskjold Eriksen, Torkild Kaland
Web
www.discoverava.com

The high-pressure washers of the AVA Master Series present a wide range of functional details, for instance a carry handle and various storage trays. Premium materials additionally facilitate work and guarantee durability. Particular focus was placed on preventing a tilting of the devices. This common problem was solved through the profile design, the shifting of the centre of gravity and the extendable front support. The pivoting hose reel also provides stability as it cushions the user's movements.

Statement by the jury
The multifunctional high-pressure washers of the AVA Master Series offer constructive ideas which facilitate work and guarantee the effortless operation of the devices.

Die Hochdruckreiniger der AVA-Master-Serie präsentieren eine ganze Reihe funktionaler Details, beispielsweise einen Tragegriff und verschiedene Ablagen. Hochwertige Materialien erleichtern die Arbeit zusätzlich und garantieren Langlebigkeit. Besonderes Augenmerk wurde darauf gelegt, ein Kippen der Geräte zu verhindern. Diese gängige Problematik wurde durch das Profil, die Verlagerung des Schwerpunktes und eine ausziehbare vordere Abstützung gelöst. Auch die schwenkbare Schlauchtrommel sorgt für Stabilität, da sie die Bewegungen des Nutzers abfedert.

Begründung der Jury
Die multifunktionalen Hochdruckreiniger der AVA-Master-Serie bieten konstruktive Ideen, die die Arbeit erleichtern und die problemlose Bedienung der Geräte garantieren.

AVA Go Series
High-Pressure Washer
Hochdruckreiniger

Manufacturer
Swantech AS, Kleppestoe, Norway
In-house design
Are-Dag Wagtskjold Eriksen
Web
www.discoverava.com

The development of this high-pressure washer focused primarily on realising a device which is as compact as possible, yet still bears the potential and functionality of larger washers. The AVA Go is an elegant solution which, with all its equipment features and integrated space for potential accessories, is completely self-contained. The device is easily stowed away and, thanks to its reduced weight, can be effortlessly operated and transported with just one hand.

Statement by the jury
The compressed use of functional elements gives the aesthetically appealing AVA Go high-pressure washer a particularly high degree of user-friendliness.

Bei der Entwicklung dieses Hochdruckreinigers ging es in erster Linie um die Verwirklichung eines Geräts, das möglichst komprimiert ist und dennoch die Funktionalität und das Potenzial größerer Reiniger hat. Der AVA Go ist eine elegante Lösung, die mit all ihren Ausstattungsmerkmalen und dem integrierten Raum für etwaiges Zubehör vollkommen autark ist. Dabei ist das Gerät einfach zu verstauen und dank seines geringen Gewichts mit einer Hand ganz leicht zu bedienen und problemlos zu transportieren.

Begründung der Jury
Der komprimierte Einsatz funktionaler Elemente verleiht dem ästhetisch reizvollen AVA Go Hochdruckreiniger eine ausgesprochene Anwenderfreundlichkeit.

RFL251R
Work Light with Laser Rangefinder
Arbeitslicht mit Laser-Entfernungsmesser

Manufacturer
AEC Lighting Solutions Co., Ltd.,
Shanghai, China
In-house design
Aixia Bian
Web
www.aeclight-reel.com

The battery-powered RFL251R combines a very bright LED work light with a laser rangefinder, resulting in a compact unit. The handy and robust device, which allows for unit conversion between feet, inches and metres, is designed for single and continuous measurements of distances up to 60 metres in the construction industry. In addition, the instrument can calculate the distance between the lowest and highest point of an object with an accuracy of 2 mm. Its data memory is able to store up to three measurements.

Statement by the jury
The design-based integration of important functions is the outstanding feature of the expedient and rugged RFL251R.

Der akkubetriebene RFL251R kombiniert ein sehr helles LED-Arbeitslicht und einen Laser-Entfernungsmesser in einer kompakten Einheit. Das handliche und robuste Gerät, das das Umrechnen zwischen Fuß, Zoll und Meter ermöglicht, ist für Einzel- und Dauermessungen bei Entfernungen bis zu 60 Meter in der Baubranche konzipiert. Das Instrument kann zudem den Abstand zwischen dem tiefsten und dem höchsten Punkt eines Objektes mit einer Abweichung von maximal 2 mm errechnen. In seinem Datenspeicher können darüber hinaus bis zu drei Messungen gespeichert werden.

Begründung der Jury
Die gestalterische Integration wichtiger Funktionen ist das herausragende Merkmal des zweckmäßigen und unempfindlichen RFL251R.

Air Flow LED Work Light
Work Light
Stirnlampe

Manufacturer
AEC Lighting Solutions Co., Ltd.,
Shanghai, China
In-house design
Aixia Bian
Web
www.aeclight-reel.com
Honourable Mention

The Air Flow LED Work Light is a combination of a headlamp and a cooling element for protective helmets. The cooling unit consists of an easy-to-use, three-stage blower. It leads warm air through a filter and releases it in a clean and cooled down state. This facilitates work in warm places in particular. The motion detector of the multifunctional headlamp allows the light to be turned on and off or facilitates the change between wide and narrow illumination through movement of the hand.

Statement by the jury
The design of this device focuses on practicability. It was conceived specially for work in hot and dark surroundings.

Air Flow LED Work Light ist eine Kombination aus Stirnlampe und Kühlelement für Schutzhelme. Die Kühlung besteht aus einem leicht zu bedienenden, dreistufigen Gebläse, bei dem warme Luft durch einen Filter geführt und anschließend gereinigt und gekühlt wieder freigegeben wird. Das erleichtert insbesondere die Arbeit an warmen Orten. Der Bewegungsmelder der multifunktionalen Stirnlampe erlaubt das An- und Ausschalten oder den Wechsel zwischen breiter und punktueller Ausleuchtung durch Handbewegung.

Begründung der Jury
Praktikabilität steht im Vordergrund bei der Gestaltung dieses Geräts. Problemorientiert wurde es insbesondere für die Arbeit in heißen und dunklen Umgebungen konzipiert.

Rig Dog™ Xtreme
Protective Gloves
Sicherheitshandschuhe

Manufacturer
Honeywell China, Shanghai, China
In-house design
SPS HUE Design Studio
Web
www.honeywell.com

These protective gloves are designed for extreme conditions and through the use of innovative features offer a high degree of ergonomics and comfort. The design is inspired by the morphology of the human hand for precise protection of the bone structure, along with simultaneous freedom of movement of the joints. The unique honeycomb structure of the impact-resistant rubber material is complimented by the multi-layered, cut-resistant and oil-repelling material on the palm surfaces. The contrast-rich colouring enhances safety in the dark.

Statement by the jury
The design of the Rig Dog Xtreme guarantees freedom of movement at a high technological level without neglecting safety aspects.

Dieser Schutzhandschuh wurde für extreme Bedingungen entwickelt und bietet durch den Einsatz innovativer Ausstattungsmerkmale ein gleichermaßen hohes Maß an ergonomischen Vorzügen und Komfort. Die Gestaltung ist vom Aufbau der menschlichen Hand inspiriert. Präziser Schutz für die Handknochen bei freier Beweglichkeit der Gelenke ist das Ergebnis. Dabei ist die einzigartige Wabenstruktur des stoßfesten Gummimaterials ebenso wichtig wie das mehrschichtige, schnittfeste und ölabweisende Material an den Handflächen. Die kontrastreiche Farbgebung sorgt für Sicherheit im Dunkeln.

Begründung der Jury
Die Formgebung des Rig Dog Xtreme garantiert auf technisch hohem Niveau Beweglichkeit, ohne dabei den Sicherheitsaspekt zu vernachlässigen.

VeriShield
Acoustic Earmuffs
Kapselgehörschutz

Manufacturer
Honeywell, Bracknell, United Kingdom
In-house design
Web
www.honeywell.com

The VeriShield hearing protectors are durable, comfortable earmuffs with a good fit and low weight. Designed with memory-foam earpads, they offer high wearing comfort, even over extended periods of time. As the risk of hearing damage due to noise is high in many industry sectors, these noise-reducing earmuffs are designed to ensure compatibility with other personal protection equipment.

Statement by the jury
The VeriShield earmuffs stand out in particular due to an impressive adaptability and integrability. They are highly suitable for everyday use.

Bei VeriShield handelt es sich um einen strapazierfähigen, bequemen Kapselgehörschutz, der mit einer guten Passform, geringem Gewicht und seinen aus Memory Foam gefertigten Ohrenkissen für hohen Tragekomfort sorgt, selbst über einen langen Zeitraum. Da das Hörschadensrisiko durch Lärm in vielen Bereichen der Industrie sehr hoch ist, ist der Gehörschutz, der über sehr gute lärmreduzierende Eigenschaften verfügt, so gestaltet, dass er mit Elementen der persönlichen Schutzausrüstung verschiedener Umgebungen kompatibel ist.

Begründung der Jury
Der Kapselgehörschutz VeriShield gefällt vor allem wegen seiner eindrucksvollen Anpassungs- und Integrationsfähigkeit und ist in hohem Maße alltagstauglich.

SecureFit™ X5000
Safety Helmet
Schutzhelm

Manufacturer
3M, Gagnef, Sweden
Design
Design Group Italia, Milan, Italy
Web
www.3m.com
www.designgroupitalia.com

This certified safety helmet allows for the use of diverse accessory parts to meet the demands of different applications in various configurations. Its reduced weight enhances safety, as does the shorter brim, which enables better visibility. The helmet's ventilation system, good fit and innovative, stabilising interior design round off the concept. The aesthetics of the helmet conveys safety, and the use of minimum material and easily separable parts simplifies recycling.

Statement by the jury
Flexibility and adaptability make the SecureFit X5000 safety helmet a versatile part of personal protective equipment.

Dieser zertifizierte Schutzhelm lässt die Verwendung diverser Zubehörteile zu, um in verschiedenen Konfigurationen den Anforderungen unterschiedlicher Anwendungen zu genügen. Sein geringes Gewicht erhöht die Sicherheit ebenso wie die Verkürzung seiner Krempe, die eine Verbesserung der Sicht mit sich bringt. Das Belüftungssystem, die gute Passform und eine innovative, stabilisierende Innenausstattung runden das Konzept ab. Die Ästhetik des Helms strahlt Sicherheit aus, und der minimale Materialeinsatz leicht voneinander zu trennender Teile vereinfacht das Recycling.

Begründung der Jury
Flexibilität und Anpassungsfähigkeit machen den Helm SecureFit X5000 zu einem vielseitig einsetzbaren Teil der persönlichen Schutzausrüstung.

Honeywell Arc Flash
Safety Harness
Auffanggurt

Manufacturer
Honeywell China, Shanghai, China
In-house design
SPS HUE Design Studio
Web
www.honeywell.com

This full body harness meets high safety standards and the unique rib structure of the waist padding provides added support. The harness is used to protect those working at height, in confined spaces or where electrical arc flash hazards are present. In order to optimise wearing comfort, scientific findings in the field of anthropometrics were adopted. The manufacturer's colours were used to guarantee good visibility and to facilitate the fastening of the harness.

Statement by the jury
The Honeywell Arc Flash harness scores with its reliable protection against electrical hazards. It also stands out with its sophisticated fit.

Dieser hohen Sicherheitsstandards genügende Ganzkörperauffanggurt, bei dem die einzigartige Rippenstruktur der Hüftpolsterung für zusätzlichen Halt sorgt, wird sowohl als Absturzsicherung in Höhen als auch bei Arbeiten in beengten Räumen eingesetzt. Über seine Grundfunktion hinaus schützt er durch seine elektrischen Isolationseigenschaften auch vor Störlichtbögen. Zur Optimierung des Tragekomforts wurden Erkenntnisse der Anthropometrie zurate gezogen. Die Herstellerfarben werden verwendet, um gute Sichtbarkeit zu garantieren und das Anlegen des Gurtes zu erleichtern.

Begründung der Jury
Der Auffanggurt Honeywell Arc Flash punktet mit seinem zuverlässigen Schutz gegen elektrische Gefährdung und besticht obendrein durch seine anspruchsvolle Passform.

Dunlop Snugboot
Safety Boots
Sicherheitsstiefel

Manufacturer
Dunlop Protective Footwear, Hevea BV, Raalte, Netherlands
In-house design
Web
www.dunlopboots.com

With their precise fit and the materials deployed, these innovative safety boots offer a high degree of wearing comfort. The design picks up three patented elements to achieve that: firstly, the four-layer, waterproof and breathable upper material Purotex; then, there is Purofort, an outer membrane with air pockets, giving the boots lightness and thermal insulation; and finally, the metal-free StabilityFix system which provides stability for the entire foot. A slip-resistant outsole rounds off the concept.

Statement by the jury
The Dunlop Snugboot succeeds in combining functional properties guaranteeing safety with a high degree of wearing comfort. In addition, it conveys a note of individuality.

Dieser innovative Sicherheitsstiefel bietet mit seiner präzisen Passform und den zum Einsatz gebrachten Materialien einen hohen Tragekomfort. Die Gestaltung greift dabei auf drei patentierte Elemente zurück: zum einen auf das vierschichtige, wasserdichte und atmungsaktive Obermaterial Purotex. Zum anderen verleiht Purofort, eine äußere Membran, dem Stiefel mit seinen Luftkammern Leichtigkeit und isoliert ihn thermisch. Und schließlich gibt das metallfreie StabilityFix System dem gesamten Fuß Stabilität. Eine rutschfeste Außensohle rundet das Konzept ab.

Begründung der Jury
Bei dem Dunlop Snugboot gelingt es, Sicherheit garantierende, funktionale Eigenschaften mit hohem Tragekomfort zu verbinden und darüber hinaus Individualität zu vermitteln.

3M™ Speedglas™ G5-01
Welding Helmet
Schweißhelm

Manufacturer
3M, Gagnef, Sweden
Design
McKinsey Design (Oskar Juhlin, Jan Puranen), Bromma, Sweden
Web
www.3m.com
www.veryday.com

The desire for an adaptable welding helmet tailored to workplace demands was the starting point in the design of the 3M Speedglas Heavy-Duty Welding Helmet G5-01. It offers comfortable lightness, compactness and strong agility at a high safety-related level. The welding filter's visibility conditions can be modified by adapting the luminous transmittance as well as the colour tone. The novel, adjustable air guidance system protects the user's eyes, face and respiratory system. In addition, integrated Bluetooth functionality ensures access to important data.

Statement by the jury
The innovative design of the 3M Speedglas G5-01 focuses on a practice-oriented concept with carefully chosen functions.

Der Wunsch nach einem anpassungsfähigen Schweißhelm, abgestimmt auf die Anforderungen am Arbeitsplatz, war der Ausgangspunkt bei der Gestaltung des 3M Speedglas G5-01. Er bietet komfortable Leichtigkeit, Kompaktheit und hohe Agilität auf einem sicherheitstechnisch hohen Niveau. Bei seinem Visier lassen sich die Sichtverhältnisse verändern, indem die Dunkelstufen auf die Bedürfnisse des Nutzers eingestellt werden können. Das neuartige, justierbare Luftführungssystem schützt Augen, Gesicht und Atemwege. Zudem garantiert die integrierte Bluetooth-Funktion den Zugang zu wichtigen Daten.

Begründung der Jury
Ein im Hinblick auf seine Funktionen gut durchdachtes, praxisnahes Konzept steht im Fokus der innovativen Gestaltung des Schweißhelms 3M Speedglas G5-01.

Cameras
Kameras

Camera accessories	Digitalkameras
Camera lenses	Filmkameras
Cameras	Kameraobjektive
Cine cameras	Kameras
Compact cameras	Kamerazubehör
Digital cameras	Kompaktkameras
Instant photography cameras	Sofortbildkameras
Surveillance cameras	Stative
Tripods	Überwachungskameras
Video cameras	Videokameras
VR cameras	VR-Kameras

ZEISS ZX1
Digital Camera
Digitalkamera

Manufacturer
Carl Zeiss AG,
Oberkochen, Germany

Design
designaffairs GmbH,
Munich, Germany

Web
www.zeiss.com
www.designaffairs.com

reddot award 2019
best of the best

Symbiotic connection
The process from choosing a motif to taking the perfect picture requires a lot of effort, even in the digital age. The ZEISS ZX1 mirrorless full-frame camera supports photographers with a concept of integrated connectivity and at the same time allows more scope for creativity. In particular, the aim of the design was a reduction towards essential elements and a simple, ergonomic operation. The result is a coherent combination of hardware and software that provides smooth access to the main functions of "Shoot", "Edit" and "Share". This symbiotic approach is also exemplified in the clear 4.3" high-resolution multitouch screen, which features a slightly bent surface that guides the user's finger intuitively through the toolbar and value settings. This screen bend allows for blind operation of the touchscreen, for example when using the viewfinder. Meanwhile, the ISO value, exposure time and aperture settings are easily accessible via hardware control elements. The camera lens delivers an impressive optical quality for outstandingly high image sharpness and excellent detailing. In addition, the camera also offers full Adobe Photoshop Lightroom CC for editing on-the-go on the screen, as well as 512 GB of internal memory and thus enough space for over 50,000 pictures in JPEG format.

Symbiotisch verbunden
Der Weg von der Wahl des Motivs bis zum perfekten Bild erfordert auch im digitalen Zeitalter viel Mühe. Die spiegellose Vollbildkamera ZEISS ZX1 unterstützt dies mit einer integrierten Konnektivität und ermöglicht zugleich mehr Spielraum für die Kreativität des Fotografen. Ziel der Gestaltung waren insbesondere eine Reduktion auf die notwendigen Elemente sowie eine einfache, ergonomische Bedienbarkeit. Das Resultat ist eine schlüssige Verbindung aus Hard- und Software, die es erlaubt, die Arbeitsschritte „Shoot", „Edit" und „Share" fließend zu tätigen. Dieser symbiotische Ansatz findet seinen Ausdruck auch in einem übersichtlichen hochauflösenden 4,3" großen Multi-Touch-Display, das mit einem angewinkelten Bereich gestaltet ist, um den Finger des Nutzers intuitiv über die Werkzeugleiste und die Einstellungswerte zu führen. Dadurch ist eine Bedienung möglich, ohne hinzusehen, beispielsweise dann, wenn der Anwender durch den Sucher blickt. Die Einstellungen von ISO-Wert, Belichtungszeit und Blende sind leicht über mechanische Bedienelemente zugänglich. Diese Kamera bietet eine beeindruckende optische Qualität des Objektivs mit gestochen scharfen Bildern in exzellenter Detailtiefe. Darüber hinaus verfügt sie über Adobe Photoshop Lightroom CC für die Bildbearbeitung auch unterwegs und ist mit einem internen Speicher von 512 GB ausgestattet, der ausreichend Platz für über 50.000 Aufnahmen im JPEG-Format bietet.

Statement by the jury
With its perfect combination of form, function and aesthetics, the ZEISS ZX1 camera is a pleasure to work with. The camera is intuitive to use and features a bent surface that projects a special tactile quality in use. Featuring professional image editing software and a high-resolution multitouch screen, its built-in connectivity provides a captivating smooth workflow from taking pictures to editing and sharing them.

Begründung der Jury
Mit ihrer perfekten Kombination aus Form, Funktion und Ästhetik vermittelt die Kamera ZEISS ZX1 dem Nutzer ein gutes Gefühl. Sie ist intuitiv bedienbar und ihre Oberfläche bietet dem Fotografen eine besondere taktile Qualität. Ausgestattet mit professioneller Software für die Bildbearbeitung und einem hochauflösenden Multi-Touch-Bildschirm, ermöglicht sie aufgrund ihrer integrierten Konnektivität einen faszinierend einfachen Workflow aus Fotografieren, Bearbeiten und Teilen.

Designer portrait
See page 46
Siehe Seite 46

COOLPIX P1000/DF-M1 Dot Sight
Camera and Dot Sight
Kamera und Punktvisier

Manufacturer
Nikon Corporation, Tokyo, Japan
In-house design
Shu Suzuki
Web
www.nikon.com

With state-of-the-art technology and an extraordinary 125× optical zoom, the low-vibration COOLPIX P1000 camera, which is equipped with a comfortable grip, offers great flexibility as well as photo and film shots of high image quality, available in raw data formats. The camera can be used for macro- and telephotography. Its operating elements are designed in such a way that all functions are accessible during zooming. The DF-M1 allows the user to line up the subject in the Dot Sight at a normal field of view to easily acquire and track it at extreme magnifications.

Modernste Technologie und ein außergewöhnlicher 125-fach-Zoom sorgen bei der mit einem bequemen Griff ausgestatteten, vibrationsarmen COOLPIX P1000 für große Flexibilität und ermöglichen Foto- und Filmaufnahmen von hoher Bildqualität im Rohdatenformat. Die Kamera kann für Makroaufnahmen ebenso verwendet werden wie für Telefotografie. Sie ist dabei so gestaltet, dass beim Zoomen auf alle Funktionen zugegriffen werden kann. Mit dem Punktvisier DF-M1 kann ein Zielpunkt platziert und so, beispielsweise Vögel oder Flugzeuge, verfolgt und in der Mitte des Bildes gehalten werden.

Statement by the jury
The COOLPIX P1000 is a technically highly advanced handheld camera which convinces with regard to ergonomics and operating comfort.

Begründung der Jury
Die COOLPIX P1000 ist eine technisch hochentwickelte Handkamera, die auch in Bezug auf Ergonomie und Bedienkomfort überzeugt.

Nikon Z Mount System
Mirrorless Camera System
Spiegelloses Kamerasystem

Manufacturer
Nikon Corporation, Tokyo, Japan
In-house design
Makoto Imamizu, Kenji Baba, Yutaka Nikaido
Web
www.nikon.com

The ergonomically balanced cameras of the Z series offer enhanced optical potential owing to their technical equipment, such as full-format sensors and an electronic viewfinder. They also facilitate high-speed serial images. The centrepiece of the series is the Z Mount and its impressively large diameter, which enables the utilisation of newer types of high-performance, full-format lenses. These lenses also guarantee that more light reaches the corners of the image field.

Die ergonomisch ausgewogenen Kameras der Z-Mount-Serie bieten dank ihrer technischen Ausstattung, wie beispielsweise Vollformatsensoren und elektronischem Sucher, ein verbessertes optisches Potenzial. Außerdem ermöglichen sie es, Serienbilder in hoher Geschwindigkeit aufzunehmen. Herzstück der Serie ist das Objektiv-Bajonettsystem, bei dem der beeindruckend große Durchmesser des Z-Bajonetts den Einsatz leistungsfähiger Vollformatobjektive neuerer Bauweise erlaubt, die garantieren, dass mehr Licht bis in die Ecken des Bildfeldes gelangt.

Statement by the jury
The cameras of the flexible Nikon Z Mount System impress with their innovative technical equipment. They also offer sound ergonomic properties.

Begründung der Jury
Die Kameras des flexiblen Nikon Z Mount System bestechen durch ihre innovative technische Ausstattung. Darüber hinaus bieten sie gute ergonomische Eigenschaften.

DC-G9
Digital Camera
Digitalkamera

Manufacturer
Panasonic Corporation, Kyoto, Japan
In-house design
Atsushi Sasaki
Web
www.panasonic.com/global/home

This highly advanced, mirrorless digital camera combines mobility and user-friendliness. The DC-G9 is so robust that it is capable of withstanding even the most adverse conditions. The pleasantly shaped housing provides an enhanced grip, and the control elements are designed in such a way that they can be handled intuitively and easily. With functional elegance, the deep-black coating of the camera highlights its function as a tool, while the red lines symbolise high performance and a passion for photography.

Statement by the jury
With regard to aesthetics, the DC-G9 convinces with its elegant black finish. At the same time, the design underscores the technical qualities of the camera.

Diese hoch entwickelte, spiegellose Digitalkamera verbindet Mobilität und Benutzerfreundlichkeit. Dabei ist die DC-G9 so widerstandsfähig, dass sie selbst widrigsten Bedingungen standhalten kann. Das angenehm geformte Gehäuse sorgt für verbesserte Griffigkeit, und die Steuerelemente sind so gestaltet, dass sie intuitiv und einfach zu handhaben sind. Die tiefschwarze Beschichtung der Kamera betont mit sachlicher Eleganz ihre Funktion als Werkzeug, während die roten Linien hohe Leistungsfähigkeit und Leidenschaft für Fotografie symbolisieren.

Begründung der Jury
Die DC-G9 überzeugt mit ihrem eleganten Schwarz in ästhetischer Hinsicht und unterstreicht damit zugleich ihre technischen Qualitäten.

DC-GX9
Digital Camera
Digitalkamera

Manufacturer
Panasonic Corporation, Kyoto, Japan
In-house design
Kouji Masano
Web
www.panasonic.com/global/home

With its solid workmanship, the DC-GX9 mirrorless system camera is designed for taking shots of streets and everyday scenes. The high-performance device is equipped with a five-axis, dual-image stabiliser to prevent camera shake. Its 20 MP sensor without low-pass filter guarantees outstanding image quality. In order to simplify taking shots from different perspectives, the viewfinder can be tilted upward by 90 degrees. In addition, the camera enables continuous high-speed shots and versatile 4K functions.

Statement by the jury
The DC-GX9 is an elegant camera with outstanding workmanship, scoring with its functionality and excellent user-friendliness.

Die DC-GX9 ist eine elegante gut verarbeitete, spiegellose Systemkamera, die für das Fotografieren von Straßen und Alltagsszenen gedacht ist. Das leistungsstarke Gerät ist mit einem Fünf-Achsen-Dual-Bildstabilisator ausgestattet, der die Fotos vor dem Verwackeln schützt. Sein 20-MP-Sensor ohne Tiefpassfilter garantiert eine sehr gute Bildqualität. Um das Fotografieren aus verschiedenen Perspektiven zu vereinfachen, lässt sich der Sucher um 90 Grad nach oben klappen. Darüber hinaus bietet die Kamera schnelle Serienaufnahmen und vielfältige 4K-Funktionen.

Begründung der Jury
Eine elegante, gut verarbeitete Kamera, die mit ihrer Funktionalität punktet und überaus anwenderfreundlich gestaltet ist.

DC-S1/DC-S1R
Digital Camera
Digitalkamera

Manufacturer
Panasonic Corporation, Kyoto, Japan
In-house design
Katsuhiro Kitade
Web
www.panasonic.com/global/home

These expressive, full-format mirrorless cameras offer high-resolution raster graphics at 47 MP in the DC-S1R model and 24 MP in the DC-S1 model, as well as fast and innovative DFD autofocus. The image sensors are spring-mounted and, together with the lens stabiliser, provide blur-free photos and videos which the devices are capable of recording in 4K HDR quality. The ergonomically balanced and robust magnesium-alloy housings protect the cameras from dust and spray, while guaranteeing flawless functionality even in sub-zero temperatures.

Statement by the jury
These technically sophisticated cameras convince with their excellent image quality. In addition, they are very robust and durable.

Diese ausdrucksstarken, spiegellosen Vollformatkameras bieten eine hochauflösende Rastergrafik von 47 MP bei der DC-S1R und 24 MP bei der DC-S1 sowie den schnellen und innovativen DFD-Autofokus. Die Bildsensoren sind beweglich gelagert und sorgen zusammen mit dem Objektiv-Stabilisator für verwacklungsfreie Fotos und Videoaufnahmen, die die Geräte in 4K-HDR-Qualität filmen können. Die aus einer Magnesiumlegierung gefertigten, ergonomisch ausgewogenen und robusten Gehäuse schützen die Kameras vor Staub und Spritzwasser und garantieren einwandfreies Funktionieren selbst bei Minustemperaturen.

Begründung der Jury
Diese technisch ausgereiften Kameras überzeugen mit ihrer exzellenten Bildqualität. Sie sind zudem sehr robust und langlebig.

PEN E-PL9
System Camera
Systemkamera

Manufacturer
Olympus Corporation, Tokyo, Japan
In-house design
Reisuke Osada
Web
www.olympus-global.com

The PEN E-PL9 is a compact system camera available in different colours. Its aesthetic appearance and accurate workmanship catch the eye. The camera delivers high-quality images and videos, and, despite its small dimensions, it offers a wide range of photographic functions. As such, aside from the built-in flashlight, the camera also includes an image stabiliser for blur-free 4K video recordings. In addition, the device is compatible with a large number of interchangeable lenses and offers built-in Wi-Fi connectivity, increasing its flexibility even further.

Statement by the jury
The PEN E-PL9 system camera captivates with an appealing appearance as well as its advanced technology and compact design.

Die PEN E-PL9 ist eine kompakte Systemkamera, die in verschiedenen Farben erhältlich ist und deren ästhetisches Erscheinungsbild und sorgfältige Verarbeitung ins Auge stechen. Sie liefert Bilder und Videos von hoher Qualität und bietet trotz ihrer geringen Maße eine Vielzahl fotografischer Funktionen. So gibt es beispielsweise neben dem eingebauten Blitzlicht auch einen Bildstabilisator, der für verwacklungsfreie 4K-Videoaufnahmen sorgt. Das Gerät ist darüber hinaus mit einer ganzen Reihe von Objektiven kompatibel und verfügt über eine Wi-Fi-Funktion, was seine Flexibilität noch erhöht.

Begründung der Jury
Die Systemkamera PEN E-PL9 besticht durch ein ansprechendes Erscheinungsbild wie auch durch ihre fortschrittliche Technik und kompakte Bauweise.

PIXII
Rangefinder Camera
Messsuchkamera

Manufacturer
PIXII, Besançon, France
In-house design
Web
pixii.fr

Pixii is a rangefinder camera with state-of-the-art design which dispenses with the display so that the user can focus on the motif without distraction when looking through the viewfinder. Thanks to its strong connectivity, images can be viewed directly on a smartphone. The camera is equipped with an electronic global shutter sensor and an M bayonet, guaranteeing high image quality and compatibility. Different settings, such as shutter speed and exposure, are controlled manually on the camera or via an app.

Statement by the jury
The user-friendly Pixii rangefinder camera convinces with its elegant appearance and state-of-the-art functionality.

Pixii ist eine zeitgenössisch gestaltete Messsuchkamera, bei der auf den Bildschirm verzichtet wurde, sodass sich der Nutzer beim Blick durch den Sucher ohne Ablenkung auf sein Motiv konzentrieren kann. Das Bild kann dafür dank guter Konnektivität direkt auf einem Smartphone gesehen werden. Die Kamera ist mit einem elektronischen Global-Shutter-Sensor und einem M-Bajonett ausgerüstet, was für gute Bildqualität und Kompatibilität sorgt. Verschiedene Einstellungen, wie Verschlusszeit oder Belichtung, lassen sich am Gerät manuell oder per App steuern.

Begründung der Jury
Die nutzerfreundliche Messsuchkamera Pixii überzeugt mit ihrem eleganten Erscheinungsbild ebenso wie mit einer zeitgemäßen Funktionalität.

Fujifilm X-T100
Digital Camera
Digitalkamera

Manufacturer
FUJIFILM Corporation, Tokyo, Japan
In-house design
Keiichiro Takahashi
Web
http://design.fujifilm.com

The X-T100 mirrorless system camera is designed for beginners with the aim of awakening their interest in a genuine camera and the pleasure associated with it. At a weight of merely 448 grams, the camera shows an appealing, timeless design. The slim, handy housing accommodates an APS-C sensor ensuring high-quality images and videos. The camera also includes an easy-to-use autofocus enabling fast and precise focusing of the motif. A three-way tilting LCD screen for selfie shots rounds off the selection.

Statement by the jury
The X-T100 reflects the successful approach of creating a camera with a classic design oriented to beginners, guaranteeing simple handling with its coherent features.

Die spiegellose Systemkamera X-T100 wendet sich an Einsteiger, deren Interesse und Gefallen an einer echten Kamera geweckt werden soll. Dabei zeigt das nur 448 Gramm schwere Gerät eine ansprechende, zeitlose Formensprache. Das schlanke, handliche Gehäuse beherbergt einen APS-C-Sensor, der qualitativ gute Bilder und Videos garantiert. Die Kamera besitzt auch einen leicht zu bedienenden Autofokus, der die schnelle und präzise Scharfstellung des Motivs erlaubt. Ein dreifach neigbarer LCD-Bildschirm, mit dessen Hilfe Selfies geschossen werden können, rundet das Bild ab.

Begründung der Jury
Mit der X-T100 ist es gelungen, eine klassisch anmutende Kamera für Einsteiger zu kreieren, die mit ihrer stimmigen Ausstattung eine einfache Handhabung garantiert.

Fujifilm X-T3
Digital Camera
Digitalkamera

Manufacturer
FUJIFILM Corporation, Tokyo, Japan
In-house design
Masazumi Imai
Web
http://design.fujifilm.com

The X-T3 mirrorless system camera belongs to the X-series generation, featuring an advanced APS-C sensor and a high-speed processor for enhanced autofocus precision and speed. The design places value on meeting international standards with regard to image quality, look and size. As such, a mix of materials was selected for the housing, while the positioning of the operating elements was optimised, giving the camera a classic charm and simplifying its operation.

Statement by the jury
The design of this mirrorless system camera succeeds in integrating highly advanced technology in a user-friendly way.

Die spiegellose Systemkamera X-T3 gehört zur Generation der X-Serie, die mit einem fortschrittlichen APS-C-Sensor und einem Hochgeschwindigkeitsprozessor aufwartet, der die Genauigkeit und Geschwindigkeit des Autofokus verbessert. Die Gestaltung legt Wert darauf, internationalen Standards bezüglich Bildqualität, Aussehen und Größe gerecht zu werden. So wird beispielsweise für das Gehäuse ein neuer Materialmix verwendet und die Positionierung der Bedienelemente ist optimiert, was der Kamera einen klassischen Charme verleiht und ihre Handhabung vereinfacht.

Begründung der Jury
Der Gestaltung dieser spiegellosen Systemkamera gelingt die anwenderfreundliche Integration hochentwickelter Technologie.

Fujifilm X-H1
Digital Camera
Digitalkamera

Manufacturer
FUJIFILM Corporation, Tokyo, Japan
In-house design
Masazumi Imai
Web
http://design.fujifilm.com

The versatile X-H1 mirrorless system camera was designed for professional photographers and videographers, which is already expressed in the dynamic lines of its robust housing. The camera is easy to operate even under difficult conditions, for instance with gloves. A superior technical level is achieved by a high-grade image sensor, an integrated image stabilisation system and enhanced video functions. A particular highlight is the silent shutter-release button for situations in which quietness is required.

Statement by the jury
The X-H1 is a high-performance, technically advanced camera for the professional field, enabling problem-free work even under difficult conditions.

Die vielseitig einsetzbare spiegellose Systemkamera X-H1 wurde für professionelle Fotografen und Videofilmer entwickelt, was sie schon äußerlich mit den dynamischen Linien ihres robusten Gehäuses zum Ausdruck bringt. Die Kamera ist selbst unter schwierigen Bedingungen, beispielsweise mit Handschuhen, gut zu bedienen. Im Inneren sorgen ein hochwertiger Bildsensor, ein integriertes Bildstabilisierungssystem sowie verbesserte Videofunktionen für ein hohes technisches Niveau. Besonders erwähnenswert ist der leise Auslöser für Situationen, in denen Stille erforderlich ist.

Begründung der Jury
Die X-H1 ist eine leistungsstarke, technisch hochwertige Kamera für den Profibereich, die problemloses Arbeiten auch unter schwierigen Bedingungen ermöglicht.

Fujifilm GFX 50R
Digital Camera
Digitalkamera

Manufacturer
FUJIFILM Corporation, Tokyo, Japan
In-house design
Keita Kamei
Web
http://design.fujifilm.com

Equipped with a sturdy, weatherproof housing, the GFX 50R is a high-performance, mirrorless medium-format camera for photo enthusiasts. Its rangefinder camera design allows the photographer to look through the viewfinder, while simultaneously keeping an eye on the motif. The strong image quality of the device guarantees good results with both studio and outdoor shots. Via Bluetooth, images can be directly transferred to a smartphone or tablet. The compact, flat camera corpus also enables enhanced mobility.

Statement by the jury
The GFX 50R is a medium-format camera optimised for mobility purposes with high image quality and very good connectivity.

Die mit einem stabilen, wetterfesten Gehäuse ausgestattete GFX 50R ist eine leistungsstarke, spiegellose Mittelformatkamera für Fotoliebhaber. Ihr Messsuchkamera-Design erlaubt es dem Fotografen durch den Sucher zu schauen und gleichzeitig das Motiv im Auge zu behalten. Die hohe Bildqualität des Gerätes garantiert gute Ergebnisse sowohl bei Studio- als auch bei Außenaufnahmen, die via Bluetooth direkt an ein Smartphone oder Tablet übertragen werden können. Der kompakte, flache Korpus der Kamera sorgt darüber hinaus für verbesserte Mobilität.

Begründung der Jury
Die GFX 50R ist eine auf Mobilität hin optimierte Mittelformatkamera, die mit hoher Bildqualität und sehr guter Konnektivität beeindruckt.

Fujifilm XF10
Digital Camera
Digitalkamera

Manufacturer
FUJIFILM Corporation, Tokyo, Japan
In-house design
Haruka Ikegame
Web
http://design.fujifilm.com

The XF10 is a compact digital camera characterised by its metal look and small size. It features an APS-C sensor which produces high-quality pictures. By using a wide-angle, fixed-focus lens, it was possible to give the housing a very slim design without forfeiting image quality in the process. The camera can thus be handled comfortably with just one hand. In addition to the main automatic functions, the XF10 is manually adjustable through a metal control ring and the touchscreen.

Statement by the jury
Due to its refined design, the XF10 captivates with its very compact dimensions and facilitates strong image quality and high operating comfort.

Die XF10 ist eine digitale Kompaktkamera, die sich durch ihre Metalloptik und geringe Größe auszeichnet. Sie verfügt über einen APS-C-Sensor, der qualitativ hochwertige Bilder hervorbringt. Durch die Verwendung eines Weitwinkel-Fixfokus-Objektivs war es möglich, das Gehäuse sehr schlank zu gestalten, ohne dabei auf Bildqualität zu verzichten. Die Kamera kann so ganz komfortabel mit einer Hand bedient werden. Neben den Hauptautomatikfunktionen kann die XF10 über einen Metallkontrollring und den Touchscreen auch manuell eingestellt werden.

Begründung der Jury
Die edel anmutende XF10 überzeugt mit ihrer sehr kompakten Bauweise und sorgt für gute Bildqualität und einen hohen Bedienkomfort.

instax SQUARE SQ20
Instant Camera
Sofortbildkamera

Manufacturer
FUJIFILM Corporation, Tokyo, Japan
In-house design
Masayuki Sakai
Web
http://design.fujifilm.com

As an instant camera, the stylish, easy-to-use instax Square SQ20 combines digital image-processing technology with the analogue world. It is equipped with an electronic 4x zoom, enabling photos to be shot at close and long range as well as in the dark. The user can change the parameters for the square-shaped photos before taking pictures as well as afterwards on the 3" display of the camera. Another feature for creatively capturing situations is the option of printing single frames from video recordings.

Statement by the jury
The instax Square SQ20 is distinguished by its vibrant design and inspiring multi-functionality. It conveys dynamics and a zest for life.

Als Sofortbildkamera verbindet die stilvoll gestaltete, leicht zu bedienende instax Square SQ20 digitale Bildverarbeitungstechnologie mit der analogen Welt. Sie ist mit einem elektronischen 4-fach-Zoom ausgestattet und lässt das Fotografieren im Nah- und Fernbereich sowie im Dunkeln zu. Der Nutzer kann die Parameter für die quadratischen Fotos sowohl vor dem Fotografieren als auch im Nachhinein an dem 3" Display der Kamera ändern. Das Drucken von Einzelbildern aus Videoaufnahmen ist eine weitere Möglichkeit, Situationen kreativ festzuhalten.

Begründung der Jury
Ihre vitale Formgebung und inspirierende Multifunktionalität zeichnen die instax Square SQ20 aus und vermitteln Dynamik und Lebensfreude.

instax SQUARE SQ6
Instant Camera
Sofortbildkamera

Manufacturer
FUJIFILM Corporation, Tokyo, Japan
In-house design
Keita Kamei
Web
http://design.fujifilm.com

The SQ6 is a purely analogue instant camera from the instax Square series. The elegant, square-shaped housing is grooved at the front and available in three colours, addressed to a broad spectrum of users. A wide range of options makes room for the user's creativity. By using double exposure, for instance, two images can be combined to one picture, or pictures can be modified by using different colour flash filters. Additional examples of the unique multi-functionality of the camera are the modes for landscape and macro shots or selfies.

Statement by the jury
The instax Square SQ6 convinces with an inventive design which invites users to creatively utilise its broad spectrum of technical options.

Die SQ6 ist eine rein analoge Sofortbildkamera der instax-Square-Reihe. Mit ihrem eleganten, an der Vorderseite geriffelten, quadratischen Gehäuse, das in drei Farbvarianten erhältlich ist, wendet sie sich an ein breites Spektrum von Anwendern. Eine Vielzahl von Möglichkeiten gibt der eigenen Kreativität Raum. So können durch Doppelbelichtung zwei Aufnahmen in einem Bild vereint oder Bilder mit farbigen Blitzfiltern verfremdet werden. Modi für Selfie-, Landschafts- oder Makroaufnahmen sind weitere Beispiele für die außergewöhnliche Multifunktionalität dieser Kamera.

Begründung der Jury
Die instax Square SQ6 überzeugt durch ihre originelle Formgebung und lädt zum kreativen Umgang mit ihrem breiten Spektrum an technischen Möglichkeiten ein.

Irix 150mm f/2.8 Macro 1:1
Full-Frame Lens for DSLR Cameras
Vollformatobjektiv

Manufacturer
TH Swiss AG, Baar, Switzerland
In-house design
Maciej Wlasnowolski
Web
www.irixlens.com

This compact macro lens was designed in collaboration with professional photographers and photography enthusiasts and offers a range of functional and technical details. Optics and mechanics are accommodated in a scratch-resistant, high-grade housing which completely protects the lens from moisture and dust. For easy handling, the lens features a rubberised focus ring equipped with an innovative locking mechanism. The fluorescent markings highlight the sophisticated black exterior, underlining the elevated quality standards of the lens.

Dieses kompakte Makroobjektiv wurde zusammen mit Profifotografen und Fotoliebhabern entwickelt und bietet eine Reihe funktionaler und technischer Details. Optik und Mechanik sind in einem kratzfesten, hochwertig verarbeiteten Gehäuse untergebracht, das vollständig vor Nässe und Staub schützt. Das Objektiv verfügt zur einfachen Handhabung über einen mit einer innovativen Arretierung ausgestatteten, gummierten Fokusring. Die fluoreszierenden Markierungen betonen das edel anmutende schwarze Äußere, das den hohen Qualitätsanspruch unterstreicht.

Statement by the jury
With loving attention to detail, this durable macro telephoto lens with its technical and functional refinements achieves a high measure of operating comfort.

Begründung der Jury
Mit Liebe zum Detail erreicht dieses widerstandsfähige Makroobjektiv dank seiner technischen und funktionalen Raffinesse einen hohen Bedienkomfort.

Fujinon Lens XF200mm F2 R LM OIS WR
Camera Lens
Kameraobjektiv

Manufacturer
FUJIFILM Corporation, Tokyo, Japan
In-house design
Keita Kamei
Web
http://design.fujifilm.com

This top-class telephoto lens, which is resistant to spray and dust, is made of a magnesium alloy and is thus both robust and relatively lightweight. It can be used without problems in bad weather or under difficult climate conditions. The premium technical equipment minimises aberration and ensures a high resolution and sharp focus with beautiful bokeh. The image stabilisation system allows for taking shots without a tripod. With this potential, the lens is well suited to sports and nature photography.

Statement by the jury
The performance features of this shapely telephoto lens characterise it as a high-tech instrument which, due to its resilience, can be used in any weather.

Dieses spritzwasser- und staubgeschützte Teleobjektiv der Oberklasse ist aus einer Magnesiumlegierung gefertigt und deshalb sowohl robust als auch verhältnismäßig leicht. Es lässt sich problemlos bei schlechtem Wetter oder klimatisch schwierigen Bedingungen einsetzen. Die technisch hochwertige Ausstattung minimiert Aberration und sorgt für eine hohe Auflösung und Bildschärfe mit schönem Bokeh. Das Bildstabilisierungssystem ermöglicht das Fotografieren ohne Stativ. Mit diesem Potenzial eignet sich das Objektiv gut für Sport- und Naturfotografie.

Begründung der Jury
Die Leistungsmerkmale dieses formschönen Teleobjektivs weisen es als High-Tech-Instrument aus, das sich dank seiner Resistenz bei jedem Wetter einsetzen lässt.

Fujinon Lens XF80mm F2.8 R LM OIS WR Macro
Camera Lens
Kameraobjektiv

Manufacturer
FUJIFILM Corporation, Tokyo, Japan
In-house design
Keita Kamei
Web
http://design.fujifilm.com

As the first XF lens with a 1:1 image scale, this macro lens is perfectly tailored to taking close-up shots. Its enhanced optical design reduces chromatic and spherical aberrations and offers a high resolution. Focusing the motif has been optimised through the utilisation of two precise focus groups and a linear motor. Together with the rich bokeh, it guarantees successful nature photographs. The intuitively operated lens is protected against water, dust and cold.

Statement by the jury
This innovative macro lens is outstandingly adapted to outdoor use. Due to its high technical performance, it offers optimised image quality.

Als das erste XF-Objektiv mit einem Abbildungsmaßstab von 1:1 ist dieses Makroobjektiv für Nahaufnahmen sehr gut geeignet. Sein verbesserter optischer Aufbau reduziert chromatische und sphärische Abbildungsfehler und bietet eine hohe Auflösung. Die Scharfstellung des Motivs wurde durch den Einsatz zweier präziser Fokusgruppen und eines linearen Motors optimiert. Zusammen mit dem attraktiven Bokeh sorgt das dafür, dass auch Naturaufnahmen gut gelingen. Das intuitiv zu bedienende Objektiv ist gegen Spritzwasser, Staub und Kälte geschützt.

Begründung der Jury
Dieses innovative Makroobjektiv ist hervorragend für den Außeneinsatz geeignet und bietet aufgrund seiner technischen Leistungsfähigkeit eine optimierte Bildqualität.

Fujinon Lens XF8-16mm F2.8 R LM WR
Camera Lens
Kameraobjektiv

Manufacturer
FUJIFILM Corporation, Tokyo, Japan
In-house design
Haruka Ikegame
Web
http://design.fujifilm.com

This wide-angle lens offers an excellent resolution for dynamic landscape and architecture photography as well as indoor shots of restaurants or hotels. The lens even enables night photographs of the stars. Its advanced design ensures that the entire zoom range is pure and unadulterated. The lens, which is splash-resistant and dustproof, can be used at temperatures down to -10 degrees centigrade. This also makes it suitable for taking shots in rough terrain. Its unmistakable look and easy handling round off the concept.

Statement by the jury
Advanced technology and the robustness required for outdoor shots are characteristic features of this user-friendly, lightweight lens.

Dieses Weitwinkelobjektiv bietet eine hervorragende Auflösung für dynamische Landschafts- und Architekturfotografie sowie für Innenaufnahmen von Restaurants oder Hotels. Sogar Nachtaufnahmen von Sternen sind möglich. Seine fortschrittliche Bauweise stellt sicher, dass der gesamte Zoombereich unverfälscht aufgenommen wird. Das Objektiv ist spritzwasser- und staubgeschützt und kann bis zu -10 Grad Celsius eingesetzt werden. So ist es auch zum Fotografieren in rauen Landschaften geeignet. Sein unverwechselbares Aussehen und eine einfache Handhabung runden das Konzept ab.

Begründung der Jury
Progressive Technik und die für Außenaufnahmen notwendige Robustheit charakterisieren dieses anwenderfreundliche, leichte Objektiv.

Fujinon Lens GF250mm F4 R LM OIS WR
Digital Camera Lens
Objektiv für Digitalkamera

Manufacturer
FUJIFILM Corporation, Tokyo, Japan
In-house design
Haruka Ikegame
Web
http://design.fujifilm.com

The GF250mm F4 R LM OIS WR is an interchangeable telephoto lens for mirrorless system cameras with a 198 mm focal length which is equivalent to a 35 mm format. It offers high-resolution performance, ensuring that each motif is reproduced realistically and with a pleasantly harmonious bokeh. The compact lens is equipped with an image stabiliser, and preset focal lengths can be called up at the push of a button. This makes it possible to take one-hand shots. In addition, the lens is protected against spray, dust and cold.

Statement by the jury
This compact interchangeable telephoto lens stands out with its authentic image quality and its excellent ergonomics and user-friendliness.

Das GF250mm F4 R LM OIS WR ist ein austauschbares Teleobjektiv für spiegellose Systemkameras, dessen Brennweite von 198 mm einem Kleinbildformat entspricht. Es bietet eine hohe Auflösungsleistung, die es ermöglicht, dass jedes Motiv wirklichkeitsgetreu und mit einem angenehm harmonischen Bokeh wiedergegeben wird. Das kompakte Objektiv ist mit einem Bildstabilisator ausgestattet, und voreingestellte Brennweiten lassen sich auf Knopfdruck aufrufen. Damit wird es möglich, mit nur einer Hand zu fotografieren. Das Gerät ist darüber hinaus gegen Spritzwasser, Staub und Kälte geschützt.

Begründung der Jury
Dieses kompakte Tele-Wechselobjektiv besticht durch seine authentische Bildqualität sowie hervorragende Ergonomie und Bedienfreundlichkeit.

UA46x9.5BERD
Broadcast Lens
Fernsehkamera-Objektiv

Manufacturer
FUJIFILM Corporation, Tokyo, Japan
In-house design
Hiroyuki Sakai
Web
http://design.fujifilm.com

The UA46x9.5BERD is a portable 4K telephoto lens for TV cameras, characterised in particular by its high-performance 46× optical zoom. With a length of merely 358 mm, the lens barrel is relatively short, simplifying handling during filming. The advanced aspherical lens features a large aperture, resulting in a maximum resolution at the image edges and keeping distortions at a minimum. It is thus possible to obtain high-resolution images in all zoom ranges.

Statement by the jury
The UA46x9.5BERD telephoto lens captivates with its user-friendly design and its excellent technical performance features.

Das UA46x9.5BERD ist ein tragbares 4K-Teleobjektiv für Fernsehkameras, das sich insbesondere durch seinen leistungsstarken, 46-fach optischen Zoom auszeichnet. Der Tubus des kompakten Objektivs ist dabei mit 358 mm Länge relativ kurz; dies vereinfacht die Handhabung beim Filmen. Das fortschrittliche asphärische Objektiv verfügt über eine große Öffnungsweite, was zu einer maximalen Auflösung an den Bildkanten führt und Verzerrungen auf ein Minimum beschränkt. Dadurch ist es möglich, hochauflösende Aufnahmen in allen Zoombereichen zu erhalten.

Begründung der Jury
Das Teleobjektiv UA46x9.5BERD besticht durch seine bedienfreundliche Gestaltung und seine hervorragenden technischen Leistungsmerkmale.

2/3" PROFESSIONAL LENS 4K LA16x8BRM
Broadcast Camera Lens
Fernsehkamera-Objektiv

Manufacturer
FUJIFILM Corporation, Tokyo, Japan
In-house design
Koji Yoshida
Web
http://design.fujifilm.com

This high-resolution 4K lens was devised for URSA Broadcast cameras, featuring a custom-tailored design. Weighing only 1.6 kg, it is very lightweight, resulting in a relatively light load on the shoulder or tripod. In order to guarantee efficient functionality both in the studio and outdoors, the LA16x8BRM, which also offers a macro function for close-up shots, is equipped with a 16x optical zoom capable of correcting flange focal distance. This keeps the range of focus consistent during zooming.

Statement by the jury
As a formally well-adapted accessory, this premium broadcast camera lens convinces with its easy handling and high performance.

Dieses hochauflösende 4K-Objektiv wurde für URSA-Broadcast-Kameras entwickelt und seine gestalterische Ausführung ist auf sie abgestimmt. Es ist mit 1,6 kg sehr leicht, sodass das Gewicht, das beim Filmen auf Schulter oder Stativ lastet, verhältnismäßig gering bleibt. Um die effiziente Funktionsfähigkeit sowohl im Studio als auch im Außeneinsatz zu gewährleisten, wurde das LA16x8BRM, das auch eine Makrofunktion für Nahaufnahmen bietet, mit einem 16-fach optischen Zoom mit Auflagemaßkorrektur ausgestattet, welche den eingestellten Schärfebereich beim Zoomen konstant hält.

Begründung der Jury
Als formal gut angepasstes Accessoire überzeugt dieses hochwertige Fernsehkamera-Objektiv durch eine einfache Handhabung und hohe Leistungsfähigkeit.

Blackmagic Pocket Cinema Camera 4K
Digital Film Camera
Digitale Filmkamera

Manufacturer
Blackmagic Design, Melbourne, Australia
In-house design
Web
www.blackmagicdesign.com

The high-resolution Pocket Cinema 4K is a professional, hand-held digital film camera with an expanded dynamic range which, with its dual-beam stereo microphones, is specifically designed for photojournalists and independent filmmakers. The compact interior of the device harbours state-of-the-art technology, with core functions readily accessible via a 5" touchscreen. The robust casing is made of a light carbon-fibre composite material, ensuring, with its balanced form and fine haptics, user-friendly handling even during one-hand operation.

Die hochauflösende Pocket Cinema 4K ist eine professionelle, digitale Spiegelreflex-Handkamera mit erweitertem Dynamikbereich, die mit ihren eingebauten Stereomikrofonen insbesondere für Fotojournalisten und unabhängige Filmemacher entwickelt wurde. Das kompakte Innere des Gerätes verbirgt modernste Technik, auf deren Kernfunktionen sich von dem 5" Touchscreen aus schnell zugreifen lässt. Das robuste Gehäuse ist aus Kohlefaserverbundwerkstoff hergestellt, dessen geringes Gewicht gemeinsam mit der ausgewogenen Form und feiner Haptik selbst bei Einhandbetrieb eine benutzerfreundliche Handhabung gewährt.

Statement by the jury
The design of the robust and elegant Pocket Cinema 4K succeeds in integrating user-friendly technical innovations at a high level.

Begründung der Jury
Bei der Gestaltung der robusten wie eleganten Pocket Cinema 4K wurden benutzerfreundliche technische Innovationen auf hohem Niveau integriert.

Vuze XR
2D/3D Pocket Camcorder
2D/3D Taschencamcorder

Manufacturer
Humaneyes Technologies Ltd.,
Neve Ilan, Israel
Design
Taga, Tel Aviv, Israel
Web
www.humaneyes.com
www.tagapro.com

The Vuze XR is a compact pocket camcorder for one-hand operation which is easy to carry while underway. It enables both 360-degree 2D and 180-degree 3D videos, with easy switching back and forth between the two modes at just one click. The device offers a resolution of 5.7K, features a full-motion video function and can also be mounted on a tripod. Recorded scenes may be directly transmitted to a smartphone, computer or VR headset.

Statement by the jury
The Vuze XR is an easy-to-use pocket camcorder which stands out with its impressive image quality and flexible connectivity.

Bei dem Vuze XR handelt es sich um einen einfach mit einer Hand zu bedienenden, kompakten Taschencamcorder, den man ohne große Probleme mitnehmen kann. Er macht es möglich, sowohl 360-Grad-2D- als auch 180-Grad-3D-Videos zu filmen und zwischen den beiden Modi mit nur einem Klick hin und her zu schalten. Dabei bietet das Gerät eine Auflösung von 5,7K, verfügt über eine Full-Motion-Videofunktion und kann zudem auf ein Stativ montiert werden. Die aufgenommenen Szenen können direkt an ein Smartphone, einen Computer oder auch ein VR-Headset gesendet werden.

Begründung der Jury
Der Vuze XR ist ein einfach zu bedienender Taschencamcorder, der durch seine beeindruckende Bildqualität und gute Konnektivität besticht.

Obsbot Tail
AI-Based Camera
KI-basierte Kamera

Manufacturer
Remo Tech Co., Ltd.,
Shenzhen, China
In-house design
Gan Lu
Web
http://remo-ai.com

The Obsbot Tail is an innovative, technically sophisticated high-resolution camera which works completely independently. This enables the user to set the scene for their activities without having to ask anyone for help. Designed in collaboration with video bloggers, street sports teams and dance groups, the camera offers different AI-based shooting modes. The device is easy to transport and can be simply placed on flat surfaces. Alternatively, it may be installed on a tripod, car or other objects. Its aesthetics is characterised by a professional high-tech look.

Statement by the jury
The intelligent, user-friendly Obsbot Tail camera convinces with futuristic aesthetics, underscoring its technical nature.

Obsbot Tail ist eine innovative, hochauflösende, technisch ausgereifte Kamera, die vollkommen selbständig arbeitet. Der Nutzer kann so seine Aktivitäten in Szene setzen, ohne jemanden um Hilfe zu bitten. Die Kamera, die in Zusammenarbeit mit Video-Bloggern, Straßensportteams und Tanzgruppen entwickelt wurde, bietet dafür verschiedene KI-basierte Aufnahmemodi. Das leicht zu transportierende Gerät kann einfach auf ebene Flächen gestellt oder aber an einem Stativ, einem Auto oder anderen Gegenständen befestigt werden. Seine Ästhetik ist von einem professionellen Hightech-Look geprägt.

Begründung der Jury
Die intelligente, benutzerfreundliche Kamera Obsbot Tail überzeugt mit einer futuristisch anmutenden Ästhetik, die ihre technische Qualität unterstreicht.

Z Cam E2 Cinematic Camera
Camera
Kamera

Manufacturer
Shenzhen ImagineVision Technology Limited,
Shenzhen, China
Design
IDING (Chengdu) Innovation Technology Ltd.
(Wanlan Luo), Chengdu, China
Web
www.z-cam.com
www.idingcn.cn

The cube-shaped E2 Cinematic Camera is a compact 4K high-resolution camera with impressive image quality. The 10 bit colour depth, 120 fps frame rate and 13 aperture stops are an expression of this high standard. In addition, the mirrorless system camera includes an MFT connection for interchangeable lenses, enabling accessories produced by different manufacturers to be used. Multiple interfaces guarantee extraordinary connectivity. A built-in stereo microphone and internal memory card round off the concept.

Statement by the jury
The expressive design of this camera reflects its high technical quality, which goes along with flexible connectivity.

Die würfelförmige Cinematic Camera E2 ist eine kompakte, hochauflösende 4K-Kamera mit beeindruckender Bildqualität. Auch ihre Farbtiefe von 10 Bit, ihre Bildfrequenz von 120 fps und die 13 Blendstufen sind Ausdruck dieses hohen Standards. Außerdem verfügt die spiegellose Systemkamera über einen MFT-Anschluss für Wechselobjektive, sodass sich Zubehör verschiedener Hersteller anschließen lässt. Zahlreiche Schnittstellen garantieren eine außergewöhnliche Konnektivität. Ein eingebautes Stereomikrofon sowie eine interne Speicherkarte runden das Konzept ab.

Begründung der Jury
Die ausdrucksstarke Form dieser Kamera spiegelt ihre hohe technische Qualität wider, die mit einer flexiblen Konnektivität einhergeht.

Magic Carpet Pro
Camera Slider
Kamera-Slider

Manufacturer
Syrp, Auckland, New Zealand
In-house design
Chris Thomson, James Allen, Sam Blok
Web
www.syrp.co.nz

The Magic Carpet Pro is a durable, quickly set-up camera slider which meets the demands of professional filmmakers and also displays appealing aesthetics. Thanks to its clever design and switchable flywheel, the easily transportable and freely expandable equipment guarantees jitter-free tracking shots and studio-quality image material even in demanding environments. When taking exterior shots, the slider enables work which is precise and focused, yet effortless as well.

Statement by the jury
Uncompromising robustness and unconditional reliability are characteristic highlights of this camera slider, which also has strong visual appeal.

Der Magic Carpet Pro ist ein widerstandsfähiger, leicht aufzubauender Kamera-Slider, der den Anforderungen professionellen Filmschaffens gerecht wird und auch in ästhetischer Hinsicht überzeugt. Das transportable und beliebig erweiterbare Ausrüstungssystem sorgt dank seiner durchdachten Gestaltung und des zuschaltbaren Schwungrads selbst mit schweren Kameras in anspruchsvollen Umgebungen für ruckelfreie Kamerafahrten und garantiert Bildmaterial in Studioqualität. Dabei ermöglicht der Slider auch bei Außenaufnahmen präzises, konzentriertes und dennoch müheloses Arbeiten.

Begründung der Jury
Kompromisslose Robustheit und unbedingte Zuverlässigkeit prägen den Charakter dieses Kamera-Sliders, der auch optisch zu gefallen weiß.

Genie 2
Camera Motion Controller
Kamera-Motion-Controller

Manufacturer
Syrp, Auckland, New Zealand
In-house design
Chris Thomson, James Allen, Sam Blok
Web
www.syrp.co.nz

The design of the compact, portable Genie 2 camera motion controller is focused on the user's needs and requirements. The controller offers the option of setting key frames and executing precisely repeatable, programmed camera movements along three axes. The technology for this is elegantly concealed, yet the points of interaction for the user are clearly accentuated. The controller is operated using the built-in display or an app. Moreover, the accessory is compatible with all common tripod and slider brands, even with custom-made camera dollies.

Statement by the jury
The Genie 2 is a compact camera accessory enabling precise camera movements, while also offering good compatibility.

Bei der Gestaltung des kompakten, portablen Kamera-Motion-Controllers Genie 2 standen die Bedürfnisse des Benutzers im Vordergrund. Der Controller bietet die Möglichkeit, Keyframes zu setzen und programmierte Kamerabewegungen auf drei Achsen präzise wiederholbar auszuführen. Die Technik hierfür ist elegant verborgen, die Interaktionspunkte für den Benutzer sind jedoch klar herausgestellt. Die Bedienung erfolgt über das eingebaute Display oder über eine App. Zudem ist das Accessoire mit allen gängigen Stativ- und Slidermarken, selbst spezialangefertigten Kamerawagen, anwendbar.

Begründung der Jury
Genie 2 ist ein kompakt gebautes Kameraaccessoire, das für präzise Kamerabewegungen sorgt und darüber hinaus über eine gute Kompatibilität verfügt.

FLO
Camera Gimbal Stabiliser
Kamera-Gimbal

Manufacturer
OCLU, Scottsdale, Arizona, USA
In-house design
Firas Kittaneh
Design
WMP Creative (Hugo Martin),
Tubney, Oxfordshire, United Kingdom
Web
shop.oclu.com
www.wmpcreative.com

The Flo is a lightweight, robust and waterproof three-axis camera gimbal stabiliser made of aluminium which was not exclusively designed for handheld use. The handgrip, which houses an internal tripod, is detachable so that the gimbal is compatible with a range of accessory parts by the manufacturer. This offers a multitude of possible configurations guaranteeing high-grade, blur-free shots. The Flo is designed for eight hours of continuous operation, or four hours when simultaneously supplying a camera with power.

Statement by the jury
With its numerous configuration options, the Flo three-axis camera gimbal stabiliser offers enormous flexibility and, in addition, meets high demands with its robustness.

Flo ist ein in leichter Aluminium-Bauweise hergestellter, robuster und wasserbeständiger 3-Achsen-Kamera-Gimbal, der nicht allein für die Verwendung als Handheld entwickelt wurde. Sein mit einem eingebauten Stativ versehener Griff ist abnehmbar, wodurch der Gimbal mit einer Reihe von Zubehörteilen des Herstellers verwendbar ist. Dies bietet eine Vielzahl möglicher Konfigurationen, die hochwertige, wackelfreie Aufnahmen gewährleisten. Flo kann für acht Stunden im Dauerbetrieb eingesetzt werden oder für vier Stunden, wenn gleichzeitig eine Kamera mit Strom versorgt wird.

Begründung der Jury
Der 3-Achsen-Kamera-Gimbal Flo bietet mit seinen zahlreichen Konfigurationsmöglichkeiten enorme Flexibilität und ist zudem durch seine Robustheit hohen Anforderungen gewachsen.

EPD-41A-D01
Broadcast Camera Accessory
Fernsehkamerazubehör

Manufacturer
FUJIFILM Corporation, Tokyo, Japan
In-house design
Hiroyuki Sakai
Web
http://design.fujifilm.com

The EPD-41A-D01 is an operating unit for adjusting the correct focus from a distance with a cable. Conceived for shooting footage from helicopters or vehicles, it is also useful for recording concerts and nature or animal images. As the modern 4K technology requires a high degree of precision, the design of the unit is geared to fast and exact operability. The star-shaped centre element guarantees easy handling of the operating unit even under difficult conditions, for instance with gloves.

Statement by the jury
The EPD-41A-D01 is a highly specialised accessory for TV cameras, providing easy handling even under adverse conditions.

Bei EPD-41A-D01 handelt es sich um eine Bedieneinheit, mit der man den richtigen Fokus aus der Entfernung über ein Kabel einstellen kann. Sie ist für das Filmen aus Hubschraubern oder Fahrzeugen gedacht, aber auch bei Konzerten, Natur- oder Tieraufnahmen nützlich. Da die moderne 4K-Technologie große Genauigkeit erfordert, ist die Gestaltung der Einheit auf schnelle und exakte Bedienbarkeit ausgelegt. Der sternförmige Mittelteil garantiert, dass sich das Bedienelement selbst unter schwierigen Bedingungen, beispielsweise mit Handschuhen, leicht handhaben lässt.

Begründung der Jury
EPD-41A-D01 ist ein hoch spezialisiertes Zubehörteil für Fernsehkameras, das selbst unter widrigen Umständen eine einfache Handhabung gewährleistet.

Fujifilm EVF-TL1
Finder Tilt Adapter
Kamerasucher-Winkeladapter

Manufacturer
FUJIFILM Corporation, Tokyo, Japan
In-house design
Masazumi Imai
Web
http://design.fujifilm.com

The EVF-TL1 tilt adapter is an accessory for the GFX medium-format camera system by Fuji. The adapter is mounted between camera body and viewfinder so that the latter can be tilted by 45 degrees in both directions on the horizontal axis, and by 90 degrees upwards on the vertical axis. This offers more flexibility when looking through the viewfinder. The plain, high-quality aluminium accessory fits with the GFX housing and is characterised by robustness. The adapter can be locked onto both axes in any position.

Statement by the jury
Adaptability and high utility value are the outstanding features of the EVF-TL1 tilt adapter.

Der Winkeladapter EVF-TL1 ist ein Zubehör für das GFX-Mittelformat-Kamerasystem von Fuji. Der Adapter wird zwischen Kameragehäuse und Sucher angebracht, sodass sich der Sucher auf der horizontalen Achse um 45 Grad in beide Richtungen und auf der vertikalen Achse um 90 Grad nach oben schwenken lässt. Das bietet mehr Flexibilität beim Blick in den Sucher. Das schlichte, qualitativ hochwertige Zubehörteil aus Aluminium passt zum GFX-Gehäuse und zeichnet sich durch Robustheit aus. Der Adapter kann auf beiden Achsen an beliebiger Stelle festgestellt werden.

Begründung der Jury
Anpassungsfähigkeit und hoher praktischer Nutzen sind die herausragenden Merkmale des Winkeladapters EVF-TL1.

GorillaPod 5K Video PRO
Video Camera Tripod
Videokamera-Stativ

Manufacturer
Vitec Imaging Solutions S.p.A.,
Cassola (Vicenza), Italy
In-house design
Noah Balmer
Web
www.manfrotto.com

The GorillaPod 5K Video Pro is a versatile tripod for video cameras with a weight of up to 4 kg. With flexible legs, it enables professional-grade videos to be shot from a large number of angles. The solid fluid head facilitates smooth pan and tilt camera movements and has a removable and foldable pan bar for extra portability. In addition, the GorillaPod is equipped with a detachable bracket mount and an arm for additional accessories such as microphones or LED lights.

Statement by the jury
The clever design of the GorillaPod 5K Video Pro video camera tripod gives it a high degree of reliability and flexibility.

GorillaPod 5K Video Pro ist ein vielseitiges Stativ für Videokameras mit einem Gewicht von bis zu 4 kg. Mit seinen flexiblen Beinen sorgt es dafür, dass aus einer Vielzahl von Blickwinkeln professionelle Videos gedreht werden können. Der stabile Fluid-Videokopf ermöglicht sanfte Schwenk- und Kippbewegungen der Kamera und verfügt über eine abnehmbare Schwenkstange, die die Beweglichkeit noch einmal erhöht. Darüber hinaus ist das GorillaPod mit einer abnehmbaren Halterung und einem Arm für zusätzliches Zubehör wie Mikrofone oder LED-Leuchten ausgestattet.

Begründung der Jury
Die durchdachte Gestaltung des Videokamera-Stativs GorillaPod 5K Video Pro verleiht ihm ein hohes Maß an Zuverlässigkeit und Flexibilität.

Gitzo Mini Traveler
Mini Tripod
Mini-Stativ

Manufacturer
Vitec Imaging Solutions S.p.A.,
Cassola (Vicenza), Italy
Design
MM Design (Alex Terzariol), Bolzano, Italy
Web
www.manfrotto.com
www.mmdesign.eu/en

Mini Traveler is dedicated to professional photographers and amateurs who use CSC/DSLR cameras with small lenses. Made of state-of-the-art carbon eXact tubes, it weighs only 265 grams and supports up to 3 kg. Its performance is very high in terms of minimum footprint, for low angle shots, when taking backstage pictures. The new Pull&Fix selector system allows to choose between two leg angles for better stability. It is available in black or in the classic Gitzo Noir Décor style.

Statement by the jury
The Mini Traveler is a small, mobile tripod with a design optimised for reliability and durability.

Mini Traveler wendet sich an professionelle Fotografen und Amateure, die CSC oder DSLR Kameras mit kleineren Objektiven benutzen. Das aus hochwertigen Carbon-eXact-Rohren bestehende Stativ ist 265 Gramm leicht und verfügt über eine Traglast von 3 kg. Mit einer geringen Stellfläche sowie der Möglichkeit aus tiefen Positionen zu fotografieren ist es beispielsweise hervorragend für den Backstage-Bereich geeignet. Das neuartige Pull&Fix System bietet zudem zwei stabile Anstellwinkel. Das Stativ ist in schwarz oder im klassischen Gitzo Noir-Décor erhältlich.

Begründung der Jury
Der Mini Traveler ist ein kleines, mobiles Stativ, dessen Gestaltung Zuverlässigkeit und Langlebigkeit optimiert.

Befree GT carbon α
Travel Tripod
Reisestativ

Manufacturer
Vitec Imaging Solutions S.p.A.,
Cassola (Vicenza), Italy
In-house design
Web
www.manfrotto.com

Befree GT carbon α is dedicated to professional photographers who need excellent performance in a particularly lightweight format. Being the perfect combination of portability and impressive strength, it supports equipment weighing up to 10 kg. Its ergonomic design enables quick and easy setup. The plate is designed to match Sony α7 and Sony α9 cameras to ensure very good grip, even in the most angled camera shots, for impressive camera stability and image sharpness.

Statement by the jury
The design of the Befree GT carbon α travel tripod is geared towards functionality and characterised by user-friendliness and good ergonomics.

Befree GT carbon α richtet sich speziell an professionellen Fotografen, die auf besonders leichtes Zubehör mit hoher Leistungsfähigkeit angewiesen sind. Als gelungene Kombination aus Mobilität und Robustheit besitzt es eine Tragkraft von 10 kg. Seine ergonomische Gestaltung ermöglicht einen schnellen Aufbau. Die Kopfplatte bietet den Sony Kameras α7 und α9 selbst beim Fotografieren aus ungewöhnlichen Winkeln sicheren Halt und Stabilität und sorgt so auch für hervorragende Bildschärfe.

Begründung der Jury
Die Gestaltung des Reisestativs Befree GT carbon α ist auf Funktionalität angelegt und zeichnet sich zudem durch Benutzerfreundlichkeit und gute Ergonomie aus.

iFootage Gazelle TA7
Tripod
Dreibeinstativ

Manufacturer
iFootage International (HK) Limited,
Hong Kong
In-house design
Xihua Zhu
Web
www.ifootagegear.com

The iFootage Gazelle TA7 tripod is made of high-grade materials guaranteeing high stability and rigidity as well as longer durability. Laid out for a load of up to 7 kg, the tripod is equipped with the patented FastBowl camera head mount and with snap locks on the tripod legs. This ensures easy setup and quick attachment, release and adjustment of the cameras used. Good processing and an appealing appearance complement the impressive functionality of the tripod.

Statement by the jury
With its high-grade processing, this photo tripod is a reliable piece of equipment which captivates with user-friendliness and striking aesthetics.

Das Dreibeinstativ iFootage Gazelle TA7 ist aus hochwertigen Materialien gefertigt, die eine gute Festigkeit und Steifigkeit aufweisen und bessere Haltbarkeit garantieren. Das für eine Last von bis zu 7 kg ausgelegte Utensil ist mit der patentierten FastBowl-Kamerakopfbefestigung und Schnappverschlüssen an den Stativbeinen ausgestattet. So ist ein einfacher Aufbau und das leichte Anbringen, Lösen und Ausrichten der verwendeten Kameras gewährleistet. Eine gute Verarbeitung und ein ansprechendes Erscheinungsbild ergänzen die beeindruckende Funktionalität des Stativs.

Begründung der Jury
Dieses hochwertig verarbeitete Fotostativ ist ein zuverlässiger Ausrüstungsgegenstand, der durch Benutzerfreundlichkeit und eine reizvolle Ästhetik besticht.

Weebill LAB
Camera Gimbal Stabiliser
Kamera-Gimbal

Manufacturer
Guilin Zhishen Information
Technology Co., Ltd.,
Guilin, China
In-house design
Zheng Bangming, Wu Caner, Ye Zilong
Web
www.zhiyun-tech.com

The Weebill LAB is an ergonomic gimbal stabiliser which prevents camera shake when shooting free-handed videos. The grip can be angled, allowing the use of the camera in different positions. It also functions as a tripod when flipped open. Additional innovations are the wireless image transmission and the ViaTouch system, supporting the monitoring, framing and parameter control of the camera. Due to the outstanding compatibility of the gimbal, it may be used in conjunction with multiple digital devices.

Statement by the jury
The Weebill LAB excites with its innovative, ergonomic design and a range of new functions. It also offers excellent compatibility.

Weebill LAB ist ein ergonomischer Kamera-Gimbal, der bei Freihand-Videoaufnahmen Unschärfen durch Verwackeln verhindert. Der Griff kann abgewinkelt werden, wodurch die Kamera in verschiedenen Positionen gehalten werden kann, oder aufgeklappt als Stativ fungieren. Weitere Innovationen sind die kabellose Bildübertragung und das ViaTouch-System, das die Überwachung, Bildeinstellung und Parametersteuerung der Kamera unterstützt. Aufgrund der hervorragenden Kompatibilität des Gimbals können eine Vielzahl digitaler Geräte mit ihm verwendet werden.

Begründung der Jury
Der Weebill LAB begeistert mit seiner innovativen, ergonomischen Gestaltung und einer Reihe neuer Funktionen sowie einer hervorragenden Kompatibilität.

Wiral© LITE
Cable Camera System
Seilkamerasystem

Manufacturer
Wiral Technologies AS,
Trondheim, Norway
In-house design
Eivind Sæter, Helle Grande, Øivind Aabye,
Osmund Bøe, Jonathan Link Selnes
Web
www.wiralcam.com

This compact, extremely mobile cable camera system features an intuitively remote-controllable direct drive motor with three speeds. The system enables time-lapse shots down to a speed of 3 metres per hour and high-speed action shots at up to 35 km/h. For simplified attachment, the Wiral Lite is equipped with the Quick-Reel cable spool system and a 50 metre long cable. The system permits the use of smartphones, action cameras and small 360-degree cameras with a weight of up to 1.5 kg.

Statement by the jury
The Wiral Lite is a reliable, intuitively operable cable camera system which offers many options thanks to its compatibility.

Dieses kompakte, äußerst mobile Seilkamerasystem verfügt über einen intuitiv fernsteuerbaren Direktantriebsmotor mit drei Geschwindigkeiten. Dabei lassen sich bei 3 Metern pro Stunde Zeitrafferaufnahmen und bei 35 km/h Actionaufnahmen machen. Um die Anbringung zu vereinfachen, ist das Wiral Lite mit dem Quick-Reel-Seilspulensystem und einer 50 Meter langen Leine ausgestattet. Mit dem System lassen sich Smartphones, Actionkameras und kleine 360-Grad-Kameras bis zu einem Gewicht von 1,5 kg problemlos verwenden.

Begründung der Jury
Wiral Lite ist ein verlässliches, intuitiv zu bedienendes Seilkamerasystem, das durch seine Kompatibilität viele Möglichkeiten bietet.

LitraPro
Camera LED Light
LED-Aufsteckleuchte

Manufacturer
Litra, San Diego, California, USA
In-house design
Scott Gant
Web
www.litra.com

The LitraPro is a compact bicolour mini light for cameras. The brightness and colour temperature can be controlled via Bluetooth by a smartphone or directly from its display. Users have the option to choose between factory or user-defined presets. The light with its robust case also allows for underwater shots and impresses in particular with regard to light performance, luminosity and beam angle. The colour-rendering index of the LitraPro, which can be used with GoPro, single-lens reflex or mirrorless system cameras as well as with a tripod, also speaks for its quality.

Statement by the jury
The technically highly advanced LitraPro camera LED light convinces with strong performance and flexibility and with a powerful design language.

LitraPro ist eine kompakte Bi-Color-Minileuchte für Kameras, bei der Helligkeit und Farbtemperatur über Bluetooth von einem Smartphone oder direkt von ihrem Display aus steuerbar sind. Dabei können Nutzer auf werkseitige oder eigene Einstellungen zurückgreifen. Die Leuchte, deren robustes Gehäuse auch Unterwasseraufnahmen zulässt, imponiert vor allem im Hinblick auf Lichtleistung, Leuchtstärke und Abstrahlwinkel. Auch der Farbwiedergabeindex der LitraPro, die mit GoPro-, Spiegelreflex- oder spiegellosen Systemkameras sowie mit einem Stativ einsetzbar ist, spricht für ihre Qualität.

Begründung der Jury
Die technisch hochentwickelte LED-Aufsteckleuchte LitraPro überzeugt mit Leistungsfähigkeit und Flexibilität sowie einer kraftvollen Formensprache.

Imp Air-Blower
Lens Cleaner
Objektivreiniger

Manufacturer
Shanghai Jieyong Technology Co., Ltd., Shanghai, China
In-house design
Haochen Wang
Web
www.51vsgo.com

The Imp Air-Blower is a cleaning accessory specifically designed to remove dust and deposits from camera lenses. It is a handy air blower which does not physically contact the lens, enabling careful and gentle cleaning without soiling the lens in the process. The elegant, dust-repellent lens cleaner features an exchangeable air filtration system which cleans the air at the inlet valve. A special counterweight prevents the air blower from rolling around on the table after it is set down.

Statement by the jury
As a functional cleaning utensil, the cleverly designed Imp Air-Blower impresses with its carefully considered user-friendliness.

Der Imp Air-Blower ist ein Reinigungszubehör, das speziell dafür gedacht ist, Staub und Ablagerungen von Kameraobjektiven zu entfernen. Er ist ein handlicher Blasebalg, der bei seiner Benutzung keinen physischen Kontakt zur Linse hat und sie dadurch schonend reinigt, ohne selbst weitere Verunreinigungen zu verursachen. Der elegante, staubabweisende Objektivreiniger verfügt über ein austauschbares Luftfiltersystem, das die Ausstoßluft am Einlassventil filtert. Des Weiteren verhindert ein Gegengewicht, dass der Blasebalg nach dem Ablegen wegrollt.

Begründung der Jury
Als funktionales Reinigungsutensil überzeugt der clever gestaltete Imp Air-Blower mit wohldurchdachter Anwenderfreundlichkeit.

Atomos Ninja V
Field Monitor-Recorder
Videomonitor und Rekorder für Außenaufnahmen

Manufacturer
Atomos,
Port Melbourne, Victoria, Australia
In-house design
Jeromy Young, Naofumi Yoneda
Web
www.atomos.com

The Ninja V is a portable video monitor and recorder which unlocks the full image capability of different cameras when connected to them. The device features an elegant aluminium polycarbonate housing and offers the option to view or play HDR image and video content, either directly or on an HDR compatible television. It is also capable of reliably storing recordings. The symbols on the display with muted colours are easily comprehensible. An expansion interface facilitates connection to local networks.

Statement by the jury
The easily operated Ninja V is a technically sophisticated device in a compact design, convincing with versatility and compatibility.

Der Ninja V ist ein mobiler Monitor und Rekorder, der das volle Potential verschiedene Kameras ausschöpft. Das Gerät verfügt über ein elegantes Aluminium-Polycarbonat-Gehäuse und bietet die Möglichkeit, Bild- und Videoinhalte in HDR-Qualität direkt oder über HDR-fähige Fernsehgeräte anzusehen oder abzuspielen. Darüber hinaus kann es Aufnahmen zuverlässig speichern. Die Symbole auf dem in gedämpften Farben gehaltenen Display sind leicht verständlich. Eine Erweiterungsschnittstelle erlaubt den Anschluss an lokale Netzwerke.

Begründung der Jury
Der einfach zu bedienende Ninja V ist ein kompakt gestaltetes, technisch ausgereiftes Gerät, das mit Vielseitigkeit und Kompatibilität besticht.

Air-Move
Cleaning Untensil
Reinigungsutensil

Manufacturer
Shanghai Jieyong Technology Co., Ltd.,
Shanghai, China
In-house design
Haochen Wang
Web
www.51vsgo.com

This cleaning utensil helps to keep the camera free from dust, thus fulfilling the requirement for the successful shooting of high-quality images. The Air-Move can be used to clean the camera both inside and out. The well-designed, exchangeable head of the blower consists of an air outlet nozzle and filter system. This ensures that no dust can enter the interior of the cleaning accessory, which is also equipped with a dust-repellent coating.

Statement by the jury
The Air-Move is an elegant cleaning accessory for cameras which inspires with its practically oriented design.

Dieses Kamerautensil hilft, die Kamera staubfrei zu halten, und schafft so die Voraussetzung für das Gelingen qualitativ hochwertiger Fotos. Der Air-Move kann eingesetzt werden, um die Kamera sowohl von außen als auch von innen zu reinigen. Der durchdacht gestaltete, austauschbare Kopf des Blasebalgs besteht dabei aus einer Luftaustrittsdüse und einem Filtersystem, das dafür sorgt, dass kein Staub in das Innere des mit einer staubabweisenden Schicht überzogenen Reinigungsaccessoires gelangen kann.

Begründung der Jury
Der Air-Move ist ein elegantes Reinigungszubehör für Kameras, das durch seine praxisnahe Gestaltung besticht.

Blackmagic Camera Control Panel
Remote Camera Control Unit
Bedienpult zur Fernsteuerung von Kameras

Manufacturer
Blackmagic Design,
Melbourne, Australia

In-house design
Blackmagic Design

Web
www.blackmagicdesign.com

reddot award 2019
best of the best

In perfect order
At large events or live concerts, multiple cameras are often used to capture footage, providing viewers with a richer experience. The Blackmagic Camera Control Panel is used for the remote control of live cameras, allowing real-time adjustments to technical settings such as iris, shutter and colour balance. Designed specifically for use within the scope of live productions like concerts and sporting events, the control panel costs considerably less than a typical single-camera system, allowing simultaneous control of up to four cameras. The iconic design vocabulary of this control panel is characterised by an impressively clear hierarchical layout of physical controls. Organised into clear and self-explanatory functional zones, it promotes intuitive operation of the most important functions. It features multi-axis joysticks with refined haptic quality for simultaneous, single-handed tuning of iris and black levels. Another huge advantage is that, unlike conventional controllers, this panel does not require fixed desk installation. It thus ensures not only efficient, flexible setups thanks to its easy portability, it also allows control in just a quarter of the space. With its elegant and balanced aesthetics and finely tuned colour scheme, the Camera Control Panel ties in seamlessly with the Blackmagic camera family.

Perfekte Ordnung
Bei Großevents oder im Rahmen von Live-Konzerten werden oftmals mehrere Kameras eingesetzt, um den Zuschauern ein umfassenderes Erlebnis zu bieten. Das Blackmagic Camera Control Panel dient der Fernsteuerung von Live-Kameras. Es erlaubt die Einstellung technischer Parameter wie Blende, Verschlusszeit und Farbbalance in Echtzeit. Speziell für Live-Produktionen wie Konzerte und Sportereignisse entworfen, ist es wesentlich kostengünstiger als ein Einzelkamerasystem, wobei es die gleichzeitige Steuerung von bis zu vier Kameras ermöglicht. Prägend für die ikonische Formensprache dieses Bedienpults ist eine beeindruckend klare hierarchische Anordnung der physischen Steuerelemente. Es ist in übersichtliche, sich selbsterklärende Funktionszonen unterteilt und gewährleistet eine intuitive Kontrolle der Funktionen. Mehrachsige Joysticks bieten eine verbesserte Haptik für die gleichzeitige, mit nur einer Hand ausführbare Einstellung von Blenden- und Schwarzwerten. Ein großer Vorteil ist zudem, dass, anders als bei herkömmlichen Controllern, keine feste Installation erforderlich ist. Dieses Bedienpult erlaubt eine effiziente, flexible Einrichtung dank seiner Tragbarkeit und benötigt nur ein Viertel der sonst üblichen Fläche. Mit seiner gleichermaßen ausgewogenen wie eleganten Ästhetik und fein abgestimmten Farbgebung fügt sich das Camera Control Panel nahtlos in die Blackmagic-Kamerafamilie ein.

Statement by the jury
In terms of design, the Blackmagic Camera Control Panel has managed to provide a perfectly structured, compact unit for the remote control of multiple live cameras. The clear form and aesthetics have successfully simplified the technological complexity and give users a sense of mastery. This portable control panel allows real-time adjustments to many technical settings. Its multi-axis joysticks are pleasing to the touch and offer intuitive hands-on camera control.

Begründung der Jury
Gestalterisch gelingt mit dem Blackmagic Camera Control Panel die Bereitstellung einer perfekt strukturierten, kompakten Einheit für die Fernsteuerung von Live-Kameras. Die klare Ästhetik und Form reduziert die Komplexität der Technologie und vermittelt Nutzern ein sicheres Gefühl. Das transportable Bedienpult ermöglicht in Echtzeit die Anpassung vieler technischer Einstellungen. Seine haptisch angenehmen, mehrachsigen Joysticks bieten dabei eine intuitive Steuerung.

Designer portrait
See page 48
Siehe Seite 48

Stellina
Smart Telescope
Intelligentes Teleskop

Manufacturer
Vaonis,
Clapiers, France

Design
Ova Design,
Ivry-sur-Seine, France

Web
www.vaonis.com
www.ovadesign.com

reddot award 2019
best of the best

Conquering new worlds
Telescopes have always had something magical about them throughout history, as the view they allow of distant worlds truly inspires the imagination. The aim of designing Stellina (Italian for "little star") has been to refine and simplify the design of a telescope, making it easier to use and opening the doors to a wider audience. Stellina has been developed as a smart and connected device that offers a simple operation and thus user-friendly experience to discover the universe: galaxies, nebulae, star clusters, the moon or the sun. This thoughtfully designed telescope offers many innovative features that go hand in hand with modern multimedia functionality. It thus automatically finds the stars and captures pictures instantly, stacking them live on a tablet or smartphone to reveal their details and colours. The Stellina app allows users to share their pictures on social media, interact with the worldwide Stellina community or learn more about astronomy through the educational content that the app provides. Combining electronics, optics and mechanics of high precision, this manually assembled device showcases a sleek and compact design that integrates a lens and an embedded computer, as well as different motors and several sensors that allow the telescope to adapt easily to changes in its environment such as rain or humidity.

Eroberung neuer Welten
Das Teleskop hatte in seiner Geschichte stets etwas Magisches an sich, denn der Blick hindurch entführt in ferne Welten und beflügelt die Phantasie. Das Ziel der Entwicklung von Stellina (italienisch für „kleiner Stern") war die gestalterische Vereinfachung und Verbesserung des Teleskops, um es einem größeren Nutzerkreis zugänglich zu machen. Stellina ist konzipiert als ein intelligentes und vernetztes Gerät, das eine einfache und benutzerfreundliche Bedienbarkeit bietet, um das Weltall zu entdecken: Galaxien, Nebel, Sternhaufen, den Mond oder die Sonne. Dieses durchdacht gestaltete Teleskop verfügt dazu über viele innovative Eigenschaften, die mit einer zeitgemäßen Multimedialität einhergehen. Es findet Sterne selbsttätig, nimmt davon sofort Bilder auf und zeigt sie live auf einem Tablet oder Smartphone in hoher Detail- und Farbtreue. Über eine dazugehörige App können Nutzer ihre Bilder in sozialen Medien teilen, mit der weltweiten Stellina-Community interagieren oder durch die von der App bereitgestellten Lerninhalte mehr über Astronomie erfahren. Hochpräzise Elektronik, Optik und Mechanik kombinierend, vereint das mit großer Sorgfalt in Handarbeit montierte Gerät in einer schlanken und kompakten Gestaltung ein Objektiv, einen integrierten Computer sowie verschiedene Motoren und Sensoren. Dadurch kann es sich an Veränderungen in seiner Umgebung wie Feuchtigkeit oder Regen gut anpassen.

Statement by the jury
Stellina embodies an aesthetically and functionally impressive interpretation of the traditional telescope. Its elegant design merges high-precision electronics, optics and mechanics forming a captivating unit. Following a fascinating approach, it provides the ability to easily find stars, to capture them in high-resolution images and to share one's individual observation results with a worldwide community via the Stellina app.

Begründung der Jury
Stellina verkörpert eine ästhetisch und funktional beeindruckende Interpretation des traditionellen Teleskops. Seine elegante Gestaltung vereint hochpräzise elektronische, optische und mechanische Elemente zu einer eindrucksvollen Einheit. Auf faszinierende Weise bietet es die Möglichkeit, Sterne problemlos zu finden, sie fotografisch mit hoher Auflösung zu erfassen und die Beobachtungsergebnisse dank der dazugehörigen Stellina-App mit einer weltweiten Community zu teilen.

Designer portrait
See page 50
Siehe Seite 50

Huddly IQ
Video Conference Camera
Videokonferenzkamera

Manufacturer
Huddly AS, Oslo, Norway
In-house design
Stein Ove Eriksen, Knut Helge Teppan,
Mats Gabriel Love Johansen,
Mona Kleven Lauritzen, Niklas Schmidt
Design
Frost Produkt AS
(Sindre Widerberg, Kjartan Vaaland,
Karin Ekwall, Sondre Frost Urstad),
Oslo, Norway
Web
www.huddly.com
www.frostprodukt.com

The Huddly IQ is an intelligent camera for video conferencing. During its design phase, practical experience flowed into the process and resulted in a high-quality device. The camera provides first-class optics and an advanced interface, accommodated in an elegant aluminium housing. The Huddly IQ offers a 150-degree field of view and a microphone of outstanding quality. Innovative processor technology allows for an analysis of the environment in order to automatically adjust different parameters, for instance the image field when the number of participants in the conference changes.

Statement by the jury
As an innovative camera for video conferencing, the Huddly IQ is strongly geared to the practical context, meeting these demands through its sophisticated technical refinements.

Die Huddly IQ ist eine intelligente Videokonferenzkamera, bei deren Entwicklung praktische Erfahrungen in ein hochwertiges Gerät eingeflossen sind. Das Ergebnis ist eine Kamera mit erstklassiger Optik und einer fortschrittlichen Schnittstelle, untergebracht in einem eleganten Aluminiumgehäuse. Huddly IQ bietet ein Sichtfeld von 150 Grad und ein hervorragendes Mikrofon. Innovative Prozessortechnik ermöglicht es, die Umgebung zu analysieren, um verschiedene Parameter, beispielsweise den Bildausschnitt bei veränderter Teilnehmerzahl, automatisch anzupassen.

Begründung der Jury
Als innovative Videokonferenzkamera zeigt die Huddly IQ einen starken Bezug zur Praxis, deren Anforderungen sie durch technische Raffinesse löst.

Flir Duo
Dual-Sensor Thermal Camera
Dual-Sensor-Wärmebildkamera

Manufacturer
FLIR Systems, Inc., Goleta, California, USA
In-house design
May Mao, Sonja Song
Web
www.flir.com

The lightweight and compact Flir Duo is a high-resolution dual-sensor camera designed for use with drones. The remotely controllable device includes a daylight and an infrared sensor for recording both images and videos. Objects can be made visible from over 100 metres away even in complete darkness, smoke and light fog. Using the MSX image-processing algorithm, the camera processes information from both sensors to attain a very sharp dual-spectrum image.

Statement by the jury
The Flir Duo is a technically and functionally sophisticated camera, which, due to its light and compact construction, lends itself to flexible use.

Die leichte und kompakte Flir Duo ist eine hochauflösende Dual-Sensor-Kamera, die für den Einsatz mit Drohnen entwickelt wurde. Das fernsteuerbare Gerät verfügt über einen Tageslicht- und einen Infrarotsensor, mit denen man sowohl Bilder als auch Videos aufzeichnen kann. Objekte werden dabei aus einer Entfernung von mehr als 100 Metern selbst bei völliger Dunkelheit, Rauchentwicklung oder leichtem Nebel erkannt. Mit Hilfe des MSX-Bildverarbeitungsalgorithmus verarbeitet die Kamera Informationen beider Sensoren zu einem hochwertigen Zweikanalbild.

Begründung der Jury
Die Flir Duo ist eine technisch wie funktional ausgereifte Kamera, die durch ihre leichte und kompakte Bauweise flexibel einsetzbar ist.

Bosma X1
Smart Home Camera
Smart-Home-Kamera

Manufacturer
BOSMA Corp., Guangzhou, China
In-house design
Jason Wong
Web
www.bosmasmarthome.com

The design of the X1 places a focus on security, which is underscored by its robust yet aesthetic look. The high-performance camera, with its wide-angle lens and night vision functionality, ensures that the user will not miss anything critical. Thanks to its good connectivity, this also holds true when the user is not at home. Different detection systems and a siren provide additional protection, and the enhanced interaction with other devices allows for the integration into new or already existing Smart Home systems.

Statement by the jury
The easy-to-use X1 Smart Home camera impresses with well-conceived functionality and an elegant appearance.

Die Gestaltung der Kamera X1 legte das Hauptaugenmerk auf das Thema Sicherheit, was durch ihr ästhetisch gelungenes, robustes Aussehen unterstrichen wird. Die leistungsstarke Kamera und das Winkelobjektiv sowie eine Nachtsichtfunktion stellen sicher, dass dem Benutzer nichts entgeht, und dank guter Konnektivität gilt das auch, wenn er nicht zu Hause ist. Verschiedene Detektionssysteme und eine Sirene sorgen für zusätzlichen Schutz, und die verbesserte Interaktion mit anderen Geräten ermöglicht die Integration in neue oder schon bestehende Smart-Home-Systeme.

Begründung der Jury
Die einfach zu bedienende Smart-Home-Kamera X1 beeindruckt mit wohldurchdachter Funktionalität und einem eleganten Erscheinungsbild.

CD2-XT
CCTV Camera
Überwachungskamera

Manufacturer
r2p GmbH, Flensburg, Germany
In-house design
Web
www.r2p.com

The CD2-XT is a cube-shaped, compact camera which delivers exploitable video footage even under poor lighting conditions thanks to its True WDR sensors. It is protected from unauthorised access by employing AES-type encryption. The camera is used in rail vehicles for surveillance and the recording of the progress of the journey. Its powder-coated aluminium housing is produced in all available RAL colours and is suitable for concealed installation. Via Wi-Fi and a flexible smartphone app, quick access to the recordings is possible.

Statement by the jury
The technically sophisticated CD2-XT surveillance camera impresses with a compact form which enables easy embedding into its environment.

Die CD2-XT ist eine würfelförmige, kompakte Kamera, die dank ihrer True-WDR-Sensoren selbst bei schlechten Lichtverhältnissen verwertbares Videomaterial liefert und durch AES-Verschlüsselung vor unbefugtem Zugriff geschützt ist. Eingesetzt wird sie in Schienenfahrzeugen zur Aufnahme und Überwachung des Fahrtverlaufs. Ihr pulverbeschichtetes Aluminiumgehäuse wird in allen RAL-Farben produziert und eignet sich für den verdeckten Einbau. Über Wi-Fi und eine flexible Smartphone-App kann schnell auf die Aufzeichnungen zugegriffen werden.

Begründung der Jury
Die technisch ausgereifte Überwachungskamera CD2-XT besticht mit ihrer komprimierten Form, durch die sie gut in ihre Umgebung eingebettet werden kann.

SX800 40xIS
Surveillance Camera
Überwachungskamera

Manufacturer
FUJIFILM Corporation, Tokyo, Japan
In-house design
Hiroyuki Sakai
Web
http://design.fujifilm.com

The SX800 40xIS is a camera designed for remote surveillance. Equipment employed for such tasks is frequently exposed to difficult conditions, such as strong winds or heat haze. In order to overcome such hindrances, the camera is equipped with a telephoto lens which is supported by high-grade image processing and stabilisation technology to ensure sufficiently strong image quality. In addition, the round, elegant housing made of anodised, resin-sealed aluminium guarantees the robustness and durability required.

Statement by the jury
With its technical qualities and evident robustness, the SX800 40xIS is perfectly equipped for the intended contexts.

Die SX800 40xIS ist eine für Fernüberwachung entwickelte Kamera. Eine bei solchen Aufgaben eingesetzte Ausrüstung ist oft schwierigen Bedingungen ausgesetzt, wie beispielsweise starkem Wind oder Hitzeflimmern. Um diese Widrigkeiten auszugleichen, ist das Gerät mit einem Telezoom ausgerüstet, der von hochwertiger Bildverarbeitungs- und Bildstabilisationstechnologie unterstützt wird, was eine ausreichend hohe Bildqualität gewährleistet. Darüber hinaus garantiert das runde, elegante Gehäuse aus schwarz eloxiertem, harzversiegeltem Aluminium die nötige Robustheit.

Begründung der Jury
Mit ihren technischen Qualitäten und der gebotenen Robustheit ist die SX800 40xIS perfekt für die ihr zugedachten Aufgaben ausgestattet.

Abus Advanced
Surveillance Camera Series
Überwachungskamera-Serie

Manufacturer
ABUS Security-Center GmbH & Co. KG,
Affing, Germany
In-house design
Web
www.abus.com

The dome cameras of the Advanced series, which are controllable via an app, include three models guaranteeing usable footage even under extreme lighting conditions. A highlight of the series is the innovative design enabling easy mounting. After attaching the baseplate, the camera module and the camera dome are mounted. This considerably reduces installation time and the risk of accidents. The dust- and waterproof housing is shock-resistant and protects against damage.

Statement by the jury
The Abus Advanced surveillance camera series convinces with its functionality. The innovative mounting option reduces installation time and enhances workplace safety.

Die über eine App steuerbaren Dome-Kameras der Advanced-Reihe bestehen aus drei Modellen, die selbst bei extremen Lichtverhältnissen zuverlässig verwertbares Bildmaterial garantieren. Hervorzuheben ist die innovative Bauart, die eine einfache Montage ermöglicht. Nach dem Anbringen der Bodenplatte werden das Kameramodul und die Kamerakuppel montiert. Das verkürzt die Montagezeit um ein Vielfaches und reduziert das Unfallrisiko. Das staub- und wasserfeste Gehäuse ist stoßfest und schützt vor Beschädigung.

Begründung der Jury
Die Überwachungskamera-Serie Abus Advanced überzeugt mit ihrer Funktionalität. Ihre innovative Möglichkeit der Montage verkürzt die Arbeitszeit und erhöht die Arbeitssicherheit.

Huawei X
IP Camera Series
Netzwerk-Kamera-Serie

Manufacturer
Huawei Technologies Co., Ltd.,
Shenzhen, China
In-house design
Guan Yu, Xiong Jian
Web
www.huawei.com

The X series consists of a range of intelligent, network-enabled surveillance cameras which are easily adaptable to various demands and used for diverse forms of data analysis. The appearance of each camera mirrors the intelligent, progressive nature of the brand and ensures that the IP67-certified, dirt-repellent, silver-grey device harmoniously integrates into its environment, particularly in the case of outdoor facilities. Smooth installation is achieved with the included mounting kits.

Statement by the jury
The Huawei X is a series of versatile surveillance cameras which convince with regard to their functionality and aesthetics.

Bei der X-Serie handelt es sich um eine Reihe intelligenter, netzwerkfähiger Überwachungskameras, die mühelos diversen Anforderungen angepasst und zu verschiedensten Datenanalysen verwendet werden können. Ihr Erscheinungsbild spiegelt die intelligente Fortschrittlichkeit der Marke wider und sorgt dafür, dass sich das IP67-zertifizierte, schmutzabweisende, silbergraue Gerät leicht in seine Umgebung, insbesondere Außenanlagen, integriert. Die Anbringung ist einfach und kann mit den mitgelieferten Montagesätzen durchgeführt werden.

Begründung der Jury
Huawei X ist eine Serie variabel einsetzbarer Überwachungskameras, die im Hinblick auf ihre Funktionalität und Ästhetik überzeugen.

CD-ICX
CCTV Camera
Überwachungskamera

Manufacturer
r2p GmbH, Flensburg, Germany
In-house design
Web
www.r2p.com

The CD-ICX is a flexible exterior camera for rail vehicles equipped with WDR technology and intelligent temperature management. It produces high-quality, full HD images and serves as a rear-view mirror substitute for door control. The camera allows for good sight of the vehicle and its environment, thus contributing to the overall safety in rail transport. The small housing with its adaptable aesthetics is laid out for rough surroundings: high speeds, extreme climate, dirt and dust.

Statement by the jury
The flexible CD-ICX surveillance camera combines robustness, functionality and the adaptive aesthetics required in public spaces.

Die CD-ICX ist eine flexible Außenkamera für Schienenfahrzeuge, die mit WDR-Technologie und intelligentem Temperaturmanagement ausgestattet ist. Sie erzeugt qualitativ hochwertige Full-HD-Bilder und dient als Rückspiegel-Ersatz zur Türkontrolle. Die Kamera gewährt dabei gute Sicht auf das Fahrzeug und seine Umgebung und trägt so zur Sicherheit im Bahnbetrieb bei. Das kleine Gehäuse mit seiner anpassungsfähigen Ästhetik ist auf raue Umgebungen ausgerichtet: hohe Geschwindigkeiten, extremes Klima, Schmutz und Staub.

Begründung der Jury
Die flexible Überwachungskamera CD-ICX verbindet Robustheit, Funktionalität und eine für den öffentlichen Raum notwendige anpassungsfähige Ästhetik.

Unisinsight IPC
Surveillance Camera Series
Überwachungskamera-Serie

Manufacturer
New H3C Technologies Co., Ltd., Hangzhou, China
In-house design
Kai Li, Zhengjun Huang
Design
Toout Design, Hangzhou, China
Web
www.h3c.com.cn
www.toout.com

The Unisinsight IPC is a series of network-compatible surveillance cameras applying artificial intelligence to meet the demands of different scenarios. With an enhanced dynamic range, the cameras function even in difficult light and contrast conditions. Their elegant form gives the product range an unmistakable look and guarantees that the cameras can also be integrated into demanding environments, which they are able to withstand due to their robust chassis.

Bei Unisinsight IPC handelt es sich um eine Serie netzwerkfähiger Überwachungskameras, bei denen künstliche Intelligenz eingesetzt wird, um den Anforderungen unterschiedlicher Szenarien gerecht zu werden. Durch eine Verbesserung des Dynamikumfangs funktionieren die Kameras auch bei schwierigen Licht- und Kontrastverhältnissen. Ihre elegante Form verleiht der Produktreihe ein unverwechselbares Gesicht und garantiert, dass sich die Kameras in anspruchsvolle Umgebungen integrieren lassen, denen sie aufgrund der robusten Gehäuse auch standhalten können.

Statement by the jury
The design of the Unisinsight IPC surveillance cameras succeeds in combining sophisticated technology with an elegant, identity-creating appearance.

Begründung der Jury
Der Gestaltung der Unisinsight-IPC-Überwachungskameras gelingt es, eine ausgefeilte Technik mit einem eleganten, identitätsstiftenden Erscheinungsbild in Einklang zu bringen.

Communication
Kommunikation

2-way radio sets	Fitnessarmbänder
Accessories	Basisstation
Activity trackers	Diktiergeräte
Base station	Funkgeräte
Conference technology	Headsets
Headsets	Konferenztechnik
Microphones	Mikrofone
Mobile phones	Mobiltelefone
Power banks	Power Banks
Routers	Router
Smart watches	Smartphones
Smartphones	Smartwatches
Tablets	Tablets
Voice recorders	VR-Brillen
VR headsets	Wearables
Wearables	Zubehör

Apple Watch Series 4
Smartwatch

Manufacturer
Apple,
Cupertino, California, USA

In-house design
Apple

Web
www.apple.com

reddot award 2019
best of the best

Personal companion
Since its debut in 2015, the Apple Watch has established itself as a new kind of personal companion that can easily be worn on the wrist. The Apple Watch Series 4 has been redesigned and re-engineered to help users stay connected even more easily, be more active and manage their health in powerful new ways. The activity tracker, for example, tracks and shows the user's daily movement in the form of three simple metrics called "Move", "Exercise" and "Stand", with the aim of motivating users to close these rings every day through corresponding activity. The Apple Watch can show how many minutes users have done a brisk activity and even measure the respective calorie consumption. In addition, it also reminds wearers with a gentle vibration that they should get up if they have been sitting for a long time, as too much sitting is unhealthy. The fourth-generation Apple Watch has been further refined in terms of technology, combining new hardware and software enhancements into a distinctive, unified form. The display is over 30 per cent larger and yet integrates seamlessly into the now thinner, smaller case, while the new interface provides more information with additional details. The watch offers many innovative capabilities in particular with regard to health precautions, including fall detection and the ability for users to easily create an electrocardiogram using the new ECG app.

Persönlicher Begleiter
Die Apple Watch steht seit ihrem Erscheinen im Jahr 2015 für eine neue Art von persönlichem Begleiter, den man unkompliziert am Handgelenk tragen kann. Die Apple Watch Series 4 wurde neu gestaltet und überarbeitet. Ziel war es, Nutzern dabei zu helfen, noch besser in Verbindung zu bleiben, aktiver zu sein und ihre Gesundheit auf leistungsfähige Weise zu überwachen. So werden beispielsweise mittels des Aktivitätstrackers die täglichen Bewegungen in Form von drei einfachen Werten dargestellt, den Aktivitätsringen „Bewegen", „Trainieren" und „Stehen", die sich bei entsprechender Tätigkeit nach und nach schließen. Die Apple Watch zeigt an, wie viele Minuten man sich zügig bewegt hat und misst dabei sogar den jeweiligen Kalorienverbrauch. Außerdem erinnert sie ihren Träger mit einer sanften Vibration daran, dass er aufstehen sollte, falls er lange Zeit gesessen hat, da zu viel Sitzen ungesund ist. Die vierte Generation der Apple Watch wurde technologisch weiterentwickelt und vereint neue Hardware- und Software-Verbesserungen in einer markanten, einheitlichen Form. Das Display ist über 30 Prozent größer und fügt sich nahtlos in das nun dünnere, kleinere Gehäuse ein, während die neue Benutzeroberfläche mehr Informationen mit zusätzlichen Details liefert. Die Uhr bietet viele innovative Funktionen, insbesondere zur gesundheitlichen Vorsorge einschließlich einer Sturzerkennung sowie der Möglichkeit, unkompliziert ein Elektrokardiogramm mittels einer neuen EKG-App zu erstellen.

Statement by the jury
The design of the Apple Watch Series 4 is an expression of consistent advancement. Overall bigger, it impresses with its balanced proportions. The watch features electronic sensors that measure the user's heartbeat and provide feedback on the daily activities, thus enabling users to realise an effective health management. Of high quality, the watch is also very comfortable to wear.

Begründung der Jury
Die Apple Watch Series 4 ist in ihrem Design Ausdruck einer in sich schlüssigen Weiterentwicklung. Insgesamt größer, beeindruckt sie durch ihre ausgewogenen Proportionen. Sie verfügt über elektronische Sensoren zur Messung des Herzschlags und gibt ein Feedback auf die Aktivitäten des Nutzers, wodurch sie ein effektives Gesundheitsmanagement ermöglicht. Qualitativ hochwertig, ist sie auch sehr angenehm zu tragen.

Xiaotiancai Watch Phone Z1
Smartwatch Phone

Manufacturer
Guangdong Genius Technology Co., Ltd.,
Changan, Guangdong Province, China
In-house design
Web
www.okii.com

This smartwatch phone with 4G technology has been designed specially for children from four to eleven years old. A clear, calm design, which at the same time generates interest, helps the confidence of younger users of the device. A button and a slot for the SIM card are located on the right side. The screen consists of 2.5D glass which supports the three-dimensional appearance of the device. Wrist straps of modern design and bright colours contribute to the lively impression.

Statement by the jury
The Xiaotiancai Watch Phone Z1 is a well-considered aid for families. Its functions conform to the user habits of children.

Medion® Life® E1800
Smartwatch

Manufacturer
MEDION AG, Essen, Germany
In-house design
Web
www.medion.com

The Medion Life E1800 smartwatch plans and monitors the user's sports activities. The heart rate control directly on the wrist renders the user independent from elaborate accessories. The 0.96" large display provides information about incoming messages on the go. Thanks to the IP68 standard, the smartwatch allows for a dive in deep water. Sleep health and sports units are enhanced in an efficient way. A clear design and intuitive user interface underline the sporty appearance of the smartwatch.

Statement by the jury
The Medion Life E1800 smartphone offers recordable information easily, thanks to which the potential in sport and exercising can be improved.

Die Smartwatch Medion Life E1800 plant und überprüft die sportlichen Trainings eines Nutzers. Die Kontrolle der Herzfrequenz direkt am Armgelenk macht diese unabhängig von aufwendigem Zubehör. Das 0,96" große Display informiert unterwegs über einkommende Nachrichten. Einen Tauchgang in tiefem Wasser ermöglicht die Smartwatch dank einem Standard von IP68. Die Schlafgesundheit wie auch die Sporteinheiten werden effizient verbessert. Eine klare Gestaltung und eine intuitiv erfassbare Benutzerschnittstelle unterstreichen die sportive Anmutung der Smartwatch.

Begründung der Jury
Die Smartwatch Medion Life E1800 bietet einfach erfassbare Informationen, dank derer sich sportliches Potenzial verbessern lässt.

TicWatch E2
Smartwatch

Manufacturer
Mobvoi US LLC, San Francisco, USA
In-house design
Xie Ke
Web
www.mobvoi.com

The TicWatch E2 is based on a proprietary AI technology which tracks the fitness and swimming activities of the user. The device also offers Wear OS by Google-Support, an integrated GPS, a pulse monitor, Google Assistant as well as 48 hours of battery life. An illuminated OLED display, a light polycarbonate design and the possibility of individually personalising watch faces and watch straps, complete the offer.

Statement by the jury
Thanks to its minimalist design, the user can concentrate on the skilfully integrated functions of the TicWatch E2.

Die TicWatch basiert auf einer patentrechtlich geschützten AI-Technologie, die proaktiv die Fitness- und Schwimmaktivitäten des Nutzers aufzeichnet. Zusätzlich stellt das Gerät Wear OS von Google-Support, ein integriertes GPS, einen Pulsmesser, Google Assistant sowie 48 Stunden Akkulaufzeit zur Verfügung. Ein leuchtendes OLED-Display, ein leichtes Polykarbonat-Design und die Möglichkeit, Zifferblättern und Uhrbänder individuell anzupassen, runden das Angebot ab.

Begründung der Jury
Dank ihres minimalistischen Designs kann sich der Benutzer auf die geschickt integrierten Funktionen der TicWatch E2 konzentrieren.

SuperCharger
Self-Charging Smartwatch
Selbstaufladende Smartwatch

Manufacturer
Sequent Ltd., Zug, Switzerland
In-house design
Adrian Buchmann
Web
www.sequent-world.com

The SuperCharger is based on a patented hybrid self-charging system. It can thus acquire energy through the user's movements, just like a classical automatic watch. The Smartwatch offers call and text notification through LED lighting and vibrations, GPS and monitors the heartbeat. A BioFeedback app gives information on calories expended, serves as pace and distance counter and displays the energy generated – all that can be read on the watch face. Case and watch straps are designed according to innovative, ergonomic and sustainable viewpoints; all components are of high-quality and recyclable materials. It synchronises with android as well as an iPhone.

Der SuperCharger basiert auf einem patentierten hybriden selbstladenden System. Dadurch kann er wie eine klassische automatische Uhr durch die Bewegung des Nutzers Energie gewinnen. Die Smartwatch bietet Anruf- und Textanzeige mittels LED-Beleuchtung und Vibration, zudem GPS und Herzschlagüberwachung. Eine BioFeedback-App informiert über den Kalorienverbrauch, dient als Schritt- und Distanzzähler und gibt die erzeugte Energie an – all das ist auf der Uhrenanzeige ablesbar. Gehäuse und Armbänder sind nach innovativen ergonomischen sowie nachhaltigen Gesichtspunkten gestaltet, alle Komponenten bestehen aus hochwertigen und wiederverwendbaren Materialien. Die Synchronisation funktioniert für Android wie auch iPhone.

Statement by the jury
A smartwatch equipped with a hybrid charging system is an exciting, innovative idea whose sustainability is convincing.

Begründung der Jury
Eine Smartwatch mit einem hybriden Ladesystem auszustatten, ist eine aufregend innovative Idee, deren Nachhaltigkeitsgedanke überzeugt.

Amazfit Verge
Smartwatch

Manufacturer
Anhui Huami
Information Technology Co., Ltd.,
Hefei, China
In-house design
Web
www.huami.com

The Amazfit Verge can hold one charge for up to five days operation. An integrated AI assistant controls other IoT devices of the product series by voice activation. In 165 cities, the device provides access to the public transport system; eleven sport modes are supported. A special outer coating keeps the straps soft and dry and thus hygienic. Due to a second colour on the case bottom the smartwatch with 1.3" AMOLED display appears particularly thin.

Statement by the jury
The good wearing properties and the many functions suitable for daily use make the smartwatch Amazfit Verge especially popular.

Mit einer Ladung bleibt die Amazfit Verge bis zu fünf Tage in Betrieb. Ein integrierter AI-Assistent steuert andere IoT-Endgeräte der Produktlinie durch Stimme. In 165 Städten verschafft das Gerät Zugang zum öffentlichen Transportsystem, elf Sportmodi werden unterstützt. Eine spezielle Oberfläche hält die Bänder weich und trocken und somit hygienisch. Durch eine zweite Farbe am Gehäuseboden erscheint die Smartwatch mit 1,3"-AMOLED-Display besonders schmal.

Begründung der Jury
Die guten Trageeigenschaften und die vielen alltagstauglichen Funktionen der Smartwatch Amazfit Verge finden besonderen Zuspruch.

LG Watch W7
Smartwatch

Manufacturer
LG Electronics, Inc., Seoul, South Korea
In-house design
Jeongguen Choi, Sea-La Park
Web
www.lg.com

The innovative smartwatch combines the up-to-date functions of Wear OS with a mechanical movement based on the Swiss model. Thus the LG Watch W7 retains the traditional hour and minute hands, the watch face is, however, digital and can be adjusted to the user's requirements. The case is of stainless steel, the bezel and the glass precisely engineered. Design of the wrist straps is reserved and harmonises well with all watch dial versions.

Statement by the jury
In the LG Watch W7, a tangible experience of the analogue combines skilfully with the contemporary functions of a digital smartwatch.

Die innovative Smartwatch kombiniert die zeitgemäßen Funktionen aus Wear OS mit einem mechanischen Uhrwerk nach Schweizer Vorbild. So verfügt die LG Watch W7 über den traditionellen Stunden- und Minutenzeiger, das Zifferblatt wird jedoch digital dargestellt und kann den individuellen Bedürfnissen des Nutzers angepasst werden. Das Gehäuse aus Edelstahl, die Lünette und das Glas sind präzise gefertigt. Die zurückhaltend gestalteten Armbänder harmonieren gut mit allen Zifferblatt-Versionen.

Begründung der Jury
In der LG Watch W7 verbindet sich geschickt das greifbare Erleben des Analogen mit den zeitgemäßen Funktionen einer digitalen Smartwatch.

TicWatch S2
Smartwatch

Manufacturer
Mobvoi US LLC, San Francisco, USA
In-house design
Xie Ke
Web
www.mobvoi.com

The smartwatch is based on Wear OS and includes a powerful, integrated GPS, a heartbeat sensor, an accelerometer and a gyroscope. The TicWatch S2 is particularly robust. It has, for example, a water resistance of 5 ATM; it is certificated to MIL-STD-810G; the case consists of durable polycarbonate and the resilient gorilla glass provides very good scratch resistance. Innovative TicMotion technology tracks activities proactively.

Statement by the jury
The TicWatch S2 surprises with its robustness, whereby it is recommended for use under extreme climatic conditions.

Die Smartwatch basiert auf Wear OS und enthält ein leistungsstarkes integriertes GPS, einen Herzfrequenzsensor, einen Beschleunigungsmesser und ein Gyroskop. Die TicWatch S2 ist besonders widerstandsfähig. So etwa ist ihre Wasserdichte-Bewertung 5 ATM, sie weist MIL-STD-810G auf, das Gehäuse besteht aus langlebigem Polycarbonat und das spannkräftige Gorilla-Glas zeigt sehr gute Kratzfestigkeit. Die innovative TicMotion-Technologie verfolgt Aktivitäten proaktiv.

Begründung der Jury
Die TicWatch S2 erstaunt durch ihre Robustheit, durch die sie sich für den Einsatz unter extremen klimatischen Bedingungen empfiehlt.

TicWatch C2
Smartwatch

Manufacturer
Mobvoi US LLC, San Francisco, USA
In-house design
Xie Ke, Yu Chen
Web
www.mobvoi.com

The TicWatch C2 is of minimalist design, with slender and elegant lines and surfaces, without impairing the Wear OS based function. The stainless steel case harmonises optically with the round watch face, and yet incorporates the internal component group of a smartwatch. Thus the TicWatch C2 offers an integrated GPS, dynamic heartbeat monitoring, accelerometer and a gyroscope.

Statement by the jury
The TicWatch C2 offers the modern functions of a smartwatch and presents very stylishly the aesthetics of a classical wristwatch.

Die TicWatch C2 ist minimalistisch gestaltet, mit schlanken und eleganten Linien und Oberflächen, ohne die auf Wear OS basierende Funktion zu beeinträchtigen. Das Gehäuse aus Edelstahl harmoniert optisch mit dem runden Zifferblatt, dennoch nimmt es die interne Komponentenbaugruppe einer Smartwatch in sich auf. So bietet die TicWatch C2 etwa ein integriertes GPS, dynamische Herzfrequenzüberwachung, Beschleunigungsmesser und Gyroskop.

Begründung der Jury
Die TicWatch C2 bietet die modernen Funktionen einer Smartwatch und präsentiert sich sehr stilvoll in der Ästhetik einer klassischen Armbanduhr.

Versa
Smartwatch

Manufacturer
Fitbit, Inc., San Francisco, USA
In-house design
Web
www.fitbit.com

Versa is a lightweight, modern and approachable everyday health and fitness smartwatch. It supports an advanced day and night heart rate tracking as well as sleep tracking and a personalised dashboard with pertinent health and activity data. All components are housed in a very thin, robotically cut, aerospace grade aluminum case that is waterproof up to 50 meters.

Statement by the jury
The Versa smartwatch combines the sensible modern functions of a fitness tracker with the practical applications in urban everyday life.

Versa ist eine leichte, moderne und ansprechende Gesundheits- und Fitness-Smartwatch für den alltäglichen Gebrauch. Sie unterstützt eine fortschrittliche Herzfrequenzmessung rund um die Uhr, Schlafüberwachung sowie eine personalisierte Armatur mit nützlichen Daten zu Gesundheit und Aktivität. Alle Komponenten sind in einem sehr dünnen, robotergeschnittenen Aluminiumgehäuse in Raumfahrtqualität untergebracht, welches bis zu einer Tiefe von 50 Metern wasserfest bleibt.

Begründung der Jury
Die Smartwatch Versa verbindet sinnvoll moderne Funktionen eines Fitness-Trackers und praktische Anwendungsmöglichkeiten im urbanen Alltag.

Charge 3
Fitness Tracker

Manufacturer
Fitbit, Inc., San Francisco, USA
In-house design
Web
www.fitbit.com

Use of high-quality materials, for example aluminium or gorilla glass deriving from space travel, assure an especially light, slim, waterproof and durable design of the fitness tracker Charge 3. The device provides motivation notifications, personalised advice and intelligent knowledge that is easy to put into practice. Additional innovation is provided by advanced heart rate sensors and an inductive button.

Statement by the jury
The fitness tracker Charge 3 is particularly appealing due to its sporty design and well-considered, innovative functions.

Der Einsatz von hochwertigen Materialen, etwa von in der Raumfahrt eingesetztem Aluminium oder Gorilla-Glas, sorgt bei dem Fitness-Tracker Charge 3 für eine besonders leichte, schlanke, wasserfeste wie auch widerstandsfähige Ausgestaltung. Das Gerät liefert tägliche Motivationsbenachrichtigungen, eine personalisierte Beratung und intelligente, einfach umsetzbare Erkenntnisse. Für zusätzliche Innovation sorgen fortschrittliche Herzfrequenz-Sensoren und eine induktive Taste.

Begründung der Jury
Der Fitness-Tracker Charge 3 spricht besonders durch seine sportive Gestaltung und wohldurchdachte, innovative Funktionen an.

Inspire
Fitness Tracker

Manufacturer
Fitbit, Inc., San Francisco, USA
In-house design
Web
www.fitbit.com

Form, colour and proportions of the Inspire fitness tracker are designed in such a way that they give it the appearance of a decorative bracelet. Operation is conveniently performed via a touchscreen. The device is watertight to a depth of 50 meters and has a battery life of up to five days. The wristbands can be exchanged easily for example against accessories of woven metal, double-wrapped Saffiano leather or printed silicone bands.

Statement by the jury
The Inspire gains merit with its touchscreen, by means of which the fitness tracker can be operated quite easily and intuitively.

Form, Farbgebung und Proportionen des Fitness-Trackers Inspire sind so gestaltet, dass er wie ein schmückendes Armband am Handgelenk anmutet. Die Bedienung erfolgt bequem über einen Touchscreen. Das Gerät ist bis zu 50 Metern Tiefe wasserfest und verfügt über eine Akkulaufzeit von bis zu fünf Tagen. Die Armbänder lassen sich ganz einfach austauschen und etwa gegen Accessoires aus Metallgewebe, doppelt gewickeltes Saffiano-Leder oder bedruckte Silikonbänder austauschen.

Begründung der Jury
Der Inspire punktet mit seinem Touchscreen, über den sich der Fitness-Tracker ganz einfach und intuitiv bedienen lässt.

Teslasuit
Full-Body Haptics Suit
Haptischer Ganzkörperanzug

Manufacturer
VR Electronics Limited,
London, United Kingdom

In-house design
Igor Buturlia

Web
www.teslasuit.io

reddot award 2019
best of the best

New way of experiencing
The well-known biologist turned philosopher Humberto R. Maturana describes reality as a learned environment constructed by us through our perceptions. The Teslasuit is a full-body interface between a user and a digital environment. It enhances virtual and augmented reality experiences by providing a sense of touch, force feedback via electric stimulation and thermal feedback. The haptic experience is supported by advanced biometric and motion capture systems. While the Teslasuit is currently only used for enterprise-internal training, the suit also has great potential in medicine, sports and gaming. Its design is highly functional, ergonomic and minimalist, complemented by precise electrode mapping that enables accurate stimulation of muscle groups. The high-tech materials and fabrics used for the suit do not restrict the user's movements and provide an optimum fit, as is also required for the correctly placed delivery of haptic stimulation. The suit's high-fidelity haptics is enabled by 80 electro-stimulation channels and five thermal feedback channels. The motion capture system is driven by ten integrated inertial measurement unit sensors. The biometric system employs the electro-stimulation channels to provide highly accurate electrocardiography and galvanic skin response data. A minicomputer control unit enables wireless operation of the suit.

Neues Erleben
Der bekannte Biologe und Philosoph Humberto R. Maturana beschreibt die Realität als erlernte Umgebung, die wir selbst erst durch Wahrnehmung erzeugen. Der Teslasuit ist eine Ganzkörper-Schnittstelle zwischen Nutzer und digitaler Umgebung. Er intensiviert das Erlebnis virtueller und erweiterter Realität, indem er über elektrische Stimulation ein Gefühl für Berührung und Krafteinwirkung sowie auch ein thermisches Feedback liefert. Seine Haptik wird dabei von fortschrittlichen biometrischen und Bewegungserfassungssystemen unterstützt. Während der Teslasuit aktuell für Unternehmensschulungen vorgesehen ist, besitzt er auch ein großes Potenzial in der Medizin, im Sport und im Gaming-Bereich. Seine Gestaltung ist hochfunktional, ergonomisch und minimalistisch. Ein präzises Elektroden-Mapping ermöglicht die zielgenaue Stimulation von Muskelgruppen. Die verwendeten Hightech-Materialien und -Stoffe des Anzugs schränken die Bewegung nicht ein und bieten eine gute Passform, die für die korrekt platzierte Übertragung der Haptik erforderlich ist. Eine naturgetreue haptische Empfindung wird durch 80 Elektrostimulationskanäle und fünf thermische Feedback-Kanäle ermöglicht. Die Bewegungserfassung wird durch zehn integrierte inertiale Messeinheiten gesteuert. Das biometrische System verwendet die Elektrostimulationskanäle, um sehr präzise elektrokardiographische Daten sowie auch Daten zur galvanischen Hautreaktion zu liefern. Eine Minicomputer-Steuereinheit erlaubt den drahtlosen Betrieb des Teslasuits.

Statement by the jury
Perfectly integrating sophisticated technology, this full-body suit delivers the feeling of becoming one with digital reality. The Teslasuit points out the future already today, because it allows users wearing it to move around easily and freely in their environment. The suit is well thought-out and well made in every aspect of its components – featuring a design that discreetly integrates the sensors and which lends it an iconic appearance.

Begründung der Jury
In diesem die anspruchsvolle Technologie perfekt integrierenden Kleidungsstück hat man das Gefühl, eins zu werden mit der digitalen Realität. Der Teslasuit zeigt uns heute schon die Zukunft auf, denn der Nutzer kann sich mit ihm einfach und frei in seiner Umgebung bewegen. Der Anzug ist in jeder seiner Komponenten durchdacht und gut verarbeitet – seine die Sensoren diskret einpassende Gestaltung verleiht ihm ein ikonisches Erscheinungsbild.

Designer portrait
See page 52
Siehe Seite 52

ThinkReality A6
Augmented Reality Headset

Manufacturer
Lenovo,
Morrisville, North Carolina, USA

In-house design
Experience Design Group

Web
www.lenovo.com

reddot award 2019
best of the best

Free interaction
At first primarily to be found only in the gaming sector, augmented reality (AR) today has conquered the work environments of more and more companies across a wide variety of different industries. The ThinkReality A6 is an innovative stereoscopic AR headset that is particularly well suited for this. It includes a lightweight head-mounted display (HMD), which weighs in at only 250 grams, and a powerful compute box that allows for over four hours of uninterrupted work in graphic-intensive AR applications. Designed specifically for extended-wear use cases, this lightweight display features soft materials that make the headset very comfortable to wear, as well as an innovative strap-tightening mechanism to quickly achieve a perfect fit for different head sizes. The ThinkReality A6 is Android certified and built for enterprise and industrial environments with water, dust, and shock protection. Thanks to its full sensor suite, it possesses advanced interaction capabilities through gestures and voice input, allowing workers to carry out their tasks and interact with the device hands-free. Thus, users are able to easily fuse digital information into their physical workspaces by pinning, interacting and collaborating with 3D digital information in the real world. This leads to a significantly improved contextual awareness and enhanced efficiency in a variety of tasks and environments.

Freie Interaktion
Ursprünglich vor allem im Gaming-Bereich präsent, hält die Arbeit in Umgebungen, die Augmented Reality (AR) nutzen, mittlerweile auch zunehmend Einzug in die Unternehmen verschiedenster Branchen. Das ThinkReality A6 ist ein innovatives, dafür sehr gut geeignetes stereoskopisches AR-Headset. Es besteht aus einem 250 Gramm leichten Head-Mounted Display (HMD) und einer leistungsstarken Recheneinheit, die mehr als vier Stunden ununterbrochenes Arbeiten in grafikintensiven AR-Anwendungen ermöglicht. Das leichte Display wurde für solch zeitaufwendige Einsätze entwickelt und ist dafür mit weichen Materialien gestaltet, die das Tragen des Headsets sehr angenehm machen. Mittels eines innovativen Spannmechanismus für den Tragebügel lässt es sich perfekt an verschiedene Kopfgrößen anpassen. Für den Einsatz auch in industriellen Umgebungen konzipiert, ist das ThinkReality A6 Android-zertifiziert sowie wasser-, staub- und stoßresistent. Dank seiner vollständigen Sensoren-Ausstattung bietet es erweiterte Interaktionsmöglichkeiten durch Gesten und Spracheingaben, sodass Anwender mit dem Gerät freihändig interagierend ihre Aufgaben ausführen können. Auf diese Weise lassen sich unkompliziert digitale Informationen in die physischen Arbeitsbereiche integrieren, indem die Nutzer digitale 3D-Informationen in die reale Welt einbringen und damit interagieren und arbeiten. Dies führt dazu, dass sich Kontextbewusstsein wie auch Effizienz in einer Vielzahl von Tätigkeiten und Bereichen entscheidend verbessern.

Statement by the jury
The design of the ThinkReality A6 augmented reality headset is truly pushing boundaries. It is ergonomic, extremely lightweight and easily adaptable to different head sizes thanks to its innovative strap-tightening mechanism. Soft and pleasant to the touch, its material properties make it comfortable to wear for a long time. Through intuitive gestures and voice commands, the headset allows users to work interactively in AR work environments.

Begründung der Jury
Die Gestaltung des Augmented-Reality-Headsets ThinkReality A6 schlägt eine neue Richtung ein. Es ist ergonomisch, außerordentlich leicht und kann sich mittels eines innovativen Spannmechanismus unterschiedlichen Kopfgrößen anpassen. Weich und angenehm in seiner Materialbeschaffenheit, lässt es sich lange Zeit komfortabel tragen. Auf intuitive Weise können Nutzer dabei in einer AR-Umgebung mit Gesten und Stimmbefehlen interagierend ausgesprochen produktiv arbeiten.

Designer portrait
See page 54
Siehe Seite 54

Mutrics M1
Smart Glasses
Intelligente Brille

Manufacturer
Mutrics Innovation Intelligence Co., Ltd.,
Shenzhen, China
Design
inDare Design Strategy Limited
(Qinglang Chen, Fengming Chen,
Yujie Chen, Shaolong Chen, Weihao Chen),
Shenzhen, China
Web
www.mutrics.com
www.indare.love
Honourable Mention

In the Mutrics M1 smart glasses, bone conduction glasses and loudspeakers are integrated. The system communicates via NFC, whereby transmission in comparison with FFC functions is interference-free. Selected text messages are converted to audio form, thus distraction, for example when driving, is avoided. If the glasses are removed, music or videos can be played via an integrated surround-stereo system.

Statement by the jury
By means of the creative appliance of bone conduction technology, the Mutrics M1 smart glasses offer surprisingly high transmission quality.

In die intelligente Brille Mutrics M1 sind Knochenleitungskopfhörer und Lautsprecher integriert. Das System kommuniziert via NFC, wodurch die Übertragung im Vergleich zu FFC störungsfreier funktioniert. Ausgewählte Textnachrichten werden in Audioform konvertiert, so wird Ablenkung etwa während einer Autofahrt vermieden. Wird die Brille abgelegt, können mittels des eingebauten Surround-Stereo-Systems Musik oder Videos abgespielt werden.

Begründung der Jury
Durch die kreative Anwendung von Knochenleitungstechnologie bietet die intelligente Brille Mutrics M1 eine erstaunlich hohe Übertragungsqualität.

Mobile Game Controller

Manufacturer
Shenzhen Ontology Design Co., Ltd.
Shenzhen, China
Design
Shenzhen Ontology Design Co., Ltd.
(Jun Biao Huang, Geng Hao Ma,
Yu Han Chen, Feng Zhi Wu, De Cheng Li),
Shenzhen, China
Web
www.manpeigame.com

In order to control games more easily and avoid hand fatigue, a smartphone is simply plugged into the Mobile Game Controller. The width can thereby be adjusted. In order to meet the demands of various types of games, three shapes of handle can be chosen. The Mobile Game Controller is low in weight and thus can be easily carried around when on the road and be used when needed.

Statement by the jury
The Mobile Game Controller supports ergonomically logical, manual operation and enhances thereby the gaming experience on a smartphone.

Um Spiele einfacher steuern zu können und Ermüdungserscheinungen der Hand zu vermeiden, wird ein Smartphone einfach in den Mobile Game Controller eingesteckt. In der Breite kann dieser dabei angepasst werden. Um den Ansprüchen unterschiedlicher Spieletypen gerecht zu werden, stehen drei Griffformen zur Auswahl. Der Mobile Game Controller hat ein geringes Gewicht und lässt sich daher gut unterwegs mitführen und bei Bedarf verwenden.

Begründung der Jury
Der Mobile Game Controller unterstützt eine ergonomisch sinnvolle Handführung und verbessert damit das Spielerlebnis auf einem Smartphone.

Tap
Wearable

Manufacturer
Sixeye Interactive, Neve Ilan, Israel
Design
Shape Products (John Liu, Jeff Wollenzien), Toronto, Canada
Web
www.tapwithus.com
www.shape-products.com
Honourable Mention

Tap is an input device worn over all five fingers. It registers hand movements and by this means enables the user to create texts on nearly all surfaces and to control a curser. It is compatible with the usual operating systems and is adaptable with many applications. Due to its light weight, small dimensions and user-friendly ergonomics, the wearable is particularly suitable for VR/AR applications as well as persons with impaired eyesight.

Statement by the jury
The wearable Tap can be used in a surprising variety of ways. It offers support for impaired sight as well as for VR/AR gaming.

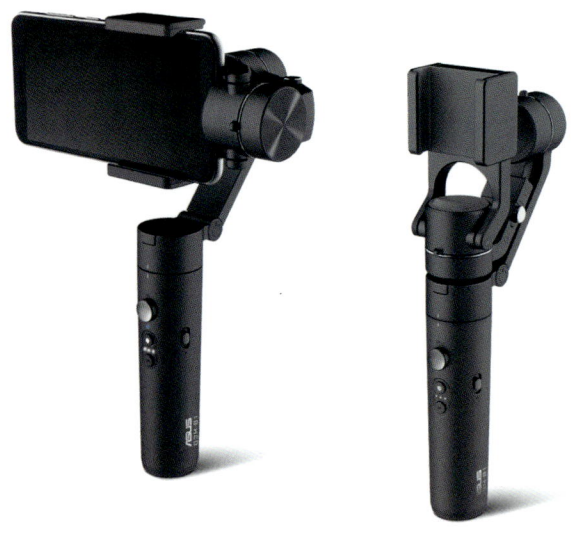

ASUS Gimbal G3M-B1
Schwebestativ

Manufacturer
Asustek Computer Inc., Taipei City, Taiwan
In-house design
Web
www.asus.com

The ASUS Gimbal G3M-B1 stabilises smartphones while filming in motion. Various control modes are available for the user, among these are a three-axial stabilising technology, horizontal panning of 360 degrees, an intelligent operational interface as well as an accompanying app. The integrated buttons support intuitive operation. The device fits easily in the pocket and can be taken everywhere.

Statement by the jury
Thanks to ASUS Gimbal G3M-B1, professional filming technology can be applied to the smartphone without complication.

Das ASUS Gimbal G3M-B1 stabilisiert Smartphones während des Filmens in Bewegung. Nutzern stehen zahlreiche Steuerungsmodi zur Verfügung, darunter eine dreiaxiale Stabilisations-Technologie, ein horizontaler Schwenk über 360 Grad, eine intelligente Betriebsschnittstelle sowie eine begleitende App. Die integrierten Tasten unterstützen eine intuitive Bedienung. Das Gerät lässt sich leicht in einer Tasche unterbringen und überallhin mitnehmen.

Begründung der Jury
Dank ASUS Gimbal G3M-B1 lässt sich professionelle Filmtechnik unkompliziert auf dem Smartphone umsetzen.

JOBY TelePod Mobile
Selfie Stick Tripod
Selfiestick-Stativ

Manufacturer
Vitec Imaging Solutions S.p.A., Cassola (Vicenza), Italy
In-house design
Noah Balmer
Web
www.manfrotto.com

This selfie stick tripod is designed for mobile use. It can be utilised as a handgrip, monopod, elevated stand or telescopic tripod. Suitable for vlogging, selfies and more, it securely holds 360 degree cameras, phones, as well as phones with 360 degree camera attachments. It allows to capture shots from a distance with the included Bluetooth Impulse remote shutter, and is compatible with a variety of different mounts.

Statement by the jury
The JOBY TelePod Mobile attracts attention due to its flexibility. Furthermore, its contemporary application options are pleasant.

Das Selfiestick-Stativ ist für die mobile Nutzung gestaltet. Es kann verwendet werden als Handgriff, normales oder erhöhtes Stativ sowie als Teleskopstativ. Etwa für Vlogging oder Selfies hält es sicher kleine 360-Grad-Kameras oder Mobiltelefone, selbst solche mit 360-Grad-Kamera-Aufsatz. Mit dem inkludierten Bluetooth-Impulse-Fremdauslöser sind Aufnahmen aus der Distanz möglich und das Gerät ist kompatibel mit einer breiten Produktpalette.

Begründung der Jury
Das JOBY TelePod Mobile zieht durch seine Flexibilität die Aufmerksamkeit auf sich. Darüber hinaus gefallen seine zeitgemäßen Einsatzmöglichkeiten.

Power+Data Kit
Powerbank and Hub
Powerbank und Hub

Manufacturer
Zimi Corporation, Nanjing, China
In-house design
Web
www.zmifi.com

This set consists of a powerbank with hub function, and a smaller data hub to support the use of laptops while travelling. In the larger unit a battery of 10,000 mAh is integrated, with which, for example mobile phones or laptops can be charged. The smaller hub offers connections for USB 3.0, USB-C, memory cards and HDMI. The clear design of the devices is complemented by textile covers at the front, offering pleasant haptics.

Statement by the jury
The Power+Data Kit proves to be a practical aid when travelling with digital devices. Its elegant design is also appealing.

Dieses Set besteht aus einer Powerbank mit Hub-Funktion und einem kleineren Daten-Hub, das auf Reisen die Nutzung von Laptops unterstützt. In dem größeren Element ist eine Batterie mit 10.000 mAh integriert, mit der z. B. Mobiltelefone oder Laptops geladen werden können. Der kleinere Hub bietet Anschlüsse für USB 3.0, USB-C-Speicherkarten und HDMI. Die klar gestalteten Geräte sind an der Frontseite mit einem Textilstoff bezogen, der eine angenehme Haptik bietet.

Begründung der Jury
Das Power+Data Kit erweist sich auf Reisen mit digitalen Geräten als praktisches Hilfsmittel. Auch seine elegante Gestaltung gefällt.

Logitech Crayon
Digital Pencil for iPad
Digitaler Zeichenstift
für das iPad

Manufacturer
Logitech, Lausanne, Switzerland
In-house design
Web
www.logitech.com

The Logitech Crayon upgrades the iPad with modern technology. It delivers sub-pixel precision, low latency and support for tilt. Thanks to palm rejection technology, the hand can rest comfortably on the iPad. Connection to the tablet is performed without pairing. Due to the flat design and an easy-to-grip surface, the pencil lies comfortably in the hand and cannot roll away. The smart tip is child-safe and can only be removed with a special tool. The rubber cap is tethered to the device and can therefore not be easily misplaced.

Statement by the jury
The Logitech Crayon is a functionally sophisticated accessory for the iPad and its clear design is appealing.

Der Logitech Crayon ergänzt das iPad durch moderne Technologie. Er bietet eine Auflösung im Subpixel-Bereich, eine niedrige Latenz und der Neigungswinkel wird erfasst. Dank Handflächenunterdrückung kann die Hand bequem auf dem iPad ruhen. Die Verbindung mit dem Tablet funktioniert ohne Pairing. Durch die flache Gestaltung und seine rutschfeste Oberfläche liegt der Stift gut in der Hand und kann außerdem nicht wegrollen. Die Spitze des Stifts ist kindersicher gestaltet und kann nur durch ein spezielles Werkzeug abgenommen werden. Die Gummikappe ist mit dem Gerät fest verbunden und geht somit nicht einfach verloren.

Begründung der Jury
Der Logitech Crayon ist eine funktional ausgereifte Ergänzung zum iPad und gefällt durch seine klare Gestaltung.

Pocket Sky
Wearable

Manufacturer
Active Wearables GmbH, Vienna, Austria
Design
Pocket Sky OG (Michael Geyer, Mark Wallerberger), Vienna, Austria
Web
www.pocket-sky.com

Pocket Sky is worn like a pair of glasses. The wearable produces a soft blue light which, similar to daylight, reduces the production of melatonin for the user. The sleep-wake rhythm, wakefulness and general well-being are improved. Pairs of magnets, plated with gold, help the arc to fold and glide into its dock. The lightweight case offers wireless charging and can easily be carried around.

Statement by the jury
By the use of blue light, the wearable Pocket Sky impressively increases the well-being of users in situations of stress affecting the biorhythm.

Pocket Sky wird wie eine Brille getragen. Das Wearable produziert ein sanftes blaues Licht, das wie natürliches Tageslicht die Produktion von Melatonin beim Nutzer vermindert. Dadurch werden der Schlaf-wach-Rhythmus, die Wachheit sowie das allgemeine Wohlbefinden verbessert. Vergoldete Magnetenpaare unterstützen, dass sich der Bogen zusammenfaltet und in seine Schale gleitet. Das Etui bietet kabelloses Laden und kann mühelos mitgenommen werden.

Begründung der Jury
Durch den Einsatz von blauem Licht steigert das Wearable Pocket Sky eindrucksvoll das Wohlbefinden in für den Biorhythmus stressreichen Situationen.

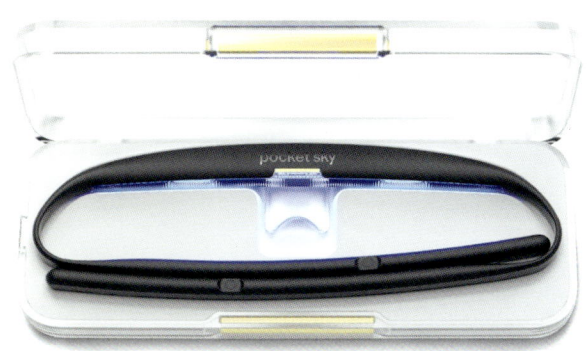

OceanMedallion™
Wearable

Manufacturer
Carnival Corporation & plc, Miami, USA
In-house design
John Padgett
Web
www.carnivalcorp.com

The OceanMedallion is a wearable that provides communication on board of cruise ships by networking with thousands of BLE and NFC supported sensors to offer passengers numerous interactive experiences. By these means, for example, food and drinks can be ordered and delivered directly to guests wherever they may be on board and check-in takes less than a minute. In addition, the device facilitates dynamic orientation and keyless access to the guests' cabins. No on-off switch, no charging or configuration is required. The device is easy to wear and water-, sand-, salt- and heat-resistant.

Statement by the jury
The innovative OceanMedallion gains merit due to its high functionality and very uncomplicated operability.

Das Wearable OceanMedallion ermöglicht eine Kommunikation an Bord von Kreuzfahrtschiffen mittels tausender BLE- oder NFC-unterstützter Sensoren, damit kann den Passagieren eine Vielzahl an interaktiven Erlebnissen geboten werden. Speisen und Getränke können etwa überall an Bord bestellt und serviert werden, der Check-in dauert weniger als eine Minute. Zudem ermöglicht das Gerät dynamische Orientierung und schlüssellosen Zugang zu den Gästezimmern. Weder ein Ein-Aus-Schalter, ein Aufladen oder ein Konfigurationsmenü sind vonnöten. Das Gerät ist unkompliziert tragbar und widerstandsfähig gegen Wasser, Sand, Salz und Hitze.

Begründung der Jury
Das innovative OceanMedallion punktet durch eine hohe Funktionalität und eine sehr unkomplizierte Bedienbarkeit.

iPhone XS
Smartphone

Manufacturer
Apple, Cupertino, California, USA
In-house design
Web
www.apple.com

Both the iPhone XS with 5.8" as well as the iPhone XS Max with 6.5" are equipped with a Super Retina display. An improved dual-camera system offers sophisticated functions for video and image; furthermore it offers an innovative 7 nm chip, particularly quick facial recognition and a wider stereo sound. In addition to the usual high-quality, stainless steel design in silver and space grey, there is a variant in gold. The glass at the front and back is particularly robust and provides increased scratch protection. Wireless charging is performed very quickly at the back.

Mit Super-Retina-Display sind sowohl das iPhone XS mit 5,8" als auch das iPhone XS Max mit 6,5" ausgestattet. Ein verbessertes Dual-Kamera-System bietet ausgefeilte Funktionen für Video und Bild, weiter stellt es einen innovativen 7-Nanometer-Chip, besonders schnelle Gesichtserkennung und weiten Stereoklang zur Verfügung. Zu den gewohnten hochwertigen Edelstahl-Ausführungen in Silber und Space Grau kommt eine Variante in Gold hinzu. Das Glas an Front und Rückseite ist besonders widerstandsfähig und bietet erhöhten Schutz gegen Kratzer. Sehr schnell gelingt das kabellose Laden über die Rückseite.

Statement by the jury
With impressive colour accuracy, high-quality engineering and selective materials, the iPhone XS meets high aesthetic expectations.

Begründung der Jury
Mit eindrucksvoller Farbgenauigkeit, hochwertiger Ausführung und ausgesuchten Materialien erfüllt das iPhone XS hohe ästhetische Erwartungen.

iPhone XR
Smartphone

Manufacturer
Apple, Cupertino, California, USA
In-house design
Web
www.apple.com

The iPhone XR integrates the technology of the iPhone XS in an all-screen design of glass and aluminium as well as an advanced LCD screen. The smartphone offers a powerful A12 bionic chip, Face ID as well as a further developed camera system, by which portrait images are created with only one lens. Due to the all-screen design, the display of the iPhone XR reaches up into the corners. The durable front glass is surrounded by an anodised aluminium frame which is available in six elegant colours. An advanced colouration process with seven coatings imparts deep, brilliant colours to the glass finish at the back.

Das iPhone XR integriert die Technologie des iPhone XS in ein All-Screen-Design aus Glas und Aluminium sowie einen fortschrittlichen LCD-Bildschirm. Das Smartphone bietet einen leistungsstarken A12-Bionic-Chip, Face ID sowie ein weiterentwickeltes Kamerasystem, bei dem Porträtaufnahmen mit nur einer Linse entstehen. Durch das All-Screen-Design reicht das Display des iPhone XR bis in die Ecken. Das stabile Frontglas ist von einem eloxierten Aluminiumrahmen umgeben, der in sechs eleganten Farben angeboten wird. Durch einen fortschrittlichen Färbeprozess in sieben Schichten zeigt das Glas-Finish auf der Rückseite tiefe, brillante Farben.

Statement by the jury
The design of the iPhone XR succeeds in combining sophisticated technology with use of high-quality materials and an expressive look.

Begründung der Jury
Der Gestaltung des iPhone XR gelingt es, eine ausgereifte Technik mit einem hochwertigen Materialeinsatz und einem ausdrucksstarken Look zu vereinen.

Mi MIX 3
Smartphone

Manufacturer
Xiaomi Inc., Beijing, China
In-house design
Liu Jia, Wang Yi
Web
www.mi.com

The display of this smartphone covers the front to 94 per cent. By means of a sliding mechanism, the high-resolution OLED display is slid downwards and uncovers a camera with flash. This function also provides other options, for instance receiving incoming calls. A fingerprint sensor is located at the back of the device. Both cameras located at the back produce images with twelve pixels. The selfie camera also provides two lenses, each with 24 and two megapixels definition. It can also be wirelessly charged.

Statement by the jury
The Mi MIX 3 smartphone convinces with its very stylish design and the high quality of the sliding function.

Das Display dieses Smartphones füllt die Frontseite zu 94 Prozent aus. Mittels magnetischem Sliding-Mechanismus wird das hochauflösende OLED-Display nach unten verschoben und eine Kamera mit Blitzlicht freigelegt. Zugleich ermöglicht diese Funktion andere Optionen, etwa Anrufe entgegenzunehmen. Ein Fingerabdrucksensor befindet sich auf der Rückseite des Geräts. Die beiden rückwärtig verbauten Kameras nehmen Bilder mit je zwölf Megapixeln auf. Die Selfie-Kamera verfügt ebenso über zwei Linsen, die je mit 24 und zwei Megapixeln auflösen. Kabelloses Aufladen ist ebenfalls möglich.

Begründung der Jury
Das Smartphone Mi MIX 3 überzeugt durch seine sehr stilvolle Gestaltung und die hochwertig ausgeführte Sliding-Funktion.

Pixel 3/Pixel 3XL
Smartphones

Manufacturer
Google LLC, Mountain View, California, USA
In-house design
Web
https://store.google.com

For the smartphones of the models Pixel 3 and Pixel 3XL, hardware, software and AI should all interrelate in a harmonised way. The OLED screen in HDR quality presents a silky surface structure, by means of which less fingerprints are left. A highly developed camera enhances images in retrospective processing and even suggests especially successful photos. The smartphones are available in the colours Just Black, Clearly White and Not Pink; each on/off button stands out in another distinctive colour.

Statement by the jury
Thanks to a harmonious design concept, the smartphones Pixel 3 und Pixel 3XL exude a carefree easiness.

Bei den Smartphones in den Ausführungen Pixel 3 und Pixel 3XL sollen Hardware, Software und AI harmonisch ineinandergreifen. Der OLED-Bildschirm in HDR-Qualität weist eine seidige Oberflächenstruktur auf, durch die weniger Fingerabdrücke zurückbleiben. Eine hochentwickelte Kamera verbessert Bilder in der Nachbearbeitung und schlägt selbst besonders gelungene Aufnahmen vor. Die Smartphones gibt es in den farblichen Ausführungen Just Black, Clearly White und Not Pink, der An-/Aus-Knopf hebt sich farblich jeweils zusätzlich ab.

Begründung der Jury
Dank eines harmonischen Gestaltungskonzepts versprühen die Smartphones Pixel 3 und Pixel 3XL eine unbekümmerte Leichtigkeit.

Mi 8 Explorer Edition
Smartphone

Manufacturer
Xiaomi Inc., Beijing, China
In-house design
Yang Jinling, Zhu Kai
Web
www.mi.com

The smartphone of the Mi 8 Explorer Edition offers an innovative dual frequency GPS and is equipped with a transparent glass cover which provides a view of the interior of the smartphone. By means of AI function, the dual camera recognises 206 scenes. Also, by means of AI technology, good images can be easily captured. Thanks to NFC, the Mi-Pay contactless payment system is available, which supports connection with over 160 urban transport systems as well as a key card.

Statement by the jury
Thanks to the many innovative functions, the Smartphone Mi 8 Explorer Edition supports a wide range of digital offers in urban areas.

Das Smartphone Mi 8 Explorer Edition bietet ein innovatives Dual Frequency GPS und verfügt über eine transparente Glasabdeckung, die einen Blick auf das Innere des Smartphones erlaubt. Mittels AI-Funktion erkennt die Dual-Kamera 206 Szenen. Ebenfalls durch AI-Technologie können auf einfachem Weg gute Bilder eingefangen werden. Dank NFC werden die Zahlungsfunktion Mi Pay, die Verbindung mit über 160 städtischen Transportsystemen sowie eine Schlüsselkarte unterstützt.

Begründung der Jury
Dank einer Vielzahl innovativer Funktionen unterstützt das Smartphone Mi 8 Explorer Edition eine breite Palette digitaler Angebote im urbanen Raum.

Pixel 3 Cases
Smartphone Cases
Smartphone-Hüllen

Manufacturer
Google LLC, Mountain View, California, USA
In-house design
Web
https://store.google.com

The knit exterior of these cases imparts to the colourfully striking on/off buttons of the Pixel 3 and Pixel 3XL phones an additional feature. Thanks to this tangible structure, the smartphone can also be easily pulled out of the pocket. The microfibre lining on the inside gives the phones protection, yet the necessary pressure on the outside for activating Google Assistant can still be applied.

Statement by the jury
These cases with their fresh look prove to be an easy to handle complement to the smartphones Pixel 3 and Pixel 3XL.

Das Strickmuster an der Außenseite dieser Hüllen verleiht den farblich auffälligen An-/Aus-Knöpfen der Smartphones Pixel 3 und Pixel 3XL einen zusätzlichen Akzent. Dank dieser spürbaren Struktur kann das Smartphone zudem leicht aus einer Tasche hervorgeholt werden. Die Mikrofaser-Auskleidung an der Innenseite verleiht den Smartphones Schutz, der notwendige Druck auf die Außenseiten zur Aktivierung von Google Assistant kann dennoch ausgeübt werden.

Begründung der Jury
Die Hüllen mit ihrem frischen Look erweisen sich als gut handhabbare Ergänzung zu den Smartphones Pixel 3 und Pixel 3XL.

LG V40 ThinQ
Smartphone

Manufacturer
LG Electronics Inc., Seoul, South Korea
In-house design
Seongjae Lim, Seala Park
Web
www.lg.com

Although the 6.4" monitor screen of the LG V40 ThinQ has a very large format, dimensions and weight are designed in such a way that the smartphone can be held comfortably in the hand. For this purpose, the glass is gently and elegantly curved. Its glass back is processed with the proprietary Silky Blast treatment. This generates pleasant metallic haptics with a luxurious appearance. The LG V40 ThinQ is equipped with three back and two front cameras.

Statement by the jury
The LG V40 ThinQ delights with its innovative material properties which impart an attractive, silky haptic to the smartphone.

Obwohl der Bildschirm des LG V40 ThinQ mit 6,4" sehr großformatig ist, sind Dimensionen und Gewicht so ausgelegt, dass sich das Smartphone bequem in der Hand halten lässt. Zu diesem Zweck ist das Glas an allen vier Seiten sanft und elegant gebogen. Das rückseitige Glas ist mit dem markeneigenen Silky-Blast-Verfahren behandelt. Dieses erzeugt eine angenehme metallische Haptik mit luxuriöser Anmutung. Das LG V40 ThinQ ist mit drei Rück- und zwei Frontkameras ausgestattet.

Begründung der Jury
Das LG V40 ThinQ begeistert durch seine innovativen Materialeigenschaften, die dem Smartphone eine ansprechende, seidenweiche Haptik verleihen.

LG G7 ThinQ
Smartphone

Manufacturer
LG Electronics Inc., Seoul, South Korea
In-house design
Hyoni Kim, Jiyoun Cha
Web
www.lg.com

When designing the LG G7 ThinQ, superfluous elements were left out to the benefit of a 6.1" QHD+ FullVision display with fully immersive effect. The front glass and metal frame are gently curved; by means of this and due to the very straight and smooth surfaces, the smartphone lies pleasantly in the hand. The display is easy to read, even in bright sunlight. The smartphone is impact-resistant, conforming to MIL-STD-810G1 as well as waterproof and dustproof in conformity with IP68.

Statement by the jury
The appearance of the LG G7 ThinQ is impressively plain and elegant at the same time and proves to be particularly sturdy.

Bei der Gestaltung des LG G7 ThinQ wurde zugunsten eines möglichst immersiv wirkenden 6,1" großen QHD+ FullVision-Displays auf überflüssige Elemente verzichtet. Frontglas und Metallrahmen sind an den Rändern sanft gebogen; dadurch sowie durch die sehr geraden und glatten Oberflächen liegt das Smartphone angenehm in der Hand. Das Display kann auch bei sehr hellem Sonnenlicht gut abgelesen werden. Das Smartphone ist stoßsicher gemäß MIL-STD-810G1 und wasser- und staubdicht gemäß IP68.

Begründung der Jury
Das LG G7 ThinQ präsentiert sich in eindrucksvoller Weise schlicht und elegant zugleich und erweist sich dabei als besonders robust.

MEIZU 15
Smartphone

Manufacturer
Meizu Technology Co., Ltd., Zhuhai, China
In-house design
Weijie Shen, Youngsu Cho
Web
www.meizu.com

The MEIZU 15 case is made of surgical stainless steel and aluminium alloy. The borders of the display are very narrow and harmonise with the overall, mainly symmetrically designed body. The device is unlocked by face recognition. A 20MP dual camera at the front enhances selfies by means of AI technology. The device is available in the elegant versions of gold, black and ceramic white.

Statement by the jury
The MEIZU 15 smartphone impresses with an optical equilibrium and the use of selective materials.

Das Gehäuse des MEIZU 15 besteht aus chirurgischem Edelstahl und einer Aluminiumlegierung. Die Displayränder sind sehr schmal und harmonieren mit dem insgesamt weitgehend symmetrisch gestalteten Körper. Entsperrt wird das Gerät mittels Gesichtserkennung. Eine 20MP-Dual-Kamera an der Frontseite verfeinert Selfies mittels AI-Technologie. Das Gerät ist in den eleganten Ausführungen Gold, Black und Ceramic White erhältlich.

Begründung der Jury
Das Smartphone MEIZU 15 beeindruckt durch eine optische Ausgewogenheit und die Verwendung ausgesuchter Materialien.

MEIZU 16th
Smartphone

Manufacturer
Meizu Technology Co., Ltd., Zhuhai, China
In-house design
Dongwei Wang, Rongmin You
Web
www.meizu.com

The MEIZU 16th offers a 6.0" AMOLED-COF screen, whereby the glass is curved at the sides and connects appealingly with the aluminium frame. This effect is emphasised by extremely narrow display borders. With a thickness of 7.3 mm, the smartphone appears relatively thin. The device is unlocked by fingerprint recognition; in order to prevent fatigue symptoms, this feature is located, for purposes of ergonomics of the thumb at the bottom of the screen and easily reached.

Statement by the jury
The design of the MEIZU 16th convinces with a high-quality screen and ergonomics that are anatomically right for the hand.

Das MEIZU 16th bietet einen 6,0"-AMOLED-COF-Bildschirm, dessen Glas an den Seiten gewölbt ist und sich harmonisch anmutend mit dem Aluminiumrahmen verbindet. Verstärkt wird dieser Effekt durch äußerst schmale Displayränder. Mit einer Stärke von 7,3 mm fällt das Smartphone verhältnismäßig schmal aus. Das Gerät wird mittels Fingerprinterkennung entsperrt; um dabei Ermüdungserscheinungen zu vermeiden, wurde diese für die Ergonomie des Daumens möglichst entgegenkommend am unteren Teil des Bildschirms platziert.

Begründung der Jury
Die Gestaltung des MEIZU 16th überzeugt mit einem hochwertigen Bildschirm und einer Ergonomie, die der Anatomie einer Hand gerecht wird.

Medion® Lifetab® X10604
Tablet

Manufacturer
MEDION AG, Essen, Germany
In-house design
Web
www.medion.com

The Medion LifeTab X10604 is a 10.1" tablet of the higher quality class. With its compact dimensions, an aluminium housing with elegant and smooth line management underlining the characteristics of the device, as well as a thickness of only 8.5 mm, it fills the gap between a smartphone and a mobile computer. The keyboard allows for comfortable text input. High-quality component parts such as the Quad-Core processor and full HD display guarantee comfortable working conditions even when working on sophisticated challenges.

Statement by the jury
Thanks to its transformability and light weight, the Medion Lifetab X10604 offers itself as an uncomplicated and functional companion.

Das Medion LifeTab X10604 ist ein 10,1"-Tablet der gehobenen Qualitätsklasse. Mit seinen kompakten Dimensionen, einem Aluminiumgehäuse mit eleganter und ruhiger Linienführung, die die Charakteristik des Geräts unterstreicht, sowie einer Gehäusestärke von nur 8,5 mm füllt es den Bereich zwischen einem Smartphone und einem mobilen Computer. Die Tastatur ermöglicht eine komfortable Texteingabe. Hochqualitative Bestandteile wie der Quad-Core-Prozessor und das Full-HD-Display sorgen für komfortable Arbeitsbedingungen auch bei anspruchsvollen Herausforderungen.

Begründung der Jury
Dank seiner Wandelbarkeit und Leichtigkeit bietet sich das Medion Lifetab X10604 als unkomplizierter und funktionaler Begleiter an.

Pixel Slate/Pixel Slate Keyboard
Tablet and Keyboard
Tablet und Tastatur

Manufacturer
Google LLC, Mountain View, California, USA
In-house design
Web
https://store.google.com

The Pixel Slate Tablet is connected to the Pixel Slate Keyboard by simply snapping it in, pairing or Bluetooth are not necessary. The back is designed in such a way that the tablet can be adjusted to any angle. Thanks to the gentle curving of all edges and corners, the unit can be easily slipped into a bag. A pleasant feel is created by matte surfaces. The round keys generate a friendly impression and are very ergonomic when typing.

Statement by the jury
The interaction of Pixel Slate and Pixel Slate Keyboard is playful to perform. Thus, a laptop is created which can be taken along when out of doors.

Das Pixel Slate Tablet wird mit dem Pixel Slate Keyboard durch simples Einrasten verbunden, Pairing oder Bluetooth sind nicht vonnöten. Der Rückenteil ist so konstruiert, dass das Tablet in jedem Winkel justiert werden kann. Dank sanfter Rundungen an allen Kanten und Ecken lässt sich die Einheit problemlos in eine Tasche stecken. Eine angenehme Haptik wird durch matte Oberflächen erzeugt. Die runden Tasten erzeugen eine freundliche Anmutung und kommen der Ergonomie beim Tippen sehr entgegen.

Begründung der Jury
Die Interaktion von Pixel Slate und Pixel Slate Keyboard gelingt spielerisch. So entsteht ein Laptop, der sich zur Mitnahme für unterwegs anbietet.

Scrolling Keyboard
Tastatur

Manufacturer
Royole Corporation, Fremont, California, USA
In-house design
Web
www.royole.com

Rolled up in its tube, the Scrolling Keyboard is only 154 mm long and fits in everyone's pocket. When pulled out it can connect to a mobile device via Bluetooth. In this way, the user has a generously dimensioned keyboard available at all times, for instance in a narrow aircraft seat or for memorising a spontaneous idea. With a single press of a button, the keyboard can be rolled back in its tube after use.

Statement by the jury
The ingenious design of this roll-up keyboard is ideal for the demands of a mobility-conscious society.

In seine Hülse eingerollt, ist das Scrolling Keyboard nur 154 mm lang und passt in jede Tasche. Wird es ausgezogen, lässt es sich via Bluetooth mit einem mobilen Endgerät verbinden. Dem Nutzer steht damit eine großzügige Tastatur jederzeit zur Verfügung, etwa in einem engen Flugzeugsitz oder um in einem Café spontan einen Gedanken festzuhalten. Durch einen einzigen Tastendruck rollt sich die Tastatur nach Gebrauch selbstständig in ihre Hülse zurück.

Begründung der Jury
Die einfallsreiche Gestaltung dieser zusammenrollbaren Tastatur wird den Anforderungen einer auf Mobilität bedachten Gesellschaft gerecht.

MIIIW Dual Mode Keyboard
Tastatur

Manufacturer
Beijing MIIIW Technology Co., Ltd.,
Beijing, China
In-house design
Miiiw Design Team
(Gaoxin Bi, Zhenhao Chen,
Lei Chen, Xiangwen Wu, Xunyu Yang)
Web
www.miiiw.com

A rubberised slot at the upper edge of this keyboard allows mobile devices to be fitted in. That way, traditional and mobile devices in an office can be interconnected. By means of a Bluetooth and a 4G button, switching between different devices is possible. Arrangement of the buttons is compatible for a PC, as well as for Mac, iOS and Android. A high-quality aluminium bottom shell stabilises the keyboard. A specific number keyboard and shortcuts assure efficient input.

Statement by the jury
The MIIIW Dual Mode Keyboard proves to be a well-considered interface between the various devices used for modern office work.

Ein gummierter Schlitz an der oberen Kante dieser Tastatur nimmt mobile Endgeräte auf. Auf diese Weise werden traditionelle und mobile Endgeräte eines Büros miteinander verbunden. Mittels einer Bluetooth- und einer 4G-Taste kann einfach zwischen den verschiedenen Geräten hin und her gewechselt werden. Die Tastengestaltung ist auf PC sowie Mac, iOS und Android ausgelegt. Ein hochwertiger Aluminiumboden stabilisiert die Tastatur. Eine eigene Nummerntastatur und Shortcuts sorgen für eine effiziente Eingabe.

Begründung der Jury
Das MIIIW Dual Mode Keyboard erweist sich als gut durchdachte Schnittstelle zwischen den unterschiedlichen Endgeräten eines modernen Bürobetriebes.

Gotek Master Wireless Keyboard with Charging Pad
Kabellose Tastatur
mit Ladepad

Manufacturer
Shenzhen Bo Yi Industrial Co., Ltd.,
Shenzhen, China
In-house design
Shenzhen Bo Yi Industrial Co., Ltd.
(Elena Balakhnova)
Web
www.rego-tech.com

The wireless keyboard connects by Bluetooth 3.0 compatible user devices such as smartphones or tablets within a range of ten metres. It is compatible with Windows, iOS and Android devices. With only one button, the user can switch back and forth between three devices. The concavely shaped keys allow quiet typing and are precisely manufactured. The wireless charging pad provides Qi-enabled smartphones or a mouse with energy.

Statement by the jury
The wireless keyboard assures ergonomically pleasant operation. In combination with charging pad and mouse it forms a coherent unit.

Die kabellose Tastatur verbindet sich mittels Bluetooth 3.0 mit kompatiblen Endgeräten wie Smartphones oder Tablets in einem Umkreis von zehn Metern. Sie ist kompatibel mit Windows-, iOS und Android-Endgeräten. Mit nur einem Knopfdruck lässt sich bequem zwischen drei Geräten hin und her wechseln. Die konkaven Tasten ermöglichen leises Tippen und sind präzise gefertigt. Das kabellose Ladepad versorgt Qi-fähige Smartphones oder die Maus mit Energie.

Begründung der Jury
Die kabellose Tastatur ermöglicht eine ergonomisch angenehme Bedienung. In Kombination mit Ladepad und Maus bildet sie eine schlüssige Einheit.

i.safe MOBILE Tablets

Manufacturer
i.safe MOBILE GmbH, Lauda-Königshofen, Germany
In-house design
Web
www.isafe-mobile.com

The series comprises the IS910.1 and the IS910.2 for use in explosion endangered areas as well as the RG910 for use in rugged industrial environments outside of those areas. The durable plastic frame supports in particular the impact-resistant and shockproof properties of the devices. They are waterproof and dustproof as well as microparticle-protected in conformity with IP68 and can withstand temperatures from -20 to 60 degrees C. Their low weight, compact dimensions as well as a hand strap at the back of the 8" tablets assure practical and secure handling.

Die Serie besteht aus dem IS910.1 und dem IS910.2 für den Einsatz in explosionsgefährdeten Bereichen sowie dem RG910 für die Nutzung in rauen Industrieumgebungen außerhalb dieser Bereiche. Der widerstandsfähige Kunststoffrahmen unterstützt insbesondere den Stoß- und Aufprallschutz der Geräte. Nach IP68 sind diese wasser- und staubdicht sowie vor Mikropartikeln geschützt und bei extremen Temperaturen von -20 bis 60 Grad C einsetzbar. Ein geringes Gewicht, kompakte Maße sowie eine Handschlaufe auf der Rückseite der 8"-Tablets gewährleisten eine praktische und sichere Handhabung.

Statement by the jury
The i.safe MOBILE Tablets stand out due to their high-quality workmanship, by means of which they assure operation even under extreme conditions.

Begründung der Jury
Die i.safe MOBILE Tablets überzeugen durch ihre hochwertige Verarbeitung, durch die sie sich auch unter Extrembedingungen bewähren.

iPad Pro
Tablet

Manufacturer
Apple, Cupertino, California, USA
In-house design
Web
www.apple.com

The new all-screen design of the iPad Pro brings the advanced Liquid Retina display to the edges of the tablet. The iPad Pro offers Face ID and a smart, powerful A12X Bionic chip. USB-C facilitates high-performance connectivity to accessories such as an external display or a camera. With Gigabit-class LTE, quick connectivity is possible while travelling. The new Apple Pencil holds to the iPad magnetically and can thus be stowed away together and wirelessly charged. For use with apps, for example Notes, a double-tap enables a quick change between tools or activates the eraser.

Das neue All-Screen-Design des iPad Pro führt das fortschrittliche Liquid-Retina-Display bis an den Rand. Das iPad Pro bietet Face ID und einen smarten, leistungsfähigen A12X-Bionic-Chip. USB-C ermöglicht eine Hochleistungsverbindung zu Zubehör wie einem externen Display oder einer Kamera. LTE der Gigabit-Klasse ermöglicht schnelle Verbindungen unterwegs. Der neue Apple Pencil hält magnetisch an dem iPad und kann so verstaut, gekoppelt und kabellos geladen werden. Beim Bearbeiten von Apps wie etwa Notes wird mittels Doppeltippen schnell zwischen Werkzeugen gewechselt oder der Radierer gewählt.

Statement by the jury
Thanks to its exciting all-screen design and use of advanced technology, the iPad Pro offers a contemporary, multi-functional work surface.

Begründung der Jury
Dank seines aufregenden All-Screen-Designs und eines fortschrittlichen Technikeinsatzes bietet das iPad Pro eine zeitgemäße, multifunktionale Arbeitsfläche.

ROG Phone
Smartphone and Accessories
Smartphone und Zubehör

Manufacturer
Asustek Computer Inc., Taipei City, Taiwan
In-house design
Web
www.asus.com

The ROG Phone with 3D glass and ultra-responsive AirTriggers, dual front stereo loudspeakers with a powerful 18:9 AMOLED display offers additional components for the gaming sector. The removable AeroActive cooler disperses the heat. By means of integration in the TwinView Dock, the ROG is converted into a dual-screen handheld console which, among others, offers an extended 6,000mAh battery and buttons with haptic feedback. The Mobile Desktop Dock connects the device with an external 4K UHD monitor.

Statement by the jury
The ROG Phone surprises with its impressive accessories enabling it to be converted into a complete gaming station.

Das ROG Phone mit 3D-Glas und reaktionsschnellen AirTriggern, dualen Front-Stereo-Lautsprechern und einem leistungsstarken 18:9-AMOLED-Bildschirm bietet zusätzliche Komponenten für den Gaming-Bereich. Der abnehmbare AeroActive Cooler leitet die Hitze ab. Durch Integration in das TwinView Dock wird das ROG Phone zu einer Dual-Screen Handheld-Konsole, die u. a. eine erweiterte 6.000-mAh-Batterie und Tasten mit haptischem Feedback bietet. Das Mobile Desktop Dock verbindet das Gerät mit einem externen 4K-UHD-Monitor.

Begründung der Jury
Das ROG Phone erstaunt durch sein beeindruckendes Zubehör, mit dem es zu einer vollwertigen Gaming-Station wird.

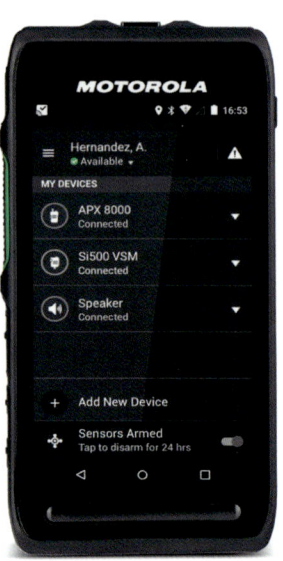

LEX L11
Smartphone and Two-Way-Radio
Smartphone und Funkgerät

Manufacturer
Motorola Solutions, Plantation, Florida, USA
In-house design
Web
www.motorolasolutions.com

The LEX L11 is a combination of traditional push-to-talk button communication and a generously dimensioned touchscreen, which can run via app and multimedia functions. In order to make use of the available radio frequency system, it can be linked to another radio device. In undercover operation it can also control a covert radio. The functions make operation for the user from the public security sector as easy and effective as possible, for example by large and intuitively controllable buttons.

Statement by the jury
Sturdiness and well-considered functions prove the particular suitability of the LEX L11 in the field responsible for public order.

Das LEX L11 ist eine Kombination aus traditioneller Sprechtasten-Kommunikation und einem großzügigen Touchscreen, auf dem Apps und multimediale Funktionen laufen können. Um das vorhandene Funkwellensystem zu nutzen, kann es sich mit einem anderen Funkgerät verbinden. Bei versteckten Operationen steuert es auch ein geheimes Funkgerät. Die Funktionen machen die Bedienung für Anwender aus dem Bereich der öffentlichen Sicherheit so leicht und effektiv wie möglich, etwa durch große und intuitiv steuerbare Tasten.

Begründung der Jury
Robustheit und durchdachte Funktionen beweisen die besondere Eignung des LEX L11 für verantwortungsvolle Bereiche der öffentlichen Ordnung.

Chocolate MM750 Feature Phone
Mobile Phone
Mobiltelefon

Manufacturer
SIMDO Technology Co., Ltd., Shenzhen, China
In-house design
Henry Shawn
Web
www.simdo.cn

The Chocolate MM750 Feature Phone is designed for the requirements of elderly people. It offers an emergency button which, however, does not have a corresponding symbol in order to avoid negative emotions among the target group. The SIM card can be removed directly via a slot at the side. The side components are seamless; access to electronic components inside is possible from the top. The housing can be held well and safely in the hand due to a matte finish with tangible structure.

Statement by the jury
From a functional viewpoint, the Chocolate MM750 Feature Phone takes the needs of elderly people sensitively into account.

Das Chocolate MM750 Feature Phone ist auf die Bedürfnisse älterer Nutzer ausgerichtet. Es bietet einen Notfallknopf, der allerdings ohne entsprechendes Symbol versehen ist, um negative Emotionen bei der Zielgruppe zu vermeiden. Die SIM-Karte kann über einen seitlichen Schlitz direkt entnommen werden. Die Seitenteile sind nahtlos ausgeführt, auf elektronische Komponenten im Inneren kann über die Oberseite zugegriffen werden. Durch eine matte Politur mit spürbarer Struktur kann das Gehäuse gut und sicher in der Hand gehalten werden.

Begründung der Jury
In funktionaler Hinsicht nimmt das Chocolate MM750 Feature Phone sehr einfühlsam auf die Bedürfnisse älterer Menschen Bedacht.

The Light Phone
Mobile Phone
Mobiltelefon

Manufacturer
Light, New York, USA
In-house design
Kaiwei Tang, Joe Hollier
Web
www.lightphone.com

The Light Phone is a slender mobile phone with the size of a credit card, with which only phone calls can be made and answered. Thus the user remains reachable without being distracted by the usual online functions. The device is connected to the smartphone by means of pairing and uses its phone number. The LED display shimmers softly out of the elegant, reduced form of matte glass.

Statement by the jury
The Light Phone has a minimalist design and is characterised by a reduced functionality which enables the user to concentrate on essential tasks.

Das Light Phone ist ein schlankes Mobiltelefon in Kreditkartengröße, mit dem man ausschließlich Anrufe tätigen und entgegennehmen kann. So bleibt der Nutzer erreichbar, ohne von den üblichen Online-Funktionen abgelenkt zu werden. Mittels Pairing ist das Gerät mit dem Smartphone verbunden und nutzt dessen Telefonnummer. In der elegant reduzierten Form aus Mattglas schimmert die LED-Anzeige sanft hervor.

Begründung der Jury
Das minimalistisch gestaltete Light Phone zeichnet sich durch eine reduzierte Funktionsweise aus, durch die sich der Nutzer auf essenzielle Aufgaben konzentrieren kann.

Card Phone KY-01L
Mobile Phone
Mobiltelefon

Manufacturer
KYOCERA Corporation, Kyoto, Japan
Design
NTT DOCOMO, Inc., Product Department, Design Management Section, Tokyo, Japan
Web
http://global.kyocera.com
www.nttdocomo.co.jp/english

This mobile phone is extremely thin, having only the size of a business card. The display uses e-paper technology. By this means, it not only saves energy but also realises miniaturisation. The colours have been chosen to give the impression of e-paper, on which the display characters appear to float. Its compact form makes it attractive, above all, for early adopters and business users.

Statement by the jury
With its surprisingly small dimensions and its sophisticated aesthetics the Card Phone KY-01L fascinates the user.

Dieses Mobiltelefon ist äußerst dünn und kommt mit den Maßen einer Visitkarte aus. Das Display ist mit E-Paper-Technologie ausgestattet. Damit lässt sich einerseits Energie sparen und sie verhilft dem Gerät zu seinem minimalistischen Format. Die gewählten Farben vermitteln den Eindruck von elektronischem Papier, auf dem die Zeichen zu fließen scheinen. Seine Kompaktheit macht das Mobiltelefon vor allem für Erstanwender und im Berufsalltag attraktiv.

Begründung der Jury
Mit seinen erstaunlich geringen Maßen und seiner raffinierten Ästhetik zieht das Card Phone KY-01L den Nutzer in seinen Bann.

NichePhone-S 4G
Mobile Phone
Mobiltelefon

Manufacturer
FutureModel Corp., Shinjuku, Tokyo, Japan
In-house design
Web
www.futuremodel.co.jp

The NichePhone-S 4G is restricted to the important functions of telephony and SMS texting. It also facilitates tethering via Wi-Fi, enabling other devices to connect with the Internet. An intuitively understood keyboard supports operation. With a thickness of only 9.5 mm, a weight of 52 grams, an aluminium reinforced back and gently rounded sides, the mobile phone exudes an elegant impression.

Statement by the jury
The NichePhone-S in an impressive way stays reduced to essentials and proves thereby to be exceptionally up-to-date.

Das NichePhone-S 4G beschränkt sich auf die wichtigen Funktionen der Telefonie und Texterstellung. Zusätzlich ermöglicht es Tethering via Wi-Fi, sodass es andere Geräte mit dem Internet verbinden kann. Eine intuitiv erfassbare Tastatur unterstützt die Bedienung. Mit einer Seitenstärke von nur 9,5 mm, einem Gewicht von 52 Gramm, einem aluminiumverstärktem Rückenteil und sanft abgerundeten Seiten strahlt das Mobiletelefon eine elegante Anmutung aus.

Begründung der Jury
Das NichePhone-S bleibt auf beeindruckende Weise auf das Wesentliche reduziert und erweist sich gerade dadurch als ausnehmend zeitgemäß.

AQUOS Zero
Smartphone

Manufacturer
SHARP Corporation, IoT Communication BU,
Sakai, Osaka, Japan
In-house design
Akira Haranaka, Yasuhiko Mano
Web
www.sharp.co.jp

By means of a light magnesium alloy for the frame and a back of Kevlar fibre, the Aquos Zero is particularly light. An arched display emphasises the slender design in the side view; from the front, the side frame is almost invisible. Moreover, the smartphone is pleasant to hold due to the rounded sides and hand fatigue is reduced. The generous display in combination with a sound quality in Dolby stereo supports a high-quality image experience.

Statement by the jury
The precisely engineered, arched display of the Aquos Zero is appealing with its elegant appearance. Its light weight is also attractive.

Durch eine leichte Magnesiumlegierung für den Rahmen und eine Rückseite aus Kevlar-Faser ist das Aquos Zero besonders leicht. Ein gebogenes Display betont das schlanke Design in der Seitenansicht, in der Frontsicht bleibt der seitliche Rahmen nahezu unsichtbar. Zudem lässt sich das Smartphone durch die gerundeten Seiten gut halten und es werden Ermüdungserscheinungen in der Hand reduziert. Das großzügige Display in Verbindung mit einer Tonqualität in Dolby Stereo unterstützt ein hochwertiges Bilderleben.

Begründung der Jury
Das präzise gefertigte, gewölbte Display des Aquos Zero gefällt mit seiner eleganten Anmutung. Darüber hinaus findet auch das geringe Gewicht Zuspruch.

AQUOS sense2
Smartphone

Manufacturer
SHARP Corporation, IoT Communication BU,
Sakai, Osaka, Japan
In-house design
Masaki Kawamura
Web
www.sharp.co.jp

With its vertically long aspect ratio of 18:9, the body of the smartphone with 5.5" IGZO-LCD screen is kept slim and it can be held easily in the hand. The display is enclosed by a very narrow frame. An apparently seamless form and chamfered corners result in a plain and yet noble design. The glass screen, a very stable metal construction and a matte, metallic colouring add up to the peaceful and elegant appearance of the Aquos sense2.

Statement by the jury
The slender body of the Aquos sense2 proves to be user-friendly. Its harmonious and coherent design is appealing.

Mit einem hochgestreckten Bildformat von 18:9 bleibt der Körper des Smartphones mit 5,5"-IGZO-LCD-Bildschirm schlank und es ist einfach in der Hand zu halten. Das Display ist von einem nur sehr schmalen Rahmen umgeben. Eine scheinbar nahtlose Formgebung und abgerundete Ecken ergeben ein schlichtes und zugleich edles Design. Der Glas-Bildschirm, eine sehr stabile Metallkonstruktion und eine mattierte metallische Farbgebung unterstützen die ruhige und elegante Anmutung des Aquos sense2.

Begründung der Jury
Der schlanke Körper des Aquos sense2 erweist sich als nutzerfreundlich. Zudem gefällt seine harmonische und stimmige Gestaltung.

AQUOS R2 compact
Smartphone

Manufacturer
SHARP Corporation, IoT Communication BU,
Sakai, Osaka, Japan
In-house design
Kazuhiro Shibata, Takashi Tanaka
Web
www.sharp.co.jp

For the design of this smartphone, special attention was paid to a compact design which lies pleasantly in the hand. The four rounded corners give the user the feel of holding the whole screen in the hand. The innovative Free Form Display has a camera integrated in the screen. The back of the 3D liquid crystal screen has been treated with a special vapour deposition process which imparts on it a clear, elegant surface finish.

Statement by the jury
The Aquos R2 compact gains merit with its ergonomically sophisticated construction, which proves to be very user-friendly.

Besonderes Augenmerk wurde bei der Gestaltung dieses Smartphones auf ein kompaktes Design gelegt, das sich gut in der Hand halten lässt. Die vier abgerundeten Ecken vermitteln dem Nutzer das Gefühl, den gesamten Bildschirm umfassen zu können. Das innovative Free-Form-Display hat im Bildschirm eine Kamera integriert. Die Rückseite des 3D-Flüssigkristallbildschirms wurde einem speziellen Gasphasenabscheidungsverfahren unterzogen, was ihr eine klare, elegante Oberfläche verleiht.

Begründung der Jury
Das Aquos R2 compact punktet mit seiner ergonomisch ausgefeilten Bauweise, die sich als sehr nutzerfreundlich erweist.

Xperia XZ3
Smartphone

Manufacturer
Sony Mobile Communications Inc.,
Tokyo, Japan
Design
Sony Corporation, Creative Center
(Yusuke Otani, Wakaba Sakai), Tokyo, Japan
Web
www.sonymobile.com
www.sony.net/design

Thanks to the highly developed technology implemented from the TV sector, with the Xperia XZ3, Internet content is provided in HDR image quality. A double-tap on the right or left side of the device activates the newly developed, user-friendly Side Sense function. It learns from user behaviour and suggests apps for the particular situation, which are also arranged in a user-friendly manner on the 6.0" sized HDR OLED display with 3D rounded surfaces.

Statement by the jury
With Side Sense each user of an Xperia XZ3 receives an individual smartphone – an impressive, innovative idea.

MotoZ4/Moto Mods
Smartphone and Accessories
Smartphone und Zubehör

Manufacturer
Motorola, Shenzhen, China
In-house design
Web
www.motorola.com.cn
www.motorola.com

Due to the accessory set Moto Mods, the functions of the MotoZ4 can be variably extended. With the Moto Insta-Share Projector, films can be projected on large screens. The Moto Smart Speaker in connection with Amazon Alexa offers personalised assistance functions. The Polaroid Insta-Share Printer reproduces photos. With the Moto Turbopower Pack, the smartphone is recharged quickly. The accessories are easily attached by means of a magnetic strip with contacts at the back.

Statement by the jury
With its extended function range by means of the clever Moto Mods, the MotoZ4 smartphone attracts attention.

FlexPai
Smartphone

Manufacturer
Royole Corporation, Fremont, California, USA
In-house design
Web
www.royole.com

Thanks to an innovative, patent technology, development succeeded in creating a fully functional AMOLED display screen which can be folded to each side in the middle. The FlexPai smartphone can be folded over 200,000 times without breaking. Integrating a cutting-edge Snapdragon processor of the series 8, the device supports high-performance AI technology and is upgradable to 5G mobile reception. The camera has a 20 MP telephoto lens and a 16 MP wide-angle lens as well as dual viewing mode for normal photos and selfies.

Statement by the jury
Thanks to its impressive, innovative, foldable display screen, this FlexPai smartphone convinces with high functionality and convenience.

Vogue
Powerbank

Manufacturer
Goui, Dubai
In-house design
Web
www.goui.com

The Vogue powerbank offers a charging capacity of 10,200 mAh. It is equipped with Qualcomm 3.0 as well as Power Delivery 3.0 technology and charges both Android devices as well as iPhones. 80 per cent of the most popular iPhones are charged in less than 35 minutes. The powerbank displays a compact form. The rubberised surface provides protection and facilitates convenient handling, creating at the same time a modern impression.

Statement by the jury
The Vogue powerbank impresses due to its short charging time and proves to be pleasantly simple to operate.

Die Powerbank Vogue bietet eine Ladekapazität von 10.200 mAh. Mit Qualcomm-3.0- und Power-Delivery-3.0-Technologie ausgestattet, lädt sie sowohl Android-Geräte wie auch iPhones. 80 Prozent der meistgenutzten Smartphones werden in weniger als 35 Minuten aufgeladen. Die Powerbank zeigt eine kompakte Form. Die gummierte Oberfläche bietet Schutz und ermöglicht eine bequeme Handhabung, zugleich verleiht sie dem Gerät eine moderne Anmutung.

Begründung der Jury
Die Powerbank Vogue beeindruckt durch eine schnelle Ladezeit und erweist sich als angenehm einfach in der Bedienung.

Venti
Powerbank

Manufacturer
Goui, Dubai
In-house design
Web
www.goui.com

The Venti powerbank provides a charging capacity of 17,000 mAh. Equipped with Qualcomm 3.0 and Power Delivery 3.0 technologies, it can supply both Android devices as well as iPhones with power. The power bank charges 80 percent of the most commonly used smartphones in under 35 minutes. With its handy form and a non-slip surface, the device is good to operate and carry around. Display of the charging status is a feature in modern colours.

Statement by the jury
High-quality technical equipment makes the Venti powerbank surprisingly versatile and efficient in use.

Eine Ladekapazität von 17.000 mAh stellt die Powerbank Venti bereit. Ausgestattet mit Qualcomm 3.0 und Power Delivery 3.0 können sowohl Android-Geräte wie auch iPhones mit Energie versorgt werden. In unter 35 Minuten lädt die Powerbank 80 Prozent der meistgenutzten Smartphones. Mit seiner handlichen Formgebung und einer rutschbeständigen Oberfläche lässt sich das Gerät gut bedienen und mitführen. Die Anzeige des Ladestatus setzt einen modischen farblichen Akzent.

Begründung der Jury
Eine hochwertige technische Ausstattung macht die Powerbank Venti erstaunlich vielseitig und effizient einsetzbar.

Prelude
Powerbank

Manufacturer
Bezalel Inc., Los Angeles, USA
In-house design
Frank Wu, Sheng-Chieh Chang
Web
www.bezalel.co

By combining the nano-suction and wireless charging technology, the powerbank Prelude can easily stick to the back of any Qi-enabled smartphone and charge even while the user is on the move. 5000mAh battery cells and fast wireless charging chipsets are integrated in a slim, durable frame. With a smooth body and gently rounded corners, the seamless design of Prelude fits very good in the hand and offers pleasant haptics.

Statement by the jury
Prelude gains merit with user-friendly functionality, thanks to which the smartphone can be used while being wirelessly charged.

Dank einer Kombination der Nano-Suction- und kabelloser Lade-Technologie, haftet die Powerbank Prelude einfach an der Rückseite jedes Qi-fähigen Smartphones, selbst wenn der Nutzer unterwegs ist. 5000-mAh-Batteriezellen und Chipsätze für schnelles kabelloses Laden sind in einen schlanken, langlebigen Körper integriert. Mit einem glatten und sanft gerundeten Gehäuse ist Prelude so gestaltet, dass es sehr gut in die Hand passt und eine angenehme Haptik bietet.

Begründung der Jury
Prelude punktet mit nutzerfreundlicher Funktionalität, dank der das Smartphone während des Ladevorgangs einsatzbereit bleibt.

PB102 Powerbank

Manufacturer
Ugreen Group Limited, Shenzhen, China
In-house design
Tuo Zhu
Web
www.ugreen.com

The PB102 Powerbank is equipped with an integrated lightning cable which is MFi certified. By means of built-in magnets, the cable slots reliably into a groove for storage. The semicircular design of this groove is ergonomic, allowing the cable to be easily removed as required. A honeycomb structure is located under the surface, giving the powerbank a pleasant and non-slip haptic and preventing scratches.

Statement by the jury
The PB102 Powerbank, with its aesthetically ambitious design attracts attention and delights with its easy handling.

In die PB102 Powerbank ist ein MFi-zertifiziertes Lightning-Kabel integriert. Mittels eingebauter Magneten rastet das Kabel zuverlässig in einer Rille ein, um es zu verstauen. Die halbrunde Gestaltung dieser Einbuchtung kommt der Ergonomie entgegen, so lässt sich das Kabel bei Bedarf einfach herauslösen. Unter der Oberfläche befindet sich eine Wabenstruktur, die der Powerbank eine angenehme und rutschfeste Haptik verleiht und Kratzern entgegenwirkt.

Begründung der Jury
Die PB102 Powerbank zieht mit einer ästhetisch anspruchsvollen Gestaltung die Blicke auf sich und erfreut durch einfaches Handling.

CP602 GoPro Powerbank

Manufacturer
Ugreen Group Limited, Shenzhen, China
In-house design
Bolin Luo, Tuo Zhu, Chen Jie
Web
www.ugreen.com

This powerbank has been developed to supply a sport camera of the GoPro Hero series with new energy while the user is on the go. At the same time, the device can charge a mobile phone. For the charging process, the GoPro battery is slotted into a side compartment. Thanks to its compact form, it is easy to transport and store in a bag next to other outdoor equipment. The surface is rubberised, so the device is pleasant to handle.

Statement by the jury
The CP602 GoPro Powerbank proves to be a well-considered construction. It is therefore well suited to demanding outdoor use.

Diese Powerbank wurde entwickelt, um eine Sportkamera der Serie GoPro Hero unterwegs mit neuer Energie versorgen zu können. Gleichzeitig kann das Gerät ein Mobiltelefon laden. Für den Ladevorgang wird der GoPro-Akku über ein Seitenfach eingeschoben. Dank seiner kompakten Form lässt es sich leicht transportieren und in einer Tasche neben anderer Outdoor-Ausrüstung verstauen. Die Oberfläche ist gummiert, dadurch lässt sich das Gerät gut handhaben.

Begründung der Jury
Die CP602 GoPro Powerbank erweist sich als durchdacht konstruiert. Sie eignet sich dabei besonders gut für den anspruchsvollen Outdoorbereich.

Xiaomi Laptop Powerbank

Manufacturer
Zimi Corporation, Nanjing, China
Design
Xiaomi Inc., Beijing, China
Web
www.zmifi.com
www.mi.com

The Xiaomi Laptop Powerbank has a very clear design that is reminiscent of a reliable cartridge. The matte surface emphasises the noble appearance, at the same time offering pleasant haptics and easing the handling of the device. With a power of 45 watts, it has quick charging protocols; laptops or a Nintendo Wii can also be supplied with energy via USB-C connection.

Statement by the jury
The Xiaomi Laptop Powerbank is attractive with its compact design which reflects the reliability of the device.

Eine sehr klare Gestaltung, die an eine zuverlässige Kartusche erinnert, weist die Xiaomi Laptop Powerbank auf. Die matte Oberfläche verstärkt diese edle Anmutung, zugleich bietet sie eine angenehme Haptik und erleichtert die Handhabung des Geräts. Bei einer Leistung von 45 Watt arbeitet es im Schnellladungsprotokoll, auch Laptops oder eine Nintendo Wii können mittels USB-C-Anschluss mit Energie versorgt werden.

Begründung der Jury
Die Xiaomi Laptop Powerbank gefällt in ihrer kompakten Gestaltung, in der sich die Zuverlässigkeit des Geräts widerspiegelt.

Powerbank PD10000

Manufacturer
Intenso International GmbH, Vechta, Germany
In-house design
Web
www.intenso-international.de

Equipped with Power Delivery and Quick Charge 3.0, the Powerbank PD10000 offers high-quality fast charging functions. The digital percent display provides information on the charge status at all times. A USB Type-C connector, a USB output and a Micro USB port make the device compatible with the latest smartphones, tablets and laptops. A connecting cable for Type-C devices is included in the package.

Ausgestattet mit Power Delivery und Quick Charge 3.0 bietet die Powerbank PD10000 hochwertige Schnellladefunktionen. Die digitale Prozentanzeige ermöglicht zu jeder Zeit eine genaue Auskunft über den Ladestatus. Ein Typ-C-USB-Anschluss, ein USB-Ausgang und ein Micro-USB-Eingang ermöglichen die Kompatibilität zu allen aktuellen Smartphones, Tablets und Laptops. Ein Kabel für die Verbindung mit Typ-C-Endgeräten ist im Lieferumfang enthalten.

Statement by the jury
The Powerbank PD10000 provides new energy to user devices surprisingly quickly. The digital display of the charge status is implemented in an optically attractive way.

Begründung der Jury
Die Powerbank PD10000 versorgt Endgeräte erstaunlich schnell mit neuer Energie. Die digitale Anzeige des Ladestatus ist optisch ansprechend umgesetzt.

Wireless Charger BA1/WA1
Kabelloses Ladepad

Manufacturer
Intenso International GmbH,
Vechta, Germany
In-house design
Web
www.intenso-international.de

Thanks to inductive charging technology the smartphone only needs to be placed on the BA1/WA1 wireless charger to re-energise it. The silver, aluminium edge is an eye-catcher, whereby the device blends in well with every interior and ambience. The matte contact surface in black or white contributes to the stylish appearance as well and also prevents the smartphone from sliding off. The BA1/WA1 wireless charger is compatible with every Qi-enabled smartphone.

Statement by the jury
The BA1/WA1 wireless charger gains merit by its stylish design which makes it an appealing accessory at home as well as in the office.

Dank induktiver Ladetechnologie lässt sich das Smartphone einfach auf den Wireless Charger BA1/WA1 auflegen, um es mit neuer Energie zu versorgen. Der silberne Aluminium-Rand bietet einen optischen Blickfang, wodurch sich das Gerät gut in jedes Wohnambiente einfügt. Auch die matte Auflagefläche in Schwarz oder Weiß setzt einen stilvollen Akzent und verhindert zusätzlich ein Abrutschen des Smartphones. Der Wireless Charger BA1/WA1 ist mit jedem Qi-fähigen Smartphone kompatibel.

Begründung der Jury
Der Wireless Charger BA1/WA1 punktet durch seine stilvolle Gestaltung, die ihn zuhause wie auch im Büro zu einem ansprechenden Accessoire macht.

Wireless Charger B1
Kabelloses Ladepad

Manufacturer
Intenso International GmbH,
Vechta, Germany
In-house design
Web
www.intenso-international.de

The Wireless Charger B1 uses inductive charging technology, by means of which the smartphone no longer needs to be connected by a cable. It is available as a permanent charging station. By simply laying it down on it, every Qi-enabled smartphone, no matter whether Android or iOS, is supplied with new energy. A Micro USB cable which is included in the set for the power supply can also be connected to a computer or laptop.

Statement by the jury
The Wireless Charger B1, which is also usable as a permanent charging station, impresses by uncomplicated handling.

Der Wireless Charger B1 arbeitet mit induktiver Ladetechnologie, somit muss das Smartphone nicht mehr an ein Kabel angeschlossen werden. Er steht als permanente Ladestation zur Verfügung. Durch einfaches Auflegen wird jedes Qi-fähige Smartphone, gleichgültig ob Android oder iOS, mit neuer Energie versorgt. Ein im Set enthaltenes Micro-USB-Kabel für die Stromversorgung lässt sich auch an einem Computer oder Laptop anschließen.

Begründung der Jury
Der auch als permanente Ladestation zu nutzende Wireless Charger B1 beeindruckt durch unkomplizierte Handhabung.

CHARGEit
Powerbank and Wireless Charger
Powerbank und kabelloses Ladegerät

Manufacturer
SACKit ApS, Aalborg, Denmark
In-house design
Web
www.sackit.eu

CHARGEit is a powerbank that wirelessly charges smartphones, loudspeakers and other mobile devices while placed on the spot marked by "X". Since the device has a USB port, users can also plug in a charging cable. It is possible to use wireless charging and cable charging at the same time. In terms of appearance, the model comes with a minimalist design: An organically rounded aluminium frame surrounds the finely structured front covered with woollen upholstery fabric in a trend colour.

Statement by the jury
The design of CHARGEit is specifically needs-orientated, scoring with high-end materials and purist aesthetics.

CHARGEit ist eine Powerbank, die Smartphones, aber auch Lautsprecher und andere tragbare Endgeräte kabellos auflädt, wenn sie auf dem mit „X" markierten Punkt platziert werden. Das Gerät ist mit einem USB-Port versehen, daher können Nutzer auch ein Ladekabel anschließen. Gleichzeitiges Aufladen mit und ohne Kabel ist möglich. Optisch setzt das Modell auf minimalistisches Design: Ein organisch abgerundeter Aluminiumrahmen umspannt die fein strukturierte Vorderseite, die mit Wollpolsterstoff in einer Trendfarbe bezogen ist.

Begründung der Jury
Die Gestaltung von CHARGEit orientiert sich gezielt an den Benutzerbedürfnissen und punktet mit Qualitätsmaterialien sowie einer puristischen Ästhetik.

HanPower Plus in
Solar Charger
Solarladegerät

Manufacturer
Hanergy Mobile Energy Holding Group Ltd., Beijing, China
In-house design
Yanxin Dai, Zhe Li
Web
www.hanergymobileenergy.com

HanPower Plus in combines solar power generation with charging. Thanks to a special folding design, the user can spread out the solar panels or pack them away, thereby saving space. The magnetic suction interface between the power generation module and the energy storage module allows independent use of both functions – so the storage element can be disconnected and used as a mobile battery. The product comes with a modern surface design which imitates the haptic qualities of leather.

Statement by the jury
The 2-in-1 solar charger offers sophisticated technology for environmentally-aware consumers in a particularly flexible design.

Stromerzeugung aus Sonnenenergie wird bei HanPower Plus in mit einer Ladefunktion kombiniert. Dank einer speziellen faltbaren Gestaltung können Nutzer je nach Bedarf die Solarpanels aufklappen oder platzsparend verstauen. Die magnetische Schnittstelle zwischen dem Modul für Stromerzeugung und dem Speichermodul erlaubt einen unabhängigen Gebrauch der beiden Funktionen, sodass das Speicherelement einfach abgetrennt und als mobiler Akku eingesetzt werden kann. Äußerlich präsentiert sich das Produkt mit einem modernen Oberflächendesign, das die Griffigkeit von Leder imitiert.

Begründung der Jury
Das 2-in-1-Solarladegerät stellt ausgeklügelte Technik für umweltbewusste Verbraucher in einer besonders flexiblen Aufmachung bereit.

Huawei Wireless Quick Charger
Wireless Charger
Kabelloses Ladepad

Manufacturer
Huawei Device (Shenzhen) Co., Ltd.,
Shenzhen, China
In-house design
Web
www.huawei.com

The Huawei Wireless Quick Charger is designed for the Mate RS and Mate 20 series. The phones are charged quickly at a maximum of ten watts, whereby the warming temperature remains low. The all-metal bottom is brushed precisely and crafted with a diamond cutting technique. A surface of attractive TPU assures good haptics. Since it weighs only 120 grams, the device can easily be carried along when travelling.

Statement by the jury
The slender construction makes the powerfully designed Huawei Wireless Quick Charger a useful travel companion.

Der Huawei Wireless Quick Charger ist für die Serien Mate RS und Mate 20 konzipiert. Die Smartphones werden bei maximal zehn Watt schnell geladen, wobei der Erwärmungsgrad niedrig bleibt. Der vollmetallische Boden ist präzise gebürstet und mit einer Technik für Diamantschliff bearbeitet. Eine Oberfläche aus attraktivem TPU sorgt für gute Haptik. Mit nur 120 Gramm Gewicht kann das Gerät gut auf Reisen mitgenommen werden.

Begründung der Jury
Die schlanke Konstruktion macht den leistungsstark gestalteten Huawei Wireless Quick Charger zu einem nützlichen Reisebegleiter

High Five
Charging Cable
Ladekabel

Manufacturer
Vonmählen GmbH, Lüneburg, Germany
Design
Emamidesign, Berlin, Germany
Web
www.vonmaehlen.com
www.emamidesign.de

The High Five compact charging cable combines five different connections and thus facilitates the charging of all popular Micro-USB and USB-C devices such as iPhone, iPad and iPod. By plugging the connectors together, the device forms a loop and can be easily attached to a key ring and thus be quickly ready for use. Flowing contours and a high-quality metal housing provide a noble impression.

Statement by the jury
High Five is attractive in its clever design which gives it a high practical value and turns the charging cable into a chic, everyday accessory.

Das kompakte Ladekabel High Five vereint fünf verschiedene Verbindungen und ermöglicht somit das Laden aller gängigen Micro-USB- und USB-C-Endgeräte sowie von iPhone, iPad und iPod. Durch Zusammenstecken der Anschlüsse wird das Gerät zu einer Schlaufe geformt und lässt sich ganz einfach etwa an einem Schlüsselbund befestigen und ist somit auch schnell einsatzbereit. Fließende Konturen und ein hochwertiges Metallgehäuse sorgen für eine edle Anmutung.

Begründung der Jury
High Five gefällt in seiner cleveren Gestaltung, die auf einen hohen Nutzwert ausgerichtet ist und zudem das Ladekabel zu einem schicken Alltagsaccessoire macht.

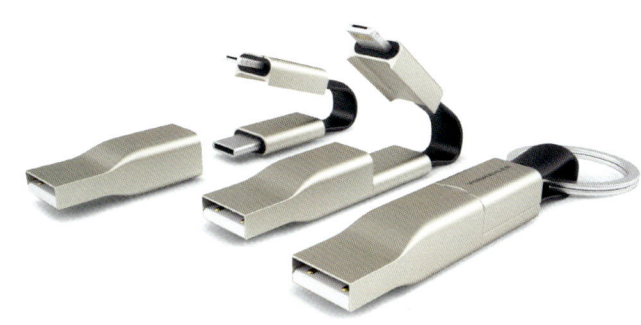

6 Port Filehub Charger
USB Charger with Data Transfer Capability
USB-Ladegerät mit Datentransfermöglichkeit

Manufacturer
Shenzhen NearbyExpress Technology Development Co., Ltd., Shenzhen, China
In-house design
Chengmin Li, Tianyu Xiao
Web
www.sunvalley-group.com/en

By means of the corresponding U-Hub app you can transfer writing and reading access from this data medium to another device. The app works for both Android and iOS systems. The smartphone or tablet are charged during the transfer. With a transfer speed of 20ms, the transfer is quicker than with usual cloud systems. Materials, symbols, light and USB connections are designed in such a manner as to be intuitively operated.

Statement by the jury
Using a charger at the same time for data transfer is an innovative idea. In this case it is convincingly efficient in its application.

Mittels der zugehörigen App U-Hub können Schreib- und Lesezugriffe von diesem Datenträger auf ein anderes Endgerät vorgenommen werden. Die App funktioniert sowohl für Android als auch iOS. Während der Datenübertragung wird das Smartphone oder Tablet aufgeladen. Mit einer Transfergeschwindigkeit von 20 ms gelingt der Transfer schneller als bei üblichen Cloud-Systemen. Materialien, Symbole, Licht und USB-Anschlüsse sind so gestaltet, dass sie intuitiv bedient werden können.

Begründung der Jury
Ein Ladegerät zugleich für den Datentransfer einzusetzen, ist eine innovative Idee. Diese ist hier überzeugend effizient verwirklicht worden.

DTEN D7
AI-Powered Video Conference Board
KI-gestütztes Videokonferenz-Board

Manufacturer
DTEN,
San Jose, California, USA

In-house design
Kent Zeng

Web
www.dten.com

reddot award 2019
best of the best

Perfectly integrated
Video conferencing has become an established practice today. The aesthetics and effectiveness of this type of communication are closely related to the capabilities provided for by design and technology. The DTEN D7 is an AI-powered video conference board that promotes an impressive combination of form and functionality. It allows video conferences to be held easily and intuitively via the 55" touchscreen. Equipped with 16 built-in directional microphones and fully integrated speakers, the 4K camera provides a high-definition, realistic face-to-face experience. In addition, using highly responsive touch technology, the D7 is also a digital whiteboard, offering easy collaboration and content sharing to support and strengthen teamwork. The D7 showcases a sleek and elegant design with well-balanced lines and weighs only 23 kg, which makes it easy to move around using the optional mobile stand. The generous screen with a horizontal bezel width of 12.9 mm projects an outstanding image quality. Thanks to wireless connectivity, the board enables a simple set-up for immediate use without extra cables. The innovative concept of this board goes hand in hand with a highly convenient, user-friendly approach.

Perfekt integriert
Videokonferenzen sind heute gelebte Praxis. Deren Ästhetik und Effektivität stehen dabei in engem Zusammenhang mit den Möglichkeiten, die Design und Technologie dafür vorgeben. Das DTEN D7 ist ein KI-gestütztes Videokonferenz-Board, das hier eine in seiner Form und Funktionalität beeindruckende Kombination darstellt. Auf unkomplizierte Weise lassen sich Videokonferenzen mit dem 55" großen Touchscreen durchführen. Ausgestattet mit 16 eingebauten Richtmikrofonen und vollständig integrierten Lautsprechern, bietet die 4K-Kamera ein hochauflösendes und realistisches Face-to-Face-Erlebnis. Der Einsatz einer hochgradig responsiven Touch-Technologie ermöglicht zudem ein einfaches Zusammenarbeiten sowie teamförderndes Teilen und Nutzen von Inhalten mit dem D7, das zugleich auch ein digitales Whiteboard ist. Gestaltet mit einer ausgewogenen Linienführung, wiegt das schlanke und elegante D7 nur 23 kg und lässt sich mithilfe eines optionalen fahrbaren Ständers auch gut bewegen. Der großzügige Bildschirm mit einer horizontalen Breite des Frontrahmens von 12,9 mm erlaubt eine ausgezeichnete Übersicht. Dank drahtloser Konnektivität ist es einfach einzurichten und ohne Verkabelung sofort einsetzbar. Das innovative Konzept dieses Boards geht einher mit einer sehr bequemen Art der Nutzung.

Statement by the jury
The clear and elegant design of the DTEN D7 integrates a myriad of different functions in a highly convincing manner. Very practical in use, the device impresses with many features tailored to satisfy high user needs. The high-quality finish harmonises well with both the design and user-friendly technology. Thus, video conferencing turns into an exciting experience. The DTEN D7 is an outstandingly convincing example of an interactive whiteboard aiming at the future.

Begründung der Jury
Der klaren und eleganten Gestaltung des DTEN D7 gelingt eine überaus schlüssige Integration seiner vielfältigen Funktionen. Es ist sehr praktikabel im Gebrauch und beeindruckt durch seine hohe Anforderungen erfüllende Ausstattung. Das hochwertige Finish harmoniert gut mit dem Design und der nutzerfreundlichen Technologie. Videokonferenzen werden so zu einem Erlebnis. Das DTEN D7 ist ein ausgesprochen überzeugendes Beispiel für ein interaktives Whiteboard der Zukunft.

Designer portrait
See page 56
Siehe Seite 56

Promethean ActivPanel Titanium
Interactive Display
Interaktives Display

Manufacturer
Promethean World Inc., Blackburn, United Kingdom
In-house design
Melanie Friar, Chris Dawson,
Blackburn, United Kingdom
Design
NetDragon Websoft Inc. (Chia Chun Hsu,
Chun Chieh Peng, Yu Chang Huang),
Fuzhou, China
Web
www.nd.com.cn
www.prometheanworld.com

With the Promethean ActivPanel Titanium data can be exchanged and processed in an interactive way during lessons. Thanks to the innovative InGlass technology, writing appears in real time and is more fluid and precise than when using conventional infrared technology. The smart signal recognition function makes it possible to correct handwritten texts or mathematical equations intuitively with the heel of the hand. Two high-performance stereo speakers on the front support transmission of educational contents and prevent learners from becoming distracted. The integrated ClassFlow learning software provides additional teaching material for different subjects.

Mit dem Promethean ActivPanel Titanium können im Unterricht Daten interaktiv getauscht und bearbeitet werden. Durch die innovative InGlass-Technologie gelingt das Schreiben verzögerungsfrei sowie flüssiger und präziser als mit traditioneller Infrarottechnologie. Durch die intelligente Signalerkennung können handschriftliche Texte oder mathematische Gleichungen intuitiv mit dem Handballen korrigiert werden. Zwei leistungsstarke frontseitige Stereo-Lautsprecher fördern das ablenkungsfreie Vermitteln der Lerninhalte. Die integrierte Lernsoftware ClassFlow stellt zusätzliches Unterrichtsmaterial für verschiedene Lernfächer bereit.

Statement by the jury
The Promethean ActivPanel Titanium produces an innovative, networked learning environment which benefits both teachers and pupils.

Begründung der Jury
Das Promethean ActivPanel Titanium erzeugt eine innovative, vernetzte Lernumgebung, die Schülern wie auch Lehrenden gleichermaßen entgegenkommt.

Rally ConferenceCam System
Video Conference System
Videokonferenzsystem

Manufacturer
Logitech, Lausanne, Switzerland
In-house design
Web
www.logitech.com

The Rally ConferenceCam System places unnecessary components out of sight and the cables are, by means of the Display Hub and Table Hub, organised in an orderly manner. An Ultra-HD camera provides sharp, accurate image quality with good colour definition and a resolution of up to 4K. Innovative RightLight technology emphasises faces and highlights the natural skin tone. RightSound assures clear and natural voice reproduction with noise suppression. Thanks to sensitive microphones, discussion partners are heard well; free-standing speakers provide good sound quality even in large rooms.

Statement by the jury
Thanks to its sophisticated functionality, the Rally ConferenceCam System supports noise-free interchange of ideas via the Internet.

CAM540
Conference Camera
Konferenzkamera

Manufacturer
AVer Information Inc.,
New Taipei City, Taiwan
In-house design
Hong-Chi Yeh
Design
BRICKR Corp. Information,
Hsinchu, Taiwan
Web
www.aver.com

The CAM540 conference camera is equipped with the auto-framing technology SmartFrame, with which everyone present in the conference room comes into sight with only one click. By means of a 4K PTZ camera, it offers reliable, sharp image quality. A smoothly rounded, half-moon shaped arm holds in its centre the camera element. It can be freely swivelled. A generous cover protects and conceals the wiring and circuitry, at the same time creating a seamless transition between camera and mounting.

Statement by the jury
The CAM540 conference camera convincingly promotes communication during meetings with online partners.

Lifesize Icon 700
Video Conference System
Videokonferenzsystem

Manufacturer
Lifesize, Inc., Austin, Texas, USA
Design
Fahrenheit Design
(Bryan Hunter, Zack Bennett,
Spencer Dodge, Mark Gilson),
Round Rock, Texas, USA
Web
www.lifesize.com
www.fhtdesign.com

The Lifesize Icon 700 is a 4K cloud service connected video system with an integrated PTZ 4K camera. High-quality 4K content can be shared at full frame-rate locally and remotely. Simple and easy operation is provided through an accompanying touchscreen. The camera lens is protected from unwanted light influence by a textured pattern. The system base has discreet ventilation slits at the sides that assure continuous cooling airflow.

Statement by the jury
The aesthetics of the Lifesize Icon 700 is elegant and user-friendly at the same time. Impressive image quality supports teamwork during video conferences.

Cisco Webex Room Kit Mini
Video Conference System
Videokonferenzsystem

Manufacturer
Cisco, Lysaker, Norway
In-house design
Web
www.cisco.com

Cisco Webex Room Kit Mini is an AI-based video conferencing system. It combines codec, camera, microphone and speakers in a single device that is compatible with any 4K display. A camera, with a 120-degree panning radius is designed for smaller offices. The integrated sensors make the unit able to take in its surroundings and provide a simple and individual user experience. The fabric cover lends the device a modern charm.

Statement by the jury
Through a design concept that elegantly conceals its technical components, the Cisco Webex Room Kit Mini promotes focus on the course of the meeting.

Cisco Webex Room Kit Mini ist ein AI-basiertes Videokonferenzsystem. In einem einzigen Gerät, das mit jedem 4K-Display kompatibel ist, sind hier Codec, Kamera, Mikrofon und Lautsprecher untergebracht. Mit einem 120-Grad-Schwenkradius ist die Kamera für kleinere Büroeinheiten konzipiert. Integrierte Sensoren nehmen das jeweilige Umfeld wahr, um ein einfaches und individualisiertes Nutzererlebnis bieten zu können. Der Einsatz von textilem Material verleiht dem Gerät einen modernen Charakter.

Begründung der Jury
Mit einem Design, das technische Komponenten geschickt verbirgt, fördert Cisco Webex Room Kit Mini die Konzentration auf den Konferenzverlauf.

Plixus Nameplate
Namensschild

Manufacturer
Televic Conference, Izegem, Belgium
Design
Made, Antwerp, Belgium
Web
www.televic-conference.com
www.haveitmade.be

The Plixus Nameplate is only 9 mm thick and displays the identity of conference participants electronically. By means of simply operated drag-and-drop software, individual layouts can be created. A button with a LED indicator provides a clear and easy request to speak function. The display of the nameplate uses E-Ink technology and causes no glare or reflection. The Plixus Nameplate has a viewing angle of 180 degrees for very good legibility.

Statement by the jury
The Plixus Nameplate proves to be an up-to-date and well-considered aid for large conferences.

Das nur 9 mm dicke Plixus Nameplate zeigt die Identität von Konferenzteilnehmern elektronisch an. Über eine einfach bedienbare Drag-and-Drop-Software können individuelle Layouts erstellt werden. Eine Taste mit LED-Anzeige gibt eine deutliche und klare Rückmeldung über die Sprechfunktion. Die Anzeige auf dem Namensschild erfolgt mittels E-Ink-Technologie und es entsteht keine Blendwirkung oder Reflexion. Das Plixus Nameplate ist im 180-Grad-Winkel einsehbar und somit sehr gut abzulesen.

Begründung der Jury
Das Plixus Nameplate erweist sich als zeitgemäßes und wohldurchdachtes Hilfsmittel bei großen Konferenzen.

LD Systems U300® Series
Wireless Microphone System
Kabelloses Funkmikrofon-System

Manufacturer
Adam Hall GmbH, Neu-Anspach, Germany
In-house design
Web
www.ld-systems.com/U300

Thanks to the easy-to-operate, one-touch frequency synchronisation of the LD Systems U300 Series, up to six wireless microphones can be used simultaneously. This gives musicians or other performers complete freedom to move around on stage. The system is simple to control, comfortable to wear and produces high-quality sound. The casings are robustly made. The microphones have a uniform shape which makes them instantly recognisable.

Statement by the jury
The wireless LD Systems U300 Series is impressive for its refined functionality and high sound quality.

Mittels einfach bedienbarer One-Touch-Frequenzsynchronisation sind bis zu sechs kabellose Mikrofone der LD Systems U300 Serie gleichzeitig einsatzbereit. Das ermöglicht Musikern oder anderen Performern völlige Bewegungsfreiheit auf einer Bühne. Das System zeichnet sich weiter durch intuitive Bedienbarkeit, hohen Tragekomfort und sehr gute Klangqualität aus. Die Gehäuse sind robust konstruiert. Eine bei allen Geräten umgesetzte Linienführung verleiht der Serie eine leicht wiedererkennbare Charakteristik.

Begründung der Jury
Die kabellose LD Systems U300 Serie beeindruckt mit einer ausgereiften Funktionalität und hoher Audioqualität.

ThinkSmart Hub 700
Conference System
Konferenzsystem

Manufacturer
Lenovo, Morrisville, North Carolina, USA
In-house design
Web
www.lenovo.com

ThinkSmart Hub 700 enables meeting participants in smaller boardrooms to communicate on equal terms. The spun aluminium cover serves as the HID control centre which can be accessed from any location at the table. The cables connecting it to the screen are hidden from the meeting participants. Connectivity is made simple through ports that users can access during the meeting.

Statement by the jury
Operation of the ThinkSmart Hub 700 is intuitive in that the meeting system is available to everybody to the same degree. That encourages team spirit.

Bei Konferenzen im kleineren Rahmen können mit dem ThinkSmart Hub 700 alle Teilnehmer gleichberechtigt kommunizieren. Die Aluminiumabdeckung dient als HID-Steuereinheit und kann von jeder Sitzposition an einem Tisch aus bedient werden. Die Kabelverbindung zum Bildschirm bleibt dem Gesichtsfeld der Teilnehmer verborgen. Anschlüsse gelingen einfach durch Ports, die während einer Konferenz von den Nutzern verwendet werden können.

Begründung der Jury
Die Bedienung des ThinkSmart Hub 700 gelingt intuitiv. Indem das System allen Teilnehmern gleichrangig offensteht, unterstützt es das Zusammengehörigkeitsgefühl.

Konftel 800
Conference Phone
Konferenztelefon

Manufacturer
Konftel AB, Umeå, Sweden
Design
Struktur Design
(Oscar Björk, Johan Gustavsson),
Umeå, Sweden
Web
www.konftel.com
www.strukturdesign.se

Clean lines in combination with a fabric cover give the Konftel 800 conference phone a look suited to an office environment that conveys efficiency and familiarity. Thanks to the innovative OmniSound technology, it produces a very natural speech quality. Three devices in a daisy chain suffice to cover even very big conference rooms. The device is easily operated using a colour touchscreen with icons as well as volume and mute buttons or by a mobile app.

Statement by the jury
The design of the Konftel 800 conference phone stands out for its distinctive use of forms and an intuitive usability.

Eine klare Linienführung in Verbindung mit einer textilen Oberflächenbespannung verleiht dem Konferenztelefon Konftel 800 eine arbeitsgerechte Anmutung, die Effizienz und zugleich Vertrautheit verdeutlicht. Mittels der innovativen OmniSound-Technologie wird ein sehr natürlicher Sprechklang erzeugt, drei Geräte in Daisy-Chain-Schaltung decken selbst sehr große Konferenzräume ab. Die Steuerung gelingt einfach über einen mit Symbolen arbeitenden farbigen Touchscreen, begleitet von Tasten für die Lautstärkeregelung und die Stummschaltung, oder über eine mobile App.

Begründung der Jury
Die Gestaltung des Konferenztelefons Konftel 800 zeichnet sich durch eine markante Formensprache und eine intuitive Bedienbarkeit aus.

6066 Subminiature Headset Microphone
Kopfbügelmikrofon

Manufacturer
DPA Microphones,
Allerød, Denmark
In-house design
Rune T. Møller
Design
Heger Design (Anders Heger),
Brønshøj, Denmark
Web
www.dpamicrophones.com
www.hegerdesign.dk

The elegantly unobtrusive 6066 Subminiature Headset Microphone was specifically developed for public performances. The ergonomic shape grips the head snugly and does not slip even during vigorous movement. The spring mechanism around the ears provides a gentle yet firm grip to ensure the device sits in place securely and comfortably. Users can easily adjust the headset while wearing so that it specifically fits the shape of their head. In addition, the powerful 3 mm microphone ensures that the performance is heard clearly by the entire audience.

Statement by the jury
The 6066 Subminiature Headset Microphone, which inconspicuously goes with a range of different styles of clothing, allows for unrestricted freedom of movement.

Das elegant unauffällige 6066 Subminiature Kopfbügelmikrofon wurde speziell für öffentliche Auftritte entwickelt. Die ergonomische Form umfasst den Kopf anschmiegsam und verrutscht auch nicht bei lebhafter Bewegung. Der Federmechanismus rund um das Ohr greift sanft und doch fest genug, um einen sicheren und bequemen Sitz des Geräts zu gewährleisten. Nutzer können das Headset während des Tragens einfach justieren und ihrer speziellen Kopfform anpassen. Zudem sorgt das leistungsstarke 3-mm-Mikrofon dafür, dass das gesamte Publikum die Darbietung klar verstehen kann.

Begründung der Jury
Das 6066 Subminiature Kopfbügelmikrofon, das sich dezent unterschiedlichen Kleidungsstilen anpasst, ermöglicht eine uneingeschränkte Bewegungsfreiheit.

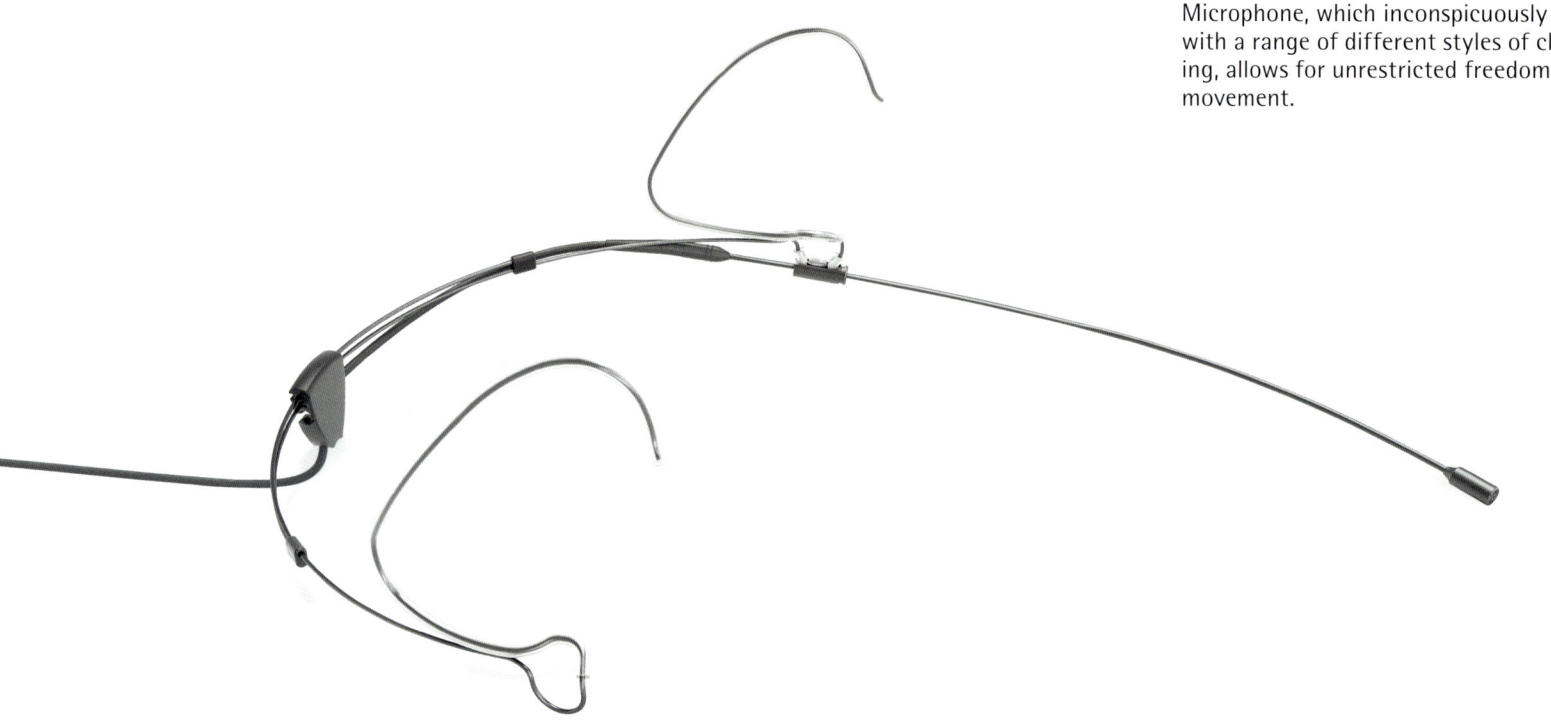

Huawei CM21
DAC Headphone Amplifier
DAC-Kopfhörerverstärker

Manufacturer
Huawei Device (Shenzhen) Co., Ltd.,
Shenzhen, China
In-house design
Web
www.huawei.com

This compact device functions as a bridge between a USB C port and the 3.5 mm headphone jack. It operates at a frequency of 384 kHz and thus provides high-resolution audio quality for anything from a smartphone to a car or a stereo. The amplifier is characterised by a very simple, clean design vocabulary in which the circular volume control creates a subtle focal point.

Statement by the jury
The attractive aesthetics and the versatility of the Huawei CM21 headphone amplifier make for a very appealing combination.

Dieses handliche Gerät dient als Adapter zwischen einem USB-C-Port und der 3,5-mm-Klinke eines Kopfhöreranschlusses und unterstützt eine 384-kHz-Frequenz. Es sorgt damit für eine Audioqualität in High-Resolution-Qualität, etwa bei einem Smartphone, im Auto oder bei einer Hi-Fi-Anlage. Der Verstärker zeigt eine sehr einfache und klare Formensprache, wobei der kreisförmige Lautstärkeregler einen dezenten Akzent setzt.

Begründung der Jury
Der Kopfhörerverstärker Huawei CM21 besticht durch seine ansprechende Ästhetik und seine vielseitigen Einsatzmöglichkeiten.

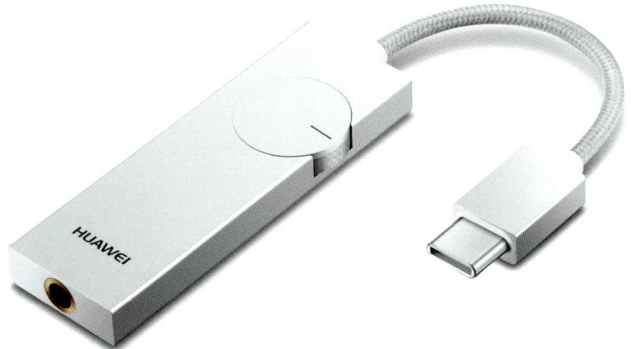

Oblong Optical Wand
Control Device for Screen Content
Steuerung für Bildschirminhalte

Manufacturer
Oblong Industries, Los Angeles, USA
In-house design
Barbara Brand, John Underkoffler
Web
www.oblong.com

The Oblong Optical Wand is a handheld pointing device used to interact with and manage data and visual digital content in immersive display environments. Because the wand's position is tracked in three dimensional space, users can employ intuitive gestures and movements to engage directly with the content displayed. The device has an ergonomic shape with balanced weight and comfortable haptic properties. Its minimal four-button touchpad allows the user to control digital content in an easy and seamless way.

Oblong Optical Wand ist ein tragbares Hand-Zeigegerät zur Interaktion und Handhabung von Daten und visuellen digitalen Inhalten in immersiven Monitor-Umgebungen. Durch die Verfolgung der Geräteposition im dreidimensionalen Raum können Nutzer intuitiv durch Gesten und Bewegungen direkt mit den angezeigten Inhalten in Kontakt treten. Das Gerät hat eine ergonomische Form mit ausgewogener Gewichtsverteilung und einer angenehmen Haptik. Sein reduziert gestaltetes Vier-Tasten-Touchpad ermöglicht Nutzern die bequeme und übergangslose Steuerung digitaler Inhalte.

Statement by the jury
With the Oblong Optical Wand, users can control digital content directly and intuitively. This lifts interaction to a new level.

Begründung der Jury
Mit dem Oblong Optical Wand können Anwender digitale Inhalte intuitiv und unmittelbar kontrollieren. Dies hebt die Interaktion auf eine neue Ebene.

Youdao
Mobile Translator
Mobiles Übersetzungsgerät

Manufacturer
NetEase Youdao Information Technology (Beijing) Co., Ltd.,
Beijing, China
In-house design
Xudong Wang
Web
www.youdao.com

This robust, adaptive translation device was designed as an easy-to-use tool to enable users to effectively communicate in a foreign language while on a vacation or business trip. The oval shape, compact size and reduced weight ensure that the Youdao rests safely and comfortably in the hand. Thanks to the integration of two microphones, the user need not focus on the speech direction. Word-search and language-learning functionality helps to facilitate the early stages of learning a new language and rounds off the overall concept.

Dieses robuste, lernfähige Übersetzungsgerät wurde als einfach zu bedienendes Hilfsmittel entwickelt, um während einer Urlaubs- oder Geschäftsreise effektiv in einer fremden Sprache zu kommunizieren. Die ovale Form, die kompakte Größe und das geringe Gewicht sorgen dafür, dass Youdao sicher und angenehm in der Hand liegt. Durch die Integration zweier Mikrofone muss sich der Nutzer nicht auf die Sprechrichtung konzentrieren. Eine Wortfindungs- und eine Sprachlernfunktion, die den Start in eine neue Sprache erleichtern sollen, runden das Konzept ab.

Statement by the jury
The Youdao mobile translator proves to be a very practical companion, thus considerably simplifying communication abroad with a range of technical refinements.

Begründung der Jury
Das mobile Übersetzungsgerät Youdao erweist sich als äußerst praktischer Begleiter, der die Verständigung im Ausland durch eine Reihe technischer Feinheiten vereinfacht.

TIGER P180
Wearable Translation Device
Tragbares Übersetzungsgerät

Manufacturer
Tinno Mobile Technology Corp., Shenzhen, China
Design
Shenzhen Tinno Wireless Technology Co., Ltd., Shenzhen, China
Wiko SAS, Marseille, France
Web
www.tinno.com
www.wikomobile.com

The wearable TIGER P180 device translates what somebody is saying into another language. It is small and slim and is therefore easy to hold and use for people of all ages. Switching between different modes is straightforward; two control knobs on either side are set into the tapered body and thus do not protrude. The display is made of 2.5D tempered glass and contrasts with the fabric-covered microphone and speaker area. The device comes in a range of fashionable colours.

Das tragbare TIGER P180 übersetzt Gesprochenes schnell in eine andere Sprache. Dank seiner schlanken Dimensionen kann es von allen Altersstufen gut in der Hand gehalten und bedient werden. Einfach gelingt ein Wechsel zwischen den verschiedenen Modi. Zwei Drehknöpfe zu beiden Seiten nehmen durch eine taillierte Formgebung an dieser Stelle keinen zusätzlichen Raum nach außen ein. Das Display in gehärtetem 2,5D-Glas steht optisch in Kontrast zu dem Mikrofon mit Textilbespannung. Das Gerät wird in mehreren trendigen Farben angeboten.

Statement by the jury
Thanks to its clear design and ease of use, the TIGER P180 makes it possible to overcome language barriers with ease.

Begründung der Jury
Dank seiner übersichtlichen Gestaltung und komfortablen Handhabung lassen sich mit dem TIGER P180 Sprachbarrieren einfach überwinden.

DS-9500
Portable Dictation Device
Portables Diktiergerät

Manufacturer
Olympus Corporation, Tokyo, Japan
In-house design
Tatsuhiko Suzuki
Web
www.olympus.eu/dictated-documented

This portable dictation device uses Wi-Fi connectivity to transfer the user's voice recordings directly to the transcription site. The smart dual microphones of the DS-9500 ensure very good noise-cancelling so that dictations can be carried out even in noisy environments. The sturdy case provides protection against damage if the device is dropped from heights of up to one-and-a-half metres. When recording, the very well-structured device is simple to operate via the slide switch located on the side.

Statement by the jury
The portable DS-9500 dictation device presents well thought-through functionality and innovative Wi-Fi connectivity in order to provide effective workflow support.

Mittels Wi-Fi sendet dieses portable Diktiergerät die Sprachaufnahme eines Nutzers direkt an die Transkriptionsstelle. Die intelligenten Dual-Mikrofone des DS-9500 sorgen für eine sehr gute Rauschunterdrückung, sodass das Diktat auch in lauter Umgebung vorgenommen werden kann. Das robuste Gehäuse schützt bei Fällen aus bis zu anderthalb Metern. Bei der Aufnahme wird das sehr klar aufgebaute Gerät einfach über den seitlichen Schiebeschalter gesteuert.

Begründung der Jury
Das portable Diktiergerät DS-9500 überzeugt durch wohldurchdachte Funktionalität und eine innovative Wi-Fi-Anbindung, mit der es den Workflow effizient unterstützt.

WAVE Two-Way Radio TLK 100
Funksprechgerät

Manufacturer
Motorola Solutions, Plantation, Florida, USA
In-house design
Web
www.motorolasolutions.com

The WAVE Two-Way Radio TLK 100 is linked to a mobile phone network. This allows for instant nationwide communication which is why the device is particularly well suited to companies with a highly dispersed workforce. The functions of the sturdy device are clearly displayed and can be understood intuitively. By doing without a screen, the user is relieved of possible distractions.

Statement by the jury
The quality of the WAVE Two-Way Radio TLK 100 stems from its deliberately minimalist construction which focuses on the essentials.

Das WAVE Two-Way Radio TLK 100 ist in ein Mobilfunknetz eingebunden. Dadurch wird der sofortige landesweite Kommunikationsaufbau möglich, weswegen sich das Gerät besonders für Unternehmen mit weit voneinander entfernt agierender Belegschaft eignet. Seine Funktionen sind klar strukturiert auf dem stabilen Gerät angezeigt und lassen sich intuitiv erfassen. Durch den Verzicht auf einen Bildschirm bleibt der Nutzer von möglichen Ablenkungen befreit.

Begründung der Jury
Die Qualität des WAVE Two-Way Radio TLK 100 liegt in seinem bewusst minimalistischen Aufbau, der sich auf das Wesentliche konzentriert.

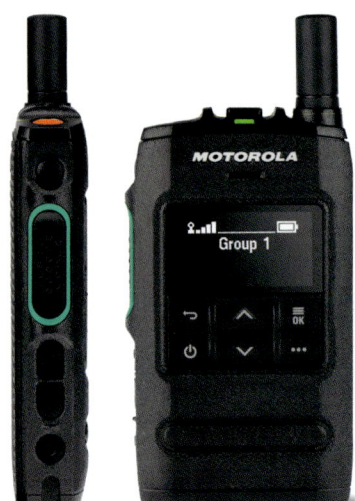

ST7500 Tetra Radio
Two-Way Radio
Funksprechgerät

Manufacturer
Motorola Solutions, Plantation, Florida, USA
In-house design
Web
www.motorolasolutions.com

Designed for efficient radio communication in the realms of public safety, transportation and industry, the ST7500 Tetra Radio is slim and light by comparison to the traditionally heavier and bulkier equipment. The sturdy construction complies with military standards as well as IP67 dust and water protection requirements. The device supports pairing via Bluetooth 4.1 Low Energy, Wi-Fi connectivity and an accelerometer.

Statement by the jury
With its impressive functionality, the ST7500 Tetra Radio is particularly well suited to the more demanding areas of industry and public order.

Für eine effiziente Kommunikation via Funk in den Bereichen öffentliche Sicherheit, Transport und Industrie dient das ST7500 Tetra Radio, das im Gegensatz zu den traditionell schweren und klobigen Geräten besonders schmal und leicht ausfällt. Die robuste Konstruktion entspricht Militärstandards und einer Schutzklasse gegen Staub und Wasser von IP67. Das Gerät unterstützt Pairing mittels Bluetooth 4.1 Low Energy, Wi-Fi-Anbindung und einen Beschleunigungsmesser.

Begründung der Jury
Durch seine beeindruckende Funktionalität eignet sich das ST7500 Tetra Radio besonders gut in verantwortungsvollen Bereichen der Industrie und öffentlichen Ordnung.

Bolero Wireless Intercom
Wireless Intercom System
Drahtloses Intercom-System

Manufacturer
Riedel Communications GmbH & Co. KG,
Wuppertal, Germany
In-house design
Jake Dodson, Christian Bockskopf
Web
www.riedel.net

This wireless intercom system provides communication for film crews and other event teams. It can support up to ten beltpacks per antenna and as many as 100 antennas simultaneously. The system includes an Advanced DECT Receiver, high-clarity voice codec, complete Artist intercom integration and simple touch & go beltpack registration. On top of all this, the device can be used in different ways, for example as a wireless beltpack, as a wireless key panel or as a two-way radio. In addition, telephone calls can also be channelled directly to the intercom channels.

Statement by the jury
Bolero Wireless Intercom is bound to impress with its carefully considered functionality and wide range of possible uses.

Das drahtlose Intercom-System dient der Kommunikation von Crews bei Filmdrehs und anderen Veranstaltungen. Bis zu zehn Beltpacks pro Antenne und bis zu 100 Antennen in einem einzigen Einsatz können unterstützt werden. Das System bietet etwa einen Advanced DECT Receiver, High-Clarity-Sprachcodec, eine komplette Artist-Intercom-Integration sowie eine einfache „Touch&Go"-Beltpack-Registrierung. Zudem bietet es unterschiedliche Einsatzmöglichkeiten als Wireless-Beltpack, drahtloses Keypanel oder als Funksprechanlage. Auch Telefonanrufe können direkt in die Intercom-Kanäle eingespeist werden.

Begründung der Jury
Bolero Wireless Intercom beeindruckt durch eine durchdachte Funktionalität und vielseitige Einsatzmöglichkeiten.

Dual Mode Intelligent Communication Terminal
Two-Way Radio
Funksprechgerät

Manufacturer
Shenzhen Eevin Technology Co., Ltd.,
Shenzhen, China
Design
Shenzhen Eevin Design Co., Ltd.
(Haibo Liao, Haopeng Xu),
Shenzhen, China
Web
www.eevin.com
www.eevindesign.com

This two-way radio is based on PNO and DMR connectivity and comes with both LTE and DMR standards. The intercom system offers useful functions such as real-time communication, vocal scheduling, image return and a one-touch alarm. IP67 as well as rubberised surfaces offer additional protection. The device furthermore supports high-frequency RFID and barcode scanning. Thanks to its combination of sharp lines and rounded edges, the device is pleasant to hold. The generous display allows for easy data entry.

Statement by the jury
An ingenious use of technology that provides numerous functions turns this two-way radio into a highly effective tool.

Dieses Funksprechgerät basiert auf PNO- und DMR-Vernetzung und verfügt über LTE- wie auch DMR-Standard. Das Gegensprechsystem bietet nützliche Funktionen wie verzögerungsfreie Kommunikation, sprachgesteuerte Zeitplanung, Image Return und One-Touch Alarm. IP67 sowie gummierte Oberflächen bieten zuverlässigen Schutz. Zudem werden hochfrequentes RFID und Barcodelesen unterstützt. Durch die Kombination aus scharfen Linien und Rundungen liegt das Gerät gut in der Hand. Das großzügige Display ermöglicht eine einfache Eingabe.

Begründung der Jury
Ein ausgeklügelter Technikeinsatz, der zahlreiche Funktionen bietet, macht dieses Funksprechgerät zu einem effizienten Arbeitsutensil.

C21
Two-Way Radio
Funksprechgerät

Manufacturer
China Mobile Communications
Group Co., Ltd., Government and Enterprise
Service Company, Beijing, China
Design
China Mobile Communications
Group Co., Ltd., Government and Enterprise
Service Company (Weiting Li), Beijing, China
Web
zhengqi.10086.cn
www.joya.cn
https://poc.10086.cn

Connectivity of the C21 two-way radio is based on a public 4G network and thus assures a stable and secure exchange of spoken information between users. Thanks to a non-slip design, a push-to-talk function and an emergency button, it is user friendly to operate. Thanks to longer battery life it can also be used reliably out of doors. The flexible attach clip avoids unpleasant pressure on the body of the wearer. An LED assures good visibility in case of emergency.

Statement by the jury
Thanks to its powerful and stable network connectivity, the C21 two-way radio offers a reliable communication service.

Die Verbindung des Funksprechgeräts C21 basiert auf einem öffentlichen 4G-Netz und sorgt so für einen stabilen und sicheren Austausch von Sprachnachrichten zwischen den Nutzern. Das Gerät lässt sich dank rutschfester Gestaltung, einer Push-to-Talk-Funktion sowie einer Notfalltaste nutzerfreundlich bedienen. Dank langer Batterielaufzeit kann es auch im Outdoorbereich zuverlässig genutzt werden. Der flexible Befestigungs-Clip vermeidet unangenehmen Druck auf den Körper des Trägers. Ein LED-Licht sorgt bei Notfällen für gute Sicht.

Begründung der Jury
Dank seiner leistungsstarken und stabilen Netzanbindung bietet das Funksprechgerät C21 zuverlässig Kommunikationsdienste.

 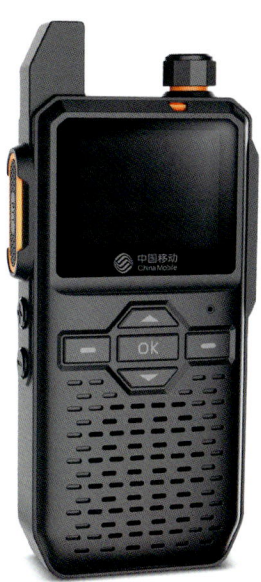

DOT 4479
Indoor Radio Unit
Indoor-Sendeeinheit

Manufacturer
Ericsson AB, Stockholm, Sweden
In-house design
Web
www.ericsson.com

DOT 4479 is an innovative small cell solution for companies that need a large amount of reliable network coverage. If there is demand for enhanced mobile broadband, machine-type communication or business-critical applications, it cannot be met by Wi-Fi or 5G base stations outside the building. This small, easy to operate indoor transmitter provides a 5G mid-band spectrum with speeds of up to 2Gbps. The device can be installed in a very short time.

Statement by the jury
The compact DOT 4479 indoor radio transmitter, which ensures reliable 5G network coverage, stands out for its sophisticated construction method.

DOT 4479 ist eine innovative Small-Cell-Lösung für Unternehmen mit hohem Bedarf an zuverlässiger Netzabdeckung. Besteht etwa die Nachfrage nach Enhanced Mobile Broadband, Machine-Type Communication oder geschäftskritischen Anwendungen, kann dies nicht mittels Wi-Fi oder 5G-Basisstationen außerhalb des Gebäudes abgedeckt werden. Diese kleine handliche Indoor-Sendeeinheit bietet 5G-Mittenfrequenz mit Geschwindigkeiten bis zu 2Gbit/s. Das Gerät lässt sich in kurzer Zeit einfach montieren.

Begründung der Jury
Die kompakt gestaltete Indoor-Sendeeinheit DOT 4479, die eine zuverlässige 5G-Netzabdeckung gewährleistet, begeistert durch ihre ausgefeilte Konstruktionsweise.

AIR 4455
Antenna for Mobile Networks
Antenne für mobile Netzwerke

Manufacturer
Ericsson AB, Stockholm, Sweden
In-house design
Industrial Design Department
Web
www.ericsson.com

As part of the Street Macro product range, this dual band antenna increases the network coverage of mobile network providers. The internal technical components have been arranged to ensure the device is very compact and flat. With a very even front and gently rounded edges, the device radiates a sense of calm and it can be enhanced with a film that matches the background. The antenna can be mounted both in a horizontal or vertical position.

Statement by the jury
The AIR 4455 dual band antenna gains merit for its discreet and space-saving style as well as its versatile installation options.

Als Teil der Produktserie Street Macro erhöht diese Dualband-Antenne die Netzabdeckung mobiler Netzbetreiber. Die technischen Komponenten sind im Inneren so angeordnet, dass das Gerät sehr schmal und kompakt ausfallen kann. Das Gerät ist an der Front sehr ebenmäßig gestaltet, mit sanft gerundeten Kanten verbreitet es eine sehr ruhige Anmutung, zugleich kann eine dem Hintergrund angepasste Folie gut darauf angebracht werden. Die Montage ist horizontal wie auch vertikal möglich.

Begründung der Jury
Die AIR 4455 Dualband-Antenne punktet mit ihrer diskreten und platzsparenden Gestaltung sowie mit ihren flexiblen Montagemöglichkeiten.

AIR 5331
Mobile Network Antenna
Mobilfunkantenne

Manufacturer
Ericsson AB, Stockholm, Sweden
In-house design
Web
www.ericsson.com

Due to innovative technology, this mobile network antenna supports the telecom industry's 5G networks on a 39 GHz bandwidth. This allows internet service providers to offer consumers high-speed, high-quality transmissions. In contrast to the usually rather clunky equipment, this antenna is compact and light, and its discreet design is visually well suited to an urban environment. Maintenance of the device is intuitive. A strong composite membrane on the front assures excellent transmission while the back focuses on thermal performance.

Statement by the jury
The AIR 5331 mobile network antenna provides strong mobile network connectivity while its design meets the contemporary requirements of urban life.

Diese Mobilfunkantenne unterstützt dank innovativer Technologie 5G-Netzwerke der Telekommunikationsindustrie auf einer Bandbreite von 39 GHz. Internetanbieter können somit den Konsumenten höchst leistungsstarke Übertragungsqualität anbieten. Im Gegensatz zu den sonst klobigen Geräten ist dieses kompakt und leicht, das unaufdringliche Design fügt sich optisch gut im urbanen Raum ein. Das Gerät erlaubte eine intuitive Wartung. Ein starker Membranverbund an der Front sorgt für hohe Transmission, während die Rückseite für den thermischen Ausgleich sorgt.

Begründung der Jury
Die Mobilfunkantenne AIR 5331 bietet eine hohe mobile Netzwerkleistung. Darüber hinaus entspricht ihre Gestaltung zeitgemäßen Ansprüchen im urbanen Raum.

AIR 6488
Mobile Network Antenna
Mobilfunkantenne

Manufacturer
Ericsson AB, Stockholm, Sweden
In-house design
Web
www.ericsson.com

AIR 6488 multiplies the capacity of a 5G mobile network through the use of massive MIMO technology. The usual situation of ugly, bulky equipment in public spaces is avoided by replacing it with a single self-contained unit. Its discreet colour allows it to blend well into such environments. A simple coupling mechanism connects individual devices in an easy and visually attractive way.

Statement by the jury
Thanks to its unobtrusive design, the AIR 6488 blends seamlessly into public spaces. Its user-friendliness also makes it appealing.

Durch AIR 6488 wird die Kapazität eines 5G-Mobilnetzwerks durch den Einsatz von Massive-MIMO-Technologie vervielfacht. Das ansonsten gewohnte Bild unschöner sperriger Installationen im öffentlichen Raum wird hier durch eine schlichte Lösung in Form einer einzelnen, in sich geschlossenen Einheit ersetzt. Durch eine unauffällige Farbgestaltung integriert sich die Einheit dezent im öffentlichen Raum. Ein einfach gestalteter Steckmechanismus verbindet einzelne Geräte unkompliziert und optisch ansprechend miteinander.

Begründung der Jury
Dank seiner zurückhaltenden Gestaltung integriert sich AIR 6488 nahtlos im öffentlichen Bereich. Zudem gefällt die Nutzerfreundlichkeit dieses Geräts.

SENCITY® Occhio MIMO Antenna

Manufacturer
HUBER+SUHNER AG, Herisau, Switzerland
Design
erfindergeist GmbH (Christian Keller),
Goldach, Switzerland
Web
www.hubersuhner.com
www.erfindergeist.ch

The SENCITY Occhio MIMO Antenna meets numerous requirements of both 5G and 4G standards. Its elegant form and sleek design is compatible with highly distinctive architecture and discretely blends in with interior decor. It enhances indoor connectivity by providing extended bandwidth and reliable availability with an innovative "smart-connect system". The convex shape, a pre-assembled self-locking adapter and a "quick-lock function" prepares for easy and secure installation.

Die SENCITY Occhio MIMO Antenna erfüllt die vielfältigen Anforderungen des 5G- und 4G-Standards. Aufgrund ihrer klaren, eleganten Formensprache und schlanken Optik fügt sie sich dezent in individuelle Raumarchitektur ein. Sie verkörpert eine neue Dimension von Indoor-Konnektivität mit erweiterter Bandbreite und zuverlässiger Verfügbarkeit mit einem innovativen Smart-Connect-System. Ihre konvexe Formgebung, ein vormontierter selbstverriegelnder Adapter und eine Quick-Lock-Funktion erleichtern die sichere Installation.

Statement by the jury
The design of the SENCITY Occhio MIMO Antenna displays both elegance and reserve. Furthermore, installation is remarkably easy.

Begründung der Jury
Die Gestaltung der SENCITY Occhio MIMO Antenna drückt gleichermaßen Eleganz und Zurückhaltung aus. Darüber hinaus gelingt die Montage denkbar einfach.

Unionvision UFO Series
Wireless Access Point

Manufacturer
Shenzhen 21g Product Design Co., Ltd.,
Shenzhen, China
In-house design
Bowen Yang, Hongzhi Zhang
Web
www.design21g.com

This wireless access point provides dual band Wi-Fi technology in 3 x 3 MIMO 802.11ac with six internal antennas. This makes it possible to operate up to 300 end devices simultaneously. Interconnection of the device also gives additional users access and allows for use in changing environments. Installation and activation are carried out with the help of plug-and-play and enables it to be managed by people who have little technical knowledge. A circular light on the edge of the simple, but elegant device indicates the operating status.

Statement by the jury
The carefully considered design of this wireless access point of the Unionvision UFO Series is impressive for its ease of use. Its elegant appearance is an additional plus point.

Dieser Wireless Access Point bietet Dual-band-Wi-Fi-Technologie in 3 x 3 MIMO 802.11ac mit sechs internen Antennen. Bis zu 300 Endgeräte können somit simultan betrieben werden. Durch Kopplung wird der Zugang auch Drittnutzern und in wechselnder Umgebung möglich. Die Installation und Inbetriebnahme erfolgt mittels Plug-and-Play und lässt sich auch von technisch weniger geübten Personen vornehmen. Eine kreisförmige Lichtanzeige am Rand des einfach-elegant geschnittenen Geräts gibt den Status an.

Begründung der Jury
Die gut durchdachte Gestaltung dieses Wireless Access Points der Unionvision UFO Serie beeindruckt durch eine einfache Bedienbarkeit. Zudem gefällt sein edles Erscheinungsbild.

RG-AP680-I
Wireless Access Point

Manufacturer
Ruijie Networks Co., Ltd., Fuzhou, China
In-house design
Chengjie Hu, Haining Huang,
Zan Huang, Xiaohui Chen
Web
www.ruijie.com.cn

The RG-AP680-I wireless access point provides secure and efficient data services outside. It works with 802.11ax technology and integrated IoT. The device can be mounted in a number of different ways and locations, for instance on lamp posts or the walls of buildings of various construction types. As the bracket and body are seamlessly connected, the device is also very secure and stable in high winds. Maintenance is carried out via Bluetooth from the ground without needing to climb to dangerous heights.

Statement by the jury
The RG-AP680-I wireless access point convinces with a both user-friendly as well as sturdy construction.

Für sicheren und effizienten Datenservice im Außenbereich sorgt der Wireless Access Point RG-AP680-I, der mit 802.11ax-Technologie arbeitet und IoT integriert. Er lässt sich sehr variabel montieren, etwa an Lichtmasten oder Hauswänden unterschiedlicher Bauart. Indem Schelle und Körper nahtlos ineinander übergehen, ist das Gerät außerdem sehr windsicher und stabil. Die Wartung funktioniert via Bluetooth vom Boden aus, sodass man sich dazu nicht in gefährliche Höhen begeben muss.

Begründung der Jury
Der Wireless Access Point RG-AP680-I überzeugt durch seine gleichermaßen nutzerfreundliche wie auch stabile Konstruktionsweise.

5G QCell Base Station

Manufacturer
ZTE Corporation, Shenzhen, China
In-house design
Huang Chun, Li Lei
Web
www.zte.com.cn

This small, easy-to-use device was designed with the idea of combining high-performance, 5G high frequency network coverage with a minimalist and friendly appearance. The sweeping vents on the back create a heat sink and give the device a rhythmic feel. The front takes the form of a convex disc whose uniformity gives the unit a sleek appearance.

Statement by the jury
The organic form of the powerful 5G QCell Base Station lends it an almost playful lightness.

Diese kleine handliche Einheit wurde nach dem Konzept gestaltet, eine leistungsstarke 5G-Hochfrequenz-Netzabdeckung bieten zu können und zugleich minimalistisch und freundlich aufzutreten. Die Hitzeableitung an der Rückseite erfolgt in Form von geschwungenen Lamellen, die dem Gerät eine rhythmische Anmutung verleihen. Die Vorderseite präsentiert sich als Scheibe mit gewölbter Oberfläche, die in ihrer Ebenmäßigkeit sehr ruhig wirkt.

Begründung der Jury
Durch ihre organische Formgebung präsentiert sich die leistungsstarke 5G QCell Base Station mit einer spielerischen Leichtigkeit.

Nokia FastMile 5G Gateway

Manufacturer
Nokia Networks, San Francisco, USA
In-house design
Nokia Design
Web
www.nokia.com

The Nokia FastMile 5G Gateway provides lightning-fast 5G broadband technology that allows up to 25 times faster surfing than with 4G. The high-end device supplies the home with reliable and fast internet access. It is very easy to set up without requiring the installation of a lot of cables. With the help of the integrated 5G New Radio interface, this ensures provision of a reliable and powerful network. The device is tubular in form with a seamless, high-gloss surface that gives it a modern and distinguished appearance.

Das Nokia FastMile 5G Gateway sorgt für ein besonders schnelles Breitbandnetz der 5G-Technologie, mit dem bis zu 25-mal schneller im Netz gesurft werden kann als mit 4G. Das hochwertige Gerät versorgt einen Haushalt mit zuverlässigem und schnellem Internet, ohne dass ein Verlegen von Kabeln vonnöten wäre und lässt sich ganz einfach installieren. Mit der innovativen Schnittstelle 5G New Radio wird ein zuverlässiges und leistungsstarkes Netzwerk zur Verfügung gestellt. Gestalterisch zeigt das Gerät eine Röhrenform mit glänzender nahtloser Oberfläche, was ihm eine moderne und edle Anmutung verleiht.

Statement by the jury
The Nokia FastMile 5G Gateway has an astoundingly high performance. The design suits both modern and more traditional surroundings equally well.

Begründung der Jury
Das Nokia FastMile 5G Gateway versetzt mit seiner enormen Leistungsstärke in Erstaunen. Das Design fügt sich in ein modernes Ambiente ebenso gut ein wie in ein traditionelles.

Nokia WiFi
Wi-Fi Gateway and Mesh Extender

Manufacturer
Nokia Networks, San Francisco, USA
In-house design
Nokia Design
Web
www.nokia.com

Nokia WiFi was developed to compensate for interference of the Wi-Fi network caused by other wireless devices. The system consists of a fiber gateway and mesh extender network that provides flexible solutions and fulfills a range of requirements. The smaller element Beacon 3 steers the network to the most powerful frequency by circumventing interference caused by neighbouring Wi-Fi channels or other devices. A mesh system comprising several beacons ensures almost seamless Wi-Fi coverage throughout the entire home. The device can identify up to 17 different sources of interference.

Nokia WiFi wurde entwickelt, um Störungen des Wi-Fi-Netzes durch andere drahtlose Endgeräte auszugleichen. Das System besteht aus einem Gateway und Mesh Extender Network, das flexible Lösungen anbietet und variable Anforderungen erfüllt. Das kleinere Element Beacon 3 lenkt das Netzwerk auf die leistungsstärkste Frequenz, indem es Überschneidungen mit anderen Wi-Fi-Kanälen oder anderen störenden Endgeräten verhindert. Ein Mesh-System aus mehreren Beacons sorgt für annähernd nahtlose Wi-Fi-Abdeckung im gesamten Zuhause. Das Gerät identifiziert bis zu 17 unterschiedliche Störungsquellen.

Statement by the jury
With its system of Wi-Fi gateway and mesh extender the Nokia WiFi guarantees almost entirely interference-free access to the internet in an innovative way.

Begründung der Jury
Auf innovative Weise ermöglicht das System aus Wi-Fi Gateway und Mesh Extender von Nokia WiFi einen nahezu störungsfreien Onlinezugang.

Beacon
Router

Manufacturer
Nokia Networks, San Francisco, USA
In-house design
Nokia Design
Web
www.nokia.com

The intelligent Beacon router ensures a stable internet network at home or in the office. The beacon steers the network to a powerful frequency of 50 Mbps by circumventing the interference caused by other Wi-Fi channels or devices. A mesh system comprising several beacons ensures almost seamless Wi-Fi coverage throughout the entire home or office. The outward appearance of Beacon is slim and seamless. The oval design imparts a modern and noble impression on the device.

Der intelligente Router Beacon sorgt für ein stabiles Netz zu Hause oder im Büro. Der Beacon lenkt das Netzwerk auf eine leistungsstarke Frequenz von bis zu 50 Mbit/s, indem er Überschneidungen mit weiteren Wi-Fi-Kanälen oder anderen störenden Endgeräten verhindert. Ein Mesh-System aus mehreren Beacons sorgt für nahezu nahtlose Wi-Fi-Abdeckung im allen Räumlichkeiten. Äußerlich zeigt sich der Beacon in einer schmalen nahtlosen Gestaltung. Die ovale Formgebung verleiht dem Gerät eine moderne und edle Anmutung.

Statement by the jury
Beacon stands out due to an efficient mesh technology and a characteristic and, at the same time, unobtrusive design.

Begründung der Jury
Beacon imponiert mit einer effizienten Mesh-Technologie und einer charakteristischen und zugleich zurückhaltenden Gestaltung.

Forerunner
Smart Hub

Manufacturer
China Mobile Group Device Co., Ltd., Beijing, China
In-house design
Yulan Cao, Chen Guo
Web
http://phone.10086.cn

The Forerunner smart hub provides more devices with access to a 5G network, whether wirelessly or via one of the various ports. VR application and full HD-Videos in the 5G or WiGig millimetre wavelength are transmitted noise-free. The chamfered corners of the device as well as the discreetly located ventilation vents support the performance of the cooling system. The screen is inclined backwards at 15 degrees and is convenient in use and operation. The device also offers a voice assistant, dual speakers as well as three microphones. Thanks to its small dimensions, it is light to transport.

Statement by the jury
The Forerunner smart hub surprises with 5G transmission, which is as fast as it is reliable. Its ergonomic, pleasant handling is also attractive.

Wi-Fi Station HW-01L
Router

Manufacturer
Huawei Device Co., Ltd.,
Shenzhen, China
Design
NTT DOCOMO, Inc., Product Department,
Design Management Section, Tokyo, Japan
Web
www.huawei.com
www.nttdocomo.co.jp/english

This mobile router offers a transmission speed of up to 1.28 Gbps. The main unit shows a clear, symmetrical design, allowing the user to carry it around in a bag and at home simply plug it into the charging station. The information on the clearly and calmly designed display is intuitively understandable. Due to the unobtrusive chromatic colouring, the device blends into any aesthetic.

Statement by the jury
Thanks to the well-proportioned design, the Wi-Fi Station HW-01L is especially suitable for carrying around. It also integrates easily with any interior.

Dieser mobile Router bietet eine Übertragungsgeschwindigkeit von bis zu 1,28 Gbit/s. Die Haupteinheit zeigt eine klare, symmetrische Gestaltung, somit lässt sie sich zum Mitführen einfach in einer Tasche transportieren und zu Hause ganz einfach in die Ladestation einsetzen. Die Informationen auf dem übersichtlich und ruhig gestalteten Display sind intuitiv erfassbar. Durch die unauffällige chromatische Farbgebung passt sich das Gerät jeder ästhetischen Gegebenheit an.

Begründung der Jury
Dank der ebenmäßigen Gestaltung eignet sich die Wi-Fi Station HW-01L besonders gut zur Mitnahme. Zudem integriert sie sich einfach in jedes Interieur.

TAG Mesh Router Station

Manufacturer
CMCC, Beijing, China
In-house design
Liu Chang
Web
zhengqi.10086.cn

The TAG Mesh Router Station divides a network into different logical segments. These individual partial network elements are smaller than the router and can be connected by means of pairing via NFC at the simple touch of a button. The separate elements manage access rights as well as sub-routing times. This makes it possible to also control the online behaviour of children. Flowing contours give the system an organic appearance.

Statement by the jury
The flowing lines of this router station convey reliability and draw attention to the central control key.

Mit der TAG Mesh Router Station wird ein Netzwerk in verschiedene logische Teilnetze segmentiert. Die einzelnen Teilnetz-Elemente sind dabei kleiner gehalten als der Router und können durch einfachen Tastendruck mittels Pairing via NFC verbunden werden. Die einzelnen Elemente steuern die Zugangsrechte sowie Sub-Routing-Zeiten. So lässt sich auch das Online-Verhalten von Kindern regeln. Fließende Formen verleihen dem System eine organische Anmutung.

Begründung der Jury
Die fließende Linienführung dieser Router-Station vermittelt Zuverlässigkeit und fokussiert den Blick auf die zentrale Steuerungstaste.

Vodafone Super WiFi
Wi-Fi Point

Manufacturer
Vodafone Group Services GmbH,
Düsseldorf, Germany
In-house design
Daniel Schubert, Anja Einwag, Yuan Liu
Design
studiomem GmbH, Munich, Germany
Web
www.vodafone.com
www.studiomem.com

This innovative Wi-Fi point provides a mesh Wi-Fi in the home, with which other devices can be connected in a smart, uncomplicated and wireless way. It implements modern design language to follow the trend of integration in the style of contemporary interior architecture. Instead of an intrusive and technically oriented approach, the Wi-Fi point with a matte anthracite-coloured surface and clear lines makes a restrained impression.

Statement by the jury
The impressive performance of the Vodafone Super WiFi with a modern design ensures effortless surfing throughout the entire home.

Dieser innovative Wi-Fi Point stellt im Heimbereich ein Mesh-Wi-Fi-Netzwerk her, mit dem sich andere Geräte smart, unkompliziert und kabellos verbinden lassen. Er realisiert eine moderne Designsprache, welche sich trendbewusst in den Stil der zeitgenössischen Innenarchitektur einfügt. Anstelle eines aufdringlichen und technoiden Auftretens setzt der Wi-Fi Point mit matt-anthrazitfarbener Oberfläche und klarer Linienführung auf eine zurückhaltende Anmutung.

Begründung der Jury
Die eindrucksvolle Leistungsfähigkeit des modern gestalteten Vodafone Super WiFi gewährleistet müheloses Surfen im gesamten Zuhause.

Telenor
Wi-Fi Router and Wi-Fi Extender

Manufacturer
Telenor Norway, Fornebu, Norway
Design
Snøhetta (Marius Myking), Oslo, Norway
Web
www.telenor.no
www.snohetta.com

In contrast to many traditional routers, this device dispenses with a technical look. The white surface of the diamond-shaped body has a vertical pattern which catches the light. The vents are hidden from view. Discreet LED lighting is only activated when prompted by the user. A minimalist metal bracket makes it possible to mount the device on the wall.

Statement by the jury
The Telenor Wi-Fi router and Wi-Fi extender exhibits a sophisticated aesthetic appearance which makes it a welcome addition to the home.

Anders als bei vielen traditionellen Routern wird hier auf ein technisches Erscheinungsbild verzichtet. Die weißen Oberflächen an dem rautenförmigen Körper sind mit einem vertikalen Muster versehen, in welchem sich das Licht widerspiegelt. Lüftungselemente bleiben vor den Augen der Nutzer verborgen. Auf Wunsch lässt sich eine zurückhaltende LED-Beleuchtung aktivieren. Eine minimalistische Metallklammer ermöglicht die Wandmontage.

Begründung der Jury
Der Telenor Wi-Fi Router und Wi-Fi Extender präsentiert sich in einer ausgereiften Ästhetik, was ihn zu einem willkommenen Wohnaccessoire macht.

5G CPE
Wireless Access Point

Manufacturer
Huawei Technologies Co., Ltd., Shanghai, China
In-house design
Web
www.huawei.com

The 5G CPE makes it possible to access both high band and low band frequencies in the living area. The system is compatible with LTE networks and supports 5G. Installation off the floor makes it particularly versatile. In this way, individual elements can be mounted on the ceiling, the wall or on posts which helps to ensure best possible network coverage. The form which gently tapers towards the top end looks both elegant and discreet. This calm appearance ensures the elements seamlessly blend into every type of setting.

Statement by the jury
The 5G CPE wireless access point stands out for its versatile installation options as well as its unobtrusive appearance.

Mit dem Huawei 5G CPE lassen sich im Wohnbereich der High-Band- wie auch der Low-Band-Frequenzbereich nutzen. Das System ist kompatibel mit LTE-Netzwerken und unterstützt 5G. Bodenfreie Installation macht es besonders vielseitig. So können die einzelnen Elemente etwa an der Decke, der Wand oder an Masten installiert werden, was wiederum die bestmögliche Netzabdeckung unterstützt. Die sich nach oben sanft verjüngende Formgebung wirkt elegant und zurückhaltend. Durch dieses ruhige Erscheinungsbild fügen sich die Elemente gut in jede Umgebung ein.

Begründung der Jury
Der Wireless Access Point 5G CPE zeichnet sich durch variable Installationsmöglichkeiten sowie ein dezentes Erscheinungsbild aus.

H3C X3 pro
Wireless Router

Manufacturer
New H3C Technologies Co., Ltd., Hangzhou, China
In-house design
Kai Li
Design
BANTUM, Shanghai, China
Web
www.h3c.com.cn
www.bantuminc.com

The H3C X3 pro wireless router was designed specially for supporting a high-grade eSports experience. Elevated incisions increase the performance of the cooling system. At the same time, together with the striking LEDs, they characterise the router as a powerful, high-speed device. It uses a Qualcomm-Gigabit dual-core CPU, offers a 512 MB memory and supports dual-band, multi-user MIMO and 802.11ac Wave 2. The device offers five GE ports and two USB 3.0 connections. Real-time applications, an intelligent broadband allocation, Wi-Fi optimisation and dual-band roaming are effectively supported.

Speziell zur Unterstützung eines hochwertigen eSports-Erlebnisses wurde der kabellose Router H3C X3 pro konzipiert. Hervorgehobene Einschnitte erhöhen die Kühlleistung. Zugleich mit den auffälligen LED-Leuchten charakterisieren sie den Router als kraftvolles Hochgeschwindigkeitsgerät. Er nutzt einen Qualcomm-Gigabit- Dual-Core-Prozessor, bietet einen 512MB-Arbeitsspeicher und unterstützt Dualband, Multi-User-MIMO und 802.11ac Wave 2. Das Gerät bietet fünf GE-Ports sowie zwei USB-3.0-Anschlüsse. Echtzeitanwendungen, eine intelligente Bandbreitenzuordnung, automatische Wi-Fi-Optimierung und Dualband-Roaming werden wirkungsvoll unterstützt.

Statement by the jury
The wireless H3C X3 pro router impresses due to its powerful appearance, which emphasises effectively its technical qualities.

Begründung der Jury
Der kabellose Router H3C X3 pro beeindruckt durch ein kraftvolles Aussehen, das seine technischen Qualitäten wirkungsvoll unterstreicht.

Nighthawk X12
Router

Manufacturer
Netgear, San Jose, California, USA
In-house design
Design
Enlisted Design, Oakland, California, USA
Web
www.netgear.com
www.enlisteddesign.com

The eye-catching and aggressive design vocabulary of the Nighthawk X12 router is inspired by the dominant appearance of a stealth fighter jet. As if to underline this image, the eight high-performance antennas are built into the wings which appear to extend seamlessly from the base of the router at an obtuse angle. The dual-band antennas efficiently amplify Wi-Fi signals to provide very secure, quick and extensive network coverage.

Statement by the jury
The Nighthawk X12 router ensures that many devices can be used concurrently without any problem. Its appearance speaks of performance.

In seiner auffälligen und aggressiv anmutenden Formensprache vergleicht sich der Router Nighthawk X12 mit dem dominanten Erscheinungsbild des gleichnamigen Tarnkappenflugzeugs. Zur Unterstreichung dieses Eindrucks sind auch seine acht leistungsstarken Antennen in die Seitenflügel integriert, die in einem stumpfen Winkel zur Bodenfläche angeordnet sind und nahtlos in diese übergehen. Die Dualband-Antennen verstärken effizient die Wi-Fi-Signale und dadurch wird eine sehr sichere, schnelle und weitläufige Netzwerkabdeckung möglich.

Begründung der Jury
Der Router Nighthawk X12 sorgt für ein problemloses Nebeneinander vieler Endgeräte. Seine Ästhetik vermittelt Leistungsstärke.

Nighthawk Pro Gaming XR700
Router

Manufacturer
Netgear, San Jose, California, USA
In-house design
Bong Gun Lee, Henry Jupille
Web
www.netgear.com

The Nighthawk Pro Gaming XR700 is a router for the highly demanding gaming sector. It is based on high-end software and hardware. A stable internet connection and decreased lag benefit the player. The outward appearance with four imposing antennas and the dynamic lines as well as colourful focal points on the exterior body accentuates the dynamic nature of the router.

Statement by the jury
The Nighthawk Pro Gaming XR700 router gives players total control of their network and therefore also their gaming experience.

Der Nighthawk Pro Gaming XR700 ist ein Router für den anspruchsvollen Gamingbereich. Dafür kommt hochwertige Software wie auch Hardware zum Einsatz. Eine stabile Internetverbindung und verringerte Übertragungsverzögerungen kommen dem Spieler entgegen. Das äußere Erscheinungsbild mit vier imposanten Antennen und einer dynamischen Linienführung sowie farblichen Akzenten unterstreicht den sportiven Charakter des Routers.

Begründung der Jury
Mit dem Router Nighthawk Pro Gaming XR700 behält der Spieler die Kontrolle über das Netzwerk und damit über sein Spielerlebnis.

Nighthawk X6 Tri-Band
Router

Manufacturer
Netgear, San Jose, California, USA
In-house design
Ed Kalubiran, Henry Jupille
Web
www.netgear.com

The Nighthawk X6 mesh extender of this router automatically connects to the best available Wi-Fi network via smart roaming. With the help of the One WiFi Name feature, the user is free to move through all the rooms in the home while maintaining a constant level of connectivity. The body of the device, with its four high-performance antennas, is reminiscent of a cut diamond. The innovative technology of the router thus receives matching visual support.

Statement by the jury
Thanks to innovative technology, the Nighthawk X6 Tri-Band router allows for unlimited internet access throughout the home.

Der Nighthawk X6 Mesh Extender dieses Routers verbindet sich mittels Smart Roaming automatisch mit dem besten zur Verfügung stehenden Wi-Fi-Netzwerk. Mittels One WiFi Name-Funktion bewegt sich der Nutzer bei gleichbleibender Verbindungsstärke frei durch alle Räume. Der Körper in Verbindung mit vier hochleistungsfähigen Antennen lässt an geschliffene Diamanten erinnern. Die innovative Technologie des Geräts wird damit auch optisch hervorgehoben.

Begründung der Jury
Dank innovativer Technologie ermöglicht der Router Nighthawk X6 Tri-Band einen uneingeschränkten Internetzugang im gesamten Wohnbereich.

Orbi Pro SRC60
Wireless Access Point

Manufacturer
Netgear, San Jose, California, USA
In-house design
Aron Han, Rose Hu
Web
www.netgear.com

Orbi Pro products are designed to cover a broad range of business environments, from small cafes and shops to larger outdoor event venues. The Orbi Pro SRC60 presents itself with a clean and simple form in a bright white, which allows it to fit into any environment. As it is attached to the ceiling, the cooling vents are hidden from view. Power and status are clearly displayed and are even visible from afar.

Statement by the jury
The Wireless Access Point Orbi Pro SRC60 demonstrates stylistic confidence through a design which is at the same time full of character and discreet.

Produkte der Serie Orbo Pro decken die Bedürfnisse einer breiten Palette an geschäftlichen Umfeldern ab, von kleinen Kaffees und Läden bis hin zu Eventanbietern mit Außenbereich. Der Orbi Pro SRC60 präsentiert sich in einfacher und schlichter Form sowie in strahlendem Weiß, sodass er sich äußerlich gut in jedem Umfeld einfügt. An der Decke montiert bleiben die Lüftungslamellen vor den Augen der Nutzer verborgen. Power und Status werden deutlich angezeigt und können auch aus weiter Distanz gut abgelesen werden.

Begründung der Jury
Stilsicherheit beweist der Wireless Access Point Orbi Pro SRC60 mit seiner charaktervollen, dabei gleichzeitig zurückhaltenden Gestaltung.

Nighthawk AX8
Router

Manufacturer
Netgear, San Jose, California, USA
Design
Enlisted Design, Oakland, California, USA
Web
www.netgear.com
www.enlisteddesign.com

The shape of the Nighthawk AX8 router is seamless and generous with flowing rounded contours. The surface material alternates between matte and glossy areas. In general, the device exudes an air of self-confidence. It comes with a high-performance 1.8GHz-quad-core processor with six Ethernet ports and achieves a connection strength of up to 2Gbps. Its innovative OFDMA technology enables several devices to be used at the same time on the same network without loss of performance.

Statement by the jury
Thanks to its extremely high Wi-Fi capability, the Nighthawk AX8 router ensures surfing, streaming, downloading and gaming without time delay.

Der Router Nighthawk AX8 zeigt eine nahtlose und großflächige Formgebung mit fließenden abgerundeten Übergängen. Das Oberflächenmaterial wechselt zwischen mattierten und glänzenden Abschnitten. Insgesamt präsentiert sich das Gerät damit in einer selbstbewussten Anmutung. Es bietet einen leistungsstarken 1,8GHz-Quadcore-Prozessor, mit sechs Ethernet-Ports gelingt eine Verbindungsstärke von bis zu 2Gbit/s. Durch die innovative OFDMA-Technologie können verschiedene Endgeräte ohne Leistungsabfall innerhalb desselben Netzwerks zeitgleich betrieben werden.

Begründung der Jury
Durch eine ausgesprochen hohe Wi-Fi-Leistung gelingt mit dem Router Nighthawk AX8 verzögerungsfreies Surfen, Streamen, Downloaden und Spielen.

Orbi Voice
Router with Smart Speaker
Router mit intelligentem Lautsprecher

Manufacturer
Netgear, San Jose, California, USA
In-house design
Aron Han, Edwin Liu
Web
www.netgear.com

Orbi Voice bundles a highly efficient mesh Wi-Fi router with a smart Alexa speaker. Loudspeakers with built-in Harman Kardon technology ensure the sound quality is exceptionally high. Voice control can be used to operate smart home devices and play music. Streaming and downloads work smoothly and easily. Outwardly, Orbi Voice uses a cylindric design vocabulary while the mix of materials – textiles, plastic and metal – gives the device a modern yet discreet appearance.

Orbi Voice bündelt einen hocheffizienten Mesh-Wi-Fi-Router mit dem intelligenten Alexa-Sprachassistenten. Für sehr gute Klangqualität sorgen Lautsprecher mit integrierter Technologie von Harman Kardon. Per Sprachsteuerung werden Smart Home-Geräte bedient und Musik wiedergegeben, Streamen und Downloads gelingen störungsfrei und einfach. Äußerlich präsentiert sich Orbi Voice in einer zylindrischen Formensprache, der Materialmix aus Textil, Kunststoff und Metall verleiht dem Gerät eine moderne und zurückhaltende Anmutung.

Statement by the jury
What makes the innovative Orbi Voice so convincing is its fascinating multifunctionality which meets the requirements of modern households.

Begründung der Jury
Der innovative Orbi Voice überzeugt durch seine faszinierende Multifunktionalität, mit der er hohe Ansprüche eines modernen Haushalts erfüllt.

M2 Hive
Wi-Fi System

Manufacturer
Mercku Inc., Waterloo, Ontario, Canada
In-house design
Ronghao Jin
Web
www.mercku.com

This Wi-Fi system consists of an M2 Wi-Fi router and many plug-in nodes. The nodes are installed around the house, creating a modular network that eliminates connectivity problems and dead spots. On this network, eighty devices can connect at the same time, while still maintaining industry-leading speed. Due to the flexibility of the system, nodes can be placed and added, depending on the structure of the house. The elements of the M2 Hive are discreetly and elegantly designed, and thus blend in well with any surroundings.

Statement by the jury
The elegantly styled Wi-Fi repeater M2 Hive assures convenience, since it creates reliable internet connectivity in the entire living area.

Satcube Ku
Satellite Communication Terminal
Satellitenkommunikationsterminal

Manufacturer
Satcube AB, Gothenburg, Sweden
Design
Shift Design & Strategy AB (Carl Hampf, Pär Bergström), Gothenburg, Sweden
Web
www.satcube.com
www.shiftdesign.se

The innovative technology of Satcube Ku is developed to tap High Throughput Satellites (HTS) to fulfill high capacity communication needs, targeting industry verticals and work places requiring broadband connectivity where only limited connectivity is available. The light weight, user-friendly device delivers quick broadband connectivity almost anywhere on earth. Its intuitive user interface makes operation very simple providing internet access in less than a minute. The compact device which meets IATA standards, weighs only eight kilogrammes and includes a specially designed battery pack for three hours of data transmission time – with battery replacement while operating.

Die innovative Technologie von Satcube Ku wurde entwickelt, um High-Throughput-Satellites (HTS) zu erschließen, um Kommunikationsanforderungen mit hoher Kapazität zu erfüllen, und richtet sich an Branchenverteiler und Arbeitsplätze, die eine Breitbandverbindung erfordern, bei der nur begrenzte Konnektivität verfügbar ist. Das leichte, benutzerfreundliche Gerät ermöglicht schnelle Breitbandverbindungen fast überall auf der Welt. Die intuitive Benutzerschnittstelle macht die Bedienung sehr einfach und bietet einen Internetzugang in weniger als einer Minute. Das kompakte Gerät, das den IATA-Standards entspricht, wiegt nur acht Kilogramm und enthält einen speziell entwickelten Akku für drei Stunden Datenübertragungszeit – mit Batteriewechsel während des Betriebs.

Statement by the jury
Satcube Ku manages to make contemporary satellite technology accessible to a wide audience in an impressively convenient way.

Begründung der Jury
Satcube Ku gelingt es in beeindruckender Weise, zeitgemäße Satellitentechnologie einem breiten Nutzerkreis zugänglich zu machen.

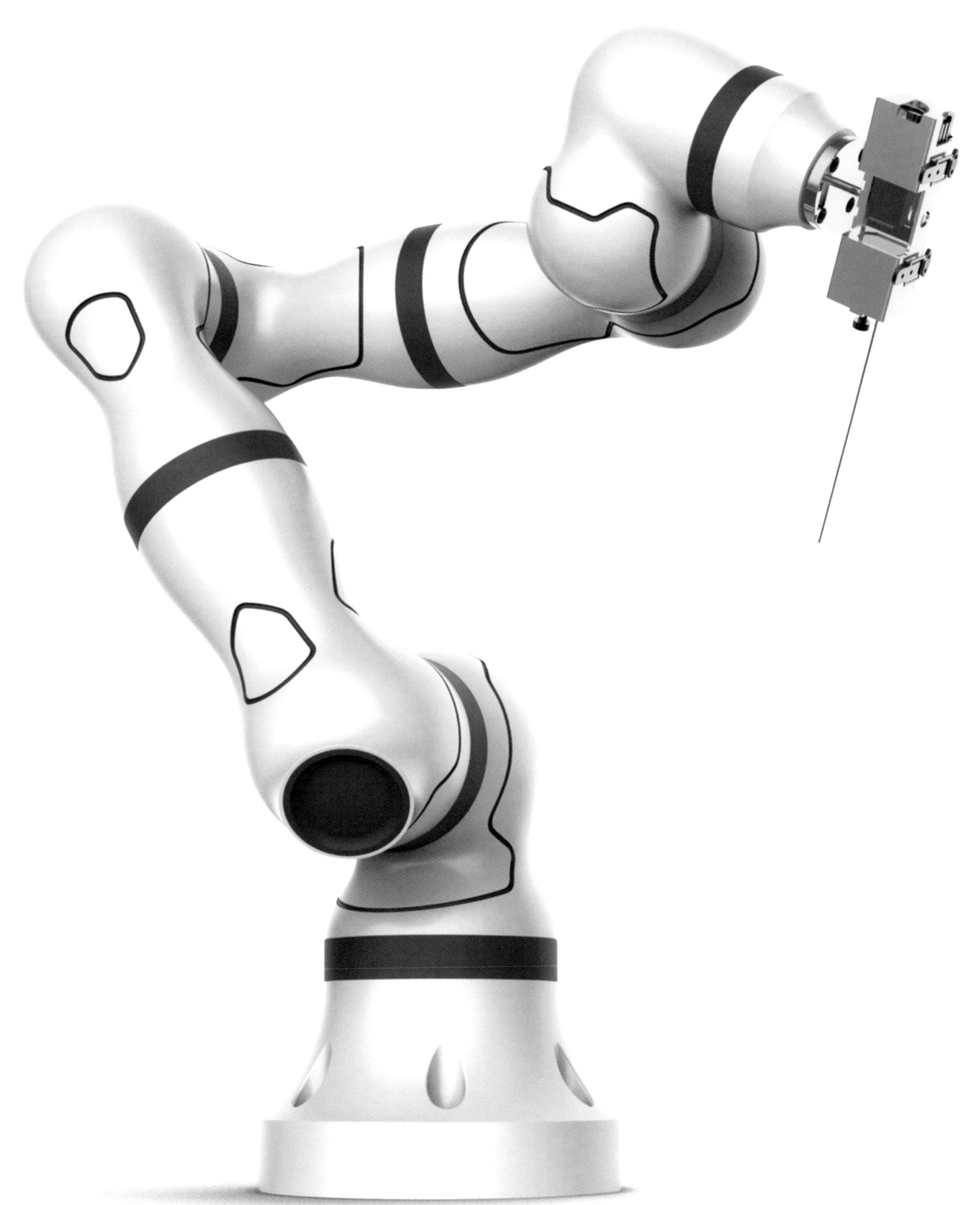

Robots
Roboter

Autonomous mobile robots   Autonome mobile Roboter
Exoskeletons   Erkundungsroboter
Exploration robots   Exoskelette
Industrial robots   Industrieroboter
Medical robots   Medizinroboter
Robotic parts   Roboterzubehör
Service robots   Serviceroboter
Toy robots   Spielzeugroboter

Hyundai Robot YL012
Collaborative Robot
Kollaborativer Roboter

Manufacturer
Hyundai Robotics,
Daegu, South Korea

In-house design
Daekyu Yun, Jongwon Kim

Design
Hyundai Heavy Industries
(Kyoungsub Bae, Jaepil Choi,
Hyundai Kim), Seoul, South Korea

Web
www.hyundai-robotics.com
www.hhi.co.kr

reddot award 2019
best of the best

Friendly colleague
Living and working side by side with robots, as described by science fiction author Isaac Asimov in his stories back in the 1940s, has become more and more of a reality today. The Hyundai Robot YL012 has been developed to directly operate in collaboration with human workers. It fascinates with a slim and organic shape, which has also reduced the robot's weight to a minimum. Thanks to its optimised structure, the pneumatic lines as well as electrical and communication wires could all be installed inside the robot's arm joints for an overall clean and smooth appearance without right angles. Boasting these innovative construction features and a remarkable work radius of 130 cm, this collaborative robot can work alongside with and close to workers without problems even in small spaces, with safety risks such as crush and collision injuries reduced significantly. The ergonomically shaped handgrip and easy-to-operate switch arrangement allows workers to interact with the robot in a quick, convenient and direct way and teach it how to work. For intuitive observation of the robot's condition from all surroundings, the YL012 has been equipped with LED flash lamps. Offering excellent mechanical performance, this industrial robot offers a payload of up to 12 kg. In addition, various input-output ports for end effectors facilitate easy and immediate application of different tools to the system.

Freundlicher Kollege
Das bereits in den 1940er Jahren von dem Science-Fiction-Autor Isaac Asimov in seinen Erzählungen beschriebene Leben und Arbeiten mit Robotern wird heute mehr und mehr Realität. Der Hyundai Robot YL012 wurde für die direkte Zusammenarbeit mit dem Menschen entwickelt. Er begeistert mit einer schlanken wie organischen Gestaltung, die auch sein Gewicht auf ein Minimum reduziert. Durch eine insgesamt optimierte Struktur konnten die Pneumatik sowie die Kabel für Elektrik und Kommunikation in den keine rechten Winkel aufweisenden Armgelenken integriert werden. Dieser kollaborative Roboter bietet damit einen bemerkenswerten Arbeitsradius von 130 cm und kann dank seiner innovativen Konstruktionsmerkmale auch in engen Umgebungen gefahrlos Seite an Seite mit Menschen zusammenarbeiten. Sicherheitsrisiken wie Quetsch- oder Kollisionsverletzungen werden deutlich verringert. Ergonomisch gestaltete Handgriffe und eine einfach zu bedienende Schalteranordnung ermöglichen den Anwendern eine schnelle, bequeme und direkte Interaktion, um den Roboter Arbeitsabläufe erlernen zu lassen. Der YL012 verfügt zudem über LED-Lampen für ein intuitives Erkennen seines Zustands in jeder Umgebung. Dieser Industrieroboter bietet eine hervorragende mechanische Leistung mit einer Nutzlast von bis zu 12 kg. Ausgestattet ist er mit mehreren Anschlüssen, was den unmittelbaren Einsatz verschiedener Werkzeuge erleichtert.

Statement by the jury
The design of the Hyundai Robot YL012 succeeds in its perfect integration of all elements. This collaborative robot showcases a fluid use of forms that lends it an open, friendly appearance. Facilitating a new approach towards human-robot interaction, it assures a high degree of workers' safety. Highly flexible in application, the robot offers an optimised work radius and a high payload. Its clear structure promotes intuitive operation.

Begründung der Jury
Der Gestaltung des Hyundai Robot YL012 gelingt die perfekte Integration aller Elemente. Dieser kollaborative Roboter zeigt eine fließende Formensprache, die ihm einen zugewandten Charakter verleiht. Seine Konstruktion begünstigt eine neue Art der Interaktion mit einem hohen Maß an Sicherheit. In einem optimierten Arbeitsradius ist er sehr flexibel und verfügt über eine hohe Tragkraft. Sein klarer Aufbau ermöglicht eine intuitive Art der Bedienung.

Designer portrait
See page 58
Siehe Seite 58

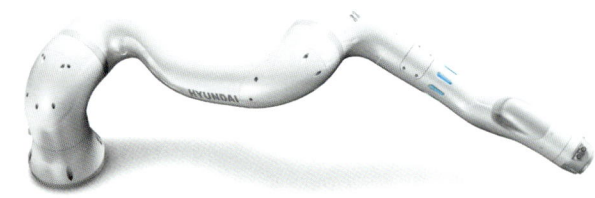

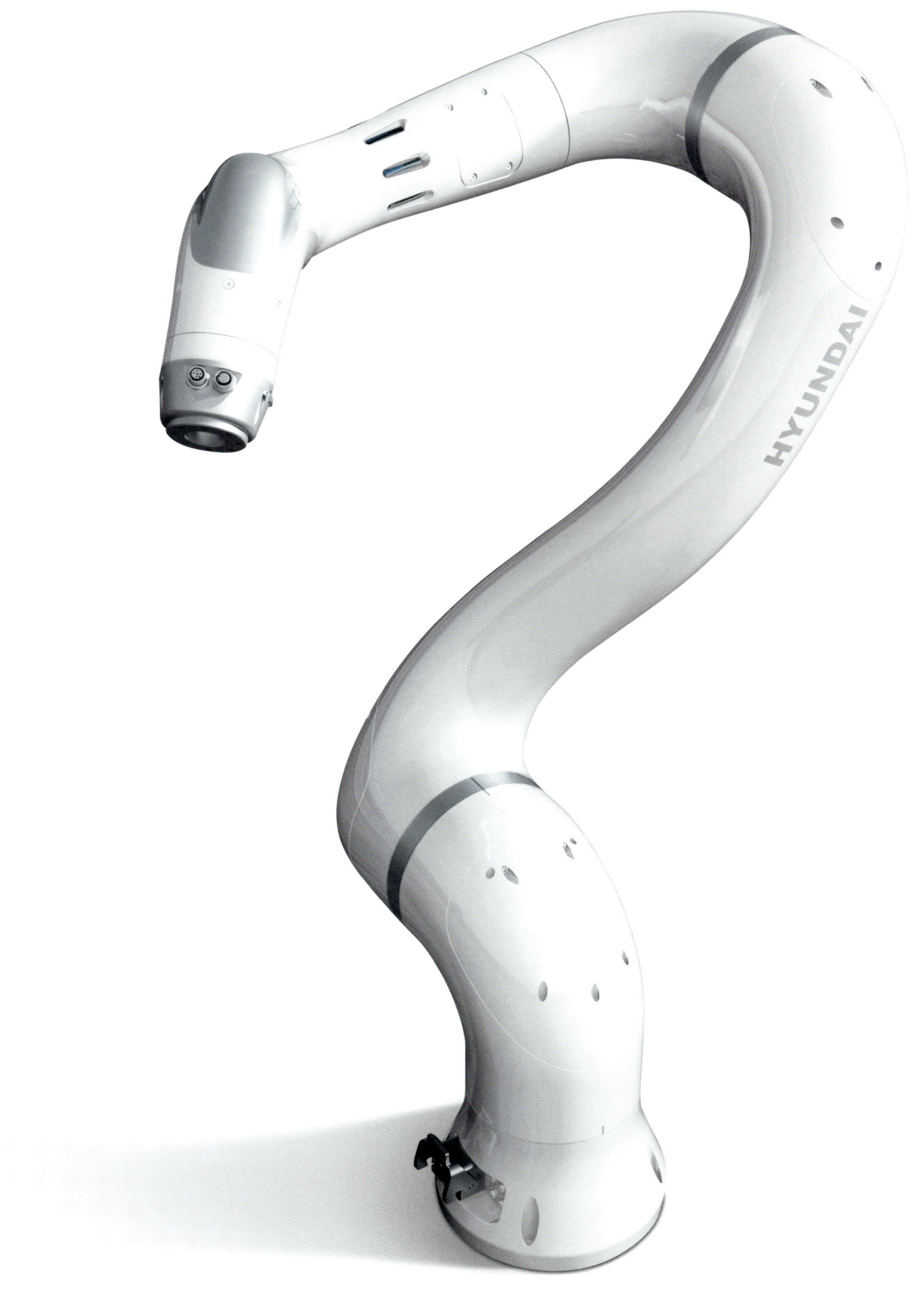

KUKA LBR iisy
Small Robot
Kleinroboter

Manufacturer
KUKA AG, Augsburg, Germany
In-house design
Markus Theiler, Melina Nasradini
Design
Selic Industriedesign (Mario Selic), Augsburg, Germany
Web
www.kuka.com
www.selic.de

The KUKA LBR iisy is a sensitive and precise robot that makes automation particularly intuitive. With a payload capacity of 3 kg and a reach of 600 mm, it is optimised for operation in narrow spaces, such as for unloading, packaging, precise mounting or difficult research and development tasks. It has joint torque sensors in all six axes, which react to minor external forces and provide certified collision protection. In order to give the robot a signature look, its appearance is characterised by gentle edges that are clearly visible but cannot be felt by the operator.

Der KUKA LBR iisy ist ein sensitiver und präziser Roboter, der die Automatisierung sehr intuitiv gestaltet. Mit einer Traglast von 3 kg und Reichweite von 600 mm ist er auf Tätigkeiten in engen Räumen optimiert, ob Bestücken, Entnehmen, Verpacken, zuverlässiges Montieren oder diffizile Arbeiten in der Forschung. Er besitzt in allen sechs Achsen Gelenkmomentensensoren, die auf geringste Kräfte von außen reagieren und zertifizierten Kollisionsschutz bieten. Um dem Roboter eine markentypische Formensprache zu verleihen, ist sein Erscheinungsbild von sanften Kanten geprägt, die gut sichtbar, aber für den Anwender nicht spürbar sind.

Statement by the jury
With its sleek and emotionally appealing design language, the small robot fulfils all critical requirements for human-robot collaboration.

Begründung der Jury
Der Kleinroboter erfüllt in seiner geschmeidigen und auch emotional ansprechenden Formensprache alle wichtigen Merkmale für die Mensch-Roboter-Kollaboration.

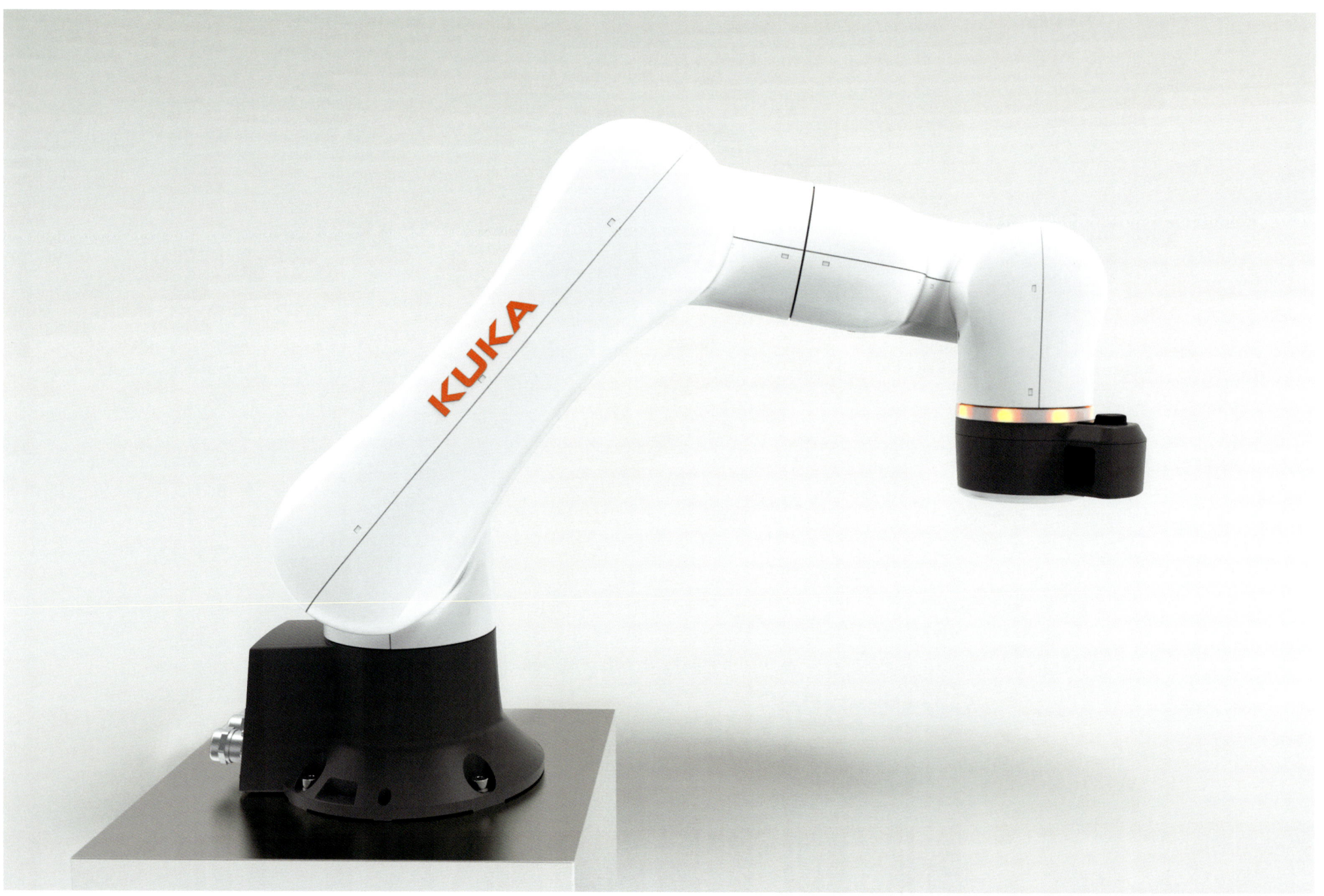

robolink® ReBeL®
Robot Arm

Manufacturer
igus GmbH, Cologne, Germany
In-house design
Web
www.igus.de

For the first time in the robolink product family, low-cost strain wave gear was used, making it possible to develop a robot with six axes. The additional sixth rotation axis allows for rotary movement of the articulated robot arm and ensures that all positions can be reached. In this model, motors, cables and control electronics can be installed in the arm. The external shell is entirely made of polymers and therefore very cost-effective and light.

Statement by the jury
The use of synthetic materials not only makes the robolink ReBeL robot arm affordable. It also creates a unique and appealing appearance.

Bei diesem Roboterarm wird erstmals in der robolink-Produktreihe ein Low-Cost-Wellgetriebe verwendet, mit dem sich 6-Achs-Roboter realisieren lassen. Die zusätzliche sechste Rotationsachse ermöglicht eine Drehbewegung des Knickarmroboters und eine vollständige Erreichbarkeit von Positionen. Bei diesem Modell lassen sich Motoren, Kabel und Steuerungselektronik im Arm verbauen. Die Außenkontur besteht vollständig aus Polymeren und ist deshalb besonders kostengünstig und leicht.

Begründung der Jury
Die Verwendung von Kunststoff macht den Roboterarm robolink ReBeL nicht nur erschwinglich, sondern schafft auch eine ganz eigene ansprechende Ästhetik.

MotoMINI
Lightweight
High-Speed Robot
Leichter Highspeed-Roboter

Manufacturer
YASKAWA Electric Corp.,
Fukuoka, Japan
In-house design
Web
www.yaskawa.co.jp

The MotoMINI combines fast cycle rates with a high degree of repeatability. This makes the six-axis robot ideal for handling small workpieces and components, but also for assembly work in small production machines. Its compact design enables space-saving installation. This robot moves components in all three directions and on all three axes within the smallest of spaces. This freedom of movement also facilitates more complex, three-dimensional handling.

Statement by the jury
Its defined, smooth contours give the MotoMINI a powerful appearance that deftly expresses its speed and precision.

Der MotoMINI verbindet schnelle Taktzahlen mit einer hohen Wiederholgenauigkeit. Damit eignet sich der 6-Achs-Roboter ideal für das Handling kleiner Werkstücke und Bauteile, aber auch für den Montageeinsatz in kleinen Produktionsmaschinen. Die kompakte Bauform erlaubt eine platzsparende Installation. Auf kleinstem Raum bewegt der Roboter die Bauteile in alle drei Richtungen und um alle drei Achsen. Diese Bewegungsfreiheit ermöglicht auch kompliziertere, dreidimensionale Handlingvorgänge.

Begründung der Jury
Seine definierten, glatten Konturen verleihen dem MotoMINI eine kraftvolle Ausstrahlung, die seiner Schnelligkeit und Präzision gekonnt Ausdruck verleiht.

Seven-Axis Intelligent Cooperative Arm
Robot Arm
Roboterarm

Manufacturer
Harbin Institute of Technology,
State Key Laboratory of Robotics and System,
Harbin, China
Luoyang Shangqi Robot Technology Co., Ltd.,
Luoyang, China
Design
Hebei Yifan Zhuopin Industrial Design Co., Ltd.,
Enjoyjob Design Studio, Shijiazhuang, China
Web
http://robot.hit.edu.cn
www.enjoyjobdesign.com

This seven-axis robot arm enables precise control of surgical instruments – regardless of where the surgeon is situated, either directly on site or at a remote location. The design places special emphasis on a friendly and simultaneously professional appearance that supports a positive perception of the robot as the surgeon's assistant. Its contours are inspired by the human arm and precisely adapted to the working environment. The shell made of carbon fibre and the metal exoskeleton ensure reduced weight and strong robustness.

Dieser 7-Achs-Roboterarm ermöglicht die präzise Steuerung chirurgischer Instrumente – egal ob der Chirurg, der den Roboter bedient, direkt vor Ort oder weit weg ist. Bei der Gestaltung wurde besonderer Wert auf ein freundliches und zugleich professionell anmutendes Erscheinungsbild gelegt, das eine positive Wahrnehmung des Roboters als dienstbaren Helfer des Chirurgen unterstützt. Seine Konturen sind dem menschlichen Arm nachempfunden und präzise auf das Arbeitsumfeld abgestimmt. Die Verkleidung aus Carbon in Verbindung mit einem Exoskelett aus Metall verleiht dem Roboter ein geringes Gewicht und hohe Festigkeit.

Statement by the jury
The proportions of this robot arm are carefully matched. Distinctive lines create an appealing futuristic appearance.

Begründung der Jury
Die Proportionen dieses Roboterarms sind sorgfältig aufeinander abgestimmt. Markante Linien sorgen für einen ansprechenden futuristischen Look.

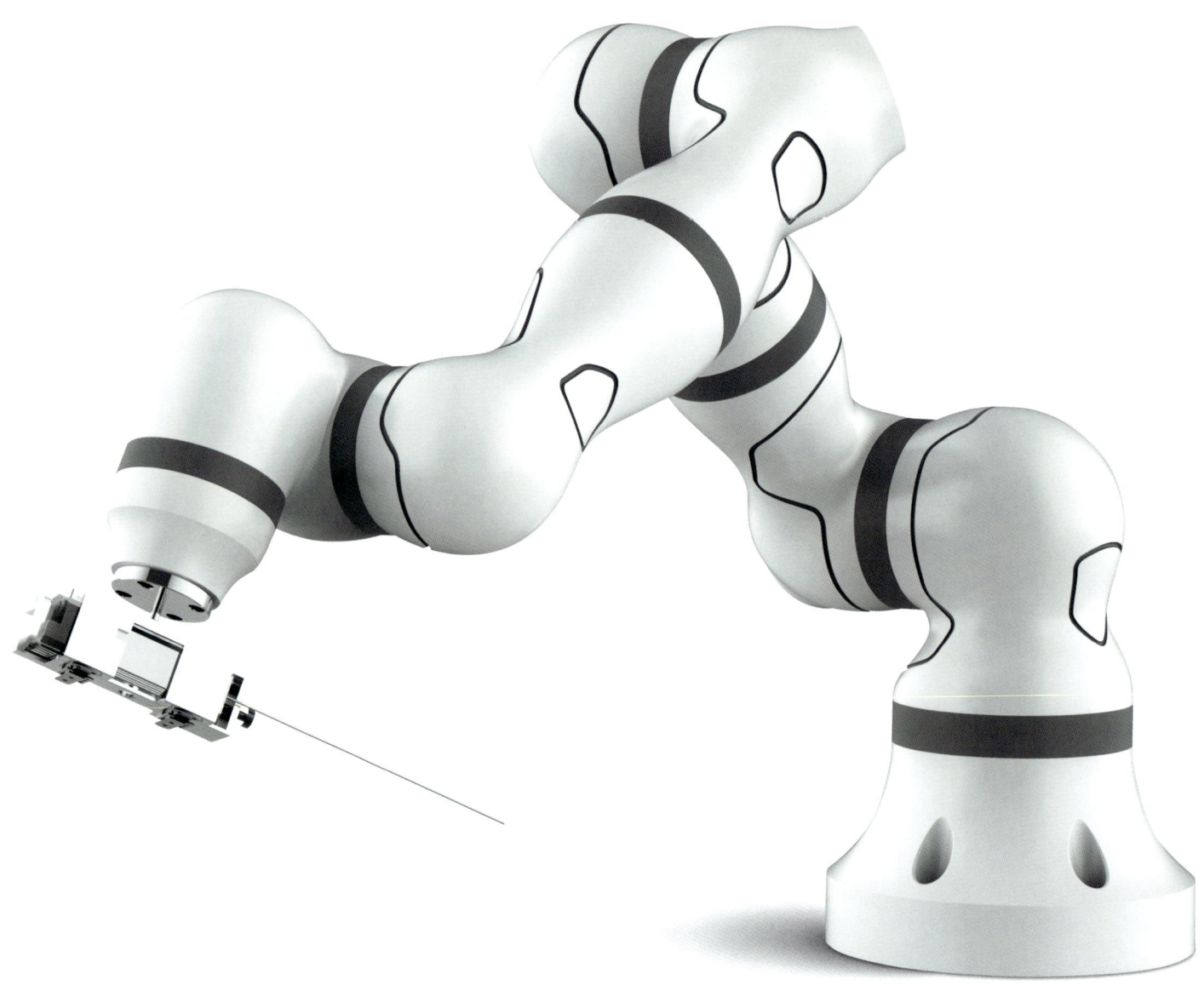

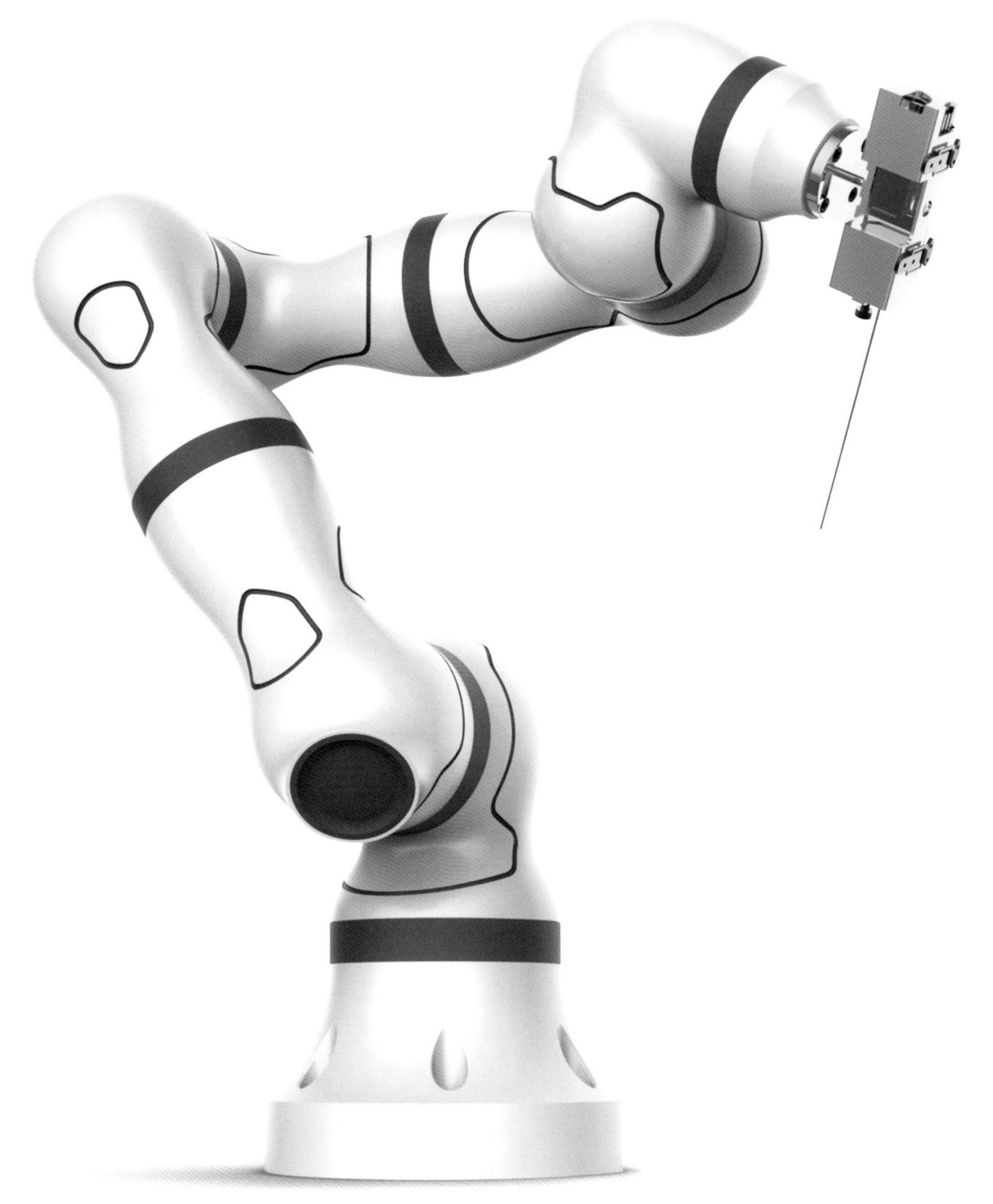

Auris Monarch
Endoscopic Robotic Platform
Endoskopie-Roboterplattform

Manufacturer
Auris Health,
Redwood City, California, USA

Design
Fjord | Accenture Interactive,
San Francisco, USA

Web
www.aurishealth.com
www.fjordnet.com

reddot award 2019
best of the best

Pioneering system
As lung cancer is the leading cause of cancer deaths worldwide, fighting it is an audacious pursuit for all disciplines involved. Auris Monarch is a solution that combines the latest advancements in robotics, user experience, software, data science and radical endoscope improvement. As the endoscope has hardly changed since the 1960s, the mission was to create a next-generation surgical robotic solution to help diagnose and fight lung cancer. The Monarch Platform offers an innovative flexible endoscopic technology that allows physicians to diagnose small, hard-to-reach peripheral nodules earlier and with greater precision. When working with Auris Health on the platform, the design focused on industrial design, design for manufacturing, user experience, user interface design, visual design and high-fidelity prototyping. The result is a surgical system that is unified by a consistent, intuitive physical and digital interface. It combines traditional endoscopic views with computer-assisted navigation based on 3D models of the patient's lung anatomy. This allows for a continuous view throughout the procedure, which is a significant improvement on existing endoscopic systems – thereby enhancing physician capabilities and improving patient outcomes.

Wegweisendes System
Da Lungenkrebs weltweit die häufigste Todesursache bei Krebs ist, stellt seine Bekämpfung eine kühne Aufgabe für alle beteiligten Disziplinen dar. Auris Monarch ist eine Lösung, die neueste Entwicklungen in Robotik, Benutzererfahrung, Software, Datenwissenschaft und eine grundlegende Endoskop-Verbesserung zusammenführt. Weil das Endoskop sich seit den 1960er Jahren kaum verändert hat, war es das Ziel, eine chirurgische Roboterlösung der nächsten Generation zu entwickeln, die bei der Diagnose und Bekämpfung von Lungenkrebs hilft. Die Monarch-Plattform bietet eine innovative, flexible Endoskopie-Technologie, die es den Ärzten erlaubt, bereits kleine, schwer erreichbare periphere Lungenknoten früher und mit größerer Präzision zu diagnostizieren. Bei der Zusammenarbeit mit Auris Health fokussierte sich die Gestaltung auf das Industriedesign, Fertigungsdesign, Nutzererleben, Interfacedesign, visuelle Design und High-Fidelity-Prototyping. Das Ergebnis ist ein chirurgisches System, das eine durch eine konsistente, intuitiv nutzbare physische und digitale Schnittstelle definierte Einheit darstellt. Es kombiniert herkömmliche endoskopische Bildergebnisse mit einer auf 3D-Modellen der Lungenanatomie des Patienten basierenden computergestützten Navigation. Dies ermöglicht eine kontinuierliche Sicht während der Untersuchung, was eine erhebliche Verbesserung im Vergleich zu üblichen Endoskopie-Systemen bedeutet. Auf diese Weise werden die ärztlichen Fähigkeiten und die Ergebnisse für die Patienten optimiert.

Statement by the jury
As an innovative robotic solution, Auris Monarch significantly enhances diagnostic options for lung cancer patients. The platform offers a user interface that impresses in particular with its display quality for a highly effective examination. The individual elements, which are also perfectly matched for high aesthetic appeal, allow for outstandingly precise procedures.

Begründung der Jury
Als innovative Roboterlösung verbessert Auris Monarch die Diagnosemöglichkeiten von Lungenkrebs-Patienten erheblich. Die Plattform bietet eine besonders in ihrer Darstellungsqualität beeindruckende Benutzerschnittstelle für eine hocheffektive Untersuchung. Die auch in ihrer ästhetischen Gestaltung perfekt aufeinander abgestimmten Elemente erlauben ein äußerst präzises Vorgehen.

Designer portrait
See page 60
Siehe Seite 60

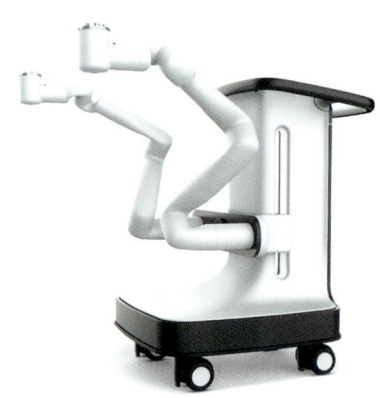

FRA
Linear Unloading Robot
Linearroboter für Entnahmeanwendungen

Manufacturer
Yushin Precision Equipment Co., Ltd., Kyoto, Japan
Design
ICI Design Institute Inc. (Yoshiaki Iida, Yayoi Kuroda), Osaka, Japan
Web
www.ype.co.jp/en
www.ici-design.co.jp

The linear robot FRA has one of the world's first active vibration stabilisation systems that enables particularly smooth movements and is intelligently connected with its environment. White LEDs indicating the on and off status make the machine seem alive. Based on computer calculations, an optimum design with maximum stiffness has been developed. Its main characteristic is the tapered shape of the main arm. The colour code with stationary parts in dark blue and moving parts in metallic blue visually distinguishes them from each other.

Der Linearroboter FRA verfügt über eines der weltweit ersten aktiven Schwingungsstabilisierungssysteme, das besonders fließende Bewegungen ermöglicht, und ist intelligent mit seiner Umgebung vernetzt. Weiße LEDs, die den Ein-/Aus-Status anzeigen, lassen die Maschine lebendig erscheinen. Mithilfe computerbasierter Berechnungen wurde eine optimale Bauform entwickelt, die maximale Steifigkeit erzielt. Charakteristisch ist hierbei die sich verjüngende Form des Hauptarms. Die stationären Teile in Dunkelblau und die beweglichen Teile in metallischem Blau sind optisch klar voneinander abgegrenzt.

Statement by the jury
Due to its optimised design structure, the linear robot provides excellent functionality. Its geometry is also a visual highlight.

Begründung der Jury
Der Linearroboter erzielt durch seine strukturoptimierte Bauweise eine exzellente Funktionalität. Seine Geometrie ist auch optisch ein Highlight.

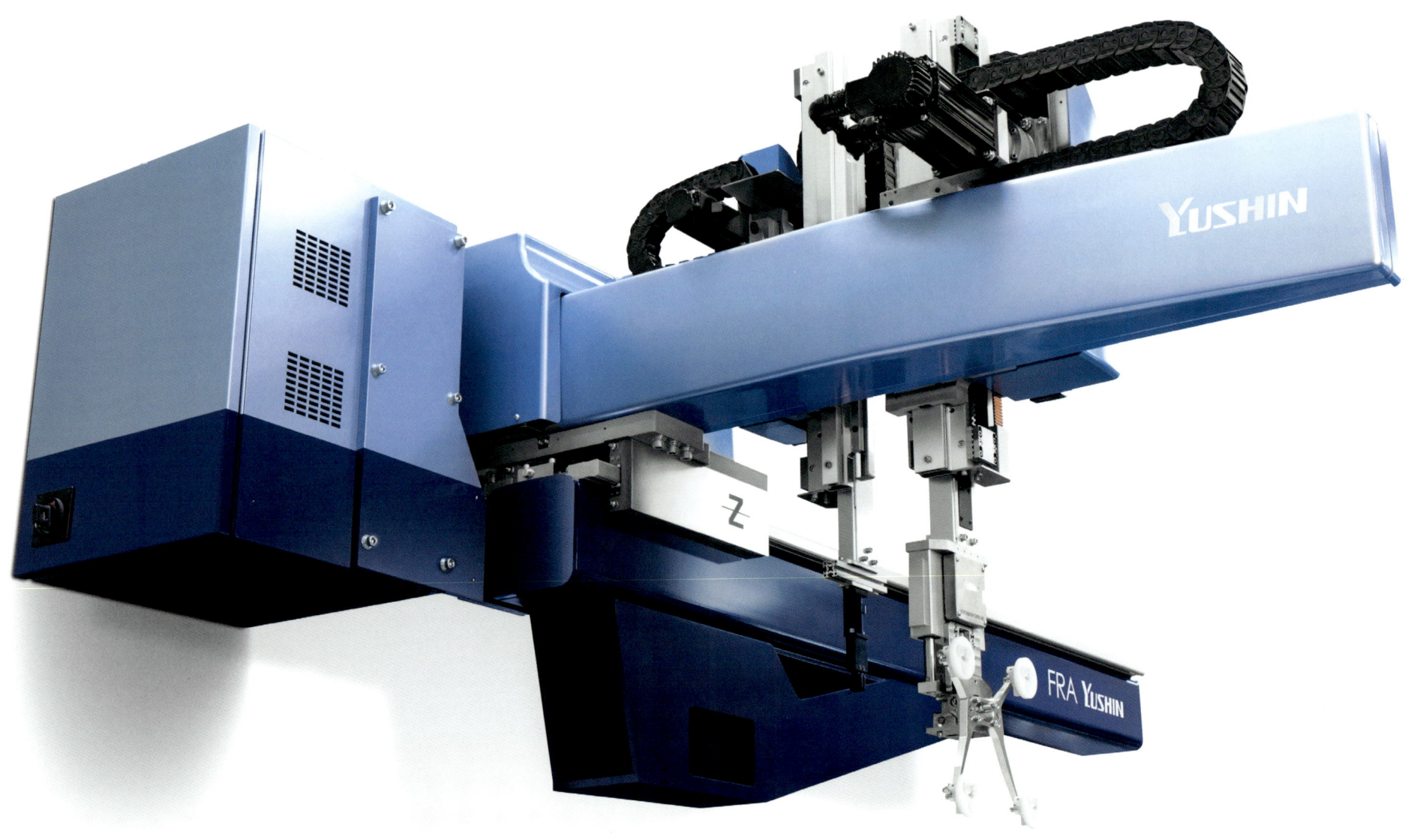

AG-95
Adaptive Gripper
Adaptiver Greifer

Manufacturer
DH-Robotics Technology Co., Ltd.,
Shenzhen, China
In-house design
Dizhou Luo
Web
www.dh-robotics.com

The gripper AG-95 can hold objects of various shapes and sizes without the fingers having to be replaced. It offers different grip types as well as precise position and pressure control, making it suitable for use with robots in various application scenarios, such as service, logistics or production. Thanks to the compact design, it features a small footprint and straightforward assembly. The gripper is programmed via a graphical user interface.

Statement by the jury
The gripper AG-95 eliminates the need to change tools and can therefore be easily integrated into any production environment.

Der Greifer AG-95 kann Objekte unterschiedlichster Form und Größe halten, ohne dass die Finger dafür ausgetauscht werden müssen. Er beherrscht verschiedene Greifarten und bietet eine präzise Positions- und Druckkontrolle. Dadurch ist der Greifer für den Einsatz an Robotern in einer Vielzahl von Anwendungsszenarien wie Service, Logistik oder Fertigung geeignet. Die kompakte Bauform erlaubt eine platzsparende, unkomplizierte Montage. Programmiert wird er über eine grafische Benutzeroberfläche.

Begründung der Jury
Der Greifer AG-95 macht einen Wechsel der Werkzeuge überflüssig und lässt sich dadurch denkbar einfach in jede Produktionsumgebung integrieren.

HRC-03
Collaborative Gripper
Kollaborativer Greifer

Manufacturer
Zimmer Group, Rheinau, Germany
In-house design
Marcel Pfeiffer
Web
www.zimmer-group.com

The HRC-03 gripper enables safe, barrier free collaboration between humans and robots. It is made of 100 per cent recycled materials and produced in a particularly environmentally friendly way. Its LED status indicator is visible from all sides. Rounded edges and limited gripping force mitigate the risk of injury. The clear, reduced design language and light colour scheme intend to eliminate reservations about collaboration with the robot.

Statement by the jury
With its gentle design and self-contained shape, the gripper communicates its high degree of operational safety at first glance.

Der Greifer HRC-03 ermöglicht eine gefahrlose, barrierefreie Mensch-Roboter-Kollaboration. Er besteht zu 100 Prozent aus Recyclingmaterialien und wird besonders umweltschonend produziert. Die LED-Statusanzeige ist von allen Seiten gut sichtbar. Die abgerundeten Kanten und eine begrenzte Greifkraft beugen Verletzungsgefahr vor. Die klare, reduzierte Formensprache und die helle Farbgebung zielen darauf, Vorbehalte des Werkarbeiters hinsichtlich der Zusammenarbeit mit dem Roboter abzubauen.

Begründung der Jury
Mit seiner sanft anmutenden Gestaltung und der in sich geschlossenen Form kommuniziert der Greifer auf den ersten Blick seine hohe Betriebssicherheit.

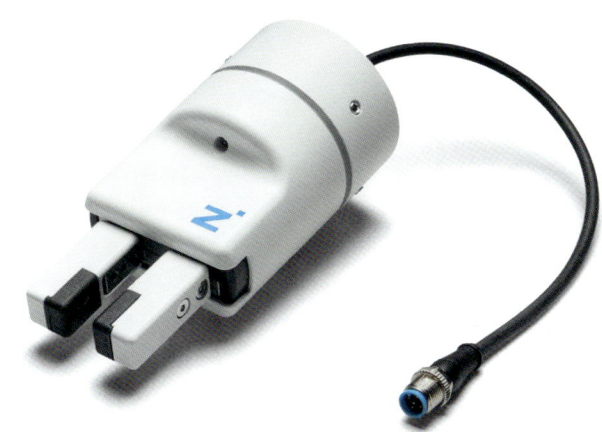

Skelex 360
Exoskeleton
Exoskelett

Manufacturer
Skelex B.V., Rotterdam, Netherlands
Design
VanBerlo, Eindhoven, Netherlands
Web
www.skelex.com
www.vanberlo.nl
Honourable Mention

Skelex 360 reduces the strain on persons performing overhead work, for instance in vehicle assembly. The exoskeleton can be put on as easily as a backpack. It is individually adjustable and allows unrestricted freedom of movement. In order to keep the weight of the exoskeleton as low as possible, no electronics or servomotors have been installed. Instead, the construction is based on intelligent carbon-fibre suspension. Due to the sophisticated fit, it only touches the body where it is inevitable.

Statement by the jury
This exoskeleton convinces with its high ergonomic wearability. It supports wearers without limiting their freedom of movement.

Skelex 360 entlastet den Träger bei Überkopfarbeiten, z. B. in der Fahrzeugmontage. Das Exoskelett wird wie ein Rucksack angelegt, lässt sich individuell anpassen und ermöglicht uneingeschränkte Bewegungsfreiheit. Um das Gewicht des Exoskeletts so gering wie möglich zu halten, wurden weder Elektronik noch Stellmotoren verbaut. Stattdessen beruht die Konstruktion auf einer intelligenten Federung aus Carbonfaser. Die hoch entwickelte Passform berührt den Körper nur dort, wo es notwendig ist.

Begründung der Jury
Überzeugend an diesem Exoskelett ist sein hoher ergonomischer Tragekomfort. Es unterstützt den Arbeiter, ohne ihn in seinen Bewegungen einzuschränken.

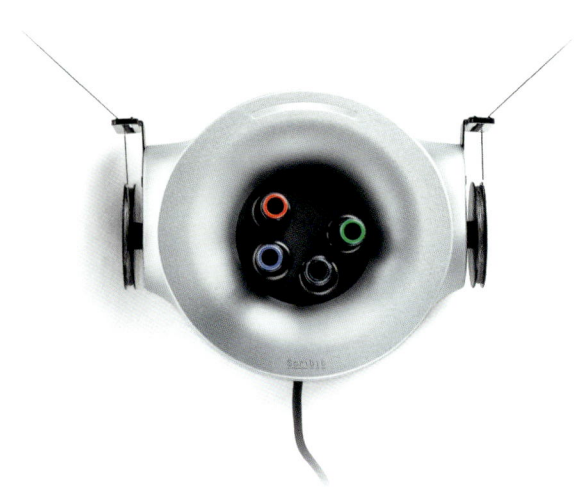

Scribit
Write and Erase Robot
Schreib- und Löschroboter

Manufacturer
Scribit, Turin, Italy
In-house design
Design
CRA Carlo Ratti Associati
(Pietro Leoni), Turin, Italy
Web
www.scribit.design

Scribit is a digital printer that can draw images and text on walls. It is suspended vertically from the wall via two guide wires and then moves independently along the drawing surface. Thanks to a special ink, the artworks can be erased at any time. The robot downloads content from the Internet and reproduces it in real time. The LED display at the top indicates whether the robot is drawing, erasing or downloading content.

Statement by the jury
Scribit ushers in a new way of creating wall designs. Plus, it is extremely easy to mount and operate.

Scribit ist eine Art digitaler Drucker für die Wand, der Bilder und Texte zeichnen kann. Dazu wird er an zwei Führungsdrähten vertikal an der Wand aufgehängt und bewegt sich dann selbständig entlang der Zeichenfläche. Dank einer speziellen Tinte können die Kunstwerke jederzeit wieder von der Wand gelöscht werden. Der Roboter kann Inhalte aus dem Internet herunterladen und in Echtzeit reproduzieren. Ob er gerade etwas zeichnet, löscht oder lädt, signalisiert die obere LED-Anzeige.

Begründung der Jury
Scribit eröffnet neue Wege der kreativen Wandgestaltung. Montage und Bedienung sind denkbar einfach und gelingen mit wenig Aufwand.

Blueye Pioneer
Underwater Drone
Unterwasserdrohne

Manufacturer
Blueye Robotics, Trondheim, Norway
In-house design
Design
EGGS Design, Oslo, Norway
Web
www.blueyerobotics.com
www.eggsdesign.com

The Blueye Pioneer is a portable, robust and easy-to-manoeuvre underwater drone that is suitable for both professional and private use. It has been designed for optimum performance even in harsh maritime environments. The camera transmits images and videos in full HD quality directly to an app. Thanks to powerful LED lights, this is possible even at sea depths of up to 150 metres. Due to its vertical architecture, the drone moves through the water with high stability.

Statement by the jury
The Blueye Pioneer displays a sophisticated design in terms of construction and technology, successfully merging inspirations from the design of contemporary research submarines.

Blueye Pioneer ist eine tragbare, robuste und einfach zu manövrierende Unterwasserdrohne, die für den Profieinsatz sowie für den Privatgebrauch geeignet ist. Sie wurde für eine optimale Leistung auch in rauen maritimen Umgebungen konzipiert. Die Kamera überträgt Bilder und Videos in Full-HD-Qualität direkt an eine App – dank leistungsstarker LED-Leuchte auch in Meerestiefen von bis zu 150 Metern. Durch ihre vertikale Bauweise bewegt sich die Drohne vollkommen stabil durchs Wasser.

Begründung der Jury
Mit gelungenen Anleihen an die Gestaltung ausgewachsener Forschungs-U-Boote zeigt sich die Konstruktion der Blueye Pioneer baulich und technisch voll ausgereift.

MR-Q3C-LE600C1(H)
Automated Guided Vehicle
Fahrerloses Transportfahrzeug

Manufacturer
Hangzhou Hikrobot Technology Co., Ltd.,
Hangzhou, China
In-house design
Web
http://en.hikrobotics.com

Based on inertial and visual sensors, this transport system autonomously moves through the warehouse and knows its own position in space. The differential drive allows this robot to move forward and backward and to rotate. In detecting obstacles, the system uses laser technology at the front and ultrasound technology at the rear. Both the front and rear are equipped with one emergency stop button each. When the battery is low, the vehicle automatically recharges itself and then returns to work.

Statement by the jury
Complex on the inside, compact on the outside – the sophisticated design of this automated guided vehicle conveys a high degree of reliability and appeal.

Basierend auf inertialen und visuellen Sensoren, bewegt sich dieses Transportsystem autonom durch die Lagerhalle und kennt die eigene Position im Raum. Der Differentialantrieb ermöglicht es dem Roboter, vorwärts und rückwärts zu fahren sowie zu drehen. Zum Erkennen von Hindernissen nutzt das System vorne Laser- und hinten Ultraschalltechnologie. Front und Heck sind jeweils mit einem Not-Aus-Knopf ausgestattet. Bei niedrigem Akkustatus lädt sich das Fahrzeug selbständig wieder auf und kehrt danach zurück an die Arbeit.

Begründung der Jury
Von innen komplex, von außen kompakt – die ausgereifte Gestaltung dieses fahrerlosen Transportfahrzeugs strahlt eine hohe Verlässlichkeit und Sympathie aus.

JEEVES
Service Robot
Serviceroboter

Manufacturer
Robotise GmbH, Munich, Germany
Design
Eckstein Design, Munich, Germany
Web
www.jeeves.robotise.eu
www.eckstein-design.com

The JEEVES robot performs transport tasks and infotainment services in hotels and nursing homes. Its appearance is characterised by flowing lines and smooth transitions. Details such as the illuminated gap between the base and the body add to the elegant overall look. Thanks to sensor technology, the robot always knows its position and can even use the lift. Its modular drawers may be individually assembled as required and simply inserted according to the plug-and-play principle.

Statement by the jury
The design of JEEVES successfully translates functionality into an approachable appearance that is immediately understood by the user.

JEEVES verrichtet Transportaufgaben und Infotainment-Services in Hotels und Pflegeeinrichtungen. Seine Erscheinung ist gekennzeichnet von fließenden Linien und sanften Übergängen. Details wie der beleuchtete Spalt zwischen Basis und Korpus ergänzen den eleganten Gesamteindruck. Dank Sensortechnik weiß der Roboter immer, wo er sich gerade befindet, und kann sogar Aufzug fahren. Seine modularen Schubladen lassen sich nach Bedarf individuell zusammenstellen und einfach per Plug-and-play einsetzen.

Begründung der Jury
Bei der Gestaltung von JEEVES ist es gelungen, seine Funktion in eine klar verständliche Form zu überführen, die sich dem Benutzer sofort erschließt.

LG B2B
Service Robot
Serviceroboter

Manufacturer
LG Electronics Inc., Seoul, South Korea
In-house design
Jinsu Kim, Taewoo Yoo,
Hyunwoo Yoo, Yousook Eun
Design
Design3 GmbH, Hamburg, Germany
Web
www.lg.com

The intelligent service robot LG B2B is available in three versions: as a porter robot, as a cart robot and as an information terminal. This makes it predestined for use in hotels and sales areas, where it enhances the atmosphere with its friendly appearance. The focus is on the user interface, which has the shape of a head with digital facial expressions, adding a human aspect to interaction with the robot. The cylindrical shape of the body underlines its stability and safe operation.

Statement by the jury
Its high degree of modularity and clear aesthetics make the LG B2B an extremely useful assistant in various service scenarios.

Der intelligente Serviceroboter LG B2B steht in drei Ausführungen zur Verfügung – als Gepäckträger, Einkaufswagen und Informationsterminal. Damit ist er prädestiniert für den Einsatz in Hotels und auf Verkaufsflächen, wo er das Ambiente durch sein freundliches Auftreten bereichert. Der Fokus liegt auf der Benutzerschnittstelle in Form eines Kopfes mit digitaler Mimik, wodurch die Interaktion mit dem Roboter vermenschlicht wird. Die zylindrische Form des Korpus unterstreicht die stabile und sichere Fahrweise.

Begründung der Jury
Seine hohe Modularität und die klare Ästhetik machen den LG B2B zum äußerst nützlichen Gehilfen in einer Vielzahl von Dienstleistungsszenarien.

NIRO Pro
Interactive Robot
Interaktiver Roboter

Manufacturer
Baidu Online Network Technology (Beijing) Co., Ltd.,
Beijing, China
In-house design
Guan Daisong, Yang Fan, Li Shiyan
Web
http://aiid.baidu.com

NIRO Pro is an interactive robot with a minimalist appearance. It features natural image and speech understanding, so that the robot can have a fluent conversation with its counterpart without the need for voice commands. In addition, the robot can imitate human motion sequences in a surprisingly authentic way and adapt them to the respective situation. Using the built-in micro laser projector, digital content such as apps or games can be projected in HD quality onto any surface and thus brought to life.

NIRO Pro ist ein interaktiver Roboter mit einem minimalistischen Äußeren. Er verfügt über ein natürliches Bild- und Sprachverstehen, wodurch er in der Lage ist, eine fließende Unterhaltung mit seinem Gegenüber zu führen, ohne die Notwendigkeit von Sprachkommandos. Darüber hinaus kann der Roboter menschliche Bewegungsabläufe verblüffend echt nachahmen und diese an die jeweilige Situation anpassen. Über den eingebauten Mikrolaserprojektor lassen sich digitale Inhalte wie Apps oder Spiele in HD-Qualität auf jede beliebige Fläche projizieren und so zum Leben erwecken.

Statement by the jury
NIRO Pro breathes new life into the world of human-robot interaction. Its look, inspired by animation design, gives the robot a charming character.

Begründung der Jury
NIRO Pro setzt neue Impulse in der Mensch-Roboter-Interaktion. Seine Gestalt, die vom Animationsdesign inspiriert ist, verleiht ihm eine liebenswerte Persönlichkeit.

Abbebot
Educational Robot
Lernroboter

Manufacturer
Shenzhen Shenxiao Technology Co., Ltd.,
Shenzhen, China
Design
Shenzhen Xivokids Design Co., Ltd.
(Jiao Ge, Guokun Liu), Shenzhen, China
Web
www.abbebot.com
www.xivodesign.com

The educational robot Abbebot has been developed especially for the Chinese market. It is designed to teach children aged three to eight years the English language in a competent, interactive way. Its game-based tutorials include exercises in listening, speaking, writing and reading, as well as pronunciation. Patented AI algorithms enable the robot to recognise physical letters and integrate them into educational games or even read stories from books.

Statement by the jury
Thanks to its cuteness, Abbebot is sure to attract the attention of children. The combination of analogue and digital elements intensifies the learning effect.

Der Lernroboter Abbebot wurde speziell für den chinesischen Markt entwickelt, um Kinder im Alter von drei bis acht Jahren auf kompetente, interaktive Weise in der englischen Sprache zu unterrichten. Das spielebasierte Lernprogramm umfasst neben dem Hören, Sprechen, Schreiben und Lesen auch die korrekte Aussprache. Patentierte KI-Algorithmen versetzen den Roboter in die Lage, physische Buchstaben zu erkennen und in die Lernspiele miteinzubeziehen oder auch Geschichten aus Büchern vorzulesen.

Begründung der Jury
Dank seiner Niedlichkeit ist Abbebot die Aufmerksamkeit von Kindern gewiss. Die Mischung aus analogen und digitalen Elementen intensiviert den Lerneffekt.

Somnox Sleep Robot
Somnox Schlafroboter

Manufacturer
Somnox, Delft, Netherlands
In-house design
Julian Jagtenberg, Stijn Antonisse,
Wouter Kooyman van Guldener,
Job Engel, Clement Heinen
Design
Royal Auping (Ine Stultjens, Jabe Faber),
Deventer, Netherlands
Web
www.meetsomnox.com
www.auping.com

The sleep robot helps people to fall asleep. It uses a specific breathing rhythm, which is automatically replicated by the person holding the robot in their arms. Via the integrated speaker, soothing sounds may be played. The shape is designed in such a way that the user adopts a natural position when cuddling with the robot. This also promotes a natural alignment of the neck and shoulders.

Statement by the jury
This sleeping robot skilfully embodies the idea of peace and comfort. It naturally blends into the sleeping environment.

Der Schlafroboter hilft dabei, leichter in den Schlaf zu finden. Er verfügt über einen spezifischen Atemrhythmus, an den sich der Benutzer automatisch anpasst, wenn er den Roboter im Arm hält. Zusätzlich lassen sich über den eingebauten Lautsprecher beruhigende Geräusche abspielen. Die Form ist so entworfen, dass der Benutzer durch das Kuscheln mit dem Roboter eine natürliche Haltung einnimmt, was gleichzeitig eine natürliche Ausrichtung des Nackens und der Schultern fördert.

Begründung der Jury
Der Schlafroboter verkörpert stilvoll die Idee von Ruhe und Geborgenheit. Er integriert sich vollkommen natürlich in die Schlafumgebung.

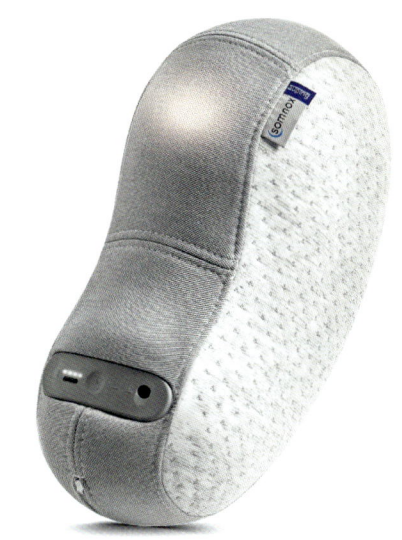

Qoobo
Therapy Robot
Therapieroboter

Manufacturer
Yukai Engineering, Tokyo, Japan
In-house design
Kosuke Tatsumi
Web
www.ux-xu.com

Qoobo is a fur-covered, pillow-shaped robot with a tail that moves in reaction to touch. The tail makes various movements, depending on how the robot is stroked. Its minimalist design highlights the importance of tail-wagging as a communication medium in animals. Qoobo was developed to interact with users based on this non-verbal, universal language, focusing on the comfort otherwise provided by real pets.

Statement by the jury
With Qoobo, everyone can benefit from the advantages of animal therapy. The design skilfully reflects an artificial creature with a perceptible presence.

Qoobo ist ein Roboter in der Form eines Fellkissens mit einem Schwanz. Dieser fängt an zu wedeln, wenn der Roboter berührt wird. Je nachdem, wie der Roboter gestreichelt wird, führt der Schwanz unterschiedliche Bewegungen aus. Das minimalistische Design unterstreicht die Bedeutung des Schwanzwedelns als wichtiges Kommunikationsmittel von Tieren. Qoobo wurde mit dem Ziel entwickelt, anhand dieser nonverbalen, universellen Sprache mit dem Benutzer zu interagieren und ihn so aufzumuntern, wie es ein echtes Haustier tun würde.

Begründung der Jury
Qoobo macht die Vorteile einer Tiertherapie für jeden nutzbar. Bei der Gestaltung ist es gelungen, ein künstliches Wesen mit einer spürbaren Präsenz zu schaffen.

SenseRover
Remote Control Vehicle
Ferngesteuertes Fahrzeug

Manufacturer
Shenzhen SenseTime Technology Co., Ltd.,
Shenzhen, China
In-house design
Hui Cheng, Feng Ni
Design
ZCO Design Co., Ltd.
(Liang Tang, Rong Zhang, Wei Xiong),
Shenzhen, China
Web
www.sensetime.com
www.zcosz.com

SenseRover is a scaled model self-driving car with all the necessary elements of a real one, including vehicle mechanisms, a visual modular unit and sensors integrated within a powerful microcomputer. Students can learn about real car mechanics and electrical engineering, machine learning, robotics and control in a realistic and also playful way. Through data collecting and augmentation, algorithm training and testing, the students are equipped with a vivid understanding of artificial intelligence.

Statement by the jury
The SenseRover enables users to experience the principles of autonomous driving in a playful way. Its realistic design adds emotional appeal to the machine.

SenseRover ist ein selbstfahrendes Modellfahrzeug mit allen Ausstattungsmerkmalen eines echten Autos. Dazu gehören die Fahrzeugmechanik, eine visuelle Moduleinheit und Sensoren, die in einem leistungsstarken Mikrocomputer integriert sind. So können Schüler die Automechanik und Elektrotechnik, maschinelles Lernen, Robotik und Steuerung auf realistische und zugleich spielerische Weise kennenlernen. Durch das Sammeln und Ergänzen von Daten, Algorithmustraining und -tests erwerben sie ein lebendiges Verständnis von KI.

Begründung der Jury
Mit dem SenseRover lassen sich die Prinzipien des autonomen Fahrens spielerisch erfahren. Sein realitätsnahes Design emotionalisiert den Anwender.

WhalesBot AI Module
Educational Robot
Lernroboter

Manufacturer
Shanghai Whalesbot Technology Co., Ltd.,
Shanghai, China
In-house design
Web
www.whalesbot.com

This educational robot from the AI Module series combines modular robot technology with artificial intelligence in an innovative way. The robot can speak, see and react to emotions and show feelings via two screens that look like a pair of eyes. This sparks interest in children and youth, thus heightening their motivation to learn. The robot meets the requirements of different age groups thanks to five different programming languages.

Statement by the jury
The educational robot impresses with its humanoid features, which add a special emotional quality to its technical dimensions.

Dieser Lernroboter der Reihe AI Module verbindet auf innovative Weise einen modularen Roboterbausatz mit künstlicher Intelligenz. Er kann sprechen, sehen und über zwei Bildschirme, die einem Augenpaar gleichen, auf Emotionen reagieren sowie selbst Gefühle zeigen. Dies weckt das Interesse von Kindern und Jugendlichen und steigert ihre Lernmotivation. Dank fünf verschiedener Programmiersprachen wird der Lernroboter den Anforderungen unterschiedlicher Altersgruppen gerecht.

Begründung der Jury
Der Lernroboter begeistert durch seine humanoiden Züge, die ihm neben seiner technischen Dimension eine besondere emotionale Qualität verleihen.

Motionblock
Programmable Robot Kit
Programmierbarer Roboterbausatz

Manufacturer
Makeblock Co., Ltd., Shenzhen, China
In-house design
Liang Wang, Mulin Li, Feng Chen
Web
www.makeblock.com

Motionblock has been designed to teach children the basics of coding, engineering and bionics. The robot kit features ten different functions. The individual blocks can be connected to each other according to a simple plug-in principle. This allows projects to be implemented in just a few steps, without limiting the imagination. For safety reasons, the blocks featuring embedded servomotors are encapsulated. Learners can control the robots with and without software.

Statement by the jury
Due to its deliberately minimalistic design, Motionblock is not overly prescriptive and thus optimally promotes the creativity of children.

Motionblock wurde konzipiert, um Kindern die Grundlagen des Kodierens, Engineerings und der Bionik zu vermitteln. Der Bausatz bietet zehn unterschiedliche Funktionen. Die einzelnen Blöcke lassen sich nach einem einfachen Steckprinzip miteinander verbinden. So können Projekte mit nur wenigen Handgriffen realisiert werden, ohne dass der Phantasie Grenzen gesetzt sind. Aus Sicherheitsgründen sind die Blöcke, in die Servomotoren integriert sind, verkapselt. Die Lernenden können die Roboter mit und ohne Software steuern.

Begründung der Jury
Motionblock macht Kindern durch die gezielt minimalistische Gestaltung nur wenig Vorgaben. Dadurch wird ihre Kreativität optimal gefördert.

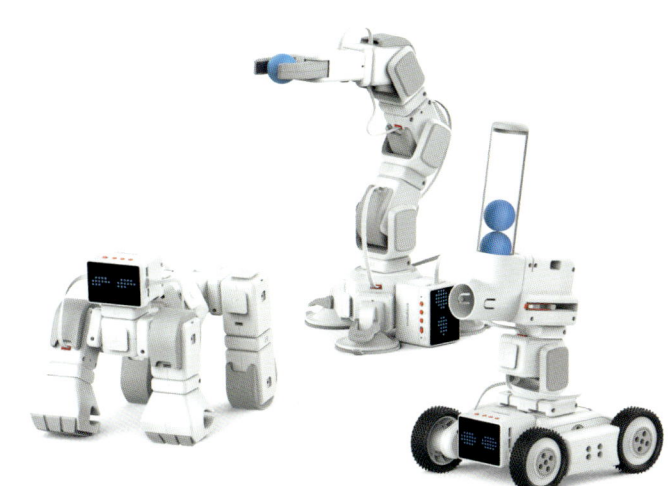

ONEBOT
Educational Robot Kit
Didaktischer Roboterbausatz

Manufacturer
Beijing AIQI Technology Co., Ltd.,
Beijing, China
In-house design
Cong Cao, Yang Zhang
Web
www.iqi-inc.com

The robot kit Onebot for children aged ten years or older combines fun with self-paced learning. It consists of more than 100 different synthetic components and more than ten electronic building elements with different functions. This makes it possible to construct a robot with sophisticated mechanical capabilities and various functions, for instance a robot that can walk or a caterpillar robot. All components feature pleasantly smooth haptics and have been specially designed for the hands of children.

Statement by the jury
Onebot impresses with a look and feel that is ideal for the target group. The striking blue-white contrasting lends the components a distinctive character.

Der Roboterbausatz Onebot für Kinder ab zehn Jahren verbindet Spielspaß mit selbständigem Lernen. Er besteht aus mehr als 100 unterschiedlichen Kunststoffbauteilen sowie mehr als zehn elektronischen Bauelementen, die es ermöglichen, einen Roboter mit anspruchsvollen mechanischen Eigenschaften und vielfältigen Funktionsmöglichkeiten zu konstruieren, z. B. einen Laufroboter oder ein Raupenfahrzeug. Alle Komponenten fühlen sich angenehm glatt an und wurden speziell für Kinderhände entworfen.

Begründung der Jury
Onebot gefällt durch seine altersgerechte Haptik und Optik. Der auffällige Blau-Weiß-Kontrast verleiht den Komponenten einen unverwechselbaren Charakter.

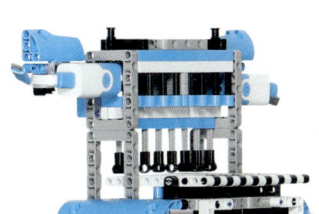 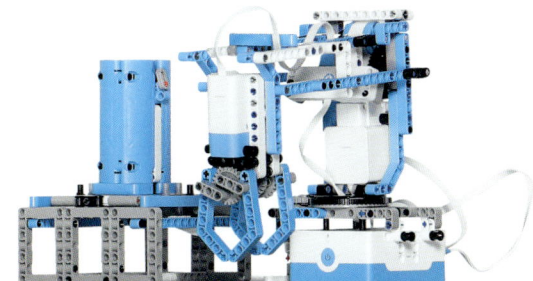 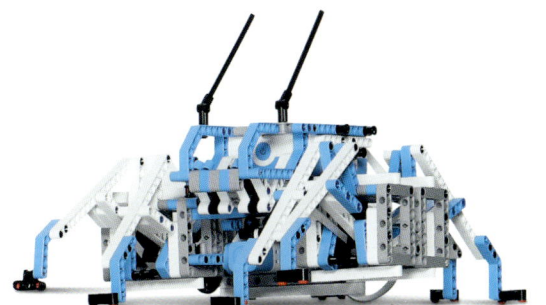 

The jury 2019
International orientation and objectivity
Internationalität und Objektivität

The jurors of the Red Dot Award: Product Design
All members of the Red Dot Award: Product Design jury are appointed on the basis of independence and impartiality. They are independent designers, academics in design faculties, representatives of international design institutions, and design journalists.

The jury is international in its composition, which changes every year. These conditions assure a maximum of objectivity. The members of this year's jury are presented in alphabetical order on the following pages.

Die Juroren des Red Dot Award: Product Design
In die Jury des Red Dot Award: Product Design wird als Mitglied nur berufen, wer völlig unabhängig und unparteiisch ist. Dies sind selbständig arbeitende Designer, Hochschullehrer der Designfakultäten, Repräsentanten internationaler Designinstitutionen und Designfachjournalisten.

Die Jury ist international besetzt und wechselt in jedem Jahr ihre Zusammensetzung. Unter diesen Voraussetzungen ist ein Höchstmaß an Objektivität gewährleistet. Auf den folgenden Seiten werden die Jurymitglieder des diesjährigen Wettbewerbs in alphabetischer Reihenfolge vorgestellt.

David Andersen
Denmark
Dänemark

David Andersen, born in 1978, graduated from Glasgow School of Art and the Fashion Design Academy in 2003. Until 2014, he developed designs for ready-to-wear clothes, shoes, perfume, underwear and home wear and emerged as a fashion designer working as chief designer at Dreams by Isabell Kristensen as well as designing couture for the royal Danish family, celebrities, artists etc. under his own name. In 2007, he debuted his collection "David Andersen". He has received many awards and grants for his designs, e.g. a grant from the National Art Foundation. David Andersen is also known for his development of sustainable clothing with his collection, Zero Waste, and has received several awards for his work on ecology and sustainable productions. David Andersen has changed his job as Vice President for Design at Rosendahl Design Group and is now working for the fur giant, KC FUR in China, as Design Director. Furthermore, David Andersen is a guest lecturer at different schools and colleges.

David Andersen, 1978 geboren, studierte an der Glasgow School of Art und der Fashion Design Academy, wo er 2003 sein Examen machte. Bis 2014 fertigte er Entwürfe für Konfektionsware, Schuhe, Parfüm, Unterwäsche und Homewear. Daraus entwickelte sich eine Karriere als Modedesigner und er begann, bei Dreams von Isabell Kristensen als Chefdesigner zu arbeiten sowie unter seinem eigenen Namen Couture für die dänische Königsfamilie, Prominente, Künstler etc. zu entwerfen. Im Jahr 2007 stellte er erstmals seine eigene „David Andersen"-Kollektion vor. Für seine Entwürfe erhielt er bereits viele Auszeichnungen und Fördergelder, darunter ein Stipendium der National Art Foundation (Nationale Kunststiftung). David Andersen hat sich auch mit „Zero Waste", einer Kollektion nachhaltiger Kleidung, einen Namen gemacht, und mehrere Auszeichnungen für seine Arbeit im Bereich von Umwelt und nachhaltiger Produktion erhalten. David Andersen hat seine ehemalige Stelle als Vizepräsident für Design bei der Rosendahl Design Group aufgegeben und ist jetzt Design Director für den riesigen Pelzkonzern KC Fur in China. Darüber hinaus ist er Gastdozent an verschiedenen Schulen und Hochschulen.

01–02
Designs of David Andersen's sustainable "Zero Waste" collection
Entwürfe aus David Andersens nachhaltiger Kollektion „Zero Waste"

01

02

"The most important thing is to be true to oneself. Never compromise unless it is a necessity."

„Das Wichtigste ist, sich selbst treu zu bleiben. Niemals Kompromisse eingehen, es sei denn, es ist absolut notwendig."

What can people surprise you with in your role as fashion designer?
Most people think that being a fashion designer is glamour, red runner and lots of parties. The fashion industry is filled with glamour, but you have to create it yourself and that is hard work.

What, in your opinion, makes for good design?
Good design must be able to stand for itself and, at the same time, do something good for the person who will carry it. The design becomes interesting when there is a good story behind and through the choice of materials, shape and colour.

What, currently, stands out especially in the fashion industry?
An incredible amount is happening. In recent years, we have worked hard to create a more sustainable approach to the way we work with our clothing. In a short time, there has been tremendous development in sustainable fashion, which is incredibly interesting to be a part of, and to work every day to do better.

Womit können Menschen Sie in Ihrer Rolle als Modedesigner überraschen?
Die meisten Menschen glauben, dass das Leben eines Modedesigners aus Glamour, roten Teppichen und vielen Partys besteht. Die Modeindustrie ist voller Glamour, doch muss man ihn selbst schaffen und das erfordert harte Arbeit.

Was macht Ihrer Meinung nach gutes Design aus?
Gutes Design muss sowohl für sich alleine funktionieren als auch für denjenigen, der es trägt, etwas Gutes tun. Design wird interessant, wenn es im Hintergrund eine gute Story gibt – und auch durch die Wahl von Materialien, Form und Farbe.

Was ist gerade besonders auffallend in der Modeindustrie?
Es geschieht wahnsinnig viel. In den letzten Jahren haben wir hart gearbeitet, um einen nachhaltigeren Ansatz für unsere Arbeit in der Modebranche zu etablieren. In relativ kurzer Zeit hat es im Bereich nachhaltiger Mode eine enorme Entwicklung gegeben. Es ist sehr interessant, Teil davon zu sein und jeden Tag zu versuchen, besser zu werden.

Prof. Masayo Ave
Japan/Germany
Japan/Deutschland

Professor Masayo Ave is the founder of the design studio MasayoAve creation and SED.Lab, Sensory Experience Design Laboratory in Berlin. The Japanese designer merges culture and disciplines and brings to bear her expertise in her sensory-based innovative design works and also in the field of design education. A graduate in architecture from Hosei University in Japan, her design career began in Milan in the early 1990s. Taking a sensorial and imaginative approach to basic design principles, her focus on material exploration and experimental design development brought her critical fame and many international design awards. In the early 2000s, Masayo Ave also became involved in the field of design education and was appointed a professor at University of Arts in Berlin, the Estonian Academy of Arts and recently at Berlin International University of Applied Sciences. As a prominent designer-teacher, she has also been dedicating her career to developing a new design education programme for children and young people that encompasses sensory-based design experiences.

Professor Masayo Ave ist Gründerin des Designstudios MasayoAve creation und des SED.Lab, einem Labor für sensorische Designforschung in Berlin. Die japanische Designerin verschmilzt Kultur mit Wissenschaftsfächern und bringt ihre Fachkenntnisse in ihre innovativen, auf Sensorik basierenden Gestaltungsprojekte ein, ebenso wie auf dem Gebiet der Designausbildung. Nach einem Architekturabschluss an der Hosei University in Japan begann sie ihre Designkarriere in Mailand in den frühen 1990er Jahren. Maßgebende Designgrundlagen ging sie mit einem sensorischen und ideenreichen Konzept an. Ihre Ausrichtung auf Rohstoffforschung und experimentelle Designentwicklung hatte das Lob der Kritiker und viele internationale Designauszeichnungen zur Folge. In den frühen 2000er Jahren fing Masayo Ave an, sich auch mit der Designausbildung zu beschäftigen, und wurde zur Professorin an der Universität der Künste in Berlin sowie an der Estländischen Kunstakademie und unlängst an der Berlin International University of Applied Sciences ernannt. Als prominente Designerin und Lehrerin hat sie sich im Laufe ihrer Karriere für die Entwicklung eines neuen Designausbildungsprogramms für Kinder und Jugendliche eingesetzt, das auch auf Sensorik basierende Designerlebnisse beinhaltet.

01 GENESI
Table light with a cover made from a washable open-cell polyester and a body in chromed steel, launched in her own collection "MasayoAve creation", 1998

Tischleuchte mit einem Lampenschirm aus waschbarem, offenporigem Polyester und einem Körper aus verchromtem Stahl, erschienen in ihrer eigenen Kollektion „MasayoAve creation", 1998

01

"My advice for young designers is to observe details of their everyday living environment with a scientific designer's eye. The answer exists there and is waiting to be discovered."

„Mein Ratschlag für junge Designer ist, die Details des täglichen Lebens mit einem wissenschaftlichen Designerauge zu betrachten. Die Antwort ist dort zu finden und wartet nur darauf, entdeckt zu werden."

How did you get into design?
By being imaginative and curious about the potential of industrial materials in relation to lifestyle culture.

What does the "MasayoAve creation" design studio stand for?
It is a cross-disciplinary platform where design projects and sensory experiences interconnect.

What, to date, has been the most exciting project of your career?
Each moment in the past projects was unforgettably exciting, but I may say the newest sensory experience design project which I am now working on is the most exciting one.

Where do you find inspiration?
Learning the fundamentals of design is to get a comprehensive understanding of one's own living environment through perceptive senses. The everyday discoveries of tiny details in nature have inspired me a lot.

Wie sind Sie zum Design gekommen?
Indem ich dem Potenzial für industrielle Materialien in Bezug auf unsere Lebenskultur mit Phantasie und Neugierde begegnet bin.

Wofür steht das Designstudio „MasayoAve creation"?
Es ist eine interdisziplinäre Plattform, die Designprojekte mit sensorischen Erlebnissen verbindet.

Was war Ihr bisher spannendstes Projekt?
Jeder Moment vergangener Projekte war unvergesslich spannend, doch kann ich sagen, dass das neueste Designprojekt für sensorische Erlebnisse, an dem ich gerade arbeite, das spannendste ist.

Woher nehmen Sie Ihre Inspiration?
Wenn man die Grundlagen der Gestaltung lernt, erwirbt man mithilfe seiner sinnlichen Wahrnehmung auch ein grundlegendes Verständnis seines Lebensraums. Die täglichen Entdeckungen kleinster Details in der Natur haben mich sehr inspiriert.

Martin Beeh
Germany
Deutschland

Martin Beeh is a graduate in Industrial Design from the Darmstadt University of Applied Sciences in Germany and the ENSCI-Les Ateliers, Paris, and completed a postgraduate course in business administration. In 1995, he became design coordinator at Décathlon in Lille/France, in 1997 senior designer at Electrolux Industrial Design Center Nuremberg and Stockholm and furthermore became design manager at Electrolux Industrial Design Center Pordenone/Italy, in 2001. He is a laureate of several design awards as well as founder and director of the renowned student design competition "Electrolux Design Lab". In the year 2006, he became general manager of the German office of the material library Material ConneXion in Cologne. Three years later, he founded the design office beeh_innovation. Martin Beeh lectured at the Folkwang University of the Arts in Essen, the University of Applied Sciences Schwäbisch Gmünd and the University of Applied Sciences Hamm-Lippstadt and was professor for design management at the University of Applied Sciences Ostwestfalen-Lippe in Lemgo from 2012 to 2015. He has furthermore developed the conference format "materials.cologne" as a dialogue platform for materials, design and innovation.

Martin Beeh absolvierte ein Studium in Industriedesign an der Fachhochschule Darmstadt und an der ENSCI-Les Ateliers, Paris, sowie ein Aufbaustudium der Betriebswirtschaft. 1995 wurde er Designkoordinator bei Décathlon in Lille/Frankreich, 1997 Senior Designer im Electrolux Industrial Design Center Nürnberg und Stockholm sowie 2001 Design Manager im Electrolux Industrial Design Center Pordenone/Italien. Er ist Gewinner diverser Designpreise und gründete und leitete den renommierten Designwettbewerb für Studierende, das „Electrolux Design Lab". Im Jahr 2006 wurde er General Manager der deutschen Niederlassung der Materialbibliothek „Material ConneXion" in Köln. Drei Jahre später gründete Martin Beeh das Designbüro beeh_innovation. Martin Beeh hatte Lehraufträge an der Folkwang Universität der Künste in Essen, an der Hochschule für Gestaltung Schwäbisch Gmünd und an der Hochschule Hamm-Lippstadt und war von 2012 bis 2015 Professor für Designmanagement an der Hochschule Ostwestfalen-Lippe in Lemgo. Darüber hinaus entwickelte er das Konferenzformat „materials.cologne" als Plattform für den Dialog zwischen Material, Design und Innovation.

01
Key visual of the
materials.cologne –
the conference for
design and innovation 2019
Initiative and project
management: beeh_innovation
Design: Büro Freiheit

Keyvisual der
materials.cologne –
Die Konferenz für
Design und Innovation 2019
Initiative und Projektleitung:
beeh_innovation
Design: Büro Freiheit

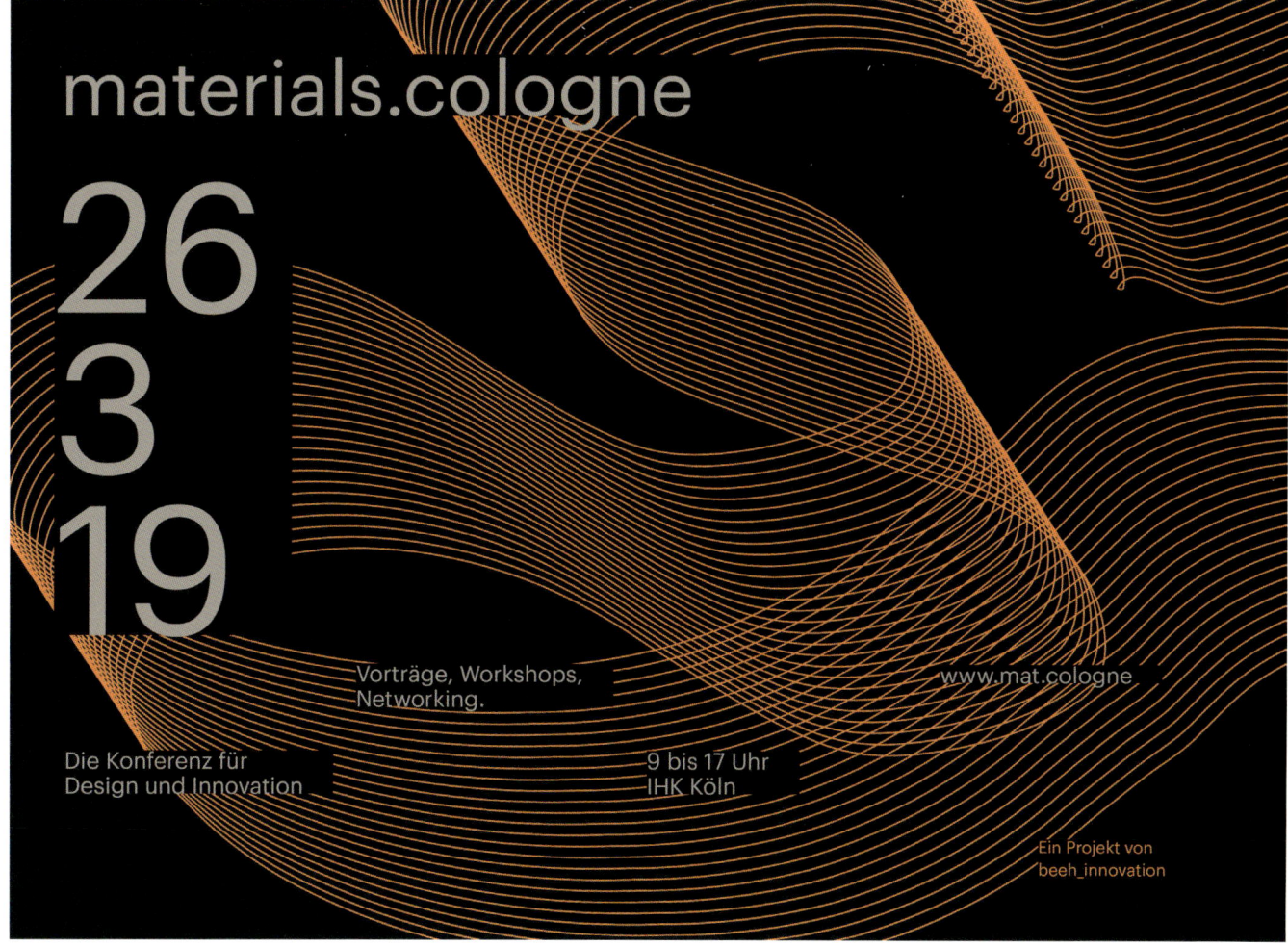

01

"Good design is as little 'visual noise' as possible: if the product comes up with a convincing solution and is easy and intuitive to use."

„Gutes Design ist so wenig ‚weißes Rauschen' wie möglich: wenn das Produkt eine überzeugende Lösung bietet und einfach und intuitiv zu benutzen ist."

With what can a product surprise you?
As a designer, design manager and design juror I evaluate if a product gives an original, human, effective and sustainable solution to an identified problem. If the product is also nice to look at and to work with, it is a good product. To make it really a pleasant surprise, the product should have more benefits and functions then you might first think.

What inspires you?
I had the chance to intensively research the design process of Ray and Charles Eames. Curiosity, experiment, a strong purpose, profoundness, patience combined with a thinking from sketch to production to user, are part of a "total design process" – together with all crafts from others that we need to integrate to create value-adding products.

Which innovations will in future influence our everyday life?
Sustainability is first, smart digital integration second. We will use and share products, not own them.

Womit kann Sie ein Produkt überraschen?
Als Designer, Designmanager und Designjuror beurteile ich ein Produkt danach, ob es eine originelle, menschliche, wirksame und nachhaltige Lösung für ein bestimmtes Problem bietet. Wenn es auch noch gut aussieht und angenehm zu handhaben ist, ist es ein gutes Produkt. Eine wirklich positive Überraschung ist es, wenn es mehr Vorteile und Funktionalitäten bietet, als man zuerst denkt.

Was inspiriert Sie?
Ich habe die Chance gehabt, den Designprozess von Ray und Charles Eames intensiv zu erforschen. Neugierde, Experimentierfreude, Zielstrebigkeit, Tiefe und Geduld, verbunden mit einem Prozess, der von der Skizze über die Herstellung bis zum Verbraucher durchdacht ist, sind Teil eines „kompletten Designprozesses" – genauso wie das Handwerk aller Beteiligten, das wir in den Prozess einfließen lassen müssen, um ein Produkt mit Mehrwert zu schaffen.

Welche Innovationen werden künftig unseren Alltag prägen?
An erster Stelle Nachhaltigkeit, dann die intelligente digitale Integration. Wir werden Produkte gemeinsam benutzen, statt sie zu besitzen.

Gordon Bruce
USA

Gordon Bruce is the owner of Gordon Bruce Design LLC and has been a design consultant for 45 years working with many multinational corporations in Europe, Asia and the USA. He has worked on a wide range of products, interiors and vehicles – from aeroplanes to computers to medical equipment to furniture. From 1991 to 1994, Gordon Bruce was a consulting vice president for the Art Center College of Design's Kyoto programme and, from 1995 to 1999, chairman of Product Design for the Innovative Design Lab of Samsung (IDS) in Seoul, Korea. In 2003, he played a crucial role in helping to establish Porsche Design's North American office. For many years, he served as head design consultant for Lenovo's Innovative Design Center (IDC) in Beijing. He recently worked with Bühler, in Switzerland, and Huawei Technologies Co., Ltd., in China. Gordon Bruce is a visiting professor at several universities in the USA and China. He has been an author for Phaidon Press, London and has written for several international design magazines. He has several products in various permanent design collections such as with MoMA, in New York City. Gordon Bruce recently received Art Center College of Design's "Lifetime Achievement Award".

Gordon Bruce ist Inhaber der Gordon Bruce Design LLC und seit mittlerweile 45 Jahren als Designberater für zahlreiche multinationale Unternehmen in Europa, Asien und den USA tätig. Er arbeitete bereits an einer Reihe von Produkten, Inneneinrichtungen und Fahrzeugen – von Flugzeugen über Computer bis hin zu medizinischem Equipment und Möbeln. Von 1991 bis 1994 war Gordon Bruce beratender Vizepräsident des Kioto-Programms am Art Center College of Design sowie von 1995 bis 1999 Vorsitzender für Produktdesign beim Innovative Design Lab of Samsung (IDS) in Seoul, Korea. Im Jahr 2003 war er wesentlich daran beteiligt, das Büro von Porsche Design in Nordamerika zu errichten. Über viele Jahre war er leitender Designberater für Lenovos Innovative Design Center (IDC) in Beijing. In letzter Zeit arbeitete er für Bühler, Schweiz, und für Huawei Technologies Co., Ltd. in China. Gordon Bruce ist Gastprofessor an zahlreichen Universitäten in den USA und in China. Er war auch als Buchautor für Phaidon Press in London und als Verfasser von Artikeln für diverse internationale Designmagazine aktiv. Einige seiner Produkte werden in verschiedenen Dauerausstellungen gezeigt, unter anderem im MoMA in New York. Kürzlich erhielt Gordon Bruce vom Art Center College of Design den Lifetime Achievement Award.

01
Recreational High-Bypass Turbofan Bi-Plane
Design concept for Industrial Design Magazine, 1984
Freizeit-Hochbypass-Mantelstromtriebwerk-Doppeldecker
Designkonzept für Industrial Design Magazine, 1984

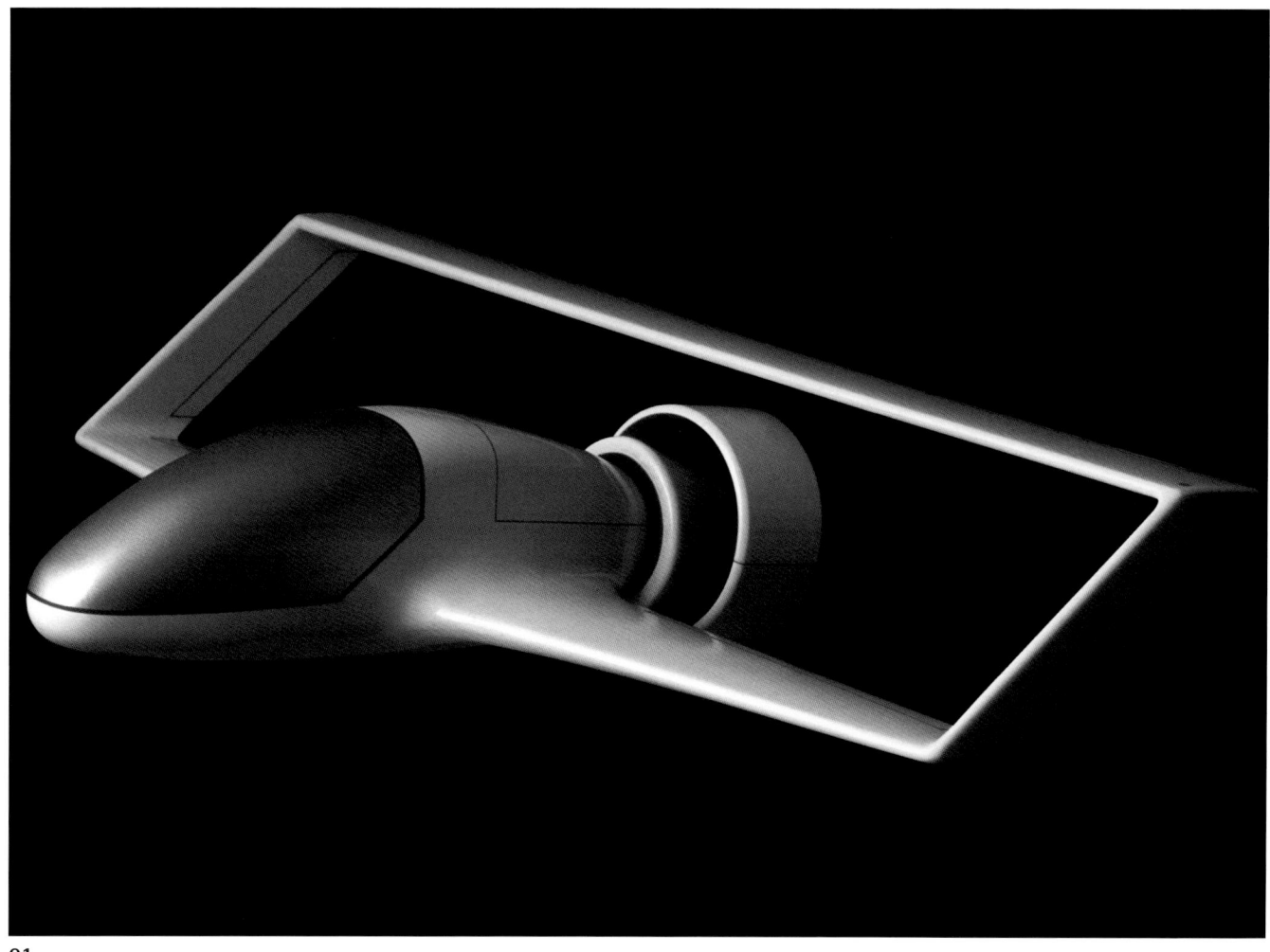
01

"Seeing design beyond professional practices, business strategies, and fashion statements, young designers need to advance their own heightened sense of design mindfulness, because design is a way of thinking about all one does in life."

„Junge Designer sollten bei Design an mehr als die berufliche Praxis, Geschäftsstrategien und Modestatements denken und einen gesteigerten Sinn für Designachtsamkeit entwickeln, da Design eine Geisteshaltung ist, mit der man alles betrachtet, was man im Leben tut."

To what do you attach particular importance when judging products?
The basis for my design judgement is similar to that of a three-legged stool where all supports need to be strong. The first leg is why is a design relevant? If this aspect is unique and pertinent to resolving problems, it brings credibility to the design idea. The second one concerns how the design conforms to the user. This gives credence to the design idea. The third leg is whether the product represents the true character of the designer or the company and embodies a design spirit, attitude and philosophy that gives it a distinctive quality.

What direction would you like product design to take in future?
There are many benefits to be gained from the products we use, as in the areas of health, safety, productivity or ecology. However, they can embody unanticipated hidden dangers as well. Just look at the downside of our civility due to the effects from smart phones and gaming upon minds and behaviour. So, future design professions need to eliminate any of the bad hidden within the good in our products.

Worauf legen Sie bei der Bewertung von Produkten besonderen Wert?
Die Basis für mein Designurteil ähnelt der Struktur eines dreibeinigen Hockers, bei dem alle drei Beine stark sein müssen. Das erste Bein ist, ob eine Gestaltung relevant ist. Wenn dieser Aspekt einzigartig und zweckdienlich ein Problem löst, ist die Designidee glaubwürdig. Das zweite Bein betrifft die Art, in der die Gestaltung auf den Nutzer eingeht. Das gibt der Designidee Überzeugungskraft. Das dritte Bein ist, ob das Produkt die wahre Natur des Designers oder des Unternehmens darstellt und den Geist, die Einstellung und die Philosophie des Designs verkörpert. Das gibt ihm eine unverkennbare Qualität.

Was wünschen Sie sich für die Zukunft des Produktdesigns?
Die Produkte, die wir benutzen, liefern uns viele Vorteile, so wie in den Bereichen Gesundheit, Sicherheit, Produktivität oder Ökologie. Allerdings können sie auch unerwartete Gefahren mit sich bringen. Nehmen Sie nur mal den Rückgang an Höflichkeit aufgrund des negativen Effekts, den Smartphones und Computerspiele auf unseren Verstand und unser Verhalten haben. Zukünftige Designberufe werden daher all das Schlechte, das in dem Guten unserer Produkte versteckt ist, beseitigen müssen.

Gisbert L. Brunner
Germany
Deutschland

Gisbert L. Brunner, born in 1947, has been working on watches, pendulum clocks and other precision timepieces since 1964. During the quartz clock crisis of the 1970s, his love for the apparently dying-out mechanical timepieces grew. His passion as a hobby collector eventually led to the first newspaper articles in the early 1980s and later to the by now more than 20 books on the topic. Amongst others, Brunner works for magazines such as Chronos, Chronos Japan, Ganz Europa, Handelszeitung, Prestige, Terra Mater, GQ and ZEIT Magazin. He also shares his expertise on Focus Online. Together with a partner, he founded the Internet platform www.uhrenkosmos.com in 2018. After the successful Watch Book I (2015) and Watch Book II (2016), the teNeues publishing house published the Watch Book Rolex, written by Gisbert L. Brunner, in June 2017. The book has appeared in German, English and French and has already been reprinted several times due to high international demand.

Gisbert L. Brunner, Jahrgang 1947, beschäftigt sich seit 1964 mit Armbanduhren, Pendeluhren und anderen Präzisionszeitmessern. Während der Quarzuhren-Krise in den 1970er Jahren wuchs seine Liebe zu den anscheinend aussterbenden mechanischen Zeitmessern. Ein leidenschaftliches Sammelhobby führte ab den frühen 1980er Jahren zu ersten Zeitschriftenartikeln und inzwischen mehr als 20 Büchern über dieses Metier. Brunner ist u. a. für Magazine wie Chronos, Chronos Japan, Ganz Europa, Handelszeitung, Prestige, Terra Mater, GQ und ZEIT Magazin tätig. Darüber hinaus stellt er seine Expertise Focus Online zur Verfügung. 2018 gründete er zusammen mit einem Partner die Internet-Plattform www.uhrenkosmos.com. Nach den erfolgreichen Publikationen Watch Book I (2015) und Watch Book II (2016) publizierte der teNeues Verlag im Juni 2017 das wiederum von Gisbert L. Brunner verfasste Watch Book Rolex in den Sprachen Deutsch, Englisch und Französisch. Aufgrund der hohen internationalen Nachfrage musste es schon mehrfach nachgedruckt werden.

01 THE WATCH BOOK – COMPENDIUM
Published by teNeues, 2019
Erschienen bei teNeues, 2019

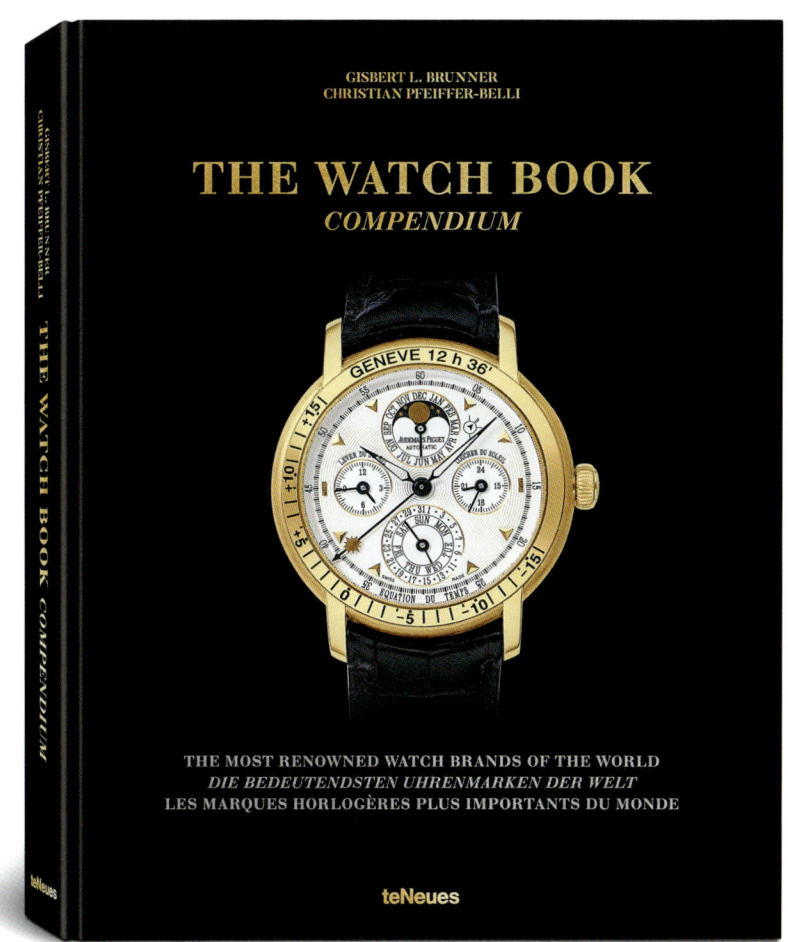

01

"The most exciting trends in the world of watches at the moment are coloured watch faces, smartwatches, bronze casings and a retro look."

„Die spannendsten Trends der Uhrenbranche sind aktuell farbige Zifferblätter, Smartwatches, Bronzegehäuse und Retrolook."

What does a watch have to offer in order to persuade you of its merits?
Naturally, it must look good, have a harmonious design and the correct signature as well as show real watchmaking quality or be truly original.

Where will the watch industry be ten years from now?
That's something nobody can really predict with any certainty as the middle and long-term impact of smartwatches is not yet clear at the moment. But one thing is sure, the traditional mechanical watch will survive.

What is the hallmark of good design?
In good, considered design, it is almost inevitable that form follows function. It is not ostentatious, but appeals instead with a classical, more reserved appearance. Nevertheless, it attracts attention. A significant aspect, where applicable, is ease of use.

How do you proceed when evaluating products?
Step by step. Firstly by screening a watch, then by examining all aspects in detail as well as its tactile properties.

Was muss eine Uhr mitbringen, um Sie zu überzeugen?
Sie muss natürlich gut aussehen, ein stimmiges Design und die richtige Signatur besitzen sowie uhrmacherische Qualität vorweisen oder besonders originell sein.

Wo wird die Uhrenbranche in zehn Jahren stehen?
Das kann niemand mit letzter Sicherheit vorhersagen, weil die mittel- und langfristigen Auswirkungen der Smartwatch momentan noch nicht absehbar sind. Aber die gute alte Mechanik wird sicher überleben.

Was kennzeichnet gutes Design?
Bei gutem, durchdachtem Design folgt die Form beinahe zwangsläufig der Funktion. Es wirkt nicht vordergründig, sondern besticht durch klassischen, eher zurückhaltenden Auftritt. Trotzdem weckt es die Aufmerksamkeit des Betrachters. Ein maßgeblicher Aspekt ist, sofern gegeben, eine intuitive Bedienbarkeit.

Wie gehen Sie bei der Bewertung von Produkten vor?
Schrittweise. Erst Screening, dann Begutachtung der Uhr aus allen Perspektiven inklusive aller Details sowie Prüfung der Haptik.

Rüdiger Bucher
Germany
Deutschland

Rüdiger Bucher, born in 1967, graduated in political science from Philipps-Universität Marburg and completed the postgraduate study course "Interdisciplinary studies on France" in Freiburg, Germany. Since 1995, he has been in charge of "Scriptum. Die Zeitschrift für Schreibkultur" (Scriptum. The magazine for writing culture) at the Verlagsgruppe Ebner Ulm publishing house where he became editorial manager of Chronos, the leading German-language special interest magazine for wrist watches in 1999. As chief editor since 2005, he has positioned Chronos internationally with subsidiary magazines and licensed editions in China, Korea, Japan and Poland. At the same time, Rüdiger Bucher established a successful corporate publishing department for Chronos. Since 2014, he has been editorial director and, in addition to Chronos, is also in charge of the sister magazines "Uhren-Magazin" (Watch Magazine), "Klassik Uhren" (Classic Watches) and the New York-based "WatchTime". Rüdiger Bucher lectures as an expert for mechanical wrist watches and is a sought-after interview partner for various media.

Rüdiger Bucher, geboren 1967, absolvierte ein Studium in Politikwissenschaft an der Philipps-Universität Marburg und das Aufbaustudium „Interdisziplinäre Frankreich-Studien" in Freiburg. Ab 1995 betreute er beim Ebner Verlag Ulm fünf Jahre lang „Scriptum. Die Zeitschrift für Schreibkultur", bevor er im selben Verlag 1999 Redaktionsleiter von „Chronos", dem führenden deutschsprachigen Special-Interest-Magazin für Armbanduhren wurde. Ab 2005 Chefredakteur, hat sich Chronos seitdem mit Tochtermagazinen und Lizenzausgaben in China, Korea, Japan und Polen international aufgestellt. Gleichzeitig baute Rüdiger Bucher für Chronos einen erfolgreichen Corporate-Publishing-Bereich auf. Seit 2014 verantwortet er als Redaktionsdirektor neben Chronos auch die Schwestermagazine „Uhren-Magazin", „Klassik Uhren" sowie die in New York beheimatete „WatchTime". Als Experte für mechanische Armbanduhren hält Rüdiger Bucher Vorträge und ist ein gefragter Interviewpartner für verschiedene Medien.

01
Chronos is available around the globe with different magazine issues and special supplements.
Mit verschiedenen Ausgaben und Sonderheften ist Chronos rund um den Globus vertreten.

01

"Good design should ensure that appearance and tactile properties evoke positive emotions and also reflect the unique characteristics of the brand."

„Gutes Design sollte optisch wie haptisch positive Emotionen hervorrufen und zugleich die besonderen Eigenheiten der Marke verkörpern."

What fascinates you about watches?
The fact that they manage to show the time with a precision of 99.99 per cent – often completely by mechanical means. Also, that the technology and design history of major brands, which are often over 150 years old, is encapsulated in such a small space.

What three qualities must a watch have in order to persuade you of its merits?
It must evoke strong emotions, be instantly recognisable, and easy and fast to read.

Where will the watch industry be five years from now?
There will be increased digitalisation and online selling will be much more established. Brands will be even more important, and, at the same time, need to keep reinventing themselves.

How do you proceed when evaluating products?
I check whether the design is new and unique, if the proportions are correct and if it is pleasant to wear. I also establish whether the design gets across the idea behind the watch and its function.

Was begeistert Sie an Uhren?
Dass sie es – oft mit rein mechanischen Mitteln – schaffen, die Zeit mit einer Präzision von 99,99 Prozent anzuzeigen. Und dass sich auf so kleinem Raum die Technik- und Designgeschichte großer, oft 150 Jahre alter Marken widerspiegelt.

Welche drei Eigenschaften muss eine Uhr mitbringen, um Sie zu überzeugen?
Sie muss starke Gefühle evozieren, unverwechselbar sowie gut und schnell ablesbar sein.

Wo wird die Uhrenbranche in fünf Jahren stehen?
Sie wird noch mehr digitalisiert und der Onlinehandel deutlich stärker etabliert sein. Marken werden noch wichtiger und müssen sich gleichzeitig immer wieder neu erfinden.

Wie gehen Sie bei der Bewertung von Produkten vor?
Ich prüfe, ob das Design neu und einzigartig ist, ob die Proportionen der Uhr stimmen und wie es sich mit der Haptik verhält. Ich untersuche, ob und wie das Design die Idee, die hinter der Uhr und ihrer Funktion steht, zur Geltung bringt.

Prof. Jun Cai
China

Jun Cai is professor at the Academy of Arts & Design, and director of the Design Management Research Lab at Tsinghua University in Beijing. He is also external reviewer for the Aalto University and Design School of Hong Kong Polytechnic University. Professor Cai has focused on research for design strategy and design management since the 1990s. Through exploration of design-driven business innovation and user-centred design thinking by theoretical and practical research, he was a consultant for more than 60 projects for among others Motorola, Nokia, LG, Boeing, Lenovo, Coway, Fiyta and Aftershockz. Furthermore, he has published papers and publications on design research, design strategy and design management.

Jun Cai ist Professor an der Academy of Arts & Design sowie Direktor des Design Management Research Lab an der Tsinghua University in Beijing. Er ist zudem externer Referent der Aalto University und der Designschule der Polytechnic University in Hongkong. Bereits seit den 1990er Jahren konzentriert sich Professor Cai auf die Forschung in den Bereichen Designstrategie und Designmanagement. Aufgrund seiner Erforschung von designorientierter Geschäftsinnovation und benutzerzentriertem Designdenken durch theoretische und praktische Forschung war er in mehr als 60 Projekten beratend tätig, unter anderem für Motorola, Nokia, LG, Boeing, Lenovo, Coway, Fiyta und Aftershockz. Außerdem hat er bereits Abhandlungen und Veröffentlichungen über Designforschung, Designstrategie und Designmanagement verfasst.

01 **Dust of Galaxy**
Lighting design
Leuchtendesign

01

"The quality of design improves the core competence of a company from market differentiation to brand recognition."
„Die Designqualität verbessert die Kernkompetenz eines Unternehmens, angefangen bei der Marktdifferenzierung bis hin zum Markenbekanntheitsgrad."

You are a professor at the Academy of Arts & Design. What advice do you give your students for their future career?
Be creative and have space in your heart for love and empathy. Be sensitive to changes in nature and always concerned with environment. A designer should have the responsibility not only to bring the beauty to the world, but also to protect our home planet.

What do you find most enjoyable about your work as a jury member?
It is exciting to see the progress of design and to witness change. I am always inspired by the work of talented designers, by their creative innovation and unique imagination.

What does a product have to offer in order to surprise you?
An experience far beyond function and an external shape that touches me inside. A really good product can be a reliable partner that only emerges when you need it.

Sie sind Professor an der Academy of Arts & Design. Welchen Rat geben Sie Ihren Studenten für ihre zukünftige Karriere?
Seid kreativ und habt in euerm Herzen Platz für Liebe und Empathie. Nehmt die Veränderungen in der Natur mit Sensibilität wahr und kümmert euch um die Umwelt. Ein Designer hat nicht nur die Aufgabe, Schönes zur Welt zu bringen, sondern ist auch für den Schutz unseres Planeten verantwortlich.

Was macht Ihnen an Ihrer Arbeit als Juror am meisten Spaß?
Es ist aufregend, den Fortschritt und die Veränderung im Design beobachten zu können. Mich inspiriert immer wieder die Arbeit der talentierten Designer, ihre kreativen Neuerungen und einzigartige Phantasie.

Was muss ein Produkt mitbringen, um Sie zu überraschen?
Ein Erlebnis, das über die Funktion hinausgeht, und eine äußere Form, die mich im Innersten berührt. Ein wirklich gutes Produkt kann ein verlässlicher Partner sein, der nur dann erscheint, wenn er gebraucht wird.

Vivian Wai-kwan Cheng
Hong Kong
Hongkong

On leaving the Kee Hong Kong Design Institute after 19 years of educational service, Vivian Cheng founded "Vivian Design" in 2014 to provide consultancy services and promote her own art in jewellery and glass. She graduated with a BA in industrial design from the Hong Kong Polytechnic University and was awarded a special prize in the Young Designers of the Year award hosted by the Federation of Hong Kong Industries in 1987, and the Governor's Award for Industry: Consumer Product Design in 1989, after joining Lambda Industrial Limited as the head of the product design team. In 1995 she finished her master's degree and joined the Vocational Training Council, teaching product design, and later became responsible for, among others, establishing an international network with design-related organisations and schools. Vivian Cheng was the International Liaison Manager at the Hong Kong Design Institute (HKDI), member of the Board of Directors of the Hong Kong Design Centre (HKDC) from 2002 to 2004, and was board member of the World Design Organization (formerly Icsid) from 2013 to 2017. Furthermore, she has been a panel member for various adjudication boards of the government and various NGOs.

Nach 19 Jahren im Lehrbetrieb verließ Vivian Cheng 2014 das Hong Kong Design Institute und gründete „Vivian Design", um Beratungsdienste anzubieten und ihre eigene Schmuck- und Glaskunst weiterzuentwickeln. 1987 machte sie ihren BA in Industriedesign an der Hong Kong Polytechnic University. Im selben Jahr erhielt sie einen Sonderpreis im Wettbewerb „Young Designers of the Year", veranstaltet von der Federation of Hong Kong Industries, sowie 1989 den Governor's Award for Industry: Consumer Product Design, nachdem sie bei Lambda Industrial Limited als Leiterin des Produktdesign-Teams angefangen hatte. 1995 beendete sie ihren Masterstudiengang und wechselte zum Vocational Training Council, wo sie Produktdesign unterrichtete und später u. a. für den Aufbau eines internationalen Netzwerks mit Organisationen und Schulen im Designbereich verantwortlich war. Vivian Cheng war International Liaison Manager am Hong Kong Design Institute (HKDI), Vorstandsmitglied des Hong Kong Design Centre (HKDC) von 2002 bis 2004 sowie Gremiumsmitglied der World Design Organization (ehemals Icsid) von 2013 bis 2017. Außerdem war sie Mitglied verschiedener Bewertungsgremien der Regierung und vieler Nichtregierungsorganisationen.

01 FIRE
Casting in Shibuichi (metal alloy)
Shibuichi-Guss (Metalllegierung)

02 AIR
Casting in silver
Silberguss

01

02

"A piece of jewellery must have value in emotion and design values, besides being well produced, well crafted and perfect inside out."

„Ein Schmuckstück muss eine Wertigkeit an Emotionen und Designwerten ausdrücken und natürlich auch hervorragend gemacht, gut ausgearbeitet und rundum perfekt sein."

What trends have caught your attention in the fashion industry?
Its currently biggest challenge is making its products sustainable. How to retain the product values and make them last over time are the biggest difficulties the fashion industry is encountering.

What do you appreciate about the evaluation process at Red Dot?
The evaluation process is very fair and the jury is given full autonomy while judging the products. Design is well respected during the course of judging and if the jury should have any doubt at all, no decision will be made until all is cleared.

What experience has had a long-term impact on your career?
The design process is never a linear equation to find a solution, but a multi-directional and there are thousands of ways to reach the destination. As such, it makes me understand that there is always another way to create an answer.

Welche Trends können Sie in der Modebranche ausmachen?
Zurzeit liegt die größte Herausforderung für die Modebranche darin, die Produkte nachhaltig zu gestalten, ihre Produktwerte zu bewahren und sicherzustellen, dass sie sich langfristig bewähren. Das sind die größten Schwierigkeiten, die die Branche überwinden muss.

Was schätzen Sie am Evaluationsprozess bei Red Dot?
Der Evaluationsprozess ist sehr fair und die Jury hat während der Bewertung der Produkte vollkommene Freiheit. Design wird während der Jurierung sehr ernst genommen. Sollte ein Juror irgendeinen Zweifel haben, wird keine Entscheidung getroffen, bis nicht alle einverstanden sind.

Welche Erfahrung prägte Ihre Karriere nachhaltig?
Der Designprozess ist keine lineare Gleichung, mit der man eine Lösung findet, sondern ein Mehrwegprozess. Denn es gibt tausend verschiedene Wege, mit denen man ans Ziel kommen kann. Ich habe gelernt, dass es immer auch einen anderen Weg gibt, um eine Antwort zu finden.

Mårten Claesson
Sweden
Schweden

Mårten Claesson was born in Lidingö, Sweden, in 1970. After studying at the Vasa Technical College in Stockholm in the department of construction engineering and at the Parsons School of Design in New York in the departments of architecture and product design, he graduated in 1994 with an MFA degree from Konstfack, the University College of Arts, Crafts and Design in Stockholm. He is co-founder of the Swedish design partnership Claesson Koivisto Rune, which is multidisciplinary in the classic Scandinavian way and which pursues the practice of both architecture and design. Mårten Claesson is also a writer and lecturer in the field of architecture and design.

Mårten Claesson wurde 1970 in Lidingö, Schweden, geboren. Nachdem er am Vasa Technical College in Stockholm im Fachbereich Bautechnik und an der Parsons School of Design in New York im Fachbereich Architektur und Produktdesign studiert hatte, schloss er 1994 sein Studium mit einem MFA-Abschluss der Konstfack, der Universität für Kunst, Handwerk und Design in Stockholm, ab. Er ist Mitgründer der schwedischen Design-Sozietät „Claesson Koivisto Rune", die im klassisch-skandinavischen Sinne multidisziplinär in Architektur und Design arbeitet. Mårten Claesson ist darüber hinaus als Autor und Dozent tätig.

01 Zander K Hotel in Bergen, Norway

"Good teamwork is flat, without hierarchy. And with a work outcome that is greater than the sum of the individuals' capacity."

„Gute Teamarbeit ist flach, ohne Hierarchie. Und das Ergebnis der Arbeit ist stärker als die Summe der individuellen Fähigkeiten."

What does a product have to offer in order to persuade you of its merits?
The product should be designed in such a way that its use becomes self-explanatory, with sound and ecological materials, in an overall quality. But above all the design has to evoke a sense of beauty.

What will the house of the future look like?
At present, the individual expression is back but many times only as a kind of pick-your-style in the marketplace. I hope to see a more genuine architecture, focusing on the essentials: spatiality and honest materials.

In 2019, Bauhaus celebrates its 100th anniversary. To what extent has this school of design influenced your work?
I read the history of Bauhaus before attending design university. When I had studied for just one year, I travelled to Dessau (and stayed in one of the studio flats) together with my two new friends, today my partners Eero Koivisto and Ola Rune. So, I guess to call Bauhaus formative would be almost an understatement.

Was muss ein Produkt mitbringen, um Sie zu überzeugen?
Das Produkt sollte so gestaltet sein, dass seine Nutzung offensichtlich ist. Es sollte aus soliden, ökologischen Materialien bestehen und rundum von einer hohen Qualität sein. Vor allem aber sollte das Design eine Empfindung von Schönheit hervorrufen.

Wie sieht das Haus der Zukunft aus?
Zurzeit erlebt die individuelle Ausdrucksform ein Comeback, doch häufig nur als eine aus dem Marktangebot gewählte Stilrichtung. Ich hoffe, dass wir mehr authentische Architektur sehen werden, die ihr Augenmerk auf das Wesentliche richtet: Räumlichkeit und ehrliche Materialien.

Das Bauhaus feiert 2019 sein 100-Jahr-Jubiläum. Inwieweit hat die Designschule Ihre Arbeit beeinflusst?
Ich habe die Geschichte des Bauhauses gelesen, bevor ich an der Universität Design studierte. Nach dem ersten Studienjahr reiste ich zusammen mit zwei neuen Freunden nach Dessau (und wohnte mit ihnen in einer der 1-Zimmer-Wohnungen). Heute sind das meine Partner, Eero Koivisto und Ola Rune. Bauhaus als nachhaltig prägend zu bezeichnen, wäre daher wohl untertrieben.

Vincent Créance
France
Frankreich

After graduating from the Ecole Supérieure de Design Industriel, Vincent Créance began his career in 1985 at the Plan Créatif agency where he became design director in 1990 and developed numerous products for high-tech and consumer markets. In 1996, he joined Alcatel as Design Director for all phone activities on an international level. In 1999, he became Vice President Brand in charge of industrial design, user experience and communications for the Mobile Phones BU. In 2004, Vincent Créance advanced to the position of Design and Corporate Communications Director of the Franco-Chinese joint-venture TCL & Alcatel Mobile Phones. In 2006, he became president and CEO of MBD Design, one of the major design agencies in France, providing design solutions in transport design and product design. Then, in 2017 he created the Design Center of the Université Paris-Saclay, bringing together 14 famous French engineering schools and research institutes, with the mission to promote design in this new ecosystem. Créance is a member of the board of directors of APCI (Agency for the Promotion of Industrial Creation), and of ENSCI (National College of Industrial Creation), and a member of the Design Strategic Advisory Board for Paris Region and for Strate College.

Vincent Créance begann seine Laufbahn nach seinem Abschluss an der Ecole Supérieure de Design Industriel 1985 bei der Agentur Plan Créatif. Hier stieg er 1990 zum Design Director auf und entwickelte zahlreiche Produkte für den Hightech- und Verbrauchermarkt. 1996 ging er als Design Director für sämtliche Telefonaktivitäten auf internationaler Ebene zu Alcatel und wurde 1999 Vice President Brand, zuständig für Industriedesign, User Experience sowie die gesamte Kommunikation für den Geschäftsbereich „Mobile Phones". 2004 avancierte Vincent Créance zum Design and Corporate Communications Director des französisch-chinesischen Zusammenschlusses TCL & Alcatel Mobile Phones. 2006 wurde er Präsident und CEO von MBD Design, einer der wichtigsten Designagenturen in Frankreich, und entwickelte Designlösungen für Transport- und Produktdesign. Im Jahr 2017 gründete er das Centre de Design der Université Paris-Saclay und vereinte 14 berühmte französische Ingenieurschulen und Forschungsinstitute in dem Bestreben, Design in diesem neuen Ökosystem zu fördern. Créance ist Vorstandsmitglied von APCI (Agency for the Promotion of Industrial Creation) und von ENSCI (National College of Industrial Design) sowie Mitglied im wissenschaftlichen Designbeirat der Region Paris und des Strate College.

01
Tram for Reims Tramway, France
The Alstom tram shows five different joyful and bubbly colours. This one in yellow has a unique design for the city of Champagne, which subliminally evokes a champagne flute.
Straßenbahn für Reims Tramway, Frankreich
Die Alstom-Straßenbahn gibt es in fünf verschiedenen freudigen und lebendigen Farbtönen. Diese Bahn in Gelb trägt ein einzigartiges Design für die Stadt Champagne, das unterschwellig an eine Champagnerflöte erinnert.

01

"An accolade gives designers and brands the feeling of playing a significant role in the great adventure of product design."

„Eine Auszeichnung gibt Designern und Marken das Gefühl, in dem großen Abenteuer des Produktdesigns eine bedeutende Rolle zu spielen."

What typifies the evaluation process at Red Dot?
The jurors come from a wide mix of continents: more than a globalised international point of view, this offers a multicultural judgement. I also very much appreciate that the independence of us jurors is not just a phrase but a precious asset.

Does a well-designed product make elaborate communication design redundant?
A brand is like an opera bringing together singers, musicians, director, scenographer, etc. – each of them must serve the same dramaturgy in harmony. When all of them resonate together, it becomes magical. Design as one of the most important communication tools must be outstanding to hold its rank in the structure.

What can consumers expect from products today?
To improve our everyday life, while preserving our future. In other words, it mostly means useful, simple and attractive products, creating respectful jobs for people, and preserving our resources.

Was macht den Evaluierungsprozess bei Red Dot aus?
Die Juroren kommen von den verschiedensten Kontinenten. Zusätzlich zu einer globalisierten, internationalen Sichtweise bedeutet das ein multikulturelles Urteil. Ich schätze außerdem ungemein, dass unsere Unabhängigkeit als Juroren nicht nur eine Phrase, sondern ein kostbares Gut ist.

Macht ein gut gestaltetes Produkt ausgeklügeltes Kommunikationsdesign überflüssig?
Eine Marke ist wie eine Oper, die Sänger, Musiker, den Intendanten, den Szenografen usw. zusammenbringt – in Eintracht muss jeder von ihnen der gleichen Dramaturgie dienen. Wenn alle harmonieren, wird es magisch. Design als eines der wichtigsten Kommunikationsinstrumente muss hervorragend sein, um in der Struktur seine Stelle bewahren zu können.

Was darf ein Konsument heutzutage von Produkten erwarten?
Dass sie den Alltag verbessern und gleichzeitig die Zukunft bewahren. Mit anderen Worten meine ich damit hauptsächlich Produkte, die nützlich, einfach und attraktiv sind, wertschätzende Arbeitsplätze für Menschen schaffen und unsere Ressourcen schonen.

Martin Darbyshire
Great Britain
Großbritannien

Martin Darbyshire founded tangerine in 1989 and under his stewardship it has developed into a global strategic design consultancy that creates award-winning solutions for internationally recognised brands such as LG, Samsung, Hyundai, Toyota, Nikon, Huawei, Virgin Australia and Cepsa. Before founding tangerine, he worked for Moggridge Associates and then in San Francisco at ID TWO (now IDEO). A design leader on the international stage, Martin Darbyshire combines his work for tangerine with a worldwide programme of keynote speeches and activities promoting the importance of design. He has served as UKT&I Ambassador for the UK Creative Industries and two terms as a board member of the World Design Organization (formerly Icsid). He was also formerly a visiting professor at Central Saint Martins. Martin Darbyshire is a trustee of the UK Design Council and a juror at the Red Dot Award and Contemporary Good Design. Moreover, the UK Creative Industries Council recognised his global export success awarding him the CIC International Award 2016.

Martin Darbyshire gründete tangerine 1989. Unter seiner Leitung entwickelte sich das Büro zu einem globalen strategischen Designberatungsunternehmen, das preisgekrönte Lösungen für weltweit anerkannte Marken wie LG, Samsung, Hyundai, Toyota, Nikon, Huawei, Virgin Australia und Cepsa entwickelt. Zuvor arbeitete er für Moggridge Associates und dann in San Francisco bei ID TWO (heute IDEO). Als ein weltweit führender Designer verbindet Martin Darbyshire seine Arbeit für tangerine mit einem globalen Programm von Keynote-Referaten und -Aktivitäten, um den bedeutenden Beitrag von Design hervorzuheben. Martin Darbyshire war für das Ministerium für Handel und Investition des Vereinigten Königreichs Botschafter des Bereichs Kreativindustrie und für zwei Amtszeiten Gremiumsmitglied der World Design Organization (ehemals Icsid). Er war zudem Gastdozent an der Central Saint Martins. Martin Darbyshire ist Kurator des UK Design Council sowie Juror des Red Dot Awards und von Contemporary Good Design. Darüber hinaus wurde er für seinen weltweiten Exporterfolg vom UK Creative Industries Council mit dem CIC International Award 2016 ausgezeichnet.

01
Gulf Air cabin
A total re-brand and new customer experience designed for the flag carrier of the Kingdom of Bahrain
Gulf-Air-Kabine
Kompletter Markenrelaunch und ein neues Kundenerlebnis, gestaltet für die Fluggesellschaft des Königreichs Bahrain

01

"Good design needs to be groundbreaking, effective and appealing."

„Gutes Design muss bahnbrechend, wirksam und ansprechend sein."

How do you proceed when evaluating products?
It's always a balance of physically experiencing something on the day and comparing it to one's present experience of comparable things. Listening to the points of view across the judges to reach a unified viewpoint is also an important step.

With what can a designer surprise you?
Achieving something really new and meaningful in a crowded market.

Where do you expect the design industry to be ten years from now?
Better understood and more appreciated.

Which three qualities do you value in a customer?
Open-mindedness. Objectivity. Curiosity.

Wie gehen Sie bei der Bewertung der Produkte vor?
Es ist immer ein Balanceakt zwischen der greifbaren physischen Erfahrung eines Produkts an dem Tag und den Erfahrungen, die man mit vergleichbaren Produkten gesammelt hat. Ein weiterer wichtiger Schritt ist es, auch die Meinungen der anderen Juroren zu erwägen, um dann einen vereinten Standpunkt zu finden.

Womit kann ein Designer Sie überraschen?
Indem er in einem überfüllten Markt etwas wirklich Neues und Sinnhaftes schafft.

Wo sehen Sie die Designbranche in zehn Jahren?
Besser verstanden und mehr geschätzt.

Welche drei Eigenschaften schätzen Sie an einem Kunden?
Aufgeschlossenheit. Objektivität. Neugier.

Katrin de Louw
Germany
Deutschland

Katrin de Louw studied interior design at Detmold School for Architecture and Interior Design. Since 1997, she has been working as an independent interior designer and design manager in the furniture industry and for manufacturers of materials. In 2006, she instigated the "servicepoint A30" trend and event forum in East Westphalia, thereby setting up a nationally leading network of material manufacturers and suppliers to the furniture industry, that discusses innovative trends in furniture and interior design and provides information on topics that are of interest to the industry. Katrin de Louw's agency "TRENDFILTER – Designzukunft für Möbel und Materialien" (future of design of furniture and materials) advises global players from industry, trade and the retail sector including Abet Laminati, BASF, Continental Group, Europlac, Koelnmesse, SURTECO GROUP, Swiss Krono Group, Westag & Getalit and and Windmöller Flooring. She is recognised as the leading trend expert for furniture, interiors and materials in German-speaking countries. She also works as a freelance author and provides comprehensive design consulting services together with her team of interior, product and graphic designers as well as marketing professionals.

Katrin de Louw studierte Innenarchitektur an der Detmolder Schule für Architektur und Innenarchitektur. Seit 1997 ist sie als selbständige Innenarchitektin und Designmanagerin der Möbelindustrie und für Materialhersteller tätig. 2006 initiierte sie mit dem Trend- und Eventforum „servicepoint A30" in Ostwestfalen das bundesweit führende Netzwerk von Materialherstellern und Möbelzulieferern, das innovative Trends im Möbel- und Raumdesign diskutiert und über branchenrelevante Themen informiert. Mit ihrem Büro „TRENDFILTER – Designzukunft für Möbel und Materialien" berät Katrin de Louw Global Player aus Industrie, Handwerk und Handel, darunter Abet Laminati, BASF, Continental Group, Europlac, Koelnmesse, SURTECO GROUP, Swiss Krono Group, Westag & Getalit und Windmöller Flooring. Sie gilt als führende Trendexpertin für Möbel, Inneneinrichtungen und Materialien im deutschsprachigen Raum, ist freie Autorin und bietet zusammen mit ihrem Team aus Innenarchitekten, Produkt- und Grafikdesignern sowie Marketingexperten umfassendes Design Consulting an.

01
New works with new materials in the spotlight: a branch of the Swiss Krono Group on the Kurfürstendamm in Berlin
Neues Arbeiten mit neuen Materialien im Fokus: die Dependance der Swiss Krono Group am Berliner Kurfürstendamm

"Materials transport emotions, because a virtual impulse cannot yet replace the experience of touch. Haptics are therefore increasingly important and will, in future, be a critical factor in the success of a product."

„Materialien sind emotionale Träger, denn haptische Erlebnisse sind mit virtuellen Impulsen noch nicht vergleichbar. Die Haptik wird also immer wichtiger und ist zukünftig mitentscheidend für den Erfolg eines Produkts."

What future innovations do you expect to see in materials and surfaces?
Particularly the combination of high-tech with sustainability will, in future, lead to ideas for new materials, their processing and uses. Waste products will also increasingly be seen as a source of raw materials. In general, more and more materials will become part of the cradle-to-cradle cycle.

Could you describe your typical day at TRENDFILTER?
Happy and varied. We have so many different projects related to materials and interior design that nothing is routine. Trend research and design consultation for national and international companies form an important part of that work, but we also carry out special exhibitions, industry events, workshops, presentations and publishing activities.

What material trends are noticeable in the furniture industry?
Aside from sustainable materials, there is a trend to use completely new materials. It is up to industry to explore fresh avenues not only in the choice of materials and their processing, but also in how they can be recycled in the future.

Welche Neuheiten erwarten Sie künftig im Bereich der Materialien und Oberflächen?
Insbesondere die Verknüpfung von Hightech und Nachhaltigkeit wird zukünftig neue Ideen für Materialien, deren Verarbeitung und Einsatzmöglichkeiten auf den Markt bringen. Auch Abfälle werden zunehmend als Rohstoffquelle wahrgenommen und generell gelangen Materialien stärker in den Cradle-to-Cradle-Kreislauf.

Wie sieht Ihr Alltag bei TRENDFILTER aus?
Fröhlich und bunt. Wir haben so viele unterschiedliche Projekte rund um das Thema „Material und Inneneinrichtung", dass nichts zur Gewohnheit wird. Dabei sind Trendrecherche und Design Consulting für nationale und internationale Unternehmen eine wichtige Säule. Aber auch Sonderschauen, Branchenevents, Workshops, Vorträge und Autorentätigkeiten gehören dazu.

Welche Materialtrends gibt es in der Möbelindustrie?
Neben dem Trend zu nachhaltigen Materialien gibt es den zu ganz neuen Materialien. Hier ist es an der Industrie, neue Wege zu gehen – sowohl bei der Materialwahl und deren Verarbeitung als auch dabei, wie Materialien zukünftig recycelt werden können.

Saskia Diez
Germany
Deutschland

After a stay in Paris in 1996, Saskia Diez began training in Germany as a goldsmith which she completed in 2000 as the local state winner. In 2001, she began studying industrial design, but at the same time worked for Christian Haas, where she designed lighting, china or paper products, as well as for Rosenthal and Konstantin Grcic. She started working under her own name in 2005 and, amongst others, designed trade fair stands for different companies before returning to jewellery work. In 2007/08, she set up her own label. Her aim was to explore the very notion of jewellery from invisible jewellery (perfume) to new ways of wearing jewellery, the use of new materials – also for handbags, sunglasses, nail varnish, etc. Saskia Diez works together with designers, companies, brands and artists including Arita Porzellan, e15, Pan and the Dreams, Uslu Airlines, Netaporter, Bevza, Kismet, Geza Schön, Mirko Borsche, Gym Yilmaz, Hermès, Viu, Stählemühle and the Julia Stoschek Collection.

Nach einem Aufenthalt in Paris 1996 begann Saskia Diez eine Ausbildung zur Goldschmiedin, die sie 2000 als Landessiegerin abschloss. 2001 nahm sie ein Studium in Industriedesign auf und arbeitete parallel bei Christian Haas, wo sie Leuchten, Geschirr oder Papeterie entwarf, bei Rosenthal und Konstantin Grcic. 2005 begann sie, unter eigenem Namen tätig zu werden, und entwarf unter anderem Messeauftritte für diverse Firmen, bevor sie zum Schmuck zurückkehrte und 2007/08 ihr eigenes Label gründete. Ihre Intention ist es, den Schmuckbegriff von unsichtbarem Schmuck (Parfum) über neue Arten, Schmuck zu tragen, bis hin zu neuen Materialien, auch für Taschen, Sonnenbrillen, Nagellack etc., auszuloten. Saskia Diez arbeitet mit Designern, Unternehmen, Marken und Künstlern zusammen, darunter Arita Porzellan, e15, Pan and the Dreams, Uslu Airlines, Netaporter, Bevza, Kismet, Geza Schön, Mirko Borsche, Gym Yilmaz, Hermès, Viu, Stählemühle sowie Julia Stoschek Collection.

01 Gold ME
Sunglasses, chained, 2016
These glasses come without edges or frame and were cut from a single piece of nylon. They were developed in cooperation with the glasses company VIU and made in Italy. The nylon makes them flexible, stable, lightweight and comfortable to wear. All metal parts of the shades have been gold-plated. The glasses themselves are lightly veiled with a gold dust finish.
Sonnenbrille mit Kette, 2016
Diese Brille hat keine Ränder und keinen Rahmen. Sie wurde aus einem einzigen Stück geschnitten, in Zusammenarbeit mit der Brillenfirma VIU entwickelt und in Italien hergestellt. Das Nylon-Material macht sie sehr flexibel, stabil, leicht und bequem zu tragen. Alle Metallteile der Brille sind vergoldet. Die Brillengläser wurden mit einem leichten Schleier aus Goldstaub versehen.

01

"What I find fascinating about jewellery is that it allows me to get very close to people. Jewellery is almost always charged with memories, life stories, love or even sorrow. It can be used to express a good deal, to strengthen oneself, adorn oneself, prepare oneself."

„An Schmuck fasziniert mich, dass ich Menschen damit sehr nahekomme. Schmuck ist fast immer aufgeladen mit Erinnerungen, Lebensgeschichten, Liebe oder auch Trauer. Mit Schmuck kann man sehr viel ausdrücken, sich stärken, schmücken, rüsten."

What jewellery do you personally like wearing?
I mostly wear a kind of "basic kit" for several months without a break: a pair of ear cuffs, rings, bracelets. Things, that I don't even take off when I go to bed. And depending on whether I am going out, how I feel, how decked out I want to be or on the occasion, I may add earrings or a necklace. I particularly like ear jewellery. It frames the face, is always visible, no matter how busy the party may be.

What distinguishes your design "signature"?
I always try to see things with a fresh pair of eyes, to extend the notion of jewellery and to push boundaries. So, it is always exciting to try out new materials or techniques. What is very important to me is that my jewellery must be wearable. It is more low-key than loud, but always distinct. I like working on a single idea, focusing on it and reducing it until I reach a point when the essence emerges.

With what can a designer surprise you?
With quirkiness, consistency, personality, intelligence.

Welchen Schmuck tragen Sie selbst gerne?
Meistens trage ich eine Art Grundausstattung mehrere Monate ununterbrochen: ein Paar Ear Cuffs, Ringe, Armreifen. Dinge, die ich dann auch zum Schlafen nicht mehr ablege. Und je nachdem, ob ich ausgehe, wie ich mich fühle, wie sehr ich geschmückt sein will oder was der Anlass ist, kommen dann noch Ohrringe oder eine Kette dazu. Ohrschmuck mag ich besonders gerne, er rahmt das Gesicht, ist immer sichtbar, egal, wie voll die Party ist.

Was kennzeichnet Ihre gestalterische Handschrift?
Ich versuche immer wieder, Dinge neu zu sehen, den Schmuckbegriff auszuweiten und Grenzen zu verschieben. So bleibt es für mich spannend, neue Materialien oder Techniken auszuprobieren. Sehr wichtig ist mir dabei: Mein Schmuck ist tragbar. Er ist eher leise als laut, aber immer klar. Ich arbeite gerne an einer einzelnen Idee, stelle sie in den Mittelpunkt und reduziere um sie herum so lange, bis sich deren Essenz herauskristallisiert.

Wie kann ein Designer Sie überraschen?
Mit Eigenheit, Schlüssigkeit, Persönlichkeit, Intelligenz.

Stefan Eckstein
Germany
Deutschland

Stefan Eckstein is the founder and CEO of ECKSTEIN DESIGN in Munich. The studio focuses on industrial, interaction and corporate industrial design. Stefan Eckstein studied industrial design at the Muthesius Academy of Fine Arts and Design in Kiel and ergonomics at the Anthropological Institute of the University of Kiel, Germany. Together with his design team, he has received many design awards in national and international competitions. Today, Stefan Eckstein is recognised as a renowned designer for industrial design. In line with his principle, "reduction to the essential leads to a better result", he has developed a user-driven approach to innovation, called "agile design development". It combines innovative concept- and development methods in a structured thought process. Stefan Eckstein has served on numerous international juries, has been a member of the Association of German Industrial Designers (VDID) for 25 years and was elected president of the Association in 2012. Under his management, the VDID CODEX was developed. Today, it serves as a model for the ethical values of the profession of industrial designers.

Stefan Eckstein ist Gründer und Geschäftsführer von ECKSTEIN DESIGN, einem Studio für Industriedesign, Interaction Design und Corporate Industrial Design in München. Er studierte Industrial Design an der Kieler Muthesius-Hochschule und Ergonomie am Anthropologischen Institut der Christian-Albrechts-Universität zu Kiel. Zusammen mit seinem Designteam erhielt er zahlreiche Auszeichnungen. Heute gehört Stefan Eckstein zu den renommierten Designern im Bereich des Industrial Designs. Gemäß seiner Philosophie „Reduzierung auf das Wesentliche führt zu einem besseren Ergebnis" entwickelte er eine nutzerorientierte Innovationsmethode, die „Agile Designentwicklung". In einem besonders strukturierten Denkprozess werden dabei innovative Konzept- und Entwicklungsphasen miteinander verbunden. Stefan Eckstein ist international als Juror tätig, seit über 25 Jahren Mitglied im Verband Deutscher Industrie Designer (VDID) und seit 2012 Präsident des Verbandes. Der VDID CODEX wurde unter seiner Leitung entwickelt und steht heute als Leitbild für die ethischen Werte des Berufsstandes.

01 METRAHIT IM XTRA
A digital multimeter is a technical hand-held measuring instrument used to monitor electrical devices in areas such as industry, communication technology, labs or outdoors. A special new feature is a replaceable battery pack which increases the operational readiness of the equipment through a reserve of charged batteries.
For GOSSEN METRAWATT, 2018.

Ein Digitalmultimeter ist ein technisches Handmessgerät für die Prüfung stromführender Geräte im professionellen Bereich wie Industrie, Kommunikationstechnik und Labor oder im Außenbereich. Besonderes Novum ist der wechselbare Akkupack, der die Einsatzbereitschaft des Geräts durch Vorhalten mehrerer geladener Akkus erhöht.
Für GOSSEN METRAWATT, 2018.

01

"Industrial design refers to the design of products, systems and an interactive product world. It makes sense of things and renders them efficient and understandable."

„Industriedesign ist die Gestaltung von Produkten, Systemen und der interaktiven Produktwelt. Es gibt den Dingen Sinn und macht sie effizient und verständlich."

Why does a back to basics approach lead to a better final result?
The term "reduction" has Latin origins. It comes from the verb "reducere" and means to lead back or bring back. In the context of the question it is today generally used to imply "limit to the essentials". This means the design focuses on usability, function and aesthetics. The clarity gained by this approach deliberately draws the attention of users to the essential features of a product or system and gives them a better designed product.

What is "agile design development"?
Agile design development is a user-oriented innovation method with a pared down structure. It links a structured iterative process to short concept and development phases in a team environment. The customer is always an important element of the design process. In this way, internal and external expertise are brought together.

Warum führt die Reduzierung auf das Wesentliche zu einem besseren Ergebnis?
Der Begriff „Reduktion" hat seinen Ursprung im Lateinischen. Er kommt von „reducere" und bedeutet „zurückführen". Im heutigen Gebrauch ist jedoch eher die Begrenzung auf das Wesentliche als Kernaussage gemeint. Auf diese Weise wird über die Gestaltung mehr Aufmerksamkeit auf Usability, Funktion und Ästhetik gerichtet. Durch die so gewonnene Überschaubarkeit wird der User auf das Wesentliche eines Produkts oder Systems gelenkt und bewusst geführt und bekommt so ein besser gestaltetes Produkt.

Was ist „Agile Designentwicklung"?
Agile Designentwicklung ist eine nutzenorientierte Innovationsmethode mit schlanker Struktur. Sie verbindet einen strukturierten Iterationsprozess mit kurzen Konzept- und Entwicklungsphasen im Team. Der Kunde ist dabei stets ein wichtiger Teil des Designprozesses, und so werden interne und externe Kompetenzen gebündelt.

Robin Edman
Sweden
Schweden

In 2017, Robin Edman founded the Robin Edman Innovation company and has since been working as an independent design consultant. He was previously, from 2001 onwards chief executive of SVID, the Swedish Industrial Design Foundation. After studying industrial design at Rhode Island School of Design, he joined AB Electrolux Global Design in 1981 and parallel to this started his own design consultancy. In 1989, Robin Edman joined Electrolux North America as vice president of Industrial Design for Frigidaire and in 1997, moved back to Stockholm as vice president of Electrolux Global Design. Throughout his entire career he has worked towards promoting a better understanding of users, their needs and the importance of design in society at large. His engagement in design-related activities is reflected in the numerous international jury appointments, speaking engagements, advisory council and board positions he has held. Robin Edman served on the board of the World Design Organization (formerly Icsid) from 2003 to 2007, the last term as treasurer. From 2015 to 2017, he has been the president of BEDA (Bureau of European Design Associations).

Robin Edman gründete 2017 das Unternehmen „Robin Edman Innovation" und ist seitdem selbständig als Designberater tätig. Zuvor war er seit 2001 Firmenchef der SVID, der Swedish Industrial Design Foundation. Nach einem Industriedesign-Studium an der Rhode Island School of Design kam er 1981 zu AB Electrolux Global Design und startete parallel seine eigene Unternehmensberatung für Design. 1989 wechselte Edman zu Electrolux North America als Vizepräsident für Industrial Design für Frigidaire und kehrte 1997 als Vizepräsident von Electrolux Global Design nach Stockholm zurück. Während seiner gesamten Karriere setzte er sich für ein besseres Verständnis für Nutzer und ihre Bedürfnisse ebenso ein wie für die Bedeutung von Design in der Gesellschaft insgesamt. Sein Engagement in designbezogenen Aktivitäten spiegelt sich in zahlreichen Jurierungsberufungen sowie in Rednerverpflichtungen und Positionen in Gremien sowie Beratungsausschüssen wider. Von 2003 bis 2007 war Robin Edman Mitglied im Vorstand der World Design Organization (ehemals Icsid), in der letzten Amtsperiode als Schatzmeister. Von 2015 bis 2017 war er Präsident von BEDA (Bureau of European Design Associations).

01
The company re:innovation specialises in design-driven innovation in supporting management in businesses and the public sector to grow, become more efficient and better serve their customers. Presently working with start-ups to multinationals.

Das Unternehmen re:innovation ist auf gestaltungsorientierte Innovation spezialisiert, die Führungskräfte von Unternehmen und staatlichen Behörden dabei unterstützt, zu expandieren, wirtschaftlicher zu werden und ihre Kunden besser zu versorgen. Aktuell arbeitet re:innovation sowohl mit Start-ups als auch mit multinationalen Konzernen zusammen.

re:innovation

01

"Design as a driver of societal and cultural change has the power to transform human behaviour and can radically change the way we perceive, execute and develop our products, services and systems."

„Design als Träger gesellschaftlichen und kulturellen Wandels hat die Kraft, menschliches Verhalten zu verändern, und verwandelt auch die Art, wie wir unsere Produkte, Dienstleistungen und Systeme sehen, erschaffen und entwickeln."

Please name three features of good design:
Good design consists of the integration of functional, emotional and social utilities. A product, service, process or strategy needs to include all three: the way it works, how do I feel about using it and what do other people say. Not until all three get together in a sustainable way, is it good design.

How important is user friendliness in a product?
Extremely important! Without a focus on the users and the way the products are perceived, used and discarded of, a product will never reach its full potential and achieve success.

To what extent do well designed products make our everyday life easier?
To a very high extent! A product that fulfils human desires and caters to the functional, emotional and societal needs will deliver at its best without hardly being noticed. The best designed products deliver way beyond expectations – in a way as if it was the most natural thing in the world.

Bitte nennen Sie drei Merkmale guten Designs:
Gutes Design besteht aus der Integration funktionaler, emotionaler und sozialer Leistungen. Ein Produkt – wie auch eine Dienstleistung, ein Prozess oder eine Strategie – muss alle drei einbeziehen: wie das Produkt funktioniert, wie ich mich fühle, wenn ich das Produkt verwende, und was andere Leute darüber sagen. Erst wenn alle drei nachhaltig im Einklang sind, ist es gutes Design.

Wie wichtig ist die Benutzerfreundlichkeit eines Produktes?
Extrem wichtig! Wenn Nutzer und die Art, in der Produkte gesehen, verwendet und entsorgt werden, nicht im Mittelpunkt stehen, wird ein Produkt nie sein ganzes Potenzial ausschöpfen und Erfolg erzielen.

Inwieweit erleichtern gut gestaltete Produkte unseren Alltag?
Enorm! Ein Produkt, das die Sehnsüchte von Menschen erfüllt und auf ihre funktionalen, emotionalen und sozialen Bedürfnisse eingeht, leistet sein Bestes, wenn es kaum bemerkt wird. Die am besten gestalteten Produkte liefern weit mehr als erwartet – fast so, als sei es das Natürlichste der Welt.

Prof. Lutz Fügener
Germany
Deutschland

Professor Lutz Fügener began his studies at the Technical University Dresden, where he completed a foundation course in mechanical engineering. He then transferred to the Burg Giebichenstein University of Art and Design in Halle/Saale, Germany, where he obtained a degree in industrial design in 1995. In the same year, he became junior partner of Fisch & Vogel Design in Berlin. Since then, the firm (today called "studioFT") has increasingly specialised in transportation design. Two years after joining the firm, Lutz Fügener became senior partner and co-owner. In 2000, he was appointed as Professor of Transportation Design/3D Design by Pforzheim University and there chairs the prestigious BA degree course in transportation design. Lutz Fügener is also active as an author and journalist for a number of different daily newspapers, weekly magazines and periodicals, as well as blogs in which he writes on mobility-related design topics.

Professor Lutz Fügener absolvierte ein Grundstudium in Maschinenbau an der Technischen Universität Dresden und nahm daraufhin ein Studium für Industrial Design an der Hochschule für Kunst und Design, Burg Giebichenstein, in Halle an der Saale auf. Sein Diplom machte er im Jahr 1995. Im selben Jahr wurde er Juniorpartner von Fisch & Vogel Design in Berlin. Seit dieser Zeit spezialisierte sich das Büro (heute „studioFT") mehr und mehr auf den Bereich „Transportation Design". Zwei Jahre nach seinem Einstieg wurde Lutz Fügener Seniorpartner und gleichberechtigter Mitinhaber des Büros. Im Jahr 2000 wurde er von der Hochschule Pforzheim auf eine Professur für Transportation Design/3D-Gestaltung berufen und ist Leiter des renommierten BA-Studiengangs für Fahrzeugdesign. Lutz Fügener ist als Autor und Journalist für verschiedene Tageszeitungen, Wochenmagazine, Periodika und Blogs tätig und schreibt über Themen des Designs im Zusammenhang mit Mobilität.

01 BEE
An autonomous vehicle for Continental
Ein autonomes Fahrzeug für Continental

01

"In the future, automotive designers must address a wider set of issues and focus more intensely on other areas in the design world where they can intersect such as User Experience Design (UX) and fields dominated by engineering."

„Fahrzeugdesigner müssen sich in Zukunft thematisch breiter aufstellen und Schnittstellen zu designinternen Bereichen wie User-Experience-Design (UX) sowie vom Ingenieurwesen bestimmten Feldern intensivieren."

With what can a car surprise you?
As cars are so complex, there are many different ways. The spectrum ranges from successful, aesthetic proportions to the outstanding design of form and material through to an obvious, functionally convincing overall concept.

What challenges will automotive designers have to deal with in future?
The attempted global commercialisation of cars is currently challenged by the increasingly heterogeneous development of the markets. While the impact of production, distribution and use of cars on the environment has led to tremendous pressure in Europe, the largest international market in the Far East is clamouring for larger vehicles such as SUVs. Another challenge is the automation of cars which is taking fundamentally different approaches in the USA, Europe and China. Predictions for future car purchase behaviour also pose a major challenge, not least for designers. New ways of using vehicles require different cars. Emotional aspects of driving are also under debate and are increasingly shifting to the topic of personal mobility.

Womit kann ein Auto Sie überraschen?
Dank seiner Komplexität auf sehr verschiedene Art und Weise. Das Spektrum reicht von gelungenen, ästhetischen Proportionen über eine hohe Gestaltungsqualität in Form und Material bis zum sinnfälligen, funktional überzeugenden Gesamtkonzept.

Welche Herausforderungen müssen Automobildesigner künftig meistern?
Gegen die möglichst weltweite Vermarktung von Automobilen steht derzeit eine zunehmend heterogene Entwicklung der Märkte. Während hierzulande der Druck in Bezug auf die Auswirkungen von Herstellung, Verteilung und Nutzung auf die Umwelt groß ist, verlangt der größte internationale Markt in Fernost eher voluminöse Automobile im SUV-Format. Dazu kommt die Automatisierung des Fahrens, die in USA, Europa und China grundlegend andere Ansätze zeigt. Auch Prognosen zum Verhalten künftiger Fahrzeugkäufer stellen nicht zuletzt Designer vor große Herausforderungen. Neue Nutzungskonzepte verlangen andere Fahrzeuge. Emotionale Aspekte des Fahrens stehen zur Debatte bzw. verlagern sich zunehmend in Bereiche der individuellen Mobilität.

Hideshi Hamaguchi
USA/Japan

Hideshi Hamaguchi graduated with a Bachelor of Science in chemical engineering from Kyoto University. Starting his career with Panasonic in Japan, Hamaguchi later became director of the New Business Planning Group at Panasonic Electric Works, Ltd. and then executive vice president of Panasonic Electric Works Laboratory of America, Inc. In 1993, he developed Japan's first corporate Intranet and also led the concept development for the first USB flash drive. Hideshi Hamaguchi has over 15 years of experience in defining strategies and decision-making, as well as in concept development for various industries and businesses. As Executive Fellow at Ziba Design and CEO at monogoto, he is today considered a leading mind in creative concept and strategy development on both sides of the Pacific and is involved in almost every project this renowned business consultancy takes on. For clients such as FedEx, Polycom and M-System he has led the development of several award-winning products.

Hideshi Hamaguchi graduierte als Bachelor of Science in Chemical Engineering an der Kyoto University. Seine Karriere begann er bei Panasonic in Japan, wo er später zum Direktor der New Business Planning Group von Panasonic Electric Works, Ltd. und zum Executive Vice President von Panasonic Electric Works Laboratory of America, Inc. aufstieg. 1993 entwickelte er Japans erstes Firmen-Intranet und übernahm zudem die Leitung der Konzeptentwicklung des ersten USB-Laufwerks. Hideshi Hamaguchi verfügt über mehr als 15 Jahre Erfahrung in der Konzeptentwicklung sowie Strategie- und Entscheidungsfindung in unterschiedlichen Industrien und Unternehmen. Als Executive Fellow bei Ziba Design und CEO bei monogoto wird er heute als führender Kopf in der kreativen Konzept- und Strategieentwicklung auf beiden Seiten des Pazifiks angesehen und ist in nahezu jedes Projekt der renommierten Unternehmensberatung involviert. Für Kunden wie FedEx, Polycom und M-System leitete er etliche ausgezeichnete Projekte.

01 Cintiq 24HD
for Wacom, 2012
für Wacom, 2012

01

"Innovation I would define as unprecedented, controversial, yet achievable."

„Ich würde Innovation als etwas noch nie Dagewesenes, Kontroverses, jedoch Erreichbares definieren."

What inspired you to create the USB stick?
Rather than the problem itself, I was inspired by the biases of professionals trying to solve the problem on effective data storage.

What was the most important moment of your career to date?
I feel like I am inspired by every single detail around me, every day. The sensitivity towards these perpetual inspirations took me here where I am today.

With what can a designer surprise you?
With a sense of unease which has been carefully designed for viewers to feel in an unexpected way.

What do you pay particular attention to when evaluating products?
I look for beautiful intentions behind each design.

Was inspirierte Sie zum USB-Stick?
Eher als das Problem an sich inspirierten mich die Vorurteile der Fachleute, die versuchten, das Problem der effektiven Datenspeicherung zu lösen.

Was war der bedeutendste Moment Ihrer bisherigen Karriere?
Ich habe den Eindruck, dass jedes noch so kleine Detail in meiner Umgebung mich inspiriert – jeden Tag. Die Sensibilität für diese ständigen Inspirationen hat mich dorthin gebracht, wo ich heute bin.

Womit kann ein Designer Sie überraschen?
Mit einem Gefühl der Unruhe, das vom Designer bewusst hervorgerufen wird, damit Betrachter das Produkt auf unerwartete Weise erleben.

Worauf achten Sie bei der Bewertung von Produkten?
Ich suche bei jedem Design nach den schönen Absichten, die hinter der Gestaltung stecken.

Prof. Renke He
China

Professor Renke He, born in 1958, studied civil engineering and architecture at Hunan University in China. From 1987 to 1988, he was a visiting scholar at the Industrial Design Department of the Royal Danish Academy of Fine Arts in Copenhagen and, from 1998 to 1999, at North Carolina State University's School of Design. Renke He is dean and professor of the School of Design at Hunan University and is also director of the Chinese Industrial Design Education Committee. Currently, he holds the position of vice chair of the China Industrial Design Association.

Professor Renke He wurde 1958 geboren und studierte an der Hunan University in China Bauingenieurwesen und Architektur. Von 1987 bis 1988 war er als Gastprofessor für Industrial Design an der Royal Danish Academy of Fine Arts in Kopenhagen tätig, und von 1998 bis 1999 hatte er eine Gastprofessur an der School of Design der North Carolina State University inne. Renke He ist Dekan und Professor an der Hunan University, School of Design, sowie Direktor des Chinese Industrial Design Education Committee. Er ist derzeit zudem stellvertretender Vorsitzender der China Industrial Design Association.

01
Scarf design with traditional Dong minority brocade patterns for the New Channel Design & Social Innovation Programme.
Design: School of Design of Hunan University, China.
Schaldesign mit traditionellen Brokatmustern der Dong-Minderheit für das New Channel Design & Social Innovation Programme.
Gestaltung: Designschule der Hunan-Universität, China.

01

"For the young generation of designers global warming and sustainable development will be real challenges and responsibilities."
„Für die jüngere Designergeneration sind der Klimawandel und eine nachhaltige Entwicklung die wirklichen Herausforderungen und Aufgabenbereiche."

What qualities must a well-designed product have?
High functionality, a well-designed human-machine relationship, eco-friendliness and aesthetic attractiveness.

What do you pay particular attention to when evaluating products?
In our digital age, technology becomes more and more complicated in many product designs. Interactive design is the key issue when evaluating products. Good interactive design makes for a good user experience – the most important value of design.

What would the ideal design apprenticeship look like, in your opinion?
Learning by doing is a long tradition in the design profession. Practice makes perfect is still an important rule in design education. In my opinion, the ideal design apprenticeship is a platform or system which encourages students to join design teams in design studios or companies in order to practice real projects under the guidance of skilled designers.

Welche Qualitäten muss ein gut gestaltetes Produkt aufweisen?
Eine hohe Funktionalität, eine gut gestaltete Schnittstelle zwischen Mensch und Maschine, Umweltfreundlichkeit und ästhetischen Reiz.

Worauf legen Sie bei der Bewertung von Produkten besonderen Wert?
In unserem digitalen Zeitalter wird die Technik in vielen Produktdesigns immer komplizierter. Die interaktive Gestaltung ist bei der Bewertung von Produkten der zentrale Punkt. Eine gute interaktive Gestaltung führt zu einem guten Nutzererlebnis – der wichtigste Beitrag von Design.

Wie sähe die ideale Designlehre für Sie aus?
„Learning by Doing" hat in der Designbranche schon lange Tradition. Die wichtige Regel „Übung macht den Meister" gilt in der Designausbildung auch heute noch. Meiner Meinung nach ist die ideale Designlehre eine Plattform oder ein System, das Studenten anregt, Teil eines Designteams in einem Designstudio oder einem Unternehmen zu werden, damit sie wirkliche Projekte unter der Anleitung sachkundiger Designer ausführen können.

Prof. Carlos Hinrichsen
Chile

Professor Carlos Hinrichsen graduated as an industrial designer in Chile in 1982 and earned his master's degree in engineering in Japan in 1991. Currently, he is Vice-Chancellor of Academic Affairs of INACAP Polytechnic and University, the largest in the country. At present, Chile is in transition from an efficiency-based towards an innovation-based economy where INACAP contributes with actions and initiatives to achieve this important aim for the country, mixing research, innovation, business, design and engineering spheres. From 2007 to 2009, Carlos Hinrichsen was president of the World Design Organization (formerly Icsid) and currently serves as senator within the organisation. In 2010, he was honoured with the distinction "Commander of the Order of the Lion of Finland". From 2014 to 2016, he was dean of the Faculty of Business, Engineering and Digital Arts at the Gabriela Mistral University in Santiago and from 2016 to 2017, he was the Senior Managing Coordinator of Engineering Design in the School of Engineering in the P. Universidad Católica de Chile. For more than three decades he has led interdisciplinary teams to enable corporations, educational and other institutions to gain leadership and competitive positioning.

Professor Carlos Hinrichsen machte 1982 seinen Abschluss in Industriedesign in Chile und erhielt 1991 seinen Master der Ingenieurwissenschaft in Japan. Aktuell ist er Rektor für Studienangelegenheiten an der INACAP Fachhochschule und Universität, der größten im Land. Zurzeit befindet sich Chile im Übergang von einer effizienzbasierten zu einer innovationsbasierten Wirtschaft, in der INACAP mit Maßnahmen und Initiativen dazu beiträgt, dieses wichtige Landesziel durch eine Mischung aus Forschung, Innovation, Handel, Design und Ingenieurwesen zu erreichen. Von 2007 bis 2009 war Carlos Hinrichsen Präsident der World Design Organization (ehemals Icsid) und dient heute als Senator innerhalb der Organisation. 2010 wurde er mit der Auszeichnung „Commander of the Order of the Lion of Finland" geehrt. Von 2014 bis 2016 war er Dekan der Fakultät für Handel, Ingenieurwesen und Digitale Künste an der Gabriela-Mistral-Universität in Santiago und von 2016 bis 2017 leitender geschäftsführender Koordinator für Engineering Design an der P. Universidad Católica de Chile. Seit mehr als drei Jahrzehnten leitet er interdisziplinäre Teams, um Unternehmen, Bildungsinstituten und anderen Organisationen zu helfen, eine marktführende und starke Wettbewerbsposition zu erlangen.

01
The INACAP Polytechnic and University is a learning ecosystem with technology-based study programmes, distributed in 26 campuses throughout Chile. In this scenario, the Fablab INACAP is part of the largest network of rapid prototyping labs in the country, promoting interdisciplinarity and active learning with a focus on innovation, entrepreneurship, applied research and development.
Die Universität INACAP ist ein lernendes Ökosystem mit technologiegestützten Studiengängen, die auf 26 Campus-Standorten in ganz Chile angeboten werden. In dieser Konstellation ist Fablab INACAP Teil des größten Netzwerks an Rapid-Prototyping-Laboratorien im Land und fördert Interdisziplinarität sowie aktives Lernen mit einem Schwerpunkt auf Innovation, Unternehmergeist, angewandter Forschung und Entwicklung.

01

"As a child, I realised that good design contributes to human beings' happiness, and over the years I confirmed that impression. Design also needs to be sustainable in its social, economic and environmental dimensions."

„Als Kind habe ich festgestellt, dass gutes Design zum Glücksgefühl der Menschen beitragen kann. Mit den Jahren hat sich dieser Eindruck bestätigt. Design muss allerdings ebenfalls aus sozialer, wirtschaftlicher und ökologischer Sicht nachhaltig sein."

What do you pay particular attention to when evaluating products?
I focus on the unique or particular way of responding to the needs and requirements of end users, as well as how this product responds to what we know today as a circular economy. Besides, I try to recognise the relationship between design and quality, and identify which of the products fit their purpose best.

What trends have you noticed in the design industry?
In a world where new technologies are modelling, transforming the industry, business and society in which we live every day, I see trends as an effort by design solutions at the level of products, services or experiences to capture value in these changing processes, and as a means of adding value for multiple users with new requirements and changing demands, who now expect an almost instantaneous response, due to the changes and speed of response generated by the impact of the digital transformation.

Worauf legen Sie bei der Bewertung von Produkten besonderen Wert?
Ich achte auf die einzigartige oder besondere Art und Weise, wie ein Produkt auf die Bedürfnisse und Anforderungen der Benutzer eingeht, und auf das, was wir heute als Kreislaufwirtschaft bezeichnen. Außerdem versuche ich, das Verhältnis von Gestaltung zu Qualität zu erkennen und zu erfassen, welche Produkte ihren Zweck am besten erfüllen.

Welche Trends können Sie in der Designbranche identifizieren?
In einer Welt, in der neue Technologien die Industrie, den Handel und die Gesellschaft, in der wir jeden Tag leben, formen und umwandeln, sehe ich Trends als einen Versuch an, aus diesen Änderungsprozessen mithilfe von Designlösungen in der Form von Produkten, Dienstleistungen und Erlebnissen Wert zu schöpfen. Sie bieten ebenfalls einen Mehrwert für eine Vielzahl von Nutzern mit neuen Anforderungen und wechselnden Bedürfnissen, die aufgrund der durch die digitale Transformation verursachten Veränderungen und Reaktionsgeschwindigkeit eine fast sofortige Reaktion erwarten.

Simon Husslein
Germany/Switzerland
Deutschland/Schweiz

Simon Husslein was born in Werneck, Germany, in 1976 and studied industrial design from 1995 to 2000 at Darmstadt University of Applied Sciences. From 2000 to 2005, he worked closely with his mentor and friend Hannes Wettstein at Wettstein's studio in Zurich. From 2005 to 2007, he completed a master's degree in Design Products at the London Royal College of Art. Subsequently, he led a number of projects in London and Shanghai and lectured at Shanghai's Tongji University. Between 2008 and 2014, he put his mark on a large number of projects at the Studio Hannes Wettstein in Zurich where he was creative director and member of the executive committee. In 2015, he founded the Atelier Simon Husslein. Simon Husslein develops products, furniture, installations and spatial design. Since 2017, he has been professor of interior architecture at Geneva School of Art and Design, HEAD – Geneva, Switzerland.

Simon Husslein, geboren 1976 in Werneck, Deutschland, studierte von 1995 bis 2000 Industrial Design an der Fachhochschule Darmstadt. Von 2000 bis 2005 arbeitete er eng mit seinem Mentor und Freund Hannes Wettstein in dessen Zürcher Studio zusammen. Von 2005 bis 2007 absolvierte er ein Masterstudium in Design Products am Royal College of Art in London. Danach betreute er eigene Projekte in London und Shanghai und unterrichtete an der Tongji University in Shanghai. Zwischen 2008 und 2014 prägte er als Creative Director und Mitglied der Geschäftsleitung eine Vielzahl der Projekte des Studios Hannes Wettstein in Zürich. 2015 gründete er das Atelier Simon Husslein. Simon Husslein entwickelt Produkte, Möbel, Installationen und Raumgestaltungen. Seit 2017 ist er Professor für Interior Architecture an der Geneva School of Art and Design, HEAD – Genf, Schweiz.

01 Minimatik
Wristwatch for NOMOS
Glashütte/SA Roland
Schwertner KG

Armbanduhr für NOMOS
Glashütte/SA Roland
Schwertner KG

01

"If good design is the result of a meticulous design process, then it stands a much better chance of maintaining its position in the market for a very long time."

„Gutes Design als Resultat eines sorgfältigen Designprozesses erhöht die Chance signifikant, dass sich ein Produkt überdurchschnittlich lange in seinem Marktumfeld behaupten kann."

What do you pay particular attention to when evaluating products?
A watch has many different features that must add up and make a whole. In the case of a new model, one of the questions that arises concerns the authenticity of the concept. In general, I pay a good deal of attention to the use of detailing. How has the transition between the strap and the body of the watch been managed? Does the design of the casing harmonise with the surface treatment? Do the various elements have a common design typology? Only when the design is consistent and well implemented in all aspects is it worth an award.

What distinguishes your design "signature"?
Precision, emotion and the pursuit of the archetype.

What matters when it comes to teamwork?
If the mix of personalities is right, the team can achieve great things.

Worauf legen Sie bei der Bewertung von Produkten besonderen Wert?
Bei einer Uhr gibt es sehr viele unterschiedliche Aspekte, die als Ganzes stimmen müssen. Bei einer Neukreation stellt sich beispielsweise die Frage der Authentizität des Entwurfs. Generell achte ich sehr auf den Umgang mit Details: Wie verläuft der Übergang zwischen Bandanschluss und Gehäuse? Wurde die Gehäusegestaltung mit der Veredelungstechnologie der Oberflächen schlüssig abgestimmt? Haben die verschiedenen Elemente eine gemeinsame Gestaltungstypologie? Nur wenn das Design auf allen Ebenen konsequent und gut umgesetzt wurde, verdient es eine Auszeichnung.

Was kennzeichnet Ihre gestalterische Handschrift?
Präzision, Emotionalität und die Suche nach dem Archetypus.

Worauf kommt es bei Teamarbeit an?
Wenn die Mischung aus Persönlichkeiten stimmt, kann im Team Großes erreicht werden.

Qiong Er Jiang
China

Qiong Er Jiang, founder of lifestyle brand SHANG XIA, is an internationally renowned designer. After many years studying in Europe, she brings a cosmopolitan approach and multi-cultural experience to her designs. As artistic director and CEO of SHANG XIA, she combines traditional crafts with contemporary design. Her works received wide acclaim and distinguished design awards at national and international level, being collected by world-class museums like British Museum, Musée Guimet and Musée des Arts Décoratifs. In 2011, Forbes named Qiong Er Jiang as one of the 25 most influential Chinese in "Global Fashion and Lifestyle". Furthermore, she was honoured several times in recognition of her contribution to the cultural exchange between China and France.

Qiong Er Jiang, Gründerin der Lifestyle-Marke SHANG XIA, ist eine international renommierte Designerin. Nachdem sie mehrere Jahre in Europa studiert hat, verfolgt sie bei ihren Entwürfen einen weltoffenen und multikulturellen Ansatz. Als Artistic Director und CEO von SHANG XIA kombiniert sie traditionelles Handwerk mit zeitgenössischem Design. Ihre Arbeiten haben sowohl auf nationaler als auch auf internationaler Ebene große Anerkennung und angesehene Auszeichnungen erhalten. Außerdem werden sie in Museen von Weltrang wie dem British Museum, dem Musée Guimet und dem Musée des Arts Décoratifs gesammelt. 2011 zählte Forbes Qiong Er Jiang zu den 25 einflussreichsten Chinesen im Bereich „Global Fashion und Lifestyle". Darüber hinaus wurde sie mehrere Male für ihren Beitrag zum kulturellen Austausch zwischen China und Frankreich geehrt.

01 GARDEN
Round Box in red Bo Luo lacquer with gold inlay. The red and gold lidded box is inspired by the traditional Chinese Cuan Pan vessel sets, signifying happiness and completeness.
Runde Schachtel mit roter Bo-Luo-Lackarbeit und goldenen Intarsien. Die Schachtel mit dem rot-goldenen Deckel wurde von den traditionellen chinesischen Cuan-Pan-Gefäße-Sets inspiriert und symbolisiert Glück und Vollkommenheit.

01

"My experience in Europe offered me the chance to see my own culture from another angle. The opportunity to twist my views in this unique way offered a positive influence in the creations of my designs."

„Meine Erfahrungen in Europa haben mir erlaubt, meine eigene Kultur aus einer anderen Perspektive zu sehen. Diese Gelegenheit, meine Sichtweise auf so eine einzigartige Weise umzustellen, hat sich positiv auf mein gestalterisches Schaffen ausgewirkt."

What does a product have to offer in order to surprise you?
Emotion, emotion and emotion. Of course, the emotion can come from the material of the product, craftsmanship, design concept, or cultural background story. And it may even come from all of these things combined!

What distinguishes your design "signature"?
My design encapsulates an encounter, or a dialogue, between: tradition and modernity, craft and technology, functionality and emotion, past and future. There is true emotion put into and captured through my designs.

Why is the cultural exchange between different nations valuable?
From my understanding, though the nations are different, the culture is fundamentally the same: it's about love and beauty. The cultural exchange can be conveyed through expression and style to portray "beauty", while feeling and understanding this allows for deeper "emotion". The diversity of these translations enriches our lives and makes it meaningful.

Was muss ein Produkt mitbringen, um Sie zu überzeugen?
Emotion, Emotion und noch mal Emotion! Selbstverständlich kann diese Emotion von dem Material des Produkts, seiner Handwerkskunst, dem Gestaltungskonzept oder dem kulturellen Hintergrund ausgehen. Es kann sogar eine Verschmelzung aller dieser Quellen sein.

Was kennzeichnet Ihre gestalterische Handschrift?
Mein Design bringt eine Begegnung, einen Dialog zwischen Tradition und Moderne, Handwerk und Technik, Funktionalität und Gefühl, Vergangenheit und Zukunft auf den Punkt. In meinen Gestaltungen steckt ehrliche Emotion.

Warum ist der kulturelle Austausch zwischen verschiedenen Nationen wichtig?
Nach meiner Auffassung unterscheiden sich Nationen zwar, doch ist die Kultur prinzipiell die gleiche: Es geht immer um Liebe und Schönheit. Der kulturelle Austausch kann durch eine Stilrichtung und eine Ausdrucksform, die „Schönheit" darstellt, vermittelt werden. Wenn man das versteht und spürt, ist das „emotionale Erlebnis" stärker. Die Vielfalt dieser Interpretationen bereichert unser Leben und gibt ihm Bedeutung.

Prof. Cheng-Neng Kuan
Taiwan

In 1980, Professor Cheng-Neng Kuan earned a master's degree in Industrial Design (MID) from the Pratt Institute in New York. He is currently a chair professor and served as the vice president of Shih-Chien University, Taipei, Taiwan, from 2008 to 2017. With the aim of developing a more advanced design curriculum in Taiwan, he founded the Department of Industrial Design, in 1992. He served as department chair until 1999. Moreover, Cheng-Neng Kuan founded the School of Design in 1997 and had served as the dean from 1997 to 2004 and as the founding director of the Graduate Institute of Industrial Design from 1998 to 2007. He had also held the position of the 16th chairman of the board of China Industrial Designers Association (CIDA), Taiwan. His fields of expertise include design strategy and management as well as design theory and creation. Having published various books on design and over 180 research papers and articles, he is an active member of design juries in his home country and internationally. He is a consultant to major enterprises on product development and design strategy.

1980 erwarb Professor Cheng-Neng Kuan einen Masterabschluss in Industriedesign (MID) am Pratt Institute in New York. Derzeit ist er Lehrstuhl-Professor und war von 2008 bis 2017 Vizepräsident der Shih-Chien University in Taipeh, Taiwan. 1992 gründete er mit dem Ziel, einen erweiterten Designlehrplan zu entwickeln, das Department of Industrial Design in Taiwan. Bis 1999 war Cheng-Neng Kuan Vorsitzender des Instituts. Darüber hinaus gründete er 1997 die School of Design, deren Dekan er von 1997 bis 2004 war. Von 1998 bis 2007 war er Gründungsdirektor des Graduate Institute of Industrial Design. Zudem war er der 16. Vorstandsvorsitzende der China Industrial Designers Association (CIDA) in Taiwan. Seine Fachgebiete umfassen Designstrategie, -management, -theorie und -kreation. Neben der Veröffentlichung verschiedener Bücher über Design und von mehr als 180 Forschungsarbeiten und Artikeln ist er aktives Mitglied von Designjurys in seiner Heimat sowie auf internationaler Ebene. Zudem ist er als Berater für Großunternehmen im Bereich Produktentwicklung und Designstrategie tätig.

01 Plier
A piece of furniture for an open space, designed by Lin-Huei Hwang, can be transformed into a screen panel or bar table. This project was selected as a winner of Taiwan's Young Pin Design Award 2017.

Ein Möbelstück für ein Freigelände, von Lin-Huei Hwang gestaltet. Es kann als eine Leinwand oder als ein Bartisch verwendet werden. Dieses Projekt wurde zu einem Gewinner des Young Pin Design Award 2017 in Taiwan gekürt.

01

"Good design needs to bring inspiring emotional satisfaction right to the target users."

„Gutes Design muss seiner Zielgruppe direkte, inspirierende und emotionale Befriedigung bieten."

With what can a product surprise you?
A composition of concept and language that seems unfamiliar to me yet opens up a new design horizon.

How do you proceed when evaluating products?
By seeing and thinking if the first impression offers design reasons that convince me of its excellence.

What message would you like to give your students for their future career?
Keep exploring the messages of lifestyle changes, and use your design to give it a specific meaning.

What challenges will designers have to meet in future?
Facing unprecedented ecological crisis, we designers have to rethink the spirit of brands with regard to human welfare.

Womit kann ein Produkt Sie überraschen?
Mit einer Kombination aus Konzept und Formensprache, die mir unbekannt ist und mir einen neuen Designhorizont eröffnet.

Wie gehen Sie bei der Bewertung der Produkte vor?
Indem ich sehe und überlege, ob der erste Eindruck Gründe für das Design liefert, die mich von seiner Vortrefflichkeit überzeugen.

Welche Botschaft möchten Sie Ihren Studenten mit auf den Weg geben?
Weiterhin die Botschaften aufzuspüren, die aus den Veränderungen im Lebensstil hervorgehen, und ihren Gestaltungskonzepten eine bestimmte Bedeutung zu verleihen.

Welchen Herausforderungen müssen sich Designer künftig stellen?
In Anbetracht der beispiellosen ökologischen Krise müssen wir Designer den Sinn von Marken in Bezug auf das Gemeinwohl überdenken.

Steve Leung
Hong Kong
Hongkong

Born and bred in Hong Kong, Steve Leung is a leading international architect, interior and product designer. His works reflect the projects' unique characters with his contemporary touch, taking inspirations from Asian culture and arts. Honoured as the Winner of 19th Andrew Martin International Interior Designer of the Year Award, his projects have been credited with more than 130 international corporate and design awards. He established his own architectural and urban planning consultancy in 1987, later restructured into Steve Leung Architects Ltd. (SLA) and Steve Leung Designers Ltd. (SLD). In 2018, SLD Group was listed on the Main Board of the Hong Kong Stock Exchange. Headquartered in Hong Kong with five branches in Beijing, Shanghai, Guangzhou, Shenzhen and Tianjin and with 600 dedicated designers and professionals, the Group is one of the largest interior design practices in Asia. Steve Leung is enthusiastically engaged in the design industry as the current President of the International Federation of Interior Architects/Designers (IFI) and as one of the founders of "C-Foundation", committed in actively promoting the development of the design profession in Asia and worldwide.

Steve Leung, in Hongkong geboren und aufgewachsen, ist ein führender internationaler Architekt, Innenarchitekt und Produktdesigner. Seine Arbeit spiegelt die einzigartigen Eigenschaften der Projekte wider und gibt ihnen einen zeitgemäßen Schliff, der von fernöstlicher Kultur und Kunst inspiriert ist. Steve Leung ist Gewinner des 19. Andrew Martin International Interior of the Year Award und wurde fernerhin mit mehr als 130 weiteren internationalen Unternehmens- und Designauszeichnungen gekürt. Er gründete 1987 seine eigene Beratungsagentur für Architektur und Städtebau und strukturierte sie später in Steve Leung Architects Ltd. (SLA) und Steve Leung Designers Ltd. (SLD) um. 2018 wurde die SLD Group im Hauptsegment an der Hongkonger Börse notiert. Mit Hauptsitz in Hongkong und fünf Niederlassungen in Beijing, Shanghai, Guangzhou, Shenzhen und Tianjin sowie 600 engagierten Designern und Fachleuten ist die Gruppe eines der größten Innenarchitekturbüros in Asien. Steve Leung engagiert sich mit Begeisterung in der Designindustrie – als der derzeitige Präsident der International Federation of Interior Architects/Designers (IFI) und als einer der Gründer der „C-Foundation", die aktiv zur Förderung des Designberufs in Asien und weltweit beiträgt.

01 Fusital – H377 Series SL Duemilasedici
The door handle collection in collaboration with Fusital is based on a contemporary minimalist design inspired by the bold geometry of Chinese traditional brass hardware and antique door lockset.

Die in Zusammenarbeit mit Fusital produzierte Türgriff-Kollektion basiert auf einem zeitgemäßen, minimalistischen Gestaltungskonzept, das seine Inspiration in der auffallenden Geometrie traditioneller chinesischer Messingwaren und antiker Türschlösser findet.

"I'm happy that by being a part of this jury, the passion and joy of creation can be passed on to many more designers, globally."

„Ich freue mich, dass ich als Mitglied der Jury die Gelegenheit habe, die Leidenschaft und die Freude am Gestalten an viele weitere Designer zu vermitteln, und das international."

What was the deciding moment of your career?
It was establishing my own studio at 30 and restructuring it to do both architecture and interior design in 1997. I started developing business in Mainland China three years after. It was a life changing moment and I'm thankful that it created interesting and rewarding chapters in the years after.

Are there noticeable differences between customers with different backgrounds?
Clients have different needs and preferences and are influenced by distinctive cultural and lifestyle features. But eventually design is about life, and life is about people, living and experience. In the end, original ideas that respond to people's fundamental needs functionally and more so psychologically will be the most sought-after designs, inspiring a positive change in daily life.

Was war der entscheidende Moment Ihrer Karriere?
Es war die Gründung meines eigenen Studios im Alter von 30 Jahren und dann in 1997 die Umstellung auf sowohl Architektur als auch Innenarchitektur. Drei Jahre später habe ich damit begonnen, das Geschäft in Festlandchina aufzubauen. Es war der Punkt, an dem sich mein Leben verändert hat, und ich bin dankbar dafür, dass es mir in den Jahren danach noch interessante und bereichernde Kapitel beschert hat.

Erkennen Sie Unterschiede zwischen Kunden verschiedener Herkunft?
Kunden haben unterschiedliche Bedürfnisse und Vorlieben und werden von ihren verschiedenen kulturellen Eigenheiten und Lebensformen beeinflusst. Letztlich befasst sich Design aber mit dem Leben und im Leben geht es um Menschen – darum, wie sie leben, und um die Erlebnisse, die sie haben. Am Ende werden originelle Ideen, die funktional und besonders psychologisch auf die grundlegenden Bedürfnisse von Menschen eingehen, die begehrtesten Gestaltungen sein und einen positiven Wandel im Alltag bewirken.

Dr. Thomas Lockwood
USA

Dr. Thomas Lockwood is co-author of the books "Innovation by Design" (2017) and "The Handbook of Design Management" (2011) as well as author of "Design Thinking" (2009), "Corporate Creativity" (2009), and "Building Design Strategy" (2008). He received a PhD, an MPhil and an MBA in Design Management after a BA in Business and Design. Thomas Lockwood is recognised as a thought leader at integrating design and innovation practice into business, and building great design and UX organisations. In 2011, he formed Lockwood Resource, an international consulting and recruiting firm specialising in design and innovation leadership. Previously, he was president of the Design Management Institute (DMI) from 2005 to 2011, a visiting professor at Pratt University, and from 1996 to 2005 a corporate design director at Sun Microsystems and StorageTek, among others. He created high-tech skiwear for the US Olympic Nordic Ski Team, corporate design programmes for Fortune 500 organisations and internationally led conferences and workshops.

Dr. Thomas Lockwood ist Co-Autor der Bücher „Innovation by Design" (2017) und „The Handbook of Design Management" (2011) sowie Autor von „Design Thinking" (2009), „Corporate Creativity" (2009) und „Building Design Strategy" (2008). Nach einem Bachelorabschluss in Unternehmensdesign und Gestaltung machte er seinen MPhil und MBA und promovierte in Designmanagement. Thomas Lockwood gilt als ein Vordenker für die Integration von Design und Innovation in der Wirtschaft und für den Aufbau starker Design- und UX-Unternehmen. 2011 gründete er Lockwood Resource, eine internationale Beratungs- und Personalvermittlungsfirma, die sich auf Design und Innovationsführerschaft spezialisiert hat. Zuvor war er u. a. Präsident des Design Management Institute (DMI) von 2005 bis 2011, Gastprofessor an der Pratt University sowie von 1996 bis 2005 Corporate Design Director bei Sun Microsystems und StorageTek. Er entwickelte Hightech-Skibekleidung für das Olympic Nordic Ski Team der USA sowie Corporate-Design-Programme für Fortune-500-Unternehmen und leitete internationale Kongresse und Workshops.

01 Innovation by Design
"Innovation by Design" explores the integration of innovation, design and corporate culture, and presents the ten ways leaders can develop cultures of innovation.
„Innovation by Design" erforscht die Integration von Innovation, Design und Unternehmenskultur und präsentiert die zehn Wege, mit denen Führungskräfte eine Kultur der Innovation aufbauen können.

02 Design Thinking
"DesignThinking" explores points of view, techniques, methods, and hands-on case studies from international thought leaders.
„DesignThinking" untersucht die Blickweise, Kniffe, Methoden und praktischen Fallstudien internationaler Vordenker.

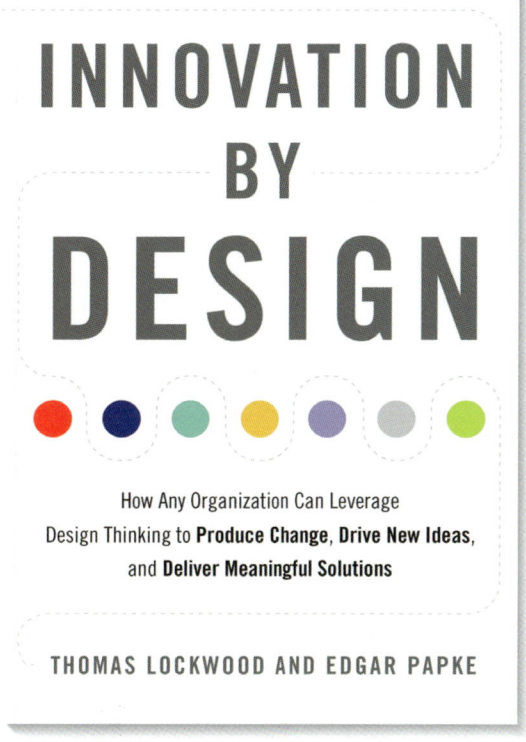

01

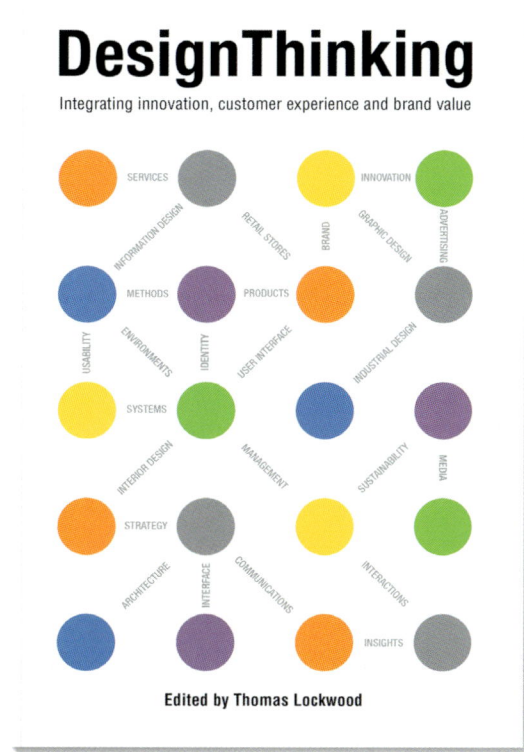

02

"Good design solves problems perfectly."
„Gutes Design löst Probleme perfekt."

In your opinion, what would the world look like without innovation?
It would probably look more like the animal kingdom. It is impossible to know what animals think, but as an outsider, I would imagine them to be more content, more peaceful and more observant. Innovation is what advances our societies.

How can a company become an innovation leader in its sector?
By reaching beyond technology innovation and embracing a strategy of open innovation. This requires a shift in focus from sales and what a company can make to a focus on what people actually need. The path means embracing design thinking and human centred design, in order to solve the right problems.

What development could significantly improve our world?
An app to create world peace! Truly, if we all could all just accept one another as we are, rather than imposing our doctrines and individual agendas upon others.

Wie sähe eine Welt ohne Innovation Ihrer Meinung nach aus?
Sie würde wahrscheinlich mehr dem Tierreich ähneln. Es ist unmöglich zu wissen, was Tiere denken, doch als Außenstehender stelle ich mir vor, dass sie zufriedener, ruhiger und aufmerksamer sind. Innovation ist der Motor, der unsere Gesellschaften vorantreibt.

Wie wird man als Unternehmen zum Innovationsführer seiner Branche?
Indem man mehr als nur technische Innovation erzielt und sich eine Strategie der offenen Innovation zu eigen macht. Das erfordert eine Verlagerung des Schwerpunktes weg vom Vertrieb und dem, was ein Unternehmen herstellen kann, hin zu dem, was Menschen wirklich brauchen. Das erreicht man, wenn man auf Designdenken und eine menschenorientierte Gestaltung umstellt, um so die richtigen Probleme zu lösen.

Welche Entwicklung könnte unsere Welt maßgeblich verbessern?
Eine App, die Weltfrieden schafft! Ehrlich, wenn wir einander nur alle akzeptieren könnten, so wie wir sind, anstatt einander unsere Dogmen und persönlichen Einstellungen aufzudrücken.

Wolfgang K. Meyer-Hayoz
Switzerland
Schweiz

Wolfgang K. Meyer-Hayoz studied mechanical engineering, visual communication and industrial design and graduated from the Stuttgart State Academy of Art and Design. After a number of years as an in-house designer in industry, he founded the Meyer-Hayoz Design Engineering Group in 1985. The multiple award-winning company works in the fields of medical engineering, biotechnology, life sciences as well as on the design of machines, robots and other appliances. The company also advises start-ups as well as multinationals in the areas of design strategy, industrial design, user-interface design, temporary architecture and communication design. From 1987 to 1993, Wolfgang K. Meyer-Hayoz was honorary president of the Swiss Design Association (SDA). He serves as jury member on international design panels and is a member of the Association of German Industrial Designers (VDID) and the Swiss Management Society (SMG). In addition, he is a member of the group of supporters for the Institute of Marketing at the University of St. Gallen and chairs change management and turnaround projects in the field of design strategy.

Wolfgang K. Meyer-Hayoz absolvierte Studien in Maschinenbau, Visueller Kommunikation sowie Industrial Design mit Abschluss an der Staatlichen Akademie der Bildenden Künste in Stuttgart. Nach Jahren als Inhouse-Designer in der Industrie gründete er 1985 die Meyer-Hayoz Design Engineering Group. Das vielfach international ausgezeichnete Unternehmen ist in Medizintechnik, Biotechnologie, Life Sciences sowie Maschinen-, Robotik- und Gerätedesign tätig und berät Start-up-Unternehmen ebenso wie Weltmarktführer in den Kompetenzbereichen Design Strategy, Industrial Design, User Interface Design, Temporary Architecture und Communication Design. Von 1987 bis 1993 führte Wolfgang K. Meyer-Hayoz ehrenamtlich als Präsident die Swiss Design Association (SDA). Er engagiert sich als Juror in internationalen Designgremien, ist Mitglied im Verband Deutscher Industrie Designer (VDID) und der Schweizerischen Management Gesellschaft (SMG) sowie aktives Mitglied im Förderkreis des Instituts für Marketing der Universität St. Gallen und moderiert Change-Management- und Turnaround-Projekte im designstrategischen Bereich.

01 Multitron
Incubation shaker for the reliable and easy cultivation of micro-organisms and cell cultures, for Infors AG, Switzerland
Inkubationsschüttler für die zuverlässige und komfortable Kultivierung von Mikroorganismen und Zellkulturen, für Infors AG, Schweiz

02 ICM 710/PCM 710
Range of compact control units for burglar alarms, for Securiton AG, Switzerland
Kompakte Bediengeräteserie für Einbruchmeldeanlagen, für Securiton AG, Schweiz

01

02

"It takes time, conviction and mutual esteem to develop a strategic direction for companies through design – our customers need to understand that design services cannot be produced quickly like in a pressure cooker."

„Die strategische Ausrichtung von Unternehmen durch gestalterische Arbeit benötigt Zeit, Überzeugung und stets die gegenseitige Wertschätzung – unsere Kunden müssen also verstehen, dass Designleistungen nicht wie aus einem Schnellkochtopf zu haben sind."

How do you keep reinventing yourself as a designer?
I have always been an inquisitive person. New materials, technologies, possibilities for the use of things and their application to new business models have always fascinated and motivated me to think a step further in the spirit of anticipation.

Where do you find the energy for your impressive commitment to your profession?
I am convinced that designers have a very fine and pronounced sense of intuition so that they notice changes and upheavals in society early on. The awareness and recognition of these changes gives us designers the unique opportunity to develop new solutions, first conceptually and later physically. For me, this process is a "source of energy".

What makes your work so exciting?
Every job is new and different. Every customer has their own specific requests and every company champions new values and value propositions in its own way. It never gets boring!

Wie erfinden Sie sich als Designer immer wieder neu?
Ich war schon immer ein sehr neugieriger Mensch. Neue Materialien, Technologien, Nutzungsmöglichkeiten und deren Anwendung für neue Geschäftsmodelle haben mich immer fasziniert und angespornt, noch einen Schritt weiter zu denken, im Sinne der Antizipation.

Woher schöpfen Sie die Energie für Ihr großes berufliches Engagement?
Ich bin überzeugt, dass Gestalter ein sehr feines und ausgeprägtes Gespür haben und daher Veränderungen und Umbrüche in unserer Gesellschaft früh wahrnehmen. Das Bewusstsein und Erkennen dieser Veränderungen gibt uns als Gestaltern gleichzeitig die einzigartige Chance, hieraus neue Lösungsansätze erst gedanklich und dann physisch zu entwickeln. Diesen Prozess empfinde ich als permanenten „Energiespender".

Was macht Ihren Beruf so spannend?
Jede Aufgabe ist neu und anders. Jeder Kunde hat seine spezifischen Wünsche und jedes Unternehmen vertritt auf seine Weise immer wieder neue Werte und Wertvorstellungen. Langeweile kommt hierdurch nie auf!

Prof. Jure Miklavc
Slovenia
Slowenien

Professor Jure Miklavc graduated in industrial design from the Academy of Fine Arts in Ljubljana, Slovenia, and has nearly 20 years of experience in the field of design. He started his career working as a freelance designer, before founding his own design consultancy, Studio Miklavc. Studio Miklavc works in the fields of product design, visual communications and brand development and is a consultancy for a variety of clients from the industries of light design, electronic goods, user interfaces, transport design and medical equipment. Sports equipment designed by the studio has gained worldwide recognition. From 2013 onwards, the team has been working for the prestigious Italian motorbike manufacturer Bimota. Designs by Studio Miklavc have received many international awards and have been displayed in numerous exhibitions. Jure Miklavc has been involved in design education since 2005 and is currently a lecturer and head of industrial design at the Academy of Fine Arts and Design in Ljubljana.

Professor Jure Miklavc machte seinen Abschluss in Industrial Design an der Academy of Fine Arts and Design in Ljubljana, Slowenien, und verfügt über nahezu 20 Jahre Erfahrung im Designbereich. Er arbeitete zunächst als freiberuflicher Designer, bevor er sein eigenes Design-Beratungsunternehmen „Studio Miklavc" gründete. Studio Miklavc ist in den Bereichen Produktdesign, Visuelle Kommunikation und Markenentwicklung sowie in der Beratung zahlreicher Kunden der Branchen Lichtdesign, Elektronische Güter, Benutzeroberflächen, Transport-Design und Medizinisches Equipment tätig. Die von dem Studio gestalteten Sportausrüstungen erfahren weltweit Anerkennung. Seit 2013 arbeitet das Team für den angesehenen italienischen Motorradhersteller Bimota. Studio Miklavc erhielt bereits zahlreiche Auszeichnungen sowie Präsentationen in Ausstellungen. Seit 2005 ist Jure Miklavc in der Designlehre tätig und aktuell Dozent und Head of Industrial Design an der Academy of Fine Arts and Design in Ljubljana.

01 Carefoot
Integral project of building a brand, corporate identity, products and communication for children's shoes by Austrian company Alpvent. The solution incorporates a convenient size measuring system with an app.

Umfassendes Projekt für den Aufbau der Marke, Corporate Identity, Produkte und Kommunikation der Kinderschuhe der österreichischen Firma Alpvent. Die Lösung schließt ein praktisches App-basiertes Messsystem für Schuhgrößen ein.

01

"I hope that in ten years, product design will be more involved with the real solutions for environmental problems. Designers will also be more connected to the field of robotics and artificial intelligence."

„Ich hoffe, dass sich das Produktdesign in zehn Jahren mehr mit den wirklichen Lösungen für Umweltprobleme auseinandersetzt. Designer werden sich auch mehr mit dem Bereich der Robotertechnik und künstlichen Intelligenz befassen."

What constitutes good design?
Good design is usually a consequence of emotional intelligence and transforms technical innovation in a way that is understandable, pleasant and enjoyable for the user and is not invasive for the environment. Good design is also more than just a summary of different parameters – in the best scenarios it influences us in such a way that it changes the way in which we live to the positive.

What distinguishes your design "signature"?
My design signature is more about the process and approach rather than some typical formal language. I believe in design viewed in context. In that respect I would say that "empathy" is the focus of my work – towards users, environment, technology and identity.

What message would you like to give young designers for their future careers?
I would want to encourage them to be extra curious and sensitive to real needs and to the environment.

Was macht gutes Design aus?
Gutes Design ist generell das Ergebnis emotionaler Intelligenz und verwandelt technische Innovation derart, dass sie für den Nutzer verständlich, angenehm und erfreulich ist, ohne die Umwelt zu belasten. Gutes Design ist auch mehr als die Summe verschiedener Parameter. In den besten Fällen beeinflusst es uns dahingehend, dass es unser Leben positiv verändert.

Was kennzeichnet Ihre gestalterische Handschrift?
Meine gestalterische Handschrift findet sich eher in dem Prozess und Ansatz als in einer charakteristischen Formensprache wieder. Ich glaube an eine Gestaltung, die im Kontext betrachtet werden sollte. In dieser Hinsicht würde ich sagen, dass „Empathie" im Fokus meiner Arbeit steht – Empathie für Nutzer, die Umwelt, Technik und Identität.

Welche Botschaft möchten Sie jungen Designern mit auf den Weg geben?
Ich würde sie dazu ermutigen, besonders neugierig zu sein – und sensibel für echte Bedürfnisse und die Umwelt.

Adriana Monk
Switzerland
Schweiz

Adriana Monk studied product design at the Art Center College of Design in La Tour-de-Peilz, Switzerland, and graduated from Pasadena, USA, beginning her career at the BMW Group Designworks/USA. She subsequently established herself as the automotive industry's leading interior designer for luxury brands such as Rolls-Royce, Jaguar and Land Rover, before pursuing her passion for yachts. In 2008, she founded Monk Design in Switzerland. The agency's focus is on boat interiors, exclusive detailing and graphic design for performance yachts, for both private clients and boats produced in series. With a balanced sense of proportions and aesthetics, Adriana Monk produces new creative solutions. Her work has won several international awards including the World Superyacht Award, Red Dot, iF and the Eurobike Design Award. She is a guest lecturer at the Royal College of Art in London and at the International University of Monaco and also a jury member at competitions like the Design & Innovation Awards of Boat International.

Adriana Monk studierte Produktdesign am Art Center College of Design in La Tour-de-Peilz, Schweiz, und machte ihren Abschluss in Pasadena, USA, bevor sie ihre Karriere bei BMW Group Designworks/USA startete. Anschließend etablierte sie sich als führende Innenarchitektin der Automobilbranche für Luxusmarken wie Rolls-Royce, Jaguar und Land Rover, bevor sie ihrer Leidenschaft für Yachten nachging. 2008 gründete sie Monk Design in der Schweiz. Der Schwerpunkt liegt auf Boot-Interieurs, exklusiven Detailausführungen und Grafikdesign für Performance-Yachten, sowohl für Privatkunden als auch für Serienboote. Mit einem ausgewogenen Sinn für Proportionen und Ästhetik gelangt Adriana Monk zu neuen, kreativen Lösungen. Ihre Arbeit wurde mehrfach international ausgezeichnet, u. a. mit dem World Superyacht Award, Red Dot, iF und dem Eurobike Design Award. Sie ist als Gastdozentin am Royal College of Art in London und der International University of Monaco sowie als Jurorin z. B. des Design & Innovation Awards von Boat International tätig.

01 monk-e-shine lamp, model L1180
Low-voltage reading lamp specifically designed for yachts, produced by Palagi Marine Lights, Italy. The double rotation axis allows for a very wide range of light direction. Clean design with no visible fixings.
Speziell für den Bootsbau gestaltete Niedervolt-Leseleuchte, hergestellt von Palagi Marine Lights, Italien. Dank der 2-Achsen-Rotation ist die Beleuchtungsmöglichkeit sehr groß. Montage ohne sichtbare Schrauben.

01

"Honesty, purity and simplicity are words that resonate with my design discipline. I believe that a design will stand the test of time if it is not only functional but also aesthetically pleasing."

„Ehrlichkeit, Reinheit und Schlichtheit sind Worte, die mit meiner Auffassung von Gestaltung in Einklang stehen. Ich glaube, dass eine Gestaltung nur dann überdauert, wenn sie sowohl funktional als auch ästhetisch überzeugt."

To what do you attach particular importance when judging products?
Judging other people's work is an honour and a very demanding task. By reading the documentation I assess if the design brief has been respected, and whether the product is unique and innovative. By using and handling the products I look for beauty and function as well as quality and the intuitive operation of the product.

Why did you decide to leave the automotive industry and pursue your passion for yachts?
After ten years designing automotive interiors for various luxury brands, I wanted to challenge my creativity. Yachts have always fascinated me: sculptural forms that glide through water. I was awestruck when I first saw a 100-foot carbon-fibre hull. I then proceeded to study naval architecture and get my sailing licence before pursuing my dream: working for Wally Yachts was the stepping stone to leave the automotive industry and open my own design studio, following my passion for yachts.

Worauf legen Sie bei der Bewertung von Produkten besonderen Wert?
Das Werk anderer beurteilen zu dürfen, ist eine Ehre und eine sehr anspruchsvolle Aufgabe. Beim Lesen der Unterlagen bewerte ich, ob die Designvorgaben respektiert wurden und ob das Produkt einzigartig und innovativ ist. Beim Benutzen und Handhaben der Produkte achte ich auf Schönheit und Funktion sowie auf Qualität und die intuitive Bedienung des Produkts.

Warum haben Sie sich dazu entschieden, die Automobilbranche zu verlassen und Ihrer Leidenschaft für Yachten nachzugehen?
Nach zehn Jahren der Gestaltung von Innenräumen für Fahrzeuge verschiedener Luxusmarken wollte ich etwas für meine Kreativität tun. Yachten haben mich schon immer fasziniert: skulpturale Formen, die durch Wasser gleiten. Als ich das erste Mal einen 100-Fuß-Schiffsrumpf aus Kohlefaser sah, war ich sprachlos. Ich habe dann erst Schiffbau studiert und einen Segelschein gemacht, bevor ich meinen Traum verwirklichen konnte: Für Wally Yachts zu arbeiten, war das Sprungbrett für den Abschied aus der Automobilbranche und erlaubte mir, meiner Leidenschaft für Yachten zu folgen und mein eigenes Designstudio aufzubauen.

Prof. Dr. Ken Nah
Korea

Professor Dr. Ken Nah graduated with a Bachelor of Science in Industrial Engineering from Hanyang University, South Korea, in 1983. He deepened his interest in Human Factors/Ergonomics by earning a master's degree from Korea Advanced Institute for Science and Technology (KAIST) in 1985. He received a Ph.D. in Engineering Design from Tufts University, Boston, in 1996. Ken Nah is also a USA Certified Professional Ergonomist (CPE), for the first time as a Korean. He is currently a professor of Design at the International Design School for Advanced Studies (IDAS), Hongik University in Seoul as well as director of the Human Experience and Emotion Research (HE.ER) Lab. Since 2002 he has been the director of the International Design Trend Center (IDTC). Ken Nah was the director general of "World Design Capital Seoul 2010". Alongside his work as a professor, he is also the senior vice-president of the Korea Federation of Design Associations (KFDA) and the Korea Association of Industrial Designers (KAID). Ken Nah has been an advisor on design policy to several ministries of the Korean government since 2000.

Professor Dr. Ken Nah graduierte 1983 an der Hanyang University in Südkorea als Bachelor of Science in Industrial Engineering. Sein Interesse an Human Factors/Ergonomie vertiefte er 1985 mit einem Masterabschluss am Korea Advanced Institute for Science and Technology (KAIST). 1996 promovierte er im Bereich „Konstruktive Gestaltung" an der Tufts University in Boston. Darüber hinaus ist Ken Nah ein in den USA zertifizierter Ergonom (CPE). Derzeit ist er Professor für Design an der International Design School for Advanced Studies (IDAS) der Hongik University in Seoul sowie Direktor des „Human Experience and Emotion Research (HE.ER)"-Labors. Seit 2002 ist er zudem Leiter des International Design Trend Centers (IDTC). Ken Nah war Generaldirektor der „World Design Capital Seoul 2010". Neben seiner Lehrtätigkeit als Professor ist er Senior-Vizepräsident der Korea Federation of Design Associations (KFDA) und der Korea Association of Industrial Designers (KAID). Seit 2000 ist Ken Nah ferner als Berater in Designpolitik für verschiedene Ministerien der koreanischen Regierung tätig.

01 SHAPL Dr. Nah Series 1
Luggage and backpack set
Koffer- und Rucksackset

01

"One trend I have noticed in current design is a seamless assimilation of 'smartness' in products to achieve maximum ease and convenience for users."

„Ein Trend, der mir im aktuellen Design aufgefallen ist, ist die nahtlose Integration von ‚Intelligenz' in Produkte, um Nutzern maximalen Komfort und Anwenderfreundlichkeit zu bieten."

What constitutes an ergonomic product?
Ergonomics, or more appropriately, Human Factors, is defined as a human-centred design discipline seeking for an optimal solution for human users in their working and living environment. Therefore, a product design based on human factors should be easy, convenient, safe, and pleasant to use physically, physiologically, and psychologically and meet emotional wants as well.

How will the product design discipline develop over the ten years to come?
I guess the next ten years will be the most turbulent years for any discipline including design due to big data, AI and convergence. Design should quickly adapt the technology, especially for generative design and engineering analysis, not to mention marketing and business. In a nutshell, design as a discipline will at the same time become general on one hand and very specific on the other hand, which will make it the most challenging and exciting area.

Was macht ein ergonomisches Produkt aus?
Ergonomie oder besser gesagt die Arbeitswissenschaft wird als eine am Menschen orientierte Gestaltungsdisziplin definiert, die versucht, eine optimale Lösung für menschliche Nutzer in ihrem Arbeits- und Lebensumfeld zu entwickeln. Daher sollte ein Produktdesign, das auf Arbeitswissenschaft beruht, einfach, komfortabel, sicher und physisch, physiologisch und psychologisch angenehm zu benutzen sein. Gleichzeitig sollte es auch emotionale Bedürfnisse erfüllen.

Wie wird sich das Produktdesign in den kommenden zehn Jahren entwickeln?
Ich tippe darauf, dass die nächsten zehn Jahre die turbulentesten Jahre in jedem Sektor sein werden, auch in der Gestaltung; und das aufgrund von Big Data, KI und Konvergenz. Design sollte die neue Technologie schnell anwenden und anpassen, besonders für generatives Design und technische Analysen, mal ganz abgesehen von Marketing und der Geschäftswelt. Kurz und gut: Design als Disziplin wird auf der einen Seite sehr allgemein werden und auf der anderen sehr spezifisch, wodurch es zu dem spannendsten, aber auch anspruchsvollsten Sektor werden wird.

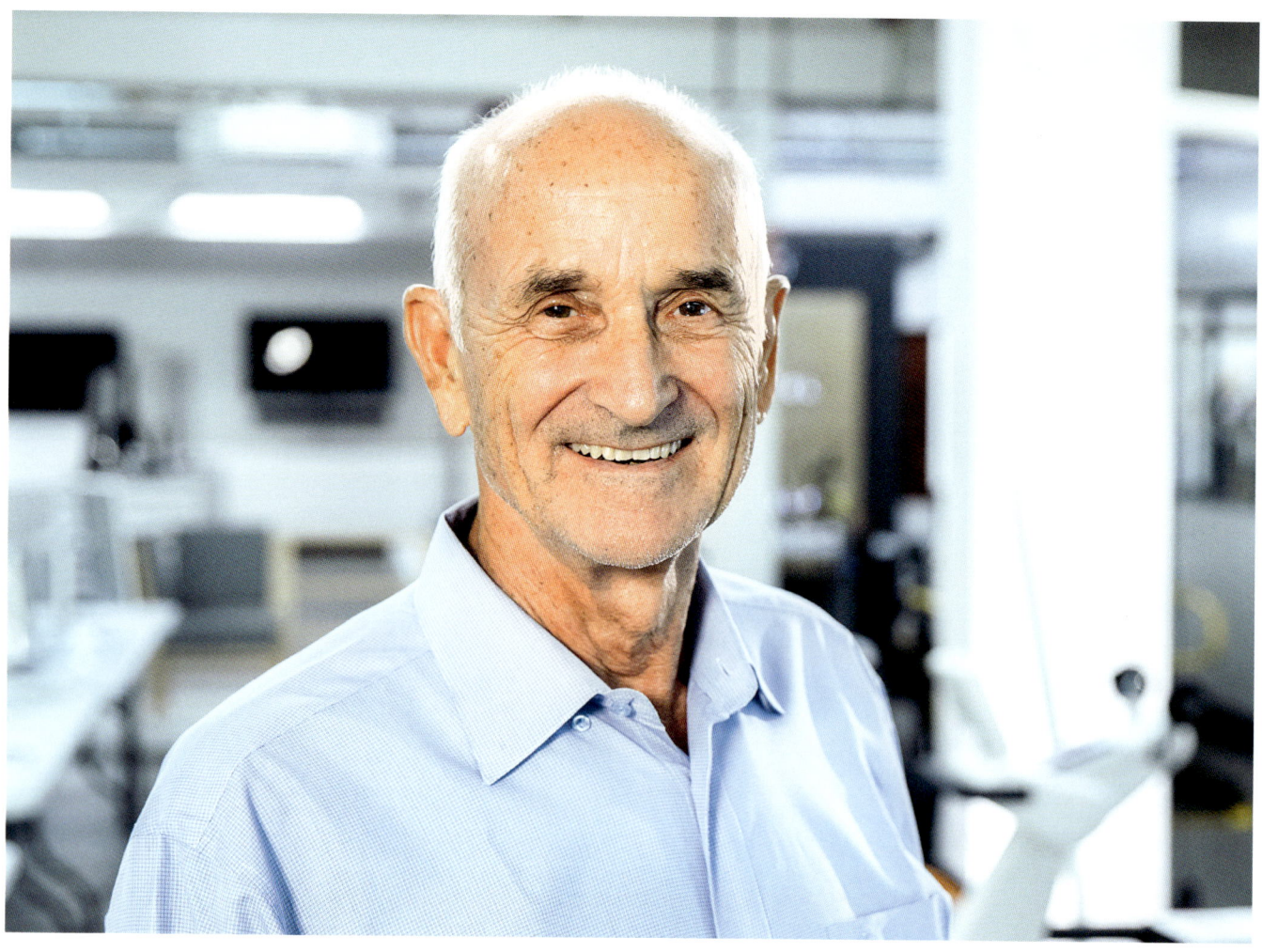

Alexander Neumeister
Germany/Brazil
Deutschland/Brasilien

Alexander Neumeister is a high-tech industrial designer, who lives both in Germany and Brazil. A graduate of the Ulm School of Design and a one-year scholarship student at the Tokyo University of Arts, he specialised in the fields of medicine, professional electronics and transportation. Among some of his best-known works are the "Transrapid" maglev trains, the German ICE trains, the Japanese Shinkansen "Nozomi 500", as well as numerous regional trains and subways for Japan, China and Brazil, and the C1 and C2 trains for the Munich underground. Aside from working on projects for large German companies, he was design consultant for Hitachi/Japan for 21 years. From 1983 to 1987, he was board member and later vice-president of the World Design Organization (formerly Icsid). In 1992, Alexander Neumeister and his team received the honorary title "Red Dot: Design Team of the Year". In 2011, he was awarded the design prize of the city of Munich and in 2015, he won the EU's "European Railway Award" in recognition of his contribution to railway design.

Alexander Neumeister arbeitet als Hightech-Industriedesigner und ist in Deutschland wie in Brasilien zu Hause. Als Absolvent der Hochschule für Gestaltung in Ulm und Stipendiat der Tokyo University of Arts für ein Jahr spezialisierte er sich auf die Bereiche Medizin, Professionelle Elektronik und Verkehr. Die Magnetschwebebahn „Transrapid", die deutschen ICE-Züge, der japanische Shinkansen „Nozomi 500", aber auch zahlreiche Regionalzüge und U-Bahnen in Japan, China und Brasilien sowie die U-Bahnen C1 und C2 für München zählen zu seinen bekanntesten Entwürfen. Neben Projekten für deutsche Großunternehmen war er 21 Jahre lang Designberater für Hitachi/Japan. Von 1983 bis 1987 war er Vorstandsmitglied und später Vizepräsident der World Design Organization (ehemals Icsid). 1992 wurden Alexander Neumeister und sein Team mit dem Ehrentitel „Red Dot: Design Team of the Year" ausgezeichnet. 2011 erhielt er den Designpreis der Landeshauptstadt München und 2015 den „European Railway Award" der EU für seine Leistungen auf dem Gebiet des Railway-Designs.

01 Series 800
Train project for Great Western Railways in the UK, where it went into operation 2017. This train works with bimodal propulsion and is driven by both electric and diesel engine power. Depending on the situation, it can be switched from one method of propulsion to the other.
Zugprojekt für die Great Western Railways im Vereinigten Königreich, wo es 2017 in Betrieb genommen wurde. Der Zug hat einen bimodalen Antrieb mit Elektro- und Dieselmotor. Je nach Situation kann er auf den einen oder anderen Antrieb umgeschaltet werden.

01

"In my opinion, good design is the successful combination of materials and function, but it also includes the ability to adapt to different environments and the exclusion of superfluous decorations."

„Gutes Design ist für mich die gelungene Kombination von Materialaufwand und Funktion. Aber auch der Verzicht auf unnötige Dekoration und die Fähigkeit, sich in Umgebungen einzuordnen."

You were responsible for the design of the ICE. What does it feel like to site in the flagship of the Deutsche Bahn?
I designed both the ICE concept train, as well as the ICE-3. My team and I created open seating areas for the design with compartments at the end of one of the carriages – with minimally greater distances between the seats in first class. The design work on the train began in 1996 and now, more than 20 years later, I still enjoy travelling in "my ICE-3". The interior has lost none of its elegance.

What would you still like to achieve professionally?
At over 75, I asked myself how many more trains I still want to design in order to be satisfied. I decided to hand my shares over to my partner and to leave N+P Industrial Design. In Germany, I still advise a former colleague, who works as a freelancer in Munich, and in Brazil I work for two companies in the electronics sector. I have never regretted the decision to step back a bit.

Sie waren für das Design des ICEs verantwortlich. Wie fühlt es sich an, in dem Flaggschiff der Deutschen Bahn zu sitzen?
Ich habe sowohl den ICE-Versuchszug wie auch den ICE-3 gestaltet. Für das Design haben mein Team und ich offene Sitzlandschaften geschaffen mit Abteilen am Ende eines Waggons – für die erste Klasse mit geringfügig größeren Sitzabständen. Das Design startete 1996 und nun, mehr als 20 Jahre danach, macht es mir immer noch Spaß, in „meinem ICE-3" zu reisen. Der Innenraum hat nichts von seiner Eleganz eingebüßt.

Was möchten Sie beruflich noch erreichen?
Mit über 75 Jahren stellte ich mir die Frage, wie viele Züge ich noch gestalten wollte, um zufrieden zu sein. Ich entschloss mich, meine Anteile an meine Partner abzugeben und aus N+P Industrial Design auszusteigen. In Deutschland berate ich noch einen ehemaligen Mitarbeiter, der sich in München selbständig gemacht hat, und in Brasilien arbeite ich für zwei Unternehmen im Elektronikbereich. Die Entscheidung, das alles zu reduzieren, habe ich nie bereut.

Ken Okuyama
Japan

Ken Kiyoyuki Okuyama, industrial designer and CEO of Ken Okuyama Design, was born in 1959 in Yamagata, Japan, and studied automobile design at the Art Center College of Design in Pasadena, California. He has worked as a chief designer for General Motors, as a senior designer for Porsche AG, and as design director for Pininfarina S.p.A., being responsible for the design of Ferrari Enzo, Maserati Quattroporte and many other automobiles. He is also known for many different product designs such as motorcycles, furniture, robots and architecture. Ken Okuyama Design was founded in 2007 and provides business consultancy services to numerous corporations. Ken Okuyama also produces cars, eyewear and interior products under his original brand. He is currently a visiting professor at several universities and also frequently publishes books.

Ken Kiyoyuki Okuyama, Industriedesigner und CEO von Ken Okuyama Design, wurde 1959 in Yamagata, Japan, geboren und studierte Automobildesign am Art Center College of Design in Pasadena, Kalifornien. Er war als Chief Designer bei General Motors, als Senior Designer bei der Porsche AG und als Design Director bei Pininfarina S.p.A. tätig und zeichnete verantwortlich für den Ferrari Enzo, den Maserati Quattroporte und viele weitere Automobile. Zudem ist er für viele unterschiedliche Produktgestaltungen wie Motorräder, Möbel, Roboter und Architektur bekannt. Ken Okuyama Design wurde 2007 als Beratungsunternehmen gegründet und arbeitet für zahlreiche Unternehmen. Ken Okuyama produziert unter seiner originären Marke auch Autos, Brillen und Inneneinrichtungsgegenstände. Derzeit lehrt er als Gastprofessor an verschiedenen Universitäten und publiziert zudem Bücher.

01 JR EAST
"Train suite Shiki-Shima"

01

"I always seek, sketch and write way before the job comes in. My hands show me the way, like a fortune teller."

„Lange bevor der Auftrag kommt, bin ich ständig auf der Suche, skizziere und schreibe. Meine Hände weisen mir den Weg, genau wie bei einem Wahrsager."

What was the development process for the Ferrari Enzo like?
Single talent doesn't make a good car. It was a miracle to gather spirited geniuses like Luca Cordero di Montezemolo and Sergio Pininfarina and to be part of the team as a designer at the very end of the last century. It will never happen again.

What advice do you most frequently give to customers?
I am a "chef" for a good design. I put up a menu, customers come, we talk, and I give a lot more than they expected with a good surprise.

What do you like about your role as consultant?
Together with the top management, we define a future vision and solutions to get there, sharing confidentiality. For that reason, we only work with one company in each industry. It's like being a family.

Wie sah der Entwicklungsprozess des Ferrari Enzo aus?
Einzelne Talente machen kein gutes Auto. Es war ein Wunder Ende des letzten Jahrhunderts, dass wir sprühende Genies wie Luca Cordero di Montezemolo und Sergio Pininfarina gewinnen konnten – und für mich als Designer, Teil des Teams sein zu können. Das wird nie wieder geschehen.

Welchen Tipp geben Sie Ihren Kunden am häufigsten?
Ich bin der „Koch" für eine gute Gestaltung. Ich stelle ein Menü zusammen, die Kunden kommen, wir reden und ich gebe ihnen sehr viel mehr als sie erwarteten, noch dazu mit einer guten Überraschung.

Was gefällt Ihnen an der Tätigkeit als Berater?
Gemeinsam mit dem Topmanagement definieren wir eine Vision für die Zukunft und die Lösungen, die uns dahinbringen werden – in strengster Vertraulichkeit. Daher arbeiten wir in jeder Branche auch nur mit einem Unternehmen. Man fühlt sich als Teil der Familie.

Simon Ong
Singapore
Singapur

Simon Ong, born in Singapore in 1953, graduated with a master's degree in design from the University of New South Wales and an MBA from the University of South Australia. He is the deputy chairman and co-founder of Kingsmen Creatives Ltd., a leading communication design and production group with 21 offices across the Asia-Pacific region, the Middle East and North America. Kingsmen has won several awards, such as the President's Design Award, Singapore Good Design Mark, SRA Best Retail Concept Award, SFIA Hall of Fame, Promising Brand Award, A.R.E. Retail Design Award and RDI International Store Design Award USA. Simon Ong is actively involved in the creative industry as chairman of the design group of Manpower, the Skills & Training Council of Singapore Workforce Development Agency. Moreover, he is a member of the advisory board of the Design Business Chamber of Singapore and Singapore Furniture Industries Council (Design). Currently, Simon Ong is a board member of the Association of Retail Environments (USA), a board director of Nanyang Academy of Fine Arts and a member of the advisory board to the School of Design & Environment at the National University of Singapore.

Simon Ong, geboren 1953 in Singapur, erhielt einen Master in Design der University of New South Wales und einen Master of Business Administration der University of South Australia. Er ist stellvertretender Vorsitzender und Mitbegründer von Kingsmen Creatives Ltd., eines führenden Unternehmens für Kommunikationsdesign und Produktion mit 21 Geschäftsstellen im asiatisch-pazifischen Raum, dem Mittleren Osten und Nordamerika. Kingsmen wurde vielfach ausgezeichnet, u. a. mit dem President's Design Award, Singapore Good Design Mark, SRA Best Retail Concept Award, SFIA Hall of Fame, Promising Brand Award, A.R.E. Retail Design Award und RDI International Store Design Award USA. Simon Ong ist als Vorsitzender der Designgruppe von Manpower, der „Skills & Training Council of Singapore Workforce Development Agency", aktiv in die Kreativindustrie involviert. Zudem ist er Mitglied des Beirats der Design Business Chamber Singapore und des Singapore Furniture Industries Council (Design). Aktuell ist Simon Ong Vorstandsmitglied der Association of Retail Environments (USA), Vorstandsvorsitzender der Nanyang Academy of Fine Arts und Mitglied des Beirats der School of Design & Environment an der National University of Singapore.

**01 Twenty3
at Formula 1 2018 Singapore
Airlines Singapore Grand Prix**
Scintillating action from the race track can be caught from full-length windows at the restaurants at Twenty3.
Das fulminante Geschehen auf der Rennstrecke kann durch die raumhohen Fenster des Twenty3-Restaurants verfolgt werden.

01

"A product that surprises me has a standout design that is simple yet well-engineered, while marrying function and aesthetics. Most importantly, it needs to be intuitive for users."

„Um mich zu überraschen, muss ein Produkt ein herausragendes Design vorweisen, das sowohl einfach als auch ausgereift ist. Gleichzeitig sollte es Funktion und Ästhetik in Einklang bringen. Am wichtigsten ist, dass es intuitiv zu benutzen ist."

What are the hallmarks of good design?
Less is more. A well-designed product that resonates with its users will let them realise that their daily lives are made better by using it whether they knew they needed it or not in the first place.

How does a product become a classic?
This status has to be earned and not claimed. The product should be able to stand the test of time amidst the changing consumer mindset and an ever increasing digitally connected world. These are products that end up representing their own category and their design becomes reason enough for users to buy the product.

Do you have a tip for young designers?
Don't lose sight that it is about the user experience (UX). You need to understand who you are designing for and how they interact and experience the product; how they use it, and the relationship the users form with the product.

Was kennzeichnet gutes Design?
Weniger ist mehr. Ein gut gestaltetes Produkt, das mit seinen Nutzern im Einklang ist, wird ihnen zeigen, dass ihr Alltag durch seine Verwendung besser wird, auch wenn sie sich vorher gar nicht bewusst waren, dass sie es brauchten.

Wie wird ein Produkt zum Klassiker?
Dieser Status will verdient sein und kann nicht einfach beansprucht werden. Das Produkt sollte sich langfristig bewähren, trotz der ständig wechselnden Einstellung der Konsumenten und der zunehmend digital vernetzten Welt. Klassiker sind Produkte, die in einer Kategorie für sich stehen und deren Design Grund genug ist, sie zu kaufen.

Haben Sie einen Tipp für junge Designer?
Nie die Benutzererfahrung (UX) aus den Augen verlieren. Sie müssen wissen, für wen sie gestalten und wie ihre Zielgruppe mit dem Produkt umgeht und es erlebt; wie sie es benutzt und welche Beziehung sie zu dem Produkt entwickelt.

Dr. Sascha Peters
Germany
Deutschland

Dr. Sascha Peters is founder and owner of the agency for material and technology HAUTE INNOVATION in Berlin. He studied mechanical engineering at the RWTH Aachen University, Germany, and product design at the ABK Maastricht, Netherlands. He wrote his doctoral thesis at the University of Duisburg-Essen, Germany, on the complex of problems in communication between engineering and design. From 1997 to 2003, he led research projects and product developments at the Fraunhofer Institute for Production Technology IPT in Aachen and subsequently became deputy head of the Design Zentrum Bremen until 2008. Sascha Peters is author of various specialist books on sustainable raw materials, smart materials, innovative production techniques and energetic technologies. He is a leading material expert and trend scout for new technologies. Since 2014, he has been an advisory board member of the funding initiative "Zwanzig20 – Partnerschaft für Innovation" (2020 – Partnership for innovation) commissioned by the German Federal Ministry of Education and Research.

Dr. Sascha Peters ist Gründer und Inhaber der Material- und Technologieagentur HAUTE INNOVATION in Berlin. Er studierte Maschinenbau an der RWTH Aachen und Produktdesign an der ABK Maastricht. Seine Doktorarbeit schrieb er an der Universität Duisburg-Essen über die Kommunikationsproblematik zwischen Engineering und Design. Von 1997 bis 2003 leitete er Forschungsprojekte und Produktentwicklungen am Fraunhofer-Institut für Produktionstechnologie IPT in Aachen und war anschließend bis 2008 stellvertretender Leiter des Design Zentrums Bremen. Sascha Peters ist Autor zahlreicher Fachbücher zu nachhaltigen Werkstoffen, smarten Materialien, innovativen Fertigungsverfahren und energetischen Technologien und zählt zu den führenden Materialexperten und Trendscouts für neue Technologien. Seit 2014 ist er Mitglied im Beirat der Förderinitiative „Zwanzig20 – Partnerschaft für Innovation" im Auftrag des Bundesministeriums für Bildung und Forschung.

01
A special area about future food and 3D printing in the food industry on the occasion of "imm/LivingKitchen" trade fair in January 2019 in Cologne
Sonderfläche zu Future Food und 3D-Druck im Ernährungsbereich anlässlich der „imm/LivingKitchen"-Messe im Januar 2019 in Köln

"I believe the most exciting recent development to be 4D printing and the resulting potential for programmable materials. With the help of an exterior impulse, components can change their own shape."

„Der 4D-Druck und die damit zusammenhängenden Potenziale programmierbarer Materialien empfinde ich als die spannendste Entwicklung der letzten Jahre. Mithilfe eines äußeren Impulses können sich Bauteile damit selbsttätig verformen."

What are key activities of your HAUTE INNOVATION agency?

I founded HAUTE INNOVATION with the aim of speeding up the transfer of innovations in materials into marketable products. In the meantime, we have become established as a trend agency for future technologies. Our customers come from the automotive, furniture and construction industries.

What is your objective as a designer?

We don't work as classical designers, but rather carry out trend analyses for our customers and initiate innovation processes. To this end, we organise exhibitions on disruptive technology. For example, we were responsible for a special area at the "imm/LivingKitchen" trade fair in Cologne about future food and 3D printing in the food industry.

Was sind die wichtigsten Aktivitäten Ihrer Agentur HAUTE INNOVATION?

Ich habe HAUTE INNOVATION mit dem Ziel gegründet, Materialinnovationen schneller in marktfähige Produkte zu überführen. In der Zwischenzeit werden wir als Trendagentur für Zukunftstechnologien wahrgenommen und haben Kunden in der Automobil-, Möbel- und Bauindustrie.

Welches Ziel verfolgen Sie als Designer?

Wir arbeiten nicht als klassische Designer, sondern setzen für unsere Kunden Trendanalysen um und initiieren Innovationsprozesse. In diesem Zusammenhang gestalten wir Ausstellungen zu disruptiven Technologien. Hier haben wir zur „imm/LivingKitchen"-Messe in Köln beispielsweise eine Sonderfläche zu Future Food und 3D-Druck im Ernährungsbereich verantwortet.

Dirk Schumann
Germany
Deutschland

Dirk Schumann, born in 1960 in Soest, studied product design at Münster University of Applied Sciences. After graduating in 1987, he joined oco-design as an industrial designer, moved to siegerdesign in 1989, and was a lecturer in product design at Münster University of Applied Sciences until 1991. In 1992, he founded his own design studio "Schumanndesign" in Münster, developing design concepts for companies in Germany, Italy, India, Thailand and China. For several years now, he has focused on conceptual architecture, created visionary living spaces and held lectures at international conferences. Dirk Schumann has taken part in exhibitions both in Germany and abroad with works that have garnered several awards, including the Gold Prize (Minister of Economy, Trade and Industry Prize) in the International Design Competition, Osaka; the Comfort & Design Award, Milan; the iF product design award, Hanover; the Red Dot Design Award, Essen; the Focus in Gold, Stuttgart; as well as the Good Design Award, Chicago and Tokyo. In 2015, he founded Schumann&Wang in Xiamen City, the Chinese subsidiary of Schumanndesign.

Dirk Schumann, 1960 in Soest geboren, studierte Produktdesign an der Fachhochschule Münster. Nach seinem Abschluss 1987 arbeitete er als Industriedesigner für oco-design, wechselte 1989 zu siegerdesign und war bis 1991 an der Fachhochschule Münster als Lehrbeauftragter für Produktdesign tätig. 1992 eröffnete er in Münster sein eigenes Designstudio „Schumanndesign", das Designkonzepte für Unternehmen in Deutschland, Italien, Indien, Thailand und China entwickelt. Seit einigen Jahren beschäftigt er sich mit konzeptioneller Architektur, entwirft visionäre Lebensräume und hält Vorträge auf internationalen Kongressen. Dirk Schumann nimmt an Ausstellungen im In- und Ausland teil und wurde für seine Arbeiten mehrfach ausgezeichnet, u. a. mit dem Gold Prize (Minister of Economy, Trade and Industry Prize) des International Design Competition, Osaka, beim Comfort & Design Award, Mailand, dem iF product design award, Hannover, dem Red Dot Design Award, Essen, dem Focus in Gold, Stuttgart, sowie dem Good Design Award, Chicago und Tokio. 2015 gründete er mit Schumann&Wang in Xiamen City die chinesische Dependance von Schumanndesign.

01
Washbasin and fittings
for JOMOO China
Waschbecken und Armatur
für JOMOO China

01

"Good design is characterised by maximum practical value for the user, sensitive management of resources, durable design, emotion and a clear brand identification."
„Gutes Design zeichnet sich durch größtmöglichen Gebrauchswert für den Benutzer, einen sensiblen Umgang mit Ressourcen, langlebiges Design, Emotionalität und klare Identifizierbarkeit der Marke aus."

What do you design at "Schumanndesign"?
Products with sophisticated functionality for a range of industries. We have often long-standing relationship with international companies in the sanitary, medical and communication technology industries as well as in mechanical and plant engineering. The resulting products are the consequence of close, personal cooperation with customers. I particularly value the international nature of our work and the associated awareness of cultural diversity and values.

How did you come to open a branch office in Xiamen City?
It all started at the "Design Business Week", organised by Red Dot in 2013 in Xiamen, where we first made contact with companies from Xiamen City and other Chinese industrial centres. This led to concrete projects in 2015. As Xiamen is also a centre for the sanitary industry, it seemed natural for us to establish a branch office there. Our operations in southern China have also led to interesting projects and overarching activities in Beijing and Shanghai.

Was gestalten Sie bei „Schumanndesign"?
Produkte mit hohem Anspruch an ihre Funktionalität für unterschiedliche Branchen. Die oft langfristigen Kooperationen mit internationalen Unternehmen liegen in den Bereichen Sanitär, Medizin- und Kommunikationstechnik sowie Maschinen- und Anlagenbau. Die Produkte entstehen in engen, individuellen Kooperationen mit den Kunden, wobei ich die Internationalität und das damit zusammenhängende Verständnis für kulturelle Vielfalt und Werte sehr schätze.

Wie kam es dazu, dass Sie eine Dependance in Xiamen City eröffnet haben?
Der Ursprung geht letztlich auf die von Red Dot 2013 veranstaltete „Design Business Week" in Xiamen zurück, auf der es zu ersten Kontakten zu Unternehmen aus Xiamen City und anderen Industriestandorten in China und 2015 zu konkreten Projekten kam. Da auch Xiamen einen Schwerpunkt im Sanitärbereich hat, war es naheliegend, eine Dependance vor Ort zu etablieren. In der Folge unserer Tätigkeiten in Südchina haben sich auch interessante Projekte und übergreifende Aktivitäten in Beijing und Shanghai ergeben.

Prof. Song Kee Hong
Singapore
Singapur

Professor Song Kee Hong has worked with some of the world's most notable brands, including Dell, Epson, HP, Intel, Lenovo, P&G, Philips, Sanyo, Sennheiser and WelchAllyn, and he has received more than twenty international design awards for his work. His recent portfolio of cross-disciplinary design work spans diverse industries – from consumer electronics to mission-critical domains in healthcare, industrial and security for government systems. Song Kee Hong is currently a deputy head at the Industrial Design Division, National University of Singapore. He is also the design director of Design Exchange. He has over two decades of design experience, including work at global innovation consultancy Ziba and at HP.

Professor Song Kee Hong hat für einige der namhaftesten Marken der Welt gearbeitet, darunter Dell, Epson, HP, Intel, Lenovo, P&G, Philips, Sanyo, Sennheiser und WelchAllyn. Für seine Arbeit wurde er in mehr als zwanzig internationalen Designwettbewerben ausgezeichnet. Zu seinen jüngeren interdisziplinären Projekten zählen Aufträge für verschiedene Branchen von der Unterhaltungselektronik bis hin zu entscheidenden Bereichen wie dem Gesundheitswesen, der Industrie und staatlichen Sicherheitssystemen. Zurzeit ist Song Kee Hong stellvertretender Leiter der Industrial Design Division an der National University of Singapore und gleichzeitig Designdirektor von Design Exchange. Er blickt auf mehr als zwei Jahrzehnte Designerfahrung zurück, die Tätigkeiten bei der globalen Innovations-Unternehmensberatung Ziba und bei HP einschließt.

01 HP Deskjet 9600 Series
Printer
Drucker

01

"Good consumer product design can be very demanding in terms of balancing stunning aesthetics with good user experience."

„Gutes Design für Konsumgüter kann sehr anspruchsvoll darin sein, beeindruckende Ästhetik mit guter Benutzererfahrung in Einklang zu bringen."

To what extent does your work as a designer in the consumer electronics industry differ from your work as a designer in the healthcare sector?
Although much of the technical process such as configuring component layout and ergonomics are similar, that's where the similarity ends. The main differences are in the user scenario and operating environment. When I designed an emergency ambulance, my team had to ride in one to real cases and understand all the critical needs of both the crew and patient; all design decisions are driven by these needs.

What do you like about being a jury member?
Besides the opportunity to view and try thousands of designs from around the world, I like to meet and share experience and insights with my peers from around the world. Always amusing to see that we're so different and yet so similar at the same time!

Inwiefern unterscheidet sich die Arbeit als Designer in der Unterhaltungselektronik von der Tätigkeit als Gestalter im Gesundheitswesen?
Obwohl ein Großteil der technischen Verfahren, z. B. die Anordnung der verschiedenen Komponenten und die ergonomische Gestaltung, sich ähneln, hört die Gemeinsamkeit da auch schon auf. Die Hauptunterschiede betreffen die Nutzungssituation und die Betriebsumgebung. Als ich dabei war, einen Notarztwagen zu gestalten, musste mein Team in einem Krankenwagen zu echten Notfällen mitfahren, um die maßgeblichen Bedürfnisse sowohl des Einsatzteams als auch der Patienten zu verstehen. Alle Designentscheidungen werden von diesen Bedürfnissen gesteuert.

Was gefällt Ihnen an Ihrer Tätigkeit als Juror?
Abgesehen von der Gelegenheit, tausende Gestaltungsprojekte aus der ganzen Welt zu sehen, gefällt mir, dass ich Kolleginnen und Kollegen aus der ganzen Welt treffen und Erfahrungen und Erkenntnisse mit ihnen austauschen kann. Es ist immer amüsant zu sehen, wie sehr wir uns unterscheiden und gleichzeitig doch ähneln!

Dick Spierenburg
Netherlands
Niederlande

Dick Spierenburg, born in 1953, studied architecture at Delft University of Technology and Interior & Product Design at the Royal Academy of Art in The Hague. He worked at the Dutch manufacturer Castelijn for over fifteen years, as managing and creative director. In 1995, he set up and managed three leading permanent interior design exhibitions in Amsterdam, NIC, Pakhuis Amsterdam and Post CS. Parallel to these activities Dick Spierenburg established KBDS with Dutch designer Karel Boonzaaijer in 2001 designing for Arco, Artifort, Castelijn, Gelderland, Hollands Licht, Minotti Italia, Montis and Moroso. In 2009, he founded his own studio. In Germany, he co-ordinated the initiative for a design and interior showroom for international brands "Design Post", and was appointed creative consultant and in 2011 creative director to imm cologne. Since 2014, Dick Spierenburg has been consulting the trade fair Orgatec, and has been focusing on the design of exhibitions such as for the MAKK museum and presentation spaces for Thonet, Linak or Oase.

Dick Spierenburg, 1953 geboren, studierte Architektur an der Technischen Universität Delft sowie Innenarchitektur und Produktdesign an der Königlichen Kunstakademie in Den Haag. Danach arbeitete er mehr als 15 Jahre als Geschäftsführer und Creative Director für den niederländischen Hersteller Castelijn. 1995 baute er drei führende permanente Innenarchitektur-Ausstellungen in Amsterdam, NIC, Pakhuis Amsterdam und Post CS, auf, die er danach auch leitete. Gleichzeitig gründete er gemeinsam mit dem holländischen Designer Karel Boonzaaijer im Jahr 2001 KBDS und gestaltete für Arco, Artifort, Castelijn, Gelderland, Hollands Licht, Minotti Italia, Montis und Moroso. 2009 eröffnete er sein eigenes Designstudio. In Deutschland organisierte er die Initiative „Design Post", ein Design- und Innenarchitektur-Showroom für internationale Marken, und wurde zum Creative Consultant benannt. 2011 wurde er Creative Director der imm cologne. Seit 2014 berät Dick Spierenburg die Fachmesse Orgatec und konzentriert sich auf die Gestaltung von Ausstellungen, u. a. für das MAKK Museum, und von Ausstellungsräumen für Thonet, Linak und Oase.

01 Pure Editions Club at imm cologne 2019

The 2019 design for the Editions Club shows an exciting contrast between volume and lightness: a high cross vault is suggested, but built with paper thin walls. Only a few materials were used to reach the special effect of an intimate room. A stretched hospitality space, serene and light, with an impressive perspective as scenery for seating areas.

Das Design für den Editions Club von 2019 weist einen spannenden Kontrast zwischen Volumen und Leichtigkeit auf: Angedeutet wird ein hohes Kreuzgewölbe, das aus papierdünnen Wänden besteht. Es wurden nur wenige Materialien verwendet, um den besonderen Effekt eines intimen Raumes zu erzeugen. Ein geräumiger Hospitality-Bereich, ruhig und hell, mit einer eindrucksvollen Perspektive als Kulisse für die Sitzecken.

01

"Next to a rational approach, all senses should be taken in consideration when judging a product. Visual and tactile aspects as well as sounds and smells can make the difference."

„Zusätzlich zu einem rationalen Ansatz sollten bei der Bewertung eines Produkts auch alle Sinne ins Spiel kommen. Optische und haptische Aspekte, Klänge und Gerüche können den Unterschied ausmachen."

With what can a piece of furniture persuade you of its merits?

With an innovative character: new possibilities in use and appealing visual aspects. A new product must earn its place with its concept, materialisation, options for use, look & feel and sustainable qualities.

To what extent has the "Bauhaus" movement influenced you?

The principles of Bauhaus have left many traces both in my education and in my work. It is good to question every step you take in the design process but letting intuition speak is equally important. We should not overestimate the influence of Bauhaus in the present time. The world has changed in the last 100 years. Design and architecture should lead and not follow when it comes to societal change and development.

Womit kann ein Möbelstück Sie überzeugen?

Mit einem innovativen Charakter: neuen Möglichkeiten der Anwendung und ansprechenden optischen Eigenschaften. Ein neues Produkt muss seinen Platz verdienen – mit Konzept, Materialisierung, Anwendungsmöglichkeiten, Optik und Haptik und nachhaltigen Eigenschaften.

Stichwort „Bauhaus": Inwieweit beeinflusste die Kunstschule Sie?

Die Bauhaus-Prinzipien haben sowohl in meiner Ausbildung als auch in meiner Arbeit nachhaltige Spuren hinterlassen. Es ist gut, jeden Schritt, den man im Gestaltungsprozess macht, zu hinterfragen. Es ist allerdings genauso wichtig, die Intuition zu Wort kommen zu lassen. Wir sollten den Einfluss des Bauhauses allerdings nicht überschätzen. Die Welt hat sich in den letzten 100 Jahren verändert. Design und Architektur sollten im Wandel der Gesellschaft und bei Entwicklungen führen und nicht folgen.

Leon Sun
China

Leon Sun is Chief Content Officer and Editorial Director of the international home and lifestyle magazine ELLE DECORATION China. He is journalist with over a decade of experience in the interior design industry. By introducing the latest global design and trends into the Chinese market, he actively promotes the development of the domestic interior industry. Amongst others, he realised the special topics "Oriental Gene", "Asia Now" and "Rong He" at ELLE DECORATION China. Furthermore, he is judge of the EDIDA International Design Awards and Vice President of the China Gold Idea Design Award. Graduating in Visual Communication from the Shanghai Donghua University, Leon Sun started his career as Visual Director at ELLE DECORATION China in 2006. From 2011 to 2014, he was Visual Director at AD China.

Leon Sun ist Chief Content Officer und Editorial Director des internationalen Wohn- und Lifestyle-Magazins ELLE DECORATION China. Er ist Journalist mit mehr als einem Jahrzehnt Erfahrung im Sektor Inneneinrichtung. Indem er die international aktuellsten Gestaltungen und Trends auf dem chinesischen Markt vorstellt, unterstützt er die Entwicklung der heimischen Einrichtungsbranche aktiv. Unter anderem realisierte er die Themenspecials „Oriental Gene", „Asia Now" und „Rong He" bei ELLE DECORATION China. Darüber hinaus ist er Juror des EDIDA International Design Awards und Vice President des China Gold Idea Design Awards. Mit einem Abschluss in Visual Communication von der Shanghai Donghua University begann er seine Karriere 2006 als Visual Director bei ELLE DECORATION China. Von 2011 bis 2014 war er Visual Director bei AD China.

01 2019 China Interior Design Annual
ELLE DECORATION China released the 2019 China Interior Design Annual, a special selection of interior design projects. The top designers Tony Chi, Steve Leung, Alan Chan and André Fu reviewed the submitted works and leading designers like Kengo Kuma, Yabu Pushelberg, Kenya Hara and Neri&Hu Studio shared their insights on excellent China interior designs in all relevant categories.

ELLE DECORATION China ist Herausgeber des 2019 China Interior Design Annual, einer Sonderauswahl von Innenarchitekturprojekten. Die Topdesigner Tony Chi, Steve Leung, Alan Chan und André Fu haben die eingereichten Arbeiten begutachtet, während führende Designer wie Kengo Kuma, Yabu Pushelberg, Kenya Hara und Neri&Hu Studio ihre Einblicke in herausragende chinesische Innenarchitekturprojekte in allen relevanten Kategorien vermitteln.

01

"A good designer is always curious. He is an expert in exploring the unknown, creating new things and revealing his unique perspective in the way in which he interprets life and the world through his works."

„Ein guter Designer ist immer neugierig. Er ist Experte im Erforschen von Unbekanntem, im Schaffen von Neuem und im Darstellen seiner einzigartigen Sichtweise, in der er das Leben und die Welt mit seiner Arbeit interpretiert."

What constitutes good design?
Design is about solving problems and offering better services to people. Therefore, a good design is a tool that makes people's life better.

To what do you attach particular importance when judging products?
Firstly, to creativity and innovations in ideas, formats or materials; secondly, to workability and its way of solving problems and considering physical or psychological needs. Thirdly, to the look and whether it immediately catches your eye and, fourthly, to friendliness: a product needs to reflect the relationship between humans and objects and to be environmentally friendly.

Where will the design industry be ten years from now?
Our life will advance along with technological developments which allow us to dream bigger. However, design will evolve in different directions due to its diversity, interacting with technologies, culture and art.

Was macht gutes Design aus?
Bei Design geht es darum, Probleme zu lösen und Menschen einen besseren Service zu bieten. Daher ist gutes Design ein Hilfsmittel, das Menschen das Leben erleichtert.

Worauf legen Sie bei der Bewertung von Produkten ein besonderes Augenmerk?
Erstens auf die Kreativität und die Innovationen, die ein Produkt in Idee, Format und Materialien bietet; zweitens auf Praktikabilität und die Art, in der es Probleme löst und auf physische und psychische Bedürfnisse eingeht. Drittens auf den Look und ob es sofort die Augen auf sich zieht und, viertens, auf die Freundlichkeit – ein Produkt sollte die Beziehung zwischen Mensch und Objekt widerspiegeln und umweltfreundlich sein.

Wo wird die Designbranche in zehn Jahren stehen?
Unser Leben wird mit den technischen Entwicklungen voranschreiten und uns erlauben, größere Träume zu träumen. Design wird sich aufgrund seiner Vielfalt allerdings in verschiedene Richtungen entwickeln und mit Technik, Kultur und Kunst zusammenwirken.

Kazuo Tanaka
Japan

Kazuo Tanaka graduated in 1983 from Tokyo University of the Arts, majored in industrial design. He is president and CEO of the GK Design Group Incorporated, a comprehensive freelance design office in Japan founded in 1952 by Kenji Ekuan. Kazuo Tanaka has been elected president of the Japan Industrial Designers Association (JIDA) and taking on many kinds of activities since 2013. In 2007, he was elected member of the board of directors of the World Design Organization (formerly Icsid) and has been active, also as a regional adviser, in many international programmes. Kazuo Tanaka has also been serving as a board member of Japan Institute of Design Promotion (JDP), and a member of the study group on the relation between industrial competitiveness and design by the Japan Patent Office (JPO) of the Ministry of Economy, Trade and Industry (METI). He also has been involved as a juror in many international design promotion activities and was awarded the Good Design Award Prime Minister Prize, the SDA Grand Prize and many other awards.

Kazuo Tanaka absolvierte sein Studium des Industriedesigns 1983 an der Tokyo University of Arts. Er ist Präsident und CEO der GK Design Group Incorporated, eines übergreifenden unabhängigen Designstudios in Japan, das 1952 von Kenji Ekuan gegründet wurde. Kazuo Tanaka wurde zum Präsidenten der Japan Industrial Designers Association (JIDA) ernannt und geht seit 2013 mehreren Tätigkeiten nach. 2017 wurde er zum Vorstandsmitglied der World Design Organization (ehemals Icsid) gewählt und ist seitdem auch auf regionaler Ebene beratend in vielen internationalen Projekten aktiv. Kazuo Tanaka ist ebenfalls als Vorstandsmitglied des Japan Institute of Design Promotion (JDP) tätig und Mitglied der Studiengruppe zur Beziehung zwischen industrieller Wettbewerbsfähigkeit und Design des Japanischen Patentbüros (JPO) des Ministeriums für Wirtschaft, Handel und Industrie (METI). Als Juror nahm er an einer Vielzahl internationaler Designwettbewerbe teil und erhielt den Good Design Award Prime Minister Prize, den SDA Grand Prize und viele weitere Auszeichnungen.

01 fugan
Fugan Suijo, shipping line of
the Toyama Prefecture, 2015
Fugan Suijo, Schifffahrtsgesell-
schaft der Toyama-Präfektur, 2015

01

"When evaluating products, I first of all prove their functionally, then their aesthetic excellence and social conviction. I then try to see if the product is pioneering by putting these views together."

„Bei der Bewertung von Produkten teste ich zuerst ihre Funktionalität, dann ihre ästhetische Qualität und soziale Überzeugung. Danach versuche ich herauszufinden, ob das Produkt bahnbrechend ist und alle diese Eigenschaften vereint."

Please describe good design:
Good design is the thing that provides excellent social, cultural and economic value. Today's design is evaluated for its comprehensiveness.

What constitutes good teamwork?
While each member has different professions and ideas, each member's deep understanding of his role in the common mission constitutes teamwork.

What does the Red Dot Award represent in your opinion?
The Red Dot Award has always been pointing towards the direction in which design should be heading in changing times. I firmly believe that it has an essential and invariable value.

How do you imagine the future of design?
New technologies and services have been changing the future of design. At the same time, the cultural nature of design, unchanged since the twentieth century, may also become more brilliant.

Beschreiben Sie bitte gutes Design:
Gutes Design ist das, was hervorragenden sozialen, kulturellen und wirtschaftlichen Wert schafft. Design wird heute nach seiner Vollständigkeit beurteilt.

Was macht gute Teamarbeit aus?
Obwohl jedes Teammitglied unterschiedliche Fachkenntnisse und Ideen hat, macht die tiefgründige Kenntnis seiner Rolle in der gemeinsamen Aufgabe die Teamarbeit aus.

Wofür steht der Red Dot Award für Sie?
Der Red Dot Award war schon immer wegweisend für die Richtung, die Design in wechselvollen Zeiten einschlagen soll. Ich bin fest davon überzeugt, dass der Red Dot Award einen maßgeblichen und konstanten Wert hat.

Wie stellen Sie sich die Zukunft des Designs vor?
Neue Technologien und Dienstleistungen beeinflussen die Zukunft des Designs. Gleichzeitig mag der kulturelle Charakter des Designs, der seit dem 20. Jahrhundert unverändert ist, noch fulminanter werden.

Nils Toft
Denmark
Dänemark

Nils Toft is the founder and managing director of Designidea. With offices in Copenhagen and Beijing, the multiple internationally awarded studio works in the key fields of sustainable energy solutions, consumer electronics, medical devices and design psychology, as well as taking on projects in business development, design strategy and exhibition design. Nils Toft graduated as an architect and designer from the Royal Danish Academy of Fine Arts in Copenhagen in 1986 and started his career as an industrial designer, joining the former Christian Bjørn Design in 1987, an internationaly active design studio in Copenhagen. Within a few years, he became a partner of CBD and, as managing director successfully ran the business until 2010. Nils Toft's work has recently been focused on understanding and measuring how people are impacted by design. By measuring physiological parameters such as heart rate, eye movements, neurological activity and electro dermal activity, it is possible to unveil a test person's emotional condition as well as their psychological reactions in relation to products, environments and services.

Nils Toft ist der Gründer und Geschäftsführer von Designidea. Mit Niederlassungen in Kopenhagen und Beijing arbeitet das international mehrfach ausgezeichnete Studio hauptsächlich in den Bereichen Erneuerbare Energien, Unterhaltungselektronik, Medizintechnik und Designpsychologie. Das Studio übernimmt ebenfalls Projekte in den Bereichen Geschäftsentwicklung, Designstrategie und Ausstellungsdesign. Nils Toft machte seinen Abschluss als Architekt und Designer 1986 an der Royal Danish Academy of Fine Arts in Kopenhagen und begann seine Karriere als Industriedesigner 1987 bei dem damaligen Christian Bjørn Design, einem international operierenden Designstudio in Kopenhagen. Innerhalb weniger Jahre wurde er Partner bei CBD und leitete das Unternehmen erfolgreich bis 2010 als Managing Director. In letzter Zeit hat Nils Toft sich in seiner Arbeit auf das Verständnis und Messen der Wirkung von Design auf Menschen konzentriert. Wenn man physiologische Parameter wie z. B. Pulsschlag, Augenbewegung, neurologische sowie elektrodermale Aktivität misst, ist es möglich, emotionale und psychologische Reaktionen der Versuchsperson auf Produkte, die Umgebung und Dienstleistungen zu erkennen.

01 Wittenborg 95
High-quality semi-automatic coffee machines
Hochwertige halbautomatische Kaffeemaschinen

01

"My professional goal is to continually be curious, always seeking new challenges and chasing a continuously moving goal post."

„Mein professionelles Ziel ist es, immer neugierig zu sein, immer neue Herausforderungen zu suchen und ein ständig wechselndes Ziel zu verfolgen."

What does the "Designidea" company stand for?
Designidea is based on the philosophy that in all companies there are great ideas waiting to be discovered and with the help of good designers can be turned into great products.

What, to date, has been the most exciting project of your career?
I have been fortunate enough to work on many different types of exiting projects and that is what has made my career exiting. I am driven by my curiosity and new projects – challenges are what excites me the most.

How do you proceed when evaluating products?
I verify whether the design is of a high quality and clearly expresses the intended idea behind the product.

With what can a designer surprise you?
I am positively surprised and full of admiration when I see a technical product with many constraints that, because of a great design by a talented designer, appears so clear and obvious, that your only response is, "of course".

Wofür steht Ihr Unternehmen „Designidea"?
Designidea basiert auf der Philosophie, dass es in allen Unternehmen großartige Ideen gibt, die nur darauf warten, entdeckt und mithilfe guter Designer in großartige Produkte verwandelt zu werden.

Was war das bisher spannendste Projekt Ihrer Karriere?
Ich habe das Glück, an vielen verschiedenen aufregenden Projekten beteiligt gewesen zu sein. Das ist es, was meine Karriere so spannend macht. Mich treiben Neugier und neue Projekte an. Am aufregendsten finde ich neue Herausforderungen.

Wie gehen Sie bei der Bewertung von Produkten vor?
Ich prüfe, ob die Gestaltung qualitativ hochwertig ist und klar die Intention hinter dem Produkt zum Ausdruck bringt.

Womit kann ein Designer Sie überraschen?
Ich bin positiv überrascht und voller Bewunderung, wenn ich ein technisches Produkt mit vielen Features sehe, das dank eines großartigen Gestaltungskonzepts von einem talentierten Designer so klar und einleuchtend erscheint, dass man nur „na klar" denken kann.

Prof. Danny Venlet
Belgium
Belgien

Professor Danny Venlet was born in 1958 in Victoria, Australia, and studied interior design at Sint-Lukas, the Institute for Architecture and Arts in Brussels. Back in Australia in 1991, Venlet started to attract international attention with large-scale interior projects such as the Burdekin hotel in Sydney and Q-bar, an Australian chain of nightclubs. His design projects range from private mansions, lofts, bars and restaurants all the way to showrooms and offices of large companies. The interior projects and the furniture designs of Danny Venlet are characterised by their contemporary international style. He says that the objects arise from an interaction between art, sculpture and function. These objects give a new description to the space in which they are placed – with respect, but also with relative humour. Today, Danny Venlet teaches his knowledge to students at the Royal College of the Arts in Ghent.

Professor Danny Venlet wurde 1958 in Victoria, Australien, geboren und studierte Interior Design am Sint-Lukas Institut für Architektur und Kunst in Brüssel. Nachdem er 1991 wieder nach Australien zurückgekehrt war, begann er, mit der Innenausstattung großer Projekte wie dem Burdekin Hotel in Sydney und der Q-Bar, einer australischen Nachtclub-Kette, internationale Aufmerksamkeit zu erregen. Seine Designprojekte reichen von privaten Wohnhäusern über Lofts, Bars und Restaurants bis hin zu Ausstellungsräumen und Büros großer Unternehmen. Die Innenausstattungen und Möbeldesigns von Danny Venlet sind durch einen zeitgenössischen, internationalen Stil ausgezeichnet und entspringen, wie er sagt, der Interaktion zwischen Kunst, Skulptur und Funktion. Seine Objekte geben den Räumen, in denen sie sich befinden, eine neue Identität – mit Respekt, aber auch mit einer Portion Humor. Heute vermittelt Danny Venlet sein Wissen als Professor an Studenten des Royal College of the Arts in Gent.

01 L-Hop 2
Toilet roll holder with integrated light for the company Dark
Toilettenrollenhalter mit integriertem Licht für die Firma Dark

01

"Cultural exchange among designers is important to discover what other cultures have to offer and what solutions they have – in order to help us challenge our cultural dogmas."

„Der kulturelle Austausch zwischen Designern ist wichtig, um herauszufinden, was andere Kulturen zu bieten und welche Lösungen sie gefunden haben – das sollte uns helfen, unsere kulturellen Dogmen zu hinterfragen."

Is there a way of instantly recognising your designs? What are their distinguishing features?
My work is sometimes described as organic behaviouristic minimalism. Organic curves are beautiful and sensual but I believe one should use them sparingly. I am also a follower of the ideas of Wabi-Sabi, "the beauty of imperfection". I believe that the distinguishing features of my work are objects that move away from encrusted habits or customs and are therefore often behavioural change makers.

Unpretentious or grandiose – what do you prefer and why?
I would say unpretentious grandiosity would be my preference. Something is grandiose when it does not scream it out loud.

What are the essential features of a well-designed piece of furniture?
Excellence of execution, exceptional concept, emotionally capturing, elegant solution of a problem, environmentally friendly. Well-designed furniture should aim to have most of these E-factors.

Woran sind Ihre Gestaltungen zu erkennen? Was zeichnet sie aus?
Meine Arbeit wird manchmal als organisch behavioristischer Minimalismus bezeichnet. Organische Rundungen sind schön und sinnlich, doch bin ich der Meinung, dass man sie sparsam einsetzen sollte. Ich bin auch ein Anhänger der Ideen von Wabi-Sabi, „der Schönheit des Unvollkommenen". Ich glaube, dass die kennzeichnenden Merkmale meiner Arbeit Objekte sind, die sich von verkrusteten Gewohnheiten oder Gebräuchen entfernt haben und daher häufig zu „Änderungsgestaltern" des Verhaltens werden.

Schlicht oder pompös – was bevorzugen Sie und warum?
Ich würde sagen, dass ich eine Vorliebe für schlichten Prunk habe. Etwas, das pompös ist, ohne es zu laut kundzutun.

Was muss ein gut gestaltetes Möbelstück mitbringen?
Eine ausgezeichnete Umsetzung, ein herausragendes Konzept, es sollte emotional fesseln, eine elegante Lösung für ein Problem bieten und umweltfreundlich sein. Gut gestaltete Möbelstücke sollten einen Großteil dieser Eigenschaften aufweisen.

Dr. Joseph Francis Wong
Hong Kong
Hongkong

Dr. Joseph Francis Wong joined the Hong Kong Design Institute as the Vice Principal in 2017. Prior to this, he was Associate Professor at the City University of Hong Kong, where he taught architectural design and theory for 19 years. Joseph Francis Wong received a Bachelor of Arts in Architecture from Berkeley, a Master of Architecture from MIT and a Doctor of Education from Leicester. He is a Fellow of the Hong Kong Institute of Architects, where he was part of the Board of Internal Affairs and the Board of Educational Affairs and chaired the Environment and Sustainable Design Committee. His research on open building and spatial/visual field analysis has been presented and published in many conferences and journals, including Design Studies, Habitat International, Journal of Architecture as well as Environment and Planning B. In recognition of his contribution to design education, Joseph Francis Wong was awarded the Berkeley Prize International Fellowship in 2014.

2017 trat Dr. Joseph Francis Wong dem Hong Kong Design Institute als Vice Principal bei. Zuvor war er als Associate Professor an der City University of Hong Kong tätig, wo er 19 Jahre lang architektonische Gestaltung und Theorie lehrte. Er machte einen Bachelor of Arts in Architektur in Berkeley, einen Master of Architecture am MIT und einen Doctor of Education in Leicester. Joseph Francis Wong ist Fellow des Hong Kong Institute of Architects, wo er Teil des Board of Internal Affairs und des Board of Educational Affairs war und dem Environment and Sustainable Design Committee vorsaß. Seine Forschung über offene Gebäude und räumliche/visuelle Feldanalyse wurde in vielen Konferenzen und Zeitschriften vorgestellt und veröffentlicht, so in Design Studies, Habitat International, Journal of Architecture sowie Environment and Planning B. In Anerkennung seines Beitrags zur Designlehre erhielt Joseph Francis Wong 2014 den Berkeley Prize International Fellowship.

01 Kai Tak District Cooling Plant, Hong Kong
In collaboration with Andrew Lee King Fun & Associates Architects Ltd., Hong Kong
In Zusammenarbeit mit Andrew Lee King Fun & Associates Architects Ltd., Hongkong

01

"Innovation is a well-considered solution to a problem redefined through rigorous research."

„Innovation ist eine wohlüberlegte Lösung für ein Problem, das durch gründliche Recherche neu definiert wurde."

What does a product have to offer in order to persuade you of its merits?
Simplicity and user considerations. A good product does not need to attempt too much; it's more preferable to do one thing or a few things really well than too many things above average. It must also be clear and sensible about actual usage by users.

How do you proceed when evaluating products?
I would go straight for it, try to understand and use the product before reading the instructions. That's my first criterion. Next, I would correlate design intentions to the actual design itself. The product should definitely stand out in terms of elegant integration of look and feel to functionality.

Was muss ein Produkt mitbringen, um Sie zu überzeugen?
Einfachheit und eine Berücksichtigung der Nutzer. Ein gutes Produkt sollte nicht versuchen, zu viel zu leisten. Es ist besser, eine Sache oder ein paar Dinge richtig gut zu machen, als zu viele Dinge über dem Durchschnitt. Das Produkt sollte auch klar und vernünftig in Bezug auf die Anwendung durch den Nutzer sein.

Wie gehen Sie bei der Bewertung von Produkten vor?
Ich gehe ganz direkt vor und versuche, das Produkt zu verstehen und zu benutzen, bevor ich die Anleitung lese. Das ist mein erstes Kriterium. Als Nächstes versuche ich, den Zusammenhang zwischen Designintention und dem eigentlichen Design zu erkennen. Das Produkt sollte auf jeden Fall aus der Masse hervorstechen – in einer eleganten Integration von Optik, Haptik und Funktionalität.

Alphabetical index manufacturers and distributors
Alphabetisches Hersteller- und Vertriebs-Register

3M
Page/Seite 198–199

Shenzhen 21g Product Design Co., Ltd.
Page/Seite 283

Shenzhen 55° Innovation Technology Co., Ltd.
Page/Seite 154

700Kids (Shenzhen) Technology Co., Ltd.
Page/Seite 89

A

ABUS Security-Center GmbH & Co. KG
Page/Seite 228

ACERA
Brand LIVEN
Page/Seite 153

Active Wearables GmbH
Page/Seite 247

AEC Lighting Solutions Co., Ltd.
Page/Seite 197

Beijing AIQI Technology Co., Ltd.
Page/Seite 313

Anaori Carbon Co., Ltd.
Page/Seite 134–135

Apple
Page/Seite 232–233, 248–249, 257

Asko Appliances AB
Page/Seite 115

Asustek Computer Inc.
Page/Seite 246, 258

Atomos
Page/Seite 221

Shenzhen Atuman Precision Machinery Technology Co., Ltd.
Page/Seite 193

Auris Health
Page/Seite 304–305

AVer Information Inc.
Page/Seite 271

Aydya Limited
Page/Seite 142

B

BA KE Technologies (Dongguan) Co., Ltd.
Page/Seite 86

BabyBjörn AB
Page/Seite 101

Bahama GmbH
Page/Seite 174

Baidu Online Network Technology (Beijing) Co., Ltd.
Page/Seite 310

Beijing Dynamics
Page/Seite 93

Shenzhen Beite Industry Design Co., Ltd.
Page/Seite 87

BERG Toys B.V.
Page/Seite 88

BergHOFF Worldwide
Page/Seite 136

HTS BeSafe AS
Page/Seite 76

Bezalel Inc.
Page/Seite 262

BK Cookware BV
Page/Seite 140

Blackmagic Design
Page/Seite 214, 222–223

Blueye Robotics
Page/Seite 308

Shenzhen Bo Yi Industrial Co., Ltd.
Page/Seite 255

Bodum AG
Page/Seite 156–157

BONECO AG
Page/Seite 116

Shenzhen Booyue Daily Necessities Co., Ltd.
Page/Seite 94

BORRN UK
Page/Seite 100, 103

Robert Bosch Hausgeräte GmbH
Page/Seite 125

Robert Bosch Power Tools GmbH
Page/Seite 119, 168, 193

BOSMA Corp.
Page/Seite 227

Brainchildren GmbH
Page/Seite 160

Britax Römer Kindersicherheit GmbH
Page/Seite 77

BSH Home Appliances (China) Co., Ltd.
Page/Seite 112

C

Cangshan Cutlery Company
Page/Seite 143

Carnival Corporation & plc
Page/Seite 247

Casa Vigar S.L.
Page/Seite 130

Check Roots s.r.o.
Page/Seite 142

China Mobile Communications Group Co., Ltd., Government and Enterprise Service Company
Page/Seite 279

China Mobile Group Device Co., Ltd.
Page/Seite 287

Cisco
Page/Seite 272

CMCC
Page/Seite 288

colarty GmbH & Co. KG
Page/Seite 147

Coway
Page/Seite 117

Cybex GmbH
Page/Seite 68, 77

Cycleurope Sverige AB
Page/Seite 89

D

DH-Robotics Technology Co., Ltd.
Page/Seite 307

Dibbern GmbH
Page/Seite 148

Diono
Page/Seite 79

DPA Microphones
Page/Seite 274

Dreamfarm
Page/Seite 141

DreBo Werkzeugfabrik GmbH
Page/Seite 187

DTEN
Page/Seite 268–269

Dunlop Protective Footwear Hevea BV
Page/Seite 199

E

Ecovacs Robotics Co., Ltd.
Page/Seite 122

Shenzhen Eevin Technology Co., Ltd.
Page/Seite 279

Eilong Enterprise Co., Ltd.
Page/Seite 156

AB Electrolux
Page/Seite 116, 124

Elesa S.p.A.
Page/Seite 190–191

Enfant Terrible Design AB
Page/Seite 80–81

Ericsson AB
Page/Seite 280–281

Eva Solo A/S
Page/Seite 162

Everdure by Heston Blumenthal
Page/Seite 171

Everybot Inc.
Page/Seite 119

Extremis NV
Page/Seite 174

F

fischerwerke GmbH & Co. KG
Page/Seite 187

Fiskars Brands Inc.
Page/Seite 169

Fiskars Finland Oy Ab
Page/Seite 166–168

Fitbit, Inc.
Page/Seite 239

Flexa4Dreams A/S
Page/Seite 82

FLIR Systems, Inc.
Page/Seite 226

FLSK Products GmbH
Page/Seite 155

Flyaway Designs
Page/Seite 84

Flying Tiger Copenhagen Zebra A/S
Page/Seite 91

Freudenberg Home and Cleaning Solutions GmbH
Page/Seite 123

FUJIFILM Corporation
Page/Seite 208–210, 212–213, 217, 227

FutureModel Corp.
Page/Seite 259

Fuyu Blue and White Rice-Pattern Porcelain Co., Ltd.
Page/Seite 159

G

GARDENA GmbH
Page/Seite 170

Gemometrics AB
Page/Seite 195

Guangdong Genius Technology Co., Ltd.
Page/Seite 234

Goodbaby Child Products Co., Ltd.
Page/Seite 88

Google LLC
Page/Seite 250–251, 254

Goui
Page/Seite 262

Groupe SEB
Page/Seite 143

H

Häfele GmbH & Co KG
Page/Seite 186

Haier Group
Page/Seite 110–111

Adam Hall GmbH
Page/Seite 272

Hanergy Mobile Energy Holding Group Ltd.
Page/Seite 266

Harbin Institute of Technology State Key Laboratory of Robotics and System
Page/Seite 302–303

Paul Henke GmbH & Co. KG
Page/Seite 186

Hangzhou Hikrobot Technology Co., Ltd.
Page/Seite 308

Hilti Corporation
Page/Seite 178, 181–183, 192

höfats GmbH
Page/Seite 171

Hoffmann GmbH Qualitätswerkzeuge
Page/Seite 190

Honeywell
Page/Seite 198

Honeywell China
Page/Seite 194, 198–199

Taizhou Howawa Baby Products Co., Ltd.
Page/Seite 103

Anhui Huami Information Technology Co., Ltd.
Page/Seite 237

Huawei Device (Shenzhen) Co., Ltd.
Page/Seite 267, 274, 288

Huawei Technologies Co., Ltd.
Page/Seite 228, 289

HUBER+SUHNER AG
Page/Seite 282

Huddly AS
Page/Seite 226

Humaneyes Technologies Ltd.
Page/Seite 215

Husqvarna AB (publ.)
Page/Seite 171

Hyundai Robotics
Page/Seite 298–299

I

Ideo Group LLC
Page/Seite 68

iFootage International (HK) Limited
Page/Seite 219

igus GmbH
Page/Seite 301

IKEA of Sweden
Page/Seite 174

iloom
Page/Seite 84

Shenzhen ImagineVision Technology Limited
Page/Seite 215

inDare Design Strategy Limited
Page/Seite 96

Intenso International GmbH
Page/Seite 264–265

Interia
Page/Seite 82

iRobot
Page/Seite 120–121

i.safe MOBILE GmbH
Page/Seite 256

J

JANUS et Cie
Page/Seite 175

Shanghai Jieyong Technology Co., Ltd.
Page/Seite 220–221

JJOBI Company
Page/Seite 98–100

Joie Children's Products Co., Ltd.
Page/Seite 64–67, 74–75

Joolz by Milk Design B.V.
Page/Seite 70

K

KAHLA/Thüringen Porzellan GmbH
Page/Seite 163

W. F. Kaiser u. Co. GmbH
Page/Seite 141

Messermacher Kappeller GmbH
Page/Seite 144–145

Alfred Kärcher SE & Co. KG
Page/Seite 118

Guangzhou Kemei Commodity Co., Ltd.
Page/Seite 153

Kingclean Electric Co., Ltd.
Page/Seite 126–127

Alphabetical index manufacturers and distributors
Alphabetisches Hersteller- und Vertriebs-Register

Kitchen King Limited
Page/Seite 128

Konftel AB
Page/Seite 273

KUKA AG
Page/Seite 300

KYOCERA Corporation
Page/Seite 259

L

LARQ
Page/Seite 150–151

Lässig GmbH
Page/Seite 105

Leica Geosystems AG
Page/Seite 193

Lenovo
Page/Seite 242–243, 273

LG Electronics Inc.
Page/Seite 237, 252, 309

Lifesize, Inc.
Page/Seite 271

LifeStraw
Vestergaard S.A.
Page/Seite 162

Light
Page/Seite 259

Like-it Co., Ltd.
Page/Seite 141

Ling Technology Co., Ltd.
Page/Seite 94

Guangdong Linkfair Group Co., Ltd.
Page/Seite 136

LISLEI, Lda
Page/Seite 87

Litra
Page/Seite 220

Little Swan
Page/Seite 112–114

Logitech
Page/Seite 247, 271

M

Makeblock Co., Ltd.
Page/Seite 313

Guangdong Master Group Co., Ltd.
Page/Seite 138–139

Max-Inf Baby Products Co., Ltd.
Baby First
Page/Seite 76

MEDION AG
Page/Seite 235, 254

Meizu Technology Co., Ltd.
Page/Seite 253

Mercku Inc.
Page/Seite 294

Microduino
Page/Seite 93

Beijing MIIIW Technology Co., Ltd.
Page/Seite 255

Minh Long I Co., Ltd.
Page/Seite 149

Mobvoi US LLC
Page/Seite 235, 238

MODU ApS
Page/Seite 93

Monit Corp.
Page/Seite 78

Morus Technology (Shenzhen) Co., Ltd.
Page/Seite 115

Motorola
Page/Seite 261

Motorola Solutions
Page/Seite 258, 278

Hangzhou Mr. Bond Technology Co., Ltd.
Page/Seite 116

Mukako
Page/Seite 84

Mutrics Innovation Intelligence Co., Ltd.
Page/Seite 244

Mymuro Ltd.
Page/Seite 91

N

Shenzhen NearbyExpress Technology Development Co., Ltd.
Page/Seite 97, 267

NetEase Youdao Information Technology (Beijing) Co., Ltd.
Page/Seite 276

Netgear
Page/Seite 291–293

New H3C Technologies Co., Ltd.
Page/Seite 229, 290

Nikon Corporation
Page/Seite 204–205

Nokia Networks
Page/Seite 284–286

Nude
Page/Seite 161, 163

Nuna International BV
Page/Seite 69, 72–73, 79

O

Oblong Industries
Page/Seite 275

OCLU
Page/Seite 217

Olymp & Olipa GmbH
Page/Seite 83, 85

Olympus Corporation
Page/Seite 207, 278

Shenzhen Ontology Design Co., Ltd.
Page/Seite 244

P

Panasonic Appliances Washing Machine
Page/Seite 108–109

Panasonic Corporation
Page/Seite 206

Philips
Page/Seite 100, 103, 117, 125

Pigeon
Page/Seite 102

PIXII
Page/Seite 207

Plant Fiber International Incorporation
Page/Seite 160

Plastika Skaza d.o.o.
Page/Seite 129

Positec Technology
Page/Seite 180

Promethean World Inc.
Page/Seite 270

Q

Quinny
Dorel Juvenile
Page/Seite 70

R

r2p GmbH
Page/Seite 227–228

RAK Porcelain Europe
Page/Seite 147

Remo Tech Co., Ltd.
Page/Seite 215

Richartz GmbH
Page/Seite 188–189

Riedel Communications GmbH & Co. KG
Page/Seite 279

Robotise GmbH
Page/Seite 309

Rösle GmbH & Co. KG
Page/Seite 159

Hangzhou Rosou Electronic Technology Co., Ltd.
Page/Seite 117

Rotho Kunststoff AG
Page/Seite 130

Royole Corporation
Page/Seite 255, 261

Ruijie Networks Co., Ltd.
Page/Seite 283

S

SACKit ApS
Page/Seite 266

Sahm GmbH & Co. KG
Page/Seite 161

Samwoo Instrument, Inc.
Page/Seite 131

Satcube AB
Page/Seite 295

Scribit
Page/Seite 308

Groupe SEB
Page/Seite 143

Senserna A/S
Page/Seite 101

Shenzhen SenseTime Technology Co., Ltd.
Page/Seite 312

Sequent Ltd.
Page/Seite 236

Serial Future Visions, Inc.
Norlan
Page/Seite 160

Luoyang Shangqi Robot Technology Co., Ltd.
Page/Seite 302–303

SharkNinja
Page/Seite 125

SHARP Corporation
IoT Communication BU
Page/Seite 260

Shenzhen Shenxiao Technology Co., Ltd.
Page/Seite 311

SIMDO Technology Co., Ltd.
Page/Seite 258

Sixeye Interactive
Page/Seite 245

Skelex B.V.
Page/Seite 307

Somnox
Page/Seite 311

Sony Mobile Communications Inc.
Page/Seite 261

SOOIBE Intelligent Technology (Hangzhou) Co., Ltd.
Page/Seite 87

Stone (Shanghai) Juvenile Product Co., Ltd.
Page/Seite 71

Xiamen Stoneware Technology Co., Ltd.
Page/Seite 95

Suomi
Page/Seite 101

Swantech AS
Page/Seite 196

Syrp
Page/Seite 216

T

Table Noir A/S
Page/Seite 146

Tanya Ceramic
Page/Seite 149

Techtronic Industries (Dongguan) Co., Ltd.
Page/Seite 179

Telenor Norway
Page/Seite 289

Televic Conference
Page/Seite 272

TENZ GmbH
Page/Seite 184–185

TH Swiss AG
Page/Seite 211

Tiger Corporation
Page/Seite 136

Tinno Mobile Technology Corp.
Page/Seite 277

Tobi Kindermöbel GmbH
Page/Seite 82

Jingdezhen Tongzao Trade Co., Ltd.
Page/Seite 158

Toolex AB
Page/Seite 191

Top Profit Manufacturing Co., Ltd.
Page/Seite 129

TrêsDê, Lda
Page/Seite 90

U

uccellino
Page/Seite 148

Ugreen Group Limited
Page/Seite 263

Urban Iki
OGK Europe BV
Page/Seite 78

Shenzhen UVLED Optical Technology Co., Ltd.
Shenzhen UV Guard Technology Co., Ltd.
Page/Seite 131

V

Vaonis
Page/Seite 224–225

Villeroy & Boch AG
Page/Seite 149

Vitec Imaging Solutions S.p.A.
Page/Seite 218, 246

Vodafone Group Services GmbH
Page/Seite 288

Vonmählen GmbH
Page/Seite 267

Vorwerk Elektrowerke GmbH & Co. KG
Page/Seite 123

VR Electronics Limited
Page/Seite 240–241

W

Robert Welch Designs Ltd.
Page/Seite 156

Shanghai Whalesbot Technology Co., Ltd.
Page/Seite 312

Wiha Werkzeuge GmbH
Page/Seite 187

Winsol
Page/Seite 172–173

Wiral Technologies AS
Page/Seite 219

WMF Group GmbH
Page/Seite 152

Norbert Woll GmbH
Page/Seite 137

Wuro GmbH & Co. KG
Page/Seite 186

X

X Block ApS
Page/Seite 91

Xiaomi Inc.
Page/Seite 70, 89, 115, 250–251

Xiamen XiaoPaoDan Technology
Page/Seite 158

Jieyang Xingcai Industrial Co., Ltd.
Page/Seite 153

Hangzhou Xingshangzhongzhi Clothing Co., Ltd.
Page/Seite 105

Alphabetical index manufacturers and distributors
Alphabetisches Hersteller- und Vertriebs-Register

Y

YAHUI Fashion & Technology
(Shanghai) Co., Ltd.
Page/Seite 104

YASKAWA Electric Corp.
Page/Seite 301

Hefei Yiso Product Design Co., Ltd.
Page/Seite 152

Shenzhen Yuanguanghao Electronics Co., Ltd.
Page/Seite 95

Yukai Engineering
Page/Seite 311

Yushin Precision Equipment Co., Ltd.
Page/Seite 306

Z

Carl Zeiss AG
Page/Seite 202-203

Guilin Zhishen Information Technology Co., Ltd.
Page/Seite 219

Zimi Corporation
Page/Seite 246, 263

Zimmer Group
Page/Seite 307

Hangzhou ZT Model Co., Ltd.
Page/Seite 92

ZTE Corporation
Page/Seite 283

Alphabetical index designers
Alphabetisches Designer-Register

3D Connection
Page/Seite 101

Shenzhen 21g Product Design Co., Ltd.
Page/Seite 283

Shenzhen 55° Innovation Technology Co., Ltd.
Page/Seite 154

700Kids (Shenzhen) Technology Co., Ltd.
Page/Seite 89

A

Øivind Aabye
Wiral Technologies AS
Page/Seite 219

Above Agency AB
Page/Seite 101

ABUS Security-Center GmbH & Co. KG
Page/Seite 228

ACERA
Brand LIVEN
Page/Seite 153

AEC Lighting Solutions Co., Ltd.
Page/Seite 197

Beijing AIQI Technology Co., Ltd.
Page/Seite 313

AKS Design Studio
Page/Seite 153

James Allen
Syrp
Page/Seite 216

Tony Andersson
Toolex AB
Page/Seite 191

Stijn Antonisse
Somnox
Page/Seite 311

Apple
Page/Seite 232-233, 248-249, 257

Asko Appliances AB
ASKO Design Centre
Page/Seite 115

Asustek Computer Inc.
Page/Seite 246, 258

Atomos
Page/Seite 221

Shenzhen Atuman Precision Machinery Technology Co., Ltd.
Page/Seite 193

Royal Auping
Page/Seite 311

AVer Information Inc.
Page/Seite 271

AVVIO GmbH & Co KG
Page/Seite 184-185

Aydya Limited
Page/Seite 142

B

BA KE Technologies (Dongguan) Co., Ltd.
Page/Seite 86

Kenji Baba
Nikon Corporation
Page/Seite 205

BabyBjörn AB
Page/Seite 101

Kyoungsub Bae
Hyundai Heavy Industries
Page/Seite 298-299

Bahama GmbH
Page/Seite 174

Baidu Online Network Technology (Beijing) Co., Ltd.
Page/Seite 310

Elena Balakhnova
Shenzhen Bo Yi Industrial Co., Ltd.
Page/Seite 255

Balance Design
Page/Seite 158

Hazal Balasar
Nude
Page/Seite 163

Noah Balmer
Vitec Imaging Solutions S.p.A.
Page/Seite 218, 246

Markus Bangerter
Flexa4Dreams A/S
Page/Seite 82

Lovorika Banovic
Flying Tiger Copenhagen
Zebra A/S
Page/Seite 91

BANTUM
Page/Seite 290

Shanghai Baotung Tech Co., Ltd.
Page/Seite 70

Nadia Bartels-Wijstma
BK Cookware BV
Page/Seite 140

Shenzhen Beite Industry Design Co., Ltd.
Page/Seite 87

Zack Bennett
Fahrenheit Design
Page/Seite 271

BERG Toys B.V.
Page/Seite 88

BergHOFF Worldwide
Page/Seite 136

Pär Bergström
Shift Design & Strategy AB
Page/Seite 295

Gemma Bernal
Page/Seite 147

Allen Bertelsen
Kitchen King Limited
Page/Seite 128

Jamie Bertelsen
Kitchen King Limited
Page/Seite 128

HTS BeSafe AS
Page/Seite 76

Bezalel Inc.
Page/Seite 262

Gaoxin Bi
Beijing MIIIW Technology Co., Ltd.
Miiiw Design Team
Page/Seite 255

Aixia Bian
AEC Lighting Solutions Co., Ltd.
Page/Seite 197

Marc Binder
Rotho Kunststoff AG
Page/Seite 130

Oscar Björk
Struktur Design
Page/Seite 273

BK Cookware BV
Page/Seite 140

Blackmagic Design
Page/Seite 214, 222-223

Sam Blok
Syrp
Page/Seite 216

Blond Ltd.
Page/Seite 100, 103

Blueye Robotics
Page/Seite 308

Shenzhen Bo Yi Industrial Co., Ltd.
Page/Seite 255

Christian Bockskopf
Riedel Communications GmbH & Co. KG
Page/Seite 279

Helena Boddenberg
Villeroy & Boch AG
Page/Seite 149

Osmund Bøe
Wiral Technologies AS
Page/Seite 219

Christoph Böhler
Böhler GmbH
Corporate Industrial Design
Page/Seite 190

Hangzhou Bole Industrial Design
Page/Seite 116

Jeremy Bond
Mymuro Ltd.
Page/Seite 91

BONECO AG
Page/Seite 116

Shenzhen Booyue Daily Necessities Co., Ltd.
Page/Seite 94

Robert Bosch Hausgeräte GmbH
Page/Seite 125

Robert Bosch Power Tools GmbH
Page/Seite 193

BOSMA Corp.
Page/Seite 227

Bradshaw Home
Page/Seite 143

Barbara Brand
Oblong Industries
Page/Seite 275

BRANDIS Industrial Design
Page/Seite 125

BRICKR Corp. Information
Page/Seite 271

Britax Römer Kindersicherheit GmbH
Page/Seite 77

Marcus Brunner
Rotho Kunststoff AG
Page/Seite 130

BSH Home Appliances (China) Co., Ltd.
Page/Seite 112

Adrian Buchmann
Sequent Ltd.
Page/Seite 236

Igor Buturlia
VR Electronics Limited
Page/Seite 240-241

C

Cangshan Cutlery Company
Page/Seite 143

Cong Cao
Beijing AIQI Technology Co., Ltd.
Page/Seite 313

Yulan Cao
China Mobile Group Device Co., Ltd.
Page/Seite 287

Carnival Corporation & plc
Page/Seite 247

Carozzeria Kawai
Page/Seite 134-135

Casa Vigar S.L.
Page/Seite 130

Luca Casini
Luca Casini Design Studio
and Casini Studio Industrial Design
Page/Seite 123

Alessandro Cereda
Tatic Designstudio S.r.l.
Page/Seite 168

Jiyoun Cha
LG Electronics Inc.
Page/Seite 252

Liu Chang
CMCC
Page/Seite 288

Sheng-Chieh Chang
Bezalel Inc.
Page/Seite 262

Feng Chen
Makeblock Co., Ltd.
Page/Seite 313

Prof. Chen Feng
Stone (Shanghai) Juvenile Product Co., Ltd.
Page/Seite 71

Fengming Chen
inDare Design Strategy Limited
Page/Seite 96, 244

Jie Chen
Hefei Yiso Product Design Co., Ltd.
Page/Seite 152

Lei Chen
Beijing MIIIW Technology Co., Ltd.
Miiiw Design Team
Page/Seite 255

Pengfei Chen
Jingdezhen Tongzao Trade Co., Ltd.
Page/Seite 158

Qinglang Chen
inDare Design Strategy Limited
Page/Seite 96, 244

Shaolong Chen
inDare Design Strategy Limited
Page/Seite 96, 244

SK Chen
Morus Technology (Shenzhen) Co., Ltd.
Page/Seite 115

Weihao Chen
inDare Design Strategy Limited
Page/Seite 244

Xiaohui Chen
Ruijie Networks Co., Ltd.
Page/Seite 283

Yu Chen
Mobvoi US LLC
Page/Seite 238

Yu Han Chen
Shenzhen Ontology Design Co., Ltd.
Page/Seite 244

Yujie Chen
inDare Design Strategy Limited
Page/Seite 96, 244

Zhenhao Chen
Beijing MIIIW Technology Co., Ltd.
Miiiw Design Team
Page/Seite 255

Hui Cheng
Shenzhen SenseTime Technology Co., Ltd.
Page/Seite 312

Chi-Ya Chien
Eilong Enterprise Co., Ltd.
Page/Seite 156

China Mobile Communications Group Co., Ltd.,
Government and Enterprise Service Company
Page/Seite 279

China Mobile Group Device Co., Ltd.
Page/Seite 287

Youngsu Cho
Meizu Technology Co., Ltd.
Page/Seite 253

Jaepil Choi
Hyundai Heavy Industries
Page/Seite 298-299

Jeongguen Choi
LG Electronics Inc.
Page/Seite 237

Huang Chun
ZTE Corporation
Page/Seite 283

Cisco
Page/Seite 272

CMCC
Page/Seite 288

colarty GmbH & Co. KG
Page/Seite 147

Coway
Page/Seite 117

CRA Carlo Ratti Associati
Page/Seite 308

David Crafoord
McKinsey Design
Page/Seite 101

Cybex GmbH
Page/Seite 68

D

D'Andrea & Evers Design
Page/Seite 76

Likun Dai
Hefei Yiso Product Design Co., Ltd.
Page/Seite 152

Yanxin Dai
Hanergy Mobile Energy Holding Group Ltd.
Page/Seite 266

Chris Dawson
Promethean World Inc.
Page/Seite 270

399

Alphabetical index designers
Alphabetisches Designer-Register

Roseanne de Bruin
Designerscope Limited
Page/Seite 186

Wim de Bruin
Designerscope Limited
Page/Seite 186

Robyn de Bruin-Judge
Designerscope Limited
Page/Seite 186

Philippe de la Coussaye
Groupe SEB
Page/Seite 143

Design + Industry
Page/Seite 171

Design Group Italia
Page/Seite 198

Design To Product Ltd.
Page/Seite 103

Design3 GmbH
Page/Seite 309

designaffairs GmbH
Page/Seite 202–203

Designerscope Limited
Page/Seite 186

Deutsche Lufthansa AG
Page/Seite 148

DH-Robotics Technology Co., Ltd.
Page/Seite 307

Diono
Page/Seite 79

Daniel Dockner
Robert Bosch Hausgeräte GmbH
Page/Seite 125

Spencer Dodge
Fahrenheit Design
Page/Seite 271

Jake Dodson
Riedel Communications GmbH & Co. KG
Page/Seite 279

Studio Doms AB
Page/Seite 195

Wukun Dong
YAHUI Fashion & Technology (Shanghai) Co., Ltd.
Page/Seite 104

DPA Microphones
Page/Seite 274

Dreamfarm
Page/Seite 141

DreBo Werkzeugfabrik GmbH
Page/Seite 187

Christina Driessen
Lässig GmbH
Page/Seite 105

DTEN
Page/Seite 268–269

Dunlop Protective Footwear
Hevea BV
Page/Seite 199

E

Eckstein Design
Page/Seite 309

Ecovacs Robotics Co., Ltd.
Ecovacs Design Team
Page/Seite 122

Shenzhen EEDesign Co., Ltd.
Page/Seite 131

Shenzhen Eevin Design Co., Ltd.
Page/Seite 279

EGGS Design
Page/Seite 308

Eilong Enterprise Co., Ltd.
Page/Seite 156

Anja Einwag
Vodafone Group Services GmbH
Page/Seite 288

Peter Ejvinsson
McKinsey Design
Page/Seite 101

Karin Ekwall
Frost Produkt AS
Page/Seite 226

Elbe Eichhorn
Page/Seite 159

AB Electrolux
Page/Seite 116, 124

Elesa S.p.A.
Page/Seite 190–191

Arman Emami
Emami Design
Page/Seite 160, 267

Enfant Terrible Design AB
Page/Seite 80–81

Job Engel
Somnox
Page/Seite 311

Enlisted Design
Page/Seite 291–292

erfindergeist GmbH
Page/Seite 282

Ergo Design
Page/Seite 68

Ericsson AB
Page/Seite 280–281

Stein Ove Eriksen
Huddly AS
Page/Seite 226

Oliver Erritzøe
X Block ApS
Page/Seite 91

Yousook Eun
LG Electronics Inc.
Page/Seite 309

Everybot Inc.
Page/Seite 119

F

Jabe Faber
Royal Auping
Page/Seite 311

Fahrenheit Design
Page/Seite 271

Bin Feng
Microduino
Page/Seite 93

Shaohai Feng
Shenzhen Yuanguanghao Electronics Co., Ltd.
Page/Seite 95

fischerwerke GmbH & Co. KG
Page/Seite 187

Fiskars Brands Inc.
Page/Seite 169

Fiskars Finland Oy Ab
Page/Seite 166–168

Fitbit, Inc.
Page/Seite 239

Manfred Fitsch
BONECO AG
Page/Seite 116

Fjord | Accenture Interactive
Page/Seite 304–305

Flexa4Dreams A/S
Page/Seite 82

FLIR Systems, Inc.
Page/Seite 226

FLSK Products GmbH
Page/Seite 155

Flyaway Designs
Page/Seite 84

Flying Tiger Copenhagen
Zebra A/S
Page/Seite 91

Benjamin Folkmann Hansen
Table Noir A/S
Page/Seite 146

FORM bureau
Page/Seite 82

Freudenberg Home and Cleaning Solutions GmbH
Page/Seite 123

Melanie Friar
Promethean World Inc.
Page/Seite 270

Sondre Frost Urstad
Frost Produkt AS
Page/Seite 226

FUJIFILM Corporation
Page/Seite 208–210, 212–213, 217, 227

Michael Fürstenberg
Britax Römer Kindersicherheit GmbH
Page/Seite 77

Lisa Furuland-Kotsianis
Enfant Terrible Design AB
Page/Seite 80–81

FutureModel Corp.
Page/Seite 259

G

Scott Gant
Litra
Page/Seite 220

Tian Gao
Shenzhen EEDesign Co., Ltd.
Page/Seite 131

GARDENA GmbH
Page/Seite 170

Jiao Ge
Shenzhen Xivokids Design Co., Ltd.
Page/Seite 311

Thomas Gemperle
Tatic Designstudio S.r.l.
Page/Seite 168

Guangdong Genius Technology Co., Ltd.
Page/Seite 234

Michael Geyer
Pocket Sky OG
Page/Seite 247

Gigodesign d.o.o.
Page/Seite 129

Mark Gilson
Fahrenheit Design
Page/Seite 271

Theo Ginman
MODU ApS
Page/Seite 93

Goodbaby Child Products Co., Ltd.
Page/Seite 88

Google LLC
Page/Seite 250–251, 254

Gorenje Design Studio
Page/Seite 115

Goui
Page/Seite 262

Helle Grande
Wiral Technologies AS
Page/Seite 219

Alexander Gransbury
Dreamfarm
Page/Seite 141

Groupe SEB
Page/Seite 143

Jiawei Gu
Ling Technology Co., Ltd.
Page/Seite 94

Roger Gu
YAHUI Fashion & Technology (Shanghai) Co., Ltd.
Page/Seite 104

Guan Daisong
Baidu Online Network Technology (Beijing) Co., Ltd.
Page/Seite 310

Chen Guo
China Mobile Group Device Co., Ltd.
Page/Seite 287

Miaojun Guo
Hefei Yiso Product Design Co., Ltd.
Page/Seite 152

Zhihui Guo
Hefei Yiso Product Design Co., Ltd.
Page/Seite 152

Johan Gustavsson
Struktur Design
Page/Seite 273

Hans Gutter
HTS BeSafe AS
Page/Seite 76

H

Laura Haas
Tatic Designstudio S.r.l.
Page/Seite 119

Haier Innovation Design Center
Page/Seite 110–111

Adam Hall GmbH
Page/Seite 272

Carl Hampf
Shift Design & Strategy AB
Page/Seite 295

Aron Han
Netgear
Page/Seite 292–293

Hanergy Mobile Energy Holding Group Ltd.
Page/Seite 266

Xiong Hao
Kurz Kurz Design China
Page/Seite 136

Akira Haranaka
SHARP Corporation
IoT Communication BU
Page/Seite 260

Jiabin He
Ling Technology Co., Ltd.
Page/Seite 94

Anders Heger
Heger Design
Page/Seite 274

Clement Heinen
Somnox
Page/Seite 311

Matthias Helfert
Alfred Kärcher SE & Co. KG
Page/Seite 118

Malin Henrikson
BabyBjörn AB
Page/Seite 101

Patrick Heutschi
Tatic Designstudio S.r.l.
Page/Seite 119

Hangzhou Hikrobot Technology Co., Ltd.
Page/Seite 308

Alison Hill
LifeStraw
Vestergaard S.A.
Page/Seite 162

Hilti Corporation
Page/Seite 178, 181–183, 192

höfats GmbH
Page/Seite 171

Ralf Holleis
Cybex GmbH
Page/Seite 68

Joe Hollier
Light
Page/Seite 259

Michel Holper
Joolz by Milk Design B.V.
Page/Seite 70

Honeywell
Page/Seite 198

Honeywell China
SPS HUE Design Studio
Page/Seite 194, 198–199

Xiao Hong
Ling Technology Co., Ltd.
Page/Seite 94

Taizhou Howawa Baby Products Co., Ltd.
Page/Seite 103

Philip Howieson
Dreamfarm
Page/Seite 141

David Howse
Kitchen King Limited
Page/Seite 128

Chia Chun Hsu
NetDragon Websoft Inc.
Page/Seite 270

Alphabetical index designers
Alphabetisches Designer-Register

Chengjie Hu
Ruijie Networks Co., Ltd.
Page/Seite 283

Gang Hu
Hefei Yiso Product Design Co., Ltd.
Page/Seite 152

Rose Hu
Netgear
Page/Seite 292

Zhefeng Hu
Hefei Yiso Product Design Co., Ltd.
Page/Seite 152

Anhui Huami Information Technology Co., Ltd.
Page/Seite 237

Haining Huang
Ruijie Networks Co., Ltd.
Page/Seite 283

Jinbo Huang
Ling Technology Co., Ltd.
Page/Seite 94

Jun Biao Huang
Shenzhen Ontology Design Co., Ltd.
Page/Seite 244

Pei Wen Huang
Guangzhou Kemei Commodity Co., Ltd.
Page/Seite 153

Weijun Huang
Roci Design Technology Co., Ltd.
Page/Seite 93

Yao Yao Huang
Shenzhen Beite Industry Design Co., Ltd.
Page/Seite 87

Yu Chang Huang
NetDragon Websoft Inc.
Page/Seite 270

Zan Huang
Ruijie Networks Co., Ltd.
Page/Seite 283

Zhengjun Huang
New H3C Technologies Co., Ltd.
Page/Seite 229

Huang Zhirong
LINKFAIR Industrial Design Center
Page/Seite 136

Huawei Device (Shenzhen) Co., Ltd.
Page/Seite 267, 274

Huawei Technologies Co., Ltd.
Page/Seite 228, 289

Huddly AS
Page/Seite 226

Bryan Hunter
Fahrenheit Design
Page/Seite 271

Husqvarna AB (publ.)
Page/Seite 171

Junghoo Hwang
JJOBI Company
Page/Seite 98–100

Hyundai Heavy Industries
Page/Seite 298–299

Hyundai Robotics
Page/Seite 298–299

I

ICI Design Institute Inc.
Page/Seite 306

Idenova BV Industrial Design
Page/Seite 78

Ideo Group LLC
Page/Seite 68

Idesign
Page/Seite 89

IDING (Chengdu) Innovation Technology Ltd.
Page/Seite 215

iFootage International (HK) Limited
Page/Seite 219

igus GmbH
Page/Seite 301

Yoshiaki Iida
ICI Design Institute Inc.
Page/Seite 306

IKEA of Sweden
Page/Seite 174

Haruka Ikegame
FUJIFILM Corporation
Page/Seite 209, 212–213

iloom
Page/Seite 84

Masazumi Imai
FUJIFILM Corporation
Page/Seite 208, 217

Makoto Imamizu
Nikon Corporation
Page/Seite 205

inDare Design Strategy Limited
Page/Seite 96, 244

Intenso International GmbH
Page/Seite 264–265

iRobot
Page/Seite 120–121

i.safe MOBILE GmbH
Page/Seite 256

J

Julian Jagtenberg
Somnox
Page/Seite 311

Robert Jensen
Milwaukee Tool
Page/Seite 179

Liu Jia
Xiaomi Inc.
Page/Seite 250

Xiong Jian
Huawei Technologies Co., Ltd.
Page/Seite 228

Wei Jiang
Hefei Yiso Product Design Co., Ltd.
Page/Seite 152

Chen Jie
Ugreen Group Limited
Page/Seite 263

Shanghai Jieyong Technology Co., Ltd.
Page/Seite 220–221

Chang Jin
Hangzhou Rosou Electronic Technology Co., Ltd.
Page/Seite 117

Ronghao Jin
Mercku Inc.
Page/Seite 294

Yang Jinling
Xiaomi Inc.
Page/Seite 251

JJOBI Company
Page/Seite 98–100

Mats Gabriel Love Johansen
Huddly AS
Page/Seite 226

Victor Johansson
Above Agency AB
Page/Seite 101

Joie Children's Products Co., Ltd.
Page/Seite 64–67, 74–75

Joolz by Milk Design B.V.
Page/Seite 70

Oskar Juhlin
McKinsey Design
Page/Seite 199

Henry Jupille
Netgear
Page/Seite 291

K

Kabinet 01 d.o.o.
Page/Seite 129

Zhu Kai
Xiaomi Inc.
Page/Seite 251

Thomas Kaiser
höfats GmbH
Page/Seite 171

Torkild Kaland
Swantech AS
Page/Seite 196

Ed Kalubiran
Netgear
Page/Seite 291

Keita Kamei
FUJIFILM Corporation
Page/Seite 209–210, 212

Kanae Design Labo
Page/Seite 136

Kang Zhen Hui
ACERA
Brand LIVEN
Page/Seite 153

Richard Kappeller
Messermacher Kappeller GmbH
Page/Seite 144–145

Umut Sinan Karaca
Nude
Page/Seite 161

Alfred Kärcher SE & Co. KG
Page/Seite 118

Masaki Kawamura
SHARP Corporation
IoT Communication BU
Page/Seite 260

Xie Ke
Mobvoi US LLC
Page/Seite 235, 238

Christian Keller
erfindergeist GmbH
Page/Seite 282

Thomas Keller
Page/Seite 143

Guangzhou Kemei Commodity Co., Ltd.
Page/Seite 153

Uwe Kemker
Vorwerk Elektrowerke GmbH & Co. KG
Page/Seite 123

Sevgi Kes
Nude
Page/Seite 163

Bong Yun Kim
Everybot Inc.
Page/Seite 119

Hyoni Kim
LG Electronics Inc.
Page/Seite 252

Hyundai Kim
Hyundai Heavy Industries
Page/Seite 298–299

Jinsu Kim
LG Electronics Inc.
Page/Seite 309

Jongwon Kim
Hyundai Robotics
Page/Seite 298–299

Tae Wan Kim
Everybot Inc.
Page/Seite 119

Kingclean Electric Co., Ltd.
Page/Seite 126–127

Katsuhiro Kitade
Panasonic Corporation
Page/Seite 206

Kitchen King Limited
Page/Seite 128

Firas Kittaneh
OCLU
Page/Seite 217

Marcel Klamer
Klamer Productdesign
Page/Seite 188–189

Mona Kleven Lauritzen
Huddly AS
Page/Seite 226

Ernst Köhler
WMF Group GmbH
Page/Seite 152

Koncern Design Studio
Page/Seite 77

Kong Zhi
Haier Innovation Design Center
Page/Seite 110–111

Wouter Kooyman van Guldener
Somnox
Page/Seite 311

Ryuichi Kozeki
RKDS
Page/Seite 141

Raphael Krug
BSH Home Appliances (China) Co., Ltd.
Page/Seite 112

KUKA AG
Page/Seite 300

Yayoi Kuroda
ICI Design Institute Inc.
Page/Seite 306

Kurz Kurz Design China
Page/Seite 136

L

Lesley Lai
Top Profit Manufacturing Co., Ltd.
Page/Seite 129

Pascal Laraignou
X Block ApS
Page/Seite 91

LARQ
Page/Seite 150–151

Johan Larsvall
Idesign
Page/Seite 89

Claudia Lässig
Lässig GmbH
Page/Seite 105

Bong Gun Lee
Netgear
Page/Seite 291

Hyebin Lee
Monit Corp.
Page/Seite 78

Jeonghoon Lee
Monit Corp.
Page/Seite 78

Sanghyun Lee
JJOBI Company
Page/Seite 98–100

Li Lei
ZTE Corporation
Page/Seite 283

Lenovo
Page/Seite 242–243, 273

Pietro Leoni
CRA Carlo Ratti Associati
Page/Seite 308

LG Electronics Inc.
Page/Seite 237, 252, 309

Chengmin Li
Shenzhen NearbyExpress Technology Development Co., Ltd.
Page/Seite 267

De Cheng Li
Shenzhen Ontology Design Co., Ltd.
Page/Seite 244

He Chun Li
Shenzhen Beite Industry Design Co., Ltd.
Page/Seite 87

Jingzhe Li
Kingclean Electric Co., Ltd.
Page/Seite 126–127

Joey Li
700Kids (Shenzhen) Technology Co., Ltd.
Page/Seite 89

Kai Li
New H3C Technologies Co., Ltd.
Page/Seite 229, 290

Li Li
Hangzhou Xingshangzhongzhi Clothing Co., Ltd.
Page/Seite 105

Mulin Li
Makeblock Co., Ltd.
Page/Seite 313

Li Shenghua
Haier Innovation Design Center
Page/Seite 110

Alphabetical index designers
Alphabetisches Designer-Register

Li Shiyan
Baidu Online Network Technology
(Beijing) Co., Ltd.
Page/Seite 310

Weiting Li
China Mobile Communications Group Co., Ltd.,
Government and Enterprise Service Company
Page/Seite 279

Xi Li
Microduino
Page/Seite 93

Zhe Li
Hanergy Mobile Energy Holding Group Ltd.
Page/Seite 266

Zhi Li
Xiamen Stoneware Technology Co., Ltd.
Page/Seite 95

Jinlong Lian
Goodbaby Child Products Co., Ltd.
Page/Seite 88

Guoxing Liang
Guangdong Master Group Co., Ltd.
Page/Seite 138–139

Liang Jianxiu
LINKFAIR Industrial Design Center
Page/Seite 136

Yanming Liang
Guangdong Master Group Co., Ltd.
Page/Seite 138–139

Youlai Liang
Shenzhen NearbyExpress Technology
Development Co., Ltd.
Page/Seite 97

Haibo Liao
Shenzhen Eevin Design Co., Ltd.
Page/Seite 279

LifeStraw
Vestergaard S.A.
Page/Seite 162

Light
Page/Seite 259

Willem Lijmbach
Freudenberg Home and Cleaning
Solutions GmbH
Page/Seite 123

Seongjae Lim
LG Electronics Inc.
Page/Seite 252

Alex Lin
AKS Design Studio
Page/Seite 153

Huahui Lin
inDare Design Strategy Limited
Page/Seite 96

Zizhe Lin
AKS Design Studio
Page/Seite 153

Kristian Lindberg-Poulsen
Senserna A/S
Page/Seite 101

Ling Technology Co., Ltd.
Page/Seite 94

Jonathan Link Selnes
Wiral Technologies AS
Page/Seite 219

LINKFAIR Industrial Design Center
Page/Seite 136

LISLEI, Lda
Page/Seite 87

Piero Lissoni
Lissoni Associati
Page/Seite 175

Litra
Page/Seite 220

Little Swan
Page/Seite 112–114

Chang Qing Liu
Shenzhen Beite Industry Design Co., Ltd.
Page/Seite 87

Prof. Dehua Liu
Shenzhen UVLED Optical Technology Co., Ltd.
Shenzhen UV Guard Technology Co., Ltd.
Page/Seite 131

Edwin Liu
Netgear
Page/Seite 293

Guokun Liu
Shenzhen Xivokids Design Co., Ltd.
Page/Seite 311

John Liu
Shape Products
Page/Seite 245

Qing Song Liu
Shenzhen Beite Industry Design Co., Ltd.
Page/Seite 87

Taorong Liu
Shenzhen 55° Innovation Technology Co., Ltd.
Page/Seite 154

Yuan Liu
Vodafone Group Services GmbH
Page/Seite 288

LKKer Technology Co., Ltd.
Page/Seite 159

Logitech
Page/Seite 247, 271

Yue Long
Kurz Kurz Design China
Page/Seite 136

Nils Löventorn
Idesign
Page/Seite 89

Gan Lu
Remo Tech Co., Ltd.
Page/Seite 215

LÚCID Design Agency
Page/Seite 130

Bolin Luo
Ugreen Group Limited
Page/Seite 263

Dizhou Luo
DH-Robotics Technology Co., Ltd.
Page/Seite 307

Wanlan Luo
IDING (Chengdu) Innovation Technology Ltd.
Page/Seite 215

Ellen Lynghed
Above Agency AB
Page/Seite 101

M

Da Ma
BA KE Technologies (Dongguan) Co., Ltd.
Page/Seite 86

Geng Hao Ma
Shenzhen Ontology Design Co., Ltd.
Page/Seite 244

Made
Page/Seite 272

Jean Luc Madier
LifeStraw
Vestergaard S.A.
Page/Seite 162

Kyoung Hwa Maeng
Coway
Page/Seite 117

Mait Mahlapuu
GARDENA GmbH
Page/Seite 170

Makeblock Co., Ltd.
Page/Seite 313

Yasuhiko Mano
SHARP Corporation
IoT Communication BU
Page/Seite 260

Roberto Manzari
Studio Volpi S.r.l.
Page/Seite 116

May Mao
FLIR Systems, Inc.
Page/Seite 226

Hugo Martin
WMP Creative
Page/Seite 217

Kouji Masano
Panasonic Corporation
Page/Seite 206

Guangdong Master Group Co., Ltd.
Page/Seite 138–139

Andreas Mathieson
Messermacher Kappeller GmbH
Page/Seite 144–145

Matuschek Design & Management
Page/Seite 181–182, 192

McKinsey Design
Page/Seite 101, 199

MEDION AG
Page/Seite 235, 254

Bruno Meier
Rotho Kunststoff AG
Page/Seite 130

Meizu Technology Co., Ltd.
Page/Seite 253

James Melia
Blond Ltd.
Page/Seite 103

Mercku Inc.
Page/Seite 294

Florian Metz
BSH Home Appliances (China) Co., Ltd.
Page/Seite 112

Michael Meyer
Alfred Kärcher SE & Co. KG
Page/Seite 118

Microduino
Page/Seite 93

Beijing MIIIW Technology Co., Ltd.
Miiiw Design Team
Page/Seite 255

Milwaukee Tool
Page/Seite 179

MM Design
Page/Seite 218

Mobvoi US LLC
Page/Seite 235, 238

MODU ApS
Page/Seite 93

Rune T. Møller
DPA Microphones
Page/Seite 274

Monit Corp.
Page/Seite 78

Atsuko Mori
Tiger Corporation
Page/Seite 136

Morus Technology (Shenzhen) Co., Ltd.
Page/Seite 115

Motorola
Page/Seite 261

Motorola Solutions
Page/Seite 258, 278

Hangzhou Mr. Bond Technology Co., Ltd.
Page/Seite 116

Mukako
Mukako Team
Page/Seite 84

Jord Mulder
BERG Toys B.V.
Page/Seite 88

Simon Müller
Böhler GmbH
Corporate Industrial Design
Page/Seite 190

Marius Myking
Snøhetta
Page/Seite 146, 289

Mymuro Ltd.
Page/Seite 91

N

Yunsu Na
iloom
Page/Seite 84

Melina Nasradini
KUKA AG
Page/Seite 300

Shenzhen NearbyExpress Technology
Development Co., Ltd.
Page/Seite 97, 267

NetDragon Websoft Inc.
Page/Seite 270

NetEase Youdao Information Technology
(Beijing) Co., Ltd.
Page/Seite 276

Netgear
Page/Seite 291–293

New H3C Technologies Co., Ltd.
Page/Seite 229, 290

Vincent Ng
Techtronic Industries (Dongguan) Co., Ltd.
Techtronic Design
Page/Seite 179

Feng Ni
Shenzhen SenseTime Technology Co., Ltd.
Page/Seite 312

Martin Nichols
Snøhetta
Page/Seite 146

Scott Niedzwecki
SharkNinja
Page/Seite 125

Yutaka Nikaido
Nikon Corporation
Page/Seite 205

Nikon Corporation
Page/Seite 204–205

Pimsiri Nilkositya
Page/Seite 149

Nokia Networks
Nokia Design
Page/Seite 284–286

Novague
Page/Seite 142

NTT DOCOMO, Inc., Product Department,
Design Management Section
Page/Seite 259, 288

Nude
Page/Seite 161, 163

Nuna International BV
Page/Seite 69, 72–73, 79

Nicole Nusser
colarty GmbH & Co. KG
Page/Seite 147

O

Oblong Industries
Page/Seite 275

OCLU
Page/Seite 217

Yusuf Okhai
Aydya Limited
Page/Seite 142

Andrej Olipa
Tatiana Olipa
Olymp & Olipa GmbH
Page/Seite 83, 85

Olympus Corporation
Page/Seite 207, 278

Shenzhen Ontology Design Co., Ltd.
Page/Seite 244

Orcadesign Consultants
Page/Seite 102

Reisuke Osada
Olympus Corporation
Page/Seite 207

Nadin Ostendorf
colarty GmbH & Co. KG
Page/Seite 147

Alphabetical index designers
Alphabetisches Designer-Register

Yusuke Otani
Sony Corporation
Creative Center
Page/Seite 261

Ova Design
Page/Seite 224–225

P

John Padgett
Carnival Corporation & plc
Page/Seite 247

Debra Pally
Flyaway Designs
Page/Seite 84

Yihang Pan
SOOIBE Intelligent Technology
(Hangzhou) Co., Ltd.
Page/Seite 87

Panasonic Appliances Washing Machine
Panasonic Design Center
Page/Seite 108–109

Panasonic Corporation
Page/Seite 206

Si Hui Pang
Shenzhen Beite Industry Design Co., Ltd.
Page/Seite 87

Junghwan Park
JJOBI Company
Page/Seite 98–100

Sea-La Park
LG Electronics Inc.
Page/Seite 237

Seala Park
LG Electronics Inc.
Page/Seite 252

Roberto Pauli
Design To Product Ltd.
Page/Seite 103

Pearl Creative
Page/Seite 118

Chun Chieh Peng
NetDragon Websoft Inc.
Page/Seite 270

Marcel Pfeiffer
Zimmer Group
Page/Seite 307

Philips
Philips Design
Page/Seite 100, 103, 117, 125

Phoenix Design GmbH + Co. KG
Page/Seite 123

Pi-Design AG
Page/Seite 156–157

Pigeon
Page/Seite 102

Christian Pihale
Tobi Kindermöbel GmbH
Page/Seite 82

PIXII
Page/Seite 207

Plant Fiber International Incorporation
Page/Seite 160

Platinumdesign
Page/Seite 193

Playsteam Education Limited
Page/Seite 92

Nilas Pleje
GARDENA GmbH
Page/Seite 170

Rony Plesl
Sahm GmbH & Co. KG
Page/Seite 161

Pocket Sky OG
Page/Seite 247

Studio F. A. Porsche
Page/Seite 108–109

Positec Technology
Page/Seite 180

Promethean World Inc.
Page/Seite 270

Jan Puranen
McKinsey Design
Page/Seite 199

Q

Chang Qu
Roci Design Technology Co., Ltd.
Page/Seite 93

Quinny
Dorel Juvenile
Page/Seite 70

R

r2p GmbH
Page/Seite 227–228

Jonathan Radetz
Studio Jonathan Radetz
Page/Seite 163

Elisabeth Ramel-Wåhrberg
McKinsey Design
Page/Seite 101

Jonathan Rasmussen
MODU ApS
Page/Seite 93

Martin Rauch
GARDENA GmbH
Page/Seite 170

Sruli Recht
Serial Future Visions, Inc.
Norlan
Page/Seite 160

Remo Tech Co., Ltd.
Page/Seite 215

Riedel Communications GmbH & Co. KG
Page/Seite 279

RKDS
Page/Seite 141

RND PLUS
Page/Seite 131

Colin Roberts
Fiskars Brands Inc.
Page/Seite 169

Roci Design Technology Co., Ltd.
Page/Seite 93

Pieter Roex
BergHOFF Worldwide
Page/Seite 136

Soren Rose Studio
Page/Seite 162

Hangzhou Rosou Electronic Technology Co., Ltd.
Page/Seite 117

Rotho Kunststoff AG
Page/Seite 130

Royole Corporation
Page/Seite 255, 261

Rudolph Schelling Webermann
Product Design & Innovation Consultancy
Page/Seite 141

Ruijie Networks Co., Ltd.
Page/Seite 283

Christian Rummel
Pearl Creative
Page/Seite 118

S

SACKit ApS
Page/Seite 266

Eivind Sæter
Wiral Technologies AS
Page/Seite 219

Sahm GmbH & Co. KG
Page/Seite 161

Hiroyuki Sakai
FUJIFILM Corporation
Page/Seite 213, 217, 227

Masayuki Sakai
FUJIFILM Corporation
Page/Seite 210

Wakaba Sakai
Sony Corporation
Creative Center
Page/Seite 261

Samwoo Instrument, Inc.
Page/Seite 131

Atsushi Sasaki
Panasonic Corporation
Page/Seite 206

Paul Scheurwater
BERG Toys B.V.
Page/Seite 88

Niklas Schmidt
Huddly AS
Page/Seite 226

Felix Schneider
Alfred Kärcher SE & Co. KG
Page/Seite 118

Henrik Schneider
Senserna A/S
Page/Seite 101

Daniel Schubert
Vodafone Group Services GmbH
Page/Seite 288

Thomas Schuster
Dreamfarm
Page/Seite 141

Scribit
Page/Seite 308

Groupe SEB
Page/Seite 143

Hans-Wilhelm Seitz
Design Studio Hans-Wilhelm Seitz
Page/Seite 149

Mario Selic
Selic Industriedesign
Page/Seite 300

Senserna A/S
Page/Seite 101

Shenzhen SenseTime Technology Co., Ltd.
Page/Seite 312

Bo Seong Seo
Coway
Page/Seite 117

Sequent Ltd.
Page/Seite 236

Serial Future Visions, Inc.
Norlan
Page/Seite 160

Fei Shan
Shenzhen Beite Industry Design Co., Ltd.
Page/Seite 87

Shape Products
Page/Seite 245

SharkNinja
Page/Seite 125

SHARP Corporation
IoT Communication BU
Page/Seite 260

Henry Shawn
SIMDO Technology Co., Ltd.
Page/Seite 258

Weijie Shen
Meizu Technology Co., Ltd.
Page/Seite 253

Kazuhiro Shibata
SHARP Corporation
IoT Communication BU
Page/Seite 260

Shift Design & Strategy AB
Page/Seite 295

Viktoriia Shkliar
FORM bureau
Page/Seite 82

SIMDO Technology Co., Ltd.
Page/Seite 258

David Alan Smith
Goodbaby Child Products Co., Ltd.
Page/Seite 88

Joyce Smits
HTS BeSafe AS
Page/Seite 76

Snøhetta
Page/Seite 146, 289

Somnox
Page/Seite 311

Sonja Song
FLIR Systems, Inc.
Page/Seite 226

Sony Corporation
Creative Center
Page/Seite 261

SOOIBE Intelligent Technology
(Hangzhou) Co., Ltd.
Page/Seite 87

Stan Spangenberg
Joolz by Milk Design B.V.
Page/Seite 70

Jesse Staines
Kitchen King Limited
Page/Seite 128

Christian Stenglein
Freudenberg Home and Cleaning
Solutions GmbH
Page/Seite 123

Stone (Shanghai) Juvenile Product Co., Ltd.
Page/Seite 71

Xiamen Stoneware Technology Co., Ltd.
Page/Seite 95

Struktur Design
Page/Seite 273

studiomem GmbH
Page/Seite 288

Ine Stultjens
Royal Auping
Page/Seite 311

Sun Peng
Haier Innovation Design Center
Page/Seite 111

Sun Xiaoli
Haier Innovation Design Center
Page/Seite 110

Suomi
Suomi Design Team
Page/Seite 101

Shu Suzuki
Nikon Corporation
Page/Seite 204

Tatsuhiko Suzuki
Olympus Corporation
Page/Seite 278

Swantech AS
Page/Seite 196

Syrp
Page/Seite 216

T

Table Noir A/S
Page/Seite 146

Taga
Page/Seite 215

Keiichiro Takahashi
FUJIFILM Corporation
Page/Seite 208

Tom Tam
Shenzhen 55° Innovation Technology Co., Ltd.
Page/Seite 154

Takashi Tanaka
SHARP Corporation
IoT Communication BU
Page/Seite 260

Kaiwei Tang
Light
Page/Seite 259

Liang Tang
ZCO Design Co., Ltd.
Page/Seite 312

Prof. Yi Tang
Shenzhen UVLED Optical Technology Co., Ltd.
Shenzhen UV Guard Technology Co., Ltd.
Page/Seite 131

Mifu Tao
Shenzhen Booyue Daily Necessities Co., Ltd.
Page/Seite 94

Aleks Tatic
Tatic Designstudio S.r.l.
Page/Seite 119, 168

Kosuke Tatsumi
Yukai Engineering
Page/Seite 311

403

Alphabetical index designers
Alphabetisches Designer-Register

Techtronic Industries (Dongguan) Co., Ltd.
Techtronic Design
Page/Seite 179

Knut Helge Teppan
Huddly AS
Page/Seite 226

Alex Terzariol
MM Design
Page/Seite 218

TH Swiss AG
Page/Seite 211

Markus Theiler
KUKA AG
Page/Seite 300

Felix Thies
Vorwerk Elektrowerke GmbH & Co. KG
Page/Seite 123

Chris Thomson
Syrp
Page/Seite 216

Tiger Corporation
Page/Seite 136

Shenzhen Tinno Wireless Technology Co., Ltd.
Page/Seite 277

Tobi Kindermöbel GmbH
Page/Seite 82

Rui Tomás
TrêsDê, Lda
Page/Seite 90

Jingdezhen Tongzao Trade Co., Ltd.
Page/Seite 158

Toolex AB
Page/Seite 191

Tools Design
Page/Seite 162

Toout Design
Page/Seite 229

Top Profit Manufacturing Co., Ltd.
Page/Seite 129

TrêsDê, Lda
Page/Seite 90

Kanae Tsukamoto
Kanae Design Labo
Page/Seite 136

Alexander Turesson
GARDENA GmbH
Page/Seite 170

U

Ugreen Group Limited
Page/Seite 263

John Underkoffler
Oblong Industries
Page/Seite 275

Shenzhen UVLED Optical Technology Co., Ltd.
Shenzhen UV Guard Technology Co., Ltd.
Page/Seite 131

V

Kjartan Vaaland
Frost Produkt AS
Page/Seite 226

Nicholas Vallo
Fiskars Brands Inc.
Page/Seite 169

Erik van der Veer
HTS BeSafe AS
Page/Seite 76

Okke van Mourik
HTS BeSafe AS
Page/Seite 76

VanBerlo
Page/Seite 307

Vanderveer Designers
Page/Seite 70

Gwenn Vanthournout
Winsol
Page/Seite 172–173

Villeroy & Boch AG
Page/Seite 149

Vitec Imaging Solutions S.p.A.
Page/Seite 218, 246

Vodafone Group Services GmbH
Page/Seite 288

Studio Volpi S.r.l.
Page/Seite 116

Vorwerk Elektrowerke GmbH & Co. KG
Page/Seite 123

VR Electronics Limited
Page/Seite 240–241

W

Are-Dag Wagtskjold Eriksen
Swantech AS
Page/Seite 196

Reiner Wallbaum
Elbe Eichhorn
Page/Seite 159

Mark Wallerberger
Pocket Sky OG
Page/Seite 247

Dongwei Wang
Meizu Technology Co., Ltd.
Page/Seite 253

Haochen Wang
Shanghai Jieyong Technology Co., Ltd.
Page/Seite 220–221

Liang Wang
Makeblock Co., Ltd.
Page/Seite 313

Mandy Wang
Hangzhou Bole Industrial Design
Page/Seite 116

Xi Wang
Ling Technology Co., Ltd.
Page/Seite 94

Xiaonan Wang
Jingdezhen Tongzao Trade Co., Ltd.
Page/Seite 158

Xudong Wang
NetEase Youdao Information Technology (Beijing) Co., Ltd.
Page/Seite 276

Yong Wang
Shenzhen Beite Industry Design Co., Ltd.
Page/Seite 87

Zhenshan Wang
Microduino
Page/Seite 93

Christian Wassermann
höfats GmbH
Page/Seite 171

Masahiro Watanabe
Tiger Corporation
Page/Seite 136

Carsten Weber
BSH Home Appliances (China) Co., Ltd.
Page/Seite 112

Emery Weber
Fiskars Brands Inc.
Page/Seite 169

Robert Welch Designs Ltd.
Robert Welch Design Team
Page/Seite 156

Cornelia Werth
Britax Römer Kindersicherheit GmbH
Page/Seite 77

Shanghai Whalesbot Technology Co., Ltd.
Page/Seite 312

Sindre Widerberg
Frost Produkt AS
Page/Seite 226

Wiha Werkzeuge GmbH
Page/Seite 187

Ola Wihlborg
IKEA of Sweden
Page/Seite 174

Wiko SAS
Page/Seite 277

Winsol
Page/Seite 172–173

Wiral Technologies AS
Page/Seite 219

Maciej Wlasnowolski
TH Swiss AG
Page/Seite 211

WMF Group GmbH
Page/Seite 152

WMP Creative
Page/Seite 217

Norbert Woll GmbH
Page/Seite 137

Jeff Wollenzien
Shape Products
Page/Seite 245

Jason Wong
BOSMA Corp.
Page/Seite 227

Lewis Wong
AKS Design Studio
Page/Seite 153

Steve Woodall
Kitchen King Limited
Page/Seite 128

Wu Caner
Guilin Zhishen Information Technology Co., Ltd.
Page/Seite 219

Feng Zhi Wu
Shenzhen Ontology Design Co., Ltd.
Page/Seite 244

Frank Wu
Bezalel Inc.
Page/Seite 262

Wu Shangkai
LINKFAIR Industrial Design Center
Page/Seite 136

Xiangwen Wu
Beijing MIIIW Technology Co., Ltd.
Miiiw Design Team
Page/Seite 255

Dirk Wynants Design Works
Page/Seite 174

X

X Block ApS
Page/Seite 91

Henglu Xia
Taizhou Howawa Baby Products Co., Ltd.
Page/Seite 103

Tianyu Xiao
Shenzhen NearbyExpress Technology Development Co., Ltd.
Page/Seite 97, 267

Xiaomi Inc.
Page/Seite 70, 89, 115, 250–251, 263

Hangzhou Xingshangzhongzhi Clothing Co., Ltd.
Page/Seite 105

Wei Xiong
ZCO Design Co., Ltd.
Page/Seite 312

Shenzhen Xivokids Design Co., Ltd.
Page/Seite 311

Haopeng Xu
Shenzhen Eevin Design Co., Ltd.
Page/Seite 279

Ya Xu
Xiamen Stoneware Technology Co., Ltd.
Page/Seite 95

Zuo Xu
Kurz Kurz Design China
Page/Seite 136

Zhou Xuqi
BSH Home Appliances (China) Co., Ltd.
Page/Seite 112

Y

YAHUI Fashion & Technology (Shanghai) Co., Ltd.
Page/Seite 104

Roy Yan
Morus Technology (Shenzhen) Co., Ltd.
Page/Seite 115

Bowen Yang
Shenzhen 21g Product Design Co., Ltd.
Page/Seite 283

Yang Fan
Baidu Online Network Technology (Beijing) Co., Ltd.
Page/Seite 310

Xunyu Yang
Beijing MIIIW Technology Co., Ltd.
Miiiw Design Team
Page/Seite 255

YASKAWA Electric Corp.
Page/Seite 301

Ye Zilong
Guilin Zhishen Information Technology Co., Ltd.
Page/Seite 219

Hong-Chi Yeh
AVer Information Inc.
Page/Seite 271

Axe Yi
Morus Technology (Shenzhen) Co., Ltd.
Page/Seite 115

Wang Yi
Xiaomi Inc.
Page/Seite 250

Hebei Yifan Zhuopin Industrial Design Co., Ltd.
Enjoyjob Design Studio
Page/Seite 302–303

Hefei Yiso Product Design Co., Ltd.
Page/Seite 152

Naofumi Yoneda
Atomos
Page/Seite 221

Hyunwoo Yoo
LG Electronics Inc.
Page/Seite 309

Taewoo Yoo
LG Electronics Inc.
Page/Seite 309

Narae Yoon
JJOBI Company
Page/Seite 98–100

Koji Yoshida
FUJIFILM Corporation
Page/Seite 213

Rongmin You
Meizu Technology Co., Ltd.
Page/Seite 253

Jeromy Young
Atomos
Page/Seite 221

Guan Yu
Huawei Technologies Co., Ltd.
Page/Seite 228

Shenzhen Yuanguanghao Electronics Co., Ltd.
Page/Seite 95

Yukai Engineering
Page/Seite 311

Daekyu Yun
Hyundai Robotics
Page/Seite 298–299

Z

ZCO Design Co., Ltd.
Page/Seite 312

Kent Zeng
DTEN
Page/Seite 268–269

Ansheng Zhang
Xiamen Stoneware Technology Co., Ltd.
Page/Seite 95

Chuanzhu Zhang
Hefei Yiso Product Design Co., Ltd.
Page/Seite 152

Hongzhi Zhang
Shenzhen 21g Product Design Co., Ltd.
Page/Seite 283

Jinping Zhang
Positec Technology
Page/Seite 180

Qiao Wei Zhang
Shenzhen Beite Industry Design Co., Ltd.
Page/Seite 87

Rong Zhang
ZCO Design Co., Ltd.
Page/Seite 312

Yang Zhang
Beijing AIQI Technology Co., Ltd.
Page/Seite 313

Yanxue Zhang
Hefei Yiso Product Design Co., Ltd.
Page/Seite 152

Zilun Zhang
Shenzhen Booyue Daily Necessities Co., Ltd.
Page/Seite 94

Alphabetical index designers
Alphabetisches Designer-Register

Zheng Bangming
Guilin Zhishen Information Technology Co., Ltd.
Page/Seite 219

Shen Zheying
Hangzhou Xingshangzhongzhi Clothing Co., Ltd.
Page/Seite 105

Guilin Zhishen Information Technology Co., Ltd.
Page/Seite 219

Haibo Zhou
Positec Technology
Page/Seite 180

Ligang Zhou
Hangzhou Bole Industrial Design
Page/Seite 116

Ruoya Zhou
Kingclean Electric Co., Ltd.
Page/Seite 126–127

Wensheng Zhou
Shenzhen UVLED Optical Technology Co., Ltd.
Shenzhen UV Guard Technology Co., Ltd.
Page/Seite 131

Zhu Bingyue
Haier Innovation Design Center
Page/Seite 111

Jing Zhu
LKKer Technology Co., Ltd.
Page/Seite 159

Tuo Zhu
Ugreen Group Limited
Page/Seite 263

Xihua Zhu
iFootage International (HK) Limited
Page/Seite 219

Yidan Zhuge
Hefei Yiso Product Design Co., Ltd.
Page/Seite 152

Zimi Corporation
Page/Seite 246

Zimmer Group
Page/Seite 307

ZTE Corporation
Page/Seite 283

Find additional award-winning products and designer portraits in the separate volumes "Living", "Working", "Enjoying".

Weitere ausgezeichnete Produkte und Designerporträts finden Sie in den Einzelbänden „Living", „Working", „Enjoying".

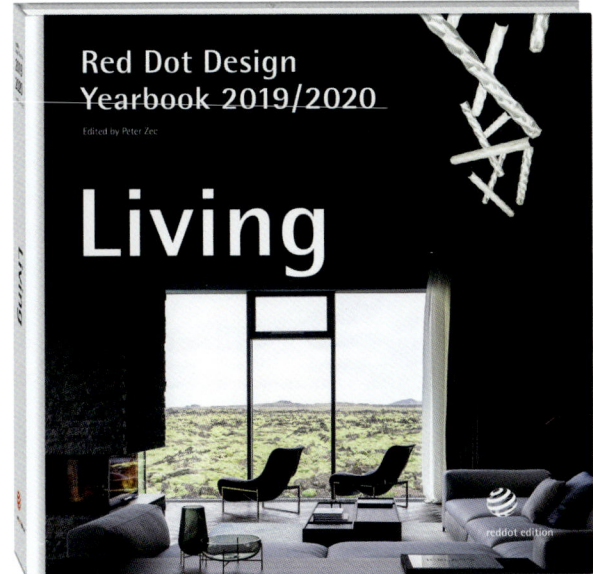 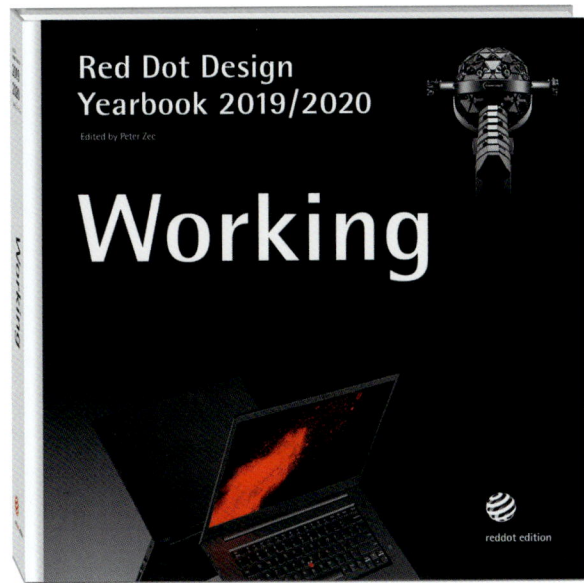 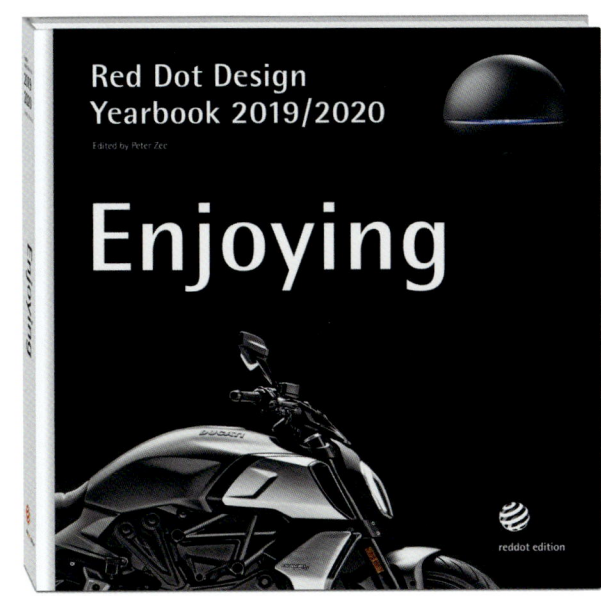

Living

Interior design
Interior Design

Living rooms and bedrooms
Wohnen und Schlafen

Kitchens
Küche

Bathrooms and sanitary equipment
Bad und Sanitär

Lighting and lamps
Licht und Leuchten

Urban design and public spaces
Urban Design und öffentlicher Raum

Working

Office
Büro

Computer and information technology
Computer- und Informationstechnik

Industrial equipment, machinery and automation
Industriegeräte, Maschinen und Automation

Materials and surfaces
Materialien und Oberflächen

Heating and air conditioning technology
Heiz- und Klimatechnik

Life science and medicine
Life Science und Medizin

Enjoying

Bicycles
Fahrräder

Vehicles
Fahrzeuge

Sports and outdoor
Sport und Outdoor

Leisure and games
Freizeit und Spiel

Entertainment
Entertainment

Spas and personal care
Wellness und Personal Care

Fashion, lifestyle and accessories
Mode, Lifestyle und Accessoires

Watches and jewellery
Uhren und Schmuck

reddot edition

Editor | Herausgeber
Peter Zec

Project management | Projektleitung
Sophie Angerer

Project assistance | Projektassistenz
Theresa Falkenberg
Ekaterina Haak
Laura-Gabriela Hellbach
Anja Lakomski
Judith Lindner
Samuel Madilonga
Vivien Mroß
Louisa Mücher
Lena Poteralla
Anamaria Sumic
Sabine Wöll
Janik Zeh

Editorial work | Redaktion
Mareike Ahlborn, Essen, Germany
Jörg Arnke, Essen, Germany
Bettina Derksen, Simmern, Germany
Eva Hembach, Vienna, Austria
Karin Kirch, Essen, Germany
Karoline Laarmann, Dortmund, Germany
Bettina Laustroer, Wuppertal, Germany
Kirsten Müller, Essen, Germany
Astrid Ruta, Essen, Germany
Martina Stein, Otterberg, Germany
Corinna Ten-Cate, Wetter, Germany

"Red Dot: Design Team of the Year"
Burkhard Jacob, Krefeld, Germany

Translation | Übersetzung
Heike Bors-Eberlein, Tokyo, Japan
Patrick Conroy, Lanarca, Cyprus
Stanislaw Eberlein, Tokyo, Japan
William Kings, Wuppertal, Germany
Kocarek GmbH (Anna Krepper, Christopher Schuster,
David Lauber), Essen, Germany
Tara Russell, Dublin, Ireland
Philippa Watts, Exeter, United Kingdom
Andreas Zantop, Berlin, Germany
Christiane Zschunke, Frankfurt am Main, Germany

Proofreading | Lektorat
Klaus Dimmler (supervision), Essen, Germany
Mareike Ahlborn, Essen, Germany
Jörg Arnke, Essen, Germany
Wolfgang Astelbauer, Vienna, Austria
Dawn Michelle d'Atri, Kirchhundem, Germany
Annette Gillich-Beltz, Essen, Germany
Sonja Illa-Paschen, London, United Kingdom
Karin Kirch, Essen, Germany
Norbert Knyhala, Castrop-Rauxel, Germany
Regina Schier, Essen, Germany
Anja Schrade, Stuttgart, Germany
SPRACHENWERFT GmbH, Hamburg, Germany

Layout | Gestaltung
Lockstoff Design GmbH, Meerbusch, Germany
Nicole Slink (supervision)
Christina Jörres
Alica Kern
Alexandra Korschefsky
Alina Laase
Stephanie Marniok
Saskia Rühmkorf

Cover | Umschlag
Idea | Idee
Burkhard Jacob, Krefeld, Germany
Implementation | Umsetzung
Lockstoff Design GmbH, Meerbusch, Germany

Photographs | Fotos
Dragan Arrigler (Carefoot, juror Jure Miklavc)

Guglielmo Galliano, Responsible Grafik & Visual
of Ferrari Design (portrait of Flavio Manzoni,
Red Dot: Design Team of the Year 2019)

Altin Manaf (GENESI, juror Masayo Ave)

Peter Molick, (product photo ReThink!, USA,
Volume Working)

Jens Passoth (designer portrait photo of Kees de Boer,
Volume Working)

Singapore GP Pte. Ltd. (Twenty3, juror Simon Ong)

Swiss Krono Group (juror Katrin de Louw)

Masafumi Yamamoto (fugan, juror Kazuo Tanaka)

Jury photographs | Jurorenfotos
eventfotograf.in, Essen, Germany
Schuchrat Kurbanov
Alex Muchnik

In-company photos | Werkfotos der Firmen

Production | Produktion
gelb+, Düsseldorf, Germany
Bernd Reinkens

Lithography | Lithografie
gelb+, Düsseldorf, Germany
Bernd Reinkens (supervision)
Wurzel Medien GmbH, Düsseldorf, Germany
Jonas Mühlenweg

Printing | Druck
Dr. Cantz'sche Druckerei Medien GmbH,
Esslingen, Germany

Bookbindery | Buchbinderei
Conzella Verlagsbuchbinderei, Pfarrkirchen, Germany

Red Dot Design Yearbook 2019/2020
Living: 978-3-89939-213-5
Doing: 978-3-89939-214-2
Working: 978-3-89939-215-9
Enjoying: 978-3-89939-216-6
Set (Living, Doing, Working & Enjoying): 978-3-89939-212-8

©2019 Red Dot GmbH & Co. KG, Essen, Germany

The Red Dot Award: Product Design
competition is the continuation of the
Design Innovations competition.
Der Wettbewerb „Red Dot Award: Product Design"
gilt als Fortsetzung des Wettbewerbs
„Design Innovationen".

All rights reserved, especially those of translation.
Alle Rechte vorbehalten, besonders die der Übersetzung
in fremde Sprachen.

No liability is accepted for the completeness
of the information in the appendix.
Für die Vollständigkeit der Angaben im Anhang
wird keine Gewähr übernommen.

Publisher & worldwide distribution |
Verlag & Vertrieb weltweit
Red Dot Edition
Design Publisher | Fachverlag für Design
Contact | Kontakt
Sabine Wöll
Gelsenkirchener Str. 181
45309 Essen, Germany
Phone +49 201 81418 22
Fax +49 201 81418 10
E-mail edition@red-dot.de
www.red-dot-edition.com
Book publisher ID no. | Verkehrsnummer
13674 (Börsenverein Frankfurt)

**Bibliographic information published
by the Deutsche Nationalbibliothek**
The Deutsche Nationalbibliothek
lists this publication in the Deutsche
Nationalbibliografie; detailed bibliographic
data are available on the Internet at
http://dnb.ddb.de
Bibliografische Information
der Deutschen Nationalbibliothek
Die Deutsche Nationalbibliothek verzeichnet
diese Publikation in der Deutschen
Nationalbibliografie; detaillierte
bibliografische Daten sind im Internet über
http://dnb.ddb.de abrufbar